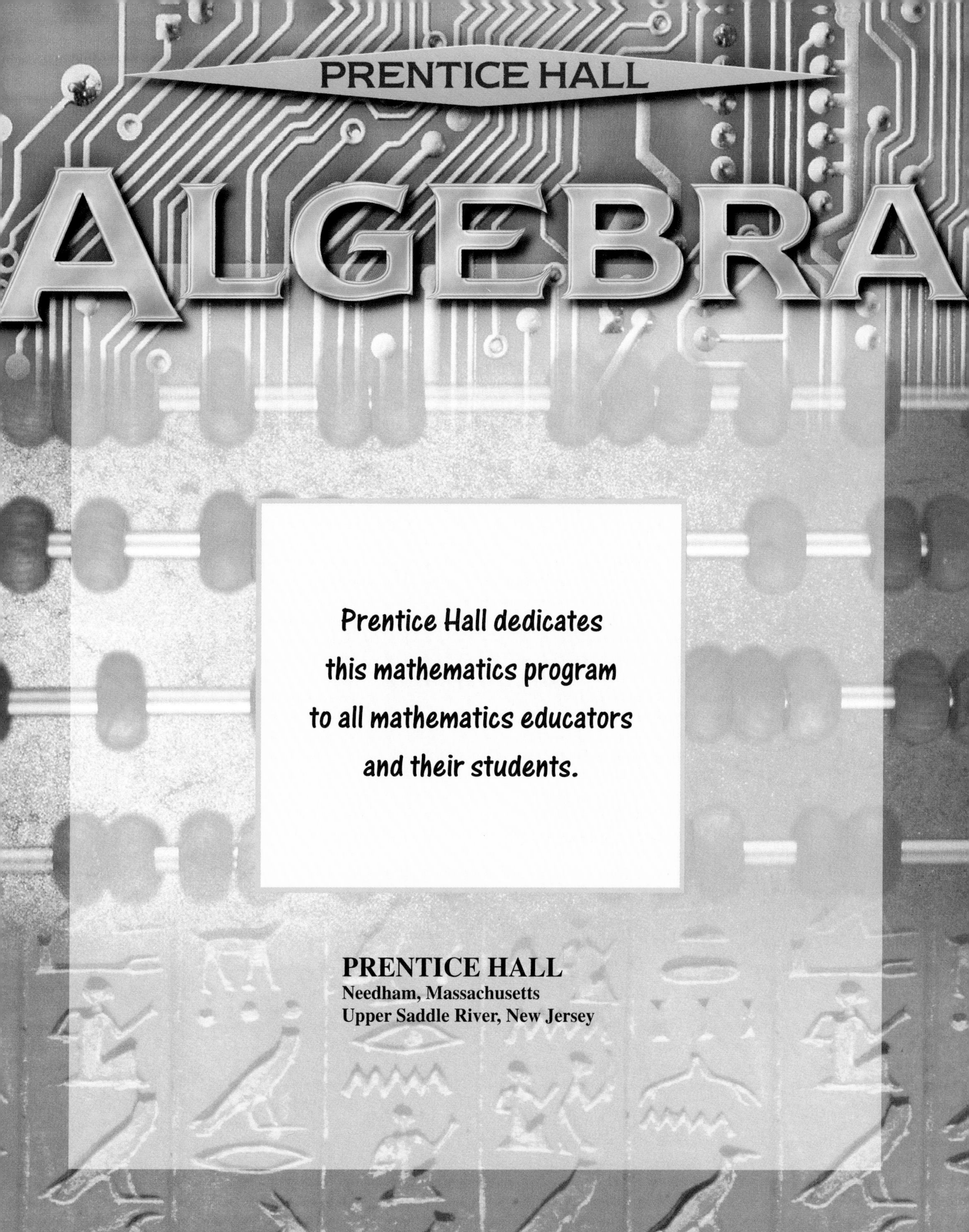

Prentice Hall dedicates this mathematics program to all mathematics educators and their students.

PRENTICE HALL
Needham, Massachusetts
Upper Saddle River, New Jersey

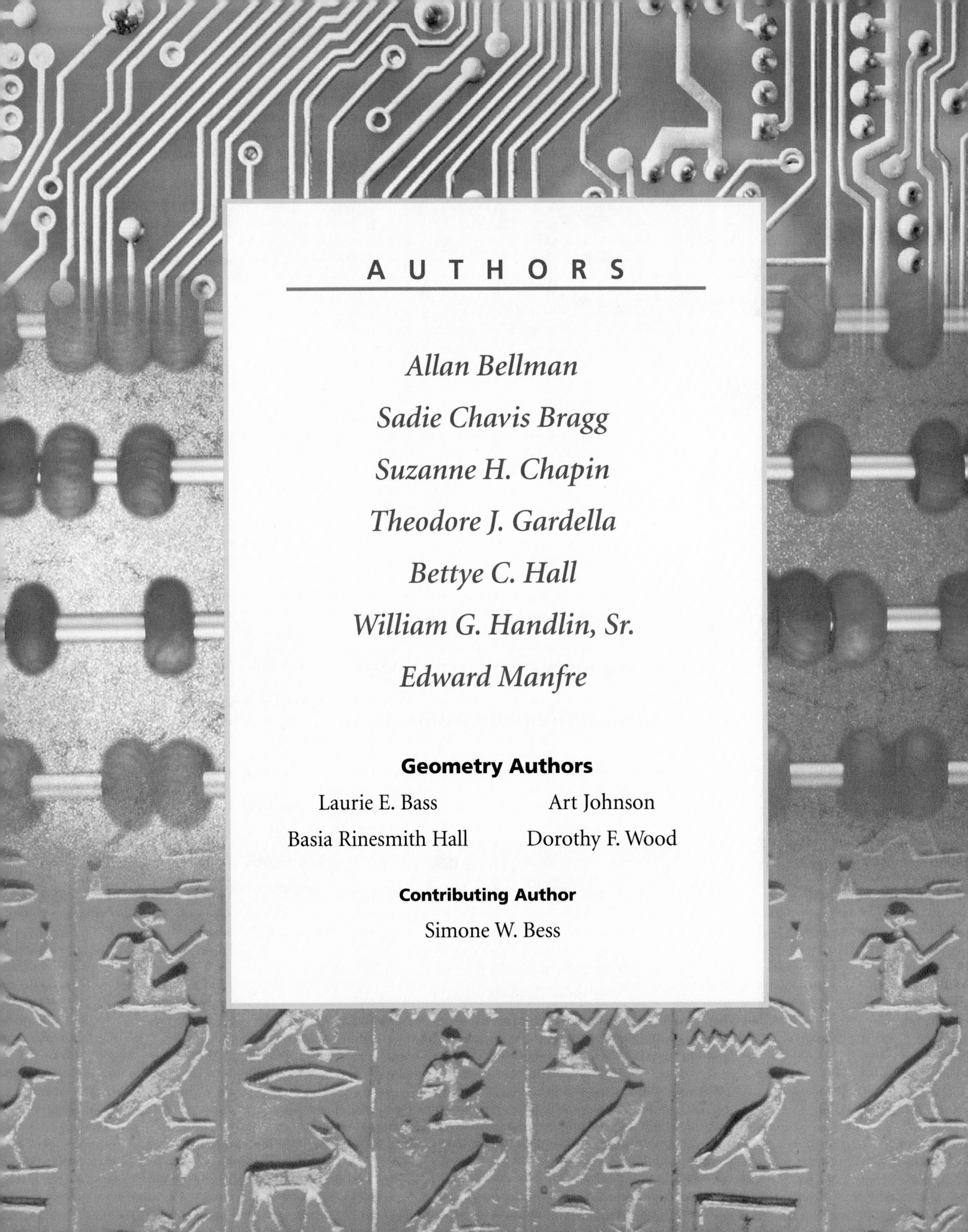

AUTHORS

Allan Bellman

Sadie Chavis Bragg

Suzanne H. Chapin

Theodore J. Gardella

Bettye C. Hall

William G. Handlin, Sr.

Edward Manfre

Geometry Authors

Laurie E. Bass

Art Johnson

Basia Rinesmith Hall

Dorothy F. Wood

Contributing Author

Simone W. Bess

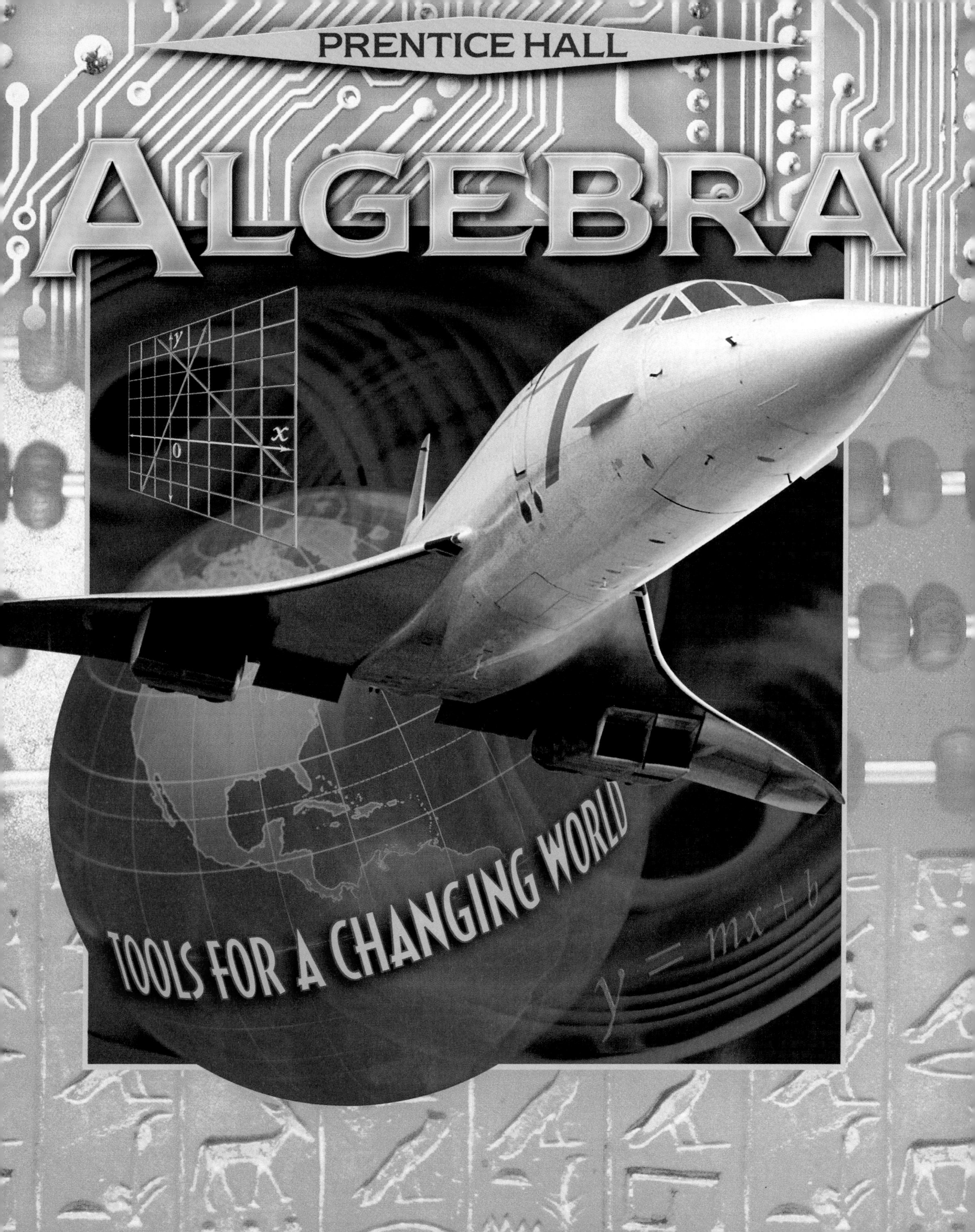

PRENTICE HALL
ALGEBRA
TOOLS FOR A CHANGING WORLD
$y = mx + b$

Authors, Algebra & Advanced Algebra

Allan Bellman
Blake High School
Silver Spring, Maryland

Sadie Chavis Bragg, Ed.D.
Borough of Manhattan
Community College
The City University of New York
New York, New York

Suzanne H. Chapin, Ed.D.
Boston University
Boston, Massachusetts

Theodore J. Gardella
Formerly, Bloomfield Hills
Public Schools
Bloomfield Hills, Michigan

Bettye C. Hall
Mathematics Consultant
Houston, Texas

William G. Handlin, Sr.
Spring Woods High School
Houston, Texas

Edward Manfre
Mathematics Consultant
Albuquerque, New Mexico

Authors, Geometry

Laurie E. Bass
The Fieldston School
Riverdale, New York

Basia Rinesmith Hall
East District
Houston Independent School District
Houston, Texas

Art Johnson, Ed.D.
Nashua High School
Nashua, New Hampshire

Dorothy F. Wood
Formerly, Kern High School District
Bakersfield, California

Contributing Author
Simone W. Bess, Ed.D.
University of Cincinnati
College of Education
Cincinnati, Ohio

Printed in the United States of America.

ISBN: 0-13-050707-5

1 2 3 4 5 6 7 8 9 10   04 03 02 01 00

REVIEWERS

Series Reviewers

James Gates, Ed.D.
Executive Director Emeritus, National Council of Teachers of Mathematics, Reston, Virginia

Vinetta Jones, Ph.D.
National Director, EQUITY 2000, The College Board, New York, New York

Algebra

John J. Brady III
Hume-Fogg High School
Nashville, Tennessee

Elias P. Rodriguez
Leander Junior High School
Leander, Texas

Dorothy S. Strong, Ed.D.
Chicago Public Schools
Chicago, Illinois

Art W. Wilson, Ed.D.
Abraham Lincoln High School
Denver, Colorado

Advanced Algebra

Eleanor Boehner
Methacton High School
Norristown, Pennsylvania

Laura Price Cobb
Dallas Public Schools
Dallas, Texas

William Earl, Ed.D.
Formerly Mathematics Education Specialist
Utah State Office of Education
Salt Lake City, Utah

Robin Levine Rubinstein
Shorewood High School
Shoreline, Washington

Geometry

Sandra Argüelles Daire
Miami Senior High School
Miami, Florida

Priscilla P. Donkle
South Central High School
Union Mills, Indiana

Tom Muchlinski, Ph.D.
Wayzata High School
Plymouth, Minnesota

Bonnie Walker
Texas ASCD
Houston, Texas

Karen Doyle Walton, Ed.D.
Allentown College of
Saint Francis de Sales
Center Valley, Pennsylvania

Staff Credits

The people who made up the *Algebra* team — representing editorial, design, marketing, page production, editorial services, production, manufacturing, technology, electronic publishing, and advertising and promotion — and their managers are listed below. Bold type denotes core team members.

Alison Anholt-White, Jackie Zidek Bedoya, **Barbara A. Bertell**, Bruce Bond, **Ellen Brown**, **Judith D. Buice**, **Kathy Carter**, Kerrie Caruso, Linda M. Coffey, Noralie V. Cox, Sheila DeFazio, Edward de Leon, Christine Deliee, **Gabriella Della Corte**, Robert G. Dunn, Barbara Flockhart, **Audra Floyd**, David Graham, Maria Green, Bridget A. Hadley, Joanne Hudson, Vanessa Hunnibell, Mimi Jigarjian, Linda D. Johnson, Elizabeth A. Jordan, Russell Lappa, Catherine Martin-Hetmansky, Eve Melnechuk, Cindy A. Noftle, Caroline M. Power, Roger E. Powers, Martha G. Smith, Kira Thaler, Robin Tiano, Christina Trinchero, **Stuart Wallace**, **Cynthia A. Weedel**, Jeff Weidenaar, Pearl B. Weinstein, Mary Jane Wolfe, Stewart Wood, David Zarowin.

We would like to give special thanks to our National Math Consultants, Ann F. Bell and Brenda Underwood, for all their help in developing this program.

Algebra & Advanced Algebra Authors

Allan Bellman is a classroom teacher at Blake High School in Silver Spring, Maryland, and is also an instructor in the Woodrow Wilson National Fellowship Foundation Outreach program for mathematics teachers. Mr. Bellman has particular expertise in the use of the graphing calculator in the classroom, and also teaches in the Teachers Teaching with Technology (T^3) professional development program. Advanced Algebra chapters 1, 2, 5, 9

Sadie Chavis Bragg, Ed.D., is Vice President of Academic Affairs at the Borough of Manhattan Community College of The City University of New York. Dr. Bragg is a member of the Conference Board of Mathematical Sciences, is President of the American Mathematical Association of Two Year Colleges, and is an active member of the Benjamin Bannecker Association. Algebra chapters 3, 6, 11 and Advanced Algebra chapter 3

Suzanne H. Chapin, Ed.D., is Professor of Mathematics Education at Boston University. Dr. Chapin also directs all mathematics professional development in a landmark Boston University/Chelsea Public Schools Partnership program, working closely with teachers, administrators, and parents to provide opportunities for all students to learn mathematics. Algebra chapters 2, 8, and the probability strand

Theodore J. Gardella, formerly of the Bloomfield Hills Public Schools, Bloomfield Hills, Michigan, was a finalist for the Michigan Presidential Award for Excellence in Science and Mathematics Teaching. Mr. Gardella is also an originator of the "Tune in Mathematics and Science" project, delivering satellite video courses for students and staff development sessions for teachers. Teacher's Editions, continuity of strands across the books, and Advanced Algebra chapter 7.

Bettye C. Hall is the former Director of Mathematics in the Houston Unified School District in Houston, Texas. Ms. Hall, admired as a "teacher's teacher" with her very practical perspective on students' and teachers' needs, is active as a mathematics consultant, speaker, and workshop leader throughout the United States. Algebra chapters 4, 7, 10 and Advanced Algebra chapters 6, 11

William G. Handlin, Sr., is a classroom teacher and Department Chairman of Technology Applications at Spring Woods High School in Houston, Texas. Awarded Life Membership in the Texas Congress of Parent and Teachers Association for his contributions to the well-being of children, Mr. Handlin is also a frequent workshop and seminar leader in professional meetings throughout the state. Advanced Algebra chapters 4, 8, 10, 12

Edward Manfre is a mathematics consultant from Albuquerque, New Mexico. Mr. Manfre has an extensive teaching background in the elementary, middle, and secondary schools, and for over twenty years has been developing educational materials that encourage thinking and self-reliance. Algebra chapters 1, 5, 9

Geometry Authors

Laurie E. Bass is a classroom teacher at the Fieldston School in Riverdale, New York. Ms. Bass has a wide base of teaching experience, ranging from grades 6 and 7 through Advanced Placement Calculus. She also has been a contributing writer of a number of publications, including software-based activities for the Algebra 1 classroom. One of her areas of special interest is geometric exploration on the computer. Chapters 2, 7, 9

Basia Rinesmith Hall, Mathematics Instructional Supervisor, East District, Houston Independent School District, Houston, Texas, is a 1992 winner of the Presidential Award for Excellence in Mathematics Teaching. Ms. Hall was a member of the NCTM Professional Teaching Standards Review Committee, served on the writing committee of the Texas Essential Knowledge Skills (TEKS), and is President of the Texas Council of Teachers of Mathematics (1996–1998). Chapters 3, 8, 11

Art Johnson, Ed.D., is a classroom teacher in Nashua High School, Nashua, New Hampshire. Dr. Johnson is a frequent speaker and workshop leader and the recipient of a number of awards, including the Tandy Prize for Teaching Excellence in 1995 and a 1992 Presidential Award for Excellence in Mathematics Teaching. He was profiled by the Disney Corporation in the American Teacher of the Year Program. Chapters 1, 6, 10

Dorothy F. Wood, formerly with the Kern High School District in Bakersfield, California, is an active member of the California Mathematics Council and a frequent presenter at their conferences. She is also a leader of middle and high school staff-development workshops sponsored by schools, districts, and county offices. As Teacher Leader and Evaluator, she serves numerous schools in the California Department of Education Mathematics Demonstration Program. Chapters 4, 5, 12

Contributing Author

Simone W. Bess, Ed.D., Adjunct Mathematics Instructor at the University of Cincinnati and Cincinnati State Technical and Community College, came to mathematics education through a career in engineering at General Electric Aircraft Engines. She is a frequent speaker at professional meetings around the country, and has special interests in integrating diversity in the classroom and supporting girls and women in mathematics careers. Dr. Bess has also been active in coordinating a number of NSF-funded programs for minority students, K–12.

Algebra Volume 2 Contents

CHAPTER 1

Tools of Algebra

Connections and Applications

Jazz Greats

Track One Records $12.00

CHAPTER 2

Functions and Their Graphs

Connections and Applications

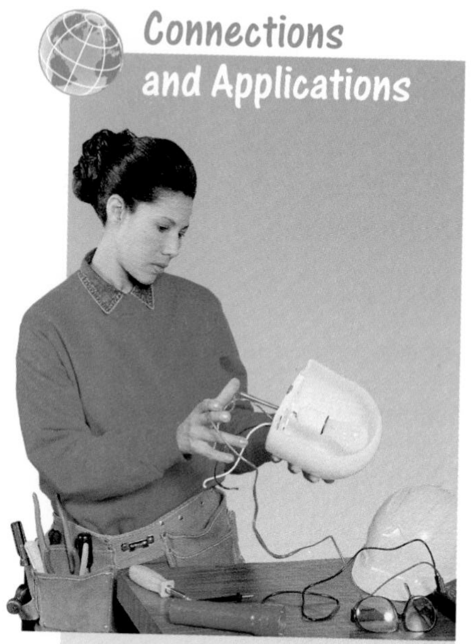

CHAPTER 3

Algebraic Concepts and Simple Equations

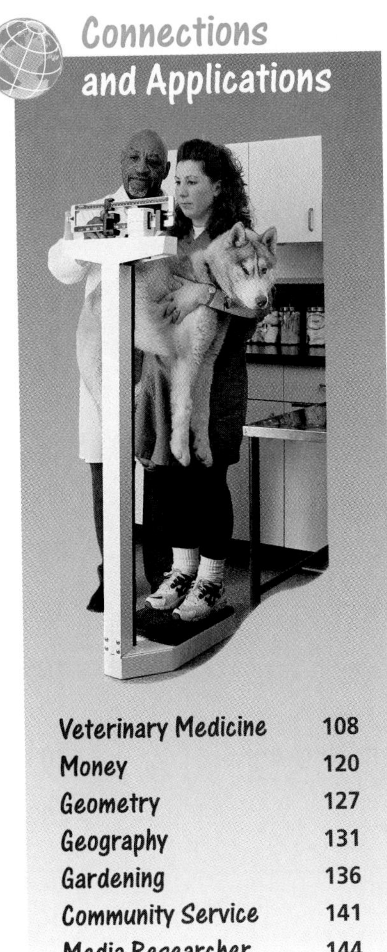

Connections and Applications

CHAPTER 4

Equations and Inequalities

Connections and Applications

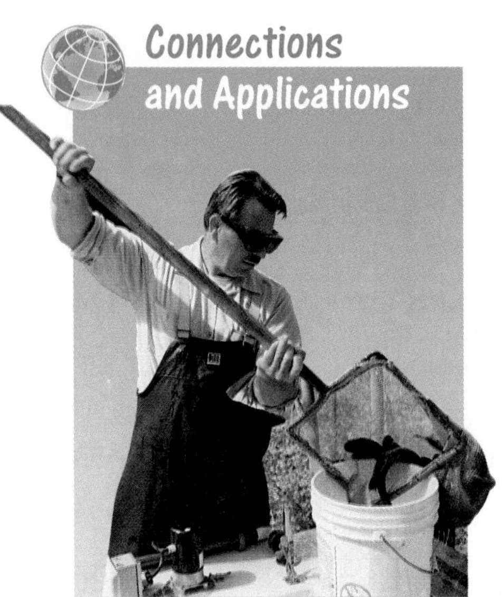

CHAPTER 5

Graphing and Writing Linear Equations

Connections and Applications

CHAPTER 6

Systems of Equations and Inequalities

Connections and Applications

CHAPTER 7

Quadratic Equations and Functions

Connections and Applications

CHAPTER 8

Exponents and Exponential Functions

Connections and Applications

CHAPTER 9

Right Triangles and Radical Expressions

Connections and Applications

CHAPTER 10

Polynomials

Connections and Applications

CHAPTER 11

Rational Expressions and Functions

Connections and Applications

To the Student

Students like you helped Prentice Hall develop this program. They identified tools you can use to help you learn now in this course and beyond. In this special "To the Student" section and throughout this program, you will find the **tools you need to help you succeed.** We'd like to hear how these tools work for you. Write us at Prentice Hall Mathematics, 160 Gould Street, Needham, MA 02494 or visit us at http://www.phschool.com.

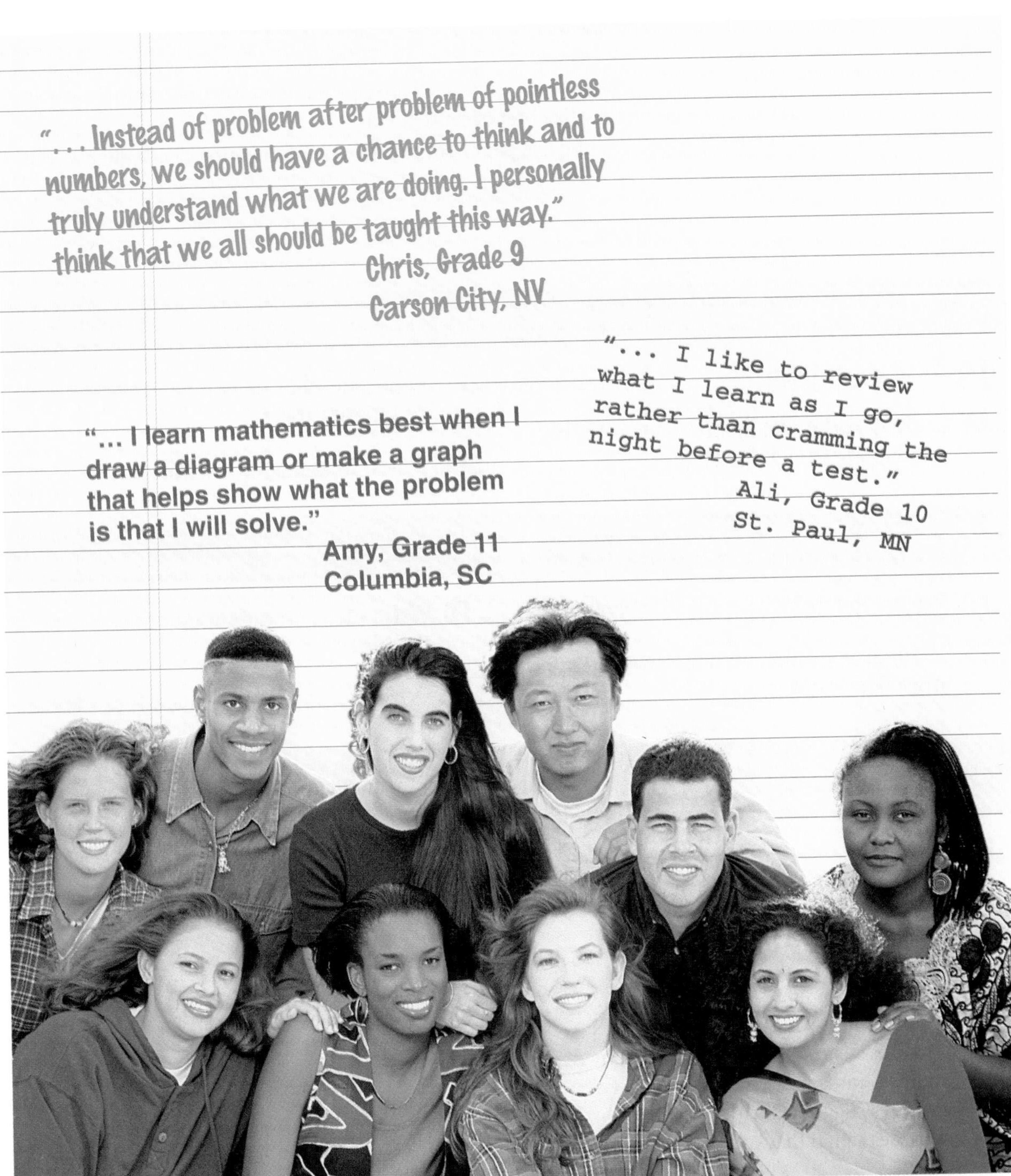

"...Instead of problem after problem of pointless numbers, we should have a chance to think and to truly understand what we are doing. I personally think that we all should be taught this way."
Chris, Grade 9
Carson City, NV
"... I like to review what I learn as I go, rather than cramming the night before a test."
Ali, Grade 10
St. Paul, MN
"... I learn mathematics best when I draw a diagram or make a graph that helps show what the problem is that I will solve."
Amy, Grade 11
Columbia, SC

To the Student: Tools to Help You Succeed

LEARN About Learning!

What comes to your mind when you hear the word **style**? Maybe it's hair style, or style of dress, or walking style. Have you ever thought about your learning style? Just like your hair or your clothes or your walk, everybody has a learning style that they like best because it works best for them. Look around you now. What do you see? Different styles … some like yours, some different from yours. That's the way it is with learning styles, too.

What's Your Best Learning Style?

I understand math concepts best when I...

- ❑ **A. Read about them.**
- ❑ **B. Look at and make illustrations, graphs, and charts that show them.**
- ❑ **C. Draw sketches or handle manipulatives to explore them.**
- ❑ **D. Listen to someone explain them.**

When I study, I learn more when I...

- ❑ **A. Review my notes and the textbook.**
- ❑ **B. Study any graphs, charts, diagrams, or other illustrations.**
- ❑ **C. Write ideas on note cards; then study the ideas.**
- ❑ **D. Explain what I know to another person.**

When I collaborate with a group, I am most comfortable when I...

- ❑ **A. Take notes.**
- ❑ **B. Make visuals for display.**
- ❑ **C. Demonstrate what I know to others.**
- ❑ **D. Give presentations to other groups or the whole class.**

Look for a pattern in your responses.
"A" responses suggest that you learn best by reading;
"B" responses indicate a visual learning style;
"C" responses suggest a tactile, or hands-on, learning style;
"D" responses signal that you probably learn best by listening and talking about what you are learning.

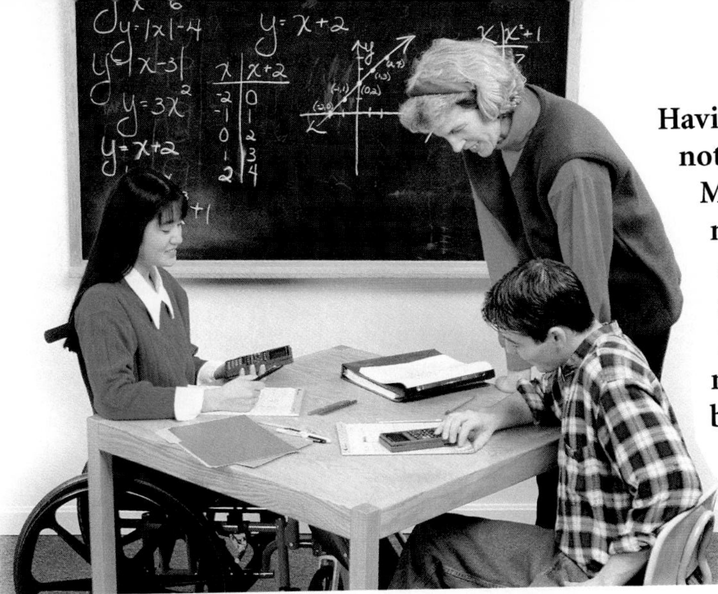

Having a preferred learning style does not limit you to using just that one. Most people learn by using a combination of learning styles. You'll be amazed by the ways that knowing more about yourself and how you learn will help you be successful — not only successful in mathematics, but successful in all your subject areas. When you know how you learn best, you will be well equipped to enter the work place.

Use this chart to help you strengthen your different learning styles.

Learning Style	Learning Tips
Learning by ***reading***	✳ Schedule time to read each day. ✳ Carry a book or magazine to read during wait time. ✳ Read what you like to read—it's OK not to finish a book.
Learning by using ***visual*** cues	✳ Visualize a problem situation. ✳ Graph solutions to problems. ✳ Let technology, such as computers and calculators, help you.
Learning by using ***hands-on*** exploration	✳ Make sketches when solving a problem. ✳ Use objects to help you solve problems. ✳ Rely on technology as a tool for exploration and discovery.
Learning by ***listening and talking***	✳ Volunteer to give presentations. ✳ Explain your ideas to a friend. ✳ Listen intently to what others are saying.

Most important, believe in yourself and your ability to learn!

What you do now...	What you do in this course...	What you do in the work place...
Learn best by using a particular learning style . . .	Example 1 Example 2 Relating to the Real World	*Choose a career that you enjoy because it is natural for you.*

Help Teamwork Work for YOU!

Each of us works with other people on teams throughout our lives. What's your job? Your job on a team, that is. Maybe you play center on your basketball team, maybe you count votes for your school elections, perhaps you help decorate the gym for a school function, or maybe you help make scenery for a community play. From relay races to doing your part of the job in the work place, teamwork is required for success.

TEAMWORK CHECKLIST

- **Break apart the large task into smaller tasks, which become the responsibility of individual group members.**
- **Treat the differences in group members as a benefit.**
- **Try to listen attentively when others speak.**

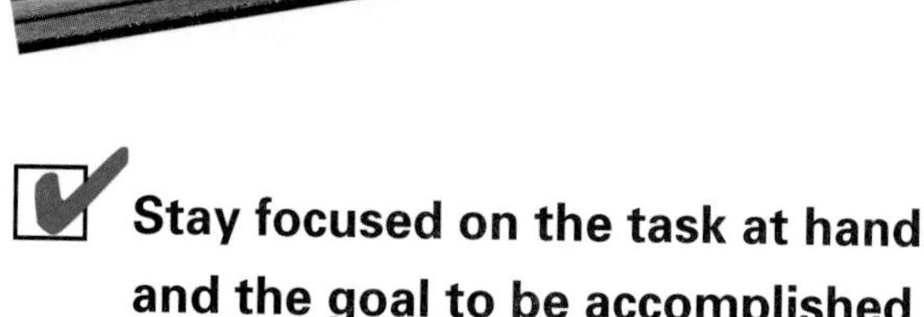

- **Stay focused on the task at hand and the goal to be accomplished.**
- **Vary the tasks you do in each group and participate.**
- **Recognize your own and others' learning styles.**
- **Offer your ideas and suggestions.**
- **Be socially responsible and act in a respectful way.**

What you do now...	What you do in this course...	What you do in the work place...
Play on a team, decorate the gym, or perform in the band...	WORK TOGETHER	*Collaborate with coworkers on projects.*

Reading + Writing + Talking + Listening:

It's All COMMUNICATION

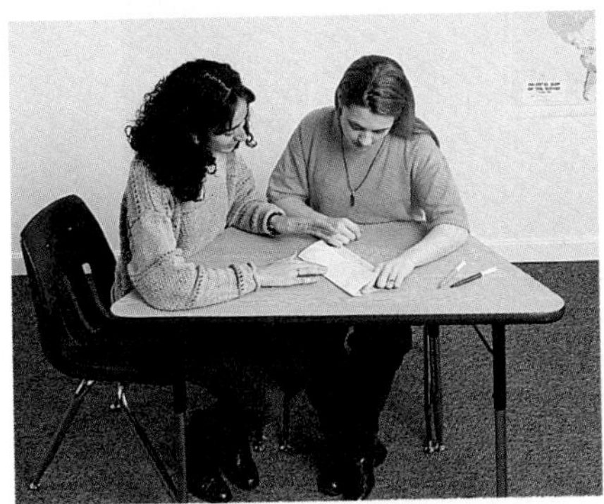

We communicate in songs. We communicate in letters. We communicate with our body movements. We communicate on the phone. We communicate in cyberspace. It's all talking about ideas and sharing what you know. It's the same in mathematics — we communicate by reading, writing, talking, and listening. Whether we are working together on a project or studying with a friend for a test, we are communicating.

Ways to Communicate What You Know and Are Able to Do

- ✔ Explain to others how you solve a problem.
- ✔ Listen carefully to others.
- ✔ Use mathematical language in your writing in other subjects.
- ✔ Pay attention to the headings in textbooks — they are signposts that help you.
- ✔ Think about videos and audiotapes as ways to communicate mathematical ideas.
- ✔ Be on the lookout for mathematics when you read, watch television, or see a movie.
- ✔ Communicate with others by using bulletin boards and chat rooms found on the Internet.

What you do now...	What you do in this course...	What you do in the work place...
Teach a young relative a sport...	THINK AND DISCUSS	***Written and verbal communication at work.***

To the Student: Tools to Help You Succeed

Solving PROBLEMS — *a* SKILL You USE Every DAY

Problem solving is a skill — a skill that you probably use without even knowing it. When you think critically in social studies to draw conclusions about pollution and its stress on the environment, or when a mechanic listens to symptoms of trouble and logically determines the cause, you are both using a mathematical problem-solving skill. Problem solving also involves logical reasoning, wise decision making, and reflecting on our solutions.

Tips for Problem Solving

Recognize that there is more than one way to solve most problems.

When solving a word problem, read it, decide what to do, make a plan, look back at the problem, and revise your answer.

Experiment with various solution methods.

Understand that it is just as important to know how to solve a problem as it is to actually solve it.

Be aware of times you are using mathematics to solve problems that do not involve computation, such as when you reason to make a wise decision.

What you do now...	What you do in this course...	What you do in the work place...
Make decisions based on changing conditions, such as weather...	 PROBLEM SOLVING	*Synchronize the timing of traffic lights to enhance traffic flow.*

To the Student: Tools to Help You Succeed

Studying for the TEST Whatever It May Be

SATs, ACTs, chapter tests, and weekly quizzes — they all test what you know and are able to do. Have you ever thought about **how** you can take these tests to your advantage? You are evaluated now in your classes and you will be evaluated when you hold a job.

Pointers for Gaining Points

- **Study as you progress through a chapter, instead of cramming for a test.**
- **Recognize when you are lost and seek help before a test.**
- **Review important graphs and other visuals when studying for a test, then picture them in your mind.**
- **Study for a test with a friend or study group.**
- **Take a practice test.**
- **Think of mnemonic devices to help you, such as Please Excuse My Dear Aunt Sally, which is one way to remember order of operations (parentheses, exponents, multiply, divide, add, subtract).**
- **Reread test questions before answering them.**
- **Check to see if your answer is reasonable.**
- **Think positively and visualize yourself doing well on the test.**
- **Relax during the test... there is nothing there that you have not seen before.**

What you do now...	What you do in this course...	What you do in the work place...
Study notes in preparation for tests and quizzes...	SELF ASSESSMENT How am I doing? Exercises ON YOUR OWN Exercises CHECKPOINT	*Prepare for and participate in a job interview.*

Review Chapter

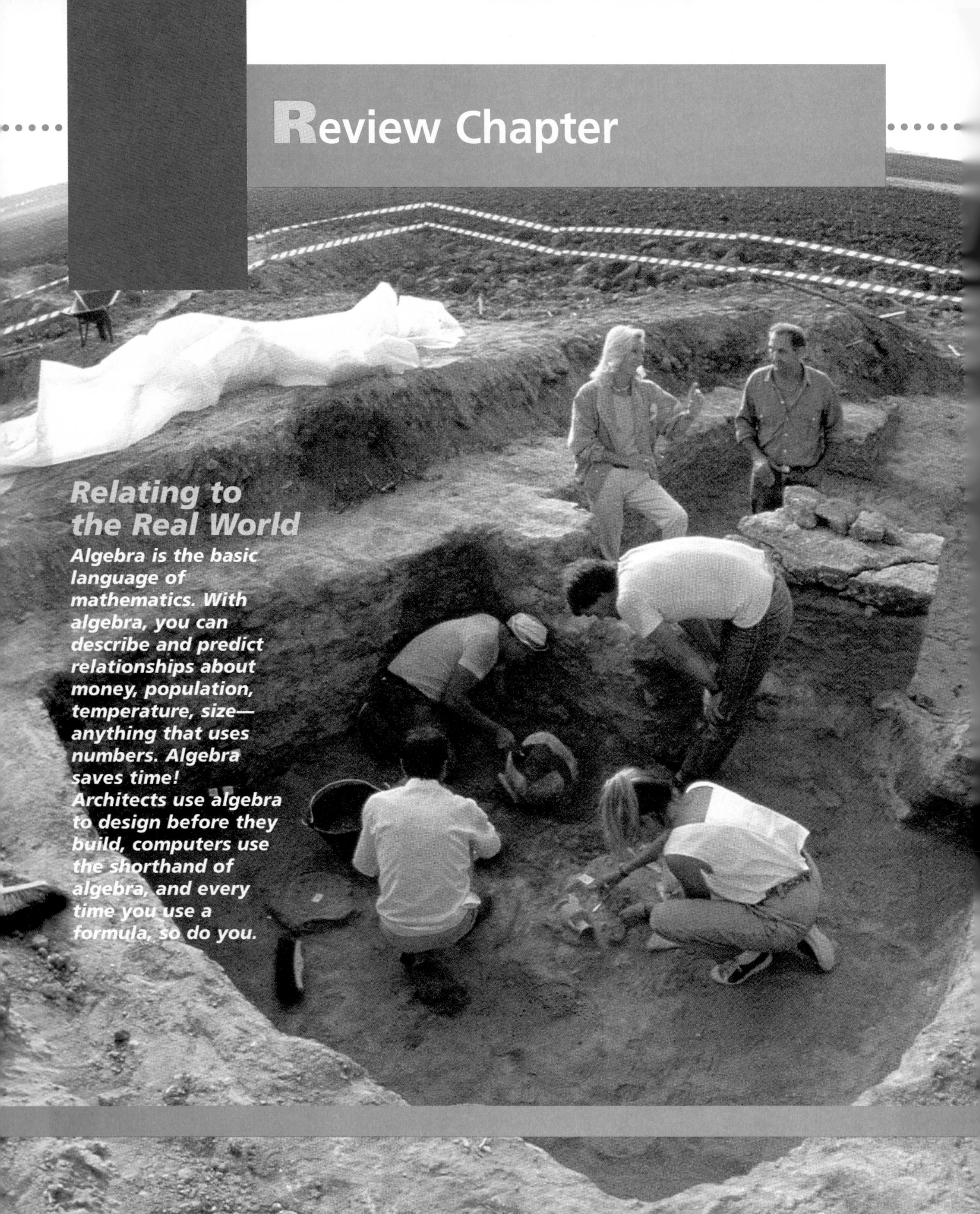

Relating to the Real World

Algebra is the basic language of mathematics. With algebra, you can describe and predict relationships about money, population, temperature, size—anything that uses numbers. Algebra saves time! Architects use algebra to design before they build, computers use the shorthand of algebra, and every time you use a formula, so do you.

Review Chapter

Math ToolboX

Skills Review

Using Properties

These properties of mathematics help you to perform arithmetic and algebraic operations.

Commutative Properties of Addition and Multiplication

For all real numbers a and b:

$a + b = b + a$ $\quad$ $a \cdot b = b \cdot a$

Examples: $2 + 3 = 3 + 2$ $\quad$ $4 \cdot 5 = 5 \cdot 4$

Associative Properties of Addition and Multiplication

For all real numbers a, b, and c:

$(a + b) + c = a + (b + c)$ $\quad$ $(a \cdot b) \cdot c = a \cdot (b \cdot c)$

Examples: $(5 + 6) + 7 = 5 + (6 + 7)$ $\quad$ $(2 \cdot 3) \cdot 4 = 2 \cdot (3 \cdot 4)$

Identity Properties of Addition and Multiplication

For every real number a:

$a + 0 = a$ and $0 + a = a$ $\quad$ $a \cdot 1 = a$ and $1 \cdot a = a$

Examples: $5 + 0 = 5$ and $0 + 5 = 5$ $\quad$ $7 \cdot 1 = 7$ and $1 \cdot 7 = 7$

Name the property that each exercise illustrates.

1. $1m = m$ **2.** $(-3 + 4) + 5 = -3 + (4 + 5)$ **3.** $3(8 \cdot 0) = (3 \cdot 8)0$

4. $2 + 0 = 2$ **5.** $np = pn$ **6.** $f + g = g + f$

Use the properties to simplify each expression.

7. $(5 \cdot 83) \cdot 2$ **8.** $47 + 39 + 3 + 11$ **9.** $25 \cdot 74 \cdot 2 \cdot 2$

10. $-5(7y)$ **11.** $8 + 9m + 7$ **12.** $4.75 + 2.95 + 1.25 + 6$

13. $6\frac{1}{2} + 4\frac{1}{3} + 1\frac{1}{2} + \frac{2}{3}$ **14.** $25 \cdot 1.7 \cdot 4$ **15.** $(3p)(4q)(6r)$

16. **Writing** Justify your answers to these questions: Is subtraction commutative? Is subtraction associative? Is division commutative? Is division associative?

1-3 Order of Operations

What You'll Learn

- Using the order of operations
- Evaluating variable expressions

...And Why

To find the total cost of items with tax

What You'll Need

- calculator

Astronaut Ellen Ochoa served on space flights in 1993 and 1994. She studied the solar corona and the effect of solar changes on Earth's environment.

WORK TOGETHER

Work with a partner.

Geometry Two formulas for the perimeter of a rectangle are $P = 2l + 2w$ and $P = 2(l + w)$.

1. Let $l = 12$ and $w = 8$. Find the perimeter of the rectangle using each formula.
2. When you used the formula $P = 2l + 2w$, did you add first or did you multiply first?
3. When you used the formula $P = 2(l + w)$, did you add first or did you multiply first?
4. Which formula do you prefer to use? Why?

THINK AND DISCUSS

Evaluating Expressions

In the Work Together activity, you used your past experience to simplify the expressions to find the perimeter. Look at this new expression and the two ways that it has been simplified.

$3 + 5 - 6 \div 2$	$3 + 5 - 6 \div 2$
$8 - 6 \div 2$	$3 + 5 - 3$
$2 \div 2$	$8 - 3$
1 ← Different results! →	5 ← This one is correct.

To avoid having two results for the same problem, mathematicians have agreed on an order for doing the operations when simplifying.

Order of Operations

1. Perform any operation(s) inside grouping symbols.
2. Simplify any term with exponents.
3. Multiply and divide in order from left to right.
4. Add and subtract in order from left to right.

5. Which operation should you do first to simplify each expression?
   a. $3 + 6 \cdot 4 \div 2$ **b.** $3 \cdot 6 - 4^2$ **c.** $3 \cdot (6 - 4) \div 2$

QUICK REVIEW

An ***exponent*** indicates repeated multiplication.

base → $3^4 = 3 \cdot 3 \cdot 3 \cdot 3$ (4 = exponent)

The base 3 is used as a factor four times.

You read 3^4 as "three to the fourth power."

You **evaluate** an expression with variables by substituting a number for each variable. Then simplify the expression using the order of operations.

Example 1 *Relating to the Real World* 

Sales Find the total cost of the sneakers shown in the ad. Use the expression at the right.

$p + r \cdot p$ — p: original price; r: sales tax rate; $r \cdot p$: sales tax

$p + r \cdot p = 59 + (0.06)59$ ← Substitute 59 for p. Change 6% to 0.06 and substitute 0.06 for r.
$= 59 + 3.54$ ← Multiply first.
$= 62.54$ ← Then add.

The total cost of the sneakers is $62.54.

6. *Calculator* Some calculators have the order of operations programmed into them. To check your calculator, use the key sequence below. Does your calculator use the order of operations? Explain.

59 [+] .06 [×] 59 [=]

Keep in mind that the base for an exponent is the number, variable, or expression directly to the left of the exponent.

Example 2

For practice with exponents, see Skills Handbook page 580.

Evaluate $3a^2 - 12 \div b$ for $a = 7$ and $b = 4$.

$3a^2 - 12 \div b = 3 \cdot 7^2 - 12 \div 4$ ← Substitute 7 for a and 4 for b.
$= 3 \cdot 49 - 12 \div 4$ ← Simplify 7^2.
$= 147 - 3$ ← Multiply and divide from left to right.
$= 144$ ← Subtract.

7. A student evaluated the expression above for $a = 8$ and $b = 6$. Her result is 94. Is her answer correct? If not, what error did she make?

8. Try This Evaluate $25 \div p + 2q^2$ for $p = 5$ and $q = 7$.

Example 3

Evaluate each expression for $c = 15$ and $d = 12$.

a. cd^2

$cd^2 = 15(12)^2$
$= 15(144)$
$= 2160$

b. $(cd)^2$

$(cd)^2 = (15 \cdot 12)^2$
$= (180)^2$
$= 32{,}400$

CALCULATOR HINT

In part (b), you can use two different key sequences to find 180^2:

180 [x^2] [ENTER] or
180 [^] 2 [ENTER] .

9. Write an expression for each phrase. Then simplify your expression.
a. four times three, squared **b.** the square of three, times four

Evaluating Expressions With Grouping Symbols

When you evaluate expressions work within the parentheses first. A fraction bar is also a grouping symbol. Do any calculations above or below a fraction bar before simplifying the fraction.

Example 4 **Relating to the Real World** 

Community Students participating in a neighborhood clean-up project are cleaning a vacant lot, which has the shape of a trapezoid. They plan to turn the vacant lot into a park. Use the expression $h\left(\frac{b_1 + b_2}{2}\right)$ to find the lot's area.

$b_1 = 100$ ft

$h = 150$ ft

$b_2 = 290$ ft

$$h\left(\frac{b_1 + b_2}{2}\right) = 150\left(\frac{100 + 290}{2}\right)$$ ← Substitute 150 for h, 100 for b_1, and 290 for b_2.

$$= 150\left(\frac{390}{2}\right)$$ ← Simplify the numerator.

$$= 150(195)$$ ← Simplify the fraction.

$$= 29{,}250$$

The area of the lot is 29,250 ft^2.

PROBLEM SOLVING

Look Back You can also use the expression $\frac{1}{2}h(b_1 + b_2)$ to find the area of a trapezoid. Explain why $h\left(\frac{b_1 + b_2}{2}\right)$ is equivalent to $\frac{1}{2}h(b_1 + b_2)$.

10. Would the result be the same if you substituted 290 for b_1 and 100 for b_2? Why or why not?

11. Describe the steps you would use to simplify $\frac{12 + 18}{3 + 9}$.

12. Explain the difference in the meaning of the expressions $5\frac{1}{6}$ and $5\left(\frac{1}{6}\right)$.

You can also use brackets [ ] as grouping symbols. When an expression has several grouping symbols, simplify the innermost expression first.

13. Try This Simplify each expression.

a. $5[4^2 + 3(2 + 1)]$ **b.** $12 + 3[18 + 5(16 - 3^2)]$

Exercises ON YOUR OWN

Simplify each numerical expression.

1. $18 + 20 \div 4$

2. $(2.4 - 1.6) \div 0.4$

3. $\frac{6 \cdot 2 - 1}{9 + 2}$

4. $(5^2 - 3)6$

5. $(10 - 2)^2$

6. $6\left(\frac{4 + 10}{2}\right)$

7. $24.6 \div 2 \cdot 4.1$

8. $25 - [2(3 + 7)]$

9. $3 \cdot 5^2$

10. $(3 \cdot 5)^2$

11. $(5^2 + 3) \div 2$

12. $\frac{(2 + 3)^2}{2}$

13. Open-ended Write an expression that includes addition, subtraction, multiplication, and parentheses. Simplify your expression.

14. a. Geometry What is the volume of the juice can at the right? The formula for the volume of a cylinder is $V = \pi r^2 h$.
b. About how many cubic inches does an ounce of juice fill?

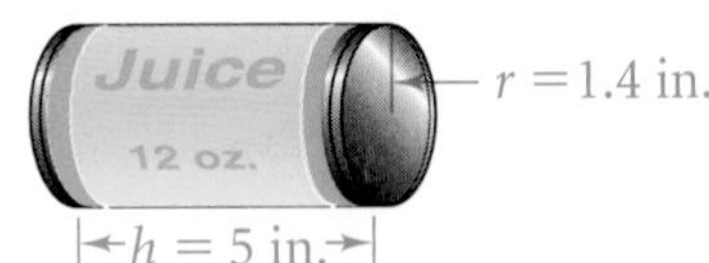

Evaluate each expression.

15. $a - 7 \cdot 2$ for $a = 15$

16. $\frac{q}{q + 8}$ for $q = 4$

17. $r + 2s$ for $r = 5.2$ and $s = 3.8$

18. $5a^2 - 4$ for $a = 3$

19. $2b^2 + 4b$ for $b = 6.3$

20. $(5x)^2$ for $x = 3$

21. $2\left(\frac{5d - 6}{3}\right)$ for $d = 9$

22. $[(5.2 + a) + 4]10$ for $a = 3.5$

23. $\frac{m^2}{m + 9}$ for $m = 6$

Use grouping symbols to make each equation true.

24. $10 + 6 \div 2 - 3 = 5$

25. $14 - 2 + 5 - 3 = 4$

26. $8 + 4 \div 3 - 1 = 10$

27. Critical Thinking Use the problem solving strategy *Guess and Test* to find two values of n that make the equation $2n = n^2$ true.

28. a. Entertainment You can use the expression $2.4t + 0.779$ to model the number of subscribers, in millions, to cable television. Copy and complete the table.
b. Statistics Use your table to draw a line graph.

Cable TV Subscribers (in millions)

Year	Subscribers
1970 ($t = 0$)	■
1980 ($t = 10$)	■
1990 ($t = 20$)	■
2000 ($t = 30$)	■

Writing **Tell if each equation is *true* or *false*. If false, use the order of operations to explain why.**

29. $3(2^3) = 6^3$

30. $2^4 = (1 + 1)^4$

31. $(4 + 5)^2 = 4^2 + 5^2$

32. Calculator Which key sequence could you use to simplify $\frac{3 + 8^2}{5}$? Explain why your choice works and the other choices do not.

A. (3 + 8) ^ 2 ÷ 5 ENTER

B. 3 + 8 ^ 2 ÷ 5 ENTER

C. (3 + 8 ^ 2) ÷ 5 ENTER

D. (3 + 8 ÷ 5 ^ 2) ENTER

Exercises MIXED REVIEW

Write each fraction as a fraction or mixed number in simplest form.

33. $\frac{4}{6}$

34. $\frac{15}{10}$

35. $\frac{27}{6}$

36. $\frac{9}{12}$

37. $\frac{12}{15}$

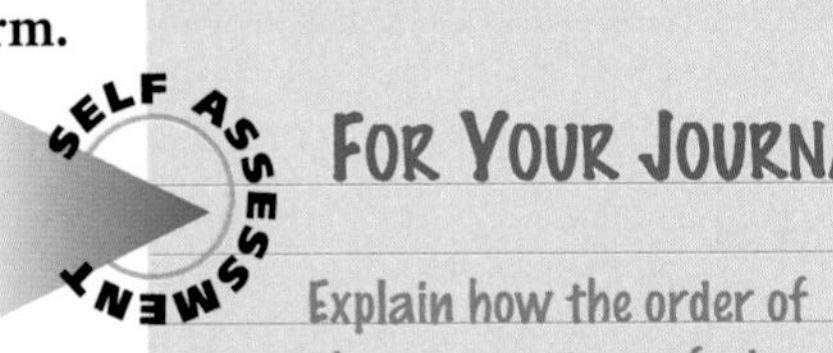

FOR YOUR JOURNAL

Explain how the order of operations prevents confusion when you are simplifying an expression.

Getting Ready for Lesson 1-4

Use the number line at the right.

38. What number corresponds to point A on the number line?

39. How far is B from zero?

40. How far is D from zero?

41. How far is C from zero?

42. How far is A from D?

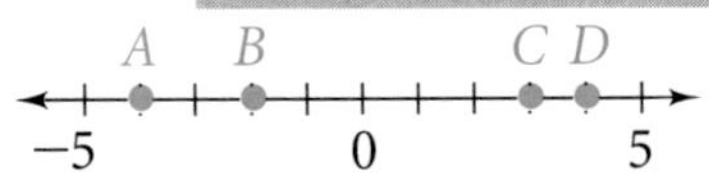

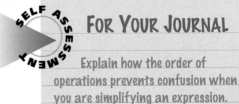

CHAPTER 1

Preparing for Standardized Tests

For Exercises 1–11, choose the correct letter.

1. Which of the following are true for the given data? 1, 2, 2, 2, 4, 4, 5, 6, 6, 7, 7
   I. mode > median **II.** mean < mode
   III. mean > median **IV.** median > mode
   A. I and III **B.** II and IV **C.** I and II
   D. III and IV **E.** I, II, and III

2. Simplify $2(5-3)^2 + 4 \div 2$.
   A. 6 **B.** 8 **C.** 10
   D. 18 **E.** None of the above

3. Evaluate $\frac{3x-(-4)}{7}$ for $x = -6$.
   A. –2 **B.** –3 **C.** 2
   D. 3 **E.** None of the above

4. You can find the distance *d* an object falls in feet for time *t* in seconds using the formula $d = 16t^2$. How far will a ball dropped out of the window of a high rise fall in 3 s?
   A. 96 ft **B.** 160 ft **C.** 144 ft
   D. 16 ft **E.** 48 ft

5. The Fuller Book Company inspects a sample of 860 books and finds that 172 books have defective bindings. What is the probability that a book has a defective binding?
   A. $\frac{1}{4}$ **B.** $\frac{1}{3}$ **C.** $\frac{1}{2}$
   D. $\frac{1}{5}$ **E.** None of the above

6. Which of the following expressions does *not* equal 27 when $x = -3$?
   A. $-x^3$ **B.** $-9x$ **C.** $-(-x)^3$
   D. $3x^2$ **E.** $24 - x$

7. Tamara's teacher allows students to decide whether to use the mean, median, or mode for their test average. Tamara will receive the highest average if she uses the mean. Which set of test scores are Tamara's?
   A. 95, 82, 76, 95, 96
   B. 79, 80, 91, 83, 80
   C. 65, 84, 75, 74, 65
   D. 100, 87, 94, 94, 81
   E. 89, 82, 84, 89, 79

8. Complete the following: $8^2 \cdot \blacksquare = 4^2$
   A. 4 **B.** 2^4 **C.** $\frac{1}{8}$ **D.** 2^3 **E.** $\frac{1}{4}$

9. Which of the following lists the numbers in order from least to greatest?
   A. $\frac{5}{6}, \frac{2}{5}, \frac{6}{7}$ **B.** $\frac{2}{5}, \frac{5}{6}, \frac{6}{7}$ **C.** $\frac{6}{7}, \frac{5}{6}, \frac{2}{5}$
   D. $\frac{2}{5}, \frac{6}{7}, \frac{5}{6}$ **E.** None of the above

Compare the boxed quantity in column A with the boxed quantity in column B. Choose the best answer.

A. The quantity in Column A is greater.
B. The quantity in Column B is greater.
C. The two quantities are equal.
D. The relationship cannot be determined on the basis of the information supplied.

	Column A	Column B
10.	-3^4	-4^3

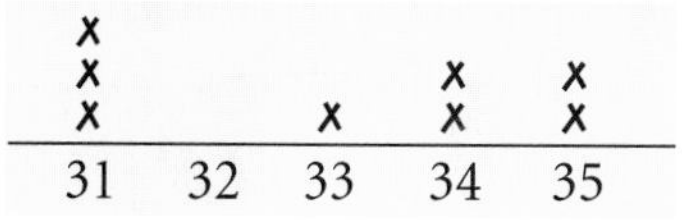

	Column A	Column B
11.	median of data in line plot	mode of data in line plot

Find each answer.

12. $\begin{bmatrix} -2 & -1 \\ 3 & 0 \end{bmatrix} - \begin{bmatrix} -1 & 2 \\ 0 & 1 \end{bmatrix}$

13. Evaluate $\frac{|x-2|}{|2x+10|}$ for $x = -4$.

14. Find $\frac{3}{8} \div \frac{5}{16}$.

15. **Writing** Use the order of operations to explain why the statement $2(5+4) = 2(5) + 4$ is false.

16. Simplify $\frac{3^2 + 3^2 + 3^2}{4^2 + 4^2 + 4^2}$.

1-6 Real Numbers and Rational Numbers

What You'll Learn

- Comparing and ordering rational numbers
- Evaluating expressions with rational numbers

...And Why

To solve real-world problems, such as converting temperatures

What You'll Need

- calculator

THINK AND DISCUSS

Comparing Rational Numbers

The Venn diagram shows the relationship of sets of numbers.

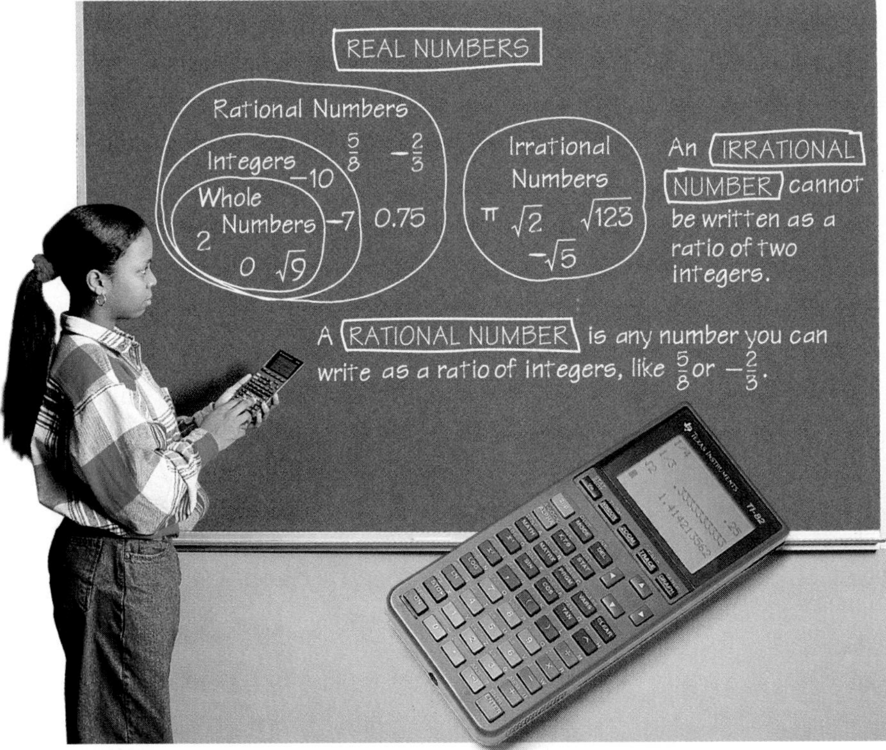

QUICK REVIEW

$\frac{1}{4} = 0.25$, which is a terminating decimal.

$\frac{1}{3} = 0.\overline{3}$, which is a repeating decimal.

Integers are rational numbers because you can write them as ratios using 1 as the denominator: $7 = \frac{7}{1}$. Rational and irrational numbers make up the set of **real numbers.**

1. Write three numbers that are rational numbers but not integers. Choose numbers different from the ones in the diagram above.
2. Show that 0.75 is a rational number by writing it as a ratio.
3. *Open-ended* Where have you used irrational numbers?
4. *Calculator* Use a calculator to find the square root of the numbers 1 through 10. Which do you think are rational? irrational?

An irrational number expressed in decimal form is a nonterminating and nonrepeating decimal. If you use a calculator to express an irrational number as a decimal, the calculator gives you a decimal approximation.

When you compare two real numbers, only one of these can be true:

$a < b$	or	$a = b$	or	$a > b$
less than		**equal to**		**greater than**

Example 1

Use a number line to compare $-\frac{1}{8}$ and $-\frac{1}{2}$.

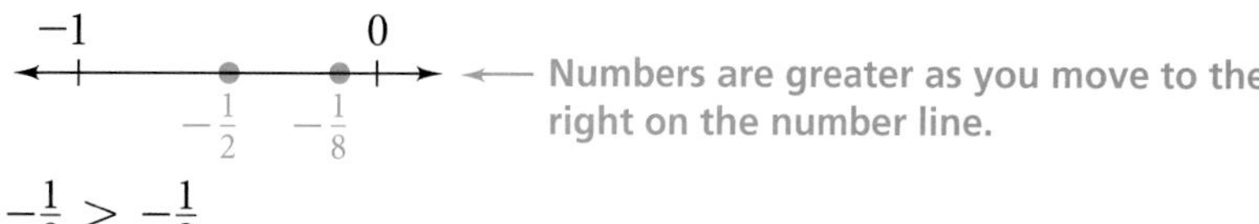

$-\frac{1}{8} > -\frac{1}{2}$

5. Rewrite the answer to Example 1 using the symbol for *less than*.
6. Critical Thinking Suppose you are comparing $-25\frac{1}{2}$ and $-25\frac{1}{8}$. Do you need a different number line from the one in Example 1 to determine which mixed number is greater? Explain.

Many ratios are not easy to compare using a number line. Another method is to write the ratios as decimals and then compare.

Example 2

Write $-\frac{3}{8}$, $-\frac{1}{2}$, and $-\frac{5}{12}$ in order from least to greatest.

Use a calculator to write the rational numbers as decimals.

$-\frac{3}{8}$	(−) 3 ÷ 8 ENTER	−.375
$-\frac{1}{2}$	(−) 1 ÷ 2 ENTER	−.5
$-\frac{5}{12}$	(−) 5 ÷ 12 ENTER	−.4166666667

$-0.5 < -0.41\overline{6} < -0.375$

From least to greatest the ratios are $-\frac{1}{2}$, $-\frac{5}{12}$, and $-\frac{3}{8}$.

7. Try This Write $\frac{1}{12}$, $-\frac{2}{3}$, and $-\frac{5}{8}$ in order from least to greatest.

Evaluating Expressions

You evaluate expressions using rational numbers by substituting and performing the indicated operations.

Example 3

Evaluate $a + 2b$ where $a = \frac{2}{3}$ and $b = -\frac{5}{8}$.

$a + 2b = \frac{2}{3} + 2\left(-\frac{5}{8}\right)$ ← Substitute the values for *a* and *b*.

$= \frac{2}{3} - \frac{5}{4}$

$= -\frac{7}{12}$

CALCULATOR HINT

You can use this key sequence:

Example 4 Relating to the Real World

For practice with fractions, see Skills Handbook pages 575–579.

Weather Use the expression $\frac{5}{9}(F - 32)$ to change from the Fahrenheit scale to the Celsius scale. What is 10°F in Celsius?

$\frac{5}{9}(F - 32) = \frac{5}{9}(10 - 32)$ ← Substitute 10 for *F*.

$= \frac{5}{9}(-22)$

≈ -12

The temperature is about −12°C.

F C
90° ?
10° ?

8. Find the Celsius temperature when the Fahrenheit temperature is 90°.

The **reciprocal,** or *multiplicative inverse,* of a nonzero number $\frac{a}{b}$ is $\frac{b}{a}$. Zero does not have a reciprocal because division by zero is undefined.

9. a. Patterns Complete the chart.

b. What is the product of a number and its reciprocal?

10. Is a number's reciprocal the same as its opposite? Explain.

Number	Reciprocal	Product
3	$\frac{1}{3}$	$3 \cdot \frac{1}{3} = ■$
$\frac{1}{5}$	$\frac{5}{1}$ or 5	$\frac{1}{5} \cdot 5 = ■$
$-\frac{2}{3}$	$-\frac{3}{2}$	$-\frac{2}{3} \cdot \left(-\frac{3}{2}\right) = ■$

You know $12 \div 3 = 12 \cdot \frac{1}{3}$. This means that dividing by a nonzero number is the same as multiplying by its reciprocal.

$$a \div \frac{b}{c} = a \cdot \frac{c}{b} \text{ for } b \neq 0 \text{ and } c \neq 0$$

Example 5

Evaluate $\frac{x}{y}$ for $x = -\frac{3}{4}$ and $y = -\frac{5}{2}$.

$\frac{x}{y} = x \div y$

$= -\frac{3}{4} \div \left(-\frac{5}{2}\right)$

$= -\frac{3}{4} \cdot \left(-\frac{2}{5}\right)$ ← Multiply by $-\frac{2}{5}$, the reciprocal of $-\frac{5}{2}$.

$= \frac{3}{10}$

11. Try This Evaluate the expression in Example 5 for $x = 8$ and $y = -\frac{4}{5}$.

Exercises ON YOUR OWN

Use <, =, or > to compare.

1. $1\frac{2}{3}$ ■ $1\frac{1}{6}$

2. $-1\frac{2}{3}$ ■ $-1\frac{1}{6}$

3. $\frac{15}{8}$ ■ $1\frac{6}{8}$

4. $\frac{3}{5}$ ■ 0.6

5. $\frac{1}{2}$ ■ $\frac{1}{4}$

6. 0.14 ■ $\frac{1}{7}$

7. $-17\frac{1}{5}$ ■ $-17\frac{1}{4}$

8. -3.02 ■ -3.002

Complete with a rational number that makes each statement true.

9. $\frac{3}{5} \cdot \blacksquare = 1$

10. $-4 \cdot \blacksquare = 1$

11. $\blacksquare \cdot \frac{7}{8} = 1$

12. $\blacksquare \cdot \left(-\frac{8}{3}\right) = 1$

Evaluate.

13. $x - \frac{3}{4}$ for $x = -1\frac{1}{4}$

14. $a - b$ for $a = -\frac{1}{2}, b = \frac{1}{5}$

15. rs for $r = \frac{2}{15}, s = 5$

16. $-p + t$ for $p = 1\frac{3}{8}, t = \frac{5}{8}$

17. $2xy$ for $x = -\frac{2}{3}, y = -\frac{3}{4}$

18. $\frac{v}{w}$ for $v = -\frac{5}{8}, w = -\frac{5}{6}$

19. ab for $a = 2\frac{1}{4}, b = -3$

20. $\frac{m}{n}$ for $m = -\frac{1}{2}, n = 5$

21. $\frac{1}{2}(q - p)$ for $q = 4, p = -\frac{1}{3}$

22. $4rs$ for $r = -3\frac{1}{4}, s = -\frac{1}{5}$

23. $b + c$ for $b = -2\frac{1}{3}, c = \frac{1}{4}$

24. $\frac{1}{5}z - y$ for $z = 1.5, y = 0.3$

Write each group of numbers in order from least to greatest.

25. $-\frac{1}{2}, -\frac{2}{3}, \frac{1}{4}$

26. $-1.5, -\frac{4}{3}, -1\frac{1}{4}$

27. $-9.7, -9\frac{7}{12}, -9\frac{3}{4}$

28. $-4.12, -4.22, -4.05$

29. **Science** Air temperature drops as altitude increases. In the formula $t = (-5.5)\left(\frac{a}{1000}\right)$, t is the approximate change in Fahrenheit temperature, and a is the increase in altitude in feet.
   a. Find the change in temperature for the balloon.
   b. Suppose the temperature is 40°F at ground level. What is the approximate temperature at the balloon?
   c. **Research** Find the height of a mountain that is near you or that you are interested in. Suppose the temperature at the base of the mountain is 80°F. What is the approximate temperature at the top of the mountain?

30. **Weather** In the formula $w = -39 + \frac{3}{2}t$, w is the approximate windchill temperature when the wind speed is 20 mi/h, and t is the actual air temperature. Find the approximate windchill temperature when the actual air temperature is 10°F and the wind speed is 20 mi/h.

Rewrite each expression using the symbol ÷, then find each quotient.

Sample $\frac{-\frac{7}{12}}{4} = -\frac{7}{12} \div 4$ ← Rewrite as $-\frac{7}{12} \div 4$.

$= -\frac{7}{12} \cdot \left(\frac{1}{4}\right)$ ← Multiply by $\frac{1}{4}$, the reciprocal of 4.

$= -\frac{7}{48}$

31. $\frac{\frac{3}{8}}{-\frac{2}{3}}$

32. $\frac{5}{\frac{4}{9}}$

33. $\frac{-\frac{5}{6}}{8}$

34. $\frac{-\frac{2}{5}}{-\frac{4}{5}}$

35. a. **Open-ended** Name a point between -2 and -3 on a number line.
   b. Name a point between -2.8 and -2.9.
   c. Name a point between $-2\frac{1}{16}$ and $-2\frac{3}{8}$.
   d. On a number line, is it possible to find a point between any two given points? Explain.

Evaluate.

36. $x + y$ for $x = \frac{13}{4}, y = -\frac{5}{2}$

37. $\frac{1}{5}(r - t)$ for $r = 6, t = -7$

38. $\frac{3}{4}w - 7$ for $w = 1\frac{1}{3}$

39. $\frac{x}{2y}$ for $x = 3.6, y = -0.4$

40. $\frac{3a}{b} + c$ for $a = -2, b = -5, c = -1$

41. $\frac{n}{m}$ for $n = -\frac{4}{5}, m = 8$

Writing **Decide if each statement is *true* or *false*. Justify your answer.**

42. All integers are rational numbers.

43. All negative numbers are integers.

44. All rational numbers are integers.

45. Some real numbers are integers.

Exercises MIXED REVIEW

For Exercises 46–48, write an equation to model each situation.

46. the cost of several movie tickets that are \$6.26 each

47. the change from a \$10 bill after a purchase

48. the total cost of an item with a shipping fee of \$3.98.

49. **Real Estate** Boulder City, Nevada, bought 107,500 acres of land in Nevada's Eldorado Valley from the United States government. The price was \$12/acre. How much did the city pay for the land?

Getting Ready for Lesson 1-7

50. **Probability** How much of the spinner is red? yellow? blue?

A Point in Time

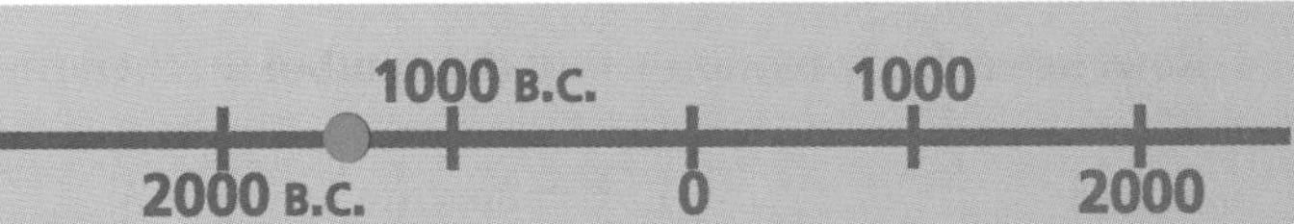

The Rhind Papyrus

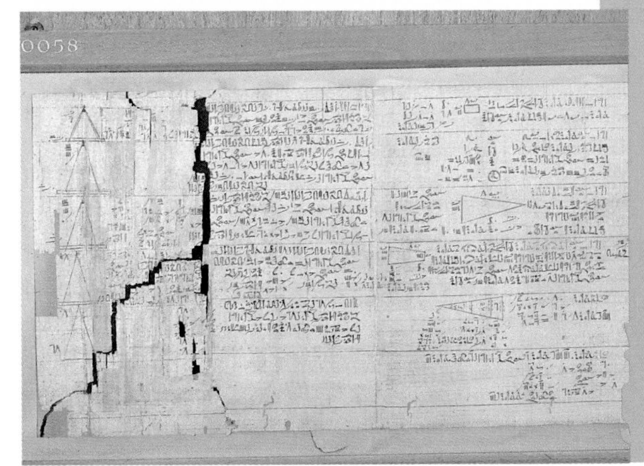

A scroll discovered in Egypt shows that Egyptians were using symbols for plus, minus, equals, and an unknown quantity over 3500 years ago. Named for the British Egyptologist A. Henry Rhind, the papyrus is 18 ft long and 1 ft wide. It is a practical handbook containing 85 problems including work with rational numbers. In the Rhind Papyrus, rational numbers are written as unit fractions. A unit fraction has 1 as its numerator. Here are some examples.

$\frac{3}{4} = \frac{1}{2} + \frac{1}{4}$ $\quad \frac{3}{8} = \frac{1}{4} + \frac{1}{8}$ $\quad \frac{21}{30} = \frac{1}{6} + \frac{1}{5} + \frac{1}{3}$

The Coordinate Plane

The **coordinate plane** is formed when two number lines intersect at right angles. The horizontal axis is the ***x*-axis** and the vertical axis is the ***y*-axis.** The axes intersect at the **origin** and divide the coordinate plane into four sections called **quadrants.**

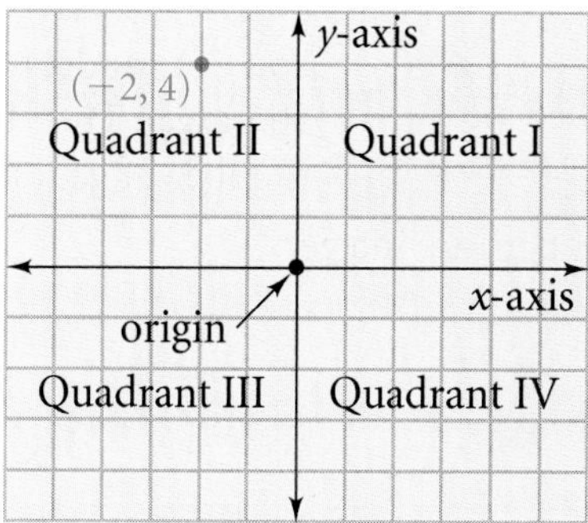

An **ordered pair** of numbers identifies the location of a point. These numbers are the **coordinates** of the point.

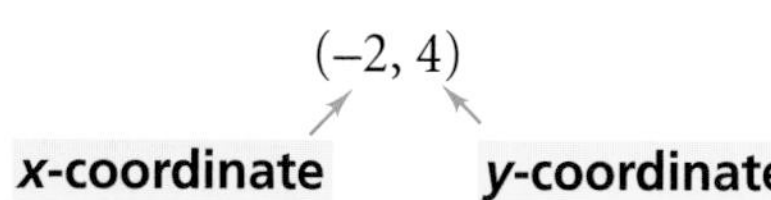

Name the point with the given coordinates in the graph at the right.

1. (2, 3) **2.** (−5, −3)

3. (−3, 2) **4.** (0, −5)

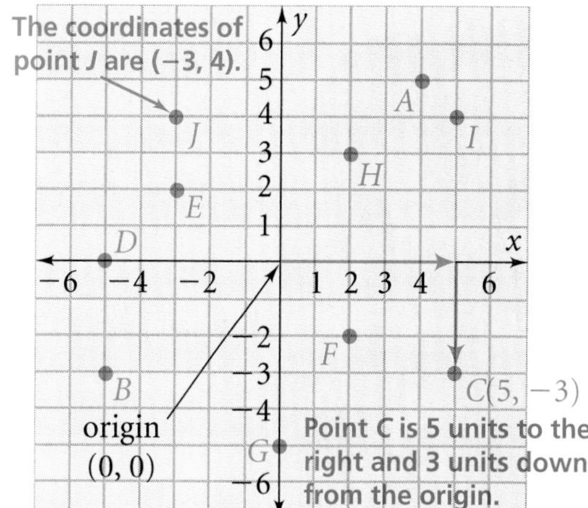

Name the coordinates of each point in the graph at the right.

5. *A* **6.** *F*

7. *D* **8.** *I*

Graph each point on a coordinate plane.

9. (3, 0) **10.** (−1, 8)

11. (−2, −3) **12.** (7, −7)

In which quadrant or on which axis would you find each point?

13. (−10, 6) **14.** (−12, 0) **15.** (8, −18) **16.** (0, 30)

17. a. Graph each point on a coordinate plane.
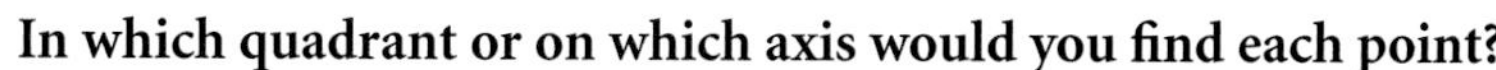
(−4, 0), (0, 1), (1, 5), (2, 1), (6, 0), (2, −1), (1, −5),(0, −1), (−4, 0)

b. Connect the points in order and describe the figure formed.

18. *Writing* Write a sentence describing the *x*- and *y*-coordinates of all points in Quadrant IV.

What You'll Learn

- Graphing a function
- Creating a table of values from a rule and a graph

...And Why

To solve problems involving electrician costs

2-6 The Three Views of a Function

THINK AND DISCUSS

You can model functions using rules, tables, and graphs. Suppose a car gets 30 mi/gal. Then the distance $d(g)$ that the car travels is a function of the number of gallons g.

Rule

$d(g) = 30g$

A function rule shows how the variables are related.

Table of Values

Gallons	Miles
g	$d(g)$
0	0
1	30
2	60
3	90

A table identifies specific values that satisfy the function.

Graph

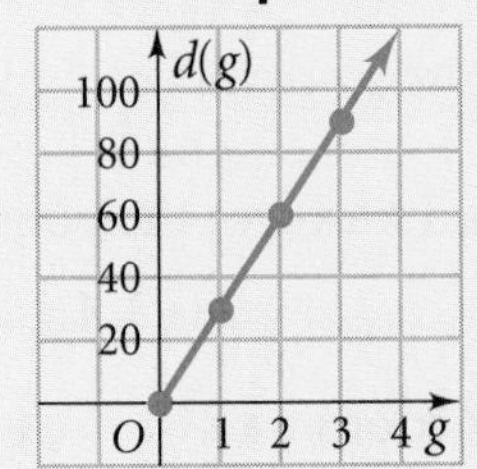

A graph gives a visual picture of the function.

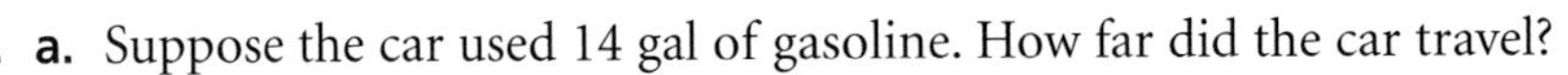

1. a. Suppose the car used 14 gal of gasoline. How far did the car travel?
   b. How did you find your answer to part (a)?
   c. Describe another method of solving the problem.

You can use a rule to model a function with a table of values and a graph.

Example 1 *Relating to the Real World*

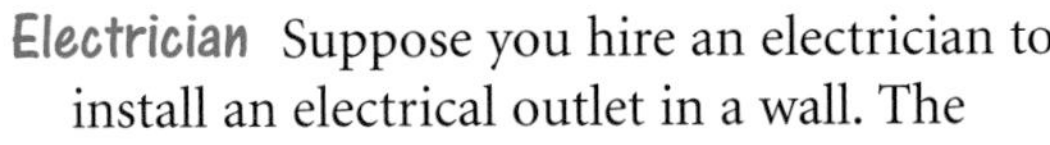

Electrician Suppose you hire an electrician to install an electrical outlet in a wall. The electrician charges \$68 for materials plus \$40 an hour for service. The total cost $C(h)$ is a function of the number of hours it takes to do the job. Use the rule $C(h) = 68 + 40h$ to make a table of values and then a graph.

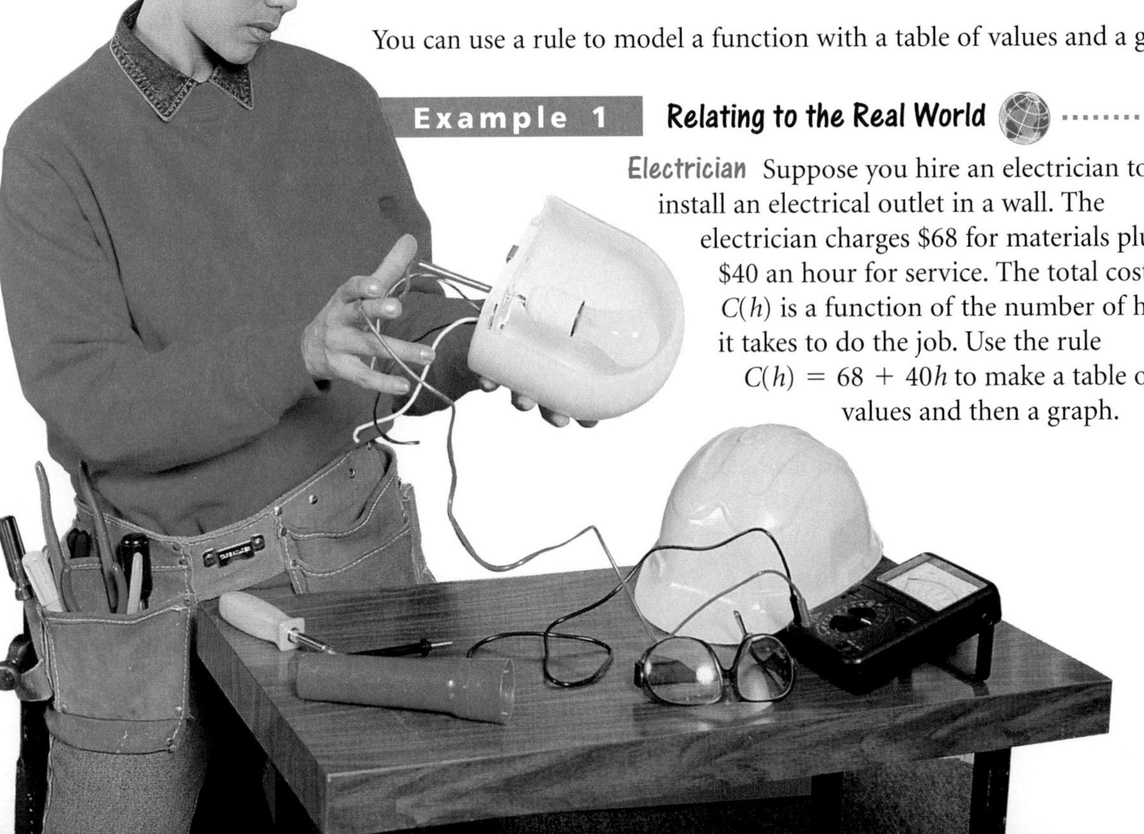

STEP 1:
Choose values for h that seem reasonable, such as 1, 2.5, 4, and 7.

STEP 2:
Input the values for h. Evaluate to find $C(h)$.

h	$C(h) = 68 + 40h$	$(h, C(h))$
1	$68 + 40(1) = 108$	$(1, 108)$
2.5	$68 + 40(2.5) = 168$	$(2.5, 168)$
4	$68 + 40(4) = 228$	$(4, 228)$
7	$68 + 40(7) = 348$	$(7, 348)$

STEP 3:
Plot the ordered pairs.

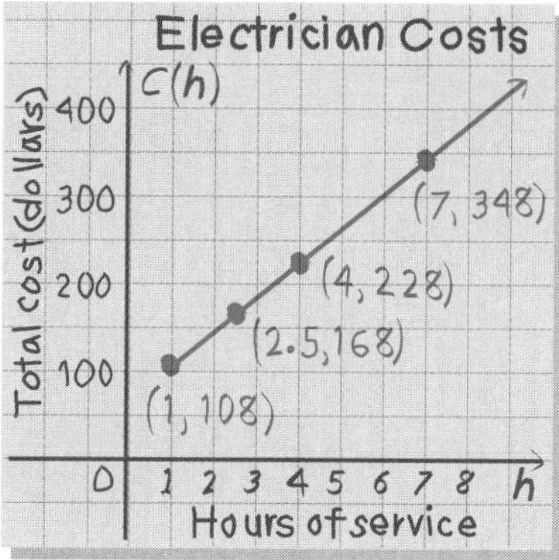

2. **a.** What is the total cost of the job if it takes $5\frac{1}{2}$ hours?
   b. Did you use the rule, the table, or the graph to answer part (a)?
3. Why are the points on the graph connected by a line?
4. Are negative values for h reasonable? Explain.
5. **Electrician** Suppose this electrician tells you the job will take 2 to 6 hours to complete. What is the range of your costs?
6. **Try This** Model each rule with a table of values and a graph.
   a. $f(x) = -3x + 5$ **b.** $f(x) = \frac{1}{2}x$

QUICK REVIEW

You can also write a function rule using "$y =$ " form. For example, $f(x) = x^2 - x - 6$ is equivalent to $y = x^2 - x - 6$.

Some functions have graphs that are not straight lines. You can graph a function as long as you know its rule.

Example 2

Graph the function $y = x^2 - x - 6$.

First, make a table of values.

x	$y = x^2 - x - 6$	(x, y)
-2	$(-2)^2 - (-2) - 6 = 0$	$(-2, 0)$
-1	$(-1)^2 - (-1) - 6 = -4$	$(-1, -4)$
0	$(0)^2 - (0) - 6 = -6$	$(0, -6)$
1	$(1)^2 - (1) - 6 = -6$	$(1, -6)$
2	$(2)^2 - (2) - 6 = -4$	$(2, -4)$
3	$(3)^2 - (3) - 6 = 0$	$(3, 0)$

Then graph the data.

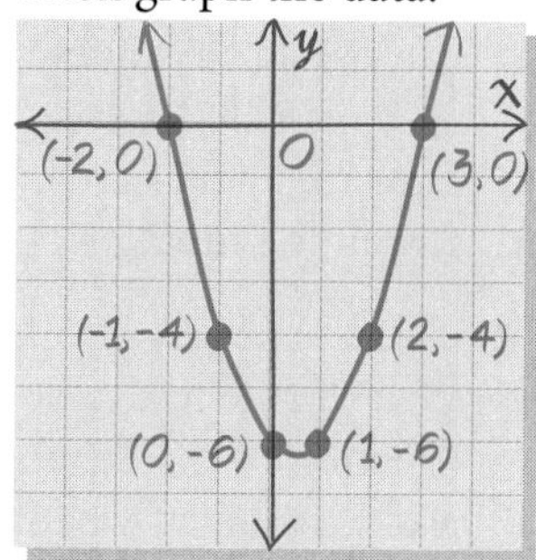

7. What advantage(s) does a rule have in describing a function?
8. **Try This** Graph each function.
   a. $y = -3x^2 + 1$ **b.** $f(x) = x^2 - 4x - 5$

You can create a table of values from a graph.

Example 3

Make a table of values for the graph below.

Use the scale of the graph to find ordered pairs.

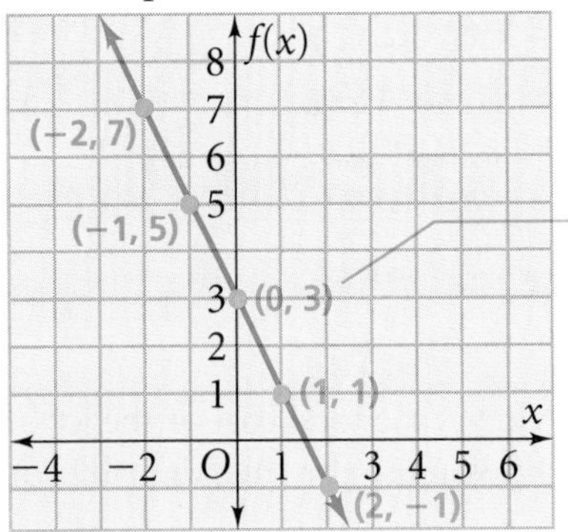

Put the ordered pairs in a table.

x	$f(x)$
−2	7
−1	5
0	3
1	1
2	−1

Exercises ON YOUR OWN

Model each rule with a table of values and a graph.

1. $y = -3x$ **2.** $y = x^2 - 4x + 4$ **3.** $f(x) = 2x - 7$ **4.** $y = 6x^2$

5. $f(x) = \frac{1}{3}x$ **6.** $f(x) = 8 - x$ **7.** $f(x) = x^2 - 2$ **8.** $y = 5 + 4x$

9. Patterns The table of values below describes the perimeter of each figure in the pattern of blue tiles at the right. The perimeter P is a function of the number of tiles t.

Number of Tiles (t)	1	2	3	4
Perimeter (P)	4	6	8	10

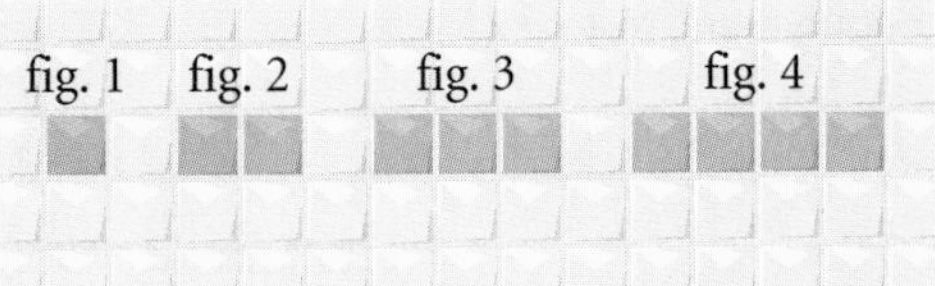

a. Choose a rule to describe the function in the table.
A. $P = t + 3$ B. $P = 4t$ C. $P = 2t + 2$ D. $P = 6t - 2$

b. How many tiles are in the figure if the perimeter is 20?

c. Graph the function.

10. Jobs Juan charges $3.50 per hour for baby-sitting.

a. Write a rule to describe how the amount of money M earned is a function of the number of hours h spent baby-sitting.

b. Make a table of values.

c. Graph the function.

d. Estimation Use the graph to estimate how long it will take Juan to earn $30.

e. Critical Thinking Do you think of baby-sitting data as discrete or continuous? Explain your reasoning.

Quick Review

Continuous data are usually measurements, such as temperatures and lengths. *Discrete data* are distinct counts, such as numbers of people or objects.

11. Conservation Use the data at the right.

a. Write a function rule for a standard shower head.

b. Write a function rule for a water-saving shower head.

c. Suppose you take a 6-min shower as recommended and use a water-saving head. How much water do you save compared to an average shower with a standard head?

d. Graph both functions on the same coordinate plane. What does the graph show you?

e. Open-ended How much water did you use during your last shower? How did you find your answer?

How Long Does Your Shower Last?

• average shower: 12.2 min

• recommended shower: 6 min

• standard head uses 6 gal/min

• water-saving head cuts water flow in half

Source: *Opinion Research Corp.*

Graph each function.

12. $f(x) = x - 2$

13. $y = -10x$

14. $y = \frac{3}{4}x + 7$

15. $f(x) = x^2$

16. $y = x^2 - 3x + 2$

17. $f(x) = x$

18. $f(x) = x^2 - 9$

19. $y = 7 - 5x$

20. $f(x) = 6x + 1$

21. $f(x) = x - 3$

22. $y = x + \frac{1}{2}$

23. $y = 3.5x$

24. $f(x) = 4x$

25. $y = 1 - x^2$

26. $f(x) = 12 - x$

27. $f(x) = -5x^2$

Make a table of values for each graph.

28.

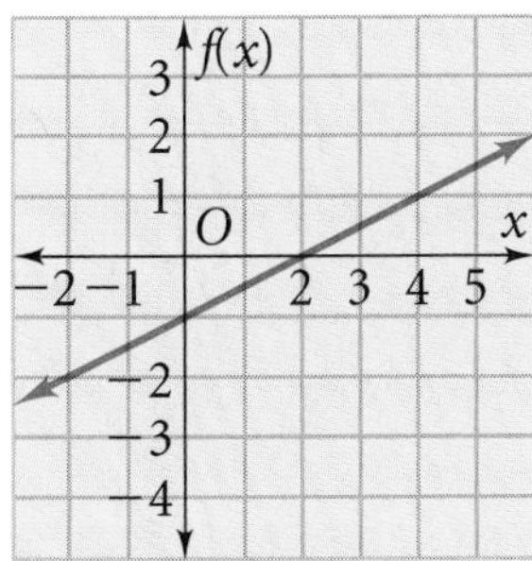

29.

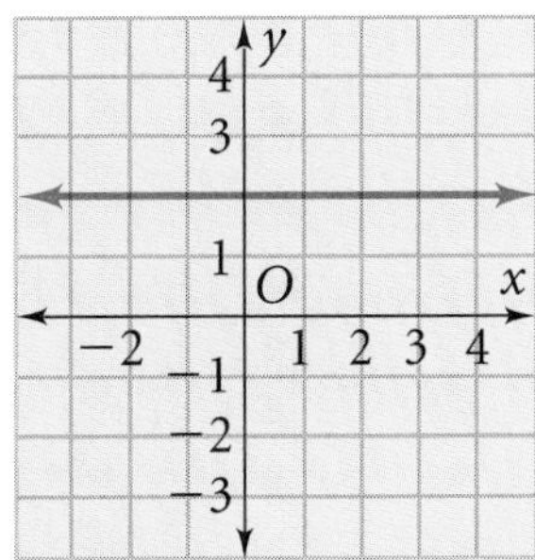

30.

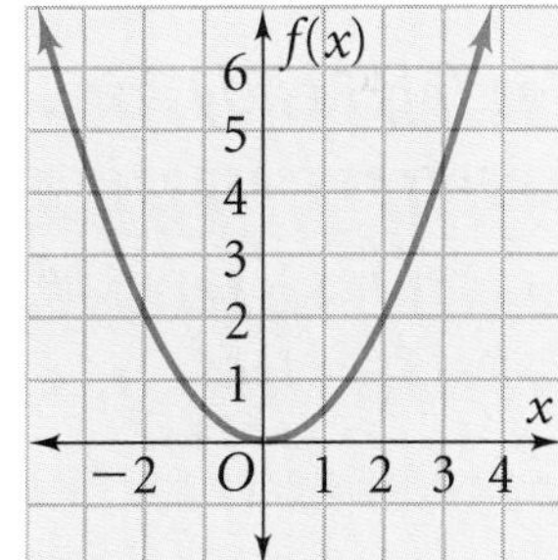

31. Communications The cost $C(a)$ of a call from Boston to Worcester, Massachusetts, is a function of the number of additional minutes a. The rule $C(a) = 0.27 + 0.11a$ closely models the cost.

a. How much will a 5-min call cost? (*Hint:* The number of additional minutes is one minute less than the length of the call.)

b. Calculator Make a table of values and graph the function.

c. Critical Thinking Suppose you don't want to spend any more than \$1.50 on this phone call. How many minutes can you talk?

32. a. Research Find the rate for weekday telephone calls in your area.

b. Write a rule to describe the cost of the call. Be sure to define your variables.

c. Calculator Make a table of values and graph the function.

33. Standardized Test Prep Which function is modeled by the table?

A. $f(x) = x - 2$

B. $f(x) = 2x + 1$

C. $f(x) = 2x$

D. $f(x) = -x + 1$

E. $f(x) = \frac{1}{2}x - 1$

x	$f(x)$
−3	−5
0	1
2	5
5	11

34. **Geometry** The function $A(l) = \frac{1}{2}l^2$ describes the area of an isosceles right triangle with leg l.

a. Make a table of values for $l = 1, 2, 3, 4$.

b. Graph the function.

35. **Writing** Suppose a student was not in class today. Describe to the student how to graph a function rule.

Exercises MIXED REVIEW

Use the scatter plot at the right.

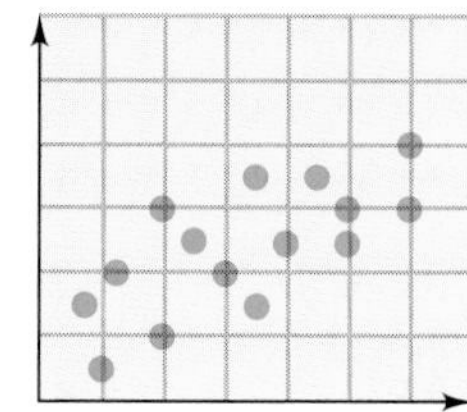

36. What kind of correlation does the scatter plot show?

37. a. **Open-ended** Describe a situation the scatter plot might represent.

b. What would you label your axes?

Find the range of each function when the domain is {–2, 0, 1, 4}.

38. $f(x) = x - 1$

39. $f(c) = 2c + 7$

40. $f(z) = \frac{1}{4}z$

41. $f(w) = -w + 2$

42. $f(t) = -2t$

Getting Ready for Lesson 2-7

Simplify each expression.

43. $-4|5|$

44. $|-5| + |-3.5|$

45. $|-8 + 4|$

46. $|-9.6|$

47. $3 - |-4|$

A Point in Time

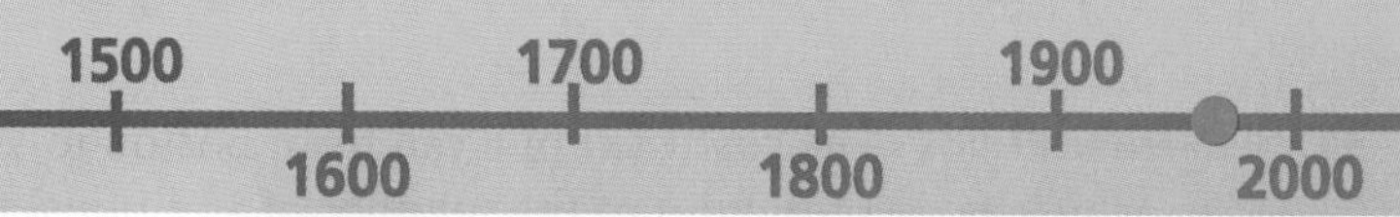

Romana Acosta Bañuelos

In 1971, Romana Acosta Bañuelos became the first Mexican American woman to hold the office of United States Treasurer. Before her appointment to this post by President Nixon, she founded and managed her own multimillion-dollar food enterprise and established the Pan American National Bank of East Los Angeles. As a highly successful businesswoman, she had to work on a daily basis with interest rates, balance sheets, investments, and other functions used in the corporate world.

CHAPTER 2

Cumulative Review

For Exercises 1–9, choose the correct letter.

1. Which line plot shows the following set of data? 0, 2, 4, 0, 5, 1, 2, 3, 5, 0, 1, 2

A.
```
X   X   X X
X X X X X X
-----------
0 1 2 3 4 5
```

B.
```
X   X
X X X     X
X X X X X X
-----------
0 1 2 3 4 5
```

C.
```
X X X X X X
X X X X X X
-----------
0 1 2 3 4 5
```

D.
```
X
X X   X
X X X X X X
-----------
0 1 2 3 4 5
```

E. None of the above

2. Which of the following expressions has a value of 48?

I. $8 + 2 \cdot 4 \cdot 3$

II. $[8 + (2 \cdot 4)] \cdot 3$

III. $(8 + 2) \cdot 4 \cdot 3$

A. I only **B.** II only **C.** II and III
D. I and III **E.** I, II, and III

3. Which of the following is a multiple of 4?
A. 3654 **B.** 8647 **C.** 19,354
D. 28,640 **E.** 78,454

4. Which spreadsheet formula can you use to find the mean of four numbers?
A. A1 + B1 + C1 + D1/4
B. A1 * B1 * C1 * D1
C. (A1 + B1 + C1 + D1) * 4
D. (A1 + B1 + C1 + D1)/4
E. A1 + B1 + C1 + D1

5. Which matrix is the difference of
$\begin{bmatrix} 8 & -7 \\ 3 & -5 \end{bmatrix} - \begin{bmatrix} 4 & 0 \\ -2 & -4 \end{bmatrix}$?

A. $\begin{bmatrix} 4 & 7 \\ 5 & 1 \end{bmatrix}$ **B.** $\begin{bmatrix} 4 & -7 \\ 1 & -1 \end{bmatrix}$

C. $\begin{bmatrix} 4 & -7 \\ 5 & -1 \end{bmatrix}$ **D.** $\begin{bmatrix} 4 & -7 \\ 1 & -9 \end{bmatrix}$

E. None of the above

6. Find the sixth term of the pattern 14, 9, 4, ...
A. –13 **B.** –11 **C.** –1 **D.** 8 **E.** –14

7. Find $f(-2)$ when $f(x) = -3x^2 + 4x$.
A. 4 **B.** –20 **C.** –4 **D.** 12 **E.** 26

8. Choose the pair of coordinates that lie on the graph shown.

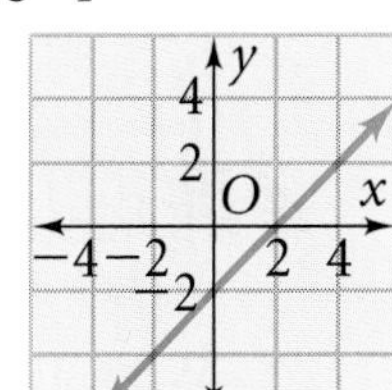

A. (–1, 1), (1, 3)
B. (–1, 2), (1, –2)
C. (–1, 3), (1, 1)
D. (–1, 2), (1, –2)
E. (–1, –3), (1, –1)

9. Compare the quantities in Column A and Column B.

Column A	Column B
$\frac{1}{2}$ of $\frac{3}{4}$	$\frac{1}{4}$ of $\frac{3}{5}$

A. The quantity in Column A is greater.
B. The quantity in Column B is greater.
C. The two quantities are equal.
D. The relationship cannot be determined on the basis of the information supplied.

For Exercises 10–12, write your answer.

10. The table shows the closing prices of a stock over a period of 5 days. Graph this relation and determine if it is a function. Is it a linear function? Explain why or why not.

Day	1	2	3	4	5
Price	12	$12\frac{1}{2}$	$12\frac{1}{4}$	13	$13\frac{1}{4}$

11. Find the range of $f(x) = |2x - 3|$ when the domain is $\{-5, -2, -1\}$.

12. Suppose you have a bag containing 3 red, 4 blue, 5 white, and 2 black marbles. One marble is selected at random.
a. Name a certain event.
b. Name an impossible event.
c. What is P(not selecting white)?
d. *Open-ended* Name an event more likely than choosing red.

Connections Jobs . . . and more

What You'll Learn

- Solving two-step equations
- Using two-step equations to solve real-world problems

...And Why

To solve problems involving money

What You'll Need

- tiles

3-2 Modeling and Solving Two-Step Equations

WORK TOGETHER

Work in pairs. To model equations, use the  tile to represent x.

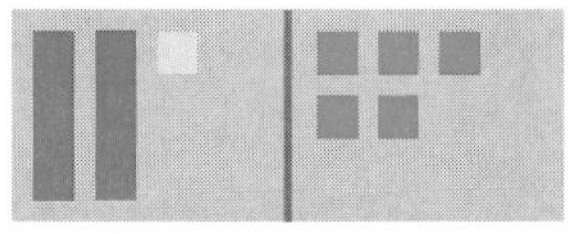

$2x + 1 = -5$

3x − 2 is the same as 3x + (−2).

$3x - 2 = 4$

QUICK REVIEW

▢ represents 1.
■ represents −1.

▢ ■ is a zero pair.

1. Write an equation for each model.
   a. 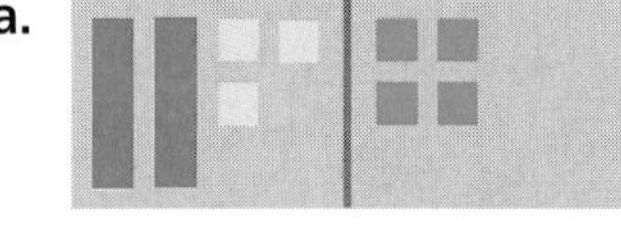
   b. 

2. Use tiles to create a model for each equation.
   a. $2x = 8$
   b. $x + 5 = -7$
   c. $4x + 3 = -5$

THINK AND DISCUSS

Using Tiles

A **two-step equation** is an equation that has two operations. You can use tiles to model and solve a two-step equation.

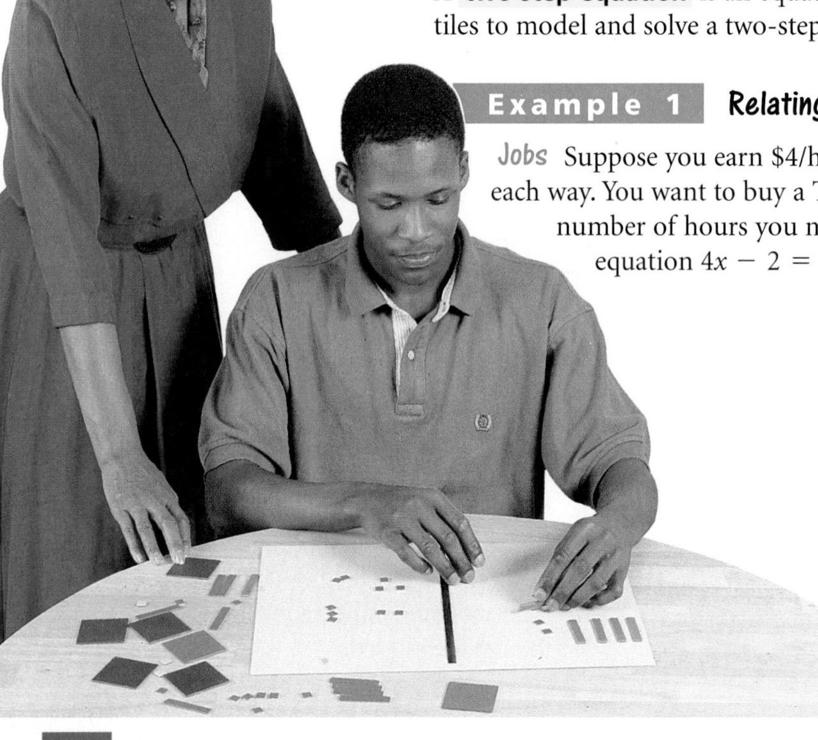

Example 1 **Relating to the Real World**

Jobs Suppose you earn \$4/h baby-sitting and pay \$1 in bus fare each way. You want to buy a T-shirt that costs \$10. To find the number of hours you must work to buy the T-shirt, solve the equation $4x - 2 = 10$.

Model the equation with tiles.

$$4x - 2 = 10$$

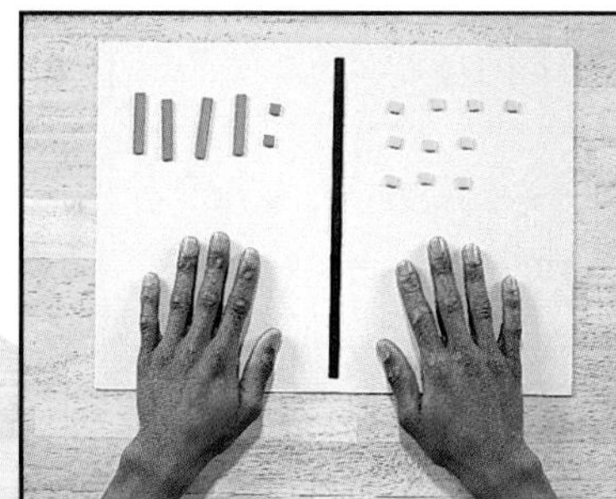

1 Add 2 to each side of the equation. $4x - 2 + 2 = 10 + 2$

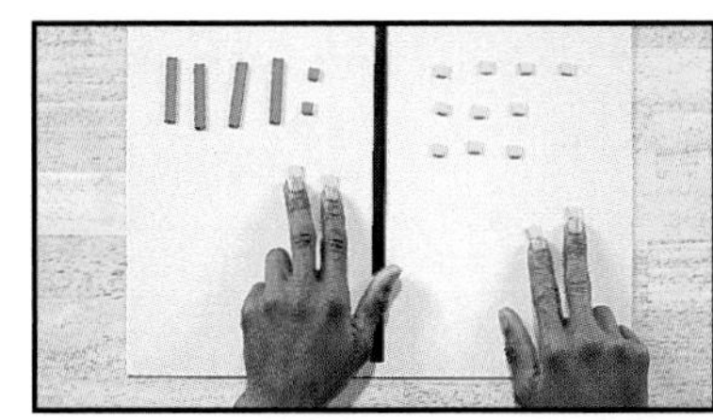

2 Simplify by removing zero pairs. $4x = 12$

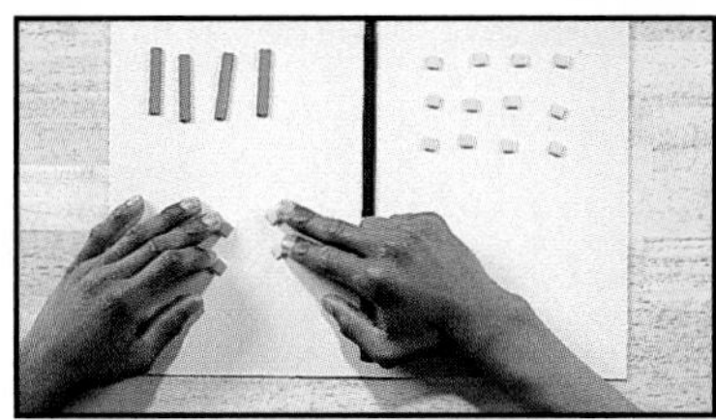

3 Divide each side into four identical groups. $\frac{4x}{4} = \frac{12}{4}$

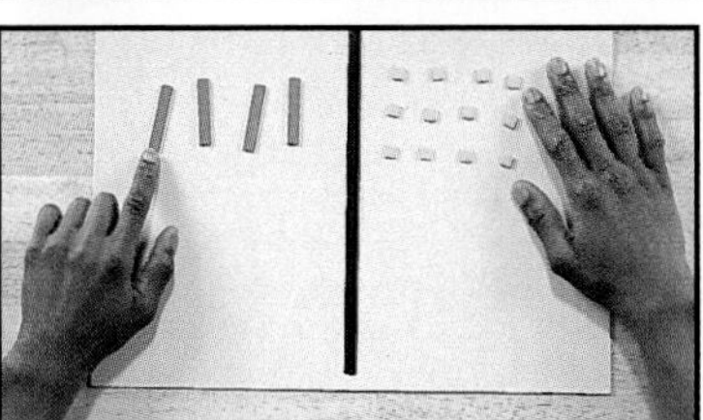

4 Solve for $1x$.

$1x = 3$

$x = 3$

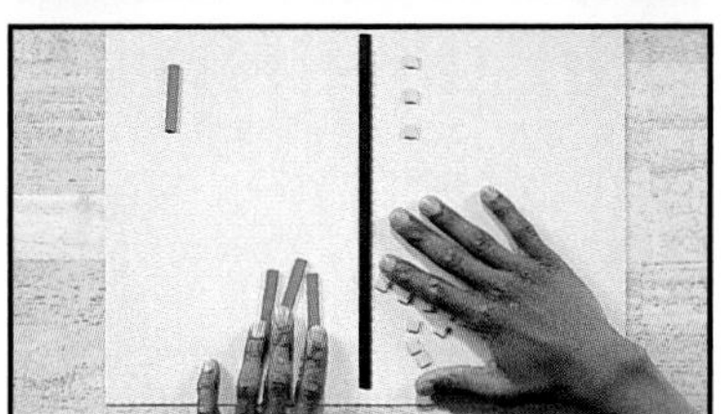

The solution is 3. You must baby-sit for 3 h to buy the T-shirt.

Check

$$4x - 2 = 10$$
$$4(3) - 2 \stackrel{?}{=} 10 \quad \leftarrow \text{Replace } x \text{ with 3.}$$
$$12 - 2 \stackrel{?}{=} 10$$
$$10 = 10 \checkmark$$

3. Which two operations were used to solve the equation? Why?

4. **Try This** Use tiles to model and solve each equation.
a. $2y - 3 = 7$ **b.** $5 = 4m + 1$ **c.** $3z - 2 = -8$

Using Properties

To help you solve equations, you can write them in different ways. The variable x means $1x$. Similarly, $-x$ means $-1x$. Subtracting a variable is the same as adding its opposite. So, you can rewrite $4 - x$ as $4 + (-x)$.

5. It takes two operations to solve the equation $-x + 7 = 12$.
a. Subtract 7 from each side of the equation.
b. Multiply each side of the equation by -1. What is the solution?

6. Solve each equation.
a. $-11 = -b + 6$ **b.** $-9 - m = -2$ **c.** $15 = 3 - x$

Example 2

Solve the equation $1 = -\frac{k}{12} + 5$.

$$1 = -\frac{k}{12} + 5$$
$$1 - 5 = -\frac{k}{12} + 5 - 5 \quad \leftarrow \text{Subtract 5 from each side.}$$
$$-4 = -\frac{k}{12}$$
$$-12(-4) = -12\left(-\frac{k}{12}\right) \quad \leftarrow \text{Multiply each side by } -12.$$
$$48 = k$$

The solution is 48.

7. **a.** Which operations would you use to solve $-4n + 20 = 36$?
   b. **Try This** Solve the equation and check your solution.

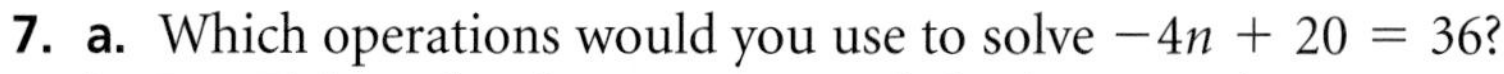

Example 3 Relating to the Real World 

Money Suppose you have \$18.75 to spend at Paradise Park. Admission is \$5.50. How many ride tickets can you buy?

Define r = number of ride tickets you can buy

Relate	entrance fee	plus	cost of ride tickets	equals	total cost
Write	5.5	+	1.5r	=	18.75

$$5.5 + 1.5r = 18.75$$
$$5.5 + 1.5r - 5.5 = 18.75 - 5.5 \quad \leftarrow \text{Subtract 5.5 from each side.}$$
$$1.5r = 13.25$$
$$\frac{1.5r}{1.5} = \frac{13.25}{1.5} \quad \leftarrow \text{Divide each side by 1.5.}$$
$$r \approx 8.8$$

You can buy 8 ride tickets.

CALCULATOR HINT

You can use a calculator to solve this equation. Write it in **calculator-ready form:** $x = (18.75 - 5.5) \div 1.5$. Use the sequence: (18.75 − 5.5) ÷ 1.5 ENTER .

8. Why should 8.8 be rounded to 8 in this situation?
9. If you buy 8 ride tickets, how much money do you have left?

Exercises ON YOUR OWN

Write an equation for each model.

1. 
2. 
3. 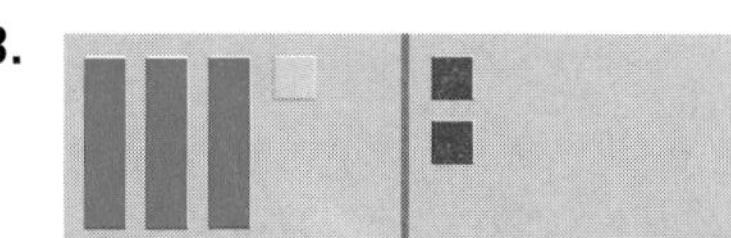

Use tiles to solve each equation.

4. $2n - 5 = 7$
5. $3 + 4x = -1$
6. $3b + 7 = -2$
7. $-10 = -6 + 2y$
8. $5y - 2 = -2$
9. $0 = 3x - 3$
10. $2z + 4 = -6$
11. $4x + 9 = 1$

Solve each equation. Check your solutions.

12. $3x + 2 = 20$
13. $-b + 5 = -16$
14. $\frac{y}{2} + 5 = -12$
15. $7 - 3k = -14$
16. $1 + \frac{m}{4} = -1$
17. $41 = 5 - 6h$
18. $1.3n - 4 = 2.5$
19. $\frac{x}{3} - 9 = 0$
20. $-t - 4 = -3$
21. $3.5 + 10m = 7.32$
22. $7 = -2x + 7$
23. $14 + \frac{h}{5} = 2$

Use an equation to model and solve each problem.

24. Farming An orange grower ships oranges in boxes that weigh 2 kg. Each orange weighs 0.2 kg. The total weight of a box filled with oranges is 10 kg. How many oranges are packed in each box?

25. Food Preparation Suppose you are helping to prepare a large meal. You can peel 2 carrots/min. You need 60 peeled carrots. How long will it take you to finish if you have already peeled 18 carrots?

26. You can find the value of each variable in the matrices at the right by writing and solving equations. For example, solving the equation $2a + 1 = 11$, you get $a = 5$. Find the values of x, y, and k.

$$\begin{bmatrix} 2a + 1 & -6 \\ -7 & -3k \end{bmatrix} = \begin{bmatrix} 11 & x - 5 \\ 5 - 2y & 27 \end{bmatrix}$$

Choose **Use a calculator, paper and pencil, or mental math to solve each equation. Check your solutions.**

27. $-y + 7 = 13$
28. $5 - b = 2$
29. $10 = 2n + 1$
30. $6 - 2p = 14$
31. $3x - 15 = 33$
32. $\frac{m}{3} - 9 = -21$
33. $14 - \frac{y}{2} = -1$
34. $\frac{x}{10} + 1.5 = 3.8$
35. $-7 = 11 + 3b$
36. $-6 + 6z = 0$
37. $\frac{a}{5} + 15 = 30$
38. $34 = 14 - 4p$
39. $4 = 4 - \frac{a}{9}$
40. $3x - 1 = 8$
41. $-8 - c = 11$
42. $\frac{m}{3} - 18 = 7$
43. $3x - 2.1 = 4.5$
44. $2 = -1 - \frac{k}{12}$
45. $\frac{m}{2} - 1.002 = 0.93$
46. $3 - 0.5c = 1.2$

47. Math in the Media You rent a car for one day. Your total bill is \$60.
    a. Estimation You estimate your mileage to be about 100 mi. Does the bill seem reasonable? Explain.
    b. Exactly how many miles did you drive?

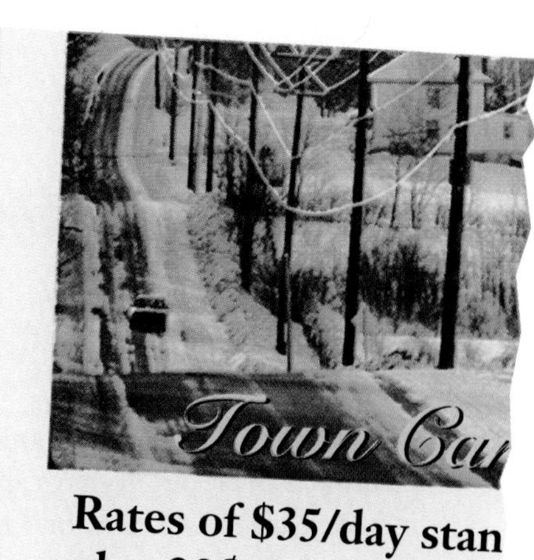

Town Ca
Rates of $35/day stan
plus 20¢/mile on all v
20 U.S. TRAVEL TODAY

48. Insurance One insurance policy pays people for claims by multiplying the claim amount by 0.8 and then subtracting \$500. If a person receives a check for \$4650, how much was the claim amount?

49. Gardening Tulip bulbs cost \$.75 each plus \$3.00 for shipping an entire order. You have \$14.00. How many bulbs can you order?

50. Open-ended Write a problem that you can model with a two-step equation. Define the variable and show the solution to the problem.

51. Critical Thinking If you multiply each side of the equation $0.24r + 5.25 = -7.23$ by 100, the result is an equivalent equation. Explain why it might be helpful to do this.

 **Write each equation in calculator-ready form and solve.**

52. $1.2x + 0.6 = 32.4$ **53.** $2.8 = 1.34 + \frac{r}{2}$ **54.** $\frac{y}{4.5} - 9 = 3.5$ **55.** $0.05n - 0.5 = 8$

56. $9.007 - b = 8.32$ **57.** $5.3 - 0.8n = 7$ **58.** $0.3z + 0.91 = -0.08$ **59.** $3 - \frac{t}{2.5} = -7.06$

60. *Temperature* The formula for converting a temperature from Celsius, C, to Fahrenheit, F, is $F = 1.8C + 32$.

a. Copy and complete the table. Round to the nearest degree.

b. *Mental Math* To convert from Celsius to Fahrenheit, you can get an estimate by using this rule: multiply the Celsius temperature by 2, then add 30. Use this strategy to convert 4°C, 15°C, and 50°C.

Fahrenheit	Celsius	Description of Temperature
212°	■	boiling point of water
■	37°	human body temperature
68°	■	room temperature
■	7°	average January high in Baltimore
■	0°	freezing point of water
19°	■	average January low in Chicago

61. *Writing* Describe a situation that you can model with the equation $185 - 15n = 110$. Explain what the variable represents.

Chapter Project

Find Out by Modeling

To make a successful budget, you need to think about savings.

- Geraldo has already saved \$40 and wants to buy a CD player for \$129 in about four months. To find how much he should save each week, he wrote $40 + 16x = 129$. Explain his equation.
- On page 113, you chose one item as the goal for your project. How much does it cost? When do you want to buy this item?
- Write and solve an equation to find how much you should save per week.

Exercises MIXED REVIEW

Solve each equation.

62. $4s = 18$ **63.** $x - 3 = 9$ **64.** $\frac{m}{5} = 3$ **65.** $-7 = n + 2$

66. In 1995, the Library of Congress had 110 million books and other items. It is projected to have about 117.2 million items in 1999. Write and solve an equation to find how many items the Library of Congress adds each year.

Getting Ready for Lesson 3-3

Simplify.

67. $8 - (-1)$ **68.** $9 - 11$ **69.** $-15 + (-5)$ **70.** $5 + (-12)$ **71.** $-6 - (-9)$

CHAPTER 3

Preparing for Standardized Tests

Choose the correct letter.

1. In which quadrants would the following points be graphed? (–2, 5) (3, –1) (5, –4) (–1, 4)
   A. I and II **B.** II and III **C.** III and IV
   D. I and IV **E.** II and IV

2. Consider the function $f(x) = x^2 - 3$. Which of the following are true?
   I. $f(1) > f(0)$ **II.** $f(2) > f(-3)$
   III. $f(2) = f(-2)$ **IV.** $f(-1) = f(3)$
   A. I only **B.** II only
   C. II and IV **D.** I and III

3. Match the graph with its equation.
   A. $f(x) = |x| + 1$
   B. $f(x) = (x + 1)^2$
   C. $f(x) = |x| + 2$
   D. $f(x) = |x| - 1$
   E. $f(x) = x - 1$

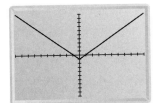

4. A store owner has a bicycle priced at $100. She raises the price 10%. During a sale, she then lowers the price 10%. What is the new price of the bicycle?
   A. $100 **B.** $101 **C.** $99
   D. $98 **E.** none of the above

5. Consider the function $f(x) = x^3 - x$. Compare the quantities in Column A and Column B.

Column A	Column B
$f(0)$	$f(-2)$

   A. The quantity in Column A is greater.
   B. The quantity in Column B is greater.
   C. The two quantities are equal.
   D. The relationship cannot be determined on the basis of the information given.

6. If $\frac{2x}{3} = 5$, $\frac{2y - 2}{4} = 3$, and $\frac{z}{2} + \frac{z}{3} = 5$, which of the following is true?
   A. $x > y$ **B.** $y < z$ **C.** $x = z$
   D. $z > x$ **E.** $x = y + z$

7. A number cube is rolled. Compare the quantities in Column A and Column B.

Column A	Column B
the probability of rolling a number 5 or greater.	the probability of rolling a number 2 or less.

   A. The quantity in Column A is greater.
   B. The quantity in Column B is greater.
   C. The two quantities are equal.
   D. The relationship cannot be determined on the basis of the information given.

8. A bag contains 10 red marbles and 20 white marbles. You draw a marble, keep it, and draw another. What is the probability of drawing two red marbles?
   A. $\frac{1}{3}$ **B.** $\frac{1}{9}$ **C.** $\frac{3}{29}$
   D. $\frac{1}{10}$ **E.** $\frac{1}{2}$

For Exercises 9–14, write your answer.

9. A table of values for the linear function $g(x)$ is given. Write an equation describing the function.

x	1	2	3	4	5	6	7
$g(x)$	−2	−1	0	1	2	3	4

10. Solve $5(x - 7) - 2x = 4$.

11. What is the median of the following values?
    –3, 7, 5, 5, –1, 0, 1, –4, 0, 1, 0

12. *Open-ended* Give an example of a real-life situation that you could model with the equation $3n + 5 = 68$. Define what the variable represents and then solve the equation.

13. Simplify $9a + 3b - 3 - 4a + 7 - 8b$.

14. *Writing* Describe the shape of the graph of each type of function: linear, quadratic, and absolute value.

3-4 Using the Distributive Property

What You'll Learn

- Using the distributive property
- Solving equations that involve the distributive property

...And Why

To solve problems involving electricity

WORK TOGETHER

Sports A high school basketball court is 84 ft long by 50 ft wide. A college basketball court is 10 ft longer than a high school basketball court.

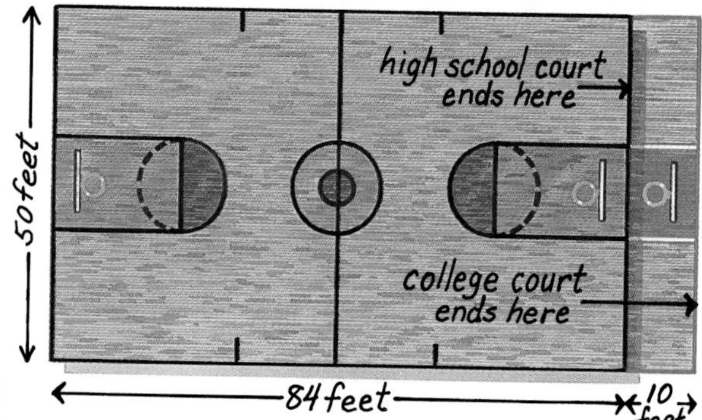

1. Work with a partner to evaluate each expression.
   a. $50(84 + 10)$ **b.** $50(84) + 50(10)$
2. Explain how each of the expressions in Question 1 represents the area of a college basketball court.

THINK AND DISCUSS

Simplifying Variable Expressions

Using two methods to find area illustrates the *distributive property*.

Distributive Property

For all real numbers a, b, and c:

$a(b + c) = ab + ac$ $(b + c)a = ba + ca$

$a(b - c) = ab - ac$ $(b - c)a = ba - ca$

Examples:

$5(20 + 6) = 5(20) + 5(6)$ $(20 + 6)5 = 20(5) + 6(5)$

$9(30 - 2) = 9(30) - 9(2)$ $(30 - 2)9 = 30(9) - 2(9)$

You can use the distributive property to simplify expressions.

$2(5x + 3) = 2(5x) + 2(3)$ $(3b - 2)\frac{1}{3} = 3b(\frac{1}{3}) - 2(\frac{1}{3})$

$= 10x + 6$ $= b - \frac{2}{3}$

To simplify an expression like $-(6x + 4)$, first rewrite it as $-1(6x + 4)$.

$$\begin{aligned} -(6x + 4) &= -1(6x + 4) \\ &= -1(6x) + (-1)(4) \\ &= -6x - 4 \end{aligned} \qquad \begin{aligned} -(-2 - 9m) &= -1(-2 - 9m) \\ &= -1(-2) - (-1)(9m) \\ &= 2 + 9m \end{aligned}$$

3. **Critical Thinking** A student rewrote $4(3x + 10)$ as $12x + 10$. Explain the student's error.

4. **Try This** Use the distributive property to simplify each expression.
a. $-3(2x - 1)$ **b.** $-(7 - 5b)$ **c.** $(3 - 8a)\frac{1}{4}$

Solving and Modeling Equations

Example 1 **Relating to the Real World** 

Shopping Posters of astronaut Sally Ride were on sale for \$3 off the regular price. Suppose you bought two posters and paid a total of \$8. Solve the equation $2(x - 3) = 8$ to find the regular price of each poster.

Model the equation with tiles.

You represent $2(x - 3)$ as two groups of tiles each containing $x - 3$. →

$2(x - 3) = 8$

Rearrange tiles and use the distributive property.

$2(x - 3) = 8$

$2x - 6 = 8$

Add six to each side.

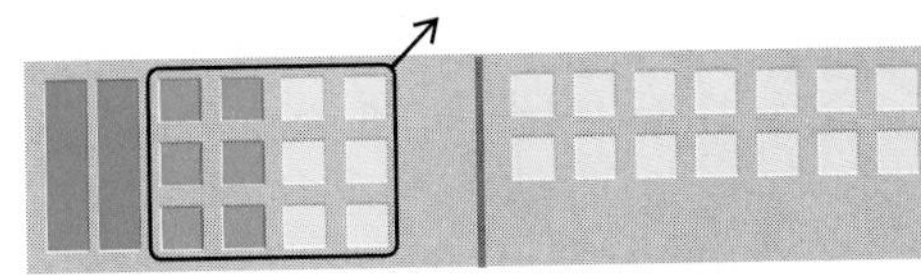

$2x - 6 + 6 = 8 + 6$

$2x = 14$

Divide each side into two identical groups.

$\frac{2x}{2} = \frac{14}{2}$

Solve for x.

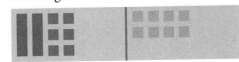

$x = 7$

Each poster regularly costs \$7.

Who? Lewis Latimer (1848–1928) was an inventor who in 1882 received a patent for his method of making a light bulb filament. He was the author of the first book on electrical lighting.

Source: *Black Achievers in Science*

5. a. Use tiles to solve the equation $3(x - 1) + x = 5$.

b. In the equation $3(x - 1) + x = 5$, is it possible to combine like terms before you use the distributive property? Explain.

You can use the distributive property to solve real-world problems.

Example 2 **Relating to the Real World** 

Electricity Several 6- and 12-volt batteries are wired so that the sum of their voltages produces a power supply of 84 volts. The total number of batteries is ten. How many of each type of battery are used?

Define $x =$ number of 6-volt batteries
$10 - x =$ number of 12-volt batteries

Relate	voltage from 6-volt batteries	plus	voltage from 12-volt batteries	equals	total voltage
Write	$6x$	$+$	$12(10 - x)$	$=$	84

$$6x + 12(10 - x) = 84$$

$$6x + 120 - 12x = 84 \quad \leftarrow \text{Use the distributive property.}$$

$$-6x + 120 = 84 \quad \leftarrow \text{Combine like terms.}$$

$$-6x + 120 - 120 = 84 - 120 \quad \leftarrow \text{Subtract 120 from each side.}$$

$$-6x = -36$$

$$\frac{-6x}{6} = \frac{-36}{-6} \quad \leftarrow \text{Divide each side by } -6.$$

$$x = 6$$

There are six 6-volt batteries.
$10 - x = 10 - 6 = 4$; there are four 12-volt batteries.

Check $6(6 \text{ volts}) + 4(12 \text{ volts}) \stackrel{?}{=} 84 \text{ volts}$
$36 \text{ volts} + 48 \text{ volts} = 84 \text{ volts}$ ✔

6. a. Suppose you let x represent the number of 12-volt batteries. Write and solve a new equation that models the problem in Example 2.

b. Do you get a different answer to the problem? Explain.

Exercises ON YOUR OWN

Write and solve each equation modeled by tiles.

1. 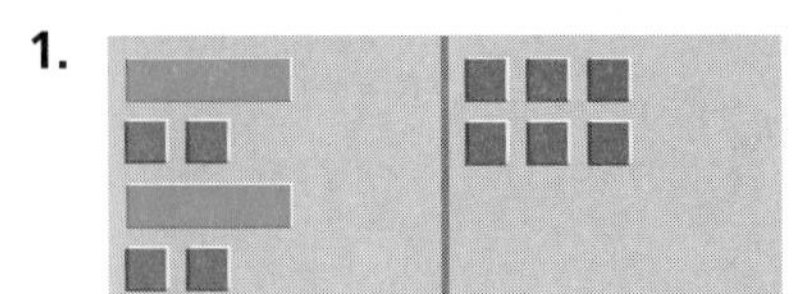

2. 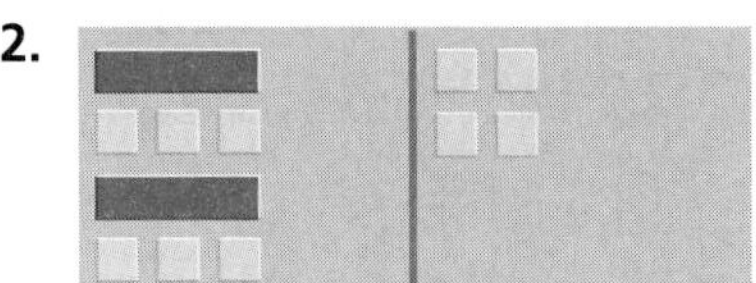

3. 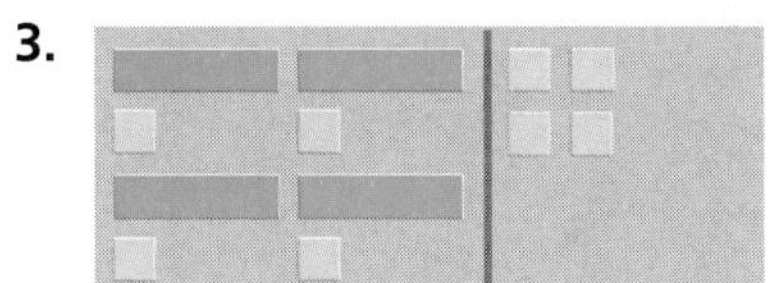

4. **Writing** In your own words, explain what the word *distribute* means.

5. **Critical Thinking** Does $2ab = 2a \cdot 2b$? Explain your answer.

Simplify each expression.

6. $7(t - 4)$
7. $-2(n - 6)$
8. $-(7x - 2)$
9. $(5b - 4)\frac{2}{5}$
10. $-2(x + 3)$
11. $\frac{2}{3}(6y + 9)$
12. $(4 - z)(-1)$
13. $(3n - 7)(6)$
14. $-(2k + 5)$
15. $-4.5(b - 3)$
16. $\frac{2}{5}(5w + 10)$
17. $(9 - 4n)(-4)$

Geometry **If a polygon has n sides, the sum of the measures of its interior angles is $(n - 2)180°$. Use this for Exercises 18–20.**

18. The sum of the measures of the interior angles of a pentagon is 540°. What is the value of x in the figure to the right?

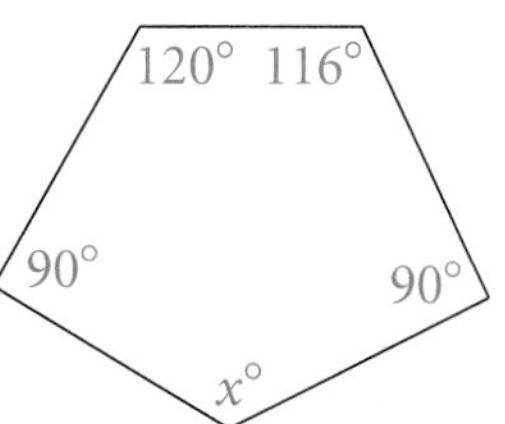

19. A polygon has seven sides. What is the sum of the measures of its interior angles?

20. The sum of the measures of the interior angles of a polygon is 1440°. Use an equation to find the number of sides of the polygon.

Solve and check each equation.

21. $2(8 + w) = 22$
22. $m + 5(m - 1) = 11$
23. $-(z + 5) = -14$
24. $0.5(x - 12) = 4$
25. $8y - (2y - 3) = 9$
26. $\frac{1}{4}(m - 16) = 7$
27. $15 = -3(x - 1) + 9$
28. $\frac{3}{4}(8n - 4) = -2$
29. $5(a - 1) = 35$
30. $6(x + 4) - 2x = -8$
31. $-3(2t - 1) = 15$
32. $-8 = -(3 + y)$
33. $0 = \frac{1}{3}(6b + 9) + b$
34. $2(1.5c + 4) = -1$
35. $n - (3n + 4) = -6$
36. $-\frac{1}{5}(10d - 5) = 9$

In Exercises 37–40, use an equation to model and solve each problem.

37. **Geography** The shape of Colorado is nearly a rectangle. The length is 100 miles more than the width. The perimeter is about 1320 mi. Find the length and width of Colorado.

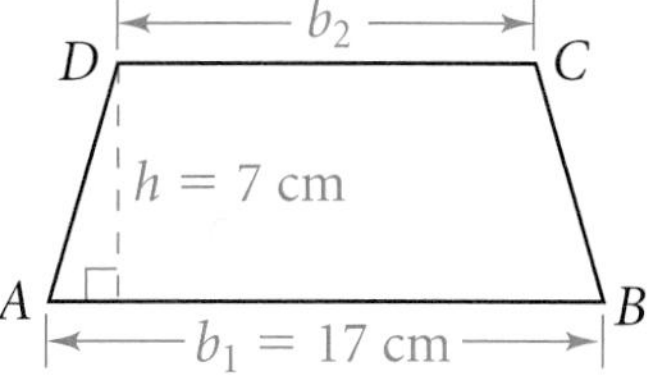

38. **Geometry** The formula for the area of a trapezoid is $A = \frac{1}{2}h(b_1 + b_2)$. The area of $ABCD$ is 98 cm^2. Find the value of b_2.

39. **Sports** A baseball team buys 15 bats for \$405. Aluminum bats cost \$25 and wooden bats cost \$30. How many of each type did they buy?

40. **Business** A company buys a copier for \$10,000. The Internal Revenue Service values the copier at $\$10{,}000(1 - \frac{n}{20})$ after n years. After how many years will the copier be valued at \$6500?

41. **Open-ended** Describe a situation where you would use the distributive property to solve a real-life problem.

42. **Standardized Test Prep** If $y = 3x - 10$, what is the value of $\frac{y}{3}$?

A. $-x + 10$ B. $x + \frac{10}{3}$ C. $x - \frac{10}{3}$ D. $-x + \frac{10}{3}$ E. $x - 10$

Mental Math **You can use mental math and the distributive property to find prices quickly. Find each price.**

43. 4($.99) **44.** 6($1.97)

45. 5($5.91) **46.** 7($29.93)

47. 3 computer games at $32.99 each

48. 4 cans of fruit punch at $.69 each

$4(2.89) = 4(3.00 - 0.11)$
$= 4(3.00) - 4(0.11)$
$= 12 - 0.44$
$= 11.56$

$ 11.56

Exercises MIXED REVIEW

Solve and check.

49. $m - 4m = 2$ **50.** $9 = -4y + 6y - 5$

51. $2t - 8t + 1 = 43$ **52.** $3.5 = 12s - 5s$

53. **Technology** Use the spreadsheet at the right.
- **a.** Write a formula for cell C2 if there are 250 million people in the United States.
- **b.** Use your formula to find the missing values in the spreadsheet to one decimal place.
- **c.** Suppose a gallon of cranberry juice costs about $4. How much do people in the United States spend on cranberry juice in one year?

Annual U.S. Fruit Juice Sales

	A	B	C
1	juice	gal (millions)	gal/person
2	orange	734	■
3	apple	213	■
4	cranberry	126	■

Source: *Florida Dept. of Citrus*

Getting Ready for Lesson 3-5

Evaluate each expression.

54. $\frac{2}{3}n + 4$ for $n = -6$ **55.** $\frac{k}{5} + \frac{2k}{7}$ for $k = -35$ **56.** $\frac{3a + 1}{4}$ for $a = 7$

Exercises CHECKPOINT

Solve and check.

1. $x - 7 = -6$ **2.** $\frac{w}{3} = 11$ **3.** $15 = 0.75v$ **4.** $2t - 1 = 4$

5. $\frac{b}{3} - 20 = 20$ **6.** $-12 - 4x + 3 = -1$ **7.** $10 = -5m - m - 2$ **8.** $3n + n - 8 = 32$

9. $-(z - 5) = -13\frac{1}{3}$ **10.** $-0.8 - y = 1.9$ **11.** $9(n + 7) = -81$ **12.** $x + 2(3 - x) = 4$

13. **Sewing** Suppose you are sewing a braid border on the edges of a quilt. The quilt is 20 in. longer than it is wide. You need 292 in. of braid to cover the edges of the quilt. What are the dimensions of the quilt?

14. Which equation has the greatest solution?
A. $\frac{m}{4} = -12$ **B.** $10 = 0.5(z + 3)$ **C.** $4w - 5w + 9 = 8.4$ **D.** $2c - 7 = 4$

3-5 Rational Numbers and Equations

What You'll Learn

- Solving equations involving rational numbers

...And Why

To solve nutrition and transportation problems

THINK AND DISCUSS

Multiplying by a Reciprocal

In Chapter 1 you learned that a rational number can be represented as a ratio of two numbers. You can use reciprocals to solve equations involving rational numbers.

Example 1 **Relating to the Real World** 

Nutrition There are about 200 mg of calcium in 1 oz of cheddar cheese. How many milligrams of calcium are in 1 c of skim milk?

Define	m = calcium (mg) in 1 c skim milk		
Relate	two-thirds calcium in 1 c skim milk	equals ↓	calcium in 1 oz cheddar cheese
Write	$\frac{2}{3}m$	$=$	200

$$\frac{2}{3}m = 200$$

$$\frac{3}{2}\left(\frac{2}{3}m\right) = \frac{3}{2}(200) \quad \leftarrow \text{Multiply each side by } \tfrac{3}{2}\text{, the reciprocal of } \tfrac{2}{3}.$$

$$m = 300$$

There are about 300 mg of calcium in 1 c of skim milk.

Check Two-thirds of the calcium in 1 c skim milk is 200.

$\frac{2}{3} \cdot 300 = 200$ ✔

1. Solve the equation in Example 1 by multiplying each side by 3 and then dividing each side by 2. Which method do you prefer? Explain.

You can also use reciprocals to solve equations like $\frac{x}{5} = -7$. Write $\frac{x}{5}$ as $\frac{1}{5}x$ and multiply each side of the equation by 5, which is the reciprocal of $\frac{1}{5}$.

2. **Try This** Solve each equation.

a. $\frac{2}{5}y = 1$ **b.** $-\frac{b}{8} = 2$ **c.** $-\frac{3}{4}x = 6$ **d.** $-2 = \frac{4c}{9}$

3. To solve $-\frac{1}{2}(3x - 5) = 7$, you can use the distributive property or you can multiply each side of the equation by –2, the reciprocal of $-\frac{1}{2}$. Explain why the second method is easier. Then solve the equation.

QUICK REVIEW

A *common denominator* of an equation is a multiple of all the denominators in the equation.

Multiplying by a Common Denominator

To simplify an equation containing a fraction, you can multiply each side by the denominator of the fraction. The resulting equation is easier to solve.

Score	Grade
90–100	A
80–89	B
70–79	C
60–69	D

Example 2 Relating to the Real World 

School Your test scores are 92 and 75. Without extra credit, can you raise your test average to an A with your next test? Explain.

Define x = your next test score

Relate average of the scores equals lowest score for an A

Write $\frac{92 + 75 + x}{3} = 90$

$$\frac{92 + 75 + x}{3} = 90$$

$$3\left(\frac{92 + 75 + x}{3}\right) = 3(90) \quad \leftarrow \text{Multiply each side by 3.}$$

$$92 + 75 + x = 270$$

$$167 + x = 270 \quad \leftarrow \text{Simplify each side.}$$

$$167 + x - 167 = 270 - 167 \quad \leftarrow \text{Subtract 167 from each side.}$$

$$x = 103$$

Without extra credit the next test cannot bring your average to an A.

CALCULATOR HINT

You can write the solution to this equation in calculator-ready form as $x = 3(90) - 92 - 75$. To calculate, use the sequence 3 × 90 − 92 − 75 ENTER .

4. ***Critical Thinking*** How is multiplying by the denominator in Example 2 similar to multiplying by a reciprocal?

To solve an equation that has two or more fractions, multiply both sides of the equation by a common denominator.

Example 3 Relating to the Real World 

Cars You fill your car's gas tank when it is about $\frac{1}{2}$ empty. Later you fill the tank when it is about $\frac{3}{4}$ empty. You bought a total of $18\frac{1}{2}$ gal of gas on those two days. About how many gallons does the tank hold?

Define x = amount of gas (gal) the tank holds

Relate gallons from first fill plus gallons from second fill equals total bought

Write $\frac{1}{2} \cdot x + \frac{3}{4} \cdot x = 18\frac{1}{2}$

$$\frac{1}{2}x + \frac{3}{4}x = 18\frac{1}{2}$$

$$4\left(\frac{1}{2}x + \frac{3}{4}x\right) = 4(18\tfrac{1}{2}) \quad \leftarrow \text{Multiply each side by 4.}$$

$$4\left(\frac{1}{2}x\right) + 4\left(\frac{3}{4}x\right) = 74 \quad \leftarrow \text{Use the distributive property.}$$

$$2x + 3x = 74 \quad \leftarrow \text{Simplify each term.}$$

$$5x = 74 \quad \leftarrow \text{Combine like terms.}$$

$$\frac{5x}{5} = \frac{74}{5} \quad \leftarrow \text{Divide each side by 5.}$$

$$x = 14.8$$

The gas tank holds about 14.8 gallons of gas.

5. What other common denominator could have been used in Example 3?

6. **Open-ended** Name a common denominator that you would use to solve each equation.

   a. $\frac{2}{3}x - \frac{5}{8}x = 26$ b. $\frac{y}{8} + \frac{y}{12} = -4$ c. $\frac{1}{2} = \frac{2}{3}b + \frac{1}{6}b$

Exercises ON YOUR OWN

Mental Math Solve each equation mentally.

1. $\frac{3}{4}y = 9$
2. $-\frac{2}{3}x = 6$
3. $-4 = \frac{2}{5}a$
4. $\frac{b}{10} = 5$
5. $\frac{-7x}{8} = \frac{7}{8}$
6. $\frac{3}{7}y = 0$
7. $-\frac{n}{8} = 6$
8. $\frac{2}{3}c = -18$

9. **Critical Thinking** Explain the error in the student's work shown at the right.

$\frac{3}{8}x - 1 = 4$
$3x - 1 = 32$
$3x = 33$
$x = 11$

10. **Jobs** Suppose you apply for a nurse's aide job that pays a \$12.90/h overtime wage. The overtime wage is $1\frac{1}{2}$ times the regular wage. What is the regular wage for the job?

11. Suppose you buy $1\frac{1}{4}$ lb of roast beef for \$5. If p = price of the roast beef per pound, which equation models this situation?

    A. $1\frac{1}{4}p = 5$ B. $p = 5 \cdot 1\frac{1}{4}$ C. $5p = 1\frac{1}{4}$ D. $p = 1\frac{1}{4} \div 5$

12. **Geography** The area of Kentucky is about 40,000 mi^2. This is about $\frac{5}{7}$ the area of Wisconsin. What is the area of Wisconsin?

13. **Sewing** Suppose you buy $\frac{5}{8}$ of a yard of fabric for \$2.50. What is the price of the fabric per yard?

Choose Use a calculator, paper and pencil, or mental math to solve each equation. Check your answers.

14. $\frac{7}{8}x = 14$
15. $-\frac{2}{9}y = 10$
16. $\frac{x}{4} + \frac{3x}{5} = 17$
17. $\frac{z}{3} = -1$
18. $\frac{5a - 1}{8} = -5\frac{1}{4}$
19. $5 = -\frac{x}{6} + \frac{x}{2}$
20. $5 = \frac{a}{6}$
21. $\frac{y + 4}{3} = -1$
22. $12 = \frac{7}{5}y$
23. $5 = -\frac{1}{3}y + \frac{2}{7}$
24. $10 = -\frac{4}{3}d$
25. $\frac{-1 - 5x}{7} = 7$
26. $\frac{2x - 1}{5} = 3$
27. $-\frac{3x}{8} = -12$
28. $\frac{6a + 4}{3} = -14$
29. $2y - \frac{3}{8}y = \frac{3}{4}$
30. $\frac{3}{4} = \frac{3 - b + 4b}{12}$
31. $-\frac{n}{2} = 30$
32. $\frac{2x}{3} + \frac{x}{2} = 7$
33. $\frac{1}{3}x + \frac{1}{6}x = 27$

Travel Solve each problem using the formula $d = r \cdot t$.

34. If you drive 65 mi/h for 3 h, how far do you drive?

35. If you drive 200 mi in $3\frac{1}{4}$ h, how fast do you drive?

36. If you drive 210 mi at 60 mi/h, how long do you drive?

37. **Work** What would the average number of hours per week have to be in the 1990s, to make the average for the three decades be 35 h/wk?

Average Work Week for Production Workers

Decade	Hours Per Week
1970s	36.4
1980s	34.9
1990s	■

38. **Writing** Explain how you can use common denominators to solve equations involving rational numbers. Give an example.

Choose Use a calculator, paper and pencil, or mental math to solve each equation. Check your answers.

39. $\frac{2x}{7} + \frac{x}{3} = -13$
40. $-\frac{1}{5}(3x + 4) = 1$
41. $\frac{2c - 1}{3} = 3$
42. $1 = \frac{a}{7} - \frac{a}{3}$
43. $-\frac{8}{11}b = 24$
44. $\frac{1}{2}(5d + 4) = 6$
45. $-1 = \frac{2x - 1}{3}$
46. $x - \frac{5x}{6} = -\frac{2}{3}$
47. $\frac{3}{8}y + \frac{2}{3}y = \frac{5}{8}$
48. $\frac{n}{60} + \frac{n}{15} = -1$
49. $\frac{7x}{3} = -21$
50. $\frac{3t}{2} - \frac{3t}{4} = \frac{3}{2}$
51. $\frac{3}{4}(2n - 5) = -1$
52. $\frac{5c - 8}{18} = \frac{2}{3}$
53. $\frac{b}{5} + \frac{5b}{3} = 2$
54. $-\frac{3t}{8} = \frac{3}{2}$

55. **Entertainment** As of 1994, the rental income for the movie *Back to the Future* was about \$105.5 million. This was about three fourths the rental income for *Home Alone.* Find the rental income for *Home Alone.*

56. **Family Budget** A family allows $\frac{1}{3}$ of its monthly income for housing and $\frac{1}{4}$ of its monthly income for food. It budgets a total of \$1050 a month for housing and food. What is the family's monthly income?

57. **School** Suppose that on an average day, you spend $\frac{1}{5}$ of your homework time on math and $\frac{1}{2}$ of your homework time on literature. The time for these subjects totals $1\frac{3}{4}$ h. How much time do you spend on your homework?

Exercises MIXED REVIEW

Solve and check each equation.

58. $8h - 3 + 2h = 7$
59. $-x + 6x = -35$
60. $5k + 6 = -14$
61. $m - 7m + 3 = 0$
62. $y + 15 + 2y = 0$
63. $c - (5c - 1) = -47$
64. $9(w - 1) = -27$
65. $2j - 6j + 5 = 1$

66. **Transportation** On Atlanta's rapid rail system, the MARTA, trains leave Airport Station every 8 min from 7:11 A.M. to 6:31 P.M.
   a. You get to Airport Station at 7:55 A.M. How long will you have to wait for a train?
   b. The ride to Doraville Station takes 41 min. When will you arrive?

Getting Ready for Lesson 3-6

Probability You have five quarters in your pocket. Their mint dates are 1987, 1991, 1989, 1994, and 1991. You pick one. Find each probability.

67. P(mint date 1987)
68. P(a quarter)
69. P(mint date 1991)
70. P(a dime)

What You'll Learn

- Solving equations with variables on both sides
- Identifying equations that have no solution or are identities

...And Why

To solve equations that model real-world situations, such as distance problems

What You'll Need

- tiles
- calculator

4-2 Equations with Variables on Both Sides

WORK TOGETHER

In Chapter 3 you used tiles and solved equations. Model each equation with tiles. Then solve.

1. $x - 4 = -9$ **2.** $-10 = 5y$ **3.** $3a + 8 = 2$ **4.** $-12 = 8 + 4b$

Now look at an equation with variables on both sides: $6x + 3 = 4x + 9$.

5. Model this equation with tiles.

6. Discuss how you might use tiles to solve the equation.

7. Use the problem solving strategy *Guess and Test* to solve the equation.

THINK AND DISCUSS

Using Tiles to Solve Equations

Some equations cannot be solved easily using the strategy *Guess and Test.* In this lesson you will learn how to solve equations with variables on both sides. First you will use tiles to help you understand the process.

Example 1

Solve the equation

$$5x - 3 = 2x + 12.$$

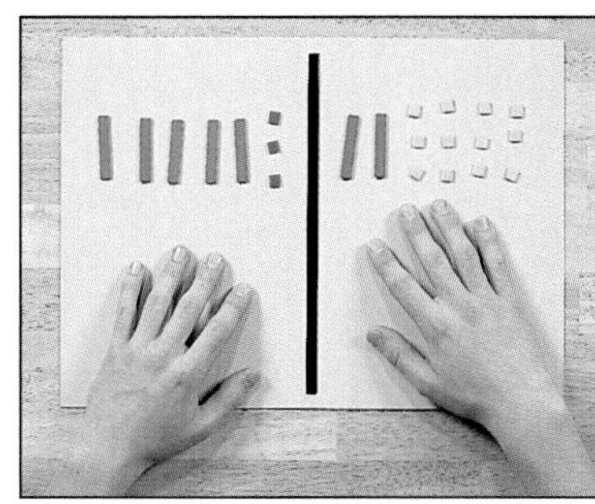

Model the equation with tiles.

$$5x - 3 = 2x + 12$$

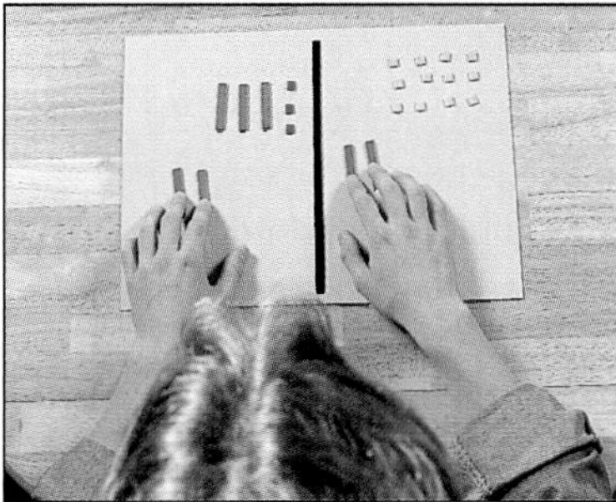

Add $-2x$ to each side, and simplify by removing zero pairs.

$$5x - 3 - 2x = 2x + 12 - 2x$$
$$3x - 3 = 12$$

QUICK REVIEW

■■ represents 0.

Add 3 to each side and simplify by removing zero pairs.

$$3x - 3 + 3 = 12 + 3$$
$$3x = 15$$

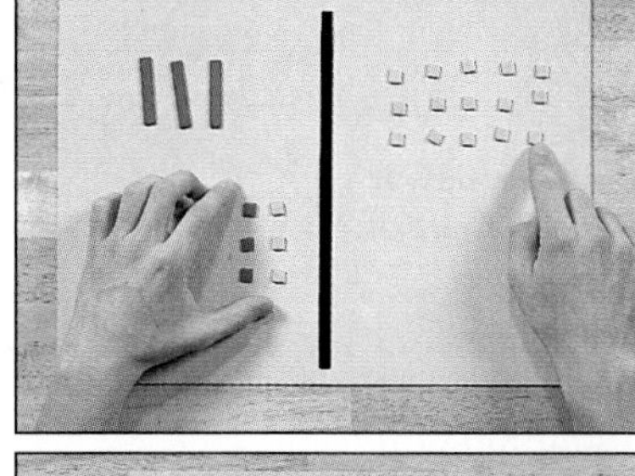

Divide each side into three identical groups.

$$\frac{3x}{3} = \frac{15}{3}$$

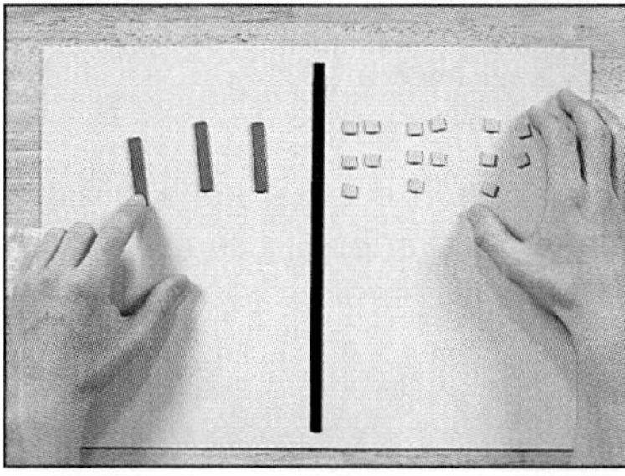

Solve for x.

$$x = 5$$

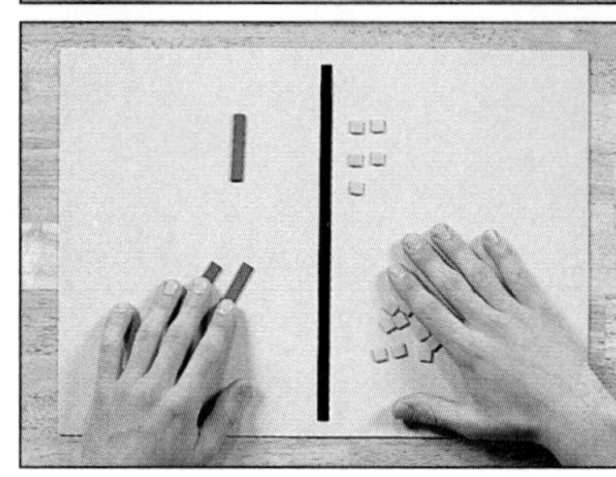

The solution is 5.

Check $5x - 3 = 2x + 12$

$5(5) - 3 \stackrel{?}{=} 2(5) + 12$ ← Substitute 5 for x.

$22 = 22$ ✓

8. Try This Use tiles to model and solve each equation.

a. $6x - 2 = x + 13$ **b.** $4(x + 1) = 2x - 2$

c. **Summarize** the steps you used to solve the equations.

Using Properties of Equality

You can use the properties of equality to get terms with variables on the same side of the equation.

Example 2

Solve $5t - 8 = 9t - 10$.

$5t - 8 + 10 = 9t - 10 + 10$ ← Add 10 to each side.

$5t + 2 = 9t$ ← Simplify each side.

$5t + 2 - 5t = 9t - 5t$ ← Subtract $5t$ from each side.

$2 = 4t$ ← Combine like terms.

$\frac{2}{4} = \frac{4t}{4}$ ← Divide each side by 4.

$\frac{1}{2} = t$ ← Simplify each side.

The solution is $\frac{1}{2}$.

GRAPHING CALCULATOR HINT

You can check your solution to Example 2 by using the TEST feature to see if $\frac{1}{2}$ is the solution of the equation.

9. **Verify** the solution of Example 2.

10. **a.** Suppose you began solving the equation in Example 2 by subtracting $9t$ from each side of the equation. Write the steps you would use to solve the equation.
    b. Compare your solution to the solution in Example 2. Does it matter that the variables are on different sides of the equal sign? Explain.

QUICK REVIEW

A formula for distance is distance = rate · time, or $d = rt$.

Equations are helpful when you solve distance problems.

Example 3 **Relating to the Real World** 

Transportation Mary and Jocelyn are sisters. They left school at 3:00 P.M. and bicycled home along the same bike path. Mary bicycled at a speed of 12 mi/h. Jocelyn bicycled at 9 mi/h. Mary got home 15 min before Jocelyn. How long did it take Mary to get home?

PROBLEM SOLVING HINT

Draw a diagram to help you visualize the conditions of the problem in Example 3.

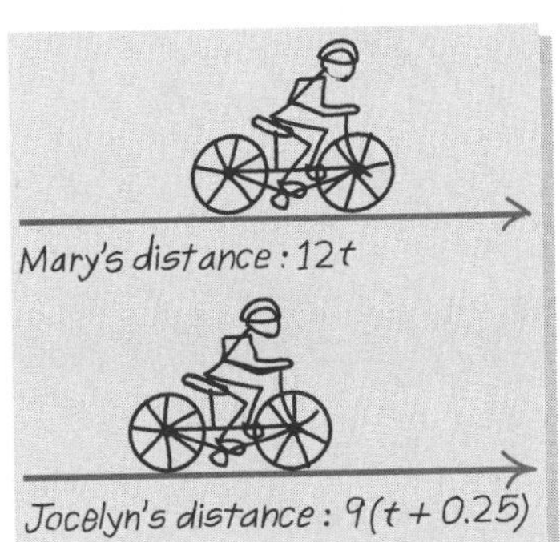

Define t = Mary's time in hours
$t + 0.25$ = Jocelyn's time in hours

Relate Mary's distance (rate · time) equals Jocelyn's distance (rate · time)

Write $12t = 9(t + 0.25)$

$12t = 9(t + 0.25)$

$12t = 9t + 2.25$ ← Use the distributive property.

$12t - 9t = 9t + 2.25 - 9t$ ← Subtract $9t$ from each side.

$3t = 2.25$ ← Combine like terms.

$\frac{3t}{3} = \frac{2.25}{3}$ ← Divide each side by 3.

$t = 0.75$ ← Use a calculator.

It took Mary 0.75 h, or 45 min, to get home.

11. **Critical Thinking** To solve the problem in Example 3, Ben wrote the equation $12t = 9(t + 15)$. What mistake did he make?

Solving Special Types of Equations

An equation has **no solution** if no value makes the equation true.

Example 4

Solve $6m - 5 = 7m + 7 - m$.

$6m - 5 = 7m + 7 - m$

$6m - 5 = 6m + 7$ ← Combine like terms.

$6m - 5 - 6m = 6m + 7 - 6m$ ← Subtract $6m$ from each side.

$-5 = 7$ Not true for any m!

This equation has no solution.

12. Is an equation that has 0 for a solution the same as an equation with no solution? Explain.

An equation that is true for every value of the variable is an **identity.**

Example 5

Solve $10 - 8a = 2(5 - 4a)$.

$$
\begin{aligned}
10 - 8a &= 2(5 - 4a) \\
10 - 8a &= 10 - 8a && \leftarrow \text{Use the distributive property.} \\
10 - 8a + 8a &= 10 - 8a + 8a && \leftarrow \text{Add } 8a \text{ to each side.} \\
10 &= 10 && \text{Always true!}
\end{aligned}
$$

This equation is true for any value of a, so the equation is an identity.

13. Could you have stopped solving the equation when you saw that $10 - 8a = 10 - 8a$? Explain.

14. **Mental Math** Without writing the steps of a solution, tell whether the equation has *one solution*, *no solution*, or is an *identity*.

a. $9 + 5a = 5a - 1$ **b.** $5a + 9 = 2a$

c. $9 + 5a = 2a + 9$ **d.** $9 + 5a = 5a + 9$

Exercises ON YOUR OWN

Write an equation for each model and solve.

1. 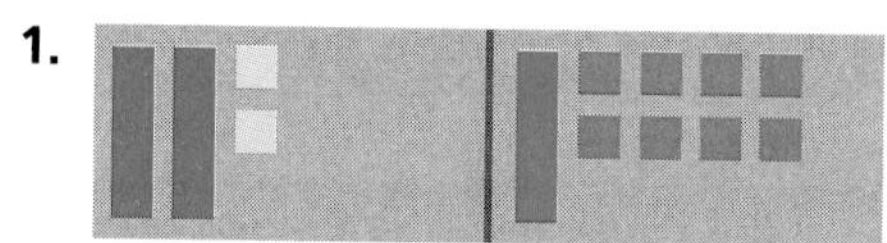

2. 

3. 

4. 

Model each equation with tiles. Then solve.

5. $4x - 3 = 3x + 4$ **6.** $5x + 3 = 3x + 9$ **7.** $8 - x = 2x - 1$

Solve and check. If the equation is an identity or if it has no solution, write *identity* or *no solution*.

8. $3(x - 4) = 2x + 6$ **9.** $4x - 7 = x + 3(4 + x)$ **10.** $5x = 3(x - 1) + (3 + 2x)$

11. $0.5y + 2 = 0.8y - 0.3y$ **12.** $6 + 3m = -m - 6$ **13.** $3t + 8 = 5t + 8 - 2t$

Critical Thinking **Find the mistake in the solution of each equation. Explain the mistake and solve the equation correctly.**

14.
$$\begin{aligned} 2x &= 11x + 45 \\ 2x - 11x &= 11x - 11x + 45 \\ 9x &= 45 \\ \frac{9x}{9} &= \frac{45}{9} \\ x &= 5 \end{aligned}$$

15.
$$\begin{aligned} 4.5 - y &= 2(y - 5.7) \\ 4.5 - y &= 2y - 11.4 \\ 4.5 - y - y &= 2y - y - 11.4 \\ 4.5 &= y - 11.4 \\ 4.5 + 11.4 &= y - 11.4 + 11.4 \\ 15.9 &= y \end{aligned}$$

Mental Math **Solve and check each equation.**

16. $5y = y - 40$

17. $7w = -7w$

18. $r + 1 = 4r + 1$

19. $6t + 1 = 6t - 8$

20. $2q + 4 = 4 - 2q$

21. $3a + 1 = 9 - a$

Choose **Use tiles, paper and pencil, calculator, or mental math to solve each equation. If appropriate, write *identity* or no *solution*.**

22. $t + 1 = 3t - 5$

23. $7y - 8 = 7y + 9$

24. $0.5k + 3.6 = 4.2 - 1.5k$

25. $2r + 16 = r - 25$

26. $\frac{3}{4}x = \frac{1}{2} + \frac{2}{3}x$

27. $\frac{1}{3}(x - 7) = 5x$

28. $0.7m = 0.9m + 2.4 - 0.2m$

29. $14 - (2q + 5) = -2q + 9$

30. $0.3t + 1.4 = 4.2 - 0.1t$

31. Find the value of each variable in the matrices. $\begin{bmatrix} 2x + 1 & a - 1 \\ w - 4 & 9y \end{bmatrix} = \begin{bmatrix} -5x - 6 & 5a \\ 3w + 4 & -3y \end{bmatrix}$

32. **Business** A toy company spends \$1500 each day on plant costs plus \$8 per toy for labor and materials. The toys sell for \$12 each. How many toys must the company sell in one day to equal its daily costs?

33. **Writing** Describe the two situations you learned about in this lesson that cannot occur when you are solving an equation with the variable on only one side of the equal sign. Give examples.

34. **Transportation** A truck traveling 45 mi/h and a train traveling 60 mi/h cover the same distance. The truck travels 2 h longer than the train. How many hours did each travel?

35. **Recreation** You can buy used in-line skates from your cousin for \$40, or you can rent them from the park. Either way you must rent safety equipment. How many hours must you skate at the park to justify buying your cousin's skates?

SKATE RENTALS
In-line skates and safety equipment $3.50/hour
Safety equipment $1.50/hour

Open-ended **Write an equation with variables on both sides for each of the following solutions.**

36. $x = 0$

37. x is a positive number.

38. x is a negative number.

39. All values of x are solutions.

40. $x = 1$

41. No values of x are solutions.

42. **a.** *Technology* Write formulas for cells B2 and C2 to evaluate the expressions at the top of Columns B and C.

b. Enter the integers from –5 to 5 in Column A. Evaluate the expressions in Columns B and C using the values in Column A.

c. What is the value in Column A when the numbers in Columns B and C are equal?

d. What equation have you solved?

e. Use a spreadsheet to solve $5.2n - 9 = 11.2n + 3$.

	A	B	C
1	x	5(x – 3)	4 – 3(x + 1)
2	–5	–40	16
3	–4	–35	13
4	–3		

43. *Geometry* $\triangle ABC$ is congruent to $\triangle DEF$. Find the lengths of the sides of $\triangle DEF$.

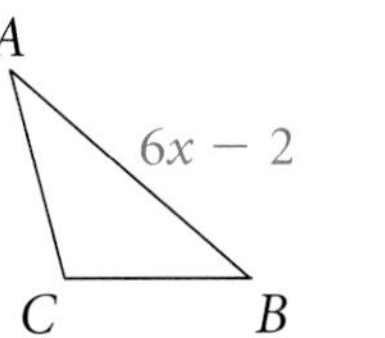

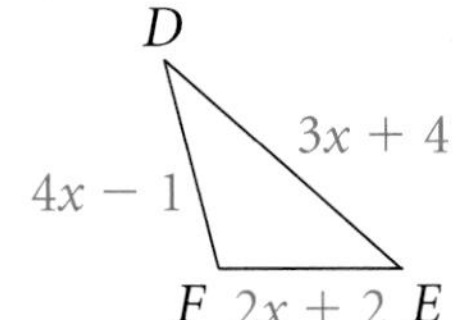

Solve each equation. Check your answers.

44. $2n - 5 = 8n + 7$

45. $3x + 4 = x + 18$

46. $3b + 5 - b = 4b$

47. $5a - 14 = -5 + 8a$

48. $4 - 6d = d + 4$

49. $-10t + 6.25 = t + 11.75$

50. $4x - 10 = x + 3x - 2x$

51. $6x = 4(x + 5)$

52. $\frac{3}{2}z - 2 = -\frac{5}{4}z - 4$

53. *Standardized Test Prep* Compare the quantities in Column A and Column B. Which statement is true for all values of x?

Column A	Column B
$5(x - 3)$	$7x - 12 - (2x + 3)$

A. The quantity in Column A is greater.
B. The quantity in Column B is greater.
C. The quantities are equal.
D. The relationship cannot be determined from the given information.

Exercises MIXED REVIEW

Solve and check each equation.

54. $-\frac{12}{14} = \frac{-9}{m}$

55. $\frac{1}{3}(h - 5) = -11$

56. $2x = 7x + 10$

57. $\frac{w}{7} = \frac{11}{10}$

58. *Money* The sales tax in Austin, Texas, is 8%. How much would you pay for three \$12 books and two \$15 books in Austin?

Getting Ready for Lesson 4-3

Simplify.

59. $|15|$

60. $|-12|$

61. $|-34|$

62. $|18 - 12|$

63. $|9 + 2|$

64. $|-12 - (-12)|$

65. $-|-19|$

66. $-|32|$

67. $-|-10 + 8|$

SELF ASSESSMENT — FOR YOUR JOURNAL

Summarize what you know about solving equations with variables on both sides by writing a list of steps for solving this type of equation.

CHAPTER 4

Cumulative Review

For Exercises 1–9, choose the correct letter.

1. Which equation does *not* have the same solution as $\frac{7}{y} = \frac{31}{36}$?

   A. $\frac{7}{31} = \frac{y}{36}$ **B.** $7 \cdot 36 = 31y$

   C. $\frac{y}{36} = \frac{7}{31}$ **D.** $\frac{36}{31} = \frac{7}{y}$

   E. $\frac{y}{7} = \frac{36}{31}$

2. Which of the following formulas correctly represent(s) the perimeter of the rectangle?

   I. $p = x + x + y + y$
   II. $p = xy$
   III. $p = 2x + 2y$

   y

   x

   A. I only **B.** II only **C.** II and III
   D. I and III **E.** I, II, and III

3. Solve $|a - 5| = 12$.

   A. 18 **B.** -12 and 12
   C. 17 and -7 **D.** -7
   E. -17 and 17

4. Solve the inequality $4x + 2 < x - 5$.

   A. $x \leq -\frac{1}{7}$ **B.** $x > \frac{7}{3}$ **C.** $x \geq -\frac{7}{3}$
   D. $x < -\frac{7}{3}$ **E.** $x < 1$

5. Of 355 people surveyed, 62% agreed with the school committee's decision. About how many people did *not* agree with the committee?

   A. 60 **B.** 140
   C. 220 **D.** 300
   E. None of the above

6. Students were asked to name their favorite type of motor vehicle. Seven preferred sport-utility vehicles, nine preferred sports cars, and five preferred luxury cars. What is the probability that a randomly selected student preferred a luxury car?

   A. $\frac{1}{3}$ **B.** $\frac{5}{21}$ **C.** $\frac{5}{16}$
   D. $\frac{3}{7}$ **E.** $\frac{2}{3}$

7. The number of subscribers to a magazine fell from 210,000 to 190,000. Find the approximate percent of decrease that this drop represents.

   A. 5% **B.** 10% **C.** 20%
   D. 90% **E.** None of the above

8. Match the graph with its absolute value inequality.

   −4 −3 −2 −1 0 1 2 3 4

   A. $|s| \leq 3$ **B.** $|s| > 3$
   C. $|s| \geq 3$ **D.** $|s| = 3$
   E. $|s| < 3$

9. Compare the quantities in Column A and Column B for $x \neq 0$.

Column A	Column B
$-\lvert x\rvert$	$\lvert -x\rvert$

   A. The quantity in Column A is greater.
   B. The quantity in Column B is greater.
   C. The two quantities are equal.
   D. The relationship cannot be determined from the information given.

For Exercises 10–13, write your answer.

10. A spinner numbered from 1 to 6 is spun. Each outcome is equally likely. Find the probability of getting an odd number. Then write this probability as a fraction, a decimal, and a percent.

11. Translate the following mathematical sentence into an equation and then solve it.
    Seventeen more than three times a number is 32.

12. **Open-ended** Use the numbers 5, –4, 9, 2, –1, and 3 to create two matrices of different sizes.

13. A CD player that normally costs $225 would cost an employee $180. What is the percent of the employee's discount?

4-7 Solving Multi-Step Inequalities

What You'll Learn

- Solving multi-step inequalities and graphing the solutions on a number line
- Using multi-step inequalities to model and solve real-world problems

...And Why

To solve inequalities that model real-world situations such as designing

THINK AND DISCUSS

Solving with Variables on One Side

When you solve equations, sometimes you need to use more than one step. The same is true when you solve inequalities.

Example 1 *Relating to the Real World*

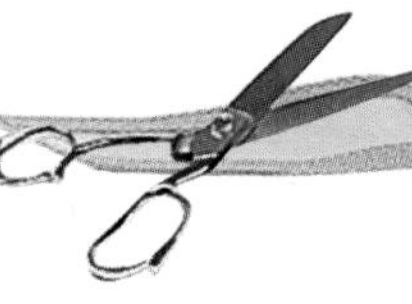

Design A school group needs a banner to carry in a parade. The narrowest street the parade is marching down measures 36 ft across, but some space is taken up by parked cars. The students have decided the length of the banner should be 18 ft. There are 45 ft of trim available to sew around the border of the banner. What is the greatest possible width for the banner?

PROBLEM SOLVING HINT

Draw a diagram.

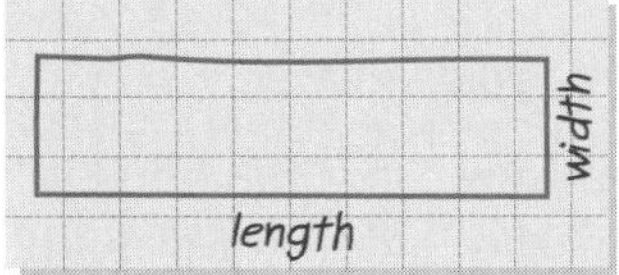

Define w = width of the banner

Relate Since the border goes around the edges of the banner, you can use the perimeter formula: $P = 2l + 2w$.

	twice the length	plus	twice the width	can be no more than	the border
Write	$2(18)$	$+$	$2w$	$\leq$	45

$$2(18) + 2w \leq 45$$

$$36 + 2w \leq 45 \quad \leftarrow \text{Simplify the left side.}$$

$$36 + 2w - 36 \leq 45 - 36 \quad \leftarrow \text{Subtract 36 from each side.}$$

$$2w \leq 9$$

$$\frac{2w}{2} \leq \frac{9}{2} \quad \leftarrow \text{Divide each side by 2.}$$

$$w \leq 4.5$$

The greatest possible width for the banner is 4.5 ft.

1. What could the model $2l + 2w > 45$ mean in the situation described in Example 1?

Sometimes solving an inequality involves the distributive property.

Example 2

Solve $2(w + 2) - 3w \geq -1$. Graph the solutions on a number line.

$$
\begin{aligned}
2(w + 2) - 3w &\geq -1 \\
2w + 4 - 3w &\geq -1 && \leftarrow \text{Use the distributive property.} \\
-1w + 4 &\geq -1 && \leftarrow \text{Combine like terms.} \\
-1w + 4 - 4 &\geq -1 - 4 && \leftarrow \text{Subtract 4 from each side.} \\
-w &\geq -5 && \leftarrow \text{Simplify.} \\
\frac{-w}{-1} &\leq \frac{-5}{-1} && \leftarrow \text{Divide each side by } -1\text{. Reverse the order of the inequality.} \\
w &\leq 5
\end{aligned}
$$

All numbers less than or equal to 5 are solutions.

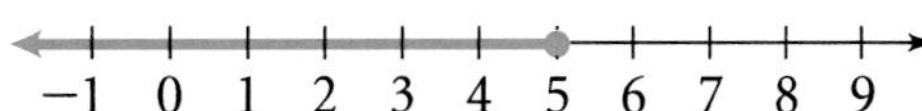

PROBLEM SOLVING

Look Back What happens if you multiply each side of $-1w \geq -5$ by -1?

2. You can check the solutions to Example 2 by substituting values into the inequality $2(w + 2) - 3w \geq -1$.
   a. Use the values 4, 5, and 6. Which values make the inequality true?
   b. Explain how part (a) serves as a check on Example 2.

Solving with Variables on Both Sides

Example 3

Solve $8z - 6 < 3z + 12$. Graph the solutions on a number line.

$$
\begin{aligned}
8z - 6 &< 3z + 12 \\
8z - 6 - 3z &< 3z + 12 - 3z && \leftarrow \text{Subtract } 3z \text{ from each side.} \\
5z - 6 &< 12 && \leftarrow \text{Combine like terms.} \\
5z - 6 + 6 &< 12 + 6 && \leftarrow \text{Add 6 to each side.} \\
5z &< 18 \\
\frac{5z}{5} &< \frac{18}{5} && \leftarrow \text{Divide each side by 5.} \\
z &< 3.6
\end{aligned}
$$

All numbers less than 3.6 are solutions.

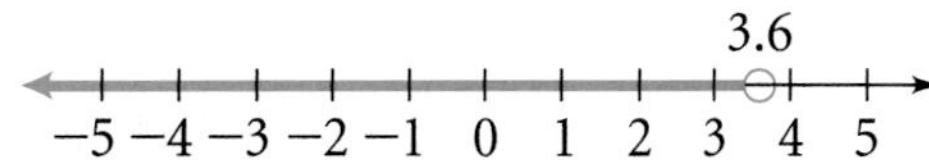

GRAPHING CALCULATOR HINT

You can check your solutions to Example 3 by using the TEST feature.

3. What happens when you replace z with 3.6 in $8z - 6 < 3z + 12$?

4. a. **Try This** Solve $3b + 12 > 21 - 2b$.
   b. Graph the solutions on a number line.

QUICK REVIEW

Equations such as $1 + 3a = 3a + 1$ are *identities.* Equations such as $2 + a = a - 2$ have *no solution.*

Like equations, some inequalities are true for all values of the variable, and some inequalities are false for all values of the variable. When an inequality is false for all values of the variable, it has no solution.

5. **Critical Thinking** Without writing the steps of a solution, tell whether the inequality is *true* or *false* for all values of the variable. **Justify** your response.
   a. $4s - 5 < 4s - 7$
   b. $4s - 5 < 3 + 4s$
   c. $4s + 6 \geq 6 + 4s$
   d. $4s + 6 > 6 + 4s$
   e. $4s - 9 < 4s$
   f. $4s \leq 4s$

Exercises ON YOUR OWN

Tell what you must do to the first inequality in order to get the second. Be sure to list *all* the steps.

1. $4j + 5 \geq 23; j \geq 4.5$
2. $2(q - 3) < 8; q < 7$
3. $8 - 4s > 16; -4s > 8$
4. $-8 > \frac{z}{-5} - 2; 30 < z$
5. $2y - 5 > 9 + y; y > 14$
6. $\frac{2}{3}g + 7 \geq 9; \frac{2}{3}g \geq 2$
7. $6 < 12 - s; s < 6$
8. $3 + 5t \geq 6(t - 1) - t; 3 \geq -6$
9. $6.2 < -r; -6.2 > r$

Match each inequality with its graph below.

10. $2x - 2 > 4$
11. $2 - 2x > 4$
12. $2x + 2 > 4$
13. $2x + 2 > 4x$
14. $-2x - 2 > 4$
15. $-2(x - 2) > 4$

A.
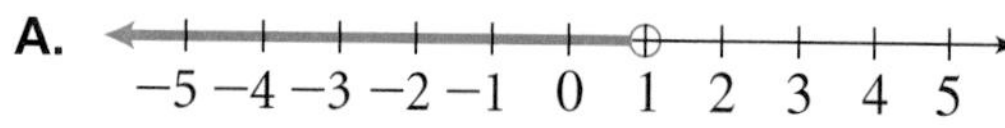

B.
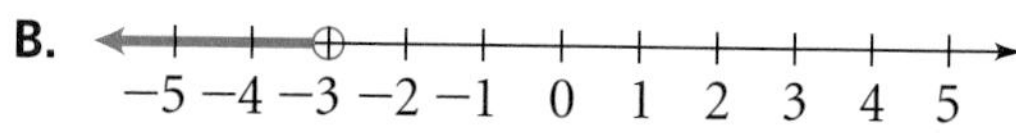

C.
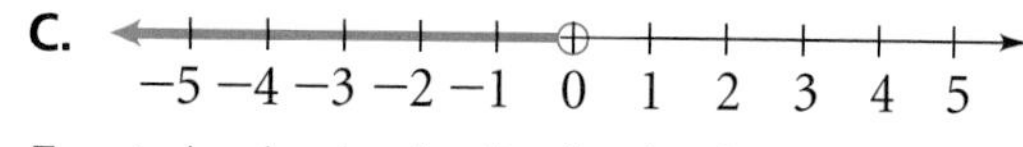

D.
−5 −4 −3 −2 −1 0 1 2 3 4 5

E.
−5 −4 −3 −2 −1 0 1 2 3 4 5

F.
−5 −4 −3 −2 −1 0 1 2 3 4 5

16. **Recreation** The sophomore class is planning a picnic. The cost of a permit to use the park is \$250. To pay for the permit, there is a fee of \$.75 for each sophomore and \$1.25 for each guest who is not a sophomore. Two hundred sophomores plan to attend. How many guests must attend in order to pay for the permit?

Solve each inequality. Graph the solutions on a number line.

17. $5 \leq 11 + 3h$
18. $3(y - 5) > 6$
19. $-4x - 2 < 8$
20. $r + 6 + 3r \geq 15 - 2r$
21. $5 - 2n \leq 3 - n$
22. $3(2v - 4) \leq 2(3v - 6)$
23. $2(m - 8) - 3m < -8$
24. $-(6b - 2) > 0$
25. $7a - (9a + 1) > 5$

26. **Writing** Suppose a friend is having difficulty solving the inequality $2.5(p - 4) > 3(p + 2)$. Explain how to solve the inequality, showing all necessary steps and identifying the properties you would use.

27. **Freight Handling** The freight elevator of a building can safely carry a load of at most 4000 lb. A worker needs to move supplies in 50-lb boxes from the loading dock to the fourth floor of the building. The worker weighs 160 lb. The cart she uses weighs 95 lb.
   a. What is the greatest number of boxes she can move in one trip?
   b. The worker must deliver 310 boxes to the fourth floor. How many trips must she make?

28. **Critical Thinking** Find a value of a such that the number line below shows all the solutions of $ax + 4 \leq -12$.

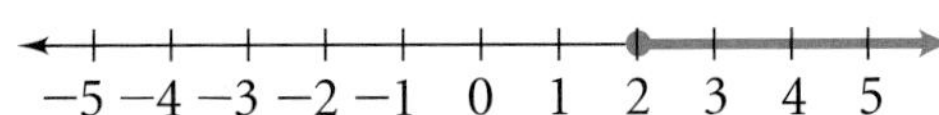

Choose **Use a calculator or paper and pencil. Solve and check each inequality.**

29. $2 - 3k < 4 + 5k$
30. $\frac{1}{2}n - \frac{1}{8} \geq \frac{3}{4} + \frac{5}{6}n$
31. $-3(v - 3) \geq 5 - 3v$
32. $8 \leq 5 - m + 1$
33. $0.5(3 - 8t) > 20(1 - 0.2t)$
34. $\frac{2}{3}d - 4 > d + \frac{1}{8} - \frac{1}{3}d$
35. $38 - k \leq 5 - 2k$
36. $\frac{4}{3}r - 3 < r + \frac{2}{3} - \frac{1}{3}r$
37. $-2(0.5 - 4s) \geq -3(4 + 3.5s)$

38. **Standardized Test Prep** Which value of n is a solution of both $2(n + 5) \geq 4$ and $3(n - 1) < 3$?
   A. -7
   B. -3
   C. 2
   D. 4
   E. none of these

39. **Open-ended** Write two different inequalities that you can solve by adding 5 and multiplying by -3. Show how to solve each inequality.

40. a. **Generalize** Solve $ax + b > c$ for x, where a is positive.
   b. Solve $ax + b > c$ for x, where a is negative.

41. **Jobs** JoLeen is a sales associate in a clothing store. Each week she earns \$250 plus a commission equal to 3% of her sales. This week she would like to earn no less than \$460. What dollar amount of clothes must she sell?

42. **Geometry** Artists often use the *golden rectangle* because it is considered to be pleasing to the eye. The length of a golden rectangle is about 1.62 times its width. Suppose you are making a picture frame in the shape of a golden rectangle. You have a 46-in. piece of wood. What are the length and width of the largest frame you can make? (Round your answers to the nearest tenth of an inch.)

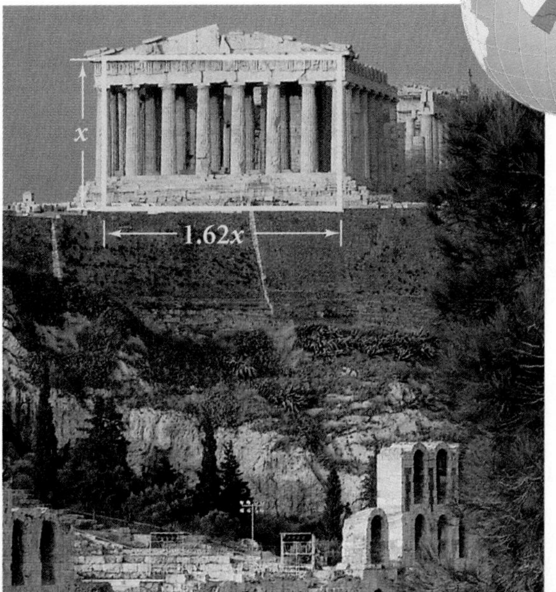

The Parthenon, an ancient Greek temple, was designed so that its dimensions form a golden rectangle.

43. *Business* Carlos plans to start a part-time word processing business out of his home. He is thinking of charging his customers \$15 per hour. The table shows his expected monthly business expenses. Write an inequality to find the least number of hours he must work in a month to make a profit of at least \$1200.

Monthly Expenses

Expense	Cost
Equipment Rental	\$490
Materials	\$45
Business Phone	\$65

Chapter Project

Find Out by Researching

Systolic blood pressure, the higher number in a blood pressure reading, is measured as your heart muscle contracts. The formula $P \leq \frac{1}{2}a + 110$ gives the normal systolic blood pressure P based on age a.

- Find your normal systolic blood pressure.
- At age 20, does 120 represent a maximum or a minimum systolic pressure? Explain.
- A blood pressure reading higher than the normal value indicates a possible need for a change in lifestyle or for special medication. Research some lifestyle changes that can help reduce high blood pressure.

Exercises MIXED REVIEW

Write an inequality to model each situation.

44. An octopus can be up to 10 ft long.

45. A hummingbird migrates more than 1850 mi.

To which family of functions does each graph belong? Explain your reasoning.

46. $y = x^2 - 3x$

47. $y = |x| - 2$

48. $y = 5x + 1$

49. $y = 9 - x^2$

50. It takes 4.5 million jasmine petals to make 450 g of jasmine oil. How many petals are needed to make 1 kg of jasmine oil?

51. *Recycling* Each year, 9.5 million vehicles are recycled.

a. About 75% of each vehicle's mass is reused. The average vehicle weighs 1.5 tons. About how many tons of materials can be reused from one vehicle?

b. How many tons of materials can be reused from all the recycled vehicles each year?

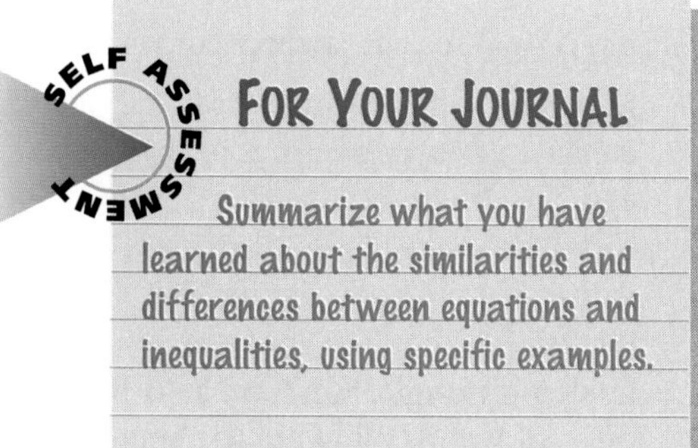

SELF ASSESSMENT
FOR YOUR JOURNAL
Summarize what you have learned about the similarities and differences between equations and inequalities, using specific examples.

Getting Ready for Lesson 4-8

Graph each pair of inequalities on one number line.

52. $c < 8; c \geq 10$

53. $t \geq -2; t \leq -5$

54. $m \leq 7; m > 12$

55. $h > 1; h < 0$

Math ToolboX

Skills Review

Dimensional Analysis

You can use conversion factors to change from one unit of measure to another. The process of analyzing units to decide which conversion factors to use is called **dimensional analysis.**

Since 60 min = 1 h, $\frac{60 \text{ min}}{1 \text{ h}}$ equals 1. You can use $\frac{60 \text{ min}}{1 \text{ h}}$ to convert hours to minutes.

$$7\,\cancel{\text{h}} \cdot \frac{60 \text{ min}}{1\,\cancel{\text{h}}} = 420 \text{ min}$$

The hour units cancel, and the result is minutes.

Sometimes you need to use more than one conversion factor.

Example

Animals A cheetah ran 300 ft in 2.92 s. What was the cheetah's speed in miles per hour?

You need to convert feet to miles and seconds to hours.

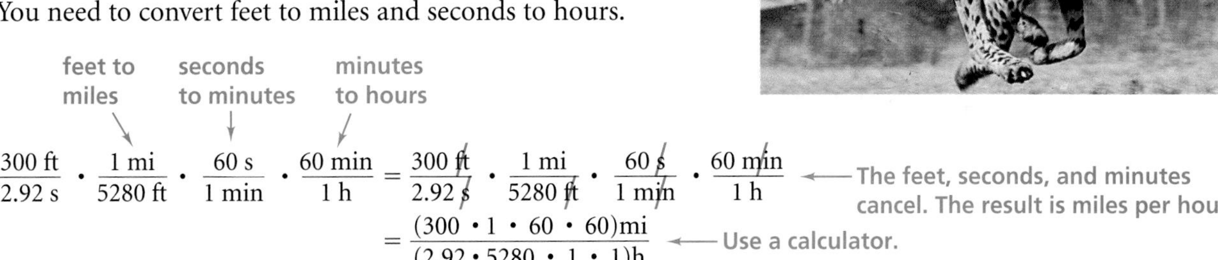

feet to miles; seconds to minutes; minutes to hours

$$\frac{300 \text{ ft}}{2.92 \text{ s}} \cdot \frac{1 \text{ mi}}{5280 \text{ ft}} \cdot \frac{60 \text{ s}}{1 \text{ min}} \cdot \frac{60 \text{ min}}{1 \text{ h}} = \frac{300\,\cancel{\text{ft}}}{2.92\,\cancel{\text{s}}} \cdot \frac{1 \text{ mi}}{5280\,\cancel{\text{ft}}} \cdot \frac{60\,\cancel{\text{s}}}{1\,\cancel{\text{min}}} \cdot \frac{60\,\cancel{\text{min}}}{1 \text{ h}}$$

The feet, seconds, and minutes cancel. The result is miles per hour.

$$= \frac{(300 \cdot 1 \cdot 60 \cdot 60)\text{mi}}{(2.92 \cdot 5280 \cdot 1 \cdot 1)\text{h}}$$

Use a calculator.

$$\approx 70 \text{ mi/h}$$

The cheetah's speed was about 70 mi/h.

Choose A or B for the correct conversion factor for changing the units.

1. quarts to gallons
A. $\frac{1 \text{ gal}}{4 \text{ qt}}$ **B.** $\frac{4 \text{ qt}}{1 \text{ gal}}$

2. ounces to pounds
A. $\frac{1 \text{ lb}}{16 \text{ oz}}$ **B.** $\frac{16 \text{ oz}}{1 \text{ lb}}$

3. inches to yards
A. $\frac{36 \text{ in.}}{1 \text{ yd}}$ **B.** $\frac{1 \text{ yd}}{36 \text{ in.}}$

Write each in the given unit or units.

4. 8 h = ■ s

5. 120 in. = ■ yd

6. \$1.85/3.25 lb = ■ ¢/oz

7. 18 qt/s = ■ gal/min

Express each in miles per hour.

8. 300 yd in 10.9 min

9. 1 mi in 3.79 min

10. 120 ft in 30 s

11. 250 mi in 45 sec

12. *Writing* Explain how you determine which conversion factors to use when changing 3 in./s to feet per minute.

5-4 Slope-Intercept Form

What You'll Learn

- Using the slope and y-intercept to draw graphs and write equations

...And Why

To investigate flag designs and real-world situations, such as salary plus commission

What You'll Need

- graphing calculator

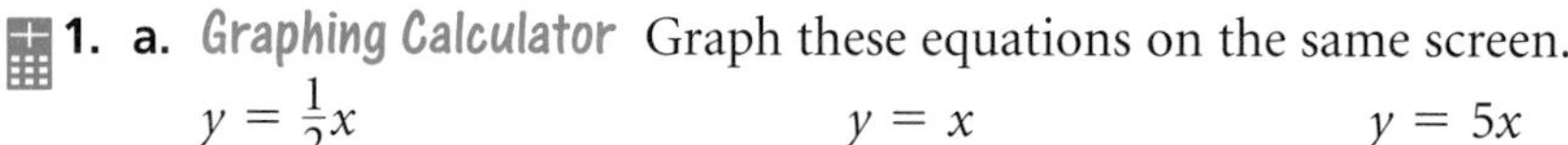

1. a. *Graphing Calculator* Graph these equations on the same screen.
$y = \frac{1}{2}x$ $\qquad$ $y = x$ $\qquad$ $y = 5x$
   b. **Generalize** How does the coefficient of x affect the graph of an equation?

2. a. *Graphing Calculator* Many national flags include designs formed from straight lines. You can use equations to model these designs. Choose values for k in the equation $y = kx$ to create a display like the one for the flag of Jamaica. Use the standard settings.

Jamaica

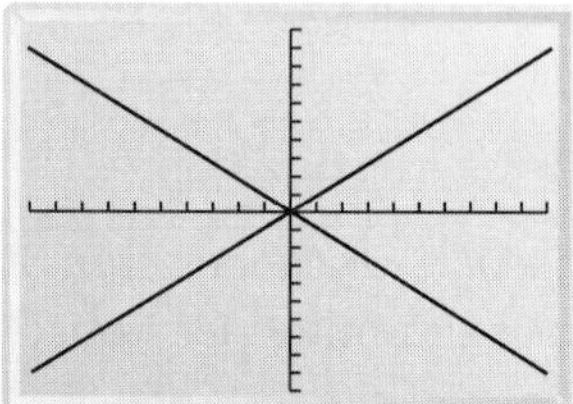

   b. What do you notice about the values of k for the lines you graphed?

3. a. *Graphing Calculator* Graph these equations on the same screen.
$y = 2x$ $\qquad$ $y = 2x + 3$ $\qquad$ $y = 2x - 4$
   b. Where does each line cross the y-axis?

Tanzania

4. Choose values for b in the equation $y = 1.1x + b$. Create a display that resembles the Tanzanian flag. Write the equations you used for your display.

5. **Generalize** What effect does the value of b have on the graph of an equation?

6. *Open-ended* Make a flag design of your own. Write the equations you use for your design.

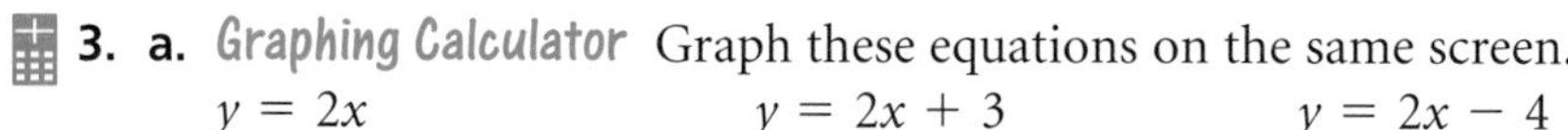

Defining Slope-Intercept Form

The point where a line crosses the y-axis is the **y-intercept.**

$y = -\frac{1}{3}x + 2$

$y = -\frac{1}{3}x$

$y = -\frac{1}{3}x - \frac{4}{3}$

7. a. What is the y-intercept of each line at the left?
   b. **Generalize** What is the connection between a line's equation and its y-intercept?

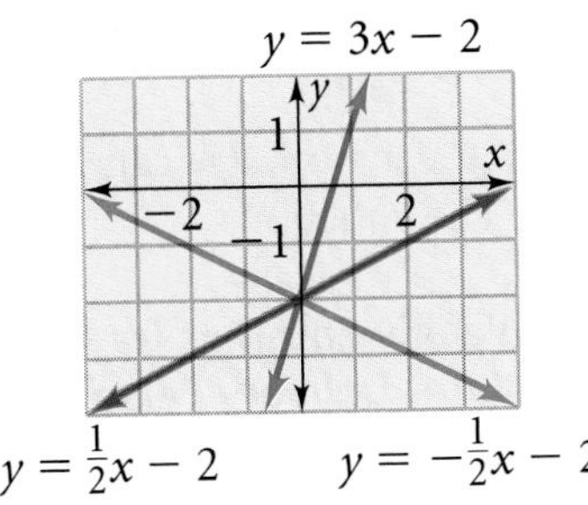

8. a. What is the slope of each line at the left?
   b. **Generalize** What is the connection between a line's equation and its slope?

In the last lesson you learned that the letter k indicates the constant of variation of a direct variation. For linear equations in general, the letter m indicates the slope and the letter b indicates the y-intercept.

Slope-Intercept Form of a Linear Equation

The **slope-intercept form** of a linear equation is $y = mx + b$.

m ↑ slope b ↑ y-intercept

9. **Try This** What are the slope and y-intercept of the line for each equation?
   a. $y = 3x - 5$ b. $y = \frac{7}{6}x + \frac{3}{4}$ c. $y = -\frac{4}{5}x$

10. **Try This** Write an equation of a line with the given slope and y-intercept.
    a. $m = \frac{2}{3}, b = -5$ b. $m = -\frac{1}{2}, b = 0$ c. $m = 0, b = -2$

You can use the slope and y-intercept to graph an equation.

Example 1

Graph the equation $y = 3x - 1$.

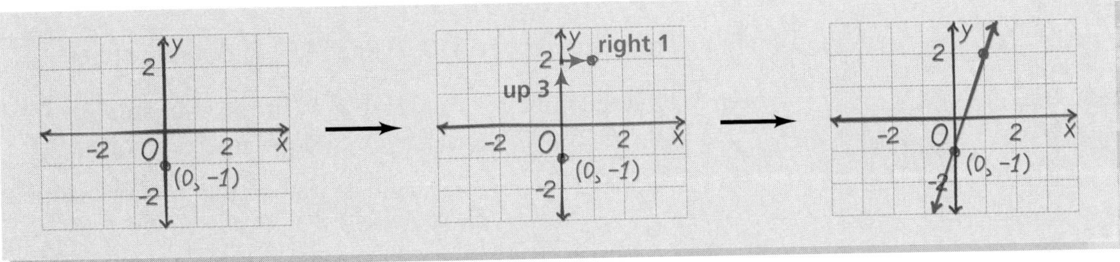

The y-intercept is -1, so plot a point at $(0, -1)$.

The slope is 3, or $\frac{3}{1}$. Use the slope to plot a second point.

Draw a line through the points.

11. **Critical Thinking** Could you find a second point by going down 3 and to the left 1? Explain.

12. **Try This** Graph $y = -\frac{3}{2}x + 2$.

You may need to rewrite a linear equation to express it in slope-intercept form.

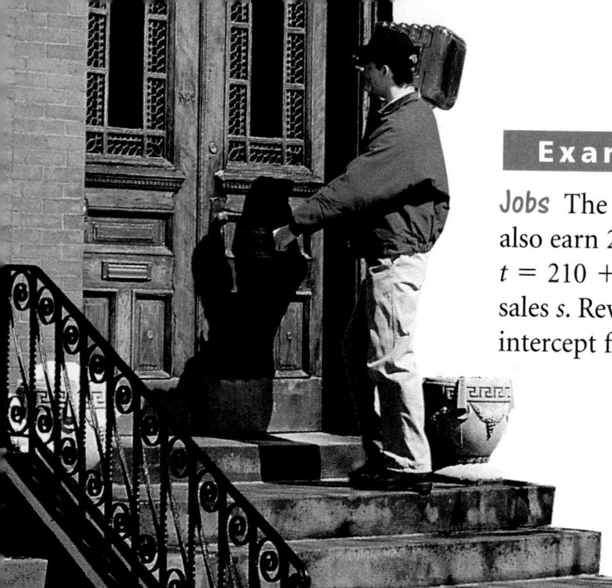

Example 2 Relating to the Real World 

Jobs The base pay of a water delivery person is \$210 per week. He can also earn 20% commission on any sales he makes. The equation $t = 210 + 0.2s$ relates total earnings t to sales s. Rewrite the equation in slope-intercept form. Then graph the equation.

$t = 210 + 0.2s$

↑ intercept ↑ slope

$t = 0.2s + 210$ ← slope-intercept form

Weekly Earnings for a Water Delivery Person

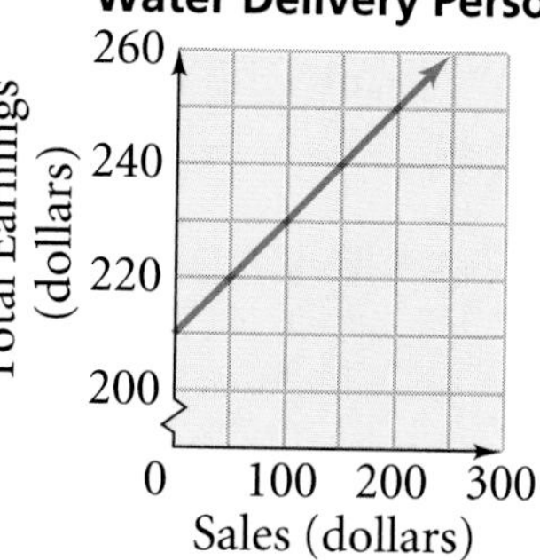

13. How would you express $t = 0.2s + 210$ using x and y in order to graph the equation on a graphing calculator? Explain.

14. Would you use the equation or the graph to find a delivery person's total earnings with sales of \$225 in one week? Why?

15. **Try This** Rewrite $y + 5 = 4x$ in slope-intercept form.

Writing Equations

Example 3

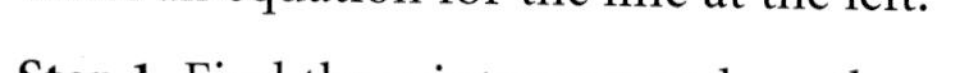

Write an equation for the line at the left.

Step 1 Find the y-intercept and another point.

The y-intercept is 2; $(0, 2)$ and $(4, -1)$ lie on the line.

Step 2 Find the slope.
Use $(0, 2)$ and $(4, -1)$.

$$\text{slope} = \frac{-1 - 2}{4 - 0} = -\frac{3}{4}$$

Step 3 Write an equation in slope-intercept form.
Substitute $-\frac{3}{4}$ for m and 2 for b.

$$y = mx + b$$
$$y = -\frac{3}{4}x + 2$$

Exercises ON YOUR OWN

Find the slope and y-intercept of each equation.

1. $y = -\frac{3}{4}x - 5$ **2.** $y = \frac{1}{2}x$ **3.** $3x - 9 = y$ **4.** $2x = y + 7$ **5.** $y = 3$

6. *Standardized Test Prep* A music store sells CDs for \$12 each. Customers may use one coupon good for \$4 off the total purchase. Suppose a customer buys n number of CDs using a coupon. Which equation models the relationship between the total cost t and the number of CDs a customer buys?

A. $t = 12n - 4$ **B.** $t = 4n - 12$ **C.** $4t = 12n$ **D.** $t = 12 - 4n$ **E.** $t = 4 - 12n$

Match the graph with the correct equation.

7. $y = x + 5$
8. $y = -\frac{5}{2}x + 5$
9. $y = -\frac{1}{2}x + 5$

I. **II.** **III.**

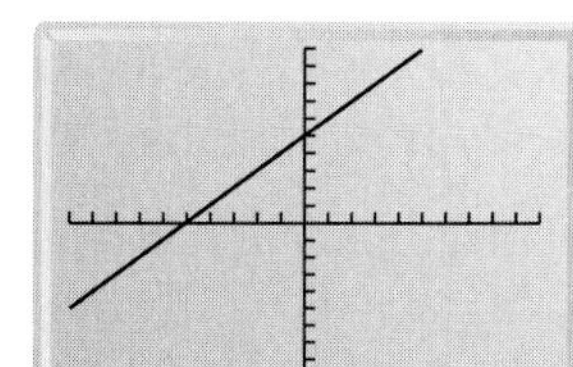

10. *Graphing Calculator* Suppose you want to graph the equation $y = \frac{5}{4}x - 3$. Enter each key sequence and display the graphs.

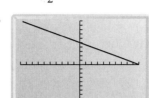

a. Y= 5 ÷ 4 X,T,θ − 3 **b.** Y= (5 ÷ 4) X,T,θ − 3

c. Which key sequence gives you the graph of $y = \frac{5}{4}x - 3$? Explain.

11. A candle begins burning at time $t = 0$. Its height is measured over a period of 30 min. The data are graphed at the right.
   a. Use the graph to find the original height of the candle.
   b. Write an equation that relates the height of the candle to the time it has been burning.
   c. How many minutes after the candle is lit will it burn out?

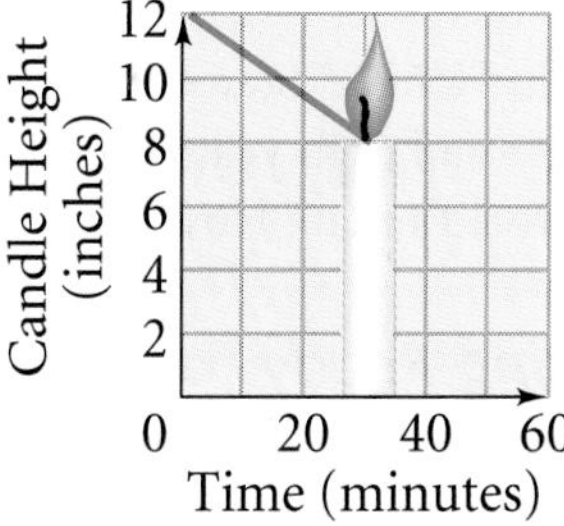

Graph each equation.

12. $y = 2x - 1$
13. $y = 5 + 2x$
14. $y - 4 = x$
15. $y + \frac{3}{4}x = 0$
16. $y = 7$
17. $y = -\frac{1}{2}x + \frac{3}{2}$
18. $y = -\frac{2}{3}x + 0$
19. $y + 3 = \frac{7}{4}x$
20. $y + x = 3$

Find the slope and y-intercept. Write an equation of each line.

21.

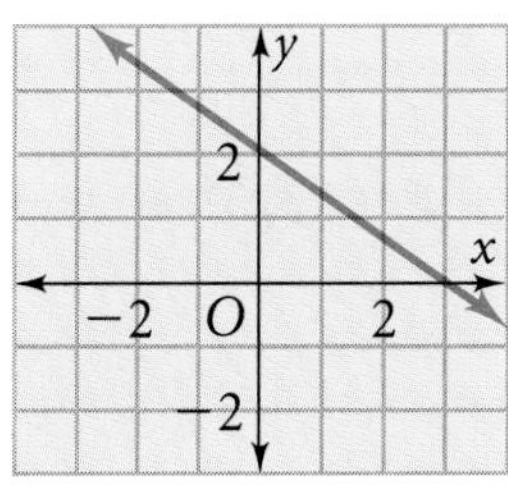

22.

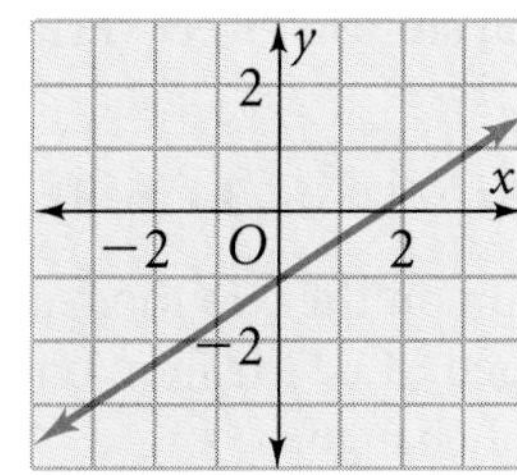

23.

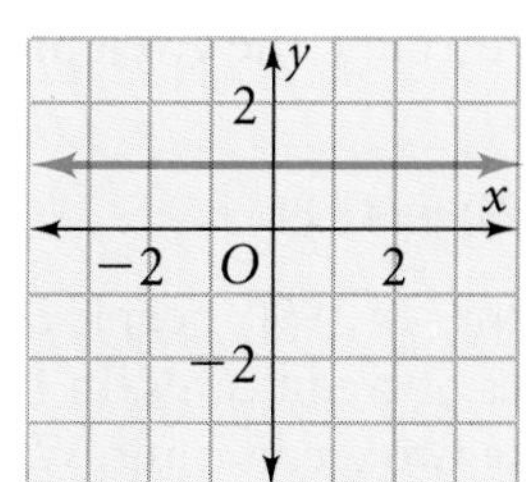

24. **Recreation** A group of mountain climbers begins an expedition with 265 lb of food. They plan to eat a total of 15 lb of food per day. The equation $r = 265 - 15d$ relates the remaining food supply r to the number of days d.
   a. Write the equation in slope-intercept form.
   b. Graph your equation.
   c. The group plans to eat the last of their food the day their expedition ends. Use your graph to find how many days the expedition will last.

25. **Open-Ended** Write an equation of your own. Identify the slope and y-intercept. Graph your equation.

26. **Writing** Explain how you would graph the line $y = \frac{3}{4}x + 5$.

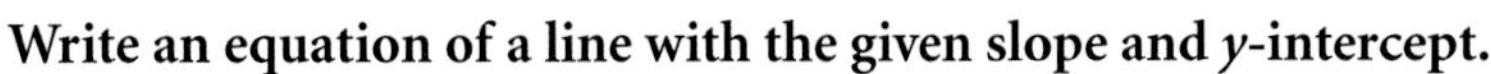

Write an equation of a line with the given slope and y-intercept.

27. $m = \frac{2}{9}, b = 3$
28. $m = 5, b = -\frac{2}{3}$
29. $m = -\frac{5}{4}, b = 0$
30. $m = 0, b = 1$

Exercises MIXED REVIEW

Find the slope of the line through each set of points.

31. $(-2, 8), (5, -1)$
32. $(4, 6), (2, -1)$
33. $(1, 2), (6, 1)$

34. The United States Postal Service delivers 177 billion pieces of mail each year. This number represents 40% of the world's mail. How many pieces are sent world-wide each year?

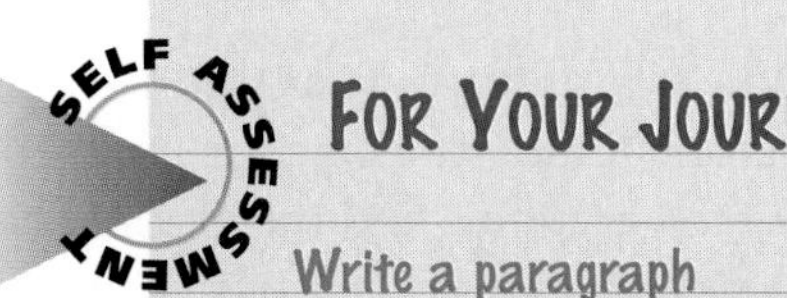

For Your Journal

Write a paragraph explaining how to use the slope and y-intercept to write an equation and to draw a graph.

Getting Ready for Lesson 5-5

Through the given point, graph a line with the given slope. Then identify the y-intercept.

35. $(2, 0); m = -1$
36. $(2, 3); m = \frac{3}{2}$
37. $(3, 2); m = \frac{1}{3}$
38. $(-2, 1); m = -\frac{5}{2}$

Exercises CHECKPOINT

Is a line through the given point with the given slope a direct variation? Explain.

1. $(4, 2); m = \frac{1}{2}$
2. $(-2, -2); m = -1$
3. $(6, 9)$; m is undefined
4. $(-3, 5); m = -\frac{5}{3}$
5. **Money** In 1990, people charged \$534 billion on the two most used types of credit cards. In 1994, people charged \$1.021 trillion on these same two credit cards. What was the rate of change?
6. **Writing** How are the graphs of $y = 3x + 5$, $y = \frac{2}{3}x + 5$, and $y = \frac{3}{5}x + 5$ alike? How are they different?

CHAPTER 5

Preparing for Standardized Tests

For Exercises 1–11, choose the correct letter.

1. A horizontal line passes through $(5, -2)$. Which other point does it also pass through?
   A. $(5, 2)$ B. $(-5, -2)$ C. $(-5, 2)$
   D. $(5, 0)$ E. none of the above

2. 180 is what percent of 60?
   A. 300% B. 50% C. 3%
   D. 500% E. 30%

3. Match the graph with its equation.

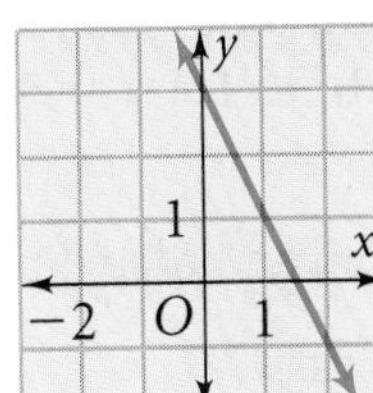

   A. $y = 2x + 3$
   B. $y = -2x + 3$
   C. $y = 2x - 3$
   D. $y = -2x - 3$
   E. none of the above

4. If $\frac{x}{3} = \frac{x+3}{5}$ and $\frac{y-7}{3} = \frac{y}{-7}$, then:
   A. $x > y$ B. $y > x$ C. $x = y$
   D. $x = 2y$ E. $y > 2x$

5. Mariko runs 800 ft in one minute. What is her approximate speed in miles per hour? (Recall: 5280 ft = 1 mi)
   A. 6 mi/h B. 8 mi/h C. 9 mi/h
   D. 12 mi/h E. 15 mi/h

6. If a, b, and c are three consecutive positive integers, which of the following could be true?
   I. $a + c < 2b$ II. $a + b < c$
   III. $a + c > 2b$ IV. $b + c > a$
   A. I only B. IV only C. I and II
   D. III and IV E. I and II

7. A line perpendicular to $y = 3x - 2$ passes through the point $(0, 6)$. Which other point lies on the line?
   A. $(9, 3)$ B. $(-9, 3)$ C. $(-9, -3)$
   D. $(9, -3)$ E. none of the above

8. Which of the following is the best estimate of the fraction $\frac{63 \cdot 123 \cdot 0.49}{6.23 \cdot 11.93}$?
   A. 50 B. 5 C. 20
   D. 250 E. 500

9. If $3x + 2 = 11$, then $5x + 1 =$ ■.
   A. 13 B. 14 C. 15 D. 16 E. 17

Compare the boxed quantity in Column A with the boxed quantity in Column B. Choose the best answer.

A. The quantity in Column A is greater.
B. The quantity in Column B is greater.
C. The two quantities are equal.
D. The relationship cannot be determined on the basis of the information supplied.

	Column A	Column B
10.	the slope of $2x - 3y = 5$	the slope of $4y - 2 = 7x$
	Use the equation $\frac{y-3}{x} = -3$.	
11.	the slope	the y intercept

Find each answer.

12. Write and solve a compound inequality for the following statement. "The sum of a number and 15 is more than 27 but less than 32."

13. Find the slope of the line that passes through $(-1, 3)$ and $(4, 6)$.

14. *Graphing Calculator* Write the equation of a trend line or the line of best fit for the data.

x	1	1	2	3	4	4	5	6
y	0	−1	1	6	8	7	12	15

15. Find two consecutive integers such that the larger is seven less than three times the smaller.

16. a. A new company employed 12 people. Two years later, it employed a total of 20 people. What was the percent of increase?
    b. If one of the 20 people retired, what would be the percent of decrease?

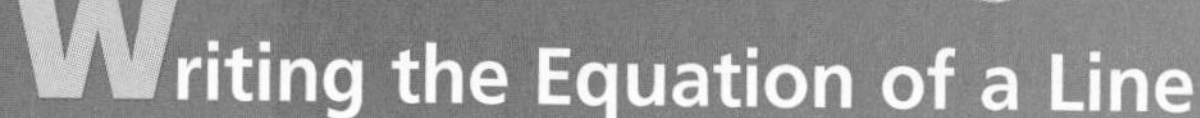

Connections Environment . . . and more

What You'll Learn

- Writing an equation given the slope and a point
- Writing an equation given two points from a graph or a table

...And Why

To write equations to investigate real-world situations, such as carbon monoxide emissions

5-5 Writing the Equation of a Line

THINK AND DISCUSS

In some real-world situations you can identify the rate of change, or slope, and an ordered pair. Then you can use the slope and ordered pair to model the situation with a linear equation.

Example 1 **Relating to the Real World** 

Environment World-wide carbon monoxide emissions are decreasing about 2.6 million metric tons each year. In 1991, carbon monoxide emissions were 79 million metric tons. Use a linear equation to model the relationship between carbon monoxide emissions and time. Let $x = 91$ correspond to 1991.

Step 1 Use the data to write the slope and an ordered pair.

slope: -2.6; ordered pair: $(91, 79)$

Step 2 Find the y-intercept using the slope and the ordered pair.

$$y = mx + b$$
$$79 = -2.6(91) + b \quad \leftarrow \text{Substitute (91, 76) for } (x, y) \text{ and } -2.6 \text{ for } m.$$
$$79 = -236.6 + b$$
$$315.6 = b$$

Step 3 Substitute values for m and b to write an equation.

$$y = mx + b$$
$$y = -2.6x + 315.6 \quad \leftarrow \text{Substitute } -2.6 \text{ for } m \text{ and } 315.6 \text{ for } b.$$

The equation $y = -2.6x + 315.6$ models the relationship between carbon monoxide emissions and time.

1. a. Using the equation in Example 1, estimate the emissions for 1990.
   b. According to this model, what will the emissions be for 2000?

2. **Try This** Write an equation of a line with slope $\frac{2}{5}$ through the point (4, –3).

You can use two points on a line to find an equation for the line. First find the slope of the line through the points. Then use the slope and one point to find the y-intercept and to write an equation of the line.

Example 2

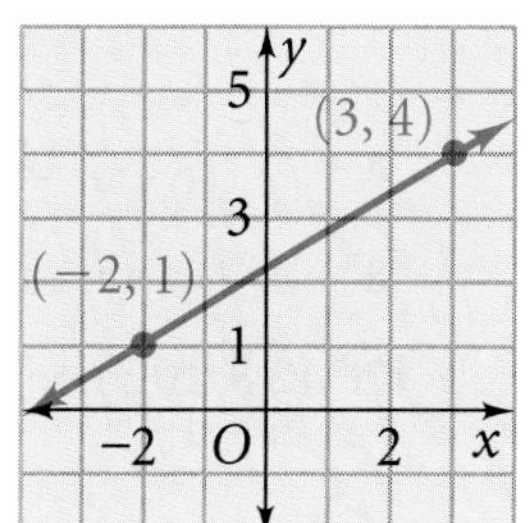

Find an equation of the line at the left.

Step 1 Use the coordinates of two points to find the slope of the line.

$$\text{slope} = \frac{y_2 - y_1}{x_2 - x_1}$$

$$= \frac{4 - 1}{3 - (-2)}$$ ← Substitute (3, 4) for (x_2, y_2) and (−2, 1) for (x_1, y_1).

$$= \frac{3}{5}$$

Step 2 Find the *y*-intercept.

$$y = mx + b$$

$$4 = \frac{3}{5}(3) + b$$ ← Substitute (3, 4) for (*x*, *y*) and $\frac{3}{5}$ for *m*. Solve for *b*.

$$4 = \frac{9}{5} + b$$

$$2\frac{1}{5} = b$$

Step 3 Substitute values in $y = mx + b$.

$$y = \frac{3}{5}x + 2\frac{1}{5}$$ ← Substitute $\frac{3}{5}$ for *m* and $2\frac{1}{5}$ for *b*.

3. Try This Find an equation of the line through (–5, 3) and (–2, –4).

You can also write a linear equation for data in tables. Two sets of data have a linear relationship if the rate of change between consecutive pairs of data is the same.

Example 3

x	*y*
−1	4
3	6
5	7
9	9

Is the relationship shown by the data linear? If it is, write an equation.

Step 1 Find the rate of change for consecutive ordered pairs.

(−1, 4) to (3, 6): $\frac{6 - 4}{3 - (-1)} = \frac{2}{4} = \frac{1}{2}$

(3, 6) to (5, 7): $\frac{7 - 6}{5 - 3} = \frac{1}{2}$

(5, 7) to (9, 9): $\frac{9 - 7}{9 - 5} = \frac{2}{4} = \frac{1}{2}$

The relationship is linear. The rate of change equals the slope. The slope is $\frac{1}{2}$.

Step 2 Find the *y*-intercept and write an equation.

$$y = mx + b$$

$$4 = \frac{1}{2}(-1) + b$$ ← Substitute (−1, 4) for (*x*, *y*) and $\frac{1}{2}$ for *m*.

$$4 = -\frac{1}{2} + b$$

$$4\frac{1}{2} = b$$ ← Add $\frac{1}{2}$ to each side of the equation.

$$y = \frac{1}{2}x + 4\frac{1}{2}$$ ← Substitute $\frac{1}{2}$ for *m* and $4\frac{1}{2}$ for *b* in $y = mx + b$.

PROBLEM SOLVING

Look Back Could you use a graph to find whether the relationship is linear? Explain.

4. *Critical Thinking* Is (−1, 4) the only ordered pair that you could use to find the *y*-intercept in Example 3? Explain.

Exercises ON YOUR OWN

Write an equation of a line through the given point with the given slope.

1. $(3, -5); m = 2$
2. $(1, 2); m = -3$
3. $(2, 6); m = \frac{4}{3}$
4. $(-1, 5); m = -\frac{3}{5}$
5. $(0, 3); m = 1$
6. $(3, 0); m = -1$
7. $(-5, 2); m = 0$
8. $(6, 7)$; m undefined
9. $(3, 3); m = -\frac{1}{4}$
10. $(5, -2); m = \frac{7}{2}$
11. $(-6, 1); m = -\frac{3}{4}$
12. $(2.8, 10.5); m = 0.25$

13. a. *Physics* Each gram of mass stretches the spring 0.025 cm. Use $m = 0.025$ and the ordered pair (50, 8.5) to write a linear equation that models the relationship between the length of the spring and the mass.
    b. *Critical Thinking* What does the y-intercept mean in this situation?
    c. What is the length of the spring for a mass of 70 g?

8.5 cm
50 g

Write an equation of a line through the given points.

14. $(3, -3), (-3, 1)$
15. $(7, 3), (2, 2)$
16. $(3, 5), (5, 3)$
17. $(-8, 2), (1, 3)$
18. $(-0.5, 2), (-2, 1.5)$
19. $(25, 100), (15, 120)$

Write an equation of each line.

20.
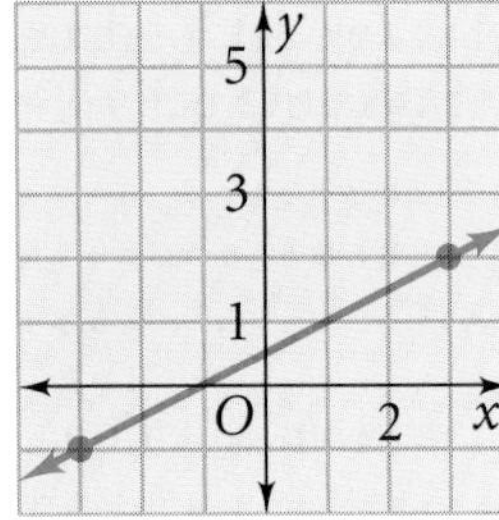

21.
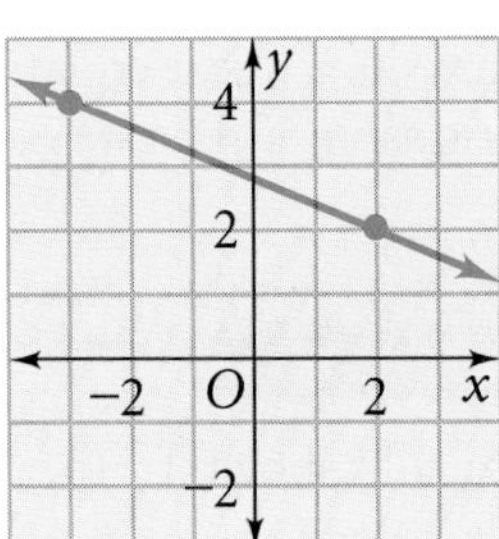

22.
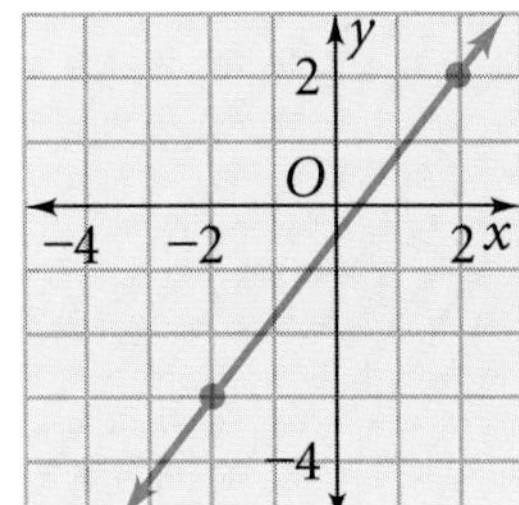

23. *Entertainment* Total receipts for motion picture theaters were \$3.9 billion in 1986. Receipts were \$6.9 billion in 1992.
    a. Write an equation to model the relationship between receipts and time in years. Let 86 correspond to 1986.
    b. Use your equation to **predict** motion picture theater receipts in the year 2010. (*Hint:* Think about the number you will use for 2010.)

Tell whether the relationship shown by the data is linear. If it is, write an equation for the relationship.

24.

x	y
−10	−7
0	−3
5	−1
20	5

25.

x	y
−4	9
2	−3
5	−9
9	−17

26.

x	y
1	7
2	8
3	10
4	13

27.

x	y
−10	−5
−2	19
5	40
11	58

28.

x	y
3	1
6	4
9	13
15	49

29. a. **Business** A taxicab ride that is 2 mi long costs \$7. One that is 9 mi long costs \$24.50. Write an equation relating cost to length of ride.

b. What do the slope and y-intercept mean in this situation?

30. **National Parks** The number of recreational visits to National Parks in the United States increases by about 9.3 million visits each year. In 1990 there were about 263 million visits.

a. Write an equation to model the relationship between the number of visits and time in years. Let 90 correspond to 1990.

b. **Open-ended** Suppose the number of recreational visits to National Parks continues to increase at the same rate. How many visits will there be this year?

Chapter Project *Find Out by Modeling*

Suppose you earn \$5.50/h at a bakery. From your first paycheck you discover that \$1.15/h is withheld for taxes and benefits. You work x hours during a five-day week and you spend \$3.75 each day for lunch.

- Write an equation for your earnings for a week after taxes and expenses.
- In this situation what does the slope represent? the y-intercept?
- How many hours must you work to earn \$120 after taxes and expenses?

Exercises MIXED REVIEW

Solve.

31. $4c < 24 + c$ 32. $\frac{t}{2} + \frac{t}{3} = 5$ 33. $-4m \geq 7$

34. $|5c| < 16$ 35. $4(3h + 2) = 5h - 3$ 36. $|2n + 5| \geq 9$

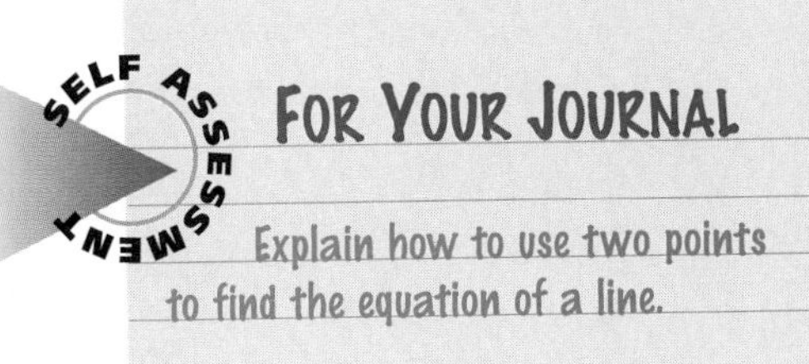

SELF ASSESSMENT
FOR YOUR JOURNAL
Explain how to use two points to find the equation of a line.

37. **Real Estate** In 1995, a new development was built near the home of Mary Davenport in Lawrence, Kansas. The appraised value of her property went from \$41,500 to \$426,870. What was the percent of change in the property's appraised value?

Getting Ready for Lesson 5-6

Determine whether each scatter plot shows *positive, negative,* or *no correlation.*

38. 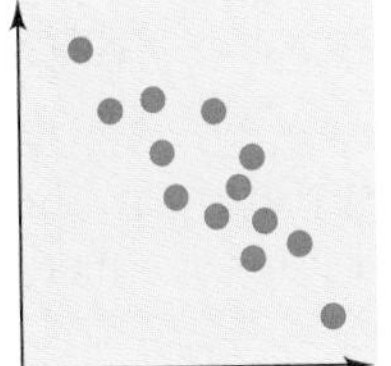

39. 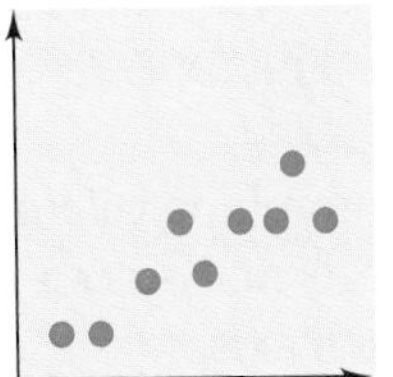

40. 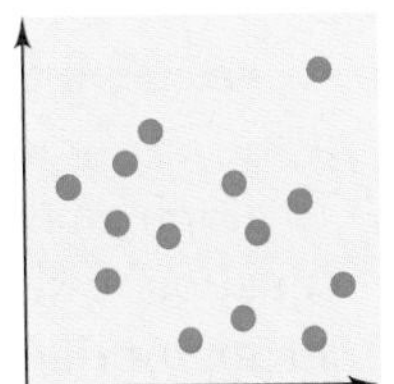

41. 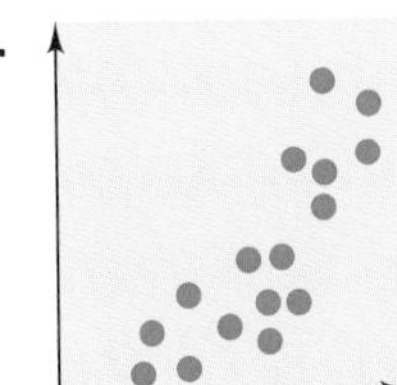

What You'll Learn

- Graphing equations using x- and y-intercepts
- Writing equations in $Ax + By = C$ form
- Modeling situations with equations in the form $Ax + By = C$

...And Why

To investigate real-world situations, such as burning calories when running and jogging

What You'll Need

- graph paper
- graphing calculator

5-7 $Ax + By = C$ Form

THINK AND DISCUSS

Graphing Equations

The slope-intercept form is just one form of a linear equation. Another form is $Ax + By = C$, which is useful in making quick graphs.

$Ax + By = C$ Form of a Linear Equation

$Ax + By = C$ is a linear equation, where A and B cannot both be zero.

$3x + 4y = 8$

To make a quick graph, you can use the x- and y-intercepts. The **x-intercept** is the x-coordinate of the point where a line crosses the x-axis.

Example 1

Graph $3x + 4y = 8$.

Step 1 To find the x-intercept, substitute 0 for y and solve for x.

$$3x + 4y = 8$$
$$3x + 4(0) = 8$$
$$3x = 8$$
$$x = \frac{8}{3}, \text{ or } 2\tfrac{2}{3}$$

The x-intercept is $2\frac{2}{3}$.

Step 2 To find the y-intercept, substitute 0 for x and solve for y.

$$3x + 4y = 8$$
$$3(0) + 4y = 8$$
$$4y = 8$$
$$y = 2$$

The y-intercept is 2.

Step 3 Plot $(2\frac{2}{3}, 0)$ and $(0, 2)$. Draw a line through the points.

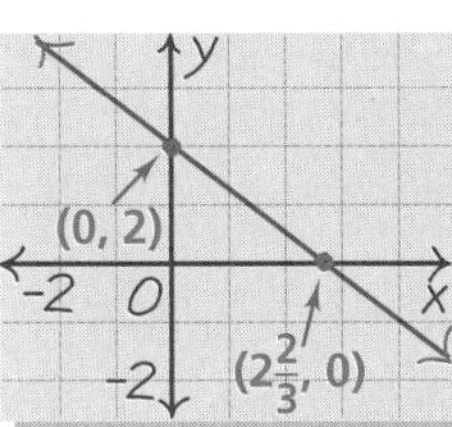

1. **Mental Math** Find the x- and y-intercept of each equation.
   a. $3x + 4y = 12$ b. $5x + 2y = -10$ c. $2x - y = 4$

To graph an equation on a graphing calculator, you must transform the equation to slope-intercept form. You can use the x- and y-intercepts to find an appropriate range for each axis.

Example 2

Graphing Calculator Graph $5x - 3y = 120$.

Step 1 Write the equation in slope-intercept form.

$$5x - 3y = 120 \quad \leftarrow \text{Solve for } y.$$
$$-3y = -5x + 120 \quad \leftarrow \text{Subtract } 5x \text{ from each side.}$$
$$y = \frac{5}{3}x - 40 \quad \leftarrow \text{Divide each side by } -3.$$

Step 2 Find the x- and y-intercepts.

$$5x - 3y = 120$$
$$5x - 3(0) = 120$$
$$5x = 120$$
$$x = 24 \quad \leftarrow x\text{-intercept}$$

From Step 1, the y-intercept is –40.

Step 3 Set the ranges to include the x- and y-axes and the intercepts. Then graph $y = \frac{5}{3}x - 40$.

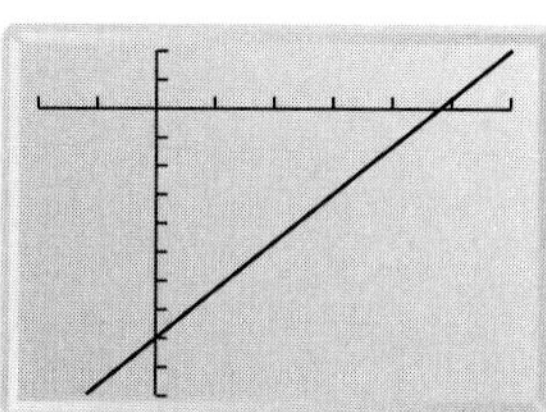

Xmin=–10 Ymin=–50
Xmax=30 Ymax=10
Xscl=5 Yscl=5

2. **Critical Thinking** What advantage is there in making Xmin less than 0 and Xmax greater than 24 for the graph on the calculator?

3. **Graphing Calculator** Graph $4x - 12y = 54$. Sketch your graph. Include Xmin, Xmax, Ymin, Ymax, and the x- and y-intercepts.

Writing Equations

You can write equations for real-world situations using the $Ax + By = C$ form.

Example 3 Relating to the Real World

Fitness When you jog, you burn 7.3 calories/min. When you run, you burn 11.3 calories/min. Write an equation to find the times you would need to run and jog in order to burn 500 calories.

Define x = minutes spent jogging $\qquad$ y = minutes spent running

Relate 7.3 × minutes jogging + 11.3 × minutes running = 500

Write $7.3x + 11.3y = 500$

4. **a.** Use the intercepts to graph the equation in Example 3, or graph the equation on a graphing calculator.

b. **Open-ended** Use your graph to estimate three different running and jogging times needed to burn 500 calories.

You can write an equation in $Ax + By = C$ form if you know the slope and one point. For a line with slope m through point (x_1, y_1), this equation is true:

$$\frac{y - y_1}{x - x_1} = m$$

Example 4

Write an equation of the line with slope $-\frac{1}{2}$ through the point $(-1, 7)$.

$\frac{y - y_1}{x - x_1} = m$ ← Use the point-slope form.

$\frac{y - 7}{x - (-1)} = -\frac{1}{2}$ ← Substitute (–1, 7) for (x_1, y_1) and $-\frac{1}{2}$ for m.

$2(y - 7) = -1(x + 1)$ ← Simplify $x - (-1)$ and cross multiply.

$2y - 14 = -x - 1$ ← Use the distributive property.

$x + 2y = 13$ ← Add x and 14 to each side in order to write $Ax + By = C$ form.

5. **Critical Thinking** How is $\frac{y - y_1}{x - x_1}$ related to the ratio for finding the slope of a line through two points?

Exercises ON YOUR OWN

Match the equation with its graph.

1. $2x + 5y = 10$
2. $2x - 5y = 10$
3. $-2x + 5y = 10$

A.

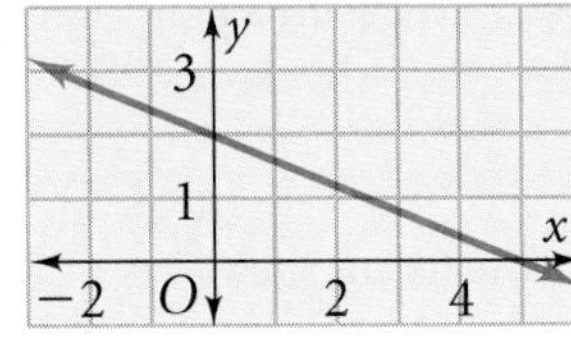

B.

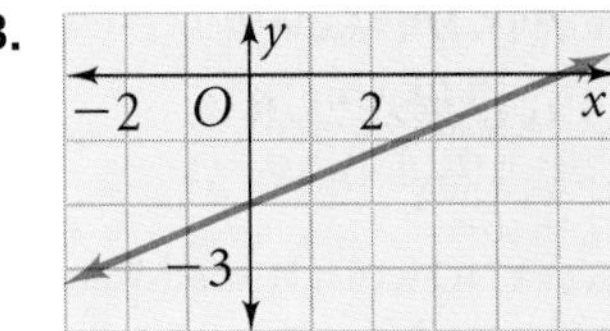

C.

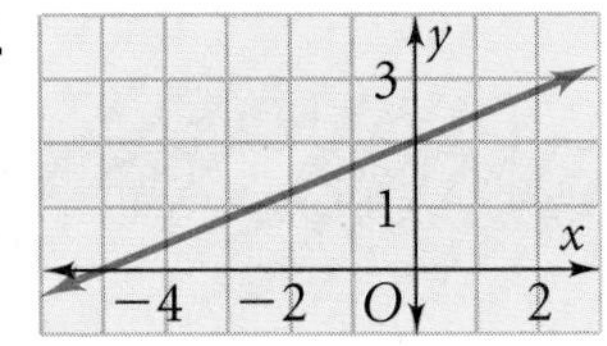

Graph each equation.

4. $x + y = 2$
5. $5x - 12y = 30$
6. $-3x + y = 6$
7. $x - y = -7$
8. $-4x + y = -6$
9. $2x + 5y = 10$
10. $2x - y = 8$
11. $-3x + 4y = 12$

12. a. **Fund Raising** Suppose your school is having a dinner to raise money for new music and art supplies. You estimate that 200 children and 150 adults will attend. Write an equation to find what ticket prices you should set to raise \$900.

    b. **Open-ended** Graph your equation. Choose three possible prices you could set for children's and adults' tickets. Explain which you think is the best choice.

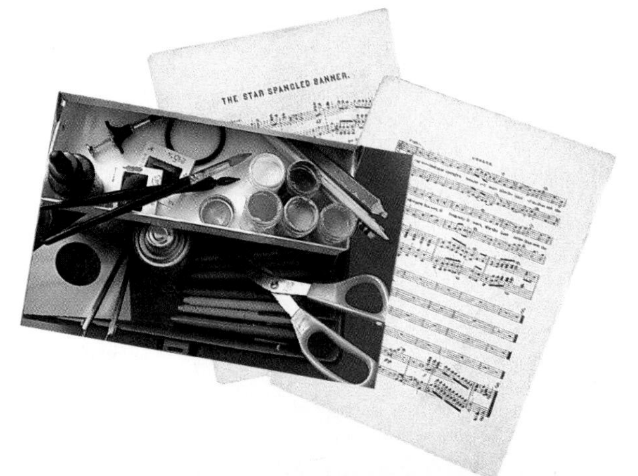

13. **Writing** Two forms of a linear equation are the slope-intercept form and the $Ax + By = C$ form. Explain when each is most useful.

14. An equation is in standard form when A, B, and C are integers for $Ax + By = C$. Write each equation in standard form.

Sample: $Ax + By = C$ Form		Standard Form	
$3.5x + 7.2y = 12$	$\longrightarrow$	$35x + 72y = 120$	$\longleftarrow$ Multiply each side by 10.

a. $3.8x + 7.2y = 5.4$ **b.** $0.5x - 0.75y = 1.25$ **c.** $\frac{2}{3}x + \frac{1}{6}y = 4$

Graphing Calculator **Graph each equation. Make a sketch of the graph. Include the x- and y-intercepts.**

15. $12x + 15y = -60$
16. $8x - 10y = 100$
17. $-5x + 11y = 120$
18. $4x - 9y = -72$
19. $-3x + 7y = -42$
20. $12x - 9y = 144$
21. $9x + 7y = 210$
22. $3x - 8y = 72$

23. **Standardized Test Prep**
    a. Write $Ax + By = C$ in slope-intercept form by solving for y.
    b. Which expression equals the slope m?
    A. $-\frac{B}{A}$ **B.** $\frac{C}{A}$ **C.** $-\frac{A}{B}$ **D.** A **E.** $\frac{C}{B}$
    c. Which expression equals the y-intercept b?
    A. $-\frac{B}{A}$ **B.** $\frac{C}{A}$ **C.** $-\frac{A}{B}$ **D.** A **E.** $\frac{C}{B}$

Write an equation in $Ax + By = C$ form for the line through the given point with the given slope.

24. $(3, -4)$; $m = 6$
25. $(4, 2)$; $m = -\frac{5}{3}$
26. $(0, 2)$; $m = \frac{4}{5}$
27. $(-2, -7)$; $m = -\frac{3}{2}$
28. $(4, 0)$; $m = 1$
29. $(5, -8)$; $m = -3$
30. $(-5, 2)$; $m = 0$
31. $(1, -8)$; $m = -\frac{1}{5}$

32. **Nutrition** Suppose you are preparing a snack mix. You want the total protein from peanuts and granola to equal 28 g.
    a. Write an equation for the protein content of your mix.
    b. Graph your equation. Use your graph to find how many ounces of granola you should use if you use one ounce of peanuts.

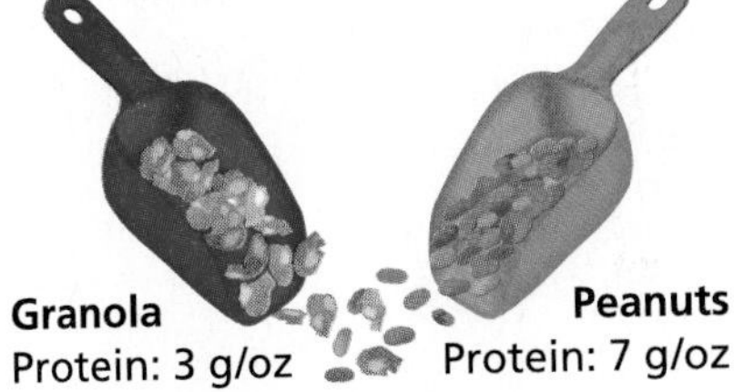

Exercises MIXED REVIEW

Probability **Find each probability.**

33. P(rolling a 2, then a 4 on a number cube)
34. P(getting heads on both coins when you toss two coins)

Getting Ready for Lesson 5-8

Graph each pair of lines on one set of axes.

35. $y = 4x + 1$
    $y = 4x - 3$
36. $y = 3x - 8$
    $y = -\frac{1}{3}x - 2$
37. $3y = 2x + 6$
    $y = \frac{2}{3}x + 4$
38. $4y = x - 8$
    $y = -4x - 1$

CHAPTER 6 Systems of Equations and Inequalities

Relating to the Real World

Often real-world problems contain more than one unknown quantity and more than one simple relationship. By writing two or more equations and solving the system, environmental and industrial planners can find the best way of assigning and using resources.

Let's Dance!

Suppose you are a member of the student council and must plan a dance. Plans include a band and refreshments. You want to keep the ticket price as low as possible to encourage students to attend.

As you work through the chapter, you will use systems of equations to analyze costs and make decisions. You will write a report detailing your choice of a band, the cost of a catering service, and what you would recommend as a ticket price.

To help you complete the project:

- **p. 274** *Find Out by Graphing*
- **p. 284** *Find Out by Calculating*
- **p. 293** *Find Out by Writing*
- **p. 299** *Find Out by Graphing*
- **p. 310** *Finishing the Project*

Math ToolboX

Problem Solving

Guess and Test

Before Lesson 6-1

You can use the *Guess and Test* strategy to solve many types of problems. First, make a guess. Then test your guess against the conditions of the problem. Use the results from your first guess to make a more accurate guess. Continue to guess and test until you find the correct answer.

Example

The ratio of boys to girls in a ninth-grade class at a high school is about 3 to 2. There are about 600 ninth-graders. How many are boys? girls?

Guess the number of boys. → Number of Boys
Subtract your guess from 600. → Number of Girls
Write the ratio and compare. → $\frac{boys}{girls}$ column

	Number of Boys	Number of Girls	$\frac{\text{boys}}{\text{girls}} \stackrel{?}{=} \frac{3}{2} = 1.5$	
First guess	400	$600 - 400 = 200$	$\frac{400}{200} = 2$	← too high, so try a lower number of boys
Second guess	350	$600 - 350 = 250$	$\frac{350}{250} = 1.4$	← too low, so try a number between 350 and 400
Third guess	375	$600 - 375 = 225$	$\frac{375}{225} = 1.\overline{6}$	← too high, so try a number between 350 and 375
Fourth guess	360	$600 - 360 = 240$	$\frac{360}{240} = 1.5$	← correct

There are about 360 ninth-grade boys and 240 ninth-grade girls.

Solve each problem.

1. Find a pair of integers with a product of 32 and a sum of 12.
2. Find a pair of integers with a sum of 114 and a difference of 2.
3. Livingston is 25 mi east of Bozeman, Montana. Lisa left Bozeman at 2:00 P.M., driving east on I-90 at 65 mi/h. Jerome left Livingston at 2:00 P.M., driving west on I-90 at 55 mi/h.
   a. At what time will Lisa pass Jerome?
   b. How far will Lisa be from Bozeman when she passes Jerome?
4. Shigechiyo Izumi of Japan lived to be one of the oldest people in the world. Carrie White was the oldest known person in the United States. Carrie lived 4 years fewer than Izumi. The sum of their ages is 236 years. How many years did each person live?
5. **Writing** Describe some advantages and disadvantages of using *Guess and Test* to solve a problem.

What You'll Learn

- Solving systems of linear equations by graphing

...And Why

To solve problems by comparing costs for services like television

What You'll Need

- graph paper
- graphing calculator

6-1 Solving Systems by Graphing

THINK AND DISCUSS

Solving Systems with One Solution

How can you show all the solutions of the linear equation $y = 2x - 3$? Graph the line, of course! Each point on the line is a solution.

Linear Equation
$y = 2x - 3$

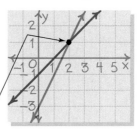

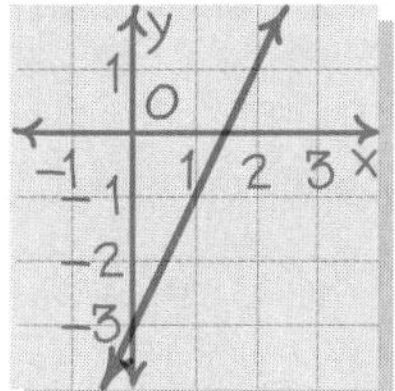

1. **Open-ended** Use the graph to write three different solutions of the equation $y = 2x - 3$. Then show that each ordered pair makes the equation true.

Two or more linear equations together form a **system of linear equations.** One way to solve a system of linear equations is by graphing. Any point common to all the lines is a **solution of the system.** So, any ordered pair that makes *all* the equations true is a solution of the system.

QUICK REVIEW

The slope-intercept form of a linear equation is $y = mx + b$, with m = slope and b = y-intercept.

Example 1

Solve the system of linear equations by graphing.

$$y = 2x - 3$$
$$y = x - 1$$

Graph both equations on the same coordinate grid.

$y = 2x - 3$: slope is 2, y-intercept is -3.
$y = x - 1$: slope is 1, y-intercept is -1.

Find the point of intersection.

The lines intersect at (2, 1), so (2, 1) is the solution of the system.

Check See if (2, 1) makes both equations true.

$y = 2x - 3$		$y = x - 1$
$1 \stackrel{?}{=} 2(2) - 3$	← Substitute (2, 1) for (x, y). →	$1 \stackrel{?}{=} 2 - 1$
$1 \stackrel{?}{=} 4 - 3$		$1 = 1$ ✓
$1 = 1$ ✓		

It checks, so (2, 1) is the solution of the system of linear equations.

2. **Try This** Solve the system $y = x + 5$. Check your solution.
$y = -4x$

3. **Critical Thinking** Do you think a system of linear equations always has exactly one solution? Draw diagrams to support your answer.

You can use the graph of a system of linear equations to solve problems.

Example 2 Relating to the Real World 

Watch Pay-Per-View!
Great Rates for Members Only:
Pay only $24/year . . .
Watch all your favorites
for ONLY $4 each!
(Non-members pay $5.50!)

Entertainment A cable company offers a "pay-per-view" club. Let $c =$ the annual cost and $n =$ the number of movies you watch in a year. Graph the system of equations below to decide whether to join the club.

Members: $c = 4n + 24$
Non-members: $c = 5.50n$

Step 1: Set an appropriate range.

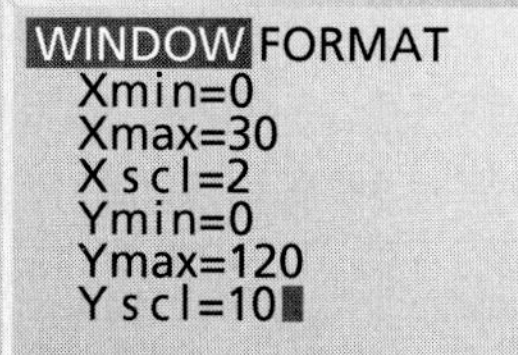

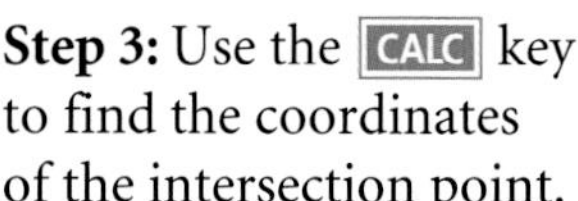

Step 3: Use the CALC key to find the coordinates of the intersection point.

Step 2: Input the equations. Let $n = x$ and $c = y$.

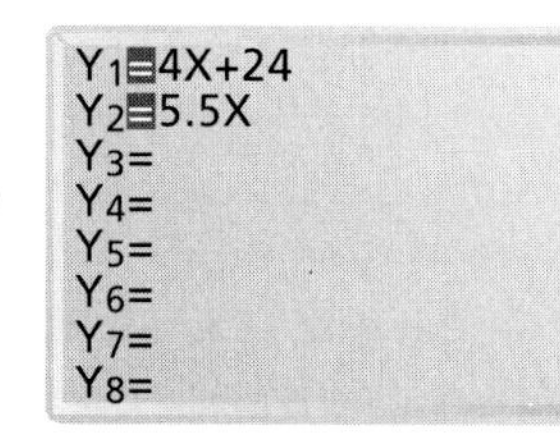

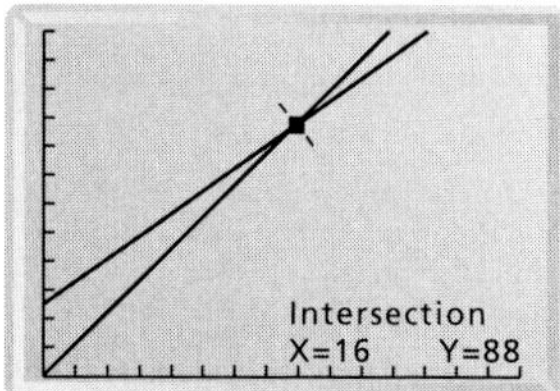

The solution of the system is (16, 88) where $(x, y) = (n, c)$.

Check See if (16, 88) makes both equations true.

$c = 4n + 24$
$88 \stackrel{?}{=} 4(16) + 24$ ← Substitute 16 for n and 88 for c. →
$88 \stackrel{?}{=} 64 + 24$
$88 = 88$ ✔

$c = 5.50n$
$88 \stackrel{?}{=} 5.50(16)$
$88 = 88$ ✔

You find that 16 movies in a year cost $88 for both members and nonmembers. If you plan to watch more than 16 movies in a year, join the club. If you plan to watch fewer than 16, do not join the club.

GRAPHING CALCULATOR HINT

You can also use the TABLE feature to find the intersection point. The ZOOM and TRACE keys will only estimate the intersection point.

PROBLEM SOLVING HINT

For Question 4, you can use *Guess and Test* or *Draw a Graph.*

4. Suppose the annual fee is $15 instead of $24. What advice would you give a friend on whether or not to join the club?

Solving Special Types of Systems

A system of linear equations has **no solution** when the graphs of the equations are parallel. There are no points of intersection, so there is no solution.

$y = -x + 1$
$y = -x - 1$

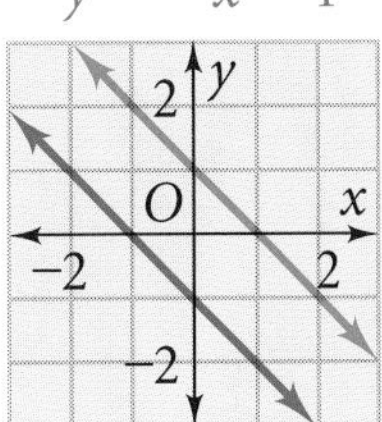

$y = 3x - 2$
$y = 3x$

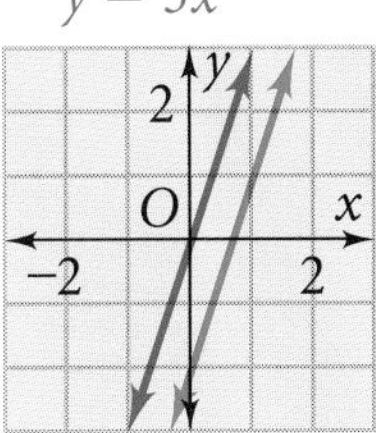

5. **Critical Thinking** Without graphing, how can you tell that a system has no solution? Give an example.

A system of linear equations has **infinitely many solutions** when the graphs of the equations are the same line. All points on the line are solutions of the system.

Example 3

Solve the system by graphing. $-4y = 4 + x$

$\frac{1}{4}x + y = -1$

First, write each equation in slope-intercept form.

$-4y = 4 + x$	$\frac{1}{4}x + y = -1$
$y = -\frac{1}{4}x - 1$	$y = -\frac{1}{4}x - 1$

GRAPHING CALCULATOR HINT

To enter an equation on a graphing calculator, you need to put it in slope-intercept form.

Then graph each equation on the same coordinate plane.

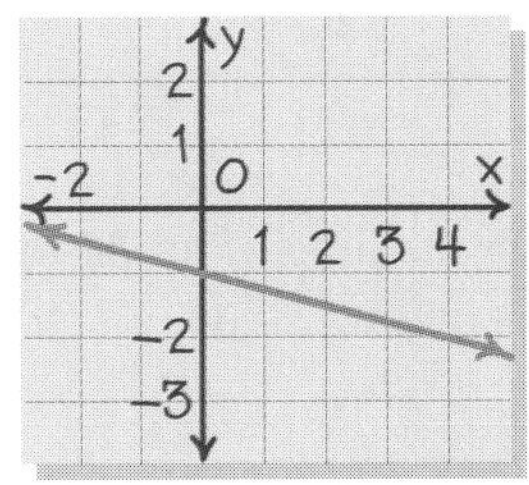

Since the graphs are the same line, the system has infinitely many solutions.

6. What do you notice about the slope-intercept form of each equation in Example 3? How could this help you solve a linear system?

7. **Try This** Solve each system by graphing.

a. $y = x$
$y = x + 6$

b. $2x + 2y = 1$
$y = -x + \frac{1}{2}$

c. $x = 1$
$x = -2$

WORK TOGETHER

PROBLEM SOLVING HINT

Start with the known information and use the strategy *Work Backward* to write an appropriate system.

Work with a partner to copy and complete the table. Your goal is to create a system of equations that satisfies the conditions given.

	System of Equations	Description of Graph	One Solution of the System	Number of Solutions
8.	■	2 intersecting lines	$(1, -5)$	■
9.	■	2 non-intersecting lines	■	■
10.	■	■	■	infinitely many

Exercises ON YOUR OWN

Graphing Calculator **Solve each system of linear equations by graphing. Sketch the graph on your paper.**

1. $y = \frac{1}{3}x + 3$
$y = \frac{1}{3}x - 3$

2. $y = x$
$y = 5x$

3. $y = 1$
$y = x$

4. $2x + y = 3$
$x - 2y = 4$

5. $3x - y = 7$
$y = 3x - 7$

6. **Number Theory** You can represent the set of nonnegative even numbers by the expression $2n$, for $n = 0, 1, 2, \ldots$. You can represent the set of nonnegative odd numbers by $2n + 1$, for $n = 0, 1, 2, \ldots$.

a. Copy and complete the table at the right.

b. Graph the system. $y = 2n$ $\quad y = 2n + 1$

c. **Writing** Why does it makes sense that this system has no solution?

n	Even Numbers $2n$	Odd Numbers $2n + 1$
0	$2(0) = 0$	$2(0) + 1 = 1$
1	■	■
2	■	■
3	■	■
4	■	■
5	■	■

Is (–1, 5) a solution of each system? Verify your answer.

7. $x + y = 4$
$x = -1$

8. $y = -x + 4$
$y = -\frac{1}{5}x$

9. $y = 5$
$x = y - 6$

10. $y = 2x + 7$
$y = x + 6$

11. Below is a retelling of an Aesop fable. Use the story to answer the questions below.

One Day, the tortoise challenged the hare to a race. The hare laughed, while bragging about how fast a runner he was. On the day of the race, the hare was so confident that he took a nap during the race. When he awoke, he ran as hard as he could, but he could not beat the slow-but-sure tortoise across the finish line.

a. The graph shows the race of the tortoise and the hare. What labels should be on each axis?

b. Which color indicates the tortoise? Which indicates the hare?

c. What does the point of intersection mean?

12. *Math in the Media* Suppose you see the two summer jobs advertised at the right. Let $x =$ the amount of sales and $y =$ money earned in a week.

Cellular Phone Sales: $y = 150 + 0.2x$
Stereo Sales: $y = 200 + 0.1x$

a. To earn the same amount of money at both jobs, how much will you need to sell in a week?

b. After talking with salespeople, you estimate weekly sales of about $600 with either job. At which job will you earn more money?

Sales Position
Salesperson Wanted
Knowledge of Cellular Phones
On-Site Sales
$150/week + 20% commission

CAREER OPPORTUNITY
Sell Stereo Equipment in
National Electronics Retail Chain!
$200/week + 10% commission

Solve each system by graphing. Write *no solution* or *infinitely many solutions* where appropriate.

13. $y = -x + 4$, $y = 2x + 1$

14. $x = 10$, $y = -7$

15. $y = 3x$, $y = 5x$

16. $y = 3x + 4$, $4y = 12x + 16$

17. $3x + y = 5$, $x - y = 7$

18. $2x - 2y = 4$, $y - x = 6$

19. $x + y = -1$, $x + y = 1$

20. $y = 1$, $3y + x = 9$

21. $y = \frac{1}{2}x - 1$, $y = -\frac{1}{2}x - 1$

22. $x + 2y = 3$, $-x = 2y - 3$

23. $y = 4x - 3$, $y = 4x + 2$

24. $y = \frac{3}{4}x - 5$, $x = 4$

Critical Thinking **Is each statement *true* or *false?* Explain your reasoning.**

25. A system of linear equations can have one solution, no solution, or infinitely many solutions.

26. If a point is a solution of a system of linear equations, it is also a solution of each linear equation in the system.

27. If a point is a solution of a linear equation, it is also a solution of any system containing that linear equation.

28. If a system of linear equations has no solution, the graphs of the lines are parallel.

PROBLEM SOLVING HINT

For Exercises 25–28, you can *Draw a Graph.*

Without graphing, decide whether the lines in each system *intersect, are parallel,* or *are the same line.* Then write the number of solutions.

29. $y = 2x$, $y = 2x - 5$

30. $x + y = 4$, $2x + 2y = 8$

31. $y = -3x + 1$, $y = 3x + 7$

32. $3x - 5y = 0$, $y = \frac{3}{5}x$

33. $2y - 10x = 2$, $y = 5x + 1$

34. $y = -4x + 4$, $y = -4x + 8$

35. $y = x + 1$, $y = \frac{1}{2}x$

36. $y = 2x + 3$, $y - 2x = 5$

Open-ended **Write a system of two linear equations with the given characteristics.**

37. one solution; perpendicular lines

38. no solutions; one equation is $y = 2x + 5$

39. one solution; (0, –4)

40. infinitely many solutions; one equation is $y = 4x$

41. **Music** Suppose you and your friends form a band, and you want to record a demo tape. Studio A rents for \$100 plus \$50/h. Studio B rents for \$50 plus \$75/h. Let $t =$ the number of hours and $c =$ the cost.

Studio A: $c = 100 + 50t$
Studio B: $c = 50 + 75t$

a. Solve the system by graphing.
b. Explain what the solution of the system means in terms of your band renting a studio.

42. **Writing** When equivalent equations form a system, there are infinitely many solutions. Explain in your own words why this is true.

Chapter Project: Find Out by Graphing

Band A charges \$600 to play for the evening. Band B charges \$350 plus \$1.25 for each ticket sold. Write a linear equation for the cost of each band. Graph each equation and find the number of tickets for which the cost of the two bands will be equal.

Estimation **Estimate the solution of each system. Use the equations to test your estimate. Adjust your estimate until you find the exact solution.**

43. $y = 6.5$
$y = x + 2$

44. $y = -4x - 10$
$y = -6$

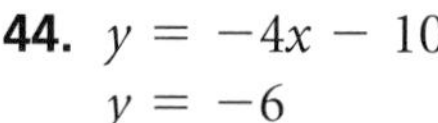

45. $y = -0.75x - 3$
$y = 0.25x - 7$

46. $y = -x - 1$
$y = x + 8$

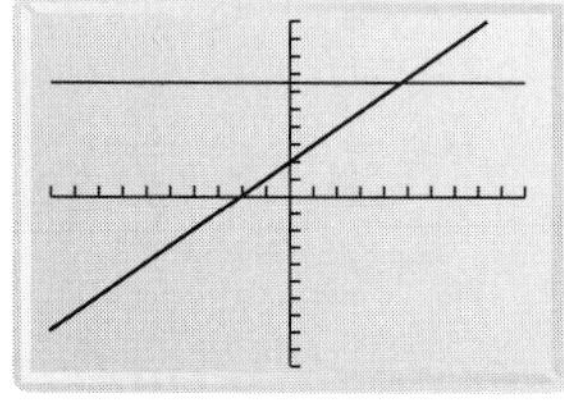

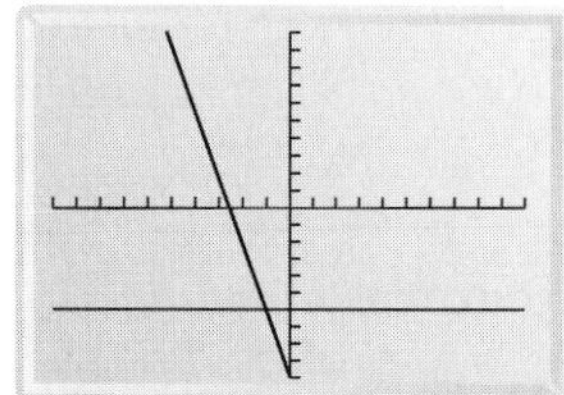

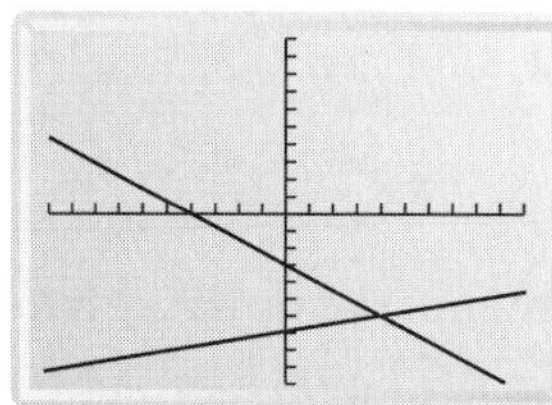

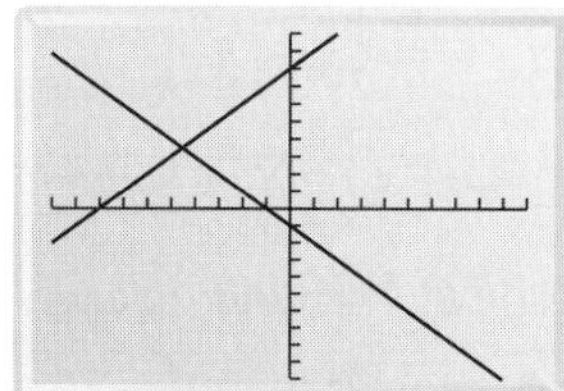

Exercises MIXED REVIEW

Probability **Find each probability for two rolls of a number cube.**

47. $P(3, \text{then } 4)$
48. $P(1, \text{then even})$
49. $P(\text{two integers})$
50. $P(\text{at least one } 1)$

Write an inequality to model each situation.

51. Polar bears can swim as fast as 6 mi/h.

52. Each eyelash is shed every 3 to 5 months.

53. a. **Geography** Cairo, Egypt, has about 18 million residents. The average population density is 130,000 people/mi^2. What is Cairo's area?
b. Cairo has $\frac{1}{4}$ of Egypt's population. What is the population of Egypt?

Getting Ready for Lesson 6-2

Solve each equation for the given variable.

54. $x - y = 3; y$
55. $\frac{1}{2}x = 4y; x$
56. $\frac{x}{2} = \frac{y}{4}; y$
57. $2x - 3y = 5; x$

6-2 Solving Systems Using Substitution

What You'll Learn

- Solving systems of linear equations by substitution

...And Why

To solve problems involving transportation

What You'll Need

- graph paper
- graphing calculator

System:
$y = x + 6.1$
$y = -2x - 1.4$

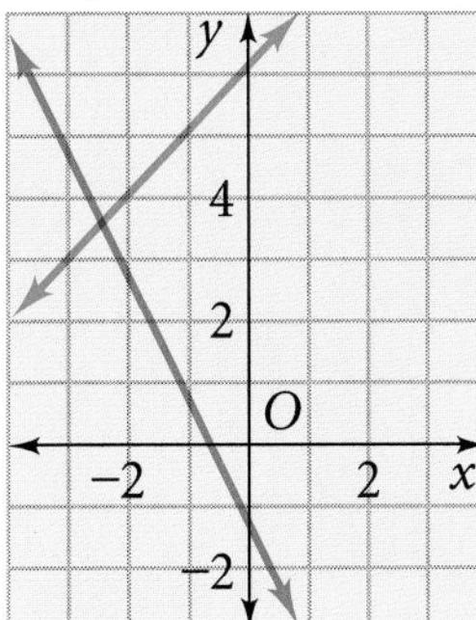

WORK TOGETHER

Work with a partner.

1. *Estimation* Use the graph at the left to estimate the solution of the system.
2. a. *Graphing Calculator* Graph the system at the left.
   b. Use the CALC or TABLE features to find the intersection point.
3. Compare your estimate to your answer in Question 2(b).
4. *Choose* Use paper and pencil or a calculator to solve each system.
   a. $y = 3x - 6$, $y = -6x$
   b. $y = x + 2.5$, $y = 2x - 0.5$
   c. $2y - x = 3$, $y = x - 2$
5. Explain why you chose the method(s) you used in Question 4.

THINK AND DISCUSS

Solving Systems with One Solution

Sometimes you won't have a graphing calculator to use. Another way to solve a system is to use substitution. **Substitution** allows you to create a one-variable equation.

Example 1

Solve the system $y = x + 6.1$ using substitution.
$y = -2x - 1.4$

$y = -2x - 1.4$ ← Start with one equation.
$x + 6.1 = -2x - 1.4$ ← Substitute $x + 6.1$ for y in that equation.
$3x = -7.5$ ← Solve for x.
$x = -2.5$

Substitute -2.5 for x in either equation and solve for y.

$y = (-2.5) + 6.1$
$y = 3.6$

Since $x = -2.5$ and $y = 3.6$, the solution is $(-2.5, 3.6)$.

Check See if $(-2.5, 3.6)$ satisfies the other equation.

$3.6 \stackrel{?}{=} -2(-2.5) - 1.4$
$3.6 \stackrel{?}{=} 5 - 1.4$
$3.6 = 3.6$ ✓

PROBLEM SOLVING

Look Back Does the solution agree with the graph of the system in the Work Together?

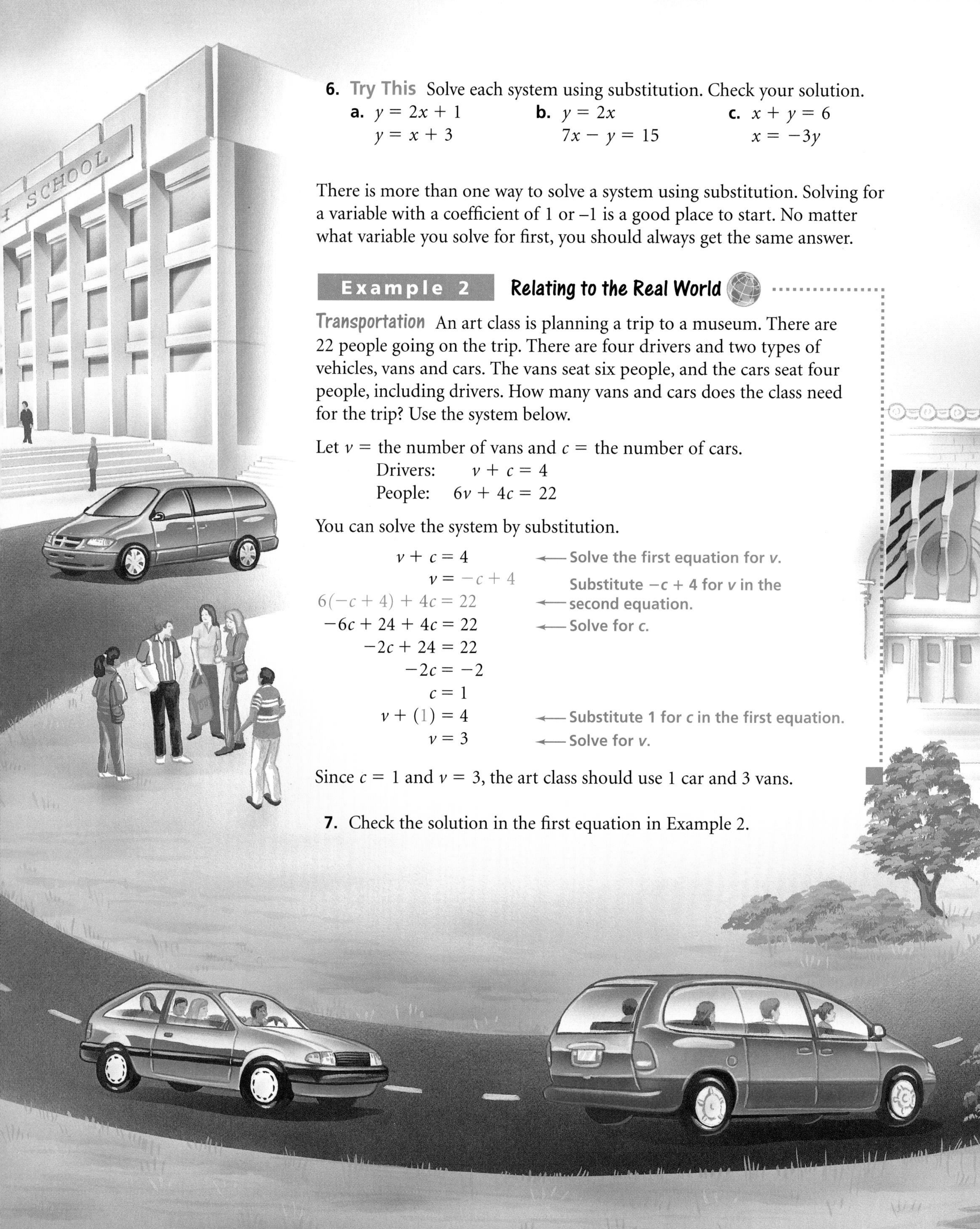

6. **Try This** Solve each system using substitution. Check your solution.

a. $y = 2x + 1$
$y = x + 3$

b. $y = 2x$
$7x - y = 15$

c. $x + y = 6$
$x = -3y$

There is more than one way to solve a system using substitution. Solving for a variable with a coefficient of 1 or –1 is a good place to start. No matter what variable you solve for first, you should always get the same answer.

Example 2 Relating to the Real World

Transportation An art class is planning a trip to a museum. There are 22 people going on the trip. There are four drivers and two types of vehicles, vans and cars. The vans seat six people, and the cars seat four people, including drivers. How many vans and cars does the class need for the trip? Use the system below.

Let v = the number of vans and c = the number of cars.

Drivers: $v + c = 4$

People: $6v + 4c = 22$

You can solve the system by substitution.

$v + c = 4$ ← Solve the first equation for v.

$v = -c + 4$

$6(-c + 4) + 4c = 22$ ← Substitute $-c + 4$ for v in the second equation.

$-6c + 24 + 4c = 22$ ← Solve for c.

$-2c + 24 = 22$

$-2c = -2$

$c = 1$

$v + (1) = 4$ ← Substitute 1 for c in the first equation.

$v = 3$ ← Solve for v.

Since $c = 1$ and $v = 3$, the art class should use 1 car and 3 vans.

7. Check the solution in the first equation in Example 2.

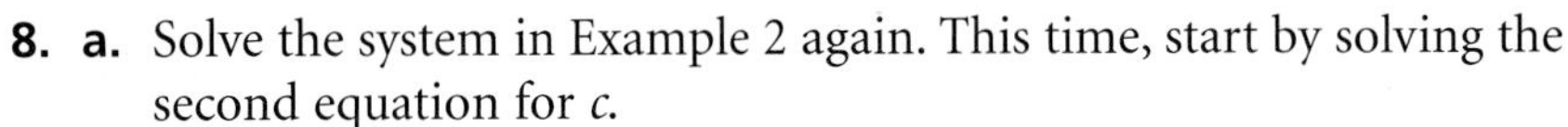

8. **a.** Solve the system in Example 2 again. This time, start by solving the second equation for *c*.
   b. **Critical Thinking** Why is this procedure more difficult?

9. Describe a possible first step for solving each system by substitution.

   a. $3x - y = 17$
   $2x + y = 8$

   b. $x + 3y = 5$
   $2x - 4y = -5$

   c. $y = -2x - 3$
   $y = x$

Solving Special Types of Systems

You can use substitution to learn that systems have *no solution* or *infinitely many solutions.*

Example 3

Solve the system using substitution. $x + y = 6$
$5x + 5y = 10$

$x + y = 6$	← Solve the first equation for *x*.
$x = 6 - y$	Substitute 6 – *y* for *x*
$5(6 - y) + 5y = 10$	← in the second equation.
$30 - 5y + 5y = 10$	← Solve for *y*.
$30 = 10$	← False!

Since $30 = 10$ is a false statement, the system has no solution.

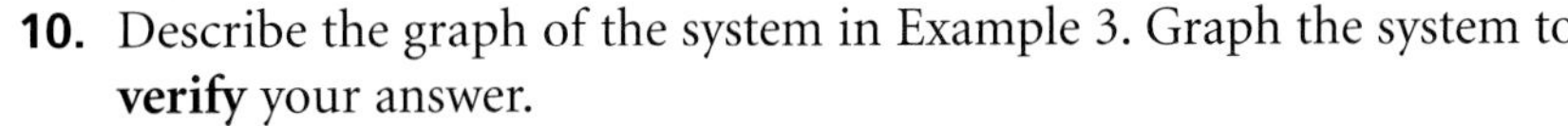

10. Describe the graph of the system in Example 3. Graph the system to **verify** your answer.

11. **Critical Thinking** How many solutions does a system of linear equations have if you get each result?
    a. a true statement, such as $2 = 2$
    b. a false statement, such as $10 = 1$
    c. a statement such as $x = 4$

12. Graphs of systems with no solution are parallel lines. What do you know about the equations of parallel lines?

13. Graphs of systems with infinitely many solutions are the same line. What do you know about the equations?

14. Without using substitution, decide whether each system has *no solution* or *infinitely many solutions.* (*Hint:* Write each equation in slope-intercept form and compare.)

    a. $3x - y = -2$
    $y = 3x + 2$

    b. $y = 4x$
    $2x - 0.5y = 0$

    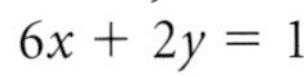

    c. $3x + y = 5$
    $6x + 2y = 1$

Exercises ON YOUR OWN

Critical Thinking **Suppose you try to solve a system of linear equations and get the following result. How many solutions does each system have?**

1. $x = 0$
2. $5 = 5$
3. $-3 = 2$
4. $n = 10$
5. $0 = 0$
6. $-8 = k$
7. $y = 6$
8. $0 = -9$

9. **Geometry** A rectangle is 4 times longer than it is wide ($l = 4w$). The perimeter of the rectangle is 30 cm ($2l + 2w = 30$). Find the dimensions of the rectangle.

10. **Internet** Suppose you want access to the Internet. With a subscription to *Access*, you pay \$7.95 per month plus \$2.95 per on-line hour. With a subscription to *Network*, you pay \$12.95 per month plus \$1.95 per on-line hour. The system below models this situation. Let $c =$ the monthly cost and $h =$ the number of on-line hours.

    Access: $c = 7.95 + 2.95h$

    Network: $c = 12.95 + 1.95h$

    a. Use substitution to solve the system.

    b. Explain how to decide which subscription to buy.

Solve each system using substitution. Write *no solution* or *infinitely many solutions* where appropriate.

11. $y = 2x$; $6x - y = 8$
12. $2x + y = 5$; $2y = 10 - 4x$
13. $y = 3x + 1$; $x = 3y + 1$
14. $x - 3y = 14$; $x - 2 = 0$
15. $2x + 2y = 5$; $y = \frac{1}{4}x$
16. $y = -3x$; $y + 3x = 2$
17. $4x + y = -2$; $-2x - 3y = 1$
18. $3x + 5y = 2$; $x + 4y = -4$
19. $y = x + 2$; $y = 2x - 1$
20. $y = 3$; $y = \frac{4}{3}x + 2$
21. $x + 4y = -3$; $2x + 8y = -6$
22. $2y = 0.2x + 7$; $3y - 2x = 2$

Estimation **Graph each system to estimate the solution. Then use substitution to find the exact solution of the system.**

23. $y = 2x$; $y = -6x + 4$
24. $y = \frac{1}{2}x + 4$; $y = -4x - 5$
25. $x + y = 0$; $5x + 2y = -3$
26. $y = 0.7x + 3$; $y = -1.5x - 7$
27. $y = 3x + 1$; $y = 3x - 2.5$

28. **Writing** Describe the advantages of using substitution to solve a system. **Justify** your answer with an example.

29. **Standardized Test Prep** Which system has no solution?

    A. $y = x + 3$; $y + 4x = -2$

    B. $2x + 2y = 1$; $y = -x + \frac{1}{2}$

    C. $y = \frac{1}{2}x + 1$; $6y - 3x = 6$

    D. $y = x + 6$; $2y - 2x = 3$

    E. $y = 2x - 1$; $y = -2x$

Mental Math **Match each system with its solution at the right.**

30. $y = x + 1$
 $y = 2x - 1$

31. $2y - 8 = x$
 $2y + 2x = 2$

32. $2y = x + 3$
 $x = y$

33. $x - y = 1$
 $x = \frac{1}{2}y + 2$

A. (3, 2)

B. (3, 3)

C. (–2, 3)

D. (2, 3)

How many solutions does each system have?

34. $3y + x = -1$
 $x = -3y$

35. $2x + 4y = 0$
 $y = -\frac{1}{2}x$

36. $y = 6x$
 $y = 3x$

37. $5x - y = 1$
 $5x - y = 7$

38. If two linear equations have the same slope and different y-intercepts, their graphs are __?__ lines. Such a system has __?__ solution(s).

39. **Agriculture** A farmer grows only soybeans and corn on his 240-acre farm ($s + c = 240$). This year he wants to plant 80 more acres of soybeans than of corn ($s = c + 80$). How many acres does the farmer need to plant of each crop?

40. **Open-ended** Write a system of linear equations with exactly one solution. Use substitution to solve your system.

Choose **Solve each system by graphing or using substitution.**

41. $y = -2x + 3$
 $y = x - 6$

42. $y = \frac{1}{4}x$
 $x + 2y = 12$

43. $y = 0$
 $4x - y = 1$

44. $x - 3y = 1$
 $2x - 6y = 2$

45. $x - y = 20$
 $2x + 3y = 0$

46. $y = -x$
 $x + y = 5$

47. $x = -2$
 $3x - 2y = 4$

48. $0.4x + 0.5y = 1$
 $x - y = 7$

Exercises MIXED REVIEW

Find the slope and y-intercept of each line.

49. $y = 7x - 4$

50. $3x + 8y = 16$

51. $y = 9x$

52. $5y = 6x - 25$

53. Write a linear function that passes through the points (2, 3) and (4, 6).

54. **Human Biology** The largest bone in the body is the femur. In a 5-ft tall woman, the femur is about 1.3 ft long. The smallest bone in the body, the stapes, is in the ear. It is only about 0.1 in. long. The femur is about how many times as long as the stapes?

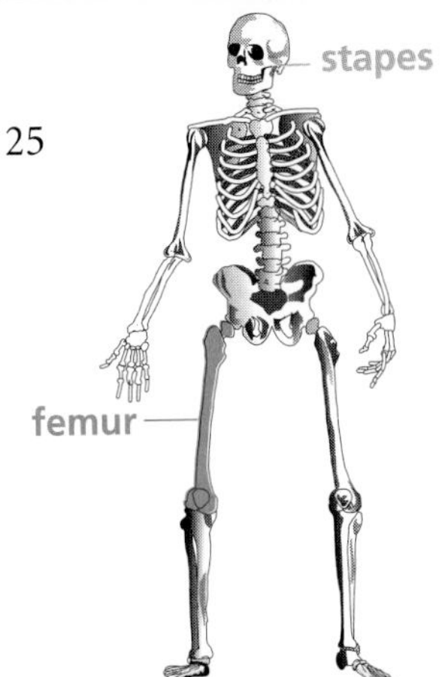

Getting Ready for Lesson 6-3

Simplify each expression.

55. $(x + 4) - 4(2x + 1)$

56. $5(2x - 3) + (7x + 15)$

57. $3(x - 2) + 6(2x + 1)$

Connections Sales . . . and more

6-3 Solving Systems Using Elimination

What You'll Learn

- Solving systems of linear equations using elimination

...And Why

To investigate real-world situations, such as sales

What You'll Need

- graph paper

QUICK REVIEW

If $a = b$ and $c = d$, then $a + c = b + d$ and $a - c = b - d$.

PROBLEM SOLVING

Look Back Why was y eliminated?

THINK AND DISCUSS

Adding or Subtracting Equations

When both linear equations of a system are in the form $Ax + By = C$, you can solve the system using **elimination.** You can add or subtract the equations to eliminate a variable.

Example 1

Solve the system using elimination. Check your solution.

$$5x - 6y = -32$$
$$3x + 6y = 48$$

First, eliminate one variable.

$$\begin{array}{r} 5x - 6y = -32 \\ 3x + 6y = 48 \\ \hline 8x + 0 = 16 \\ x = 2 \end{array}$$

← Add the equations to eliminate y.
← Solve for x.

Then, find the value of the eliminated variable.

$3x + 6y = 48$ ← Pick one equation.
$3(2) + 6y = 48$ ← Substitute 2 for x.
$6 + 6y = 48$ ← Solve for y.
$6y = 42$
$y = 7$

Since $x = 2$ and $y = 7$, the solution is (2, 7).

Check See if (2, 7) makes the other equation true.

$5(2) - 6(7) \stackrel{?}{=} -32$
$10 - 42 \stackrel{?}{=} -32$
$-32 = -32$ ✔

Example 2 Relating to the Real World

Basketball Altogether 292 tickets were sold for a high school basketball game. An adult ticket costs \$3. A student ticket costs \$1. Ticket sales were \$470. Use the system to find the number of each type of ticket sold.

number of tickets sold: $a + s = 292$
money collected: $3a + s = 470$

First, eliminate one variable.

$$\begin{array}{r} a + s = 292 \\ 3a + s = 470 \\ \hline -2a + 0 = -178 \\ a = 89 \end{array}$$

← Subtract the equations to eliminate s.
← Solve for a.

Then, find the value of the eliminated variable.

$$\begin{aligned} 89 + s &= 292 && \leftarrow \text{Substitute 89 for } a \text{ in the first equation.} \\ s &= 203 && \leftarrow \text{Solve for } s. \end{aligned}$$

There were 89 adult tickets sold and 203 student tickets sold.

1. Check the solution to Example 2.

2. Would you *add* or *subtract* the equations to eliminate a variable?

a. $a - b = 8$, $a + 2b = 5$ **b.** $-3x + 2y = 1$, $4x - 2y = -3$ **c.** $m + t = 6$, $5m + t = 14$

3. **Try This** Use elimination to solve the system in Question 2(a).

Multiplying First

To eliminate a variable, you may need to multiply one or both equations in a system by a nonzero number. Then add or subtract the equations.

Example 3 **Relating to the Real World** 

Sales Suppose your class receives $1084 for selling 205 packages of greeting cards and gift wrap. Let w = the number of packages of gift wrap sold and c = the number of packages of greeting cards sold. Use the system to find the number of each type of package sold.

total number of packages: $w + c = 205$
total amount of sales: $4w + 10c = 1084$

In the first equation, the coefficient of w is 1. In the second equation, the coefficient of w is 4. So multiply the first equation by 4. Then subtract to eliminate w.

$$\begin{aligned} w + c = 205: \quad 4w + 4c &= 820 && \leftarrow \text{Multiply each side of the first equation by 4.} \\ 4w + 10c &= 1084 \\ -6c &= -264 && \leftarrow \text{Subtract the two equations.} \\ c &= 44 && \leftarrow \text{Solve for } c. \end{aligned}$$

Find w.

$$\begin{aligned} w + c &= 205 && \leftarrow \text{Use the first equation.} \\ w + 44 &= 205 && \leftarrow \text{Substitute 44 for } c. \\ w &= 161 && \leftarrow \text{Solve for } w. \end{aligned}$$

The class sold 161 packages of gift wrap and 44 packages of greeting cards.

4. Could you have multiplied the first equation by 10 rather than 4 and then solved the system? Why or why not?

For systems with no solution or infinitely many solutions, look for the same results as you did when you used substitution.

When you solve systems using elimination, plan a strategy. A flowchart like this one may help you to decide how to eliminate a variable.

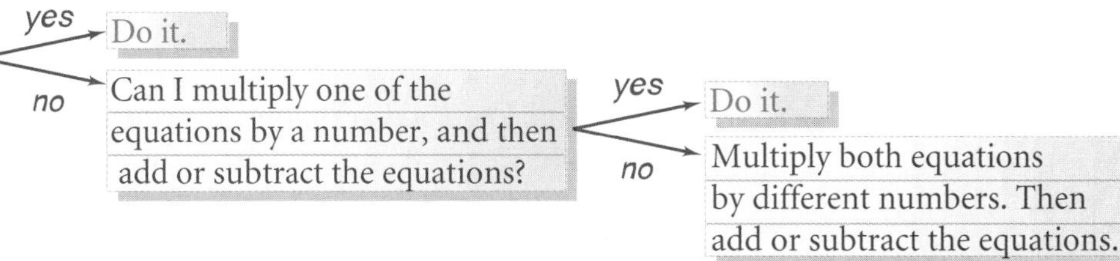

Can I eliminate a variable by adding or subtracting the given equations?
yes
Do it.
no
Can I multiply one of the equations by a number, and then add or subtract the equations?
yes
Do it.
no
Multiply both equations by different numbers. Then add or subtract the equations.

WORK TOGETHER

Work in groups.

5. Suppose you want to solve this system using elimination. $3x - 2y = 6$, $5x + 7y = 41$
   a. What would you multiply each equation by to eliminate x?
   b. What would you multiply each equation by to eliminate y?
   c. Solve the system using elimination. Be sure to check your solution.

Decide which method makes solving each system easier: graphing, substitution, or elimination. Then solve the system and explain the method you chose.

6. $-5a + 14b = 13$, $9a = 72b$

7. $3p - 8q = 4$, $9p - 4q = 5$

8. $y = \frac{2}{3}x - 1$, $y = -x + 4$

9. Describe how to solve this system using elimination. $x - 2y = 8$, $y = x + 4$

Exercises ON YOUR OWN

Describe a first step for solving each system using elimination. Then solve each system.

1. $3x - y = 21$, $2x + y = 4$

2. $3x + 4y = -10$, $5x - 2y = 18$

3. $2x - y = 6$, $-3x + 4y = 1$

4. $x - y = 12$, $x + y = 22$

5. $2r - 3n = 13$, $8r + 3n = 7$

6. $5a + 6b = 54$, $3a - 3b = 17$

7. $x + y = 6$, $x + 3y = 10$

8. $2p - 5q = 6$, $4p + 3q = -1$

9. **Business** A company orders two types of parts, brass b and steel s. One shipment contains 3 brass and 10 steel parts and costs \$48. A second shipment contains 7 brass and 4 steel parts and costs \$54. Solve the system to find the cost of each type of part. $3b + 10s = 48$, $7b + 4s = 54$

Solve each system using elimination. Check your solution.

10. $x + y = 12$
$x - y = 2$

11. $-a + 2b = -1$
$a = 3b - 1$

12. $3u + 4w = 9$
$-3u - 2w = -3$

13. $3x + 2y = 9$
$-x + 3y = 8$

14. $r - 3p = 1$
$6r - p = 6$

15. $5x + 3y = 1.5$
$-8x - 2y = 20$

16. $-2z + y = 3$
$z + 4y = 3$

17. $m - n = 0$
$m + n = 28$

18. $2k - 3c = 6$
$6k - 9c = 9$

19. $3b + 4e = 6$
$-6b + e = 6$

20. $4x = -2y + 1$
$2x + y = 4$

21. $2p - 3t = 4$
$3p + 2t = 6$

22. $3x + y = 8$
$x - y = -12$

23. $x + 4y = 1$
$3x + 12y = 3$

24. $h = 2s - 1$
$2s - h = 1$

25. $4x - 2y = 3$
$5x - 3y = 2$

26. **Writing** Explain how to solve a system using elimination. Give examples of when you use addition, subtraction, and multiplication.

27. **Electricity** Two batteries produce a total voltage of 4.5 volts ($B_1 + B_2 = 4.5$). The difference in their voltages is 1.5 volts ($B_1 - B_2 = 1.5$). Determine the voltages of the two batteries.

Critical Thinking **Do you *agree* or *disagree* with each statement? Explain.**

28. A system of linear equations written in the form $Ax + By = C$ is solved most easily by elimination.

29. A system of linear equations written in slope-intercept form, $y = mx + b$, is solved most easily by substitution.

Choose **Choose any method to solve each system.**

30. $y = x + 5$
$x + y = 1$

31. $4x - 2y = 6$
$-2x + y = -3$

32. $y = 0.25x$
$y = -4$

33. $-5x + 2y = 14$
$-3x + y = -2$

34. $y = -2x + 7$
$y = 4x - 5$

35. $y = 4$
$3x - y = 5$

36. $2x - 3y = 4$
$2x + y = -4$

37. $5x + 3y = 6$
$2x - 4y = 5$

38. **Open-ended** Write a system of linear equations that you would solve using elimination. Solve the system.

39. **Vacation** A weekend at the Beach Bay Hotel in Florida includes two nights and four meals. A week includes seven nights and ten meals. The system of linear equations below models this situation. Let n = the cost of one night and m = the cost of one meal.

Weekend: $2n + 4m = 195$
Week: $7n + 10m = 650$

a. Use elimination to solve the system.
b. What does the solution mean in terms of the prices of the room and meals?

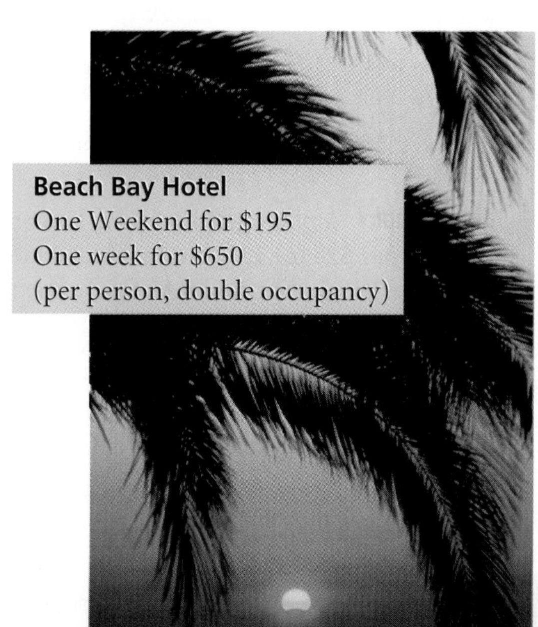

Chapter Project — Find Out by Calculating

A caterer charges a fixed cost for preparing dinner plus a cost for each person served. You know that the cost for 100 people will be \$750 and the cost for 150 people will be \$1050. Find the caterer's fixed cost and the cost per person served.

Exercises MIXED REVIEW

Write an equation of the line passing through the given points.

40. $(3, -7)$ and $(-4, 1)$ **41.** $(0, 4)$ and $(0, -7)$ **42.** $(5, -8)$ and $(9, 0)$ **43.** $(10, 2)$ and $(10, -2)$

44. *Health* In 1980, there were 400,000 cases of polio reported worldwide. From 1980 to 1993, the number of cases declined 75%. How many cases of polio were reported in 1993?

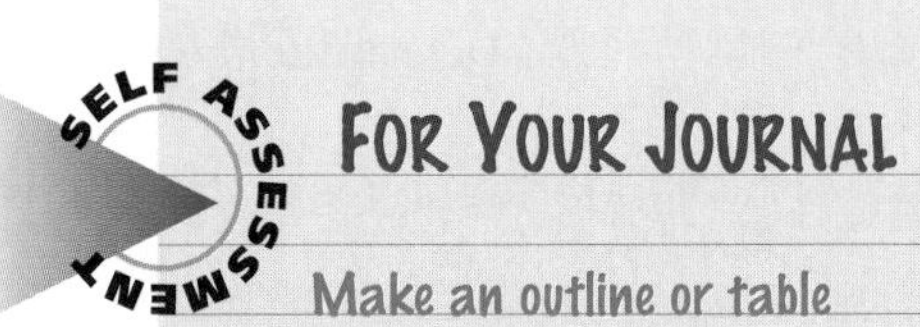

FOR YOUR JOURNAL

Make an outline or table titled "Methods for Solving Systems of Equations." Provide descriptions of procedures, helpful hints, and examples for each method.

Getting Ready for Lesson 6-4

Write an equation to model each situation.

45. Two sandwiches and a drink cost \$6.50.

46. A stack of ten paperbacks and three hardcover books is 18 in. high.

47. Five pieces of plywood and two bags of nails weigh 32 lb.

Exercises CHECKPOINT

Solve each system of equations.

1. $x + 2y = 5$
$-4x + y = 8$

2. $5x - 3y = 27$
$5x + 4y = -1$

3. $x + y = 19$
$10x - 7y = 20$

4. $6x - \frac{3}{4}y = 16$
$y = -\frac{8}{3}x$

5. *Open-ended* Write a system of equations where the solution is $x = 5$ and $y = 7$.

6. *Photography* A photographer offers two options for portraits. You can pay \$25 for 12 pictures and \$.40 for each extra print, or \$30 for 12 pictures and \$.15 for each extra print. Let $c =$ the total cost and $p =$ the number of extra prints.

first option: $c = 25 + 0.4p$
second option: $c = 30 + 0.15p$

a. Solve the system.

b. *Writing* Which option would you recommend to a friend? Explain.

Connections  Publishing . . . and more

6-4 Writing Systems

What You'll Learn

- Writing and solving systems of linear equations
- Using systems to find the break-even point

...And Why

To model real-world situations, such as publishing a newsletter

THINK AND DISCUSS

In the Math Toolbox before Lesson 6-1, the following problem was solved using the strategy *Guess and Test.*

The ratio of boys to girls in a ninth-grade class at a high school is about 3 to 2. There are about 600 ninth-graders. How many are boys? How many are girls?

You can also solve this problem using a system of linear equations.

Example 1 Relating to the Real World

Schools Use a system of linear equations to solve the problem stated above.

Define b = the number of boys
g = the number of girls

Relate	The total number of ninth-graders is 600.	The ratio of boys to girls is 3 to 2.
Write	$b + g = 600$	$\frac{b}{g} = \frac{3}{2}$

You can solve the system by substitution.

$\frac{b}{g} = \frac{3}{2}$ ← Solve the second equation for b.

$b = \frac{3}{2}g$

$b + g = 600$ ← Use the first equation.

$\frac{3}{2}g + g = 600$ ← Substitute $\frac{3}{2}g$ for b.

$\frac{5}{2}g = 600$ ← Combine like terms.

$g = 240$ ← Multiply both sides by $\frac{2}{5}$.

$\frac{b}{g} = \frac{3}{2}$ ← Use the second equation.

$\frac{b}{240} = \frac{3}{2}$ ← Substitute 240 for g.

$b = 360$ ← Multiply both sides by 240.

There are about 360 ninth-grade boys and 240 ninth-grade girls.

PROBLEM SOLVING

Look Back Which method would you prefer to solve the system: substitution, graphing, or elimination? Why?

1. **Graphing Calculator** Rewrite the system $b + g = 600$ and $\frac{b}{g} = \frac{3}{2}$ so that you could use a graphing calculator to find its solution.

QUICK REVIEW

The *break-even point* is when income equals expenses.

In Chapter 5, you found the break-even point for a business using one equation and the x-intercept of its graph. The graph shows the break-even point of two equations.

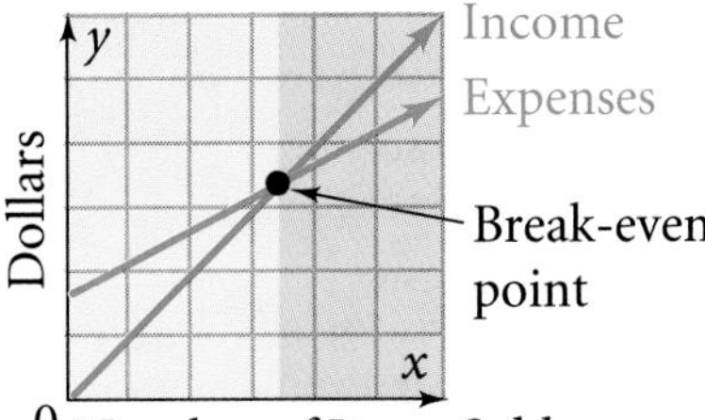

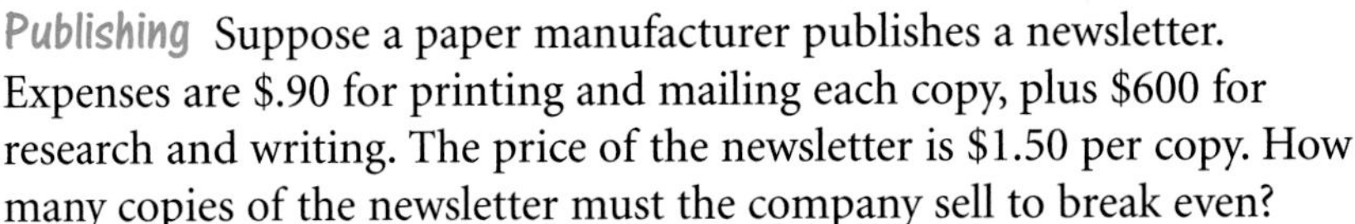

Example 2 Relating to the Real World

Publishing Suppose a paper manufacturer publishes a newsletter. Expenses are \$.90 for printing and mailing each copy, plus \$600 for research and writing. The price of the newsletter is \$1.50 per copy. How many copies of the newsletter must the company sell to break even?

Define $x =$ the number of copies
$y =$ the money for expenses or income

	Expenses	Income
Relate	\$.90 × copies printed + \$600	\$1.50 × copies sold
Write	$y = 0.9x + 600$	$y = 1.50x$

Choose a method to solve the system. Use substitution, since it is easy to substitute for y using these equations.

$$y = 0.9x + 600$$
$$y = 1.5x$$

$$1.5x = 0.9x + 600 \quad \leftarrow \text{Substitute } 1.5x \text{ for } y \text{ in the first equation.}$$
$$0.6x = 600 \quad \leftarrow \text{Subtract } 0.9x \text{ from each side.}$$
$$x = 1000 \quad \leftarrow \text{Divide each side by 0.6.}$$

To break even, the manufacturer must sell 1000 copies.

2. What are the expenses for 1000 copies? the income?

3. Critical Thinking Can the company print more than it sells, but still earn a profit? If so, give an example. If not, explain why not.

4. Try This Suppose printing and mailing expenses increase to \$1.00 for each copy. How many copies of the newsletter must the company sell at \$1.50 per copy to break even?

Exercises ON YOUR OWN

1. *Geometry* The difference of the measures of two supplementary angles is 35°. Find both angle measures.

QUICK REVIEW

The sum of the measures of supplementary angles is 180°.

2. Suppose you have just enough coins to pay for a loaf of bread priced at $1.95. You have a total of 12 coins, with only quarters and dimes.
   a. Let q = the number of quarters and d = the number of dimes. Complete: ■ + ■ = 12
   b. Complete: 0.25■ + 0.10■ = ■
   c. Use the equations you wrote for parts (a) and (b) to find how many of each coin you have.

3. Suppose you have 10 coins that total $.85. Some coins are dimes and some are nickels. How many of each coin do you have?

4. *Open-ended* Write a problem for the total of two types of coins. Then give your problem to a classmate to solve.

Choose **Solve each linear system using any method. Tell why you chose the method you used.**

5. $y = x + 2$; $y = -2x + 3$

6. $3x + 4y = -10$; $5x = 2y + 18$

7. $5y = x$; $2x - 3y = 7$

8. $3x - 2y = -12$; $5x + 4y = 2$

9. $4x = 5y$; $8x = 10y + 15$

10. $x = y - 3$; $x + 2y = 3$

11. $y = 3x$; $y = -\frac{1}{2}x$

12. $y = 2x$; $7x - y = 35$

13. *School Musical* Suppose you are the treasurer of the drama club. The cost for scripts for the spring musical is $254. The cost of props and costumes is $400. You must also pay royalty charges of $1.20 per ticket to the play's publisher. You charge $4.00 per ticket and expect to make $150 on refreshments.
    a. Write an equation for the expenses.
    b. Write an equation for the expected income.
    c. How many tickets must the drama club sell to break even?
    d. What method did you use to solve part (c)? Why?

14. *Pets* The ratio of cats to dogs at your local animal shelter is about 5 to 2. The shelter accepts 40 cats and dogs. From about how many dogs would you have to choose?

15. *Business* Suppose you invest $10,000 in equipment to manufacture a new board game. Each game costs $2.65 to manufacture and sells for $20. How many games must you make and sell before your business breaks even?

16. *Writing* Explain to a friend how to decide whether to rent a car from Auto-Rent or from Cars, Inc.

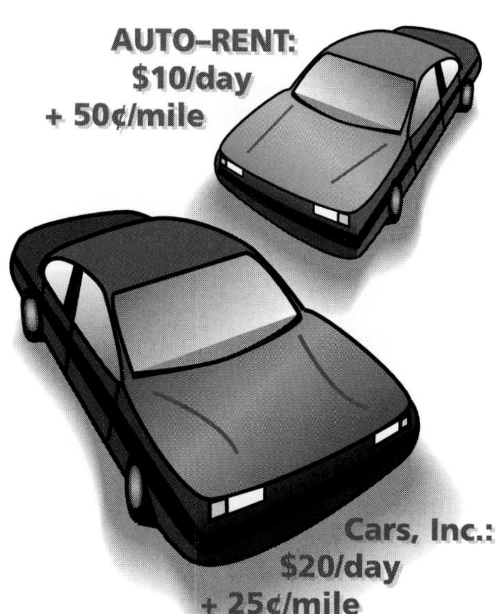

17. **Chemistry** A piece of glass with an initial temperature of 99°C is cooled at a rate of 3.5°C/min. At the same time, a piece of copper with an initial temperature of 0°C is heated at a rate of 2.5°C/min. Let $m =$ the number of minutes and $t =$ the temperature in °C. Which system models the given information?

A. $t = 99 + 3.5m$
$t = 0 + 2.5m$

B. $t = 99 - 3.5m$
$t = 0 - 2.5m$

C. $t = 99 - 3.5m$
$t = 0 + 2.5m$

D. $t = 99 + 3.5m$
$t = 0 - 2.5m$

18. Solve the system that models the situation in Exercise 17. Explain what the solution means in this situation.

Glass can be drawn into optical fibers 16 km long. One fiber can carry 20 times as many phone calls as 500 copper wires.

Without solving, what method would you choose to solve each system: *graphing, substitution,* or *elimination*? Explain your reasoning.

19. $4s - 3t = 8$
$t = -2s - 1$

20. $y = 3x - 1$
$y = 4x$

21. $3m - 4n = 1$
$3m - 2n = -1$

22. $y = -2x$
$y = -\frac{1}{2}x + 3$

23. $2x - y = 4$
$x + 3y = 16$

24. $u = 4v$
$3u - 2v = 7$

25. **Geometry** The perimeter of an isosceles triangle is 12 cm. The two sides s are each three times the length of the third side t.
   a. Write an equation for the perimeter of the triangle.
   b. Write an equation that describes the relationship between one side s and side t.
   c. Find the length of each side.

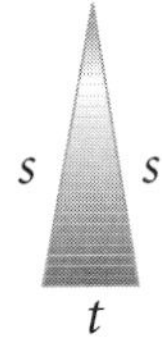

26. **Number Theory** Find two integers with a sum of 1244 and a difference of 90.

Exercises MIXED REVIEW

Solve each equation.

27. $7t + 4 = -10$

28. $j + 9 = -j - 1$

29. $|c - 4| = 21$

30. $m - 5 = -6$

31. In 1995, about $\frac{2}{3}$ of United States currency in circulation was outside the United States. There was \$390 billion in circulation. How much was in use within the United States?

Getting Ready for Lesson 6-5

Graph each equation.

32. $y = 2x + 1$

33. $y - 4 = 0$

34. $y = -\frac{2}{3}x + 1$

35. $y + 2x = -5$

6-5 Linear Inequalities

What You'll Learn

- Graphing linear inequalities

...And Why

To solve budget problems using linear inequalities

What You'll Need

- graph paper

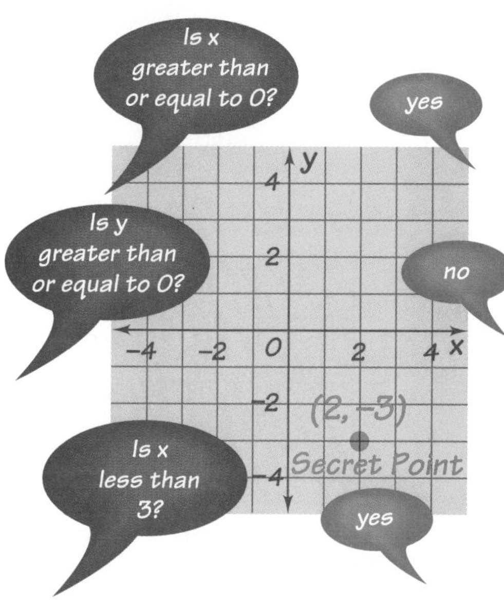

WORK TOGETHER

1. Play the game "What's the Point?" with a partner.

> **Object of the Game:** To locate a secret point on the coordinate plane by asking as few questions as possible.
>
> **How to Play:**
> - Player A chooses a secret point on the coordinate plane. Each coordinate must be an integer from -10 to 10.
> - Player B asks questions that contain the words *less than* or *greater than.* Player A answers each question with only *yes* or *no.* Count the number of questions asked until Player B names the secret point.
> - The players switch roles to complete one round of the game.
>
> **How to Win:** The player who names the point by asking fewer questions wins the round. The first player to win 3 rounds wins the game.

2. How many questions did you need to ask to locate the secret point?
3. If you were as lucky as possible, how many questions would you need to ask to locate the secret point? Explain with an example.
4. How do inequalities help you locate the secret point?
5. Describe a strategy for winning the game.

QUICK REVIEW

$<$ "less than"
$\leq$ "less than or equal to"
$>$ "greater than"
$\geq$ "greater than or equal to"

THINK AND DISCUSS

Just as you have used inequalities to describe graphs on a number line, you can use inequalities to describe regions of a coordinate plane.

Number line
$x < 1$

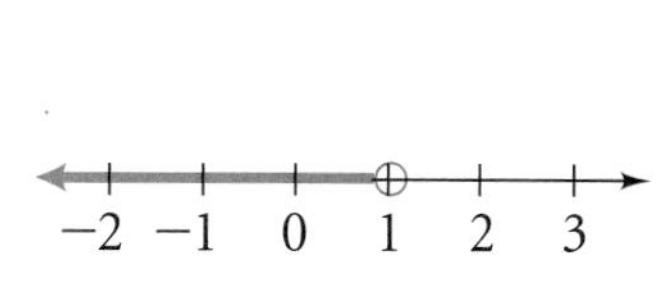

Coordinate plane
$x < 1$

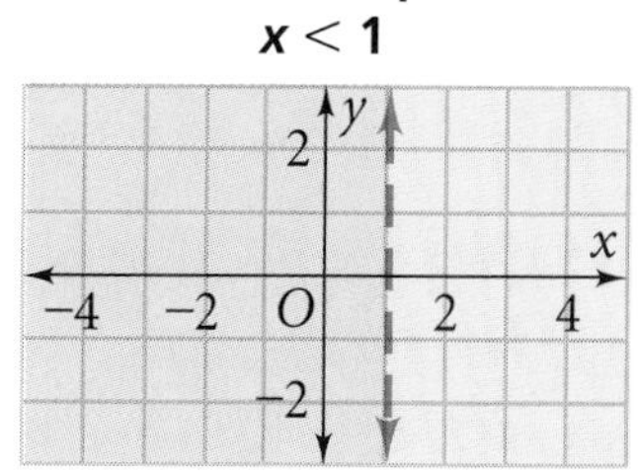

6. What do you think the graph of $y > 2$ looks like on a coordinate grid?

A **linear inequality** describes a region of the coordinate plane that has a boundary line. Every point in the region is a **solution of the inequality.**

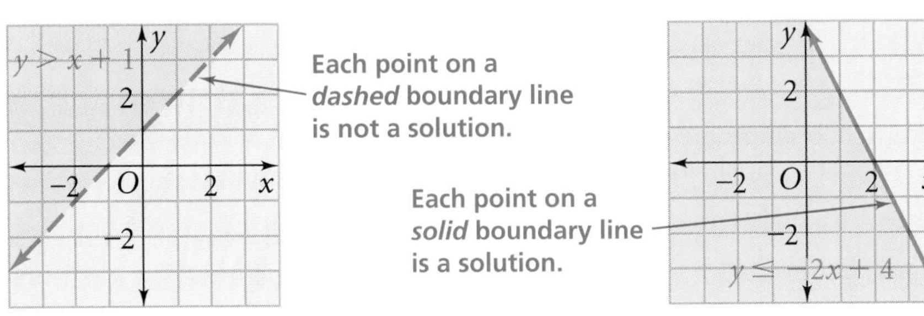

$y > x + 1$
Each point on a *dashed* boundary line is not a solution.
Each point on a *solid* boundary line is a solution.
$y \leq -2x + 4$
y
x
2
−2
O

7. Is (1, 2) a solution for either inequality shown above? Explain.

8. **Open-ended** For each inequality above, name three solutions.

Example 1

Graph $y < 2x + 3$.

First, graph the boundary line $y = 2x + 3$.

Points on the boundary line do *not* make the inequality true. Use a dashed line.

Next, test a point. Use (0, 0).

$y < 2x + 3$

$0 < 2(0) + 3$

$0 < 3$ **True**

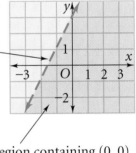

The inequality is true for (0, 0). Shade the region containing (0, 0).

9. **Try This** Graph the inequality $y \geq 2x + 3$.

10. You can test any point on the graph. Why is (0, 0) a good choice?

QUICK REVIEW

Use the slope *m* and the *y*-intercept *b* to graph an equation in the form $y = mx + b$.

PROBLEM SOLVING

Look Back Why did you test a point? Could you test the point (0, 3) to make your graph?

Sometimes it helps to rewrite the inequality to find its solution.

Example 2

Graph $2x - 5y \leq 10$.

Write the inequality in slope-intercept form.

$2x - 5y \leq 10$

$-5y \leq -2x + 10$

$y \geq \frac{2}{5}x - 2$ ← Reverse the inequality symbol.

Graph $y = \frac{2}{5}x - 2$.

Test (0, 0) in $y \geq \frac{2}{5}x - 2$.

$0 \geq (0)x - 2$

$0 \geq -2$ **True**

Shade the region containing (0, 0).

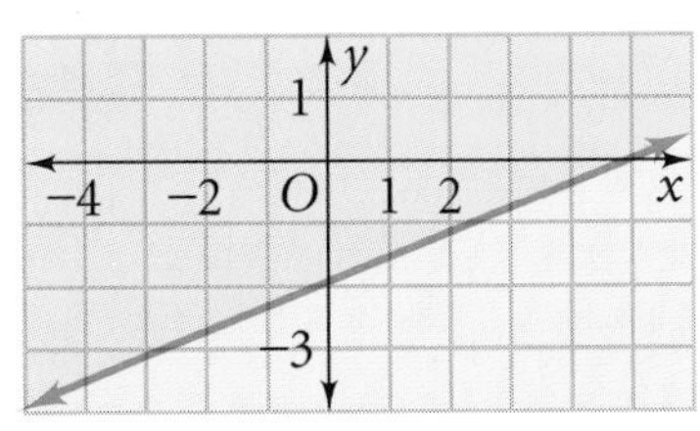

11. a. When you graphed $y \geq \frac{2}{5}x - 2$ in Example 2, did you shade *above* or *below* the line?

b. When you graphed $y < 2x + 3$ in Example 1, did you shade *above* or *below* the line?

c. Critical Thinking Both inequalities are in slope-intercept form. Make a **conjecture** about the inequality symbol and the region shaded.

d. Does your **conjecture** stay true for inequalities in $Ax + By < C$ form? Explain.

You can graph inequalities to solve real-world problems.

Example 3 *Relating to the Real World* 

Food Shopping Suppose you intend to spend no more than $12 on peanuts and cashews for a party. How many pounds of each can you buy?

QUICK REVIEW

Use the intercepts to graph an equation in the form $Ax + By = C$.

Define x = the number of pounds of peanuts
y = the number of pounds of cashews

Relate cost of peanuts + cost of cashews ≤ maximum total cost

Write $2x + 4y \leq 12$

Graph the boundary line $2x + 4y = 12$ using a solid line. Use only Quadrant I, since you cannot buy a negative amount of nuts.

Test (0, 0): $2(0) + 4(0) \leq 12$
$0 \leq 12$ True

Shade the region containing (0, 0).

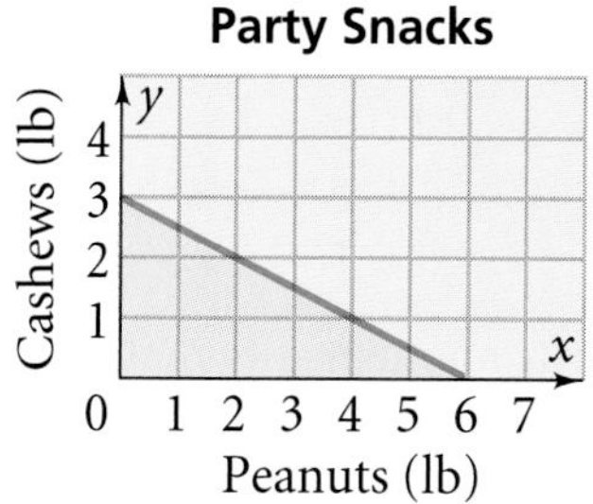

The graph shows all the possible solutions of the problem. For example, if you buy 2 lb of peanuts you can buy no more than 2 lb of cashews.

12. Which are solutions to Example 3?

A. 2 lb peanuts and 1 lb cashews
B. 6 lb peanuts and no cashews
C. 1 lb peanuts and 3 lb cashews
D. 1.5 lb peanuts and 2 lb cashews

Exercises ON YOUR OWN

Choose the linear inequality that describes each graph.

1.

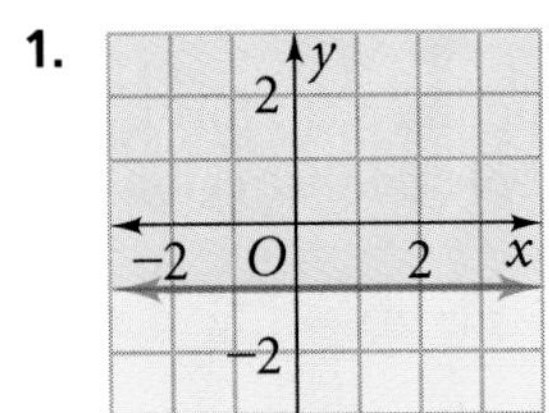
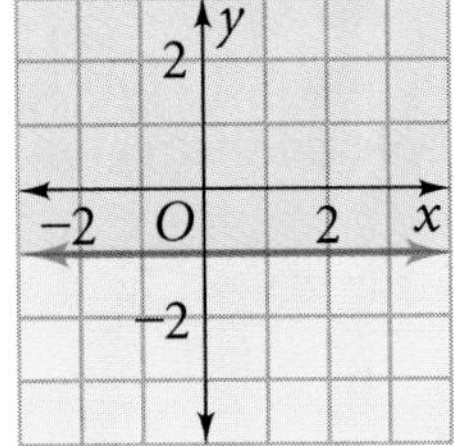

A. $y \geq -1$

B. $y \leq -1$

2.

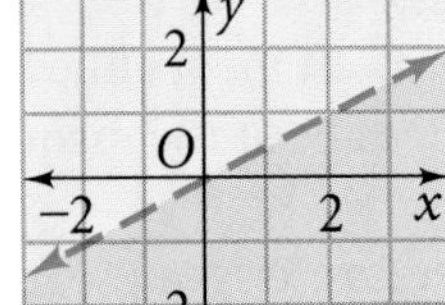

A. $y > \frac{1}{2}x$

B. $y < \frac{1}{2}x$

3.

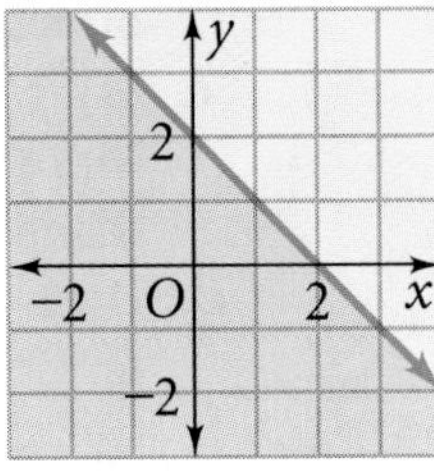

A. $x + y \geq 2$

B. $x + y \leq 2$

4.

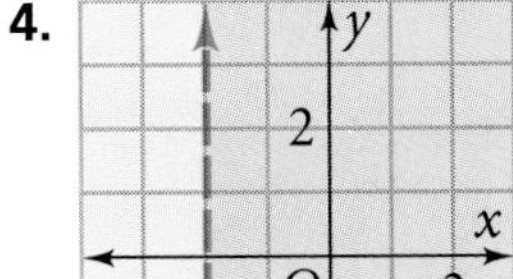

A. $x > -2$

B. $x < -2$

5. For which of the graphs in Exercises 1–4 is $(-2, -1)$ a solution?

6. **Manufacturing** A company makes backpacks. How many backpacks must the company sell to make a profit of more than $250?

  a. Write a linear inequality that describes the situation.

  b. Graph the linear inequality.

  c. Write three possible solutions to the problem.

  d. Why is "10 nylon packs and 22 canvas packs" *not* a solution?

7. **Writing** Explain why a linear inequality is useful when there are many solutions to a problem.

Graph each linear inequality.

8. $x < -2$

9. $y \geq 1$

10. $y < \frac{1}{4}x - 1$

11. $6y - 4x > 0$

12. $y < 5x - 5$

13. $y \leq 4x - 1$

14. $y > -3x + 4$

15. $y > -3x$

16. $x + y \geq 2$

17. $x + 3y \leq 6$

18. $\frac{1}{2}x + \frac{3}{2}y \geq \frac{3}{4}$

19. $y \geq \frac{1}{2}x$

20. $4y > 6x + 2$

21. $2x + 3y \leq 6$

22. $4x - 4y \geq 8$

23. $y - 2x < 2$

24. **Standardized Test Prep** Which statement describes the graph?

A. $y > x + 1$ **B.** $y < x + 1$ **C.** $y \leq x + 1$

D. $y \geq x + 1$ **E.** $y = x + 1$

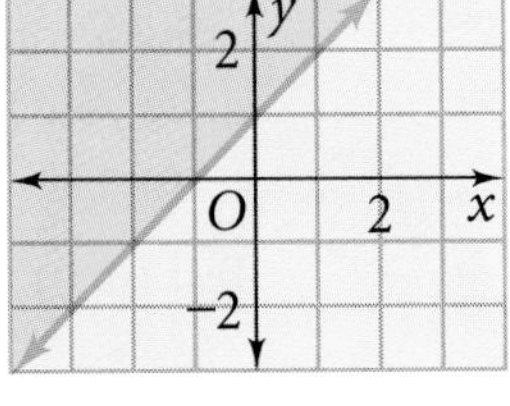

25. Write an inequality that describes the part of the coordinate plane *not* included in the graph of $y \geq x + 2$.

26. **Probability** Suppose you play a carnival game. You toss a blue and a red number cube. If the number on the blue cube is greater than the number on the red cube, you win a prize. The graph shows all the possible outcomes for tossing the cubes.

  a. Copy the graph and shade the region $b > r$.

  b. Does the shaded region include all of the winning outcomes?

  c. What is the probability that you will win a prize?

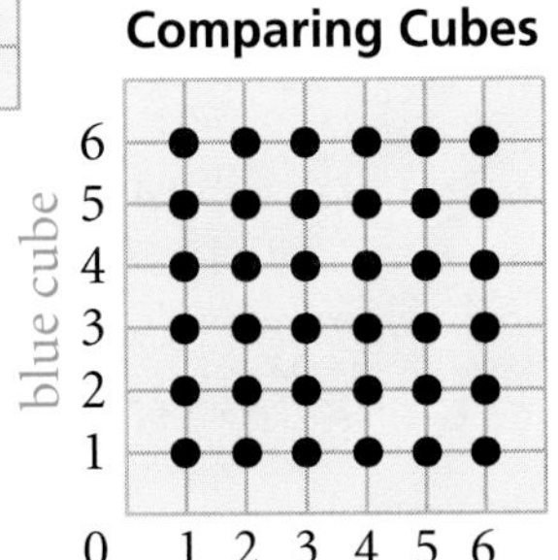

Write the inequality shown in each graph.

27. 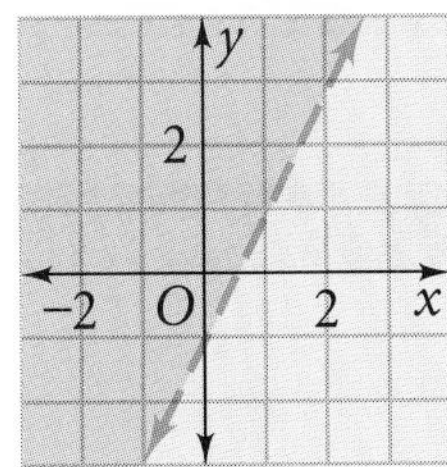

28. 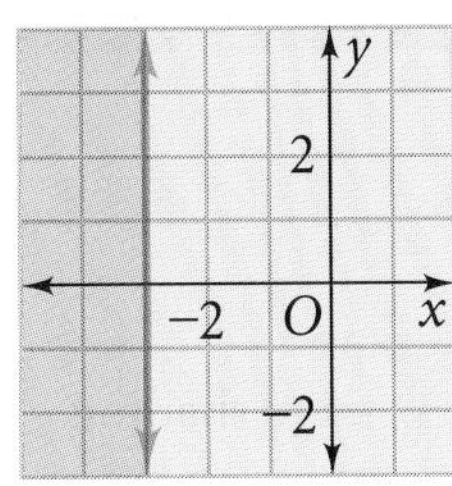

29. 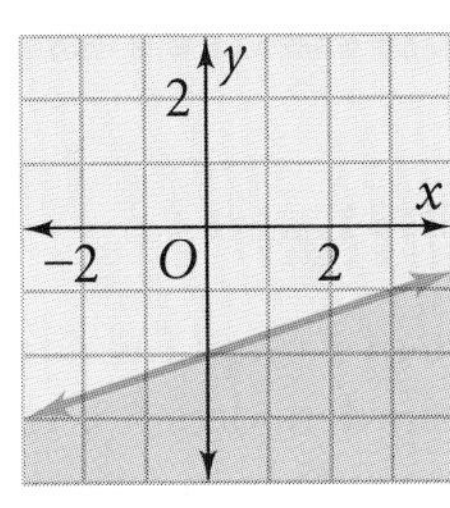

30. 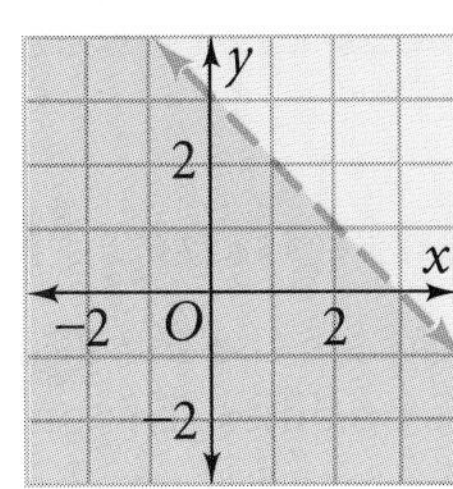

Write the linear inequality described. Then graph the inequality.

31. x is positive.

32. y is negative.

33. y is not negative.

34. x is less than y.

35. **Geometry** Suppose you have 50 ft of fencing. You want to fence a rectangular area of your yard for a garden.
    a. Use the formula for the perimeter of a rectangle to write a linear inequality that describes this situation.
    b. Graph the inequality.
    c. **Open-ended** Give two possible sizes for a square garden.
    d. Can you make the garden 12 ft by 15 ft? **Justify** your answer, using both your graph and the inequality you wrote in part (a).

Chapter Project ***Find Out by Writing***

Use your information from the Find Out questions on pages 274 and 284. Assume that 200 people will come to the dance. Write a report listing which band you would choose and the cost per ticket that you need to charge to cover expenses. Then repeat the process assuming that 300 people will come.

Is point *P* a solution of the linear inequality?

36. $y \leq -2x + 1$; $P(2, 2)$

37. $x < 2$; $P(1, 0)$

38. $y \geq 3x - 2$; $P(0, 0)$

39. $y > x - 1$; $P(0, 1)$

40. **Consumer** Suppose you are shopping for crepe paper to decorate the gym for a school dance. Gold crepe paper costs $5 per roll, and blue crepe paper costs $3 per roll. You have at most $48 to spend. How much gold and blue crepe paper can you buy? Explain your solution.

Exercises MIXED REVIEW

Find the slope of each line.

41. $y = 5x - 9$

42. $7x + 4y = 20$

43. $3y = 8x - 12$

44. $y = 8x + 1$

45. **Automobiles** The average car is parked 95% of the time. How many hours is the average car on the road each day?

Getting Ready for Lesson 6-6

Solve each system of equations.

46. $y = 2x - 3$
    $y = -4x$

47. $4y = 3x + 11$
    $y = 2x - 1$

48. $y = 5x + 2$
    $y = 4x - 6$

49. $y = 8x$
    $y = 2x + 28$

Math ToolboX

Technology

Graphing Inequalities

After Lesson 6-5

You can use the DRAW feature of a graphing calculator to graph inequalities. The order you enter data depends on whether you are shading above or below a line. When shading below Y_1, use Shade (Ymin, Y_1). When shading above Y_1, use Shade (Y_1, Ymax). You do not have to use a close parenthesis before pressing ENTER.

Example

Graph each inequality.

a. $y < 2x + 3$

Shade below Y_1 for *less than.*

b. $y > 0.5x - 1$

Shade above Y_1 for *greater than.*

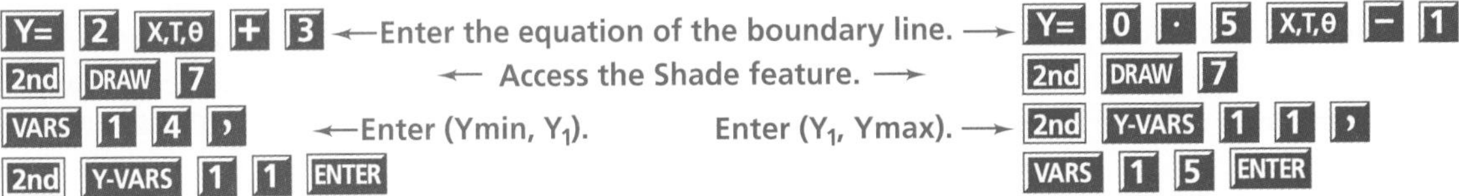

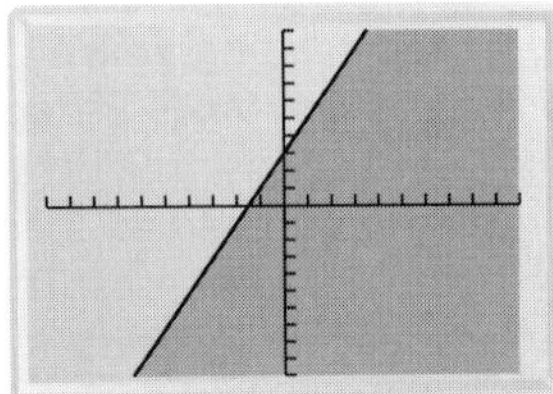

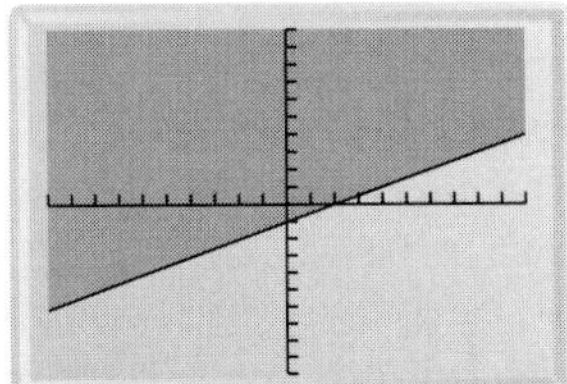

You can vary the darkness of the shading by entering an integer from 1 (dark) to 8 (light). Add a comma and the integer before pressing ENTER. The graph at the right has a darkness level of 2.

The graphing calculator does not make a distinction between a boundary line that is dotted (like *less than*) and a boundary line that is solid (like *less than or equal to*). You must decide if a boundary line should be solid or dotted when you sketch the inequality on your paper.

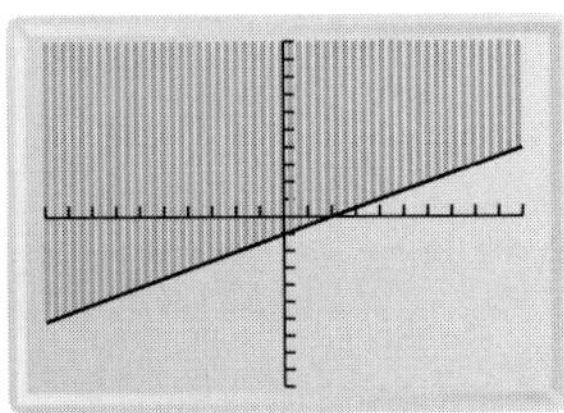

Shade(Y_1,Ymax,2)

Use a graphing calculator to graph each inequality. Sketch your graph.

1. $y < x$

2. $y > 2x + 1$

3. $y \geq -x + 3$

4. $y \leq 5$

5. $x - y \geq 4$

6. $2x + 3y \leq 12$

7. $6x - 30y < 45$

8. $x - 2y \geq 50$

9. Writing What instructions would you need to change in Example (b) to graph $y > 0.5x - 1$ using Y_2 instead of Y_1?

What You'll Learn

- Solving systems of linear inequalities by graphing

...And Why

To solve real-world problems that have many possible solutions, such as those in agriculture

What You'll Need

- graph paper
- graphing calculator

6-6 Systems of Linear Inequalities

WORK TOGETHER

Work in pairs. Explore what happens when you graph lines or linear inequalities on the same coordinate plane.

1. Can two lines be drawn with the given intersection? Support each answer with a diagram or an explanation.
   a. a point **b.** a line **c.** a region **d.** no intersection
2. Can the graphs of two linear inequalities be drawn with the given intersection? Support each answer with a diagram or an explanation.
   a. a point **b.** a line **c.** a region **d.** no intersection
3. **Summarize** your findings in Questions 1 and 2. Compare the possible intersections of two lines with the possible intersections of the graphs of two linear inequalities. What do you notice?
4. Find the possible intersections for more than two lines.
5. Find the possible intersections for the graphs of more than two linear inequalities.

THINK AND DISCUSS

Two or more linear inequalities together form a **system of linear inequalities.** Here is an example of a system that describes the shaded region of the graph. Notice that there are two boundary lines.

System of Linear Inequalities

$x \geq 2$

$y < -1$

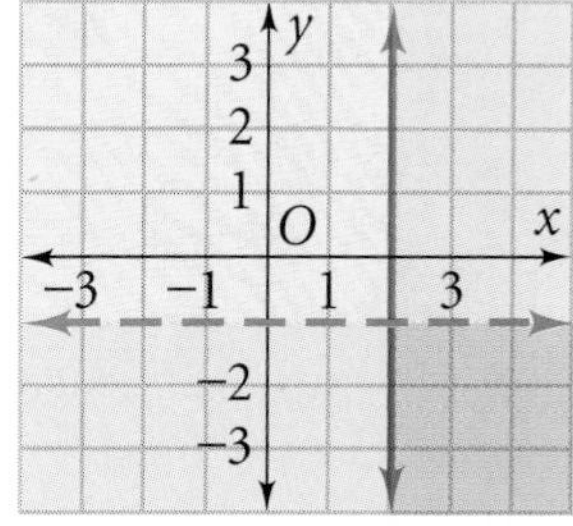

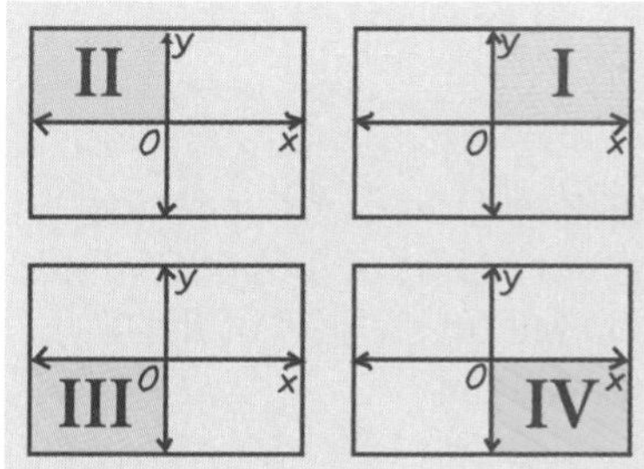

6. You can describe all the points of a quadrant with a system of linear inequalities. Match each system with a quadrant.

   A. $x > 0$, $y > 0$ **B.** $x > 0$, $y < 0$ **C.** $x < 0$, $y > 0$ **D.** $x < 0$, $y < 0$

A **solution of a system of linear inequalities** makes each inequality in the system true. The graph of a system shows all of its solutions.

Example 1 Relating to the Real World 

Animal Studies A zoo keeper wants to fence a rectangular pen for goats. The length of the pen should be at least 80 ft, and the distance around it should be no more than 310 ft. What are the possible dimensions of the pen?

Define x = width of the pen
y = length of the pen

Relate	The length	is at least	80 ft.	The perimeter	is no more than	310 ft.
Write	y	$\geq$	80	$2x + 2y$	$\leq$	310

Use slope-intercept form to graph.

$y \geq 80$
$m = 0$
$b = 80$

Test (0, 1).
$y \geq 80$
$(1) \geq 80$ **False**

Shade above.

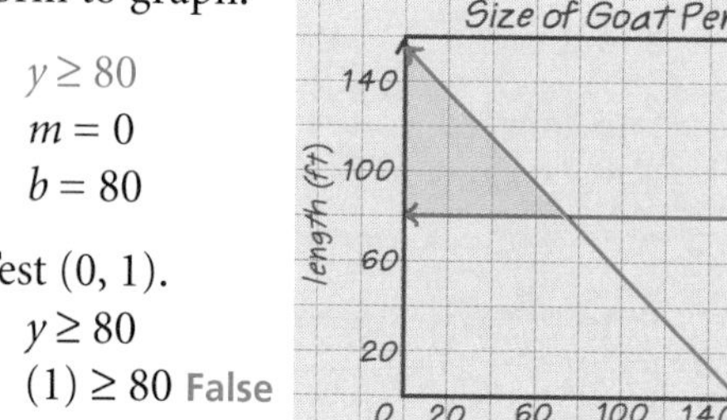

Use intercepts to graph.

$2x + 2y \leq 310$
(155, 0)
(0, 155)

Test (0, 0).
$2(0) + 2(0) \leq 310$
$0 \leq 310$ **True**

Shade below.

The solutions are all the points in the shaded region above $y = 80$ but below $2x + 2y \leq 310$.

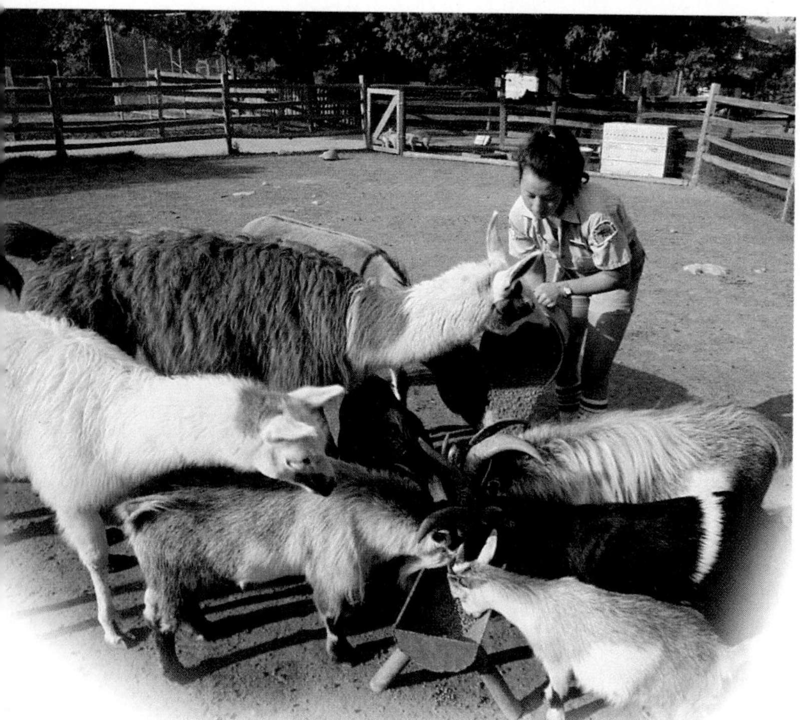

7. Give three possible dimensions (length and width) for the pen. How many solutions does this system have?

8. Why is the solution region shown only in Quadrant I?

9. **Graphing Calculator** Use the *Shade* feature to graph the system of linear inequalities in Example 1.

10. **Try This** Solve each system by graphing.
    a. $y \leq 2x + 3$
    $y \geq x - 1$
    b. $y > x$
    $x \leq 3$
    c. $x + y > -2$
    $x - y > 2$

11. **Critical Thinking** How can you decide whether or not points on boundary lines of a solution region are part of the solution of a system?

Some systems of linear inequalities do not have a solution region. The graphs of the inequalities might intersect in a line or not at all.

Example 2

Solve the system by graphing. $4y \geq 6x$
$-3x + 2y \leq -6$

Use slope-intercept form to graph.

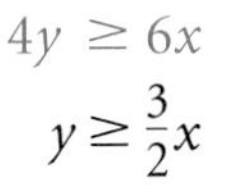

Use intercepts to graph.

$-3x + 2y \leq -6$
$(0, -3)$
$(2, 0)$

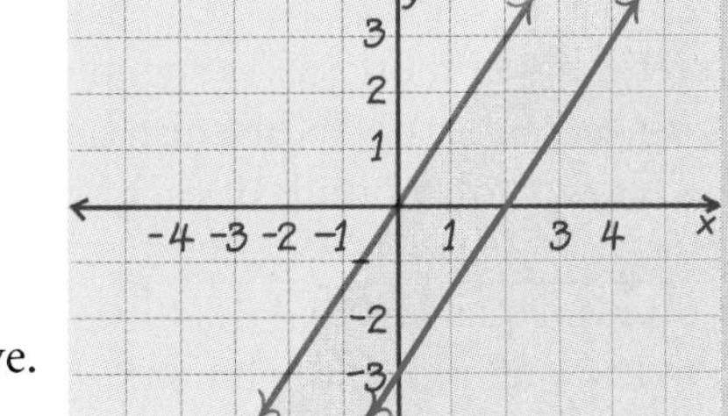

Test (0, 1).
Shade above.

Test (0, 0).
Shade below.

Since the shaded regions do not overlap, the system has no solution.

12. Explain why (0, 0) was not tested when $4y \geq 6x$ was graphed.

13. How are the boundary lines in Example 2 related?

PROBLEM SOLVING HINT

For Questions 14 and 15, first draw a diagram. Then write the inequalities.

14. a. ***Open-ended*** Write another system of two linear inequalities that has no solution.

b. Must the boundary lines be parallel? Explain.

15. ***Critical Thinking*** Write a system of linear inequalities in which the solution is a line.

Exercises ON YOUR OWN

1. ***Standardized Test Prep*** Which of these points is a solution of the system $y \leq x + 5$ and $y + x > 3$?

A. (0, 0) **B.** (−1, 4) **C.** (3, 3) **D.** (−2, 6) **E.** (2, 0)

2. Which system is represented in the graph at the right?

A. $x + y \leq 3$, $y > x - 3$
B. $x + y > 3$, $y \leq x - 3$
C. $x + y \geq 3$, $y < x - 3$
D. $x + y < 3$, $y \geq x - 3$

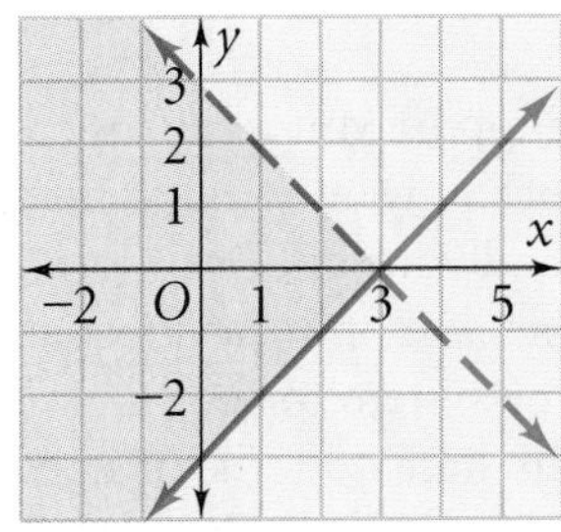

3. ***Critical Thinking*** Without graphing, explain why the point where the boundary lines intersect in the system $2x + y > 2$ and $x - y \geq 3$ is *not* a solution of the system.

4. ***Writing*** Write a problem that can be solved using the system of inequalities at the right.

$2l + 2w \leq 100$
$l \leq 30$

Solve each system of linear inequalities by graphing.

5. $x \geq 2$
$y < 4$

6. $y > 3$
$x < -1$

7. $y \leq x$
$y \geq x + 1$

8. $y > 4x + 2$
$y \leq 4$

9. $y \leq 2x + 2$
$y < -x + 1$

10. $y \geq -2x + 1$
$y < x + 2$

11. $x + y \leq 6$
$x - y < 1$

12. $y - 3x < 6$
$y > 3x + 9$

13. $x > y$
$y > 0$

14. $x + y \leq 5$
$x \geq 1$

15. $y < \frac{1}{2}x$
$y > \frac{1}{2}x - 3$

16. $-x - y \leq 2$
$y - 2x > 1$

17. **Construction** A contractor has at most \$33 to spend on nails for a project. The contractor needs at least 9 lb of finish nails and at least 12 lb of common nails. How many pounds of each type of nail should the contractor buy?
   a. Write a system of three inequalities that describes this situation.
   b. Graph the system to show all possible solutions.
   c. Name a point that is a solution of the system.
   d. Name a point that is *not* a solution of the system.

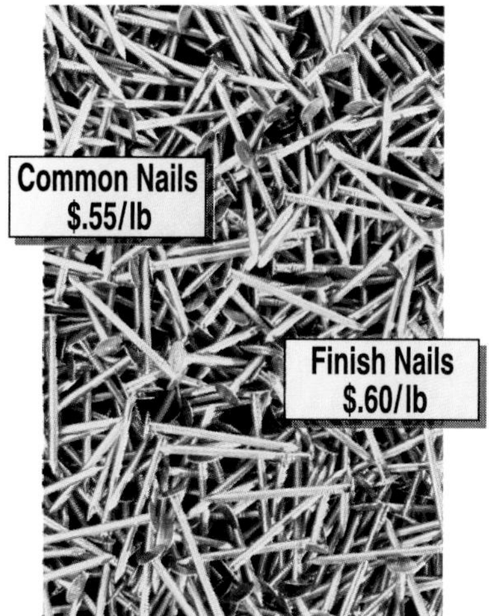

Open-ended **Write a system of linear inequalities with the given characteristics.**

18. (0, 0) is a solution.

19. Solutions are only in Quadrant II.

20. There is no solution.

21. The solution region is triangular.

22. a. Solve the system of three inequalities at the right by graphing.
    b. **Verify** your solution by testing a point from the overlapping region in all three inequalities.

$x \leq 4$
$y < x + 2$
$x + 2y \geq -2$

Geometry **For the solution region of each system of linear inequalities, (a) describe the shape, (b) find the vertices, and (c) find the area.**

23. $y \geq \frac{1}{2}x + 1$
$y \leq 2$
$x \geq -4$

24. $x \geq 1$
$x \leq 5$
$y \geq -1$
$y \leq 3$

25. $x \geq 0$
$x \leq 2$
$y \geq -4$
$y \leq -x + 2$

26. $x \geq 2$
$y \geq -3$
$x + y \leq 4$

27. **Shopping** Suppose you receive a \$50 gift certificate to the Music and Books store. You want to buy some books and at least one CD. How can you spend your gift certificate on x paperbacks and y CDs?
   a. Write a system of linear inequalities that describes this situation.
   b. Graph the system to show possible solutions to this problem.
   c. What purchase does the ordered pair (2, 6) represent? Is it a solution to your system? Explain.
   d. Find a solution in which you spend almost all of the gift certificate.
   e. What is the greatest number of paperbacks you can buy and still buy one CD?

Cityside Music and Books
All CDs
\$9.99
All books
\$5.99

Chapter Project — Find Out by Graphing

In the Find Out question on page 293, you found two ticket prices. Each price covers the cost of the dance under certain conditions. Decide what the ticket price should be. Plan for between 200 and 300 people. Graph a system of linear inequalities to show the total amount received from tickets.

Exercises MIXED REVIEW

Solve each equation.

28. $5m + 4 = 8m - 2$ **29.** $5(t + 1) = 10$ **30.** $4x = 2x + 5$ **31.** $6h - 11 = 13$

32. $3p = -\frac{3}{4}p + 5$ **33.** $-k - 7 = -3k + 1$ **34.** $\frac{3c - 1}{4} = \frac{5}{2}$ **35.** $\frac{1}{2}(t - 8) = 7$

36. a. Identify the independent and dependent variables.
b. Graph the data.
c. What scales did you use and why?

Price	Sales Tax
$1.00	$.05
$3.00	$.15
$4.00	$.20
$7.00	$.35

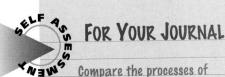

FOR YOUR JOURNAL

Compare the processes of graphing a system of linear inequalities and graphing a system of linear equations. How are they similar? How are they different?

Getting Ready for Lesson 6-7

Evaluate each formula for the given point.

37. $B = 2x + 5y$; (6, 10) **38.** $C = x + 6y$; (100, 550)

39. $P = 6x + 2y$; (200, 75) **40.** $P = 2l + 2w$; (30, 18)

Exercises CHECKPOINT

Solve each system of linear inequalities.

1. $y < -2x + 5$
$y > 3x - 1$

2. $y \geq 2x - 1$
$x \geq -5$

3. $y < 0.5x + 3$
$y \geq -x + 2.5$

4. $3x + 2y \leq 12$
$x - y < 10$

5. *Standardized Test Prep* Which of these points is a solution of the system $y \geq 4x - 1$ and $2x + 3y < 6$?
A. (3, 0) **B.** (0, 4) **C.** (4, 1) **D.** (−3, 1) **E.** (3, −4)

6. You are going out for pizza!
a. Write a system of equations for the cost of a large pizza at each restaurant.
b. Solve the system of equations. Interpret your solution.
c. *Open-ended* Where will you go for pizza? Explain your reasons.

What You'll Learn

- Solving linear programming problems

...And Why

To investigate real-world situations, such as time management

6-7 Concepts of Linear Programming

WORK TOGETHER

Suppose you are offered a part-time job. You wonder how much time you have available to work. You can use mathematics to help you organize your thoughts and make a good decision.

Work with a partner.

1. **a.** Write the different ways you spend your time during a week.
   b. Organize your list into no more than ten categories.
2. Make a personal calendar for the last week.
   a. Assign time to the categories from Question 1.
   b. How much time do you have available to work at a part-time job?
   c. Discuss what you could or could not give up in your schedule.

THINK AND DISCUSS

You can answer questions like those above by using a process called linear programming. **Linear programming** identifies conditions that make a quantity as large as or as small as possible. The variables used in the equation for the quantity have restrictions. The maximum and minimum values of the quantity occur at vertices of the graph of the restrictions.

Example 1

Use linear programming. Find the values of x and y that maximize the quantity.

Restrictions $\begin{cases} x + y \leq 8 \\ x \geq 0 \\ y \geq 3 \end{cases}$

Equation $Q = 3x + 2y$

Step 1
Graph the restrictions.

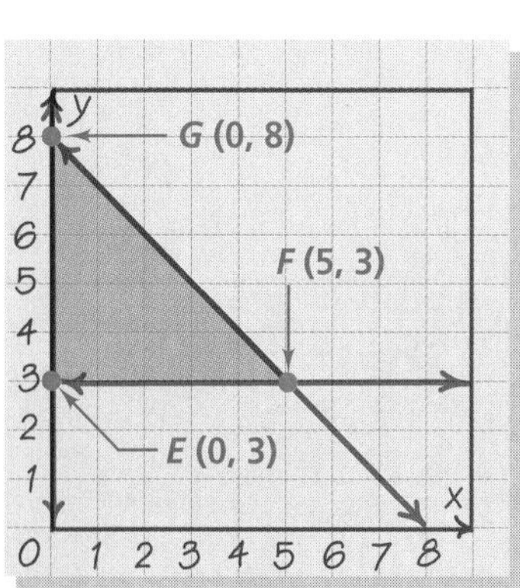

Step 2
Find coordinates of each vertex.

Step 3
Evaluate Q at each vertex.

Vertex	$Q = 3x + 2y$	
$E(0, 3)$	$Q = 3(0) + 2(3) = 6$	
$F(5, 3)$	$Q = 3(5) + 2(3) = 21$	← maximum value of Q
$G(0, 8)$	$Q = 3(0) + 2(8) = 16$	

The maximum value 21 occurs when $x = 5$ and $y = 3$.

3. Find the values of x and y that minimize the quantity in Example 1.

4. Find the value of the equation in Example 1 at each point.

a. $(1, 3)$ **b.** $(4, 3)$ **c.** $(4, 4)$ **d.** $(1, 7)$ **e.** $(3, 4)$

In the Work Together activity, you listed some restrictions you have on your time in relation to a part-time job. In the next example one student finds the best way to use her time.

Example 2 **Relating to the Real World** 

Time Management Marta plans to start a part-time job. Here are the restrictions she has found on her time for homework hours x and job hours y.

Restriction	Inequality
She has no more than 24 h/wk for homework and a job.	$x + y \leq 24$
The boss wants her to work at least 6 h/wk.	$y \geq 6$
She spends 10–15 h/wk on homework.	$x \geq 10$ $x \leq 15$

She decides that homework hours are twice as valuable as work hours. Find the best way B for Marta to split her time between homework and the job using the equation $B = 2x + y$.

Step 1
Graph the restrictions.

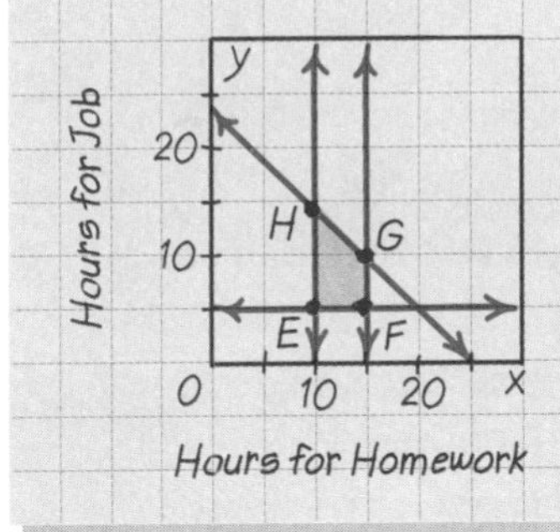

Step 2
Find the coordinates of each vertex.

Vertex
$E(10, 6)$
$F(15, 6)$
$G(15, 9)$
$H(10, 14)$

Step 3
Evaluate B at each vertex.

$\mathbf{B = 2x + y}$
$B = 2(10) + 6 = 26$
$B = 2(15) + 6 = 36$
$B = 2(15) + 9 = 39$ ← maximum value of B
$B = 2(10) + 14 = 34$

The best way for Marta to split her time each week is to spend 15 h on homework and 9 h at her job.

5. What does the point $(10, 14)$ mean in terms of homework and job time?

6. Critical Thinking For each situation, would the best solution be a *maximum value* or a *minimum value*? Explain.
   a. You are selling tomatoes and beans from your garden. You want to determine how much of each to grow for the most profit.
   b. Suppose you manage a grocery store. You can buy tomatoes from two different farmers. You consider the price of the tomatoes and transportation costs. You must decide which supplier to use.

To solve linear programming problems, you must be able to write the inequalities for the restrictions and write the equation.

Example 3 Relating to the Real World 

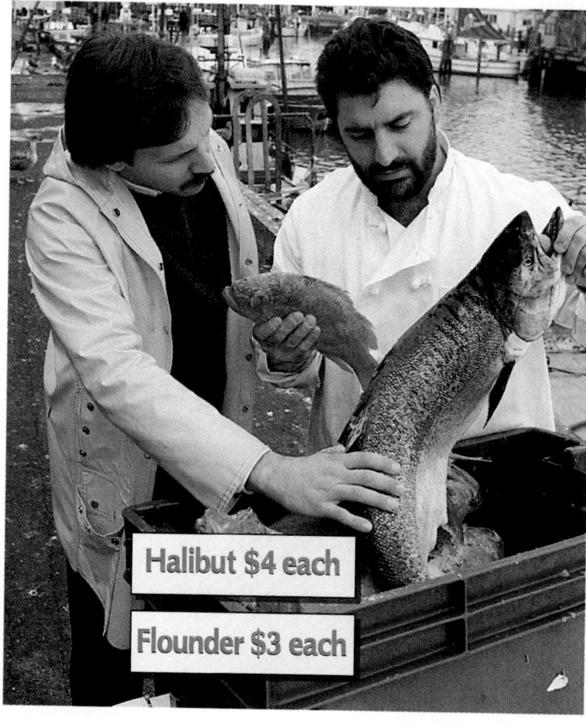

Business A seafood restaurant owner orders at least 50 fish. He cannot use more than 30 halibut or more than 35 flounder. How many of each fish should he use to minimize his cost?

Step 1 Write inequalities to describe the restrictions.

Define x = number of halibut used
y = number of flounder used

Relate	Write
He needs at least 50 fish.	$x + y \geq 50$
He cannot use more than 30 halibut.	$x \leq 30$
He cannot use more than 35 flounder.	$y \leq 35$

Step 2 Write the equation.

Define C = cost of fish

Relate cost is $4 for each halibut and $3 for each flounder

Write $C = 4x + 3y$

Step 3
Graph the restrictions.

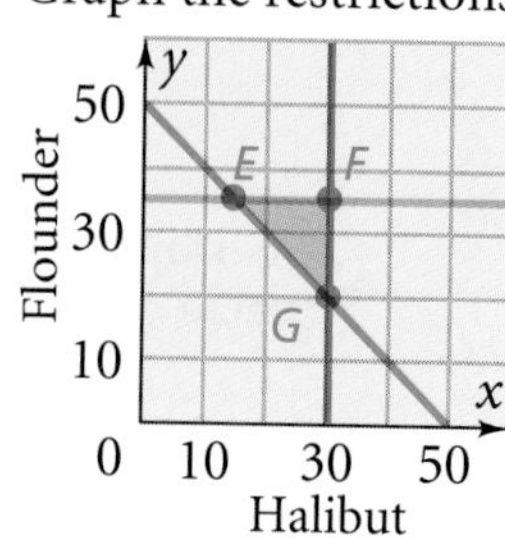

Step 4
Find the coordinates of each vertex.

Vertex
$E(15, 35)$
$F(30, 35)$
$G(30, 20)$

Step 5
Evaluate C at each vertex.

$\mathbf{C = 4x + 3y}$
$C = 4(15) + 3(35) = 165$ ← minimum value of C
$C = 4(30) + 3(35) = 225$
$C = 4(30) + 3(20) = 180$

The seafood restaurant owner should buy 15 halibut and 35 flounder to minimize his cost.

7. Try This Suppose the restaurant owner changes his order to at least 40 fish. How many of each kind should he use to minimize his cost?

Exercises ON YOUR OWN

Evaluate each equation at the points given. Which point gives the maximum value? the minimum value?

1. $Q = 3x + 5y$
(8, 0), (4, 4), (3, 5), (0, 6)

2. $B = 40x + 20y$
(0, 0), (0, 40), (15, 10), (25, 0)

3. $A = 35x + 10y$
(0, 0),(0, 10), (0, 40), (20, 10)

Find the values of x and y that maximize or minimize each quantity for each graph.

4. Maximum for
$P = x + y$

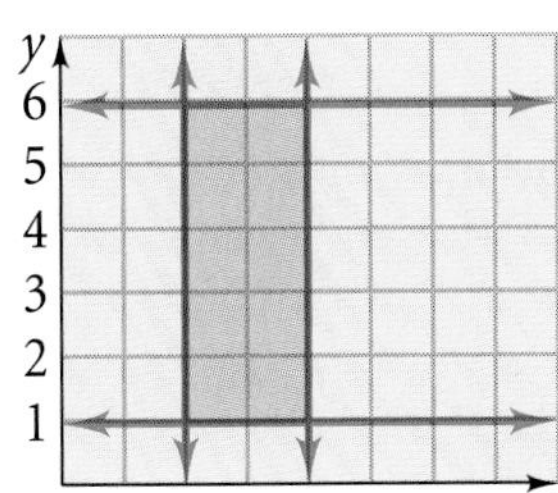

5. Maximum for
$P = 3x + 2y$

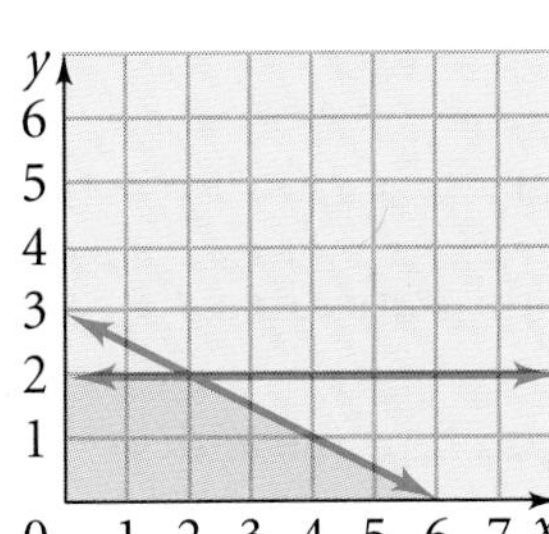

6. Minimum for
$C = 2x + 5y$

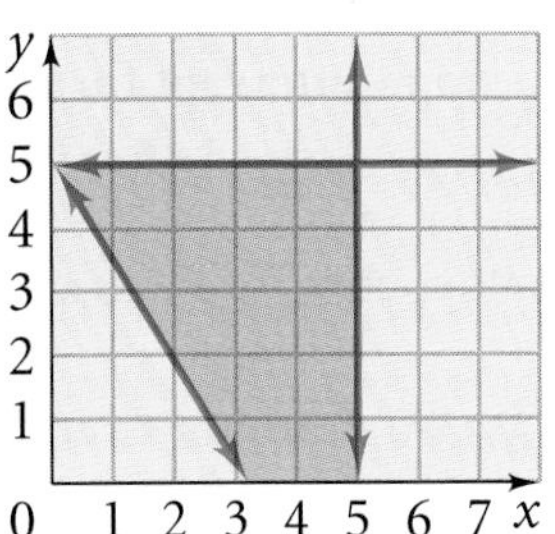

7. Minimum for
$C = \frac{1}{2}x + y$

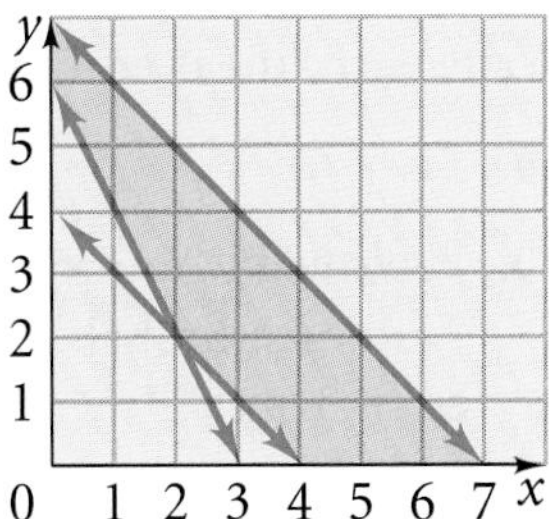

Evaluate the equation to find minimum and maximum values.

8. $x \geq 2$
$x \leq 5$
$y \geq 3$
$y \leq 6$
$A = 5x + 4y$

9. $x \geq 0$
$y \geq 0$
$x + y \leq 12$
$D = 3x + y$

10. $y \geq -x + 4$
$y \leq -2x + 10$
$x \geq 0$
$y \geq 0$
$P = 2x + 3y$

11. $y \leq -x + 8$
$y \geq 2x - 2$
$x \geq 0$
$y \geq 0$
$Q = x + y$

12. **Open-ended** Write a system of restrictions that form a trapezoid.

13. **Environment** A town is trying to find the best mix of sand and salt for treating icy roads. One consideration is cost, which they want to minimize. Sand costs \$8 per ton, and salt costs \$20 per ton. Write the equation for minimizing cost.

14. **Manufacturing** A toy manufacturer wants to minimize her cost for producing two lines of toy airplanes. Because of the supply of materials, no more than 40 Flying Bats can be built each day, and no more than 60 Flying Falcons can be built each day. There are enough workers to build at least 70 toy airplanes each day.

a. Write the inequalities for the restrictions.

b. It costs \$12 to manufacture a Flying Bat and \$8 to build a Flying Falcon. Write an equation for the cost of manufacturing the toy airplanes.

c. Use linear programming to find how many of each toy airplane should be produced each day to minimize cost.

d. **Critical Thinking** What else should the manufacturer consider before deciding how many of each toy to manufacture each day?

15. **Business** A computer company has budgeted \$6000 to rent display space at two locations for a new line of computers. Each location requires a minimum of 100 ft^2.

   a. **Writing** Explain what each inequality represents.
      Restrictions: $10x + 20y \leq 6000$, $x \geq 100$, $y \geq 100$

   b. Write an equation for the potential number of customers.

   c. Use linear programming to find the amount of space to rent at each location to maximize the number of potential customers.

Rental Locations

Location	Cost	Potential
A	\$10/ft^2	30 customers/ft^2
B	\$20/ft^2	40 customers/ft^2

Exercises MIXED REVIEW

Write each linear equation in slope-intercept form.

16. $5y = 6x - 3$
17. $4x + 8y = 20$
18. $y = 3(x - 2)$
19. $9y = 24x$

20. **Probability** You roll a number cube and toss a coin at the same time. Find each probability.

   a. $P(3 \text{ and } T)$
   b. $P(\text{odd number and } H)$
   c. $P(\text{prime and } T)$
   d. $P(6)$

Getting Ready for Lesson 6-8

To which family of functions does each function belong?

21. $y = 3x^2 - x + 6$
22. $y = |5x - 2|$
23. $y = 4x - 9$
24. $y = -7x^2 - 1$

Algebra at Work

Businessperson

Some of the goals of a business are to minimize costs and maximize profits. People in business use linear programming to analyze data in order to achieve these goals. The illustration lists some of the variables involved in operating a small manufacturing company. To solve a problem, a businessperson must identify the variables and restrictions and then search for the best possible solutions.

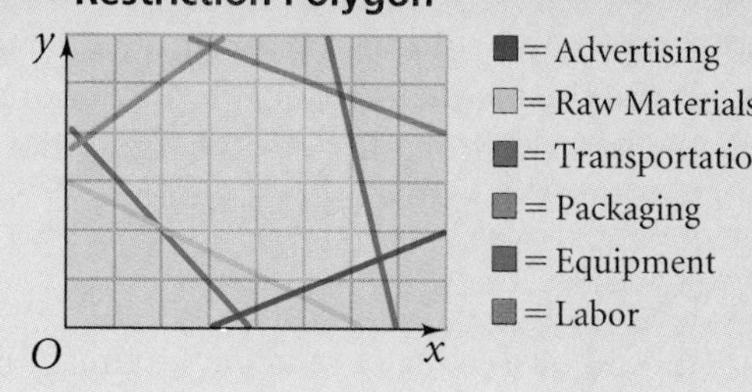

Mini Project: Work with a partner. Decide on a small business you could start. Identify the variables connected with your business and the restrictions on the variables.

What You'll Learn

- Solving systems with linear, quadratic, and absolute value equations by graphing

...And Why

To solve problems involving engineering and architecture

What You'll Need

- graphing calculator
- graph paper

6-8 Systems with Nonlinear Equations

THINK AND DISCUSS

A system of equations can include equations that are not linear. The system shown consists of a linear equation and a quadratic equation.

$$y = x + 2$$
$$y = -x^2 + 4$$

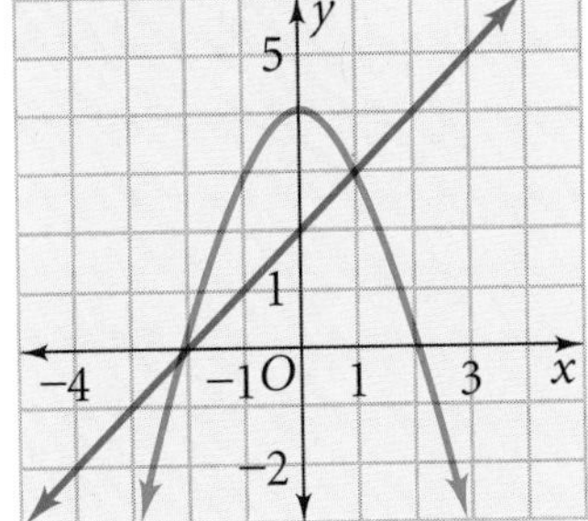

Notice that the graphs intersect at (–2, 0) and (1, 3). These two points are solutions of the system.

1. Check (–2, 0) and (1, 3) in both equations to **verify** that they are solutions of the system.

You can solve a system with a nonlinear equation by graphing.

Example 1

Solve the system of equations. $y = \frac{1}{2}x + 1$
$y = |x - 1|$

Graph each equation.

$y = \frac{1}{2}x + 1$

Use $y = mx + b$.

$m = \frac{1}{2}$

$b = 1$

$y = |x - 1|$

Make a table of values.

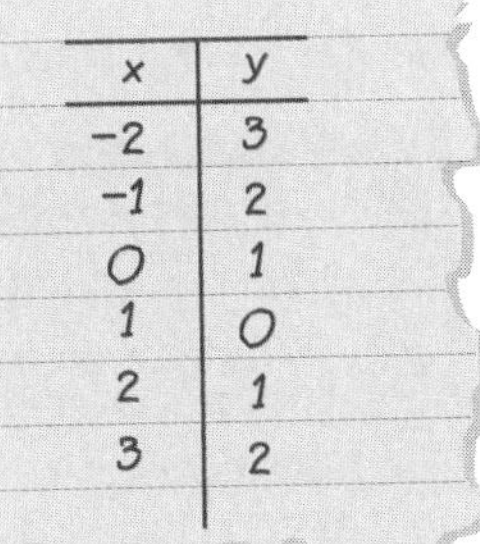

x	y
−2	3
−1	2
0	1
1	0
2	1
3	2

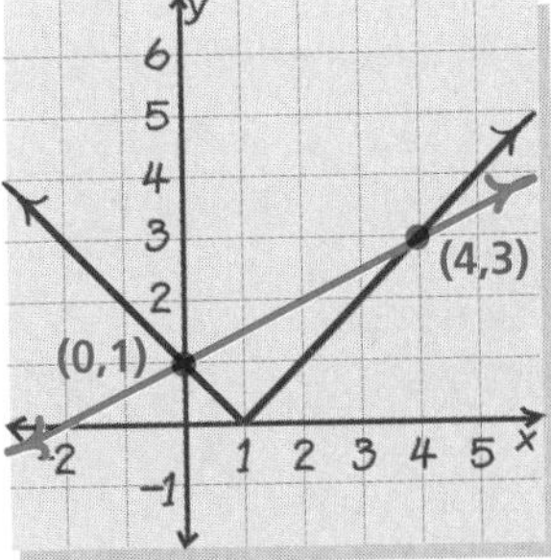

The graphs intersect at (0, 1) and (4, 3).

Check (0, 1):

$y = \frac{1}{2}x + 1$
$1 \stackrel{?}{=} \frac{1}{2}(0) + 1$
$1 \stackrel{?}{=} 0 + 1$
$1 = 1$ ✔

$y = |x - 1|$
$1 \stackrel{?}{=} |0 - 1|$
$1 \stackrel{?}{=} |-1|$
$1 = 1$ ✔

Check (4, 3):

$y = \frac{1}{2}x + 1$
$3 \stackrel{?}{=} \frac{1}{2}(4) + 1$
$3 \stackrel{?}{=} 2 + 1$
$3 = 3$ ✔

$y = |x - 1|$
$3 \stackrel{?}{=} |4 - 1|$
$3 \stackrel{?}{=} |3|$
$3 = 3$ ✔

2. **Critical Thinking** Do systems made up of one linear equation and one absolute-value equation always have two solutions? If not, what are the other possibilities? Give examples.

Some systems of nonlinear equations have no solution.

Example 2

Solve the system of equations. $y = x^2 + 3$
$y = x$

Graph each equation.

$y = x^2 + 3$
Make a table of values.

x	y
−2	7
−1	4
0	3
1	4
2	7

$y = x$
Use $y = mx + b$.
$m = 1$ $b = 0$

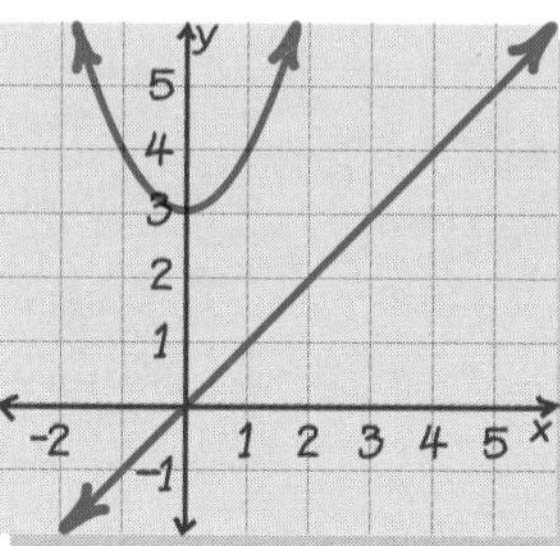

The graphs do not intersect, so the system has no solution.

3. **Try This** Solve each system.

a. $y = |x| + 2$
$y = 4x - 1$

b. $y = -x^2$
$y = x^2 - 8$

c. $y = |x - 2|$
$y = -\frac{1}{3}x + 2$

You can use a graphing calculator to solve systems with nonlinear equations.

Example 3 **Relating to the Real World**

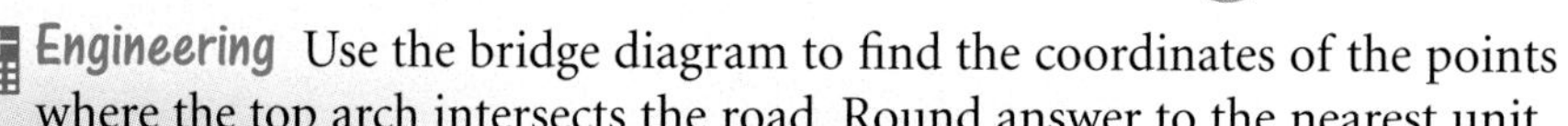

Engineering Use the bridge diagram to find the coordinates of the points where the top arch intersects the road. Round answer to the nearest unit.

Arch $y = -\frac{1}{600}x^2 + 100$
Road $y = 40$

GRAPHING CALCULATOR HINT

You can use the TABLE feature or the ZOOM and TRACE keys to estimate the intersection points.

Set an appropriate range.

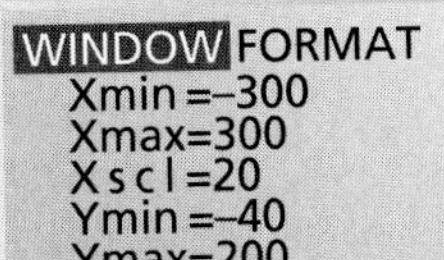

Input the equations.

Y1 = –(1/600)X²+100
Y2 = 40
Y3 =
Y4 =
Y5 =
Y6 =
Y7 =

Use the CALC key to find the coordinates of the intersection points.

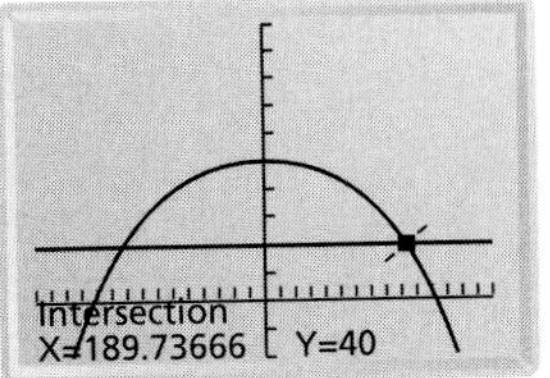

The solutions, rounded to the nearest unit, are (190, 40) and (–190, 40).

4. Each unit in Example 3 equals 1 ft. Find the length of the bridge.

Exercises ON YOUR OWN

Write the solution(s) of each system of equations. Check that each solution makes both equations of the system true.

1. $y = 2x$
$y = x^2$

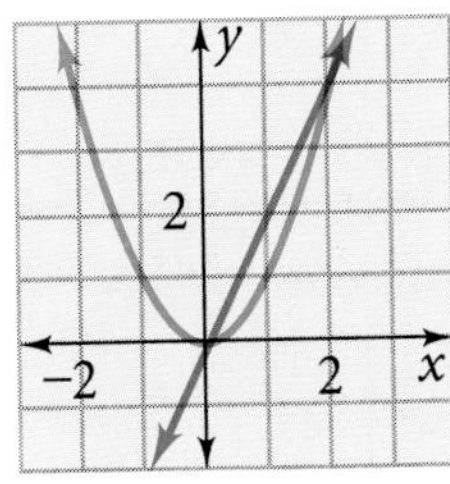

2. $y = 3$
$y = |x|$

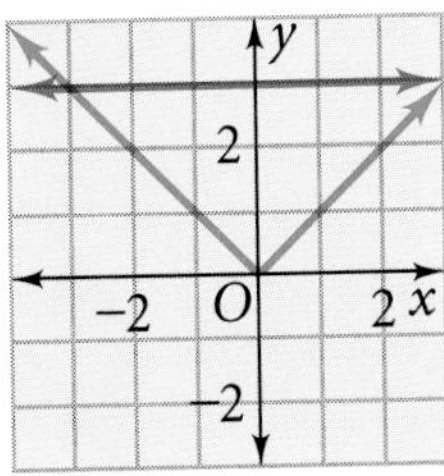

3. $y = -0.4x^2$
$y = -4x^2$

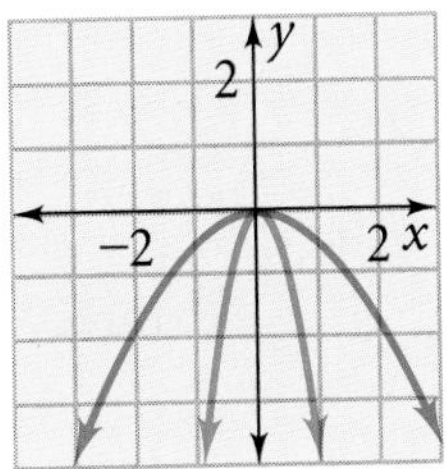

4. $y = |x|$
$y = -x + 5$

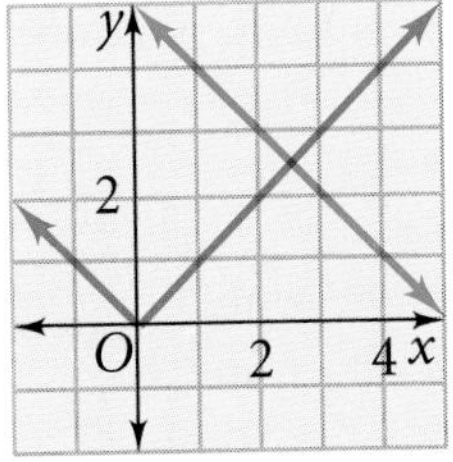

5. $y = -|x|$
$y = x^2 - 6$

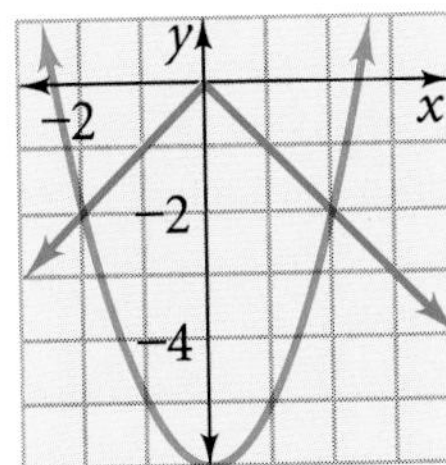

6. $y = x$
$y = -x^2$

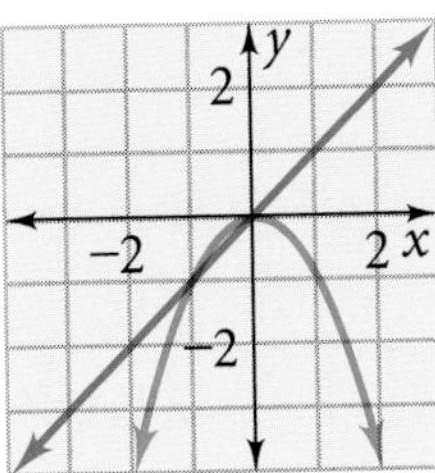

7. $y = |0.5x|$
$y = |3x| - 5$

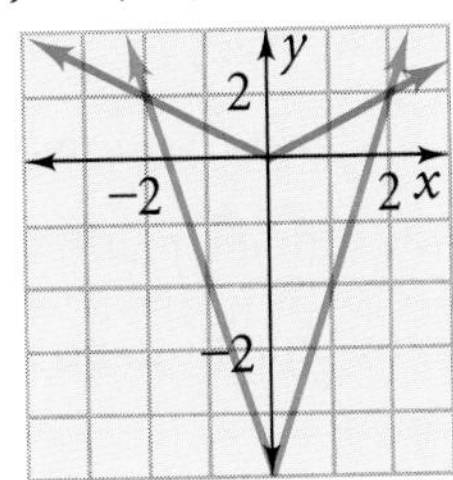

8. $y = x^2 + 2$
$y = -x^2 + 2$

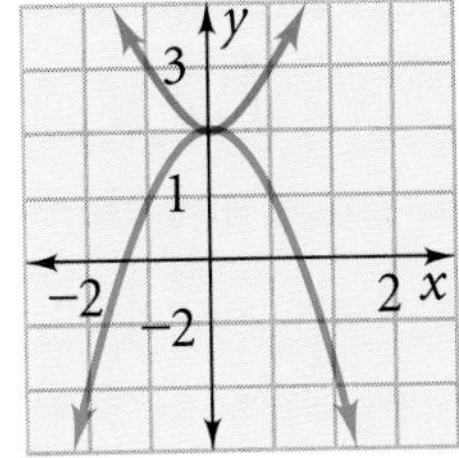

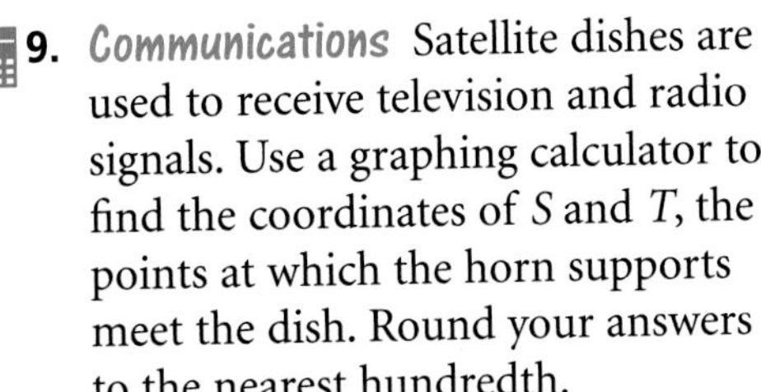

9. *Communications* Satellite dishes are used to receive television and radio signals. Use a graphing calculator to find the coordinates of *S* and *T*, the points at which the horn supports meet the dish. Round your answers to the nearest hundredth.

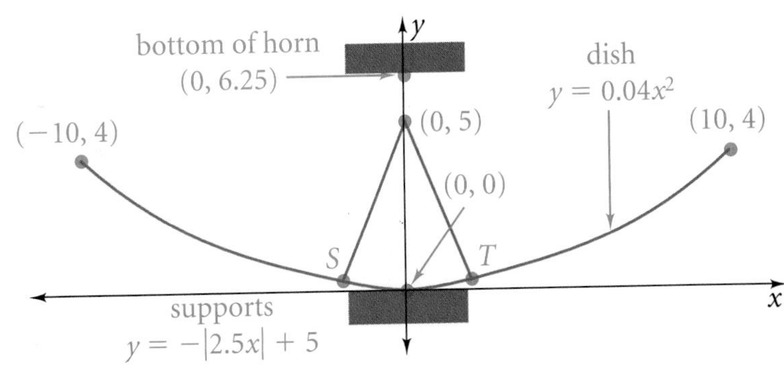

Match each system of equations with its graph. Write the solution(s) of the system.

10. $y = |x + 2|$
$y = |x - 2|$

11. $y = -2$
$y = x^2 - 3$

12. $y = 2.5x + 5$
$y = -|x - 2|$

13. $y = x^2 + 2$
$y = -\frac{1}{2}x^2$

A. 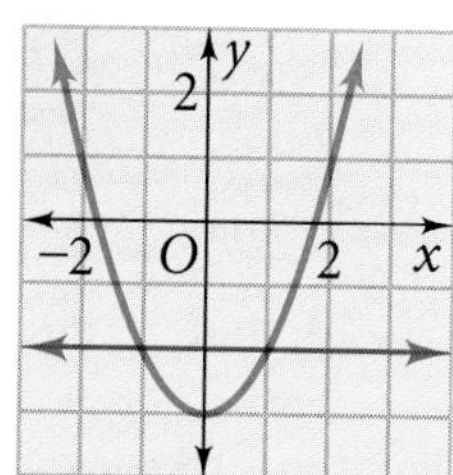

B. 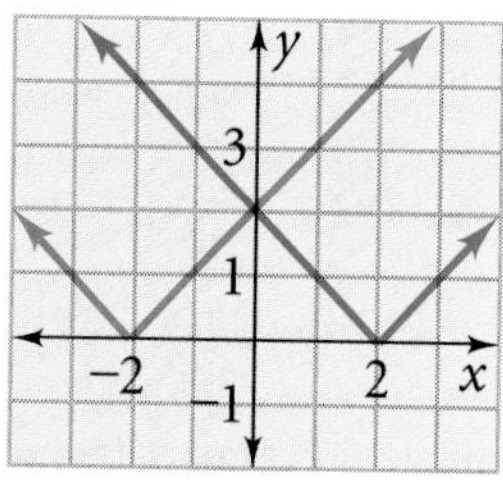

C. 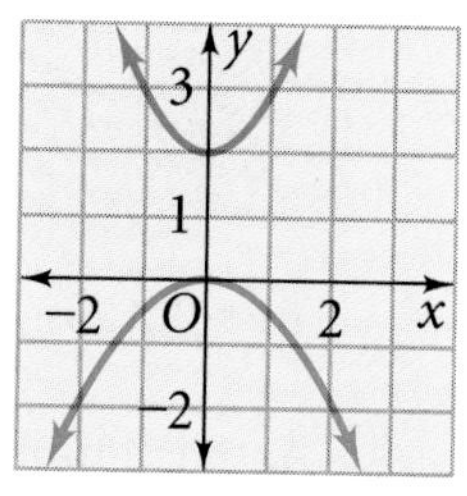

D. 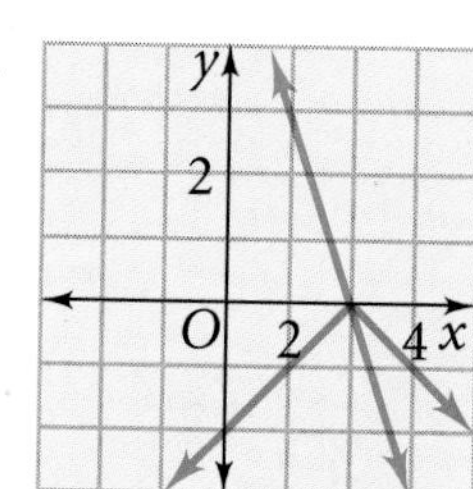

14. *Native American Art* This design was created by the Crow. The Crow are a people of the northern Great Plains of the United States. Patterns in the design can be described with a system of nonlinear equations. Find the coordinates of the points A and B.

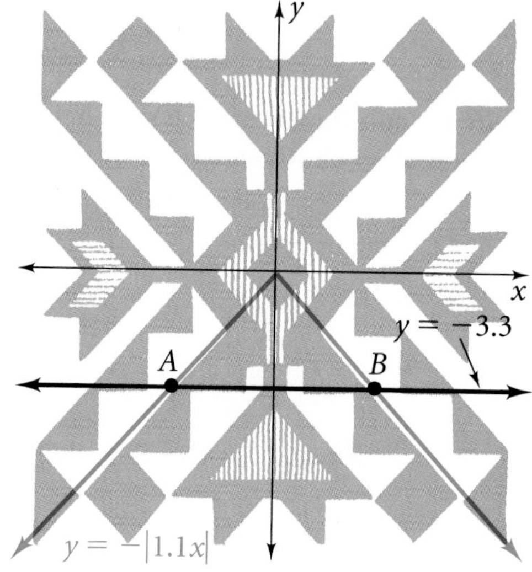

15. *Standardized Test Prep* How many solutions does this system of equations have?

$$y = \frac{1}{2}x^2$$
$$y = -|x + 3|$$

A. one **B.** two **C.** three
D. none **E.** infinitely many

Open-ended **Sketch the graph of a system of two equations with the given characteristics.**

16. two quadratic equations, no solution

17. two absolute-value equations, two solutions

18. linear equation and absolute-value equation, one solution

19. linear equation and quadratic equation, no solution

Choose **Use paper and pencil or a graphing calculator to solve each system of equations.**

20. $y = 3x - 4$
$y = -|x|$

21. $y = |x + 3|$
$y = \frac{1}{2}x$

22. $y = \frac{3}{2}x + 1$
$y = |x| + 1$

23. $y = x^2 - 1$
$y = -x + 1$

24. $y = |x|$
$y = -|x|$

25. $y = -x^2 + 2$
$y = x + 3$

26. $y = 2x$
$y = |x| + 3$

27. $y = -2x^2$
$y = |3x| - 5$

28. $y = -3$
$y = |x - 2|$

29. $y = x^2$
$y = x^2 - 2$

30. $y = |2x| - 3$
$y = |x|$

31. $y = \frac{1}{4}x^2$
$y = \frac{1}{2}x + 2$

32. a. **Architecture** The University of Illinois Assembly Hall in Urbana can be described by a system with nonlinear equations. Use a graphing calculator to find the coordinates of points S and E.
    b. Find the length of $\overline{SE}$.

33. **Writing** How can you tell if a system with nonlinear equations has any solutions?

Exercises MIXED REVIEW

34. What is 15% of 96?
35. 34 is what percent of 32?
36. What percent of 40 is 27?
37. 6 is what percent of 92?
38. What percent of 6 is 2?
39. What is 85% of 108,000?

Find each sum or difference.

40. $\begin{bmatrix} -4 & a & 5 \\ 0 & b & 4c \end{bmatrix} + \begin{bmatrix} -12 & -a & 0 \\ d & 3b & -2c \end{bmatrix}$

41. $\begin{bmatrix} 7 & x \\ 0 & -2y \\ 4z & -x \end{bmatrix} - \begin{bmatrix} x & 5 \\ 3x & -y \\ -4z & -x \end{bmatrix}$

42. **Writing** Explain the difference between the solution of an equation and the solution of a system of two equations.

43. a. **Medicine** Write a formula for cell D2 in the spreadsheet.
    b. Find the values in cells D2 and D3.

44. What is the rate of change in the total number of doctors from 1900 to 1995?

	A	B	C	D
1	Year	Number of Doctors	Population	Number of Doctors per Million People
2	1900	119,749	75,994,575	■
3	1995	638,200	263,434,000	■

PORTFOLIO

For your portfolio, choose one or two items from your work for this chapter. Here are some possibilities:
- a journal entry
- corrected work
- a Find Out question

Explain why you include each selection you make.

CHAPTER PROJECT

Finishing the Chapter Project

Questions on pages 274, 284, 293, and 299 should help you complete your project. Your report should include your analysis of the cost for refreshments and each band, depending on how many people buy tickets. Include your recommended ticket price and note any conditions under which this ticket price leads to a loss for the event. Illustrate your reasoning with graphs of linear equations and inequalities.

SOL AZTECA
CATERING FOR SPECIAL OCCASIONS

Client: Northwood High School

CHARGES

One-Time Fee
- set up
- transportation
- equipment
- staff
- clean up

Cost Per Person
- juice, soda, seltzer
- appetizers

Reflect and Revise

Present your analysis of this dance to a small group of classmates. After you have heard their analyses and presented your own, decide if your work is complete, clear, and convincing. If necessary, make changes to improve your presentation.

Follow Up

Are there other expenses you could expect to have in planning and holding this dance? Estimate them and change your recommended ticket price if necessary.

For More Information

Splaver, Bernard R. *Successful Catering*. New York: Van Nostrand Reinhold, 1991.

Watkins, Andrea and Patricia Clarkson. *Dancing Longer, Dancing Stronger: A Dancer's Guide to Improving Technique and Preventing Injury*. Princeton, New Jersey: Princeton Book Company, 1990.

CHAPTER 6

Wrap Up

Key Terms

elimination (p. 280)
infinitely many solutions (p. 271)
linear inequality (p. 290)
linear progamming (p. 300)
no solution (p. 271)
solution of a system of linear inequalities (p. 295)
solution of the inequality (p. 290)
solution of the system (p. 269)
substitution (p. 275)
system of linear equations (p. 269)
system of linear inequalities (p. 295)

How am I doing?

SELF ASSESSMENT

- State three ideas from this chapter that you think are important. Explain your choices.
- Describe the different ways you can solve systems of equations and inequalities.

Solving Systems by Graphing — 6-1

Two or more linear equations form a **system of linear equations.** You can solve a system of linear equations by graphing. Any point where all the lines intersect is the **solution of the system.**

For each graph, write the system of linear equations and its solution.

1. 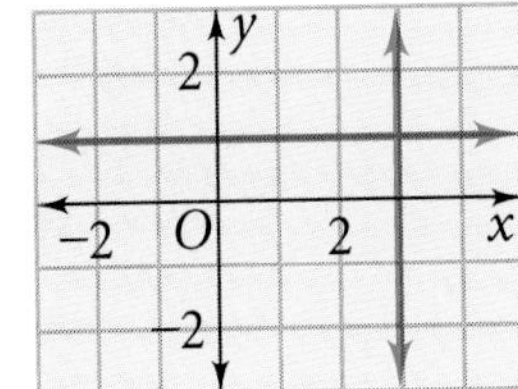

2. 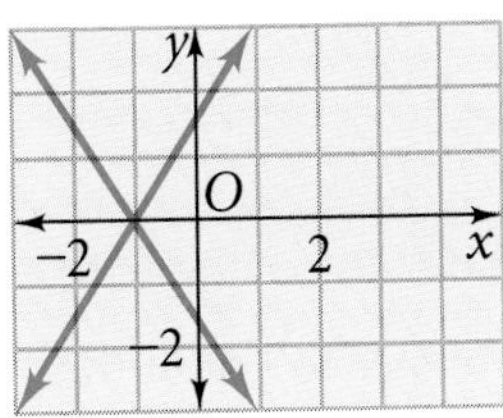

3. 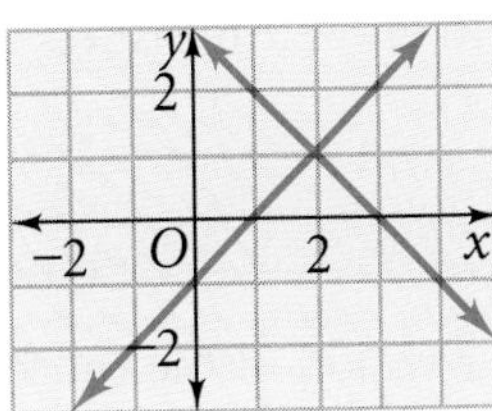

4. 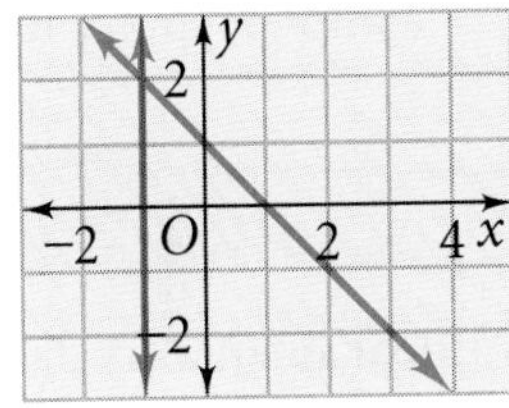

Solve each system by graphing.

5. $y = 3x - 1$
$y = -x + 3$

6. $x - y = -3$
$3x + y = -1$

7. $-x + 2y = -2$
$y = \frac{1}{2}x + 3$

8. $y = -2x + 1$
$y = 2x - 3$

Solving Systems Using Substitution — 6-2

You can also solve a system of linear equations using **substitution.** First, solve for one variable in terms of the other. Then substitute this result in either equation and solve.

Solve each system using substitution.

9. $y = 3x + 11$
$y = -2x + 1$

10. $4x - y = -12$
$-6x + 5y = -3$

11. $y = 5x - 8$
$5y = 2x + 6$

12. $8x = -2y - 10$
$2x = 4y$

13. *Writing* Explain how you determine if a system has no solution or infinitely many solutions when you solve a system using substitution.

Solving Systems Using Elimination 6-3

You can solve a system of linear equations using **elimination.** You add or subtract the equations to eliminate one variable. You can multiply one or both of the equations by a nonzero number before adding or subtracting.

Solve each system using elimination. Check your solution.

14. $y = -3x + 5$
$y = -4x - 1$

15. $2x - 3y = 5$
$x + 2y = -1$

16. $x + y = 10$
$x - y = 2$

17. $-x + 4y = 12$
$2x - 3y = 6$

Writing Systems 6-4

You can use systems of linear equations to solve word problems. First, define variables. Then model the situation with a system of linear equations.

Solve using any method. Check your solution.

18. A furniture finish consists of turpentine and linseed oil. It contains twice as much turpentine as linseed oil. If you need 16 fl oz of furniture finish, how much turpentine do you need?

19. **Geometry** The difference between the measures of two complementary angles is 36°. Find both angle measures. (*Hint:* Two angles are complementary if the sum of their measures is 90°.)

Linear Inequalities 6-5

A **linear inequality** describes a region of the coordinate plane. To graph the **solution of the inequality,** first graph the boundary line. Then test a point to shade the region that makes the inequality true.

Graph each linear inequality.

20. $y < -3x + 8$

21. $y \geq 2x - 1$

22. $y \leq 0.5x + 6$

23. $y > -\frac{1}{4}x - 2$

Systems of Linear Inequalities 6-6

Two or more linear inequalities form a **system of linear inequalities.** To find the **solution of a system of linear inequalities,** graph each linear inequality. The solution region is where all the inequalities are true.

Solve each system of linear inequalities by graphing.

24. $y \geq -4x + 1$
$y \leq 3x - 5$

25. $x - y < 10$
$x + y \leq 8$

26. $y \leq x - 3$
$y > x - 7$

27. $y < 5x$
$y \geq 0$

28. **Open-ended** Write a system of linear inequalities for which the solution region is a pentagon.

Concepts of Linear Programming 6-7

You can use **linear programming** to minimize or maximize quantities. The variables used in the equation for the quantity have restrictions. The maximum and minimum values of the equation occur at the vertices of the graph of the restrictions.

Evaluate the equation to find minimum and maximum values.

29. $x + y \leq 7$
$x + 2y \leq 8$
$x \geq 0$
$y \geq 0$
$P = 3x + y$

30. $x + 2y \leq 5$
$x \geq 0$
$y \geq 1$
$P = 2x + 3y$

31. $x + y \leq 6$
$2x + y \leq 10$
$x \geq 0$
$y \geq 0$
$P = 4x + y$

32. $x \geq 1$
$x \leq 4$
$y \geq 3$
$y \leq 6$
$P = x + 2y$

33. *Standardized Test Prep* Which point minimizes the equation $C = 5x + 2y$?

A. (4, 1) **B.** (5, 0) **C.** (2, 6) **D.** (3, 2) **E.** (1, 5)

Systems with Nonlinear Equations 6-8

You can solve systems that have linear, absolute value, and quadratic equations. Graph the equations on the same coordinate plane. Any point where the graphs intersect is a solution.

Solve each system of equations.

34. $y = x^2 - 4$
$y = -x + 2$

35. $y = |2x| - 3$
$y = x - 1$

36. $y = -x + 3$
$y = |2x - 3|$

37. $y = 2x + 6$
$y = x^2 + 3$

38. *Critical Thinking* How many solutions can a system with an absolute-value equation and a quadratic equation have? Explain.

Getting Ready for... CHAPTER 7

Find the square of each number.

39. 3 **40.** -7 **41.** 4.5 **42.** $\frac{1}{2}$ **43.** 11 **44.** -8.2

Make a table of values to graph each function.

45. $y = x^2 - 4x + 3$ **46.** $y = x^2 + x - 2$ **47.** $y = -x^2 + 4x + 5$

Evaluate the expression $b^2 - 4ac$ for the given values.

48. $a = 2, b = -5, c = 3$ **49.** $a = -7, b = 9, c = 1$ **50.** $a = 4.5, b = 8, c = 0$

51. $a = 1, b = 3, c = -2$ **52.** $a = 0.5, b = 4, c = 2.5$ **53.** $a = -8, b = -3.2, c = 5$

CHAPTER 6

Assessment

Solve each system of linear equations by graphing.

1. $y = 3x - 7$
   $y = -x + 1$

2. $4x + 3y = 12$
   $2x - 5y = -20$

Critical Thinking **Suppose you try to solve a system of linear equations using substitution and get this result. How many solutions does each system have?**

3. $x = 8$

4. $5 = y$

5. $-7 = 4$

6. $x = -1$

7. $2 = y$

8. $9 = 9$

Solve each system using substitution.

9. $y = 4x - 7$
   $y = 2x + 9$

10. $y = -2x - 1$
    $y = 3x - 16$

Solve each system using elimination.

11. $4x + y = 8$
    $-3x - y = 0$

12. $2x + 5y = 20$
    $3x - 10y = 37$

13. $x + y = 10$
    $-x - 2y = -14$

14. $3x + 2y = -19$
    $x - 12y = 19$

Write a system of equations to model each situation. Then use your system to solve.

15. *Cable Service* Your local cable television company offers two plans: basic service with one movie channel for \$35 per month, or basic service with two movie channels for \$45 per month. What is the charge for the basic service and the charge for each movie channel?

16. *Education* A writing workshop enrolls novelists and poets in a ratio of 5 to 3. There are 24 people at the workshop. How many novelists are there? How many poets?

17. You have 15 coins in your pocket that are either quarters or nickels. They total \$2.75. How many of each coin do you have?

18. *Writing* Compare solving a linear equation with solving a linear inequality. What are the similarities? What are the differences?

19. *Standardized Test Prep* Which point is *not* a solution of $y < 3x - 1$?
    A. $(2, -4)$ **B.** $(5, 7)$ **C.** $(0, -1)$
    D. $(-3, -13)$ **E.** $(4, -8)$

Solve each system by graphing.

20. $y > 4x - 1$
    $y \leq -x + 4$

21. $y \geq 3x + 5$
    $y > x - 2$

22. $y = x^2 + x + 1$
    $y = -3x + 6$

23. $y = 4x - 5$
    $y = |3x + 1|$

Open-ended **Write a system of equations with the given characteristics.**

24. two linear equations with no solution

25. a linear equation and a quadratic equation with two solutions

26. three linear inequalities with a triangular solution region

27. *Fund Raising* You are making bread to sell at a holiday fair. A loaf of oatmeal bread takes 2 cups of flour and 2 eggs. A loaf of banana bread takes 3 cups of flour and 1 egg. You have 12 cups of flour and 8 eggs.

    x = number of loaves of oatmeal bread
    y = number of loaves of banana bread
    Restrictions: $2x + 3y \leq 12$
    $2x + y \leq 8$
    $x \geq 0, y \geq 0$

    a. Explain each restriction.
    b. You will make \$1 profit for each loaf of oatmeal bread and \$2 profit for each loaf of banana bread. Write the equation.
    c. Use linear programming to find how many loaves of each type you should make to maximize profits.

CHAPTER 6

Cumulative Review

For Exercises 1–11, choose the correct letter.

1 Which of the following points are solutions of $4y - 3x \leq 8$?

I. $(0, 2)$ **II.** $(-3, \frac{1}{4})$

III. $(5, -17.6)$ **IV.** $(-4, \frac{2}{5})$

A. I only **B.** IV only **C.** I and II
D. II and IV **E.** I and III

2. Suppose you earn \$74.25 for working 9 h. How much will you earn for working 15 h?

A. \$120 **B.** \$124.50 **C.** \$127.25
D. \$123.75 **E.** none of the above

3. Which is *not* a solution of $5x - 4 < 12$?

A. -2 **B.** 3 **C.** 0 **D.** 1.8 **E.** 4

4. Which statement is true for every solution of the following system?

$$2y > x + 4$$
$$3y + 3x > 13$$

A. $x \leq -3$ **B.** $y > 1$ **C.** $x > 4$
D. $y < 5$ **E.** none of the above

5. Which of the following equations represents a vertical line through $(-7, -4)$?

A. $x = -7$ **B.** $x = 4$ **C.** $y = 7$
D. $y = -4$ **E.** none of the above

6. The function $f(x) = |x - 5|$ belongs to which family of functions?

A. linear **B.** quadratic
C. direct variation **D.** absolute value
E. none of the above

7. What is true of the graphs of the two lines $3y - 8 = -5x$ and $3x = 2y - 18$?

A. no intersection **B.** intersect at $(2, -6)$
C. intersect at $(-2, 6)$ **D.** are identical
E. none of the above

8. A scatter plot shows a positive correlation. Which of the following could be an equation of the line of best fit?

A. $y = -5x + 1$ **B.** $2x + 3y = 6$
C. $x = 16$ **D.** $y = 2x - 1$
E. none of the above

9. Which of the following is the solution of $6(4x - 3) = -54$?

A. -2.5 **B.** -3 **C.** 2.5
D. 3 **E.** none of the above

Compare the boxed quantity in Column A with the boxed quantity in Column B. Choose the best answer.

A. The quantity in Column A is greater.
B. The quantity in Column B is greater.
C. The two quantities are equal.
D. The relationship cannot be determined on the basis of the information supplied.

	Column A	Column B
10.	the y-intercept of the graph of $6y - 5x = 2$	the y-intercept of the graph of $x + 9y = 2$
11.	the slope of the line through $(2, -5)$ and $(-3, 1)$	the slope of the graph of $15y + 12x = 5$

Find each answer.

12. Write an equation of the line through $(2, -1)$ and $(3, 4)$.

13. Write an equation of the line through $(2, -3)$ that is perpendicular to the graph of $y = \frac{2}{5}x - \frac{7}{8}$.

14. Graph $-3 \leq 2x + 1 < 7$.

15. **Transportation** In 1996, the City Council of New York City voted to increase the number of taxis in the city from 11,787 to 12,187. What was the percent of increase?

16. Plumber A charges \$40 for a house call plus \$30 per hour for labor. Plumber B charges \$20 for a house call plus \$35 per hour for labor. How long must a job take before plumber A is the less expensive choice for the homeowner?

CHAPTER

7 Quadratic Equations and Functions

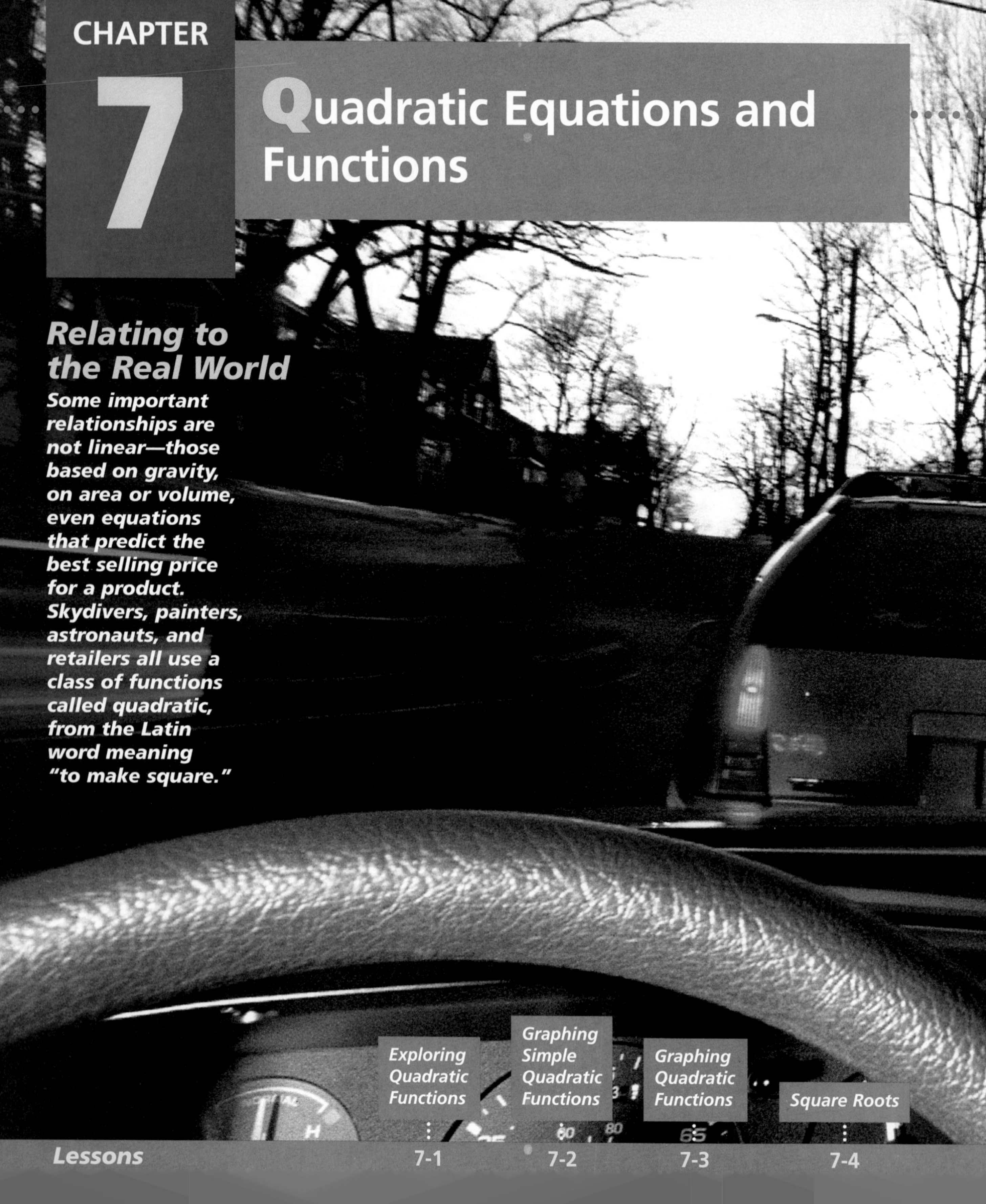

Relating to the Real World

Some important relationships are not linear—those based on gravity, on area or volume, even equations that predict the best selling price for a product. Skydivers, painters, astronauts, and retailers all use a class of functions called quadratic, from the Latin word meaning "to make square."

CHAPTER PROJECT

Full STOP Ahead

What is a safe stopping distance for cars traveling on the highway? How do accident investigators determine whether cars involved in an accident were traveling at safe speeds? There are many variables that affect how quickly a car can stop. These include the car's speed, the driver's reaction time, the type of road, and the weather conditions.

As you work through the chapter, you will use formulas to estimate safe speeds under various conditions. You will make graphs to illustrate the relationships between speed, reaction time, and stopping distance. Then, with your classmates, you will plan a skit to present what you have learned about safe highway driving.

To help you complete the project:

- **p. 331** *Find Out by Graphing*
- **p. 336** *Find Out by Calculating*
- **p. 347** *Find Out by Reasoning*
- **p. 353** *Find Out by Communicating*
- **p. 354** *Finishing the Project*

Solving Quadratic Equations 7-5

Using the Quadratic Formula 7-6

Using the Discriminant 7-7

7-1 Exploring Quadratic Functions

What You'll Learn

- Graphing quadratic functions of the form $y = ax^2$

...And Why

To understand how changing a affects the graph of a quadratic function

What You'll Need

- graphing calculator

WORK TOGETHER

Work with a partner. Complete a table of values and plot points, or use a graphing calculator set at the standard scale.

x	y
−2	■
−1	■
0	■
1	■
2	■

1. a. Graph the equations $y = x^2$ and $y = 3x^2$.
   b. How are the graphs in part (a) alike? different?
2. a. Graph the equations $y = -x^2$ and $y = -3x^2$.
   b. How are the graphs in part (a) different from the graphs in Question 1? How are they like the graphs in Question 1?

THINK AND DISCUSS

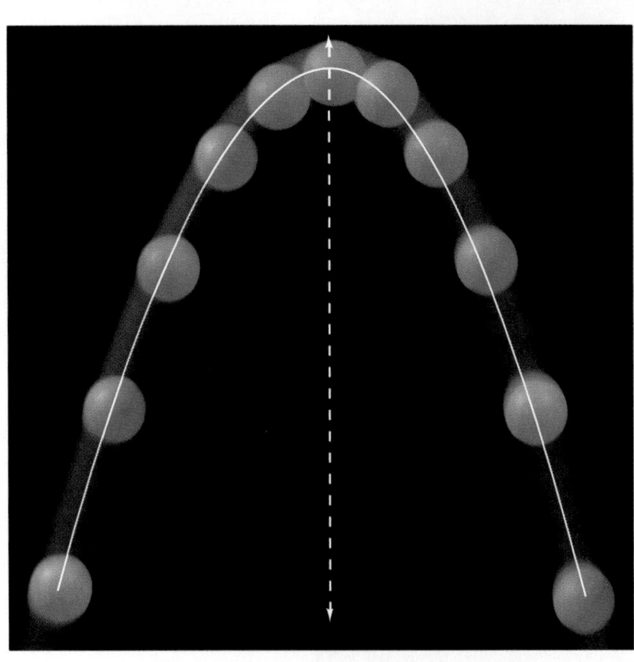

Quadratic Functions

The graphs you analyzed in the Work Together are all examples of **parabolas.** If you draw a parabola on a piece of paper, you can fold the paper down the middle of the parabola and the two sides will match exactly. The line down the middle of the parabola is the **axis of symmetry.**

3. **Try This** Trace each parabola on a sheet of paper and draw its axis of symmetry.

a.

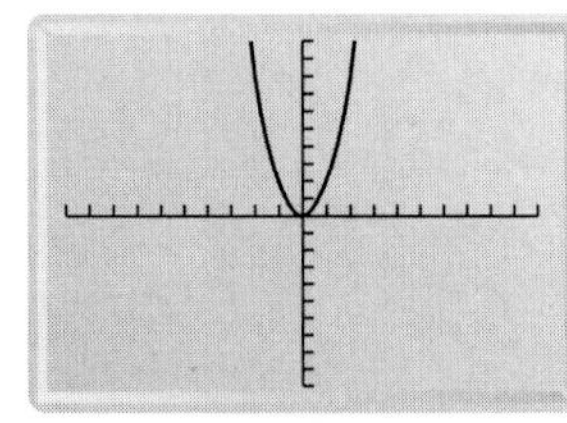

b.

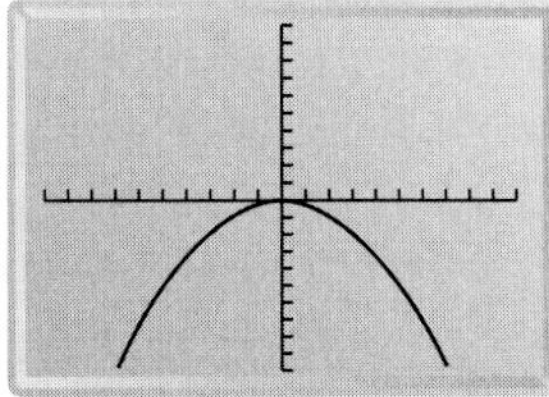

Each parabola that you have seen is the graph of a *quadratic function.*

Quadratic Function

For $a \neq 0$, the function $y = ax^2 + bx + c$ is a **quadratic function.**

Examples: $y = 2x^2$, $y = x^2 + 2$, $y = -x^2 - x - 3$

When a quadratic function is written in the form $y = ax^2 + bx + c$, it is in **standard form.**

4. Name the values of a, b, and c for each quadratic function.
a. $y = 3x^2 - 2x + 5$ **b.** $y = 3x^2$ **c.** $y = -0.5x^2 + 2x$

5. Write each quadratic function in standard form.
a. $y = 7x + 9x^2 - 4$ **b.** $y = 3 - x^2$

The Role of "a"

When you graph a quadratic function, if the value of a is positive, the parabola opens upward. If the value of a is negative, the parabola opens downward.

Example 1

Make a table of values and graph the quadratic functions $y = 2x^2$ and $y = -2x^2$.

x	$y=2x^2$	$y=-2x^2$
-3	18	-18
-2	8	-8
-1	2	-2
0	0	0
1	2	-2
2	8	-8
3	18	-18

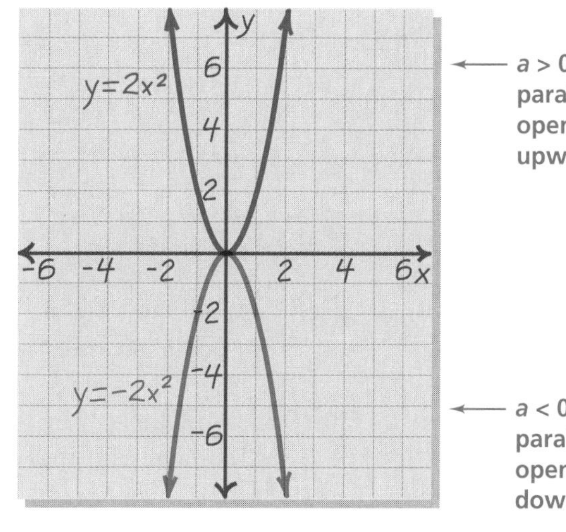

$a > 0$; this parabola opens upward.

$a < 0$; this parabola opens downward.

6. What is the axis of symmetry for the graphs in Example 1?

7. What would happen to the graph of $y = 2x^2$ if you could fold the graph over the x-axis? Explain.

The highest or lowest point on a parabola is called the **vertex** of the parabola.

When a parabola opens upward, the y-coordinate of the vertex is the **minimum value** of the function.

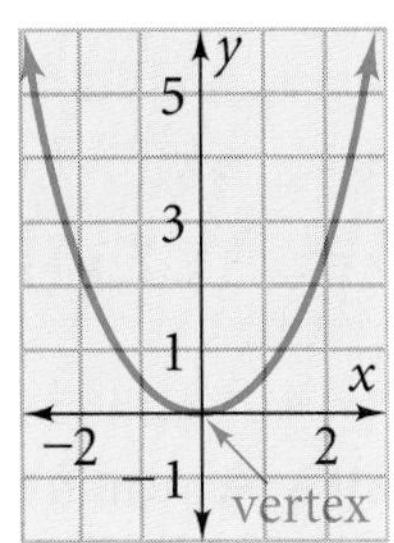

When a parabola opens downward, the y-coordinate of the vertex is the **maximum value** of the function.

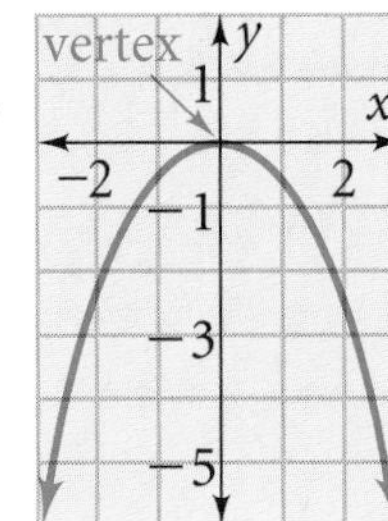

8. Answer these questions for $y = -3x^2$ and $y = 4x^2$.
   a. What is the value of a?
   b. In which direction does each graph open?
   c. Is the y-coordinate of the vertex a minimum or a maximum value of the function?

9. **Summarize** what you know so far about how the value of a affects the parabola.

The value of a also affects the width of a parabola.

Example 2

Graph $-4x^2$, $y = \frac{1}{4}x^2$, and $y = x^2$. Compare the widths of the graphs.

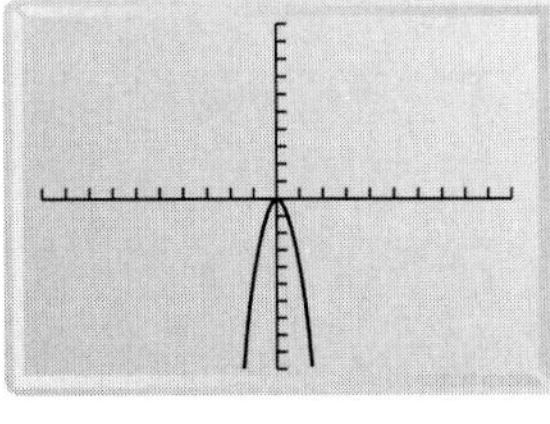

$y = -4x^2$

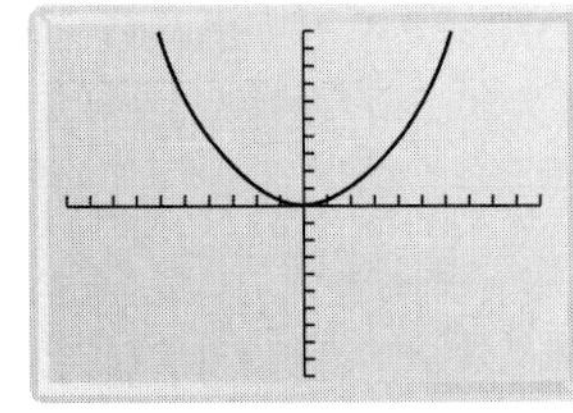

$y = \frac{1}{4}x^2$

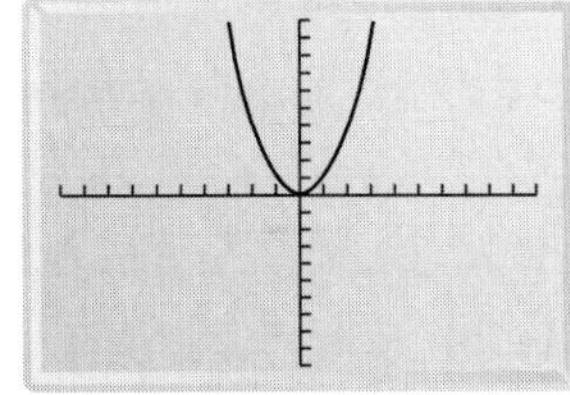

$y = x^2$

Of the three graphs, $y = \frac{1}{4}x^2$ is the widest, $y = x^2$ is narrower, and $y = -4x^2$ is the narrowest.

10. **Critical Thinking** What does the absolute value of a tell you about the width of a parabola? Use the graphs in Example 2 to explain your answer.

11. **Try This** Order each group of quadratic functions from widest to narrowest graph.
   a. $y = 2x^2, y = 3x^2, y = -5x^2$
   b. $y = \frac{3}{2}x^2, y = \frac{2}{3}x^2, y = \frac{1}{2}x^2$

Exercises ON YOUR OWN

Find the values of *a*, *b*, and *c* for each quadratic function.

1. $y = x^2 + 2x + 4$
2. $y = 2x^2$
3. $y = -x^2 - 3x - 9$
4. $y = -2x^2 + 5$

Tell whether each parabola opens *upward* or *downward* and whether the *y*-coordinate of the vertex is a *maximum* or a *minimum*.

5. $y = x^2$
6. $y = 9x^2$
7. $y = -\frac{2}{5}x^2$
8. $y = -6x^2$

Choose **Graph each quadratic function. Use either a table of values or a graphing calculator.**

9. $y = \frac{1}{2}x^2$
10. $y = 1.5x^2$
11. $y = -4x^2$
12. $y = -\frac{1}{3}x^2$
13. $y = 4x^2$
14. $y = \frac{1}{3}x^2$
15. $y = -1.5x^2$
16. $y = -\frac{1}{2}x^2$

Order each group of quadratic functions from widest to narrowest graph.

17. $y = 3x^2,\ y = x^2,\ y = 7x^2$
18. $y = 4x^2,\ y = \frac{1}{3}x^2,\ y = x^2$
19. $y = -2x^2,\ y = -\frac{2}{3}x^2,\ y = -4x^2$
20. $y = -\frac{1}{2}x^2,\ y = 5x^2,\ y = -\frac{1}{4}x^2$

Give the letter or letters of the graph(s) that make each statement true.

21. $a > 0$
22. $a < 0$
23. $|a|$ has the greatest value.
24. $|a|$ has the least value.

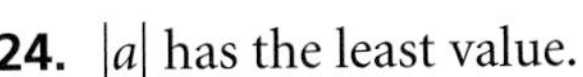

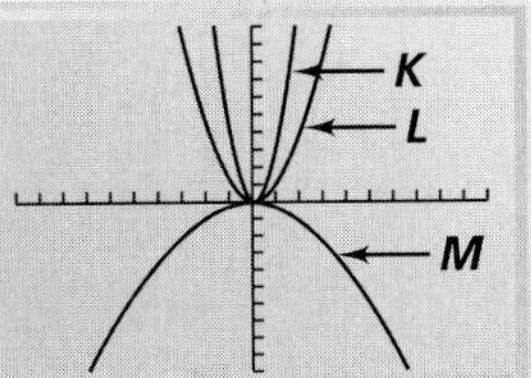

Trace each parabola on a sheet of paper and draw its axis of symmetry.

25.

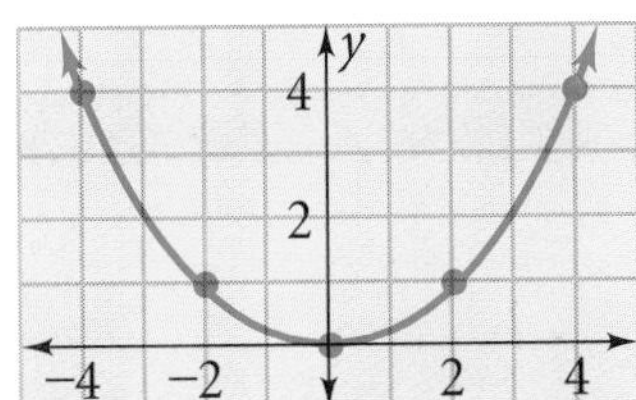

26.

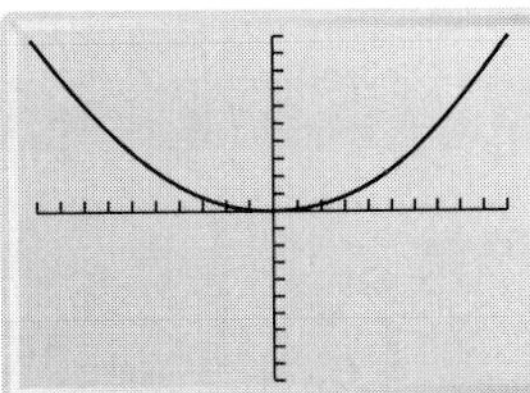

27.

28.

Writing **Without graphing, describe how each graph differs from the graph of $y = x^2$.**

29. $y = 2x^2$ **30.** $y = -x^2$ **31.** $y = 1.5x^2$ **32.** $y = \frac{1}{2}x^2$

33. **Open-ended** Give an example of a quadratic function for each description.
   a. Its graph opens upward.
   b. Its graph has the same shape as the graph in part (a), but the graph opens downward.
   c. Its graph is wider than the graph in part (b).

Match each function with its graph.

A. $y = x^2$ **B.** $y = -x^2$ **C.** $y = 3.5x^2$ **D.** $y = -3.5x^2$ **E.** $y = \frac{1}{4}x^2$ **F.** $y = -\frac{1}{4}x^2$

34. 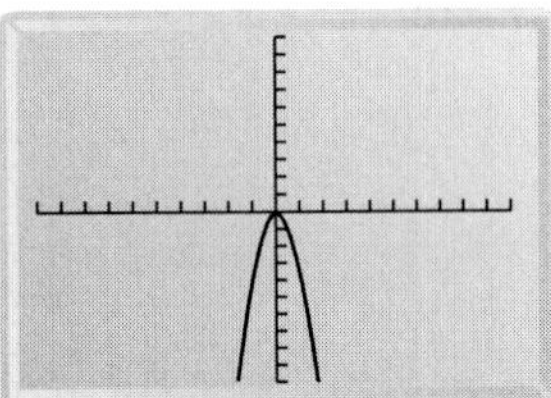

35. 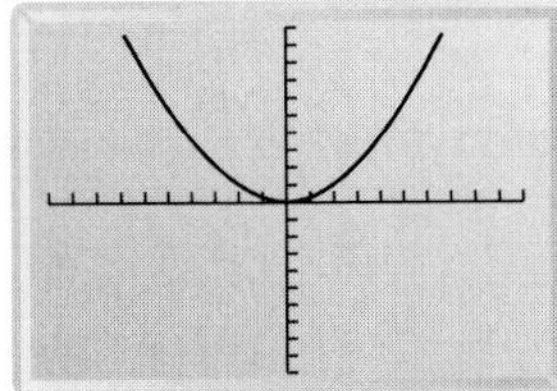

36. 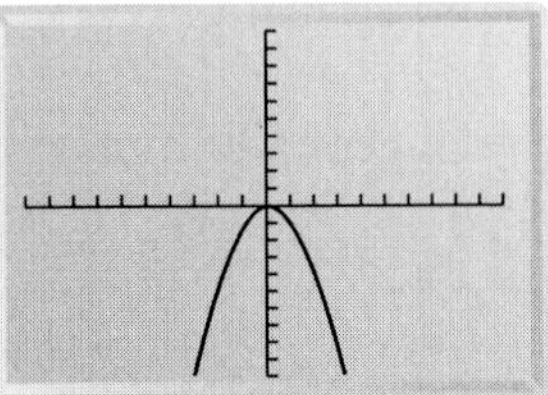

37. 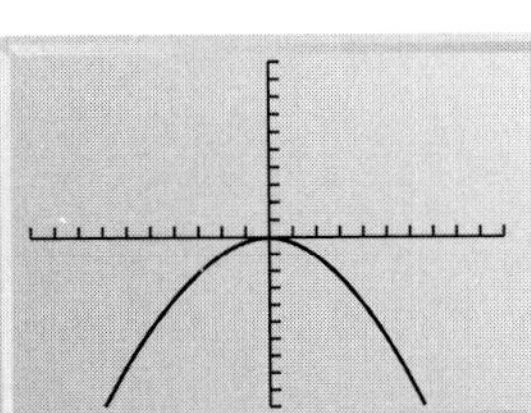

38. 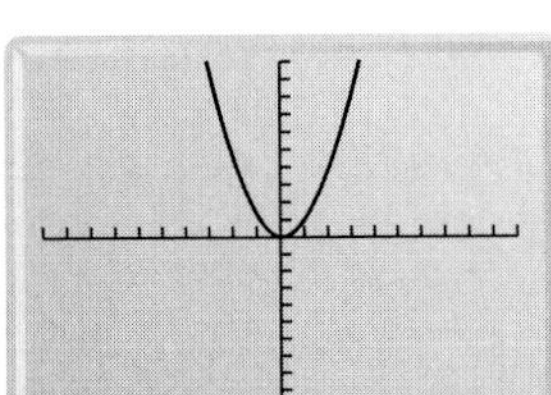

39. 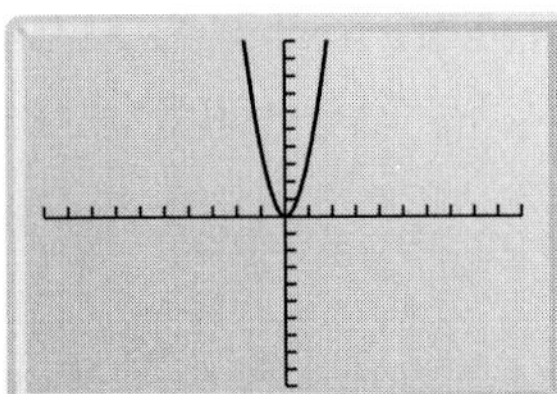

Exercises MIXED REVIEW

Find each percent of change.

40. 12 lb to 14 lb **41.** 5 ft to 7 ft **42.** \$4.50 to \$2.25

43. A Slinky® toy begins as 80 ft of wire. In 50 years of production, 3,030,000 mi of wire weighing 50,000 tons have been used.
   a. How many Slinkies have been made?
   b. How much does 1 mi of wire weigh?
   c. The 3,030,000 mi of wire could go around the equator 126 times. What is the length of the equator? What is the diameter of Earth?

FOR YOUR JOURNAL

Describe a quadratic function and its graph. Explain how the value of "a" affects the graph. Give examples of quadratic functions to support your statements.

Getting Ready for Lesson 7-2

Graph each linear equation.

44. $y = 2x$ **45.** $y = 2x - 3$ **46.** $y = 2x + 1$

Connections Nature . . . and more

7-2 Graphing Simple Quadratic Functions

What You'll Learn

- Graphing quadratic functions of the form $y = ax^2 + c$
- Graphing quadratic functions that represent real-life situations

...And Why

To understand how changing c affects the graph of a quadratic function

What You'll Need

- graphing calculator

WORK TOGETHER

Work with a partner. Use a table of values or a graphing calculator set at the standard scale.

1. **a.** Graph the quadratic functions $y = x^2$, $y = x^2 - 5$, and $y = x^2 + 1$.
   b. How are the graphs in part (a) alike? How are they different?
2. **a.** Graph the quadratic functions $y = -\frac{1}{2}x^2$, $y = -\frac{1}{2}x^2 + 4$, and $y = -\frac{1}{2}x^2 - 2$
   b. How are the graphs in part (a) alike? How are they different?

THINK AND DISCUSS

You have seen that changing the value of a in the function $y = ax^2$ affects whether the parabola opens upward or downward and how wide or narrow the parabola is. Changing the value of c in the function $y = ax^2 + c$ changes the position of the parabola.

$y = -x^2$

Example 1

Graph the quadratic functions $y = -x^2 + 3$ and $y = -x^2 - 1$. Compare them to the graph of $y = -x^2$ at the left.

Make a table of values.

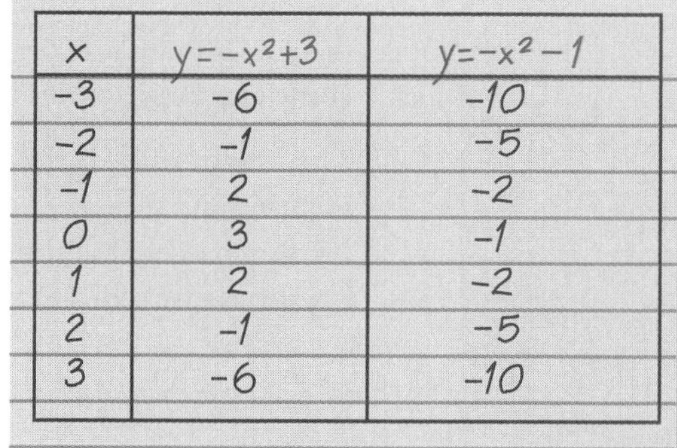

x	$y=-x^2+3$	$y=-x^2-1$
-3	-6	-10
-2	-1	-5
-1	2	-2
0	3	-1
1	2	-2
2	-1	-5
3	-6	-10

Plot the points. Connect the points to form smooth curves.

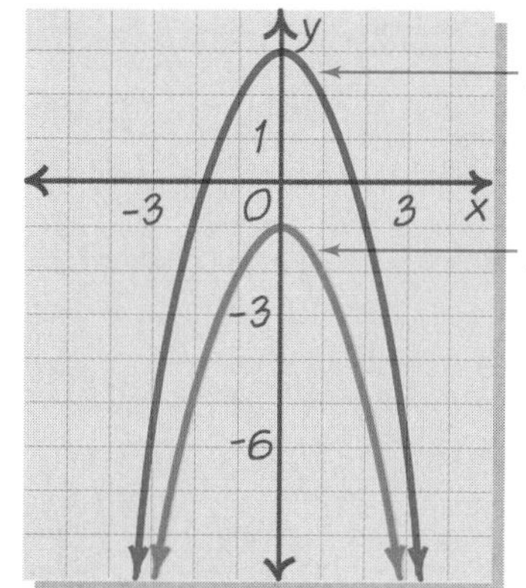

$y = -x^2 + 3$ shifts the parabola $y = -x^2$ *up* 3 units.

$y = -x^2 - 1$ shifts the parabola $y = -x^2$ *down* 1 unit.

3. **Try This** Graph $y = 2x^2$ and $y = 2x^2 - 4$. Compare the graphs.
4. **Summarize** how the graphs of $y = ax^2$ and $y = ax^2 + c$ are different and how they are alike.

5. Since the parabolas in Example 1 open downward, the *y*-coordinate of each vertex is a maximum value. Find the maximum value of each function.

When you graph a quadratic function that represents a real-life situation, you should limit the domain and range of your graph to *x*- and *y*-values that make sense in the situation.

Example 2 Relating to the Real World 

Nature Suppose you see an eagle flying over a canyon. The eagle is 30 ft above the level of the canyon's edge when it drops a stick from its claws. The function $d = -16t^2 + 30$ gives the height of the stick in feet after t seconds. Graph this quadratic function.

Graph t on the horizontal or x-axis. Graph d on the vertical or y-axis.

Choose nonnegative values of t that represent the first few seconds of the stick's fall.

Choose values for d that show the height of the stick as it falls.

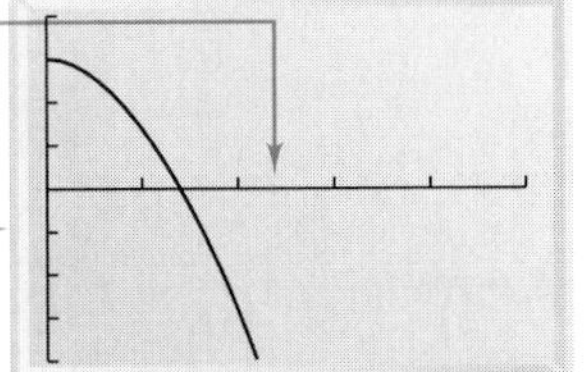

Xmin=0 Ymin=–40
Xmax=5 Ymax=40
Xscl=1 Yscl=10

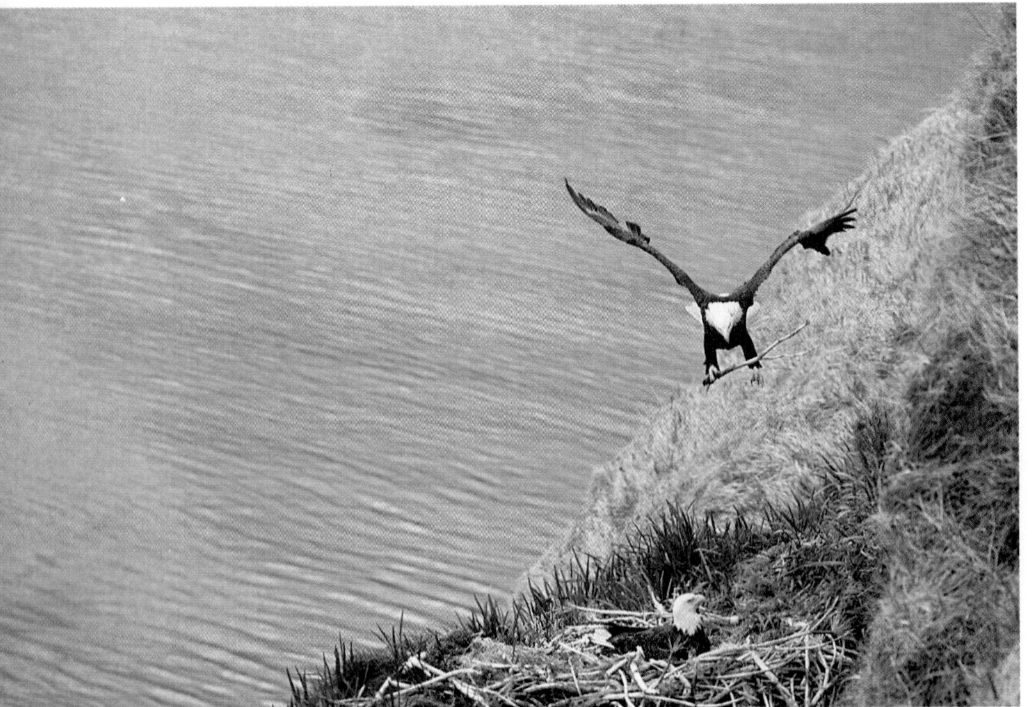

6. In Example 2, why is the domain limited to nonnegative values of t?

7. Explain why the range does not include any values greater than 30.

8. The height of the stick is represented by d. From what level is the height measured?

Exercises ON YOUR OWN

1. **Writing** Describe how the graphs of the functions $y = 5x^2$, $y = 5x^2 + 50$, and $y = 5x^2 - 90$ are alike and how they are different.

Describe whether each quadratic function has a *maximum* or *minimum*.

2. $y = x^2 - 2$
3. $y = -x^2 + 6$
4. $y = 3x^2 + 1$
5. $y = -\frac{1}{2}x^2 - 9$

Choose **Graph each quadratic function. Use either a table of values or a graphing calculator.**

6. $y = x^2 + 2$
7. $y = x^2 - 3$
8. $y = -x^2 + 4$
9. $y = -x^2 - 1$
10. $y = -2x^2 + 2$
11. $y = -2x^2 - 2$
12. $y = -\frac{1}{4}x^2$
13. $y = -\frac{1}{4}x^2 + 3$
14. $y = 4x^2$
15. $y = 4x^2 - 7$
16. $y = -1.5x^2 + 5$
17. $y = -1.5x^2 - 1$

Open-ended **Give an example of a quadratic function for each description.**

18. It opens upward and its vertex is below the origin.
19. It opens downward and its vertex is above the origin.

20. **Geometry** Suppose that a pizza must fit into a box with a base that is 12 in. long and 12 in. wide. You can use the quadratic function $A = \pi r^2$ to find the area of a pizza in terms of its radius.
    a. What values of r make sense in the function?
    b. What values of A make sense in the function?
    c. Graph the function. Use $\pi \approx 3.14$.

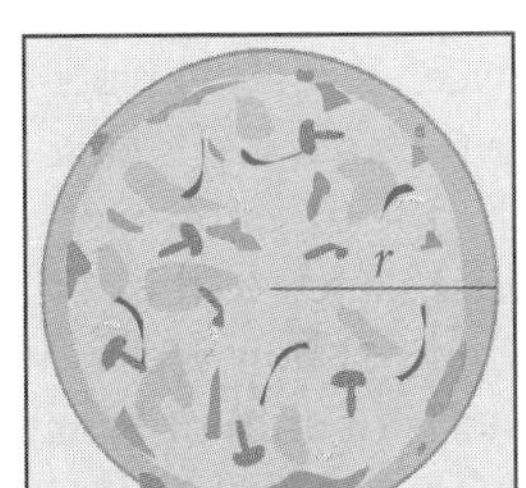

Match each function with its graph.

A. $y = x^2 - 1$
B. $y = x^2 + 4$
C. $y = -x^2 + 2$
D. $y = 3x^2 - 5$
E. $y = -3x^2 + 8$
F. $y = -0.2x^2 + 5$

21.

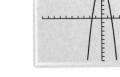

22.
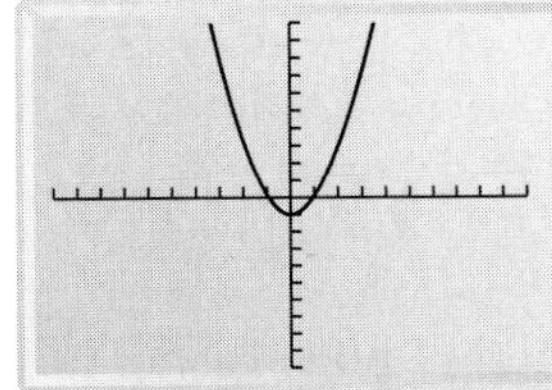

23.
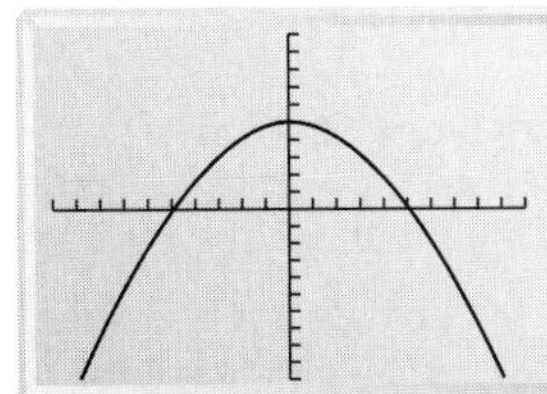

24.
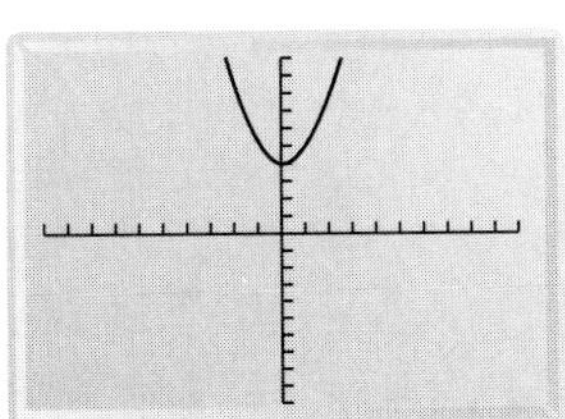

25.
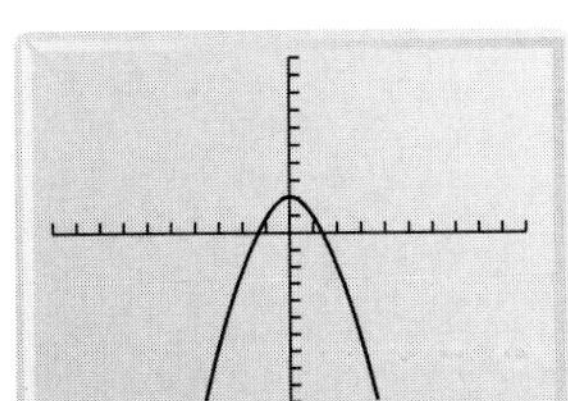

26.
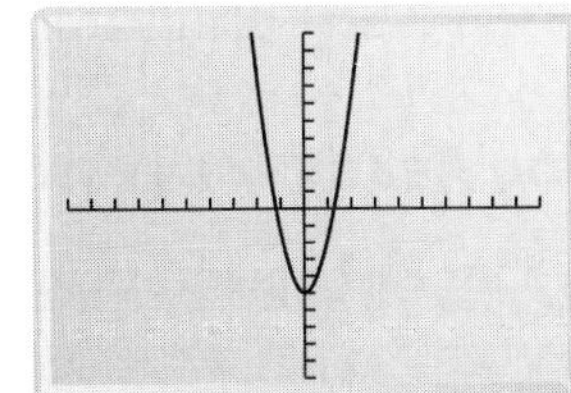

Give the letter of the parabola(s) that make each statement true.

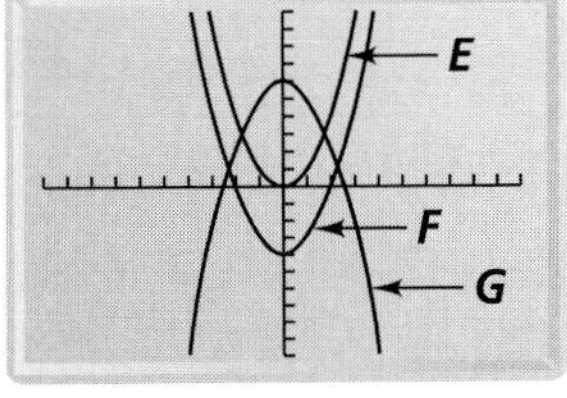

27. $c > 0$

28. $c < 0$

29. $a > 0$

30. $a < 0$

31. The function has a maximum.

32. The function has a minimum.

33. a. **Landscaping** The plan for a rectangular patio has a square garden centered in the patio with sides parallel to the sides of the patio. The patio is 20 ft long by 12 ft wide. If each side of the garden is x ft, the function $y = 240 - x^2$ gives the area of the patio in ft^2. Graph this function.

b. What values make sense for the domain? Explain why.

c. What is the range of the function? Explain why.

34. **Architecture** An architect wants to design an archway with these requirements.

- The archway is 6 ft wide and has vertical sides 7 ft high.
- The top of the archway is modeled by the function $y = -\frac{1}{3}x^2 + 10$.

a. Sketch the architect's design by drawing vertical lines 7 units high at $x = -3$ and $x = 3$ and graphing the portion of the quadratic function that lies between $x = -3$ and $x = 3$.

b. The plan for the archway is changed so that the top is modeled by the function $y = -0.5x^2 + 11.5$. Make a revised sketch of the archway.

c. **Research** Find out how arches were used by the architects of ancient Rome or during the Middle Ages.

Exercises MIXED REVIEW

Write an equation of the line perpendicular to the given line through the given point.

35. $y = 5x - 2; (7, 0)$

36. $y = -2x + 9; (3, 5)$

37. $y = 0.5x; (-8, -2)$

38. $x + y = 6; (3, 1)$

39. $y - 4x = 2; (0, 3)$

40. $y = -6x - 2; (0, 0)$

41. **Real Estate** Fox Island is a 4.5-acre island in Rhode Island. It has an assessed value of $290,400. Use a proportion to find out how much a similar 2-acre island nearby might be worth.

Getting Ready for Lesson 7-3

Find $\frac{-b}{2a}$ for each quadratic function.

42. $y = x^2 + 4x - 2$

43. $y = -8x^2 + x + 13$

44. $y = 6x^2 + x + 7$

7-3 Graphing Quadratic Functions

What You'll Learn

- Graphing quadratic functions of the form $y = ax^2 + bx + c$
- Finding the axis of symmetry and vertex
- Graphing quadratic inequalities

...And Why

To solve problems involving weather and road safety

What You'll Need

- graph paper

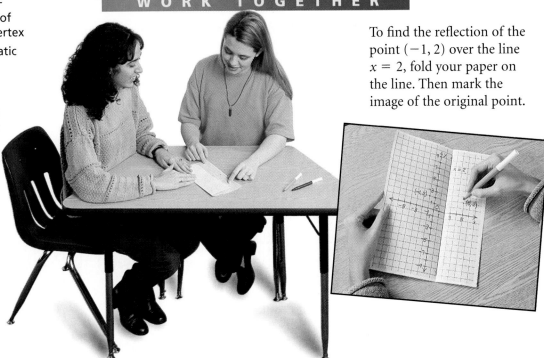

WORK TOGETHER

To find the reflection of the point $(-1, 2)$ over the line $x = 2$, fold your paper on the line. Then mark the image of the original point.

Work with a partner to find the image of each point.

1. Find the reflection over the line $x = -2$.
 a. $(-4, 5)$ **b.** $(-6, 1)$ **c.** $(2, -2)$ **d.** $(-1, 0)$ **e.** $(0, 4)$

THINK AND DISCUSS

Graphing $y = ax^2 + bx + c$

In the quadratic functions you have graphed so far, $b = 0$. When $b \neq 0$, the parabola shifts right or left. The axis of symmetry is no longer the y-axis.

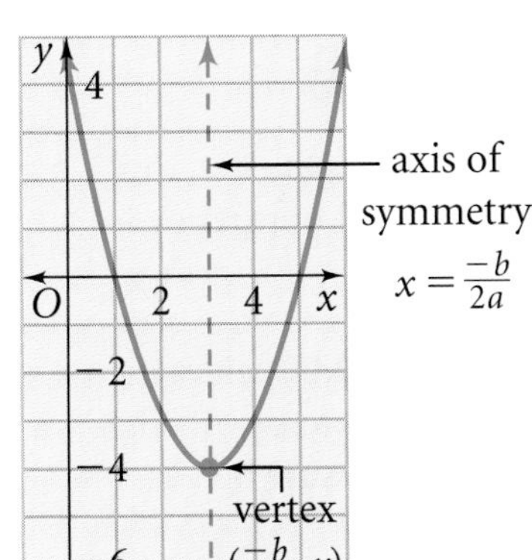

Graph of a Quadratic Function

The graph of $y = ax^2 + bx + c$, where $a \neq 0$, has the line $x = \frac{-b}{2a}$ as its axis of symmetry. The x-coordinate of the vertex is $\frac{-b}{2a}$.

The y-intercept of the graph of a quadratic function is c. This is because substituting $x = 0$ gives you the function value c. You can use the axis of symmetry and the y-intercept to help you graph the function.

Example 1

Graph the quadratic function $f(x) = 5 - 4x - x^2$.

Step 1 Find the y-intercept.

The value of c is 5, so the y-intercept of the graph is 5.

Step 2 Find the equation of the axis of symmetry and the coordinates of the vertex.

$f(x) = -x^2 - 4x + 5$ ← Write the function in standard form.

$x = -\frac{b}{2a} = -\frac{-4}{2(-1)} = -2$ ← Find the equation of the axis of symmetry.

The x-coordinate of the vertex is -2.

$f(x) = -(-2)^2 - 4(-2) + 5$ ← To find the y-coordinate of the vertex, substitute –2 for x.
$f(x) = 9$

The vertex is at $(-2, 9)$.

Step 3 Make a table of values and graph the function.

Pair each point on one side of the axis of symmetry with a point on the other side that will have the same $f(x)$ value.

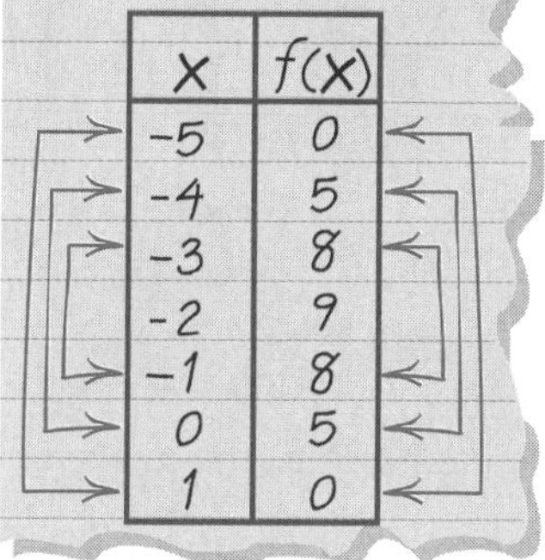

x	f(x)
-5	0
-4	5
-3	8
-2	9
-1	8
0	5
1	0

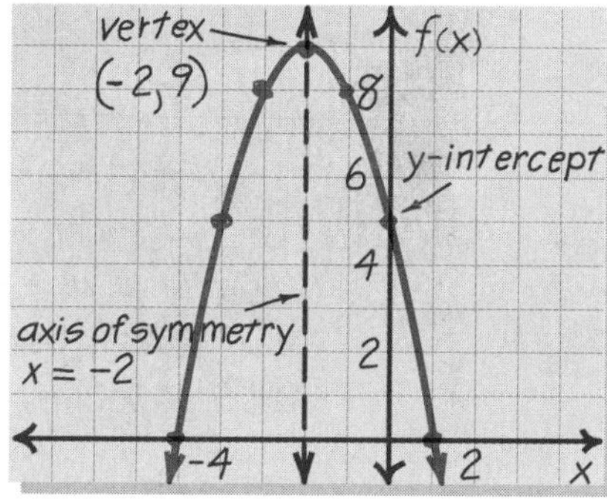

Weather balloons measure conditions in the atmosphere. About 1600 balloons a day are launched in the world.

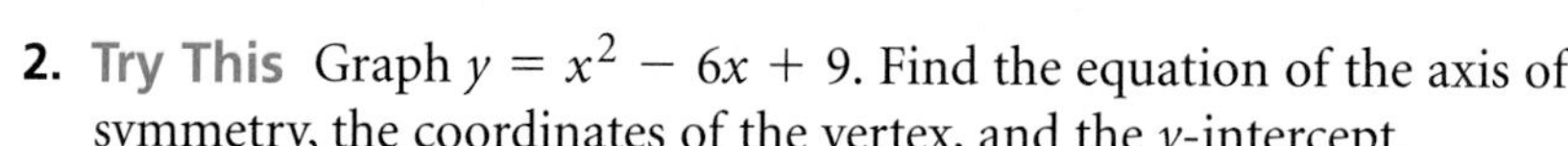

2. **Try This** Graph $y = x^2 - 6x + 9$. Find the equation of the axis of symmetry, the coordinates of the vertex, and the y-intercept.

You can use what you know about quadratic functions to find maximum or minimum values in real-world problems.

Example 2 Relating to the Real World 

Weather Meteorologists use equations to model weather patterns. This function predicts atmospheric pressure over a certain 24-hour period.

$$y = 0.005x^2 - 0.113x + 30.22$$

In the equation, x represents the number of hours after 12:00 midnight and y represents the atmospheric pressure in inches of mercury. At what time will the pressure be lowest? What will the lowest pressure be?

PROBLEM SOLVING

Look Back Use the graph of the function to check your solution.

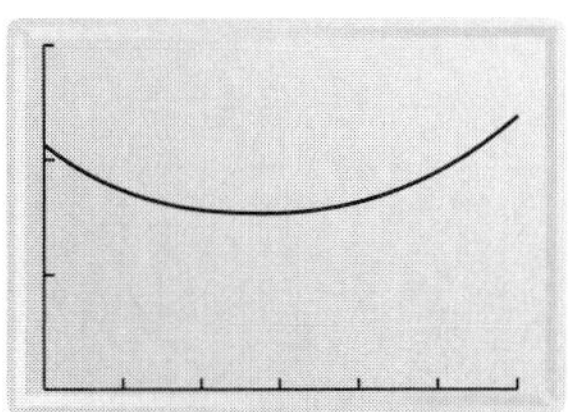

Xmin=0 Ymin=28
Xmax=24 Ymax=31
Xscl=4 Yscl=1

Since the coefficient of x^2 is positive, the curve opens upward and the y-coordinate of the vertex is a minimum.

$-\frac{b}{2a} = -\frac{-0.113}{2(0.005)} = 11.3$ ← Find the x-coordinate of the vertex.

After 11.3 hours (at 11:18 A.M.), the pressure will be at its lowest.

$y = 0.005(11.3)^2 - 0.113(11.3) + 30.22$ ← Substitute 11.3 for x.

$y = 29.58$

The minimum pressure will be 29.58 in. of mercury.

3. Why is it important to check the coefficient of the squared term when solving a real-world maximum or minimum problem?

Quadratic Inequalities

Graphing a quadratic inequality is similar to graphing a linear inequality. The curve is dashed if the inequality involves $<$ or $>$. The curve is solid if the inequality involves $\leq$ or $\geq$.

Example 3 **Relating to the Real World** 

Road Safety An archway over a road is cut out of rock. Its shape is modeled by the quadratic function $y = -0.1x^2 + 12$. Can a camper 6 ft wide and 7 ft high fit under the arch without crossing the median line?

The camper will fit if each point on it satisfies $y < -0.1x^2 + 12$. Graph the inequality $y < -0.1x^2 + 12$.

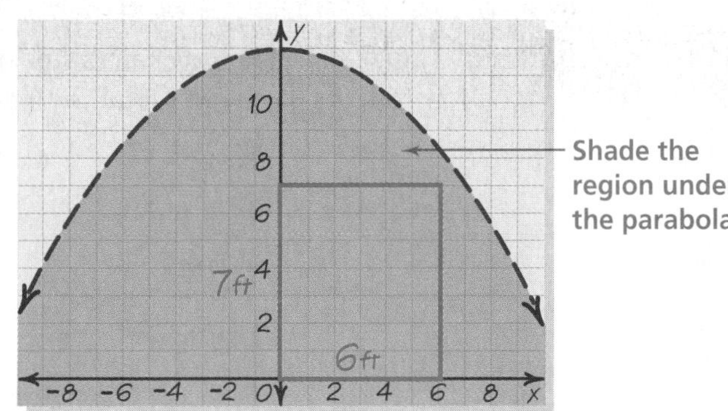

The camper should be able to fit since each point that represents the camper is in the shaded region.

4. Check the solution by showing that the values $x = 6$ and $y = 7$ satisfy the inequality $y < -0.1x^2 + 12$.

5. How does the graph of $y > -0.1x^2 + 12$ differ from the graph above?

6. *Try This* Graph $y \geq x^2 + 2x + 1$.

Exercises ON YOUR OWN

Find the equation of the axis of symmetry and the coordinates of the vertex of the graph of each function.

1. $y = 0.2x^2 + 4$
2. $y = x^2 - 8x - 9$
3. $y = 2x^2 + 4x - 5$
4. $y = 3x^2 - 9x + 5$
5. $f(x) = 4x^2 - 3$
6. $y = 3x^2 - 9$
7. $f(x) = x^2 + 4x + 3$
8. $y = 2x^2 - 6x$
9. $y = 12 + x^2$

Match each graph with its function.

A. $y = x^2 - 6x$
B. $y = x^2 + 6x$
C. $y = -x^2 - 6x$
D. $y = -x^2 + 6x$
E. $y = -x^2 + 6$
F. $y = x^2 - 6$

10. 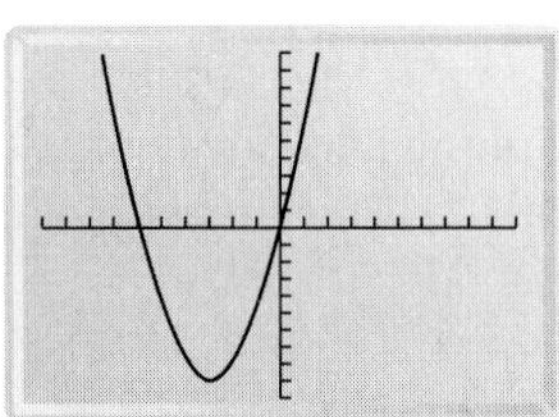

11. 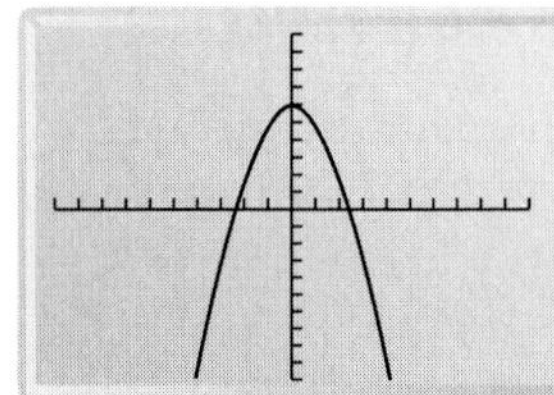

12. 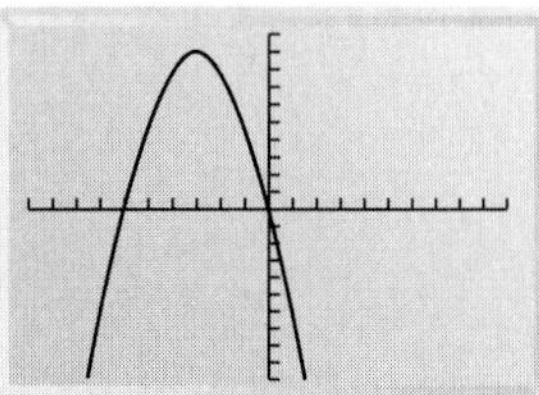

13. 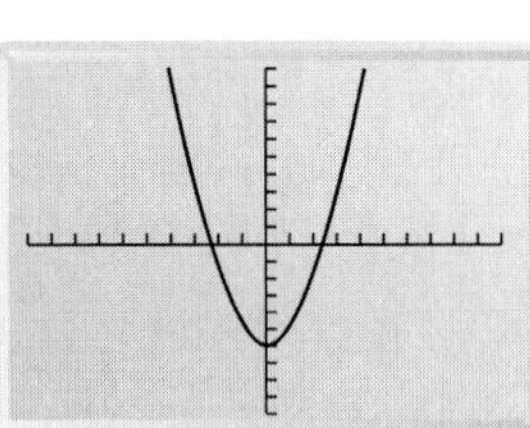

14. 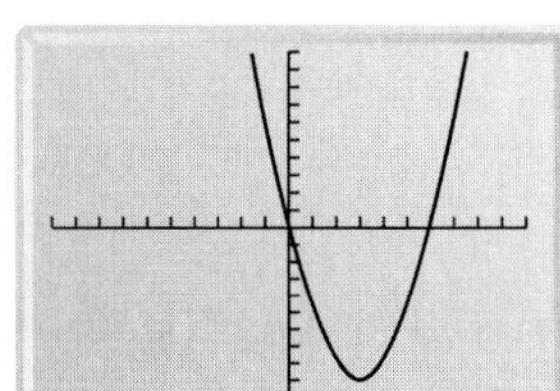

15. 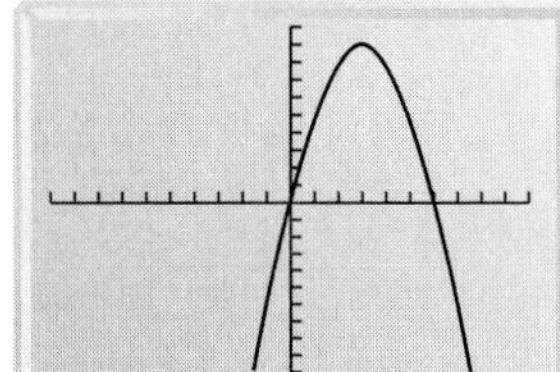

Choose **Graph each function. Use a graphing calculator or a table of values. Label the axis of symmetry, the vertex, and the *y*-intercept.**

16. $f(x) = x^2 - 6x + 8$
17. $y = -x^2 + 4x - 4$
18. $y = x^2 + 1$
19. $y = -x^2 + 4x$
20. $y = -2x^2 + 6$
21. $f(x) = 3x^2 + 6x$
22. $y = x^2 - 4x + 3$
23. $f(x) = -x^2 - 4x - 6$
24. $y = x^2 - 2x + 1$
25. $f(x) = 2x^2 + x - 3$
26. $y = x^2 + 3x + 2$
27. $y = -x^2 + 4x - 7$

28. **Fireworks** A skyrocket is shot into the air. Its altitude h in feet after t seconds is given by the function $h = -16t^2 + 128t$.
    a. In how many seconds does the skyrocket reach maximum altitude?
    b. What is the skyrocket's maximum altitude?

29. **Gardening** Suppose you have 80 ft of fence to enclose a rectangular garden. The function $A = 40x - x^2$ gives you the area of the garden in square feet where x is the width in feet. What width gives you the maximum gardening area? What is the maximum area?

30. **Writing** Explain how changing the values of a, b, and c in a quadratic function affects the graph of the function.

Graph each quadratic inequality.

31. $y > x^2$
32. $y < -x^2$
33. $y \leq x^2 + 3$
34. $y < -x^2 + 4$
35. $y \geq -2x^2 + 6$
36. $y > -x^2 + 4x - 4$
37. $y \leq x^2 + 5x + 6$
38. $y < x^2 - x - 6$
39. $y \geq 3x^2 + 6x$

Open-ended **Give a quadratic function for each description.**

40. Its axis of symmetry is to the right of the y-axis.
41. Its graph opens downward and has vertex at (0, 0).
42. Its graph lies entirely above the x-axis.

Chapter Project

Find Out by Graphing

To avoid skidding, you want to know what a safe stopping distance is. Assume you are traveling on a dry road and have an average reaction time. The formula $f(x) = 0.044x^2 + 1.1x$ gives you a safe stopping distance in feet, where x is your speed in miles per hour. Make a table of values for speeds of 10, 20, 30, 40, 50, and 60 mi/h. Then graph the function.

Exercises MIXED REVIEW

Find each probability for two rolls of a number cube.

43. P(even and odd)
44. P(7 and 5)
45. P(two odd numbers)
46. P(6 and 2)

47. a. **Rowing** The-Head-of-the-Charles Regatta is a 3 mi rowing race held annually in Cambridge, Massachusetts. In 1994, Xeno Muller won the men's singles title in 17 min, 47 s. What was his pace in mi/h? Round your answer to the nearest tenth.
    b. Muller rowed at 32 strokes/min. How many strokes did he row over the course of the race?

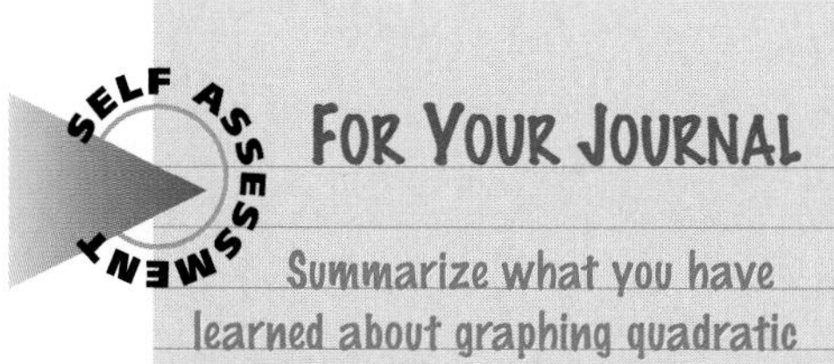

SELF ASSESSMENT
FOR YOUR JOURNAL
Summarize what you have learned about graphing quadratic functions. Include examples to support your statements.

Getting Ready for Lesson 7-4

Evaluate for $a = -1, b = 2, c = 3$, and $d = -4$.

48. a^2
49. $-a^2$
50. $-b^2$
51. dc^2
52. $(dc)^2$

What You'll Learn

- Finding square roots
- Using square roots

...And Why

To use square roots in real-world situations, such as finding the distance from a satellite to the horizon

What You'll Need

- calculator

7-4 Square Roots

THINK AND DISCUSS

Finding Square Roots

The diagram shows the relationship between squares and square roots. Every positive number has *two* square roots.

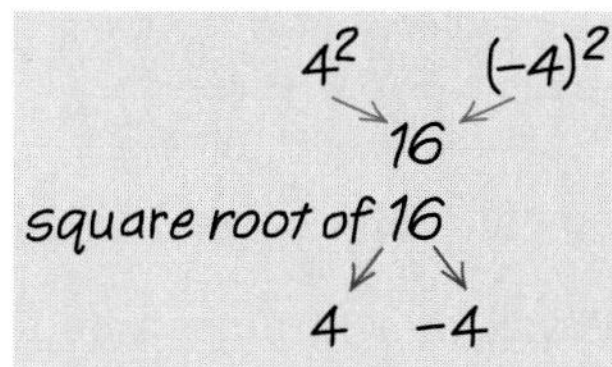

Square Root

If $a^2 = b$, then a is a **square root** of b.

Example: $4^2 = 16$ and $(-4)^2 = 16$, so 4 and -4 are square roots of 16.

A radical symbol $\sqrt{}$ indicates a square root. The expression $\sqrt{16}$ means the **principal** (or positive) **square root** of 16. The expression $-\sqrt{16}$ means the **negative square root** of 16. You can use the symbol $\pm$, read "plus or minus," to indicate both square roots.

Example 1

Simplify each expression.

a. $\sqrt{64} = 8$ ← positive square root

b. $-\sqrt{100} = -10$ ← negative square root

c. $\pm\sqrt{\frac{9}{16}} = \pm\frac{3}{4}$ ← The square roots are $\frac{3}{4}$ and $-\frac{3}{4}$.

d. $\pm\sqrt{0} = 0$ ← There is only one square root of 0.

e. $\sqrt{-16}$ is undefined ← For real numbers, the square root of a negative number is undefined.

1. **Try This** Simplify each expression.
   a. $\sqrt{49}$ b. $\pm\sqrt{36}$ c. $-\sqrt{121}$ d. $\sqrt{\frac{1}{25}}$

QUICK REVIEW

Rational and irrational numbers make up the set of *real numbers.* In decimal form, *rational* numbers terminate or repeat. *Irrational* numbers continue without repeating number patterns.

Some square roots are rational numbers and some are irrational numbers.

Rational: $\pm\sqrt{81} = \pm 9$, $-\sqrt{1.44} = -1.2$, $\sqrt{\frac{4}{9}} = \frac{2}{3} = 0.\overline{6}$

Irrational: $-\sqrt{5} = -2.23606797\ldots$, $\sqrt{\frac{1}{3}} = 0.57735026\ldots$

2. **Try This** Classify each expression as *rational* or *irrational.*
   a. $\sqrt{8}$ b. $\pm\sqrt{225}$ c. $-\sqrt{75}$ d. $\sqrt{\frac{1}{4}}$

Estimating and Using Square Roots

The squares of integers are called **perfect squares.**

consecutive integers:	1	2	3	4	5	6	7
	↓	↓	↓	↓	↓	↓	↓
consecutive perfect squares:	1	4	9	16	25	36	49

You can estimate square roots by using perfect squares and by using a calculator.

Example 2

Estimation Between what two consecutive integers is $\sqrt{14.52}$?

$\sqrt{9} < \sqrt{14.52} < \sqrt{16}$ ⟵ 14.52 is between the two consecutive square numbers 9 and 16.

$3 < \sqrt{14.52} < 4$

$\sqrt{14.52}$ is between 3 and 4.

3. Try This Between what two consecutive integers is $-\sqrt{105}$?

Example 3

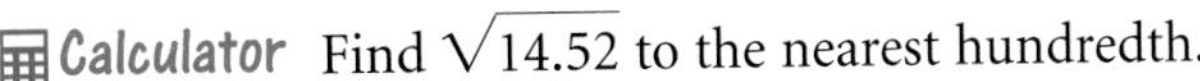

Calculator Find $\sqrt{14.52}$ to the nearest hundredth.

[√] 14.52 [ENTER] 3.810511777 ⟵ Use a calculator.

$\sqrt{14.52} \approx 3.81$

4. Critical Thinking How can you use consecutive perfect squares to mentally check calculator answers for square roots?

Example 4 **Relating to the Real World** 

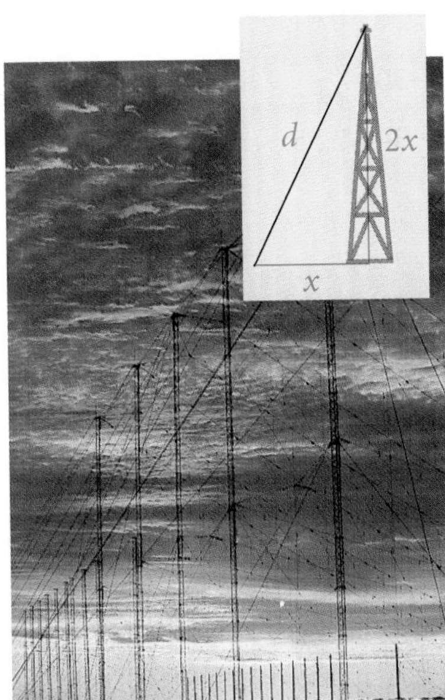

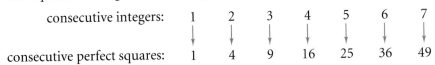

Towers A tower is supported with a wire. The formula $d = \sqrt{x^2 + (2x)^2}$ gives the length d of the wire for the tower at the left. Find the length of the wire if $x = 12$ ft.

$d = \sqrt{x^2 + (2x)^2}$

$d = \sqrt{12^2 + (2 \cdot 12)^2}$ ⟵ Substitute 12 for x.

$d = \sqrt{144 + 576}$ ⟵ Simplify.

$d = \sqrt{720}$

$d = 26.83281573$ ⟵ Use a calculator.

$d \approx 26.8$

The wire is about 26.8 ft long.

5. Try This Suppose the tower is 140 ft tall. How long is the supporting wire?

Exercises ON YOUR OWN

Find both the principal and negative square root of each number.

1. 169
2. 1.96
3. $\frac{1}{9}$
4. 900
5. 0.25
6. $\frac{36}{49}$
7. 1.21
8. 1681

Tell whether each expression is *rational* or *irrational*.

9. $\sqrt{37}$
10. $-\sqrt{0.04}$
11. $\pm\sqrt{\frac{1}{5}}$
12. $-\sqrt{\frac{16}{121}}$

Between what two consecutive integers is each square root?

13. $\sqrt{35}$
14. $\sqrt{27}$
15. $-\sqrt{245}$
16. $\sqrt{880}$

Calculator **Use a calculator to simplify each expression. Round to the nearest hundredth.**

17. $\sqrt{12}$
18. $-\sqrt{203}$
19. $\sqrt{11{,}550}$
20. $-\sqrt{150}$

21. Sports The elasticity coefficient e of a ball relates the height r of its rebound to the height h from which it is dropped. You can find the elasticity coefficient using the function $e = \sqrt{\frac{r}{h}}$.
    a. What is the elasticity coefficient for a tennis ball that rebounds 3 ft after it is dropped from a height of 3.5 ft?
    b. Critical Thinking Suppose that the elasticity coefficient of a basketball is 0.88. How high is its rebound if it is dropped 6 ft?

22. Critical Thinking What number other than 0 is its own square root?

Find the square roots of each number.

23. 0.36
24. 144
25. $\frac{25}{16}$
26. 0.01
27. 400
28. 0
29. 625
30. $\frac{9}{49}$
31. $\frac{1}{81}$
32. 1.69
33. 729
34. 2.25

35. a. Space Find the distance to the horizon from a satellite 4200 km above Earth. The formula $d = \sqrt{12{,}800h + h^2}$ tells you the distance d in kilometers to the horizon from a satellite h kilometers above Earth.
    b. Find the distance to the horizon from a satellite 3600 km above Earth.

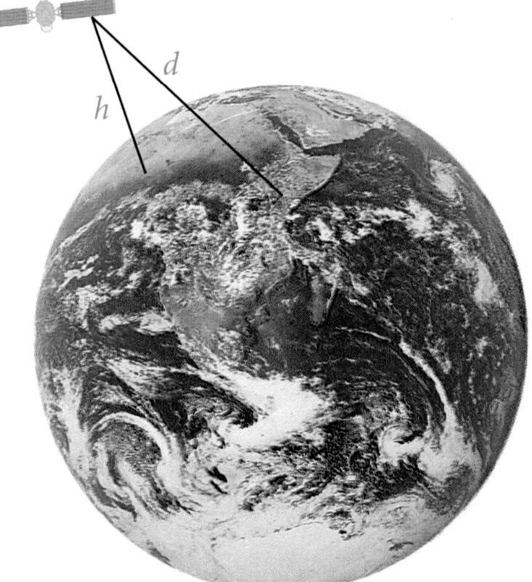

36. Standardized Test Prep If $x^2 = 16$ and $y^2 = 25$, choose the least possible value for the expression $y - x$.
    A. -1 B. 0 C. 1
    D. -9 E. -4

37. In the cartoon, to what number is the golfer referring?

from cartoon *Bound and Gagged*

Choose Use a calculator, paper and pencil, or mental math. Find the value of each expression. If the value is irrational, round to the nearest hundredth.

38. $\sqrt{441}$

39. $-\sqrt{\frac{4}{25}}$

40. $\sqrt{2}$

41. $\sqrt{\frac{1}{36}}$

42. $-\sqrt{1.6}$

43. $-\sqrt{157}$

44. $\sqrt{200}$

45. $-\sqrt{13}$

46. $\sqrt{30}$

47. $\sqrt{1089}$

48. $-\sqrt{0.64}$

49. $\sqrt{41}$

50. **Writing** Explain the difference between $-\sqrt{1}$ and $\sqrt{-1}$.

51. **Open-ended** Find two integers a and b, both between 1 and 25, such that $a^2 + b^2$ is a perfect square.

Tell whether each expression is *rational, irrational,* or *undefined.*

52. $-\sqrt{3600}$

53. $\sqrt{8}$

54. $\sqrt{-25}$

55. $\sqrt{6.25}$

56. $\sqrt{12.96}$

57. $\sqrt{129.6}$

58. $-\sqrt{12.96}$

59. $\sqrt{-12.96}$

60. **Physics** If you drop an object, the time t in seconds that it takes to fall d feet is given by $t = \sqrt{\frac{d}{16}}$.

a. Find the time it takes an object to fall 400 ft.

b. Find the time it takes an object to fall 1600 ft.

c. **Critical Thinking** In part (b), the object falls four times as far as in part (a). Does it take four times as long to fall? Explain.

Tell whether each statement is *true* or *false.* If the statement is false, rewrite it as a true statement.

61. $6 < \sqrt{38} < 7$

62. $-7 < -\sqrt{56} < -6$

63. $-4 < -\sqrt{17} < -5$

64. $3.3 \le \sqrt{10.25} < 3.4$

65. $-16 < -\sqrt{280} < -15$

66. $21 < \sqrt{436} < 22$

67. $-38 < -\sqrt{1300} < -37$

68. $-9 \le -\sqrt{72} < -8$

69. $0.1 < \sqrt{0.03} < 0.2$

Chapter Project — Find Out by Calculating

Suppose a car left a skid mark d feet long. The formulas shown will estimate the speed s in miles per hour at which the car was traveling when the brakes were applied. Use the formulas to complete the table of estimated speeds.

- Why do you think the estimates of speed do not double when the skid marks double in length?
- Based on these results, what conclusions can you make about safe following distances?

Traveling Speed		
Dry Road		$s = \sqrt{27d}$
Wet Road		$s = \sqrt{13.5d}$
Skid Mark Length (d)	**Estimated Speed (s)**	
	Dry Road	Wet Road
60 ft	■	■
120 ft	■	■

Exercises MIXED REVIEW

Solve each inequality. Graph the solution on a number line.

70. $2x > 8$ **71.** $14 < -7s$ **72.** $z - 1 \geq -1$ **73.** $-2 - b > 4$

74. $5b + 4 < -6$ **75.** $-2c \geq 5c - 1$ **76.** $8(m - 3) \leq 4$ **77.** $2 > 7 - 3t$

78. One in four residents of the United States has myopia, or nearsightedness. What is the probability that two people chosen at random are both nearsighted?

Getting Ready for Lesson 7-5

Solve each equation.

79. $3x - 14 = 27$ **80.** $4(y - 5) = 20$ **81.** $-6b + 12 = 12$ **82.** $3 - 9m = 0$

Exercises CHECKPOINT

Graph each quadratic function. Find the vertex of each parabola.

1. $y = 4x^2$ **2.** $y = 2x^2 + 7$ **3.** $y = -x^2 - 2x + 10$

Choose **Use a calculator, paper and pencil, or mental math to find the value of each square root. Round to the nearest hundredth.**

4. $\sqrt{7}$ **5.** $-\sqrt{100}$ **6.** $\sqrt{23}$ **7.** $\sqrt{144}$ **8.** $-\sqrt{150}$ **9.** $-\sqrt{\frac{1}{9}}$

10. *Writing* What does the rule for a quadratic function tell you about how the graph of the function will look?

11. *Open-ended* Give an example of a quadratic function for each of the following descriptions.
  a. Its graph opens downward. **b.** Its graph is wider than the graph of $y = \frac{1}{2}x^2 - 3$.

What You'll Learn

- Solving quadratic equations in $ax^2 = c$ form
- Finding if a quadratic equation has two solutions, one solution, or no solution

...And Why

To solve real-world problems, such as finding the radius of a pond

What You'll Need

- calculator

7-5 Solving Quadratic Equations

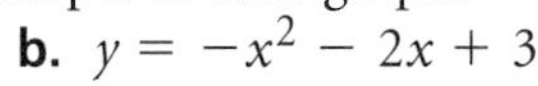

WORK TOGETHER

1. Work with a partner. Find the x-intercepts of each graph.
   a. $y = 2x - 3$
   b. $y = -x^2 - 2x + 3$

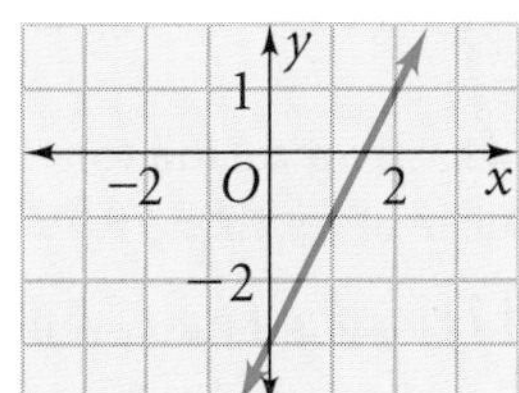

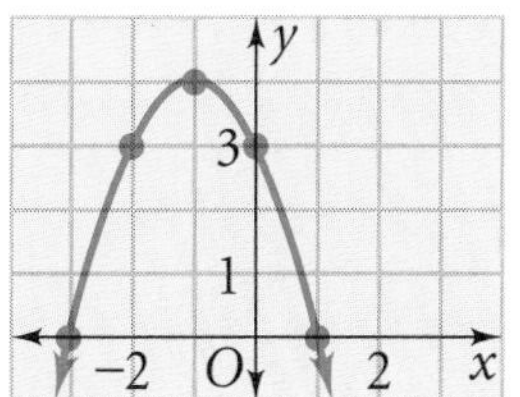

2. Use the graph in Question 1(a) to find the solution of $2x - 3 = 0$.
3. Are the x-intercepts that you found in Question 1(b) solutions of $-x^2 - 2x + 3 = 0$? Explain.
4. Graph $y = x^2 + x - 6 = 0$.
5. a. Where does the graph of $y = x^2 + x - 6$ cross the x-axis?
   b. Do the values you found in part (a) satisfy the equation $x^2 + x - 6 = 0$?

THINK AND DISCUSS

Using Square Roots to Solve Equations

In the Work Together, you investigated a quadratic equation and its related quadratic function. Any values that make the equation true are solutions.

Standard Form of a Quadratic Equation

A **quadratic equation** is an equation that can be written in **standard form**:

$$ax^2 + bx + c = 0, \text{ where } a \neq 0$$

6. Write $6x^2 = 5x - 12$ in standard form.
7. Is $5x - 3 = 0$ a quadratic equation? Why or why not?

There are two square roots for numbers greater than 0. So there are two solutions for an equation like $x^2 = 36$. You can solve equations in the form $x^2 = a$ by finding the square roots of each side.

$$x^2 = 36 \longrightarrow x = \pm 6$$

Example 1

Solve $2x^2 - 98 = 0$.

$$2x^2 - 98 = 0 + 98 \quad \longleftarrow \text{Add 98 to each side.}$$
$$2x^2 = 98$$
$$x^2 = 49 \quad \longleftarrow \text{Divide each side by 2.}$$
$$\sqrt{x^2} = \pm\sqrt{49} \quad \longleftarrow \text{Find the square roots.}$$
$$x = \pm 7$$

8. **Try This** Use a calculator to solve $x^2 - 7 = 0$. Round your solutions to the nearest tenth.

9. **Critical Thinking** Find a value for c so that the equation $x^2 - c = 0$ has 11 and -11 as solutions.

You can solve many geometric problems by finding square roots.

Example 2 Relating to the Real World 

City Planning A city is planning a circular duck pond for a new park. The depth of the pond will be 4 ft. Because of water resources, the maximum volume will be 20,000 ft^3. Find the radius of the pond. Use the equation $V = \pi r^2 h$, where V is the volume, r is the radius, and h is the depth.

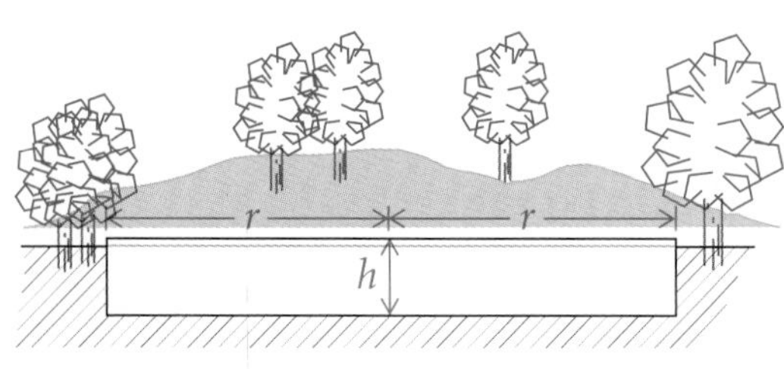

$$V = \pi r^2 h$$
$$20{,}000 = \pi r^2(4) \quad \longleftarrow \text{Substitute 20,000 for } V \text{ and 4 for } h.$$
$$\frac{20{,}000}{\pi(4)} = r^2 \quad \longleftarrow \text{Put in calculator-ready form.}$$
$$\sqrt{\frac{20{,}000}{\pi(4)}} = r \quad \longleftarrow \text{Find the principal square root.}$$
$$39.89422804 = r \quad \longleftarrow \text{Use a calculator.}$$

The pond will have a radius of about 39.9 ft.

10. *Critical Thinking* Why is the principal square root the only root that makes sense in Example 2?

11. **Justify** this step in Example 2:
If $20{,}000 = \pi r^2(4)$, then $\frac{20{,}000}{\pi(4)} = r^2$.

12. *Calculator* Which keystrokes can you use to find r in Example 2?
A. [√] [(] 20000 [÷] [(] [π] [×] 4 [)] [)] [ENTER]
B. [√] 20000 [÷] [π] [×] 4 [ENTER]

13. **a.** *Try This* Suppose the pond could have a volume of 40,000 ft^3. What will be the radius of the pond if the depth is not changed?
b. *Critical Thinking* Does the radius of the pond double when the volume doubles? Explain.

Finding the Number of Solutions

You have seen quadratic equations that have two real numbers as solutions. For real numbers, a quadratic equation can have two solutions, one solution, or no solution.

You can use a graph to find the solution(s) of a quadratic equation by finding the x-intercepts of the related quadratic function.

Example 3

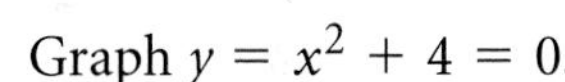

Solve each equation by graphing the related function.

a. $x^2 - 4 = 0$ — Graph $y = x^2 - 4$.

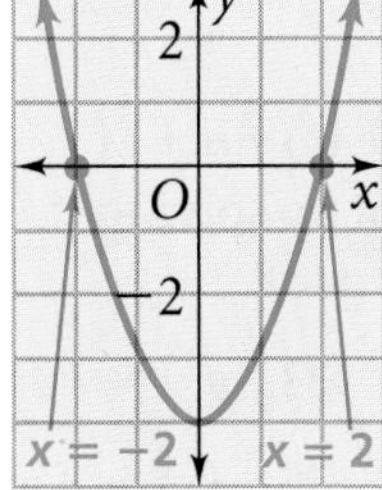

There are two solutions, $x = \pm 2$.

b. $x^2 = 0$ — Graph $y = x^2$.

There is one solution, $x = 0$.

c. $x^2 + 4 = 0$ — Graph $y = x^2 + 4 = 0$.

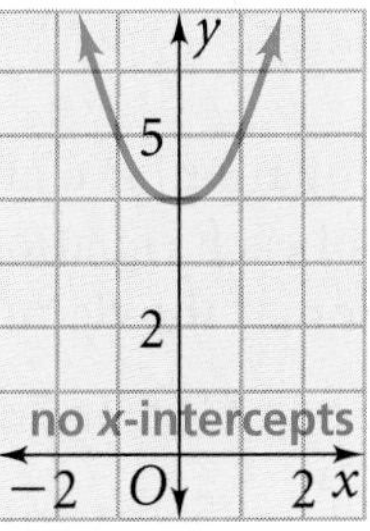

There is no solution.

14. **a.** *Critical Thinking* For what values of c will $x^2 = c$ have two solutions?
b. For what value of c will $x^2 = c$ have one solution?
c. For what values of c will $x^2 = c$ have no solution?

15. *Mental Math* Tell the number of solutions for each equation.
a. $x^2 = -36$ **b.** $x^2 - 12 = 6$ **c.** $x^2 - 15 = -15$

Exercises ON YOUR OWN

Choose **Solve each equation by graphing, using mental math, or using paper and pencil. If the equation has no solution, write *no solution.***

1. $x^2 = 4$

2. $x^2 = 49$

3. $3x^2 + 27 = 0$

4. $x^2 + 25 = 25$

5. $3x^2 - 7 = -34$

6. $x^2 - 225 = 0$

7. $49x^2 - 16 = -7$

8. $x^2 - 9 = 16$

9. $4x^2 = 25$

10. $x^2 + 36 = 0$

11. $4x^2 - 100 = -100$

12. $x^2 - 63 = 81$

13. **Critical Thinking** Michael solved $x^2 + 25 = 0$ and found the solutions -5 and 5. Explain the mistake that Michael made.

Solve each equation. Round solutions to the nearest tenth.

14. $b^2 = 3$

15. $8x^2 = 64$

16. $n^2 - 5 = 16$

17. $3m^2 + 7 = 13$

18. $2x^2 - 179 = 0$

19. $b^2 - 1 = 20$

Model each problem with a quadratic equation. Then solve.

20. **Photography** Find the dimensions of the square picture that make the area of the picture equal to 75% of the total area enclosed by the frame.

21. **Geometry** Find the radius of a sphere with surface area 160 in.^{2}. Use the formula $A = 4\pi r^2$, where A is the surface area and r is the radius of the sphere. Round your answer to the nearest tenth of an inch.

Susan La Flesche Picotte (1865–1915) was a physician and the leader of the Omaha people.

For each equation, you are given a statement about the number of solutions of each equation. If the claim is true, verify it by solving the equation. If the claim is false, write a correct statement.

22. $n^2 + 2 = 11$; there are two solutions.

23. $g^2 = -49$; there are two solutions.

24. $x^2 + 9 = 25$; there is one solution.

25. $4x^2 - 96 = 0$; there is one solution.

26. $-4r^2 = -64$; there are two solutions.

27. $4n^2 - 256 = 0$; there are two solutions.

28. $4b^2 + 9 = 9$; there are two solutions.

29. $-x^2 - 15 = 0$; there is no solution.

30. **Open-ended** Suppose you have 225 square tiles, all the same size. You can tile one surface using all the tiles. How could you tile more than one square surface using all the tiles? No surface can have only one tile.

31. **Painting** Suppose you have a can of paint that will cover 400 ft^2. Find the radius of the largest circle you can paint. Round your answer to the nearest tenth of a foot. (*Hint:* Use the formula $A = \pi r^2$.)

Physics **Use this information for Exercises 32–35.** The time t it takes a pendulum to make a complete swing back and forth depends on the length of the pendulum. This formula relates the length of a pendulum ℓ in meters to the time t in seconds.

$$\ell = \frac{2.45t^2}{\pi^2}$$

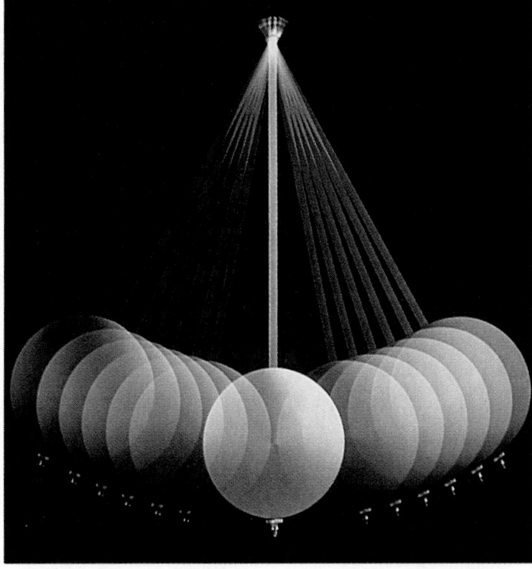

32. Find the length of the pendulum if $t = 1$ s. Round to the nearest tenth.

33. Find t if $\ell = 1.6$ m. Round to the nearest tenth.

34. Find t if $\ell = 2.2$ m. Round to the nearest tenth.

35. **Writing** You can adjust a clock with a pendulum by making the pendulum longer or shorter. If a clock is running slowly, would you lengthen or shorten the pendulum to make the clock run faster? Explain.

36. **Standardized Test Prep** Suppose that $2x^2 - 36 = x^2 - 49$. Which statement is correct?

A. The equation has two real solutions.
B. The equation has no real solutions.
C. The equation has exactly one real solution.
D. You cannot determine the number of real solutions.

Solve each equation. If the equation has no solution, write *no solution*.

37. $5x^2 + 9 = 40$

38. $2x^2 + 8x^2 + 16 = 16$

39. $8x^2 - 4 - 3x^2 + 6 = 30$

40. $x^2 + 3 - 2x^2 - 9 = 30$

41. $3x^2 - 10 + 5x^2 + 3 = 25$

42. $6x^2 + 22 + 2x^2 + 50 = 60$

Exercises MIXED REVIEW

Solve each system of equations.

43. $3x + 2y = 12$
$x - 2y = -4$

44. $-x + 4y = 18$
$3x + y = -2$

45. $0.4x - 1.2y = 24$
$1.6x + 0.6y = 15$

46. a. **Space** NASA astronauts must be between 4 ft $10\frac{1}{2}$ in. and 6 ft 4 in. tall. Russian cosmonauts must be between 5 ft $4\frac{1}{2}$ in. and 6 ft. Change these values to inches. Use a number line to graph an inequality that models each situation.

b. Use a number line to graph the heights that are acceptable for an astronaut but not acceptable for a cosmonaut.

Getting Ready for Lesson 7-6

Evaluate each expression. Round to the nearest hundredth, where necessary.

47. $\sqrt{5^2 - 15}$

48. $\sqrt{36 + 64}$

49. $\sqrt{(-4)^2 - (2)(-3)}$

50. $-3 - \sqrt{36}$

Math ToolboX | **Technology**

Finding Roots

After Lesson 7-5

The solutions of a quadratic equation are the x-intercepts of the related quadratic function. The solutions of a quadratic equation and the related x-intercepts are often called *roots of the equation* or *roots of the function.*

Example

Use a graphing calculator to solve $x^2 - 6x + 3 = 0$.

Step 1

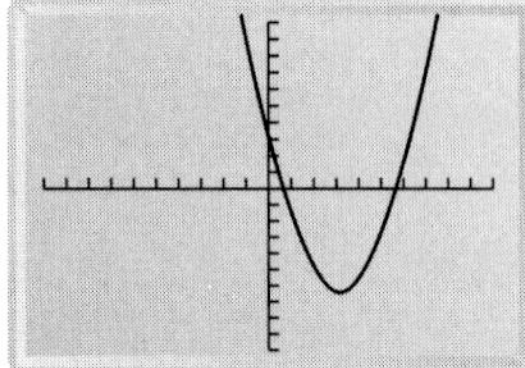

Enter $y = x^2 - 6x + 3$. Use the CALC feature. Select 2:ROOT. The calculator will plot the graph.

Step 2

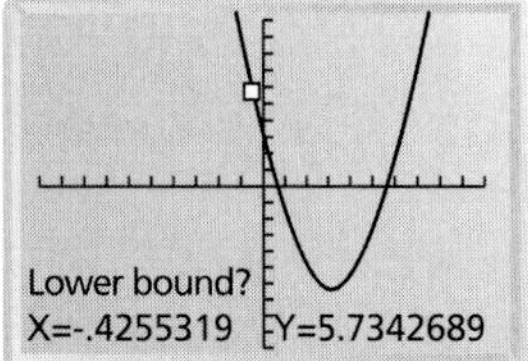

Move the cursor to the left of the first x-intercept. Press ENTER to set the lower bound.

Step 3

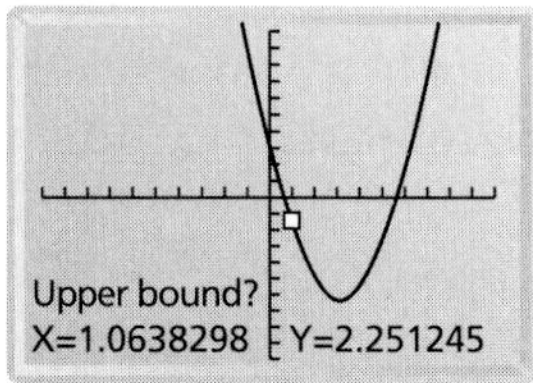

Move the cursor slightly to the right of the intercept. Press ENTER to set the upper bound.

Step 4

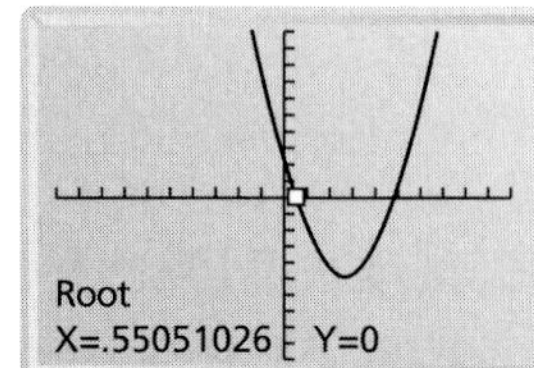

Press ENTER to display the first root, which is about 0.55.

Repeating the steps near the second intercept, you find the second root is about 5.45. So, the solutions are about 0.55 and 5.45.

Suppose you cannot see both of the x-intercepts on your graph. You can find the range for the x-axis by using the TABLE feature. The calculator screen at the right shows part of the table for $y = 2x^2 - 48x + 285$.

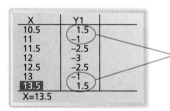

X	Y1
10.5	1.5
11	−1
11.5	−2.5
12	−3
12.5	−2.5
13	−1
13.5	1.5

X=13.5

The graph crosses the x-axis when the values for y change signs. So the range of values of x should include 10.5 and 13.5.

1. Find the x-intercepts of $y = 2x^2 - 48x + 285$.

Use a graph to solve each equation.

2. $x^2 - 6x - 16 = 0$
3. $2x^2 + x - 6 = 0$
4. $\frac{1}{3}x^2 + 8x - 3 = 0$
5. $x^2 - 18x + 5 = 0$
6. $0.25x^2 - 8x - 45 = 0$
7. $0.5x^2 + 3x - 36 = 0$
8. **Writing** Solve $3x^2 = 48$ using a calculator or paper and pencil. Explain why you chose the method you used.

What You'll Learn

- Using the quadratic formula to solve quadratic equations

...And Why

To investigate real-world situations, such as the vertical motion of model rockets

What You'll Need

- calculator

7-6 Using the Quadratic Formula

THINK AND DISCUSS

In Lesson 7-5, you solved some simple quadratic equations by finding square roots and by graphing. In this lesson, you will learn to solve any quadratic equation by using the **quadratic formula.** In Chapter 10 you will learn additional ways to solve a quadratic equation.

Quadratic Formula

If $ax^2 + bx + c = 0$ and $a \neq 0$, then $x = \frac{-b \pm \sqrt{b^2 - 4ac}}{2a}$.

Example 1

Solve $x^2 + 5x + 6 = 0$ by using the quadratic formula.

$x = \frac{-b \pm \sqrt{b^2 - 4ac}}{2a}$ ← Use the quadratic formula.

$x = \frac{-(5) \pm \sqrt{5^2 - (4)(1)(6)}}{2(1)}$ ← Substitute 1 for *a*, 5 for *b*, and 6 for *c*.

$x = \frac{-5 \pm \sqrt{1}}{2}$

$x = \frac{-5 + 1}{2}$ or $x = \frac{-5 - 1}{2}$ ← Write two solutions.

$x = -2$ or $x = -3$

The solutions are -2 and -3.

Check for $x = -2$

$(-2)^2 + 5(-2) + 6 \stackrel{?}{=} 0$

$4 - 10 + 6 \stackrel{?}{=} 0$

$0 = 0$ ✓

for $x = -3$

$(-3)^2 + 5(-3) + 6 \stackrel{?}{=} 0$

$9 - 15 + 6 \stackrel{?}{=} 0$

$0 = 0$ ✓

PROBLEM SOLVING

Look Back Could you check the solutions by graphing? Explain.

1. **Try This** Use the quadratic formula to solve $x^2 - 2x - 8 = 0$.
2. What values would you use for *a*, *b*, and *c* in the quadratic formula to solve $2x^2 = 140$?
3. How many solutions does $9x^2 - 24x + 16 = 0$ have? Explain.

When the quantity under the radical sign in the quadratic formula is not a perfect square, you can use a calculator to approximate the solutions of an equation.

Example 2

Solve $2x^2 + 4x - 7 = 0$. Round the solutions to the nearest hundredth.

$$x = \frac{-b \pm \sqrt{b^2 - 4ac}}{2a}$$ ← Use the quadratic formula.

$$x = \frac{-4 \pm \sqrt{4^2 - (4)(2)(-7)}}{2(2)}$$ ← Substitute 2 for *a*, 4 for *b*, and −7 for *c*.

$$x = \frac{-4 \pm \sqrt{72}}{4}$$

$$x = \frac{-4 + \sqrt{72}}{4} \quad \text{or} \quad x = \frac{-4 - \sqrt{72}}{4}$$ ← Write two solutions.

$$x \approx \frac{-4 + 8.485281374}{4} \quad \text{or} \quad x \approx \frac{-4 - 8.485281374}{4}$$ ← Use a calculator.

$x \approx 1.12$ or $x \approx -3.12$

The solutions are approximately 1.12 and −3.12.

Check Graph the related function $y = 2x^2 + 4x - 7$. Use the *ROOT* option to find the *x*-intercept.

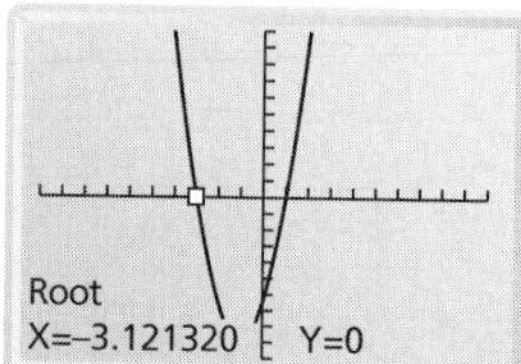

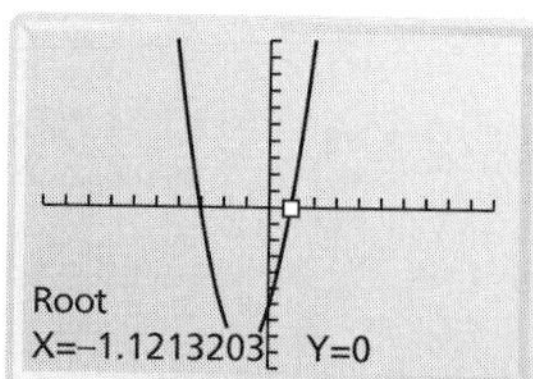

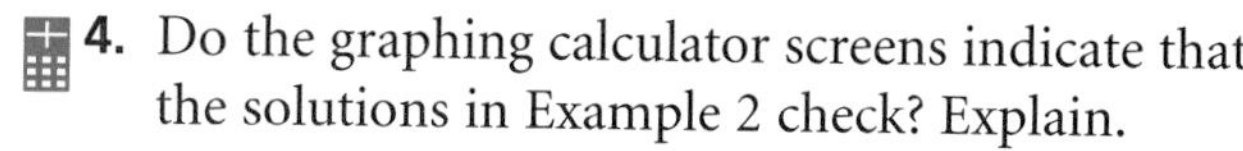

4. Do the graphing calculator screens indicate that the solutions in Example 2 check? Explain.

5. Try This Find the solutions of $-3x^2 + 5x - 2 = 0$. Round to the nearest hundredth.

The quadratic formula is important in physics when finding vertical motion. When an object is dropped, thrown, or launched either straight up or down, you can use the **vertical motion formula** to find the height of the object.

Vertical motion formula: $h = -16t^2 + vt + s$
h is the height of the object in feet.
t is the time it takes an object to rise or fall to a given height.
v is the starting velocity in feet per second.
s is the starting height in feet.

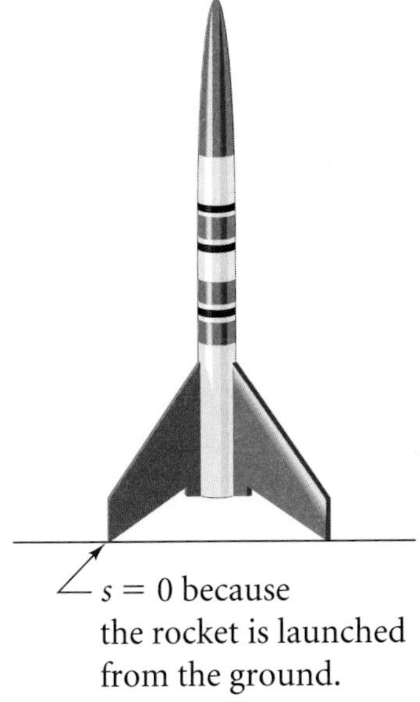

$s = 0$ because the rocket is launched from the ground.

Example 3 Relating to the Real World 

Model Rockets Members of the science club launch a model rocket from ground level with starting velocity of 96 ft/s. After how many seconds will the rocket have an altitude of 128 ft?

$h = -16t^2 + vt + s$ ← Use the vertical motion formula.

$128 = -16t^2 + 96t + 0$ ← Substitute 128 for h, 96 for v, and 0 for s.

$0 = -16t^2 + 96t - 128$ ← Subtract 128 from each side.

$$x = \frac{-b \pm \sqrt{b^2 - 4ac}}{2a}$$ ← Use the quadratic formula.

$$t = \frac{-(96) \pm \sqrt{(96)^2 - (4)(-16)(-128)}}{2(-16)}$$ ← Substitute -16 for a, 96 for b, and -128 for c.

$$t = \frac{-96 \pm \sqrt{9216 - 8192}}{-32}$$ ← Simplify.

$$t = \frac{-96 \pm \sqrt{1024}}{-32}$$

$$t = \frac{-96 + 32}{-32} \text{ or } t = \frac{-96 - 32}{-32}$$ ← Write two solutions and simplify.

$t = 2$ or $t = 4$

The rocket is 128 ft above the ground after 2 s and after 4 s.

6. **Critical Thinking** Use a diagram to explain how the rocket could have an altitude of 128 ft at two different times.

7. a. **Try This** In Example 3, after how many seconds of flight does the rocket have an altitude of 80 ft?
   b. **Critical Thinking** Estimate the number of seconds it will take the rocket to reach its maximum height. Explain how you made your estimate.

Exercises ON YOUR OWN

Write each equation in standard form.

1. $3x^2 - 10 = -13x$
2. $4x^2 = 144x$
3. $x^2 - 3x = 2x + 7$
4. $5x^2 = -7x - 8$
5. $-12x^2 + 25x = 84$
6. $-x^2 + 9x = 4x - 12$

Use the quadratic formula to solve each equation. Round solutions to the nearest hundredth when necessary.

7. $6x^2 + 7x - 5 = 0$
8. $3x^2 - 3x - 1 = 0$
9. $6x^2 - 130 = 0$
10. $x^2 + 6x + 8 = -1$
11. $5x^2 - 4x = 33$
12. $3x^2 = 6x + 4$
13. $9x^2 - 5x = 0$
14. $7x^2 = 13$
15. $2x^2 + 3x - 1 = 0$
16. $2x^2 - 12 = 11x$
17. $2x^2 + 5x + 3 = 0$
18. $4x^2 = 12x - 9$

19. **Population** The function below models the United States population P in millions since 1900, where t is the number of years after 1900.

$$P = 0.0089t^2 + 1.1149t + 78.4491$$

a. **Open-ended** Use the function to estimate the United States population the year you graduate from high school.
b. Estimate the United States population in 2025.
c. Use the function to **predict** the year in which the population reaches 300 million.

20. **Recreation** Suppose you throw a ball in the air with a starting velocity of 30 ft/s. The ball is 5 ft high when it leaves your hand. After how many seconds will it hit the ground? Use the vertical motion formula $h = -16t^2 + vt + s$.

Choose **Use any method you choose to solve each equation.**

21. $2t^2 = 72$
22. $3x^2 + 2x - 4 = 0$
23. $5b^2 - 10 = 0$
24. $3x^2 + 4x = 10$
25. $x^2 = -5x - 6$
26. $m^2 - 4m = -4$
27. $d^2 - d - 6 = 0$
28. $13n^2 - 117 = 0$
29. $3s^2 - 4s = 2$
30. $5b^2 - 2b - 7 = 0$
31. $15x^2 - 12x - 48 = 0$
32. $4t^2 = 81$

33. **Writing** Compare how you solve the linear equation $mx + b = 0$ with how you solve the quadratic equation $ax^2 + bx + c = 0$.

34. **Open-ended** Give an example of a quadratic equation that is easier to solve by finding the square roots of each side than by using the quadratic formula or by graphing. Explain your choice.

35. **Math in the Media** Use the data at the right. Suppose that a cleaner at the top of the Gateway Arch drops a cleaning brush. Use the vertical motion formula $h = -16t^2 + vt + s$.

a. What is the value of s, the starting height?
b. What is the value of h when the brush hits the ground?
c. The starting velocity is 0. Find how many seconds it takes the brush to hit the ground.

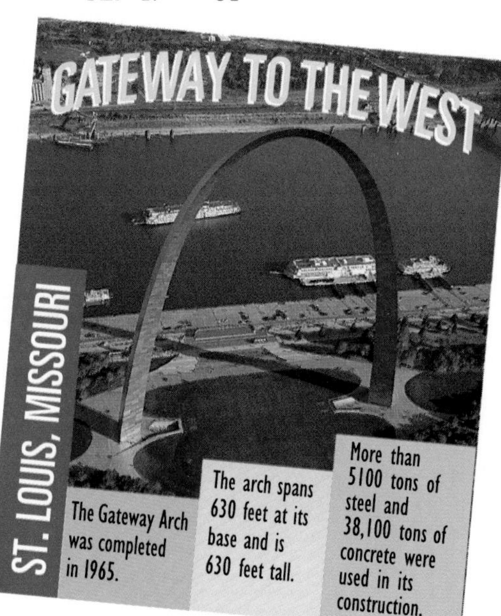

GATEWAY TO THE WEST
ST. LOUIS, MISSOURI
The Gateway Arch was completed in 1965.
The arch spans 630 feet at its base and is 630 feet tall.
More than 5100 tons of steel and 38,100 tons of concrete were used in its construction.

Chapter Project: Find Out by Reasoning

The formula $d = 0.044s^2 + 1.1s$ relates the maximum speed s in miles per hour that you should travel in order to be able to stop in d feet. Suppose you have 150 ft (about 10 car lengths) between your car and the car in front of you. Find the maximum speed you should travel.

Exercises MIXED REVIEW

Find each probability for two rolls of a number cube.

36. P(a 2 and a 6)

37. P(two odds)

38. P(two 5's)

39. P(two fractions)

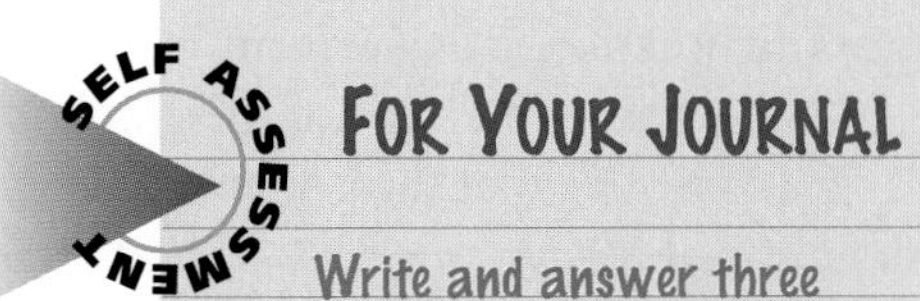

Write and answer three questions that review what you learned about quadratic equations in this chapter.

40. a. *Transportation* A commuter train has a 150-ton locomotive and 70-ton double-decker passenger cars. Write a linear function for the weight of a train with c passenger cars.

b. How much does a train with 7 passenger cars weigh?

Getting Ready for Lesson 7-7

For each equation, find the value of $b^2 - 4ac$.

41. $2x^2 + 3x - 4 = 0$

42. $3x^2 + 2x + 1 = 0$

43. $x^2 + 2x - 5 = 0$

44. $3x^2 - 6x = 5$

45. $2x^2 - 5x = 3$

46. $2x^2 + 3 = 7x$

Exercises CHECKPOINT

Solve each equation.

1. $x^2 - 16 = 49$

2. $8x^2 + 1 = 33$

3. $x^2 - 120 = 1$

Use the quadratic formula to solve each equation.

4. $x^2 - 4x + 3 = 0$

5. $5x^2 + 3x - 2 = 0$

6. $4x^2 = 14x - 3$

7. *Standardized Test Prep* Which expression could you use to solve $2x^2 + 5 = 3x$?

A. $\dfrac{-5 \pm \sqrt{5^2 - (4)(2)(3)}}{4}$

B. $\dfrac{-3 \pm \sqrt{3^2 - (4)(2)(5)}}{4}$

C. $\dfrac{-(-3) \pm \sqrt{(-3)^2 - (4)(2)(-3)}}{4}$

D. $\dfrac{-(-3) \pm \sqrt{(-3)^2 - (4)(2)(5)}}{4}$

Math ToolboX

Problem Solving

Work Backward

After Lesson 7-6

Sometimes you can solve a problem by working backward. To write a quadratic function from its graph, you need to find the x- and y-intercepts.

Example

Work backward to write the equation of the quadratic function shown in the graph.

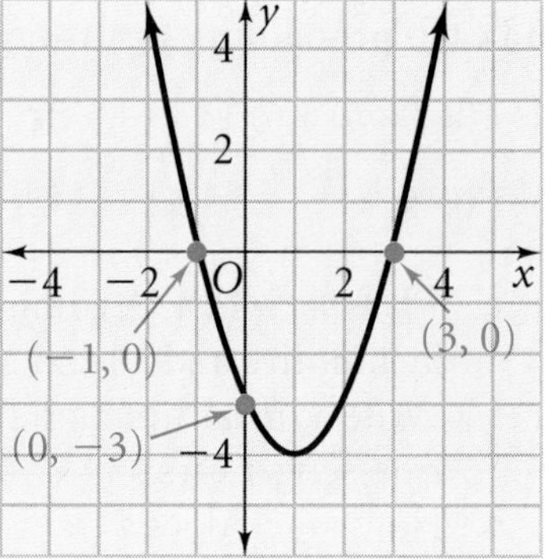

A quadratic function is in the form $y = ax^2 + bx + c$ $(a \neq 0)$. Since the y-intercept of the graph is -3, you know that $c = -3$. Notice that the graph has x-intercepts at -1 and 3. Substitute the points $(-1, 0)$ and $(3, 0)$ into $y = ax^2 + bx - 3$. The result is a system of equations.

$$\begin{aligned} y &= ax^2 + bx - 3 \\ 0 &= a(-1)^2 + b(-1) - 3 \\ 0 &= a - b - 3 \\ a - b &= 3 \end{aligned} \qquad \begin{aligned} y &= ax^2 + bx - 3 \\ 0 &= a(3)^2 + b(3) - 3 \\ 0 &= 9a + 3b - 3 \\ 9a + 3b &= 3 \\ 3a + b &= 1 \end{aligned}$$

When you solve the system of equations, you find that $a = 1$ and $b = -2$.

$$\begin{aligned} a - b &= 3 \\ 3a + b &= 1 \end{aligned}$$

The equation of the graph above is $y = x^2 - 2x - 3$.

Work backward to find the equation of each graph.

1.

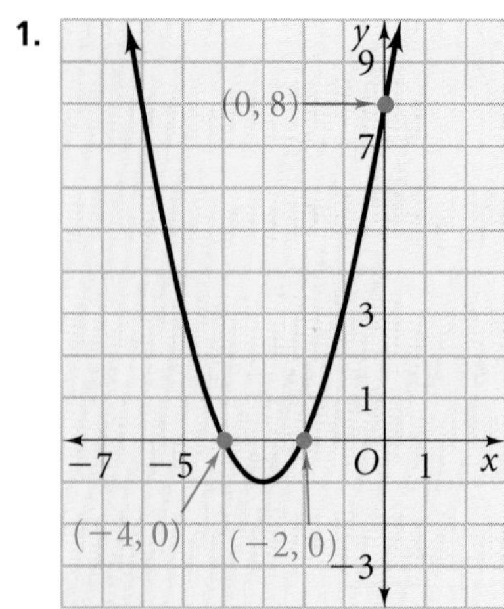

2.

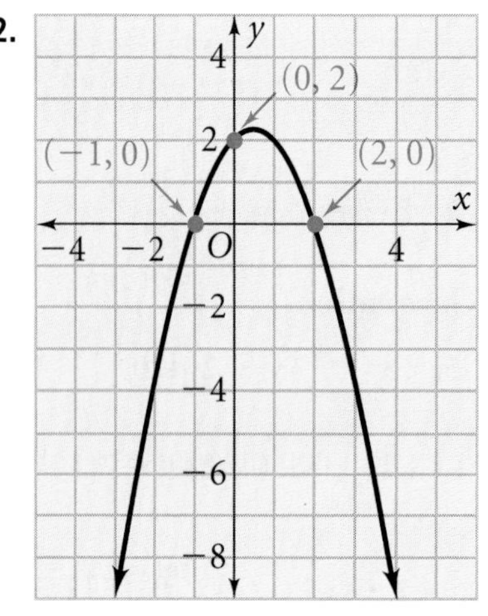

3.

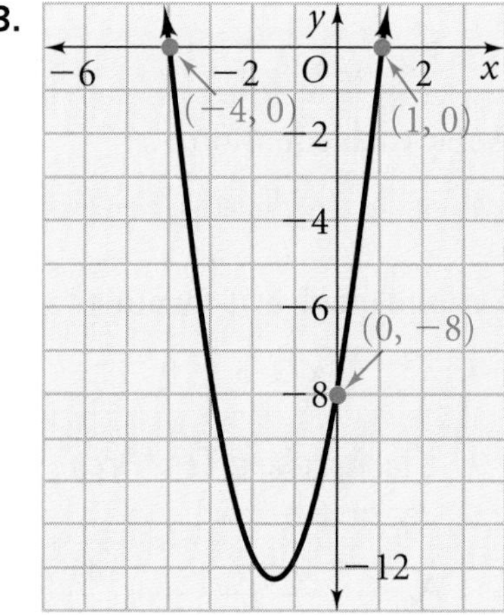

4. Writing Explain why this method would not be ideal for all graphs.

What You'll Learn

- Using the discriminant to find the number of solutions of a quadratic equation

...And Why

To solve physics and home improvement problems

What You'll Need

- graphing calculator

7-7 Using the Discriminant

WORK TOGETHER

Work with a partner.

1. Each equation is in the form of $ax^2 + bx + c = 0$. Find the value of the expression $b^2 - 4ac$ for each equation.
   a. $x^2 + 2x + 5 = 0$ **b.** $-3x^2 + 2x - 1 = 0$ **c.** $\frac{1}{2}x^2 + x + 4 = 0$

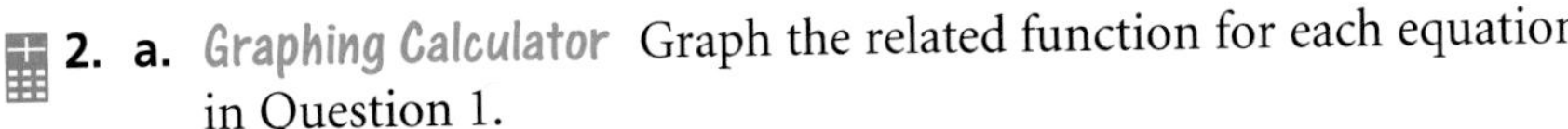

2. **a.** *Graphing Calculator* Graph the related function for each equation in Question 1.
   b. How many x-intercepts do these graphs have?
   c. How many solutions do the equations in Question 1 have?
3. **Generalize** Based on Questions 1 and 2, complete this statement: For an equation in which $b^2 - 4ac$ ■ 0, the equation has ■ solutions.

THINK AND DISCUSS

In the Work Together activity, you investigated the discriminant of three quadratic equations. The quantity $b^2 - 4ac$ is called the **discriminant** of a quadratic equation. The discriminant is part of the quadratic formula.

$$x = \frac{-b \pm \sqrt{b^2 - 4ac}}{2a} \quad \longleftarrow \text{the discriminant}$$

The graph of the related function of a quadratic equation gives you a picture of what happens when a discriminant is positive, 0, or negative.

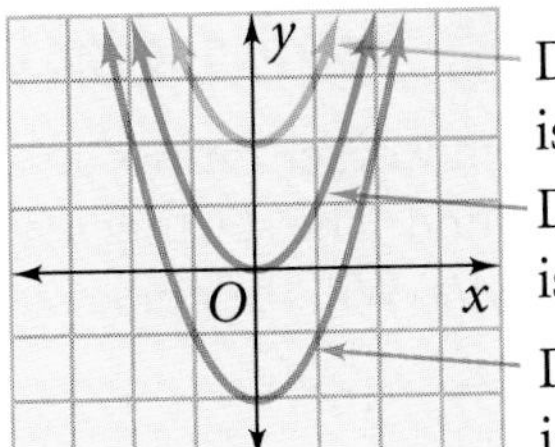

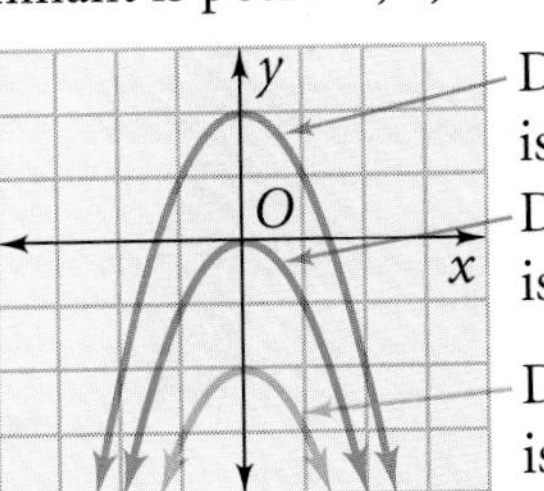

4. How many solutions will an equation have if the discriminant is positive? Explain.
5. How many solutions will an equation have if the discriminant is 0? Explain.
6. How many solutions will an equation have if the discriminant is negative? Explain.
7. Does the direction a graph opens affect the number of solutions found by using the discriminant?

Property of the Discriminant

For the quadratic equation $ax^2 + bx + c = 0$ where a $\neq 0$, the value of the discriminant tells you the number of solutions.

Discriminant	Number of Solutions
$b^2 - 4ac > 0$	two solutions
$b^2 - 4ac = 0$	one solution
$b^2 - 4ac < 0$	no solution

Example 1

Find the number of solutions of $3x^2 - 5x = 1$.

$3x^2 - 5x - 1 = 0$ ← Write in standard form.

$b^2 - 4ac = (-5)^2 - (4)(3)(-1)$ ← Substitute for a, b, and c.

$= 25 - (-12)$

$= 37$

Since $37 > 0$, the equation has two solutions.

8. *Graphing Calculator* Check the result in Example 1 by graphing the related function $y = 3x^2 - 5x - 1$.

9. *Try This* Find the number of solutions of $x^2 = 2x - 3$.

10. *Critical Thinking* Kenji claimed that the discriminant of $2x^2 + 5x - 1 = 0$ had the value 17. What error did he make?

Example 2 **Relating to the Real World**

Physics A construction worker throws an apple toward a fellow worker who is 25 ft above ground. The starting height of the apple is 5 ft. Its starting velocity is 30 ft/s. Will the apple reach the second worker?

$h = -16t^2 + vt + s$ ← Use the vertical motion formula.

$25 = -16t^2 + 30t + 5$ ← Substitute 25 for h, 30 for v, and 5 for s.

$0 = -16t^2 + 30t - 20$ ← Write in standard form.

$b^2 - 4ac = (30)^2 - 4(-16)(-20)$ ← Evaluate the discriminant.

$= 900 - 1280$

$= -380$

The discriminant is negative. The apple will not reach the second worker.

11. **Try This** Suppose the first construction worker in Example 2 goes up to the next floor. He then throws the apple at a starting height of 17 ft and starting velocity of 30 ft/s. Will the apple reach the second worker?

Exercises ON YOUR OWN

For which discriminant is each graph possible?

1. 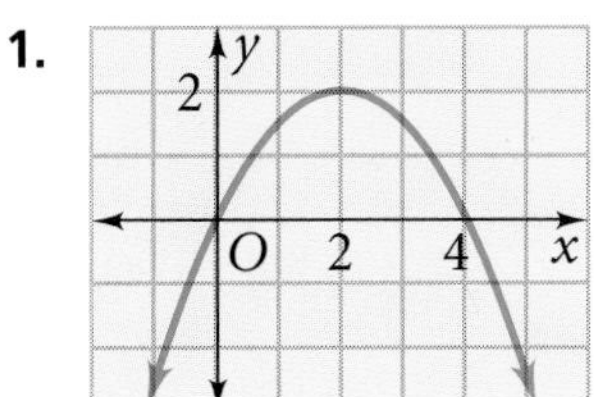

2. 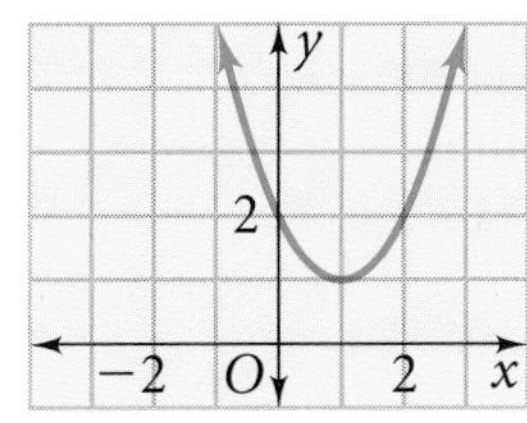

3. 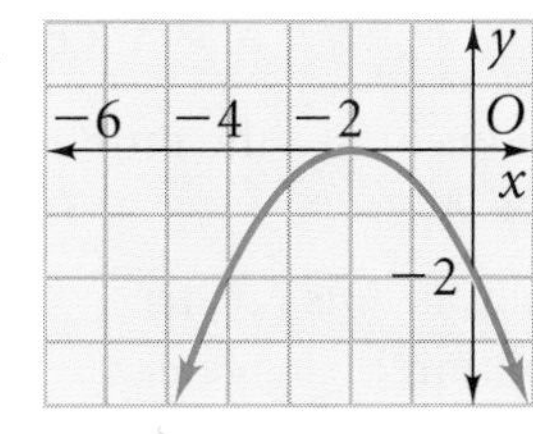

A. $b^2 - 4ac = 0$

B. $b^2 - 4ac = -2$

C. $b^2 - 4ac = 5$

Mental Math **Find the number of solutions of each equation.**

4. $x^2 - 3x + 4 = 0$
5. $x^2 - 6x + 9 = 0$
6. $x^2 + 4x - 2 = 0$
7. $x^2 - 1 = 0$
8. $x^2 - 2x - 3 = 0$
9. $x^2 + x = 0$
10. $2x^2 - 3x + 4 = 0$
11. $2x^2 + 4x = -15$
12. $x^2 - 7x + 6 = 0$
13. $x^2 + 2x + 1 = 0$
14. $4x^2 + 5x = -2$
15. $x^2 - 8x = -12$

16. **Open-ended** Write a quadratic equation that has no solution.

17. **Home Improvements** The Reeves family garden is 18 ft long and 15 ft wide. They want to modify it according to the diagram at the right. The new area is modeled by the equation $A = -x^2 + 3x + 270$.
   a. What value of x, if any, will give a new area of 280 ft^2?
   b. Is there any value of x for which the garden has an area of 266 ft^2? Explain.

18. **Writing** How can you use the discriminant to write a quadratic equation that has two solutions?

19. **Physics** Suppose the equation $h = -16t^2 + 35t$ models the altitude a football will reach t seconds after it is kicked. Which of the following altitudes are possible?
   A. $h = 16$ ft
   B. $h = 25$ ft
   C. $h = 30$ ft
   D. $h = 35$ ft

20. Find the value of the discriminant and the solutions of each equation.
   a. $x^2 - 6x + 5 = 0$
   b. $x^2 + x - 20 = 0$
   c. $2x^2 - 7x - 3 = 0$

21. **Critical Thinking** Use your results to Question 20. When the discriminant is a perfect square, are the solutions rational or irrational? Explain.

Find the number of *x*-intercepts of each function.

22. $y = x^2 - 6x + 5$

23. $y = 2x^2 + 4x - 3$

24. $y = x^2 + 2x + 9$

25. $y = -x^2 - 2x$

26. $y = x^2$

27. $y = 3x^2 - 2x + 5$

28. $y = 8x^2 - 2x - 45$

29. $y = -x^2 - 2$

30. $y = -x^2$

31. *Standardized Test Prep* Compare the quantities in Column A and Column B.

Column A	Column B
the number of solutions of $35 = 20x^2 - 15x + 47$	the number of solutions of $15x + 7 = 0$

A. The quantity in Column A is greater.
B. The quantity in Column B is greater.
C. The quantities are equal.
D. The relationship cannot be determined from the information given.

For each function, decide if its graph crosses the *x*-axis. For those that do, find the coordinates of the points at which they cross.

32. $y = x^2 - 2x + 5$

33. $y = 2x^2 - 4x + 3$

34. $y = 4x^2 + x - 5$

35. $y = -3x^2 - x + 2$

36. $y = x^2 - 5x + 7$

37. $y = 2x^2 - 3x - 5$

38. For the equation $x^2 + 4x + k = 0$, find all values of k such that the equation has each number of solutions.

a. none **b.** one **c.** two

39. *Electrical Engineering* The function $P = 3i^2 - 2i + 450$ models the power P in an electric circuit with a current i. Can the power in this circuit ever be zero? If so, at what value of i?

40. *Business* An apartment rental agency uses the formula $I = 5400 + 300n - 50n^2$ to find its monthly income I based on renting n number of apartments. Will the agency's monthly income ever be $7000? Explain.

41. *Computer* You can use a spreadsheet like the one at the right to find the discriminant for each value of b shown in column A.

a. What spreadsheet formula would you use to find the value in cell B2? in cell C2?

b. Describe the integer values of b for which $x^2 + bx + 1 = 0$ has solutions.

c. Describe the integer values of b for which $x^2 + bx + 2 = 0$ has no solution.

	A	B	C
1	b	x^2 + bx + 1 = 0	x^2 + bx + 2 = 0
2	−3	■	■
3	−2	■	■
4	−1	■	■
5	0	■	■
6	1	■	■
7	2	■	■
8	3	■	■

Chapter Project — Find Out by Communicating

Work with a group of your classmates to plan a skit that will present what you have learned about safe distances in driving. Illustrate the relationships among reaction time, road conditions, speed, and stopping distances.

Exercises MIXED REVIEW

Solve each system by graphing.

42. $4x + y \leq 5$
$3x - 2y > 10$

43. $-6x - 3y \geq 8$
$y > -9$

44. $x < 7$
$-3x + 7y \geq 0$

45. $y = 3x - 2$
$y = -x + 6$

Evaluate each function for $x = 3$.

46. $f(x) = \frac{1}{2}x + 3$

47. $g(x) = \frac{x + 3}{2}$

48. $h(x) = 3 - x$

49. $f(x) = -x - 1$

50. *Geology* Mount Shishalding is a 9372-ft tall volcano on Unimak Island, Alaska. In 1995 it erupted and sent up a 35,000-ft plume of ash. How far above sea level did the ash reach?

PORTFOLIO

Select one or two items from your work for this chapter. Consider:
- cooperative work
- work you found challenging
- diagrams, graphs, or charts

Explain why you have included each selection that you make.

A Point in Time

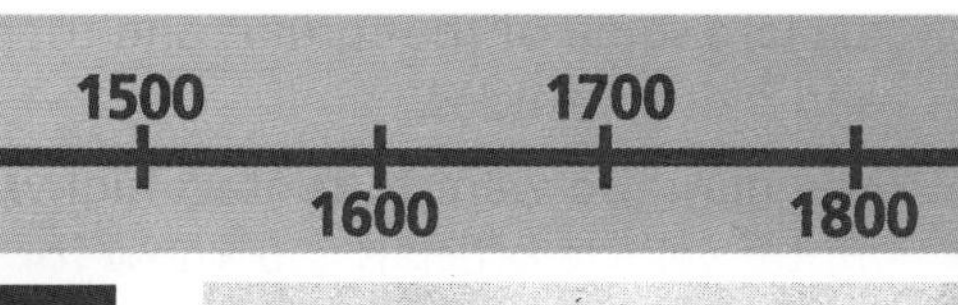

Juan de la Cierva

In 1923, Juan de la Cierva (1895–1936) designed the first successful autogyro, a rotor-based aircraft. The autogyro had rotating blades to give the aircraft lift, a propeller for forward thrust, and short, stubby wings for balance. Autogyros needed only short runways for takeoff and could descend almost vertically.

By hinging the rotor blades at the hub, de la Cierva allowed each blade to respond to aerodynamic forces. This was a significant contribution in the development of the modern helicopter.

De la Cierva's work on problems of lift and gravity, like the work of aeronautical engineers of today, involved quadratic functions.

Finishing the Chapter Project

Questions on pages 331, 336, 347, and 353 should help you to complete your project. Gather together all the data you compiled as you worked on the project. Include the equations you analyzed and your graphs. Discuss your conclusions about safe driving, stopping distance, road conditions, and so on with your classmates. Then, as a group, plan and rehearse your skit.

Reflect and Revise

Present your skit to a small group of classmates. After you have heard their comments, decide if your presentation is clear and convincing. If needed, make changes to improve your skit for the rest of the class.

Follow Up

If you have access to a commercial online service or the Internet, explore some of the forums and user groups that are related to driving and motor vehicles.

You may also want to contact highway patrol officers or registry of motor vehicle officials you know for information about the habits of drivers. Ask them what errors or violations are most common.

For More Information:

Highway Safety: Motorcycle helmet laws save lives and reduce costs to society. A Report to Congressional Requesters. Washington, D.C.: U.S. General Accounting Office, 1991.

Hewett, Joan. *Motorcycle on Patrol.* New York: Clarion Books, 1986.

Ross, Daniel Charles. "Ford F150." *Car and Driver* (January 1996): 134.

Saperstein, Robert. *Surviving an Auto Accident.* Ventura, California: Pathfinder Publishers, 1994.

CHAPTER 7

Wrap Up

Key Terms

axis of symmetry (p. 318)
discriminant (p. 349)
maximum value (p. 320)
minimum value (p. 320)
negative square root (p. 332)
parabola (p. 318)
perfect squares (p. 333)
principal square root (p. 332)
quadratic equation (p. 337)
quadratic formula (p. 343)
quadratic function (p. 319)
square root (p. 332)
standard form of a quadratic equation (p. 337)
standard form of a quadratic function (p. 319)
vertex (p. 320)
vertical motion formula (p. 344)

How am I doing?

- State three ideas from this chapter that you think are important. Explain your choices.

- Describe the different ways you can solve quadratic equations.

Exploring Quadratic Functions 7-1

A function of the form $y = ax^2 + bx + c$ is a **quadratic function**. The shape of its graph is a **parabola.** The **axis of symmetry** of a parabola divides the parabola into two congruent halves.

The **vertex** of a parabola is where the axis of symmetry intersects the parabola. When a parabola opens downward, the y-coordinate of the vertex is a **maximum value** of the function. When a parabola opens upward, the y-coordinate of the vertex is a **minimum value** of the function.

The value of a determines whether the parabola opens upward or downward and how wide or narrow it is.

Open-ended **Give an example of a quadratic function for each of the following descriptions.**

1. Its graph opens downward.
2. Its graph opens upward.
3. Its vertex is at the origin.
4. Its graph is wider than $y = x^2$.

Graphing Simple Quadratic Functions 7-2

Changing the value of c in a quadratic function $y = ax^2 + c$ shifts the parabola up or down. The value of c is the y-intercept of the graph.

Graph each quadratic equation.

5. $y = \frac{2}{3}x^2$
6. $y = -x^2 + 1$
7. $y = x^2 - 4$
8. $y = 5x^2 + 8$

State whether each function has a *maximum* or *minimum* value.

9. $y = 4x^2 + 1$
10. $y = -3x^2 - 7$
11. $y = \frac{1}{2}x^2 + 9$
12. $y = -x^2 + 6$

Graphing Quadratic Functions 7-3

The graph of $y = ax^2 + bx + c$, where $a \neq 0$, has the line $x = \frac{-b}{2a}$ as its axis of symmetry. The x-coordinate of the vertex is $\frac{-b}{2a}$.

Graph each function. Label the axis of symmetry and the vertex.

13. $y = -\frac{1}{2}x^2 + 4x + 1$ **14.** $y = -2x^2 - 3x + 10$ **15.** $y = x^2 + 6x - 2$

Graph each quadratic inequality.

16. $y \leq 3x^2 + x - 5$ **17.** $y > 2x^2 + 6x - 3$ **18.** $y \geq -x^2 - x - 8$

Square Roots 7-4

If $a^2 = b$, then a is a **square root** of b. The **principal** (or positive) **square root** of b is indicated by $\sqrt{b}$. The **negative square root** is indicated by $-\sqrt{b}$. The squares of integers are called **perfect squares.**

Tell whether each expression is *rational* or *irrational.*

19. $\sqrt{86}$ **20.** $-\sqrt{1.21}$ **21.** $\pm\sqrt{\frac{1}{2}}$ **22.** $\sqrt{64}$ **23.** $\sqrt{2.55}$ **24.** $-\sqrt{\frac{4}{25}}$

Find the value of each expression. If the value is irrational, round your answer to the nearest hundredth.

25. $\sqrt{9}$ **26.** $-\sqrt{47}$ **27.** $\sqrt{0.36}$ **28.** $\sqrt{140}$ **29.** $-\sqrt{1}$ **30.** $\sqrt{196}$

31. Standardized Test Prep What is the principal square root of 2.25?
A. 15 **B.** 1.5 **C.** -15 **D.** -1.5 **E.** 0.15

Solving Quadratic Equations 7-5

A **quadratic equation** can be written in the **standard form** $ax^2 + bx + c = 0$, where $a \neq 0$. Quadratic equations can have two, one, or no real solutions. You can solve some quadratic equations by taking the square root of each side, or by finding the x-intercepts of the related quadratic function.

If the statement is true, verify it by solving the equation. If it is false, write a true statement.

32. $x^2 - 10 = 3$; there is one solution. **33.** $3x^2 = 27$; there are two solutions.

Solve each equation. If the equation has no solution, write *no solution.*

34. $6(x^2 - 2) = 12$ **35.** $-5m^2 = -125$ **36.** $9(w^2 + 1) = 9$ **37.** $3r^2 + 27 = 0$

38. Geometry The area of a circle is given by the formula $A = \pi r^2$. Find the radius of a circle with area 16 in.^{2} to the nearest tenth of an inch.

Using the Quadratic Formula 7-6

You can solve a quadratic equation using the **quadratic formula**.

If $ax^2 + bx + c = 0$ and $a \neq 0$, then $x = \frac{-b \pm \sqrt{b^2 - 4ac}}{2a}$.

Use the quadratic formula to solve each equation. Round solutions to the nearest hundredth when necessary.

39. $4x^2 + 3x - 8 = 0$ **40.** $2x^2 - 7x = -3$ **41.** $-x^2 + 8x + 4 = 5$ **42.** $9x^2 - 270 = 0$

43. *Vertical Motion* Suppose you throw a ball in the air. The ball is 6 ft high when it leaves your hand. Use the equation $0 = -16t^2 + 20t + 6$ to find the number of seconds t that the ball is in the air.

Using the Discriminant 7-7

You can use the **discriminant** to find the number of real solutions of a quadratic equation. When a quadratic equation is in the form $ax^2 + bx + c = 0$ $(a \neq 0)$, the discriminant is $b^2 - 4ac$.

If $b^2 - 4ac > 0$, there are two solutions.
If $b^2 - 4ac = 0$, there is one solution.
If $b^2 - 4ac < 0$, there is no solution.

Evaluate the discriminant. Determine the number of real solutions of each equation.

44. $x^2 + 5x - 6 = 0$ **45.** $-3x^2 - 4x + 8 = 0$ **46.** $2x^2 + 7x + 11 = 0$

47. *Writing* Explain why a quadratic equation has one real solution if its discriminant equals zero.

Getting Ready for... CHAPTER 8

Use exponents to write each expression.

48. $3 \cdot 3 \cdot 5 \cdot 5 \cdot 5$ **49.** $8 \cdot 8 \cdot 8 \cdot x \cdot x \cdot x \cdot x$ **50.** $h \cdot h \cdot h \cdot h \cdot h \cdot w \cdot w$

Simplify each expression.

51. $5 \cdot 10^3$ **52.** $-4^3 - (-4)^3$ **53.** $8 \cdot 10^4$

54. $\frac{3^4}{3^2}$ **55.** $10(3^2 - 3^4)$ **56.** $7 \cdot 10^2 \div 10^3$

Evaluate each expression.

57. $d^2 \cdot g^2$ for $d = -2$ and $g = 3$ **58.** $7n^8 - 5n^3$ for $n = -1$ **59.** $\frac{m^3}{m^4}$ for $m = 3$

CHAPTER 7

Assessment

Match each function with its graph.

1. $y = 3x^2$
2. $y = -3x^2 + 1$
3. $y = -2x^2$
4. $y = x^2 - 3$

A. 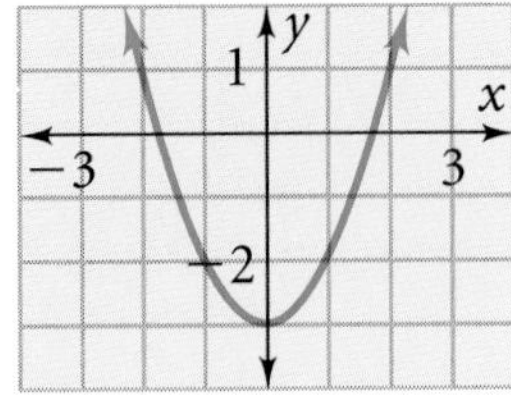

B. 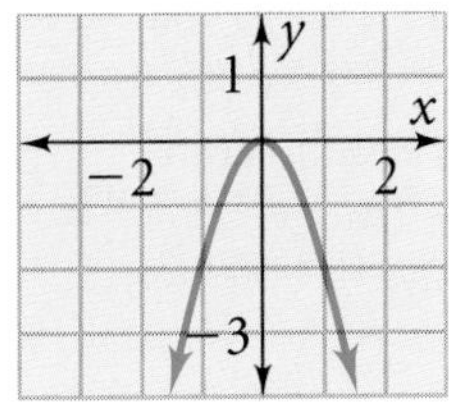

C. 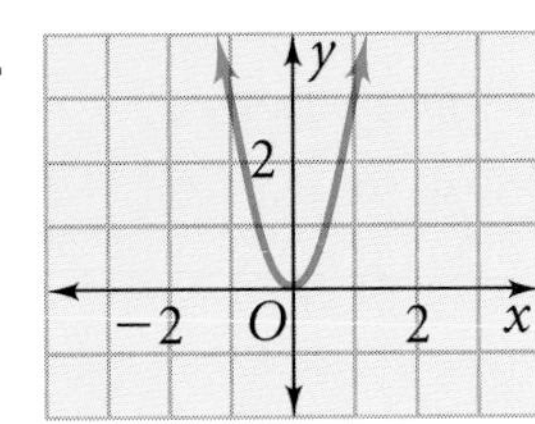

D. 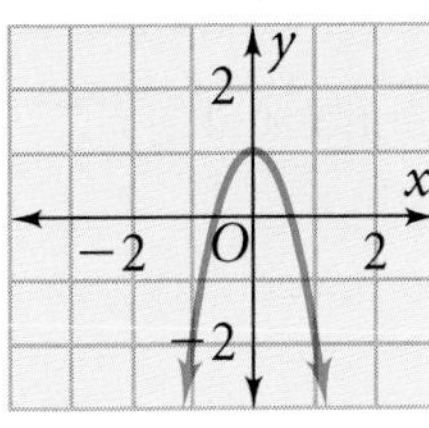

Find the coordinates of the vertex of the graph and an equation for the axis of symmetry.

5. $y = 3x^2 - 7$
6. $y = x^2 - 3x + 2$
7. $y = -2x^2 + 10x - 1$
8. $y = \frac{1}{2}x^2 + 6x$

Make a table of values and graph each function.

9. $y = x^2 - 4$
10. $y = -x^2 + 1$
11. $y = 5x^2$
12. $y = \frac{1}{2}x^2 - 2$

13. **Writing** Explain what you can determine about the shape of a parabola from its equation without graphing.

Find the number of x-intercepts of each function.

14. $y = 5x^2$
15. $y = 3x^2 + 10$
16. $y = -2x^2 + x + 7$
17. $y = x^2 - 4x$

Graph each quadratic function.

18. $y = -3x^2 - x + 10$
19. $y = \frac{1}{2}x^2 + 2x + 4$
20. $y = x^2 - 3x + 5$

Find both the principal and negative square roots of each number.

21. 1.44
22. 1600
23. $\frac{4}{9}$

Between what two consecutive integers is each square root?

24. $\sqrt{28}$
25. $\sqrt{136}$
26. $\sqrt{332}$

Use any method to solve each quadratic equation. Round solutions to the nearest hundredth.

27. $2x^2 = 50$
28. $-3x^2 + 7x = -10$
29. $x^2 + 6x + 9 = 25$
30. $-x^2 - x + 2 = 0$

31. **Open-ended** Write the equation of a parabola that has two x-intercepts and a maximum value. Include a graph of your parabola.

Model each problem with a quadratic equation. Then solve the problem.

32. **Geometry** The volume of a cylinder is given by the formula $V = \pi r^2 h$, where r is the radius of the cylinder and h is the height. A cylinder with height of 10 ft has volume 140 ft^3. What is the radius to the nearest tenth of a foot?

33. **Landscaping** The area of a rectangular patio is 800 ft^2. The length of the patio is twice the width. Find the dimensions of the patio. (*Hint*: use the formula $A = l \cdot w$.)

Evaluate the discriminant. Determine the number of real solutions of each equation.

34. $x^2 + 4x = 5$
35. $x^2 - 8 = 0$
36. $2x^2 + x = 0$
37. $3x^2 - 9x = -5$

38. **Standardized Test Prep** Find the value of k for which the equation $kx^2 - 10x + 25k = 0$ has one real root.

A. −1 **B.** 2 **C.** 3 **D.** 5 **E.** 10

CHAPTER

7 Preparing for Standardized Tests

For Exercises 1–12, choose the correct letter.

1. Choose the best approximation of the solutions of $3x^2 - 5x + 1 = 0$.
   A. 2 and -3 **B.** 1.5 and -0.5
   C. 1.5 and 1.75 **D.** -3 and 2
   E. 1.5 and 0.25

2. What is the equation of the axis of symmetry of $y = 5x^2 - 2x + 3$?
   A. $x = \frac{4}{5}$ **B.** $x = -\frac{4}{5}$ **C.** $y = \frac{4}{5}$
   D. $y = -\frac{4}{5}$ **E.** none of the above

3. Between what two consecutive integers is $\sqrt{52}$?
   A. 5 and 6 **B.** 6 and 7 **C.** 7 and 8
   D. 8 and 9 **E.** 9 and 10

4. How many solutions are there for the system $y = |x - 3|$ and $6y - x = 24$?
   A. 0 **B.** 1 **C.** 2 **D.** 3 **E.** 4

5. What are the solutions of the equation $x^2 - 6x - 11 = 0$?
   A. -8 and 3 **B.** $3 \pm 4\sqrt{5}$ **C.** 8 and -3
   D. $3 \pm 2\sqrt{5}$ **E.** none of the above

6. What is the solution of the system $-2x - 3y = -13$ and $3x + 2y = 0$?
   A. $(-2, 3)$ **B.** $(-2, -3)$ **C.** $(2, 3)$
   D. $(2, -3)$ **E.** none of the above

7. What is the maximum value of y in $y = -3x^2 - 6x - 1$?
   A. 2 **B.** -2 **C.** 1 **D.** -1 **E.** 0

8. If a line passes through $(5, 2)$ and $(-7, -1)$, its slope is between which two numbers?
   A. 0 and 1 **B.** 1 and 100
   C. -1 and -100 **D.** 0 and -1
   E. Cannot be determined from the information given.

9. What is the value of the discriminant of $0 = 3x^2 - 4x - 3$?
   A. -20 **B.** 52 **C.** 25
   D. 4 **E.** none of the above

10. If $x^2 + 4x + 4 = 49$, then
    I. $x = 5$ **II.** $x = -9$
    III. $x = \sqrt{47}$ **IV.** $x = -\sqrt{47}$
    A. I only **B.** II only **C.** III and IV
    D. I and II **E.** III only

Compare the boxed quantity in Column A with the boxed quantity in Column B. Choose the best answer.

A. The quantity in Column A is greater.
B. The quantity in Column B is greater.
C. The two quantities are equal.
D. The relationship cannot be determined on the basis of the information supplied.

	Column A	Column B
	Use $\begin{bmatrix} 6 & 1 \\ 0 & x \end{bmatrix} + \begin{bmatrix} 1 & y \\ -5 & 3 \end{bmatrix} = \begin{bmatrix} 7 & 9 \\ -5 & 6 \end{bmatrix}$.	
11.	x	y
	Use $x + y = 5$ and $2y - x = 4$.	
12.	2	x

Find each answer.

13. Find the vertex and the axis of symmetry of the graph of the equation $y = 4x^2 - 3x$.

14. Ben leaves his home 20 mi west of Boston at 10:00 A.M., traveling west by bicycle at 15 mi/h. Esmira leaves Boston by car at 12:00 noon, driving west at 55 mi/h. At what time will she pass Ben?

15. Graph the inequality $|x - 2| \leq 9$ on a number line.

16. A baker can form 2 loaves of bread in 5 min. How many loaves can the baker form in an hour?

CHAPTER 8

Exponents and Exponential Functions

Relating to the Real World

What do money in a savings account, the population of the world, and radioactive waste all have in common? You can use exponential functions to describe them and predict the future. Exponential relationships are widely used by scientists, business people, and even politicians trying to predict budget surpluses and deficits.

Lessons	8-1	8-2	8-3	8-4	8-5
	Exploring Exponential Functions	*Exponential Growth*	*Exponential Decay*	*Zero and Negative Exponents*	*Scientific Notation*

A Multiplication Property of Exponents
8-6

More Multiplication Properties of Exponents
8-7

Division Properties of Exponents
8-8

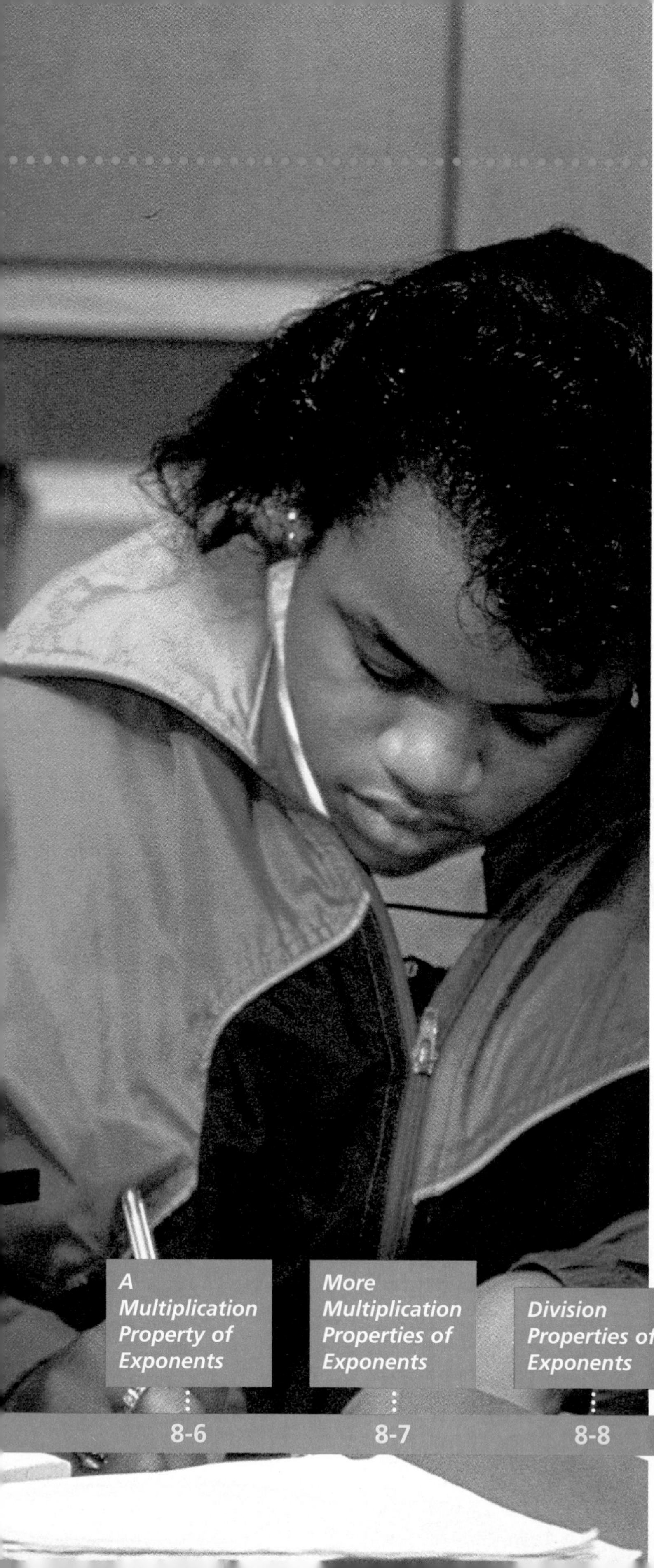

CHAPTER PROJECT

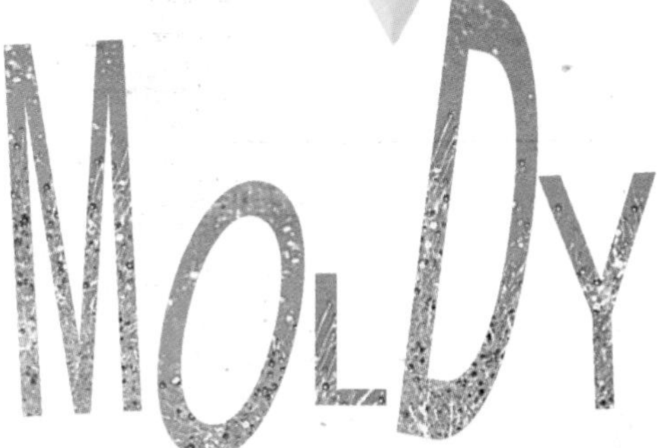

MOLDY OLDIES

You take a piece of bread from the bread bag and find that there is green mold on it. The bread was fine two days ago! You open the refrigerator to look for a snack only to see that the cheese is covered with a fuzzy white mold. So, just how fast does mold grow, anyway?

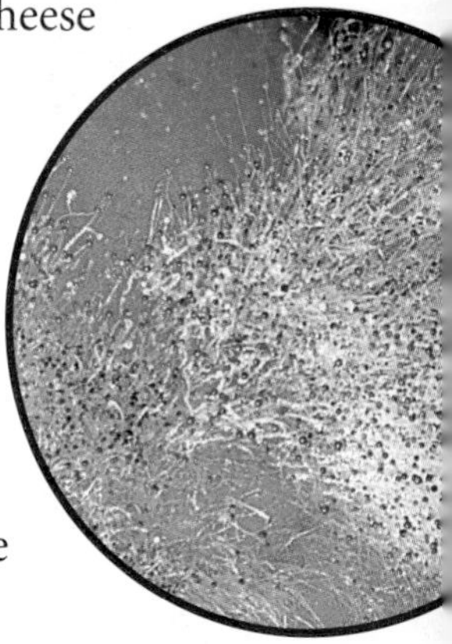

As you work through the chapter, you will grow your own mold. You will gather data, create graphs, and make predictions. As part of your research, you will plan and complete an experiment to monitor growth.

To help you complete the project:

- **p. 366** *Find Out by Doing*
- **p. 372** *Find Out by Recording*
- **p. 389** *Find Out by Graphing*
- **p. 395** *Find Out by Analyzing*
- **p. 400** *Find Out by Interpreting*
- **p. 406** *Finishing the Project*

8-1 Exploring Exponential Functions

What You'll Learn

- Examining patterns in exponential functions

...And Why

To model different patterns

What You'll Need

- notebook paper
- calculator

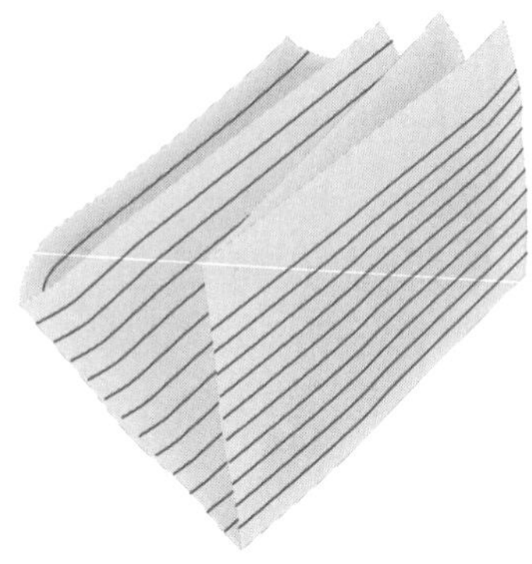

WORK TOGETHER

Work with a partner.

1. Fold a sheet of notebook paper in half. Notice that the fold line divides the paper into 2 rectangles.
2. Fold the paper in half again. Now how many rectangles are there?
3. Continue folding the paper in half until you cannot make another fold. Keep track of your results in a table like the one at the right.
4. *Patterns* What pattern do you notice in the number of rectangles as the number of folds increases? Explain.
5. Suppose you could continue to fold the paper. Extend your table to include 10 folds. How many rectangles would there be?

Number of Folds	Number of Rectangles
0	1
1	2
2	4
3	■
4	■
5	■

THINK AND DISCUSS

Exploring Exponential Patterns

The pattern that you explored in the Work Together involves repeated multiplication by 2. The table below uses exponents to show the pattern.

QUICK REVIEW

base ⟶ b^x ⟵ exponent

Number of Folds	Number of Rectangles	Pattern	Written with Exponents
0	1		
1	2	$= 2$	$= 2^1$
2	4	$= 2 \cdot 2$	$= 2^2$
3	8	$= 2 \cdot 2 \cdot 2$	$= 2^3$
4	16	$= 2 \cdot 2 \cdot 2 \cdot 2$	$= 2^4$
5	32	$= 2 \cdot 2 \cdot 2 \cdot 2 \cdot 2$	$= 2^5$

6. Use an exponent to write each number.
   a. $3 \cdot 3 \cdot 3 \cdot 3$ **b.** $(-2)(-2)(-2)$ **c.** 125

Example 1 Relating to the Real World 

Biology Suppose there are 20 rabbits on an island and that the rabbit population can triple every half-year. How many rabbits would there be after 2 years?

Time	Number of Rabbits
Initial	20
$\frac{1}{2}$ year	$20 \cdot 3 = 60$
1 year	$60 \cdot 3 = 180$
$1\frac{1}{2}$ years	$180 \cdot 3 = 540$
2 years	$540 \cdot 3 = 1620$

Use the problem-solving strategy *Make a Table*.

To triple the amount, multiply the previous half-year's total by 3.

After two years, there would be 1620 rabbits.

Rabbits were brought from Europe to Australia around 1860. The number of rabbits increased exponentially, and by 1870 there were millions of rabbits.

Evaluating Exponential Functions

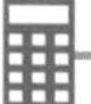

CALCULATOR HINT

To evaluate 2^n for $n = 10$, press 2 y^x 10 = or press 2 ^ 10 ENTER .

You can write the pattern you found in the Work Together as a function with a variable as an exponent. To find the number of rectangles r created by n folds, use the function $r = 2^n$. You read the expression 2^n as "2 to the nth power." The number of rectangles increases *exponentially* as the paper-folding continues.

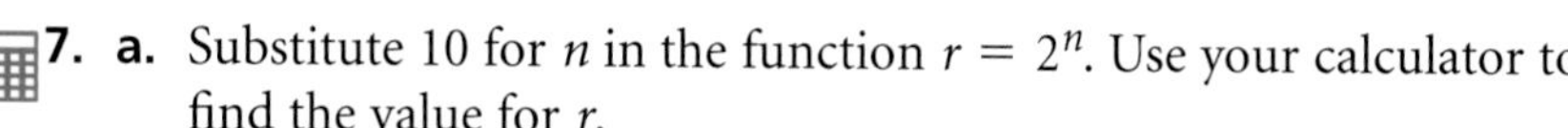

7. a. Substitute 10 for n in the function $r = 2^n$. Use your calculator to find the value for r.

b. How does your answer compare to your answer to Question 5?

The function $r = 2^n$ is an *exponential function.*

Exponential Function

For all numbers a and for $b > 0$ and $b \neq 1$, the function $y = a \cdot b^x$ is an **exponential function.**

Examples: $y = 0.5 \cdot 2^x$; $f(x) = -2 \cdot 0.5^x$

QUICK REVIEW

The order of operations is parentheses, exponents, multiplication and division, addition and subtraction.

Example 2

Evaluate each exponential function.

a. $y = 5^x$ for $x = 2, 3, 4$

x	$y = 5^x$	y
2	$5^2 = 25$	25
3	$5^3 = 125$	125
4	$5^4 = 625$	625

b. $t(n) = 4(3^n)$ for the domain $\{3, 6\}$

n	$t(n) = 4(3^n)$	$t(n)$
3	$4 \cdot 3^3 = 4 \cdot 27 = 108$	108
6	$4 \cdot 3^6 = 4 \cdot 729 = 2916$	2916

8. **Try This** Evaluate the functions $y = 6^x$ and $y = 3(2^x)$ for $x = 1, 2,$ and 3. Which function increases more quickly? Why?

Graphing Exponential Functions

The graphs of many exponential functions look alike.

Example 3 Relating to the Real World 

Technology Some photocopiers allow you to choose how large you want an image to be. The function $f(x) = 1.5^x$ models the increase in size of a picture being copied over and over at 150%. Graph the function.

Make a table of values.

x	$f(x) = 1.5^x$	$f(x)$
1	$1.5^1 = 1.5$	1.5
2	$1.5^2 = 2.25$	2.25
3	$1.5^3 = 3.375 \approx 3.4$	3.4
4	$1.5^4 = 5.0625 \approx 5.1$	5.1
5	$1.5^5 = 7.59375 \approx 7.6$	7.6

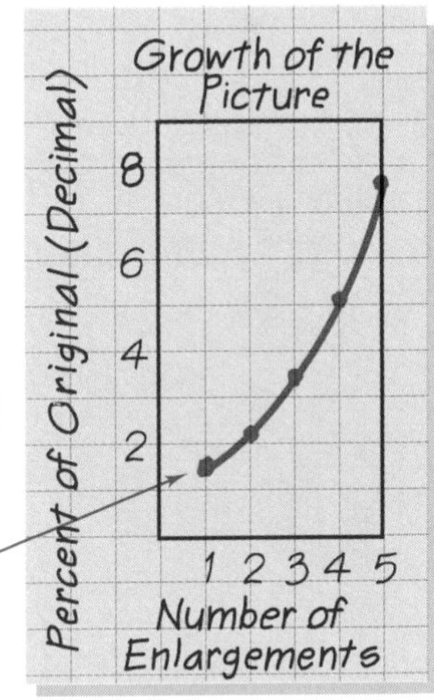

Plot the points. Connect the points with a smooth curve.

GRAPHING CALCULATOR HINT

These range values will give you a clear picture of $y = 2^x$.

Xmin = 0 Ymin = 0
Xmax = 10 Ymax = 100
Xscl = 1 Yscl = 10

9. **a. Graphing Calculator** Use your graphing calculator to graph the function $y = 2^x$.
   b. How is the graph of $y = 2^x$ similar to the graph of $f(x) = 1.5^x$? How is it different?

Exercises ON YOUR OWN

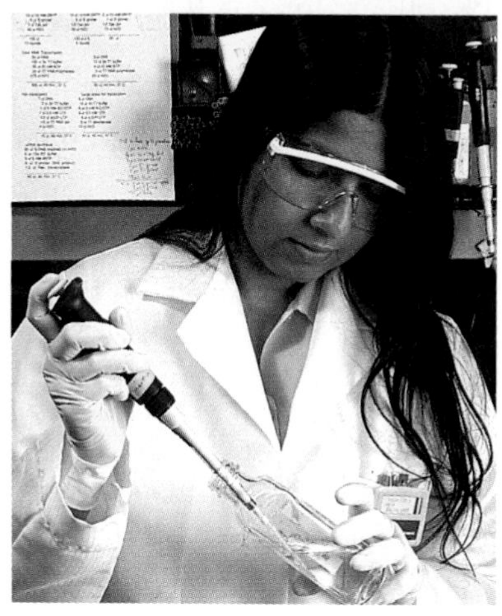

1. **Patterns** Bacteria in a laboratory culture can double in number every 20 min. Suppose a culture starts with 75 cells. Copy, complete, and extend the table to find when there will be more than 30,000 bacteria cells.

Time	Number of 20-min Time Periods	Pattern	Number of Bacteria Cells
Initial	0	75	75
20 min	1	$75 \cdot 2$	$75 \cdot 2^{■} = 150$
40 min	■	$75 \cdot 2 \cdot 2$	$75 \cdot 2^{■} = 300$
■	■	■	$75 \cdot 2^{■} = 600$
■	■	■	$75 \cdot 2^{■} =$ ■

2. **Finance** An investment of $10,000 doubles in value every 13 years. How much is the investment worth after 52 years? after 65 years?

Which function is greater at the given value?

3. $y = 5^x$ and $y = x^5$ at $x = 5$
4. $f = 10 \cdot 2^t$ and $f = 200 \cdot t^2$ at $t = 7$
5. $f(x) = 2^x$ and $f(x) = 100x^2$ at $x = 10$
6. $y = 3^x$ and $y = x^3$ at $x = 4$

Evaluate each function for the domain {1, 2, 3, 4, 5}. Is the function *increasing, decreasing,* or *neither?*

7. $f(x) = 4^x$
8. $c = a^3$
9. $h(x) = 1^x$
10. $f(x) = 5 \cdot 4^x$
11. $y = 0.5^x$
12. $y = \left(\frac{2}{3}\right)^x$
13. $g(x) = 4 \cdot 10^x$
14. $d = 100 \cdot 0.3^t$
15. **Standardized Test Prep** A population of 6000 doubles in size every 10 years. Which equation relates the size of the population y to the number of 10-year periods x?
    A. $y = 6000 \cdot 10^x$ **B.** $y = 6000 \cdot 2^x$ **C.** $y = 10 \cdot 2^x$ **D.** $y = 2 \cdot 10^x$ **E.** $y = 2 \cdot 6000^x$
16. **Graphing Calculator** Graph the functions $y = x^2$ and $y = 2^x$ on the same set of axes.
    a. What happens to the graphs between $x = 1$ and $x = 3$?
    b. **Critical Thinking** How do you think the graph of $y = 6^x$ would compare to the graphs of $y = x^2$ and $y = 2^x$?
17. **Writing** **Analyze** the range for the function $f(x) = 500 \cdot 1^x$ using the domain {1, 2, 3, 4, 5}. Explain why the restriction $b \neq 1$ is included in the definition of an exponential function.
18. **Ecology** In 50 days, a water hyacinth can generate 1000 offspring (the number of plants is multiplied by 1000). How many hyacinth plants could there be after 150 days?

Evaluate each expression.

19. $50 \cdot x^5$ for $x = 0.5$

20. $50{,}000 \cdot m^3$ for $m = 1.1$

21. $0.0125 \cdot c^4$ for $c = 2$

22. **Open-ended** Select one of the exponential functions from this lesson.
   a. What number is multiplied repeatedly in your example?
   b. As the exponent increases, tell whether the outputs of your function increase, decrease, or do neither.

23. Match each table with the function that models the data.

Table I

x	y
1	3
2	6
3	9
4	12

Table II

x	y
1	3
2	9
3	27
4	81

Table III

x	y
1	1
2	8
3	27
4	64

Functions:
A. $y = 3x$
B. $y = x^3$
C. $y = 3^x$

24. **Critical Thinking** Why don't two 150% enlargements on a photocopier produce the same size picture as one 300% enlargement?

25. **Patterns** The base in the function $y = (-2)^x$ is a negative number.
   a. Make a table of values for the domain $\{1, 2, 3, 4, 5, 6\}$.
   b. What pattern do you see in the outputs?
   c. **Critical Thinking** Is $y = (-2)^x$ an exponential function? **Justify** your answer.

Graph each function.

26. $y = 3^x$

27. $y = 3\left(\frac{3}{2}\right)^x$

28. $y = 1.5^x$

29. $y = \frac{1}{4} \cdot 2^x$

30. $y = 0.1 \cdot 2^x$

31. $y = 10^x$

Chapter Project *Find Out by Doing*

Gather the materials for your project: $\frac{1}{16}$ in. or 1 mm graph paper, a packet of unflavored gelatin, a flat dish or plate, a small piece of unprocessed cheese, and plastic wrap.

- Decide where you will keep your dish. A warm, humid place is best for growing mold.
- Cut the graph paper to cover the bottom of the dish. Follow the directions on the gelatin packet. Cover the graph paper with about $\frac{1}{8}$ in. of gelatin. Add the cheese to the gelatin. Leave the dish uncovered overnight; then cover tightly with the plastic wrap.

Exercises MIXED REVIEW

Solve each equation.

32. $5(g - 1) = \frac{1}{2}$

33. $t^2 + 3t - 4 = 0$

34. $|m - 7| = 9$

35. $x^2 - 5x + 6 = 0$

36. **Books** The smallest book in the Library of Congress is *Old King Cole.* Each square page has area $\frac{1}{25}$ in.^{2}. How wide is one page?

Getting Ready for Lesson 8-2

Find the range of each function for the domain $\{1, 2, 3, 4, 5\}$.

37. $y = 2^x$

38. $y = 4 \cdot 2^x$

39. $y = 0.5 \cdot 2^x$

40. $y = \frac{3}{2} \cdot 2^x$

41. $y = 3 \cdot 2^x$

42. How are the functions in Exercises 37–41 alike? How are they different?

Connections: Savings. . . and more

8-2 Exponential Growth

What You'll Learn

- Modeling exponential growth
- Calculating compound interest

...And Why

To solve problems involving medical costs and finance

What You'll Need

- calculator

QUICK REVIEW

A 10% increase in an amount means you have 110% of the original amount. To find 110%, multiply by 1.1.

Time	Job A	Job B
Start	$5.00	$4.80
6 mo	■	■
1 yr	■	■

WORK TOGETHER

Jobs Suppose you are offered a choice of two jobs. Job A has a starting wage of $5.00/h, with a $.50 raise every 6 months. Job B starts at $4.80/h, with a 10% raise every 6 months. Work with a partner.

1. How do you find the new wage after each raise for Job A?
2. In Job B, each new wage is 110% of the previous wage. How do you find each new wage for Job B?
3. Organize the wages for each job in a table like the one at the left. Show wages from the start of the job through the raise at three years. Round each wage to the nearest cent.
4. a. *Patterns* Which wage pattern involves repeated multiplication?
   b. Which wage pattern results in a linear function?
5. Which graph represents the wages for Job A? for Job B?
6. When would you prefer to have Job A? Job B? Explain.

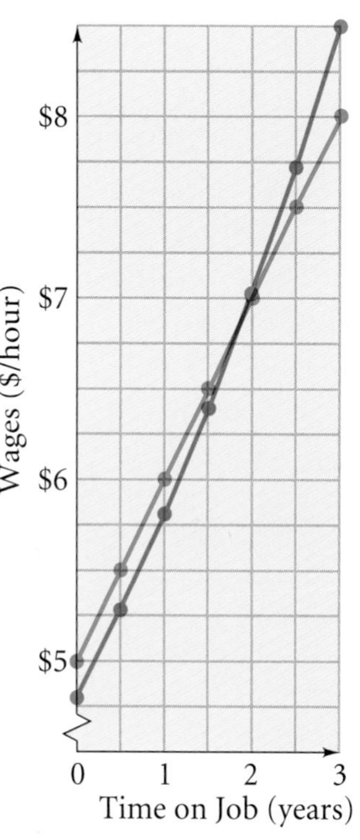

THINK AND DISCUSS

Modeling Exponential Growth

You can use an exponential function to show how the wages for Job B grow.

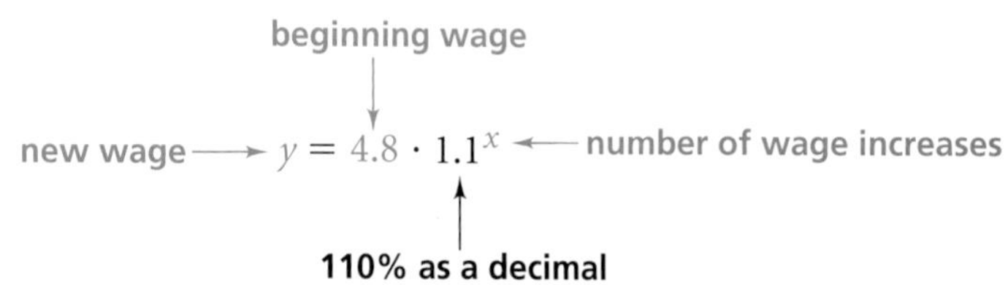

Because multiplying over and over by 1.1 causes the wage to increase, this kind of exponential function is an example of *exponential growth.*

Exponential Growth

For $a > 0$ and $b > 1$, the function $y = a \cdot b^x$ models **exponential growth.**

$y = a \cdot b^x$ — starting amount: a; number of increases: x; the base, called the **growth factor**: b

Example: $y = 1000 \cdot 2^x$

When you use exponential functions to model real-world situations, you must identify the initial amount a and the growth factor b. To show growth, b must be greater than 1.

7. Suppose the population of a city is 50,000 and is growing 3% each year.
   a. The initial amount a is ■.
   b. The growth factor b is 100% + 3%, which is 1 + ■ = ■.
   c. To find the population after one year, you multiply ■ · 1.03.
   d. Complete the equation to find the population after x years.
   $$y = ■ \cdot ■^{■}$$
   e. Use your equation to find the population after 25 years.

Example 1 ***Relating to the Real World***

Medical Care Since 1985, the daily cost of patient care in community hospitals in the United States has increased about 8.6% per year. In 1985, hospital costs were an average of \$460 per day.

a. Write an equation to model the cost of hospital care.
b. Use your equation to find the approximate cost per day in 1995.

a. Use an exponential function to model repeated percent increases.

Relate $y = a \cdot b^x$

Define x = the number of years since 1985
y = the cost of hospital care at various times
b = 100% plus 8.6% of the cost = 108.6% = 1.086
a = initial cost in 1985 = \$460

Write $y = 460 \cdot 1.086^x$ ← Substitute values for the initial amount a and the growth factor b.

b. 1995 is 10 years after 1985, so solve the equation for $x = 10$.

$y = 460 \cdot 1.086^{10}$ ← Substitute.
$= 1049.677974$

The average cost per day in 1995 was about \$1050.

CALCULATOR HINT

To evaluate $460 \cdot 1.086^{10}$ press 460 [×] 1.086 [^] 10 [ENTER].

8. **Try This** **Predict** the cost per day for the year 2000.

PROBLEM SOLVING HINT

For Questions 9 and 10, use the *Guess and Test* strategy.

9. Find the first year in which the predicted cost per day will be greater than \$2000.

10. The cost per day more than doubled between 1985 and 1995. Using the function from Example 1, about how long will it take to double the 1995 cost per day?

Finding Compound Interest

QUICK REVIEW

Principal is the amount of money you put in a bank account. *Interest* is the amount the bank pays you for letting it use your money.

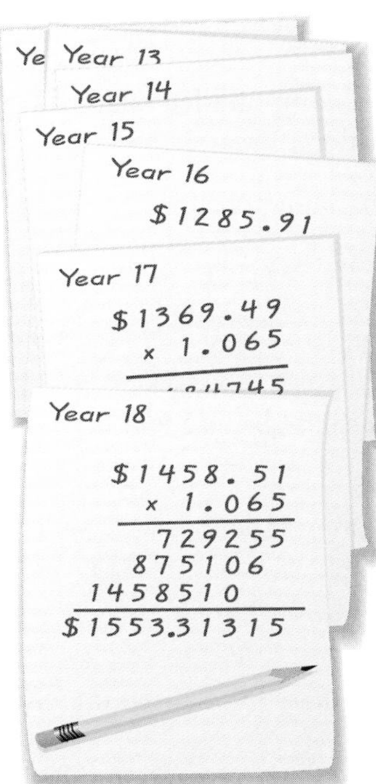

When a bank pays interest on both the principal *and* the interest an account has already earned, the bank is paying **compound interest.** An **interest period** is the length of time over which interest is calculated. Compound interest is an exponential growth situation.

Example 2 **Relating to the Real World** 

Savings Suppose your parents deposited \$500 in an account paying 6.5% interest, compounded annually (once a year), when you were born. Find the account balance after 18 years.

Relate $y = a \cdot b^x$ ← Use an exponential function.

Define $x =$ the number of interest periods

$y =$ the balance at various times

$a = 500$ ← initial deposit

$b = 1.065$ ← 100% + 6.5% = 106.5% = 1.065

Write $y = 500 \cdot 1.065^x$

$= 500 \cdot 1.065^{18}$ ← Once a year for 18 years is 18 interest periods. Substitute 18 for x.

$= 1553.32719$

The balance after 18 years will be \$1553.33.

11. **Try This** Suppose the interest rate on the account was 8%. How much would be in the account after 18 years?

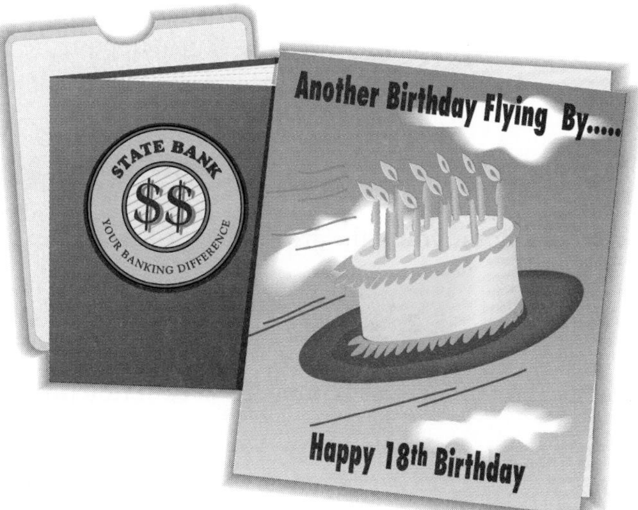

Banks sometimes pay compound interest more than once a year. When they use shorter interest periods, the interest rate for each period is also reduced.

Annual Interest Rate of 8%

Compounded	Periods per Year	Rate per Period
annually	1	8% every year
semi-annually	2	$\frac{8\%}{2}$ = 4% every 6 months
quarterly	4	$\frac{8\%}{4}$ = 2% every 3 months
monthly	12	$\frac{8\%}{12}$ = $0.\overline{6}$% every month

12. In an account that pays 6.5% interest, what is the interest rate if the interest is compounded quarterly? monthly?

Example 3

Suppose the account in Example 2 paid interest compounded quarterly instead of annually. Find the account balance after 18 years.

Relate $y = a \cdot b^x$ ← Use an exponential function.

Define x = the number of interest periods (quarters)
y = the balance at various times
$a = 500$ ← initial deposit
$b = 1 + \frac{0.065}{4}$ ← There are 4 interest periods in 1 year, so divide the interest into four parts.
$= 1.01625$

Write $y = 500 \cdot 1.01625^x$
$= 500 \cdot 1.01625^{72}$ ← 18 • 4 = 72 interest periods in 18 years
$= 1595.916716$ ← Use a calculator.

The balance after 18 years will be $1595.92.

13. a. How many interest periods per year are there for an account with interest compounded daily?

b. Try This Suppose the account above paid interest compounded daily. How much money would be in the account after 18 years?

Exercises ON YOUR OWN

Identify the initial amount a and the growth factor b in each exponential function.

1. $g(x) = 20 \cdot 2^x$ **2.** $y = 200 \cdot 1.0875^x$ **3.** $y = 10{,}000 \cdot 1.01^x$ **4.** $f(t) = 1.5^t$

What repeated percent of increase is modeled in each function?

5. $r = 70 \cdot 1.5^n$ **6.** $f(t) = 30 \cdot 1.095^t$ **7.** $y = 1000 \cdot 1.04^x$ **8.** $y = 2^x$

Write the growth factor used to model each percent of increase in an exponential function.

9. 4% **10.** 5% **11.** 3.7% **12.** 8.75% **13.** 0.5% **14.** 15%

Write an exponential function to model each situation. Tell what each variable you use represents.

15. A population of 130,000 grows 1% per year

16. A price of $50 increases 6% each year

17. A deposit of $3000 earns 5% annual interest compounded monthly.

18. Writing Would you rather have $500 in an account paying 6% interest compounded quarterly or $750 in an account paying 5.5% compounded annually? **Summarize** your reasoning.

19. Education The function $y = 355 \cdot 1.08^x$ models the average annual cost y (in dollars) for tuition and fees at public two-year colleges. The variable x represents the number of years since 1980.

a. What was the average annual cost in 1980?

b. What is the average percent increase in the annual cost?

c. Find the average annual cost for 1990.

d. Open-ended **Predict** the average annual cost for the year you plan to graduate from high school.

20. History The Dutch bought Manhattan Island in 1626 for $24 worth of merchandise. Suppose the $24 had been invested in 1626 in an account paying 4.5% interest compounded annually. Find the balance today.

21. Standardized Test Prep An investment of $100 earns 5% interest compounded annually. Which expression represents the value of the investment after 10 years?

A. $10 \cdot 100^5$ **B.** $100 \cdot 0.05^{10}$ **C.** $100 \cdot 10^{0.05}$

D. $10 \cdot 100^{1.05}$ **E.** $100 \cdot 1.05^{10}$

22. a. Math in the Media Write an equation to model the sales of workstation computers since 1987.

b. Use your model to find the total sales in 1995.

Workstations Replace Supercomputers

Workstations–sophisticated computers that sit on a desktop–are replacing larger mainframe computers in industry. Since 1987, sales of workstation computers in industry have increased about 30% per year. In 1987, sales totaled about $3 billion.

Graph the function represented in each table. Then tell whether the table represents a *linear function* or an *exponential function*.

23.

x	y
1	20
2	40
3	60
4	80

24.

x	y
1	3
2	9
3	27
4	81

25.

x	y
1	6
2	12
3	24
4	48

26.

x	y
1	3
2	9
3	15
4	21

Tell whether each graph is a *linear function*, an *exponential function*, or *neither*. Justify your reasoning.

27. 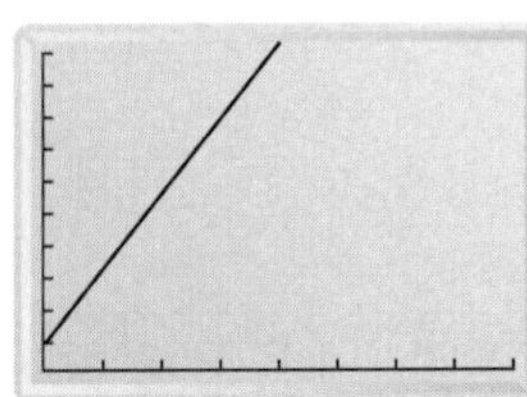

28. 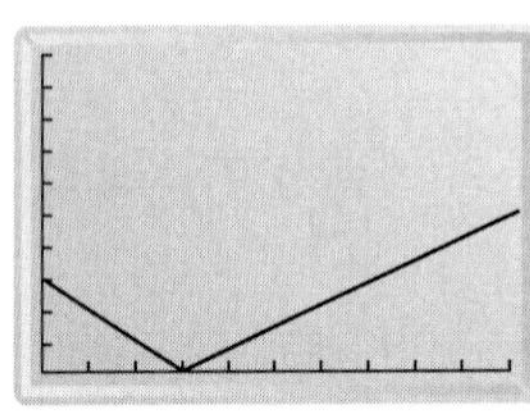

29. 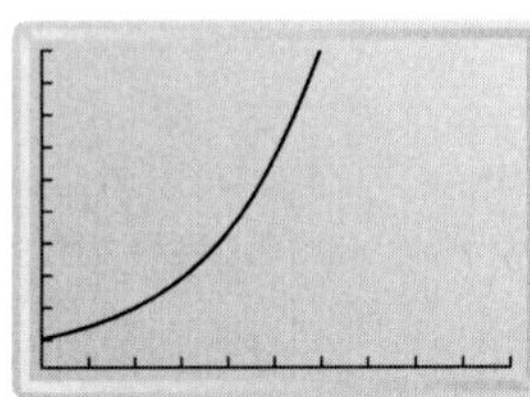

30. Statistics Since 1970, the population of Virginia has grown at an average annual rate of about 1.015%. In 1970, the population was about 4,651,000.

a. Graphing Calculator Write and graph a function to model population growth in Virginia since 1970.

b. Estimate the population of Virginia in 1980 and 1990.

c. **Predict** the population of Virginia in the years 2000 and 2025.

Write an exponential function to model each situation. Find each amount after the specified time.

31. \$20,000 principal
3.5% compounded
quarterly10 years

32. \$30 principal
4.5% compounded daily
2 years

33. \$2400 principal
7% compounded annually
10 years

34. \$2400 principal
7% compounded monthly
10 years

Chapter Project ***Find Out by Recording***

Count the number of graph paper squares covered by mold once a day for 10 days. Record the mold growth. (Don't worry if you don't see any mold for the first few days.)

Exercises MIXED REVIEW

Find the vertex of each parabola. Identify it as a *maximum* or a *minimum*.

35. $y = 3x^2 + 2x - 8$

36. $y = \frac{1}{2}x^2 - 5x + 1$

37. $y = 4x^2 - 11$

38. a. History The boardwalk in Atlantic City was 1 mi long and 12 ft wide when it was built in 1870. What was its area in square feet?

b. In 1995, the boardwalk was 4.5 mi long and up to 60 ft wide. What could be its maximum area in square feet?

c. About how many times larger was the boardwalk in 1995 than in 1870?

Getting Ready for Lesson 8-3

Simplify each expression.

39. $\left(\frac{1}{2}\right)^2$

40. 0.5^4

41. $\left(\frac{3}{4}\right)^1$

42. 0.9^3

43. 0.98^2

44. $\left(\frac{5}{6}\right)^2$

What You'll Learn

- Modeling exponential decay
- Using half-life models

...And Why

To solve problems involving population and radioactive decay

What You'll Need

- calculator

8-3 Exponential Decay

THINK AND DISCUSS

In Lesson 8-2 you used the exponential function $y = a \cdot b^x$ to model growth. You can also use it to model decay. The difference between growth and decay is the value of b, the base. With growth, b is greater than 1. With decay, b is between 0 and 1 and is called the **decay factor.**

Exponential Decay

For $a > 0$ and $0 < b < 1$, the function $y = a \cdot b^x$ models **exponential decay.**

Example: $y = 5 \cdot \left(\frac{1}{2}\right)^x$

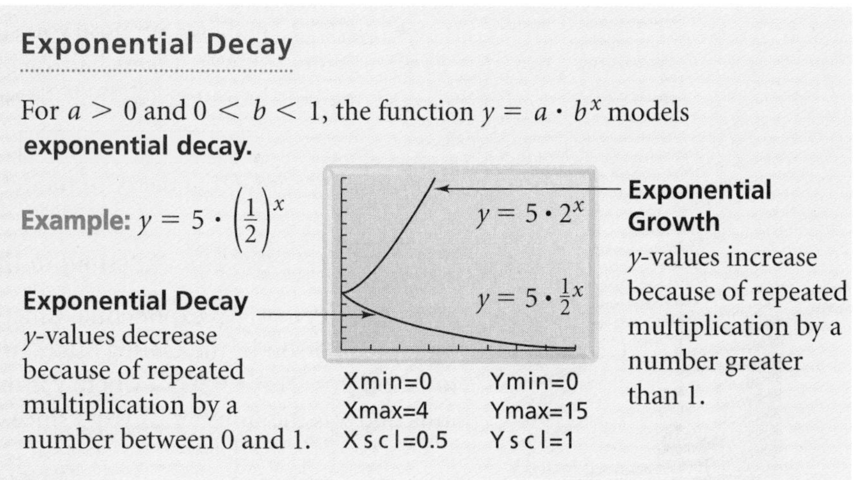

$y = 5 \cdot 2^x$
$y = 5 \cdot \frac{1}{2}^x$
Exponential Decay
y-values decrease because of repeated multiplication by a number between 0 and 1.
Exponential Growth
y-values increase because of repeated multiplication by a number greater than 1.
Xmin=0
Xmax=4
Xscl=0.5
Ymin=0
Ymax=15
Yscl=1

You can use an exponential function to model the decay of a radioactive substance.

Who? **Marie Curie (1867–1934) was born in Poland. She received Nobel Prizes in physics and chemistry for her pioneering work with radioactive elements. The *curie* is named for Marie Curie.**

Example 1 Relating to the Real World

Medicine To treat some forms of cancer, doctors use radioactive iodine. Use the graph to find how much iodine-131 is left in a patient eight days after the patient receives a dose of 20 mCi (millicuries).

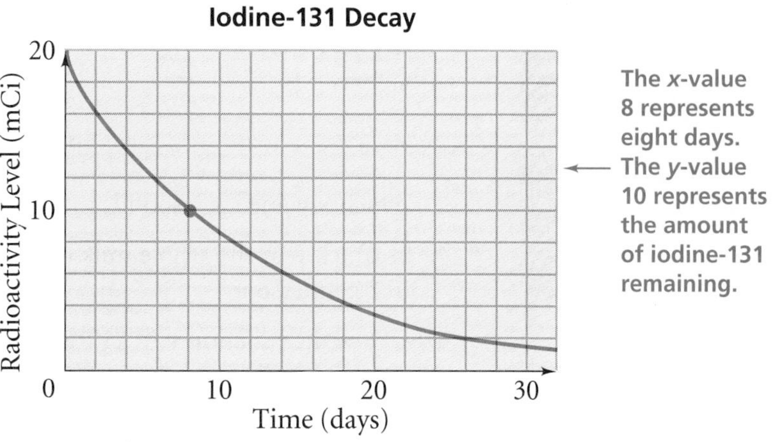

Iodine-131 Decay
Radioactivity Level (mCi)
Time (days)
0
10
20
30
10
20
The x-value 8 represents eight days. The y-value 10 represents the amount of iodine-131 remaining.

After eight days, there are 10 mCi of iodine-131 left.

1. **Try This** Use the graph in Example 1 to find the amount of iodine-131 left after 24 days.

The *half-life* of a radioactive substance is the length of time it takes for one half of the substance to decay.

2. **a.** How long does it take for half of the 20 mCi dose in Example 1 to decay? How much is left?
   b. Use your answer to part (a). How long does it take for half of that amount to decay? How much is left?
   c. What is the half-life of iodine-131?
   d. How many half-lives of iodine-131 occur in 32 days?
   e. **Critical Thinking** Suppose you start with a 50 mCi sample of iodine-131. What is its half-life? How much iodine-131 is left after one half-life? after two half-lives?

You can use exponential decay to model other real-world situations.

Example 2 **Relating to the Real World** 

Consumer Trends An exponential function models the amount of whole milk each person in the United States drinks in a year. Graph the function $y = 21.5 \cdot 0.955^x$, where y is the number of gallons of whole milk and x is the number of years since 1975.

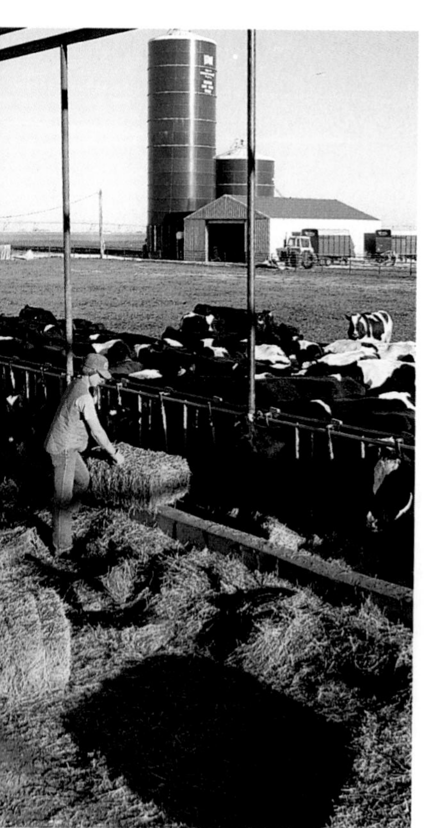

Make a table of values.

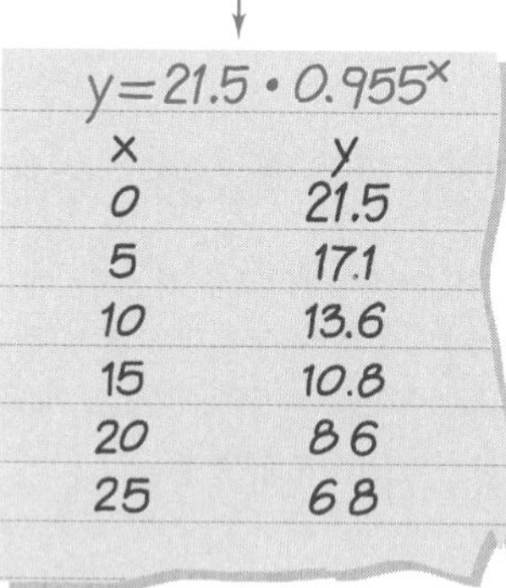

$y = 21.5 \cdot 0.955^x$

x	y
0	21.5
5	17.1
10	13.6
15	10.8
20	8 6
25	6 8

Graph the points. Draw a smooth curve through the points.

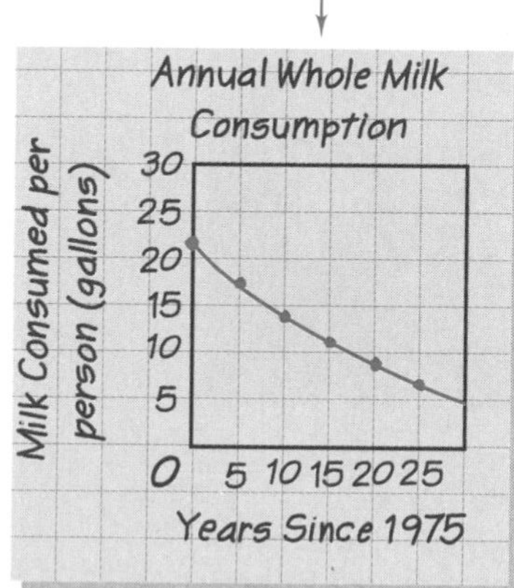

3. Which x-value corresponds to the year 1995?

4. In which year did whole milk consumption fall to about 10.8 gal/person?

5. **a.** Use the function $y = 21.5 \cdot 0.955^x$ and your calculator to **predict** whole milk consumption for the year 2010.
   b. **Open-ended** Use the function to **predict** whole milk consumption 10 years from now.

Example 3

Consumer Trends Use the equation $y = 21.5 \cdot 0.955^x$ to find the annual percent of decrease in whole milk consumption in the United States.

$0.955 = 95.5\%$ ← Change the decay factor to a percent.

$100\% - 95.5\% = 4.5\%$ ← Subtract.

Whole milk consumption is decreasing by 4.5% per year.

6. **Try This** What percent of decrease does each decay factor model?
   a. 0.75 **b.** 0.4 **c.** 0.135 **d.** 0.0074

7. By what number would you multiply 15 to decrease it
   a. by 6%? **b.** by 12%? **c.** by 3.5%? **d.** by 53.9%?

8. Suppose an initial population of 10,000 people decreases by 2.4% each year. Write an exponential function in the form $y = \blacksquare \cdot \blacksquare^x$ to model the population y after x years have passed.

Exercises ON YOUR OWN

Identify each function as *exponential growth* or *exponential decay*.

1. $y = 0.68 \cdot 2^x$ **2.** $y = 2 \cdot 0.68^x$ **3.** $y = 68 \cdot 2^x$ **4.** $y = 68 \cdot 0.2^x$

Identify the decay factor in each function.

5. $y = 5 \cdot 0.5^x$ **6.** $f(x) = 10 \cdot 0.1^x$ **7.** $g(x) = 100 \cdot \left(\frac{2}{3}\right)^x$ **8.** $y = 0.1 \cdot 0.9^x$

Find the percent of decrease for each function.

9. $r = 70 \cdot 0.9^n$ **10.** $f(t) = 45 \cdot 0.998^t$ **11.** $r = 50 \cdot \left(\frac{1}{2}\right)^n$ **12.** $y = 1000 \cdot 0.75^x$

Use the graph to estimate the half-life of each radioactive substance.

13.

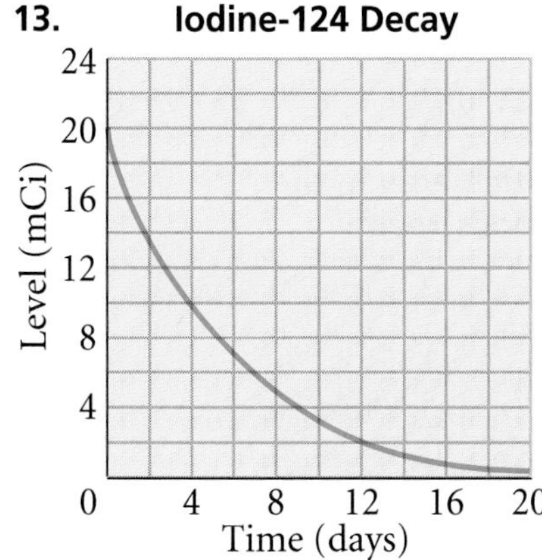

14.

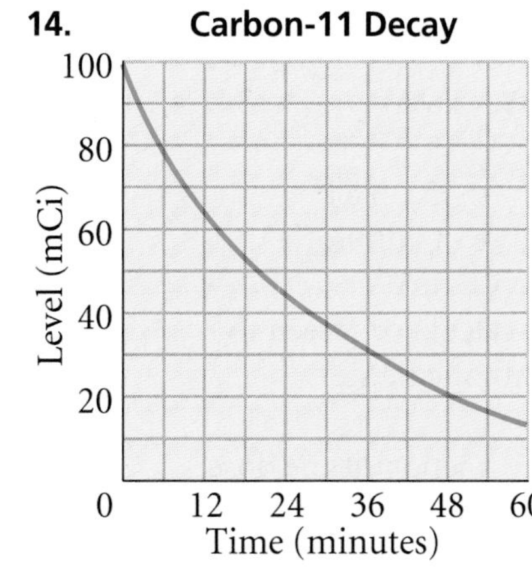

15.

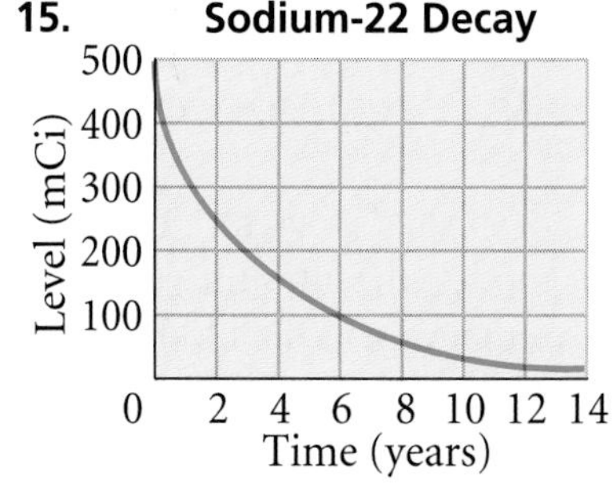

Choose **Use a graphing calculator or make a table of values to graph each function. Label each graph as *exponential growth* or *exponential decay.***

16. $f(x) = 100 \cdot 0.9^x$

17. $s = 64 \cdot \left(\frac{1}{2}\right)^n$

18. $g = 8 \cdot 1.5^x$

19. $y = 3.5 \cdot 0.01^x$

20. $y = 2 \cdot 10^x$

21. $g(x) = \left(\frac{1}{10}\right) \cdot 0.1^x$

22. $f = 10 \cdot 0.1^x$

23. $y = \frac{2}{5} \cdot \left(\frac{1}{2}\right)^x$

24. $y = 0.5 \cdot 2^x$

25. **Writing** Describe a situation that can be modeled by the equation $y = 100 \cdot 0.9^x$.

Write an exponential function to model each situation. Find each amount after the specified time.

26. 3,000,000 initial population
1.5% annual decrease
10 years

27. $900 purchase
20% loss in value each year
6 years

28. $10,000 investment
12.5% loss each year
7 years

29. **Statistics** In 1980, the population of Warren, Michigan, was about 161,000. Since then the population has decreased about 1% per year.

a. Write an equation to model the population of Warren since 1980.

b. **Estimation** Estimate the population of Warren in 1990.

c. Suppose the current trend continues. **Predict** the population of Warren in 2010.

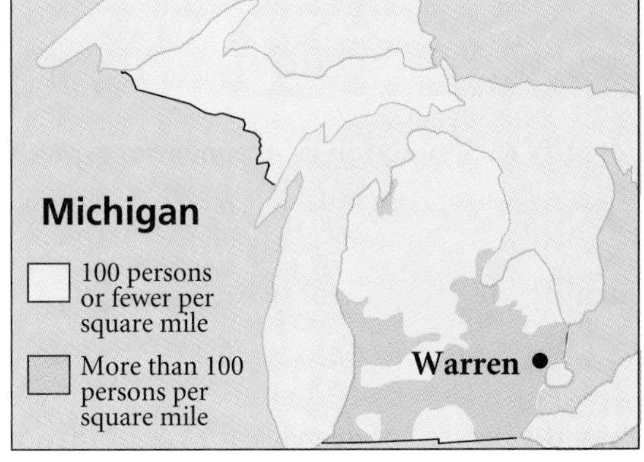

30. a. **Open-ended** Write two exponential decay functions, one with a base near 0 and one with a base near 1.

b. Find the range of each function using the domain {1, 2, 3, 4}.

c. Graph each function.

Calculate the decay factor for each percent of decrease.

31. 3%

32. 70%

33. 2.6%

34. 4.75%

35. 0.7%

36. 23.4%

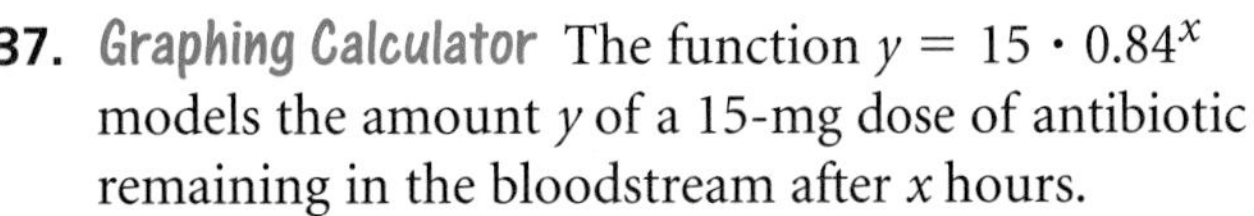

37. **Graphing Calculator** The function $y = 15 \cdot 0.84^x$ models the amount y of a 15-mg dose of antibiotic remaining in the bloodstream after x hours.

a. **Estimation** Study the graphing calculator screen to estimate the half-life of this antibiotic in the bloodstream.

b. Use your estimate to **predict** the fraction of the dose that will remain in the bloodstream after 8 hours.

c. **Verify** your prediction by using the function to find the amount of antibiotic remaining after 8 hours.

Antibiotic Decay in the Bloodstream

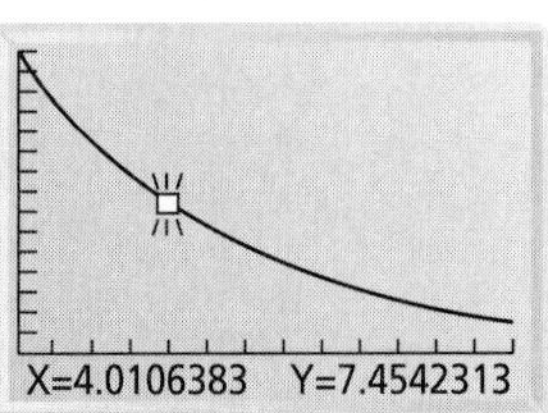

Xmin=0 Ymin=0
Xmax=13 Ymax=15

How many half-lives occur in each length of time?

38. 2 days (1 half-life = 8 h)

39. 300 years (1 half-life = 75 yr)

Exercises MIXED REVIEW

Solve.

40. $3 = |x - 7|$

41. $2 - x > 5$

42. $\frac{t}{3} - \frac{t}{6} = 15$

43. $j^2 + 3 = 12$

44. Biology A mouse's heart beats 600 times/min. The average mouse lives about 3 yr. About how many times does the average mouse's heart beat in its lifetime?

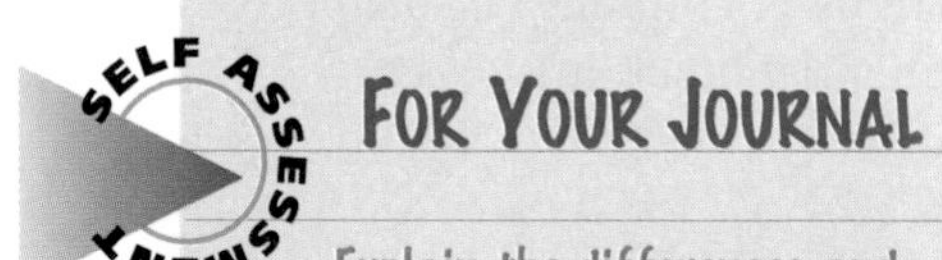

Explain the differences and similarities between exponential growth and exponential decay. Give an example of each.

Getting Ready for Lesson 8-4

Complete each expression.

45. $\frac{1}{2^2} = \frac{1}{\blacksquare}$

46. $\frac{8}{27} = \frac{2^{\blacksquare}}{3^{\blacksquare}}$

47. $\frac{2^2}{4^2} = \frac{\blacksquare}{\blacksquare} = \blacksquare$

Exercises CHECKPOINT

Write an exponential function to model each situation. Find each amount after the specified time.

1. \$65,000 initial market value
3.2% annual increase
15 years

2. 200,000 initial population
5% loss each year
20 years

3. \$300 initial value
doubles every 10 years
50 years

4. Standardized Test Prep From 1790 to 1860, the population of the United States grew slowly but steadily from 4 million. Which exponential function is the most likely model for the population p in the years after 1790?

A. $p = 4 \cdot 2.6^x$ **B.** $p = 4 \cdot 1.03^x$ **C.** $p = 4 \cdot 0.98^x$ **D.** $p = 4 \cdot 3^x$ **E.** $p = 0.98 \cdot 4^x$

Graph each function. Label each graph as *exponential growth* or *exponential decay.*

5. $y = \left(\frac{9}{10}\right) \cdot 2^x$

6. $f(x) = 5 \cdot 0.5^x$

7. $y = 2 \cdot \left(\frac{3}{2}\right)^x$

8. Open-ended Suppose you have \$1000 to deposit into a savings account for your education. One account pays 6.7% compounded annually. Another account pays 5% compounded monthly.

a. Which account would you choose? Consider the length of time you would leave the money in the account. **Summarize** your reasoning.

b. Calculate how much will be in the account if you close it when you are 18.

Math ToolboX

Technology

Fitting Exponential Curves to Data

After Lesson 8-3

In Chapter 5, you learned how to find a line of best fit for a set of data. Some data sets are better modeled by exponential functions. A graphing calculator makes it easy to graph exponential functions for a set of data.

U.S. Sales of Compact Discs

Year	Millions of CDs
1987 ↔ 7	102.1
8	149.7
9	207.2
10	286.5
11	333.3
12	407.5
13	495.4
1994 ↔ 14	662.1

Example

Use a graphing calculator to graph the data and find the best-fitting exponential function $y = a \cdot b^x$.

Step 1: Use the STAT feature to enter the data. Let 1980 correspond to $x = 0$.

Step 2: Use the STAT PLOT feature to graph the data in a scatter plot.

Step 3: Find the equation for the best-fitting exponential function. Press STAT ▶ ALPHA A ENTER to get the ExpReg equation.

```
ExpReg
y=a*b^x
a=19.82510651
b=1.287856937
r=.9908425236
```

Step 4: Graph the function. Press Y= CLEAR VARS 5 ▶ ▶ 7 to enter the ExpReg results. Press GRAPH to display the data and the function together.

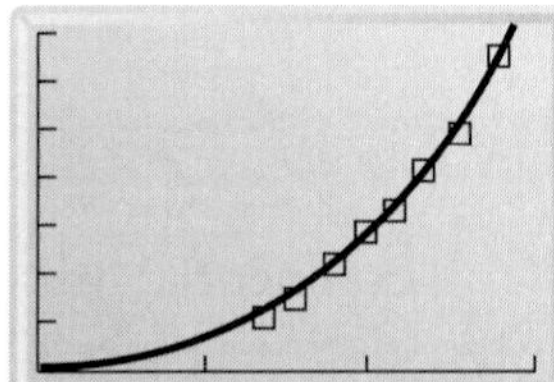

Xmin=0 Ymin=0
Xmax=15 Ymax=700
Xscl=5 Yscl=100

Use a graphing calculator to write the exponential function that fits each set of data. Sketch the graph of the function and show the data points.

1. **U.S. Movie Earnings.** Let 1980 correspond to $x = 0$.

Year	1986	1987	1988	1989	1990	1991	1992
Billions of Dollars	23.8	27.8	31.2	35.0	38.1	41.1	43.8

2. **U.S. Homes Heated by Coal.** Let 1950 correspond to $x = 0$.

Year	1950	1960	1970	1980	1991
Percent of Homes	33.8	12.2	2.9	0.4	0.3

3. a. The table gives the population of New Mexico at various times. Use the best-fitting exponential function to **predict** the population of New Mexico in 2010.
   b. *Writing* Explain how the r-value affects your answer to part (a).

Population of New Mexico (millions)

1970	1.017
1980	1.303
1985	1.438
1990	1.515
1994	1.654

What You'll Learn

- Evaluating and simplifying expressions in which zero and negative numbers are used as exponents

...And Why

To analyze exponential functions over a broader domain

What You'll Need

- graphing calculator

8-4 Zero and Negative Exponents

WORK TOGETHER

Work with a partner to copy and complete the table. Replace each box with a whole number or a fraction in lowest terms.

$y = 2^x$	$y = 5^x$	$y = 10^x$
$2^2 = 4$	$5^2 = 25$	$10^2 = 100$
$2^1 = 2$	$5^1 = 5$	$10^1 = 10$
$2^0 = ■$	$5^0 = ■$	$10^0 = ■$
$2^{-1} = ■$	$5^{-1} = ■$	$10^{-1} = ■$
$2^{-2} = ■$	$5^{-2} = ■$	$10^{-2} = ■$

1. You can describe what happens in the first column of the table as division by 2. What happens in the other columns of the table?

```
Xmin=-3
Xmax=3
Xscl =1
Ymin=0
Ymax=100
Yscl =10
```

2. a. Graph the three functions on your calculator. Use the range values at the left. Sketch the graphs.
   b. At what point do the three graphs intersect?
3. a. What pattern do you notice in the row containing 0 as an exponent?
   b. Use your calculator to calculate other numbers to the zero power. What do you notice?
4. Copy and complete each expression.
   a. $2^{-1} = \frac{1}{■} = \frac{1}{2^{■}}$ b. $2^{-2} = \frac{1}{■} = \frac{1}{2^{■}}$ c. $2^{-3} = \frac{1}{■} = \frac{1}{2^{■}}$
5. *Critical Thinking* Look for a pattern in your answers to Question 4. Does this pattern hold true for the other columns? Explain.

THINK AND DISCUSS

Using Zero and Negative Integers as Exponents

The pattern you saw in Question 3 is an important property of exponents.

Zero as an Exponent

For any nonzero number a, $a^0 = 1$.

Examples: $5^0 = 1$; $(-2)^0 = 1$; $\left(\frac{3}{8}\right)^0 = 1$; $1.02^0 = 1$

Notice that 0 is excluded as a base. The expression 0^0 is undefined, just as the expressions $\frac{2}{0}$ and $\frac{0}{0}$ are undefined.

Example 1 Relating to the Real World 

Population Growth The function $f(t) = 1000 \cdot 2^t$ models an initial population of 1000 insects that doubles every time period t. Evaluate the function for $t = 0$. Then describe what $f(0)$ represents in the situation.

$$f(0) = 1000 \cdot 2^0 \quad \leftarrow \text{Substitute 0 for } t.$$
$$= 1000 \cdot 1 \quad \leftarrow 2^0 = 1$$
$$= 1000$$

The value of $f(0)$ represents the initial population of insects. This makes sense because when $t = 0$, no time has passed.

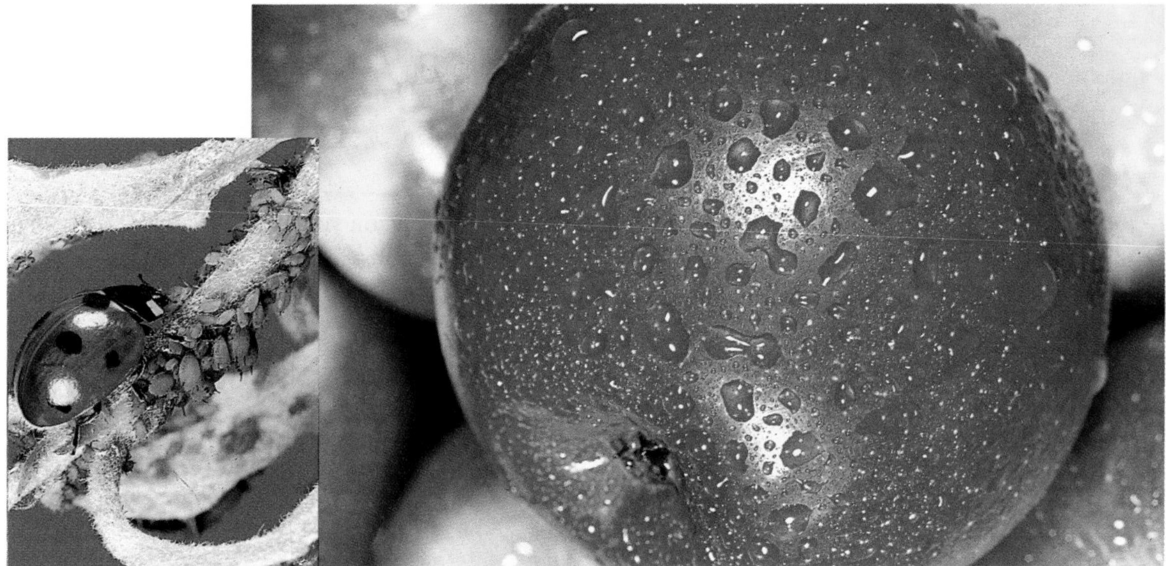

A large aphid population can destroy an apple orchard's produce. One way of controlling the aphids is to release ladybugs into the orchard, where they feed on the apple aphid colonies.

The pattern from Questions 4 and 5 illustrates another important property.

Negative Exponents

For any nonzero number a and any integer n, $a^{-n} = \frac{1}{a^n}$.

Examples: $6^{-4} = \frac{1}{6^4}$ and $7^{-1} = \frac{1}{7^1}$

Example 2

Write each expression as a simple fraction.

a. 4^{-3}

$4^{-3} = \frac{1}{4^3}$ ← definition of a negative exponent

$= \frac{1}{64}$

b. $(-3)^{-2}$

$(-3)^{-2} = \frac{1}{(-3)^2}$

$= \frac{1}{9}$

Quick Review

Unless grouping symbols are used, exponents operate on only one factor.

$-4^2 = -(4 \cdot 4) = -16$

$(-4)^2 = -4 \cdot -4 = 16$

$2x^3 = 2 \cdot x \cdot x \cdot x$

$(2x)^3 = 2x \cdot 2x \cdot 2x$

6. Try This Write each expression as a simple fraction.

a. 3^{-4} **b.** $(-7)^0$ **c.** $(-4)^{-3}$ **d.** 7^{-3} **e.** -3^{-2}

You can use what you know about rewriting the expression a^{-n} to see how the values of a^n and a^{-n} are related.

$$a^n \cdot a^{-n} = a^n \cdot \frac{1}{a^n}$$
$$= \frac{a^n}{1} \cdot \frac{1}{a^n} = 1$$

Therefore, a^n and a^{-n} are *reciprocals.*

7. **Verify** that a^n and a^{-n} are reciprocals by evaluating each product.
   a. $3^2 \cdot 3^{-2}$ **b.** $2^4 \cdot 2^{-4}$ **c.** $5^3 \cdot 5^{-3}$

8. Write the reciprocal of each number in two ways: as a simple fraction and using a negative exponent.
   a. 10^1 **b.** 10^2 **c.** 1000 **d.** 10,000

9. Write each expression as a decimal.
   a. 10^{-3} **b.** $3 \cdot 10^{-2}$ **c.** $-5 \cdot 10^{-4}$ **d.** 10^{-6}

Example 3

Rewrite each expression so that all exponents are positive.

a. $4yx^{-3} = 4y\left(\frac{1}{x^3}\right)$ ← **definition of negative exponent**

$= \frac{4y}{x^3}$

b. $\frac{1}{w^{-4}} = 1 \div w^{-4}$ ← **rewrite using a division symbol**

$= 1 \div \frac{1}{w^4}$

$= 1 \cdot w^4$ ← **multiply by the reciprocal**

$= w^4$

10. **Try This** Complete each expression using only positive exponents.
   a. $\frac{1}{x^{-3}} = x^{\blacksquare}$ **b.** $\frac{1}{v^{-2}} = v^{\blacksquare}$ **c.** $w^{-3} = \frac{1}{w^{\blacksquare}}$ **d.** $\frac{w^{-3}}{v^{-2}} = \frac{\blacksquare^{\blacksquare}}{\blacksquare^{\blacksquare}}$

Relating the Properties to Exponential Functions

Zero and negative integer exponents allow you to understand the graph of an exponential function more completely.

Example 4

GRAPHING CALCULATOR HINT

You can generate values for a function with the TABLE key on some graphing calculators.

Graphing Calculator Graph the functions $y = 2^x$ and $y = \left(\frac{1}{2}\right)^x$ on the same set of axes. Show the functions over the domain $\{-3 \le x \le 3\}$.

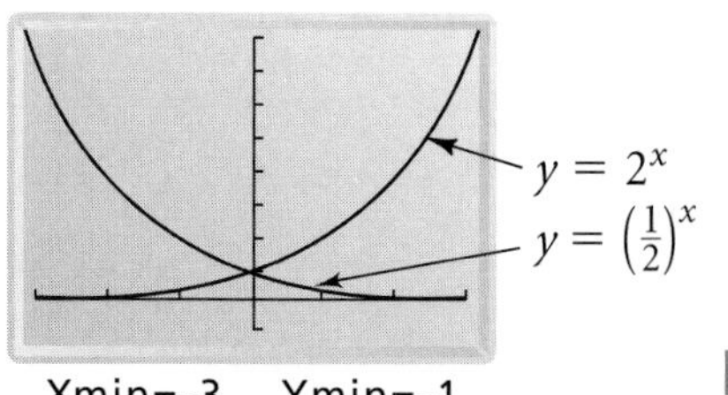

11. a. Is the value of 2^x always positive? Explain.

b. In what quadrants do the graphs of $y = 2^x$ and $y = \left(\frac{1}{2}\right)^x$ appear? Explain.

12. *Critical Thinking* The graph of $y = 2^{-x}$ is identical to one of the two graphs shown in Example 4. Use the definition of negative exponents to help decide which one. Explain.

Exercises ON YOUR OWN

Write each expression as an integer or simple fraction.

1. -2.57^0
2. 4^{-2}
3. $(-5)^{-1}$
4. $\left(\frac{2}{3}\right)^{-1}$
5. $\frac{1}{2^{-3}}$
6. 5^{-3}
7. $\left(\frac{1}{3}\right)^{-2}$
8. -3^{-4}
9. 2^{-6}
10. $(-12)^{-1}$
11. $45 \cdot (0.5)^0$
12. $\left(\frac{2}{5}\right)^{-2}$
13. $54 \cdot 3^{-2}$
14. $\left(-\frac{1}{4}\right)^{-3}$
15. $5 \cdot 10^{-2}$
16. $\frac{5^{-2}}{7^{-3}}$
17. $\frac{4^{-1}}{9^0}$
18. $\frac{(-3)^{-1}}{-2^{-1}}$

19. a. *Patterns* Complete the pattern.

$\frac{1}{5^2} = ■$ $\quad \frac{1}{5^1} = ■$ $\quad \frac{1}{5^0} = ■$ $\quad \frac{1}{5^{-1}} = ■$ $\quad \frac{1}{5^{-2}} = ■$

b. Write $\frac{1}{5^{-4}}$ using a positive exponent.

c. *Generalize* Rewrite $\frac{1}{a^{-n}}$ so that the power of a is in the numerator.

Write each expression so that it contains only positive exponents.

20. $\frac{1}{c^{-1}}$
21. $\frac{1}{x^{-7}}$
22. $3ab^0$
23. $(5x)^{-4}$
24. $\frac{5^{-2}}{p}$
25. $a^{-4}b^0$
26. $\frac{3x^{-2}}{y}$
27. $12xy^{-3}$
28. $\frac{7ab^{-2}}{3w}$
29. $5ac^{-5}$
30. $x^{-5}y^{-7}$
31. $\frac{8a^{-5}}{c^{-3}d^3}$
32. $x^{-5}y^7$
33. $\frac{7s^{-5}}{5t^{-3}}$
34. $\frac{6a^{-1}c^{-3}}{b^0}$
35. $\frac{1}{a^{-3}b^3}$
36. $\frac{c^4}{x^2y^{-1}}$
37. $\frac{mn^{-4}}{p^0q^{-2}}$

Evaluate each expression for $a = 3$, $b = 2$, and $c = -4$.

38. c^b
39. $a^{-b}b$
40. b^{-a}
41. b^c
42. $c^{-a}b^{ab}$
43. c^a

Graph each function over the domain $\{-3 \leq x \leq 3\}$.

44. $y = 2^x$
45. $f(x) = (2)^{-x}$
46. $g(x) = 0.5 \cdot 3^x$
47. $y = 1.5 \cdot (1.5)^{-x}$

Match each graphing calculator screen with the functions it displays.

48.

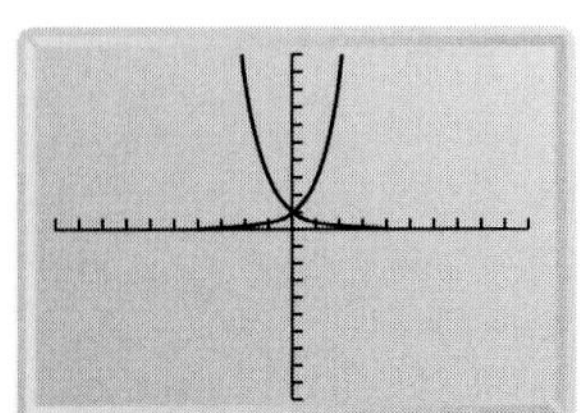

49.

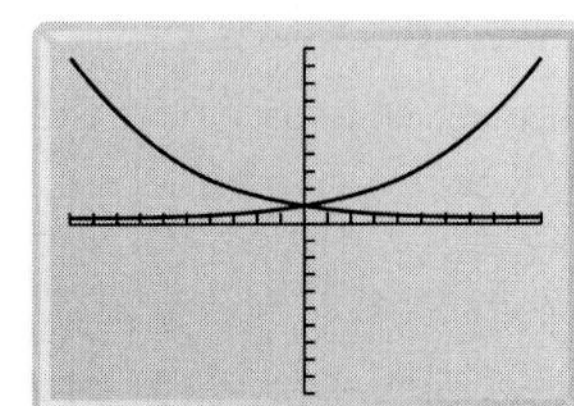

I. $y = \left(\frac{5}{4}\right)^x; y = \left(\frac{4}{5}\right)^x$

II. $y = 3^x; y = \left(\frac{1}{3}\right)^x$

III. $y = 15^x; y = \left(\frac{1}{15}\right)^x$

50. **Writing** Explain why the value of -3^0 is negative and the value of $(-3)^0$ is positive.

51. Copy and complete the table.

a	4	0.2	■	■	$\frac{7}{8}$	■
a^{-1}	■	■	3	$\frac{1}{6}$	■	0.5

Determine whether the value of each expression is *positive* or *negative.*

52. -2^2
53. $(-2)^2$
54. 2^{-2}
55. $(-2)^3$
56. $(-2)^{-3}$
57. 4^{-1}

Copy and complete each equation.

58. $2^{■} = 0.5$
59. $3xy^{■} = \frac{3x}{y^3}$
60. $\frac{x^{■}}{2y^{■}} = \frac{1}{2x^{-3}y^4}$
61. $\frac{a^{■}}{3b^{■}} = \frac{b^3}{3}$
62. $(-5)^{■} = -\frac{1}{125}$
63. $\frac{4n^{■}}{m^{■}} = \frac{4m^2}{n^3}$
64. $\frac{5x^{■}}{y^{■}} = \frac{5}{xy^2}$
65. $\frac{x^{■}}{y^{■}} = x^{-2}y^3$

66. **Standardized Test Prep** Compare the quantities in Column A and Column B.

Column A	Column B
3^x	3^{-x}

A. The quantity in Column A is greater.
B. The quantity in Column B is greater.
C. The quantities are equal.
D. The relationship cannot be determined from the information given.

67. Which expressions equal $\frac{1}{4}$?
A. 4^{-1} **B.** 2^{-2} **C.** -4^1
D. $\frac{1}{2^2}$ **E.** 1^4 **F.** -2^{-2}

68. **Open-ended** Choose a fraction to use as a value for the variable a. Find the values of a^{-1}, a^2, and a^{-2}.

69. **Research** Certain small units of length have special names. For each unit, give its length in the form $10^{■}$ meters.
a. fermi **b.** micron **c.** angstrom

70. **Botany** A botanist studying plant life on a remote island in the Pacific Ocean discovers that the number of plants of a particular species is increasing at a high rate. Each month for the next eight months, she counts the number of these plants in an acre plot of land. She then fits an exponential function to the data.
a. By what percent is the number of plants increasing each month?
b. If $x = 0$ represents the time of her initial count of the plants, what does $x = -3$ represent?
c. **Graphing Calculator** Graph the function on a graphing calculator. Use the TRACE feature to estimate when the plant was first introduced to the island. (*Hint:* Find the value of x when $y = 1$.)

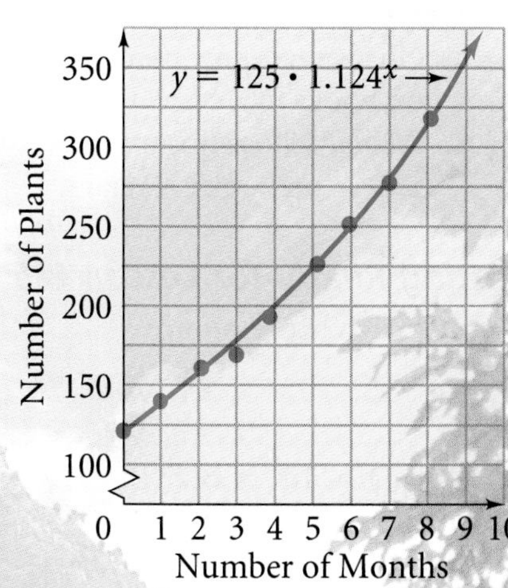

71. **Communications** Suppose you are the only person in your class who knows a story. After a minute you tell a classmate. Each minute after that, every student who knows the news tells another student (sometimes the person being told will already have heard it). In a class of 30 students, the formula $N = \frac{30}{1 + 29 \cdot 2^{-t}}$ predicts the number of people N who will have heard the news after t minutes. Find how many students will have heard your news after 2 minutes, 5 minutes, and 10 minutes.

72. **Critical Thinking** Are $3x^{-2}$ and $3x^2$ reciprocals? Explain.

Graph each pair of functions on the same set of axes over the domain $\{-3 \leq x \leq 3\}$.

73. $y = 10 \cdot 2^x; y = 20 \cdot 2^x$

74. $y = 1.2^x; y = 1.8^x$

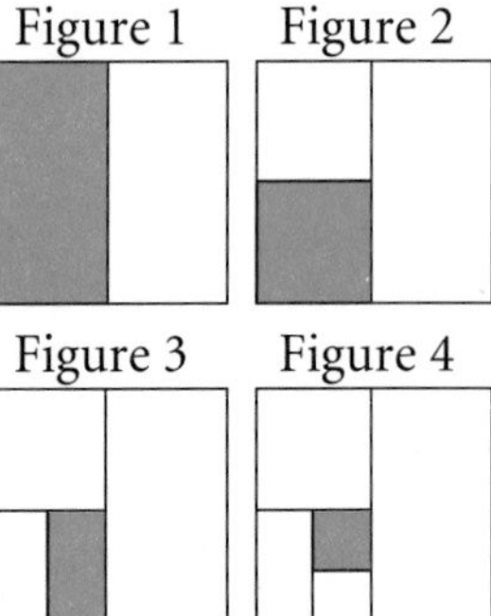

75. a. **Geometry** What fraction of each figure is shaded?
    b. Rewrite each fraction from part (a) in the form $2^{\blacksquare}$.
    c. **Patterns** Look for a pattern in your answers to part (b). Write a function that relates the figure number n to the shaded rectangle r.
    d. What portion of the square would be shaded in Figure 10?

Exercises MIXED REVIEW

Solve each system.

76. $2x + 2y = 3$
    $4x + 3y = 5$

77. $4x + y < 8$
    $2x \geq 3$

78. $3y = \frac{1}{3}|x| - 2$
    $|x| + 9y = 6$

79. Each person in Colorado spends an average of \$31.17/yr on books.
    a. Write a function to represent the amount b a group of p people spend on books in a year.
    b. On average, how much does a family of four living in Denver spend on books in a year?
    c. **Writing** Does this mean every person in Colorado spends exactly \$31.17 on books? Explain.

Getting Ready for Lesson 8-5

Simplify each expression.

80. $3.4 \cdot 10^1$

81. $7 \cdot 10^{-2}$

82. $8.2 \cdot 10^5$

83. $3 \cdot 10^{-3}$

84. $6 \cdot 10^4$

85. Write $3 \times 10^3 + 6 \times 10^1 + 7 \times 10^0 + 8 \times 10^{-1} + 5 \times 10^{-2}$ as a standard decimal number.

What You'll Learn

- Writing numbers in scientific notation
- Using scientific notation

...And Why

To calculate with very large or very small numbers

What You'll Need

- calculator

8-5 Scientific Notation

THINK AND DISCUSS

Writing Numbers in Scientific Notation

Jupiter has an average radius of 69,075 km. What is Jupiter's volume?

To answer this question, you probably want to find the formula for the volume of a sphere and use a calculator.

$V = \frac{4}{3}\pi r^3$ ← formula for the volume of a sphere

$= \frac{4}{3}\pi(69{,}075)^3$ ← Substitute 69,075 for *r*.

When you use a calculator to find the answer, the display looks something like *1.380547297E15*.

The calculator displays the answer in this form, called *scientific notation,* because the answer contains more digits than the calculator can display. Scientific notation is a kind of shorthand for very large or very small numbers.

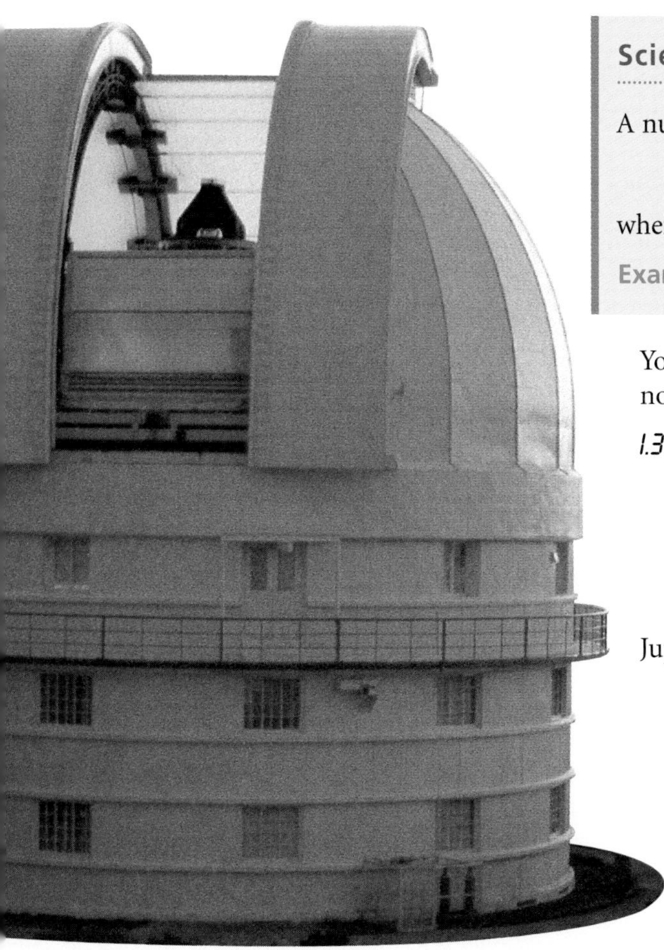

Scientific Notation

A number is in **scientific notation** if it is written in the form

$$a \times 10^n,$$

where n is an integer and $1 \leq |a| < 10$.

Examples: 3.4×10^6, 5.43×10^{13}, 9×10^{-10}

You can change a number from scientific notation into standard notation.

1.380547297E15

$\approx 1.38 \times 10^{15}$ ← scientific notation

$= 1.38 \times 1{,}000{,}000{,}000{,}000{,}000$ ← 10^{15} has 15 zeros.

$= 1{,}380{,}000{,}000{,}000{,}000$ ← standard notation

Jupiter has a volume slightly greater than 1 quintillion km^3.

1. a. **Try This** Evaluate the expression $\frac{4}{3}\pi(6000)^3$ on your calculator. What does your calculator display?
   b. Write the number in standard notation.

To write a number in scientific notation, you use a *power of 10.* A **power of 10** is an expression in the form $10^{\blacksquare}$.

2. a. Copy and complete the table.

Power of 10	$10^{\blacksquare}$	10^3	$10^{\blacksquare}$	$10^{\blacksquare}$	$10^{\blacksquare}$
Standard Notation	1,000,000	■	1	0.001	■
Unit Name	millions	■	ones	■	millionths

b. Patterns What pattern did you notice in part (a)?

3. a. Order the data in the table from least to greatest mass.

Masses of Planets (kg)

Jupiter	Saturn	Uranus	Neptune
1.9×10^{27}	5.7×10^{26}	8.7×10^{25}	1.0×10^{26}

b. **Summarize** the reasoning you used and the steps you took to order the data.

4. Physical Science Write each number in scientific notation.

a. mass of Earth's atmosphere: 5,700,000,000,000,000 tons

b. mass of the smallest insect, a parasitic wasp: 0.000 004 92 g

computer-generated image of the solar system

You can use what you know about place value and multiplication by 10 to convert from scientific notation to standard notation.

Example 1 Relating to the Real World 

Physical Science Write each number in standard notation.

a. temperature at the Sun's core: 1.55×10^6 K

b. lowest temperature ever in a lab: 2×10^{-11} K

a. $1.55 \times 10^6 = 1.550000.$ ← A positive exponent indicates a large number. Move the decimal point 6 places to the right.

$= 1{,}550{,}000$

b. $2 \times 10^{-11} = 0.00000000002.$ ← A negative exponent indicates a small number. Move the decimal point 11 places to the left.

$= 0.000\ 000\ 000\ 02$

What? One kelvin (1 K) is equal to 1°C, but the kelvin temperature scale starts at absolute zero (–273.15°C). Because nothing can be colder than absolute zero, there are no negative temperatures on the kelvin scale.

5. Try This Write each number in standard notation.

a. distance light travels in one year (one light-year): 5.88×10^{12} mi

b. highest elevation in Florida: 6.53×10^{-2} mi

6. Which numbers are *not* in scientific notation? Explain. Write each number in scientific notation.

a. 11.24×10^4 **b.** 2.004×10^{-23} **c.** -12×10^{-2}

Calculating with Scientific Notation

Standard Notation	Scientific Notation
0.0617	$6.17 \times 10^{\blacksquare}$
0.617	$6.17 \times 10^{\blacksquare}$
6.17	$6.17 \times 10^{\blacksquare}$
61.7	$6.17 \times 10^{\blacksquare}$
617	$6.17 \times 10^{\blacksquare}$
6170	$6.17 \times 10^{\blacksquare}$

7. a. Copy and complete the table at the left.

b. Patterns Look for a pattern in the exponents as you scan down the table. As you multiply a number by 10 repeatedly, the exponent in the power of 10 __?__ by ■ repeatedly.

8. Write each expression as a single power of ten.

a. $10^{12} \times 10$ **b.** 10×10^{-8} **c.** $10^{-7} \times 10$

Example 2

Mental Math Simplify $7 \times (4 \times 10^5)$. Give your answer in scientific notation.

$7 \times (4 \times 10^5) = 28 \times 10^5$ ← **Multiply whole numbers.**

$= 2.8 \times 10 \times 10^5$ ← **Write 28 as 2.8 × 10.**

$= 2.8 \times 10^6$ ← **Combine powers of 10.**

9. Try This Simplify. Give each answer in scientific notation.

a. $2.5 \times (6 \times 10^3)$ **b.** $1.5 \times (3 \times 10^4)$ **c.** $9 \times (7 \times 10^{-9})$

10. Mental Math Double each number. Give your answers in scientific notation.

a. 4×10^5 **b.** \$6.3 million **c.** 1.2×10^{-3}

11. You express 1 billion as 10^9. Explain why you express 436 billion as 4.36×10^{11}.

Most calculators have a key labeled [EE] or [EXP] that allows you to enter a number in scientific notation.

Example 3 Relating to the Real World

Telecommunications In 1993, 436 billion telephone calls were placed by 130 million United States telephone subscribers. What was the average number of calls placed per subscriber?

$\frac{\text{436 billion calls}}{\text{130 million subscribers}} = \frac{4.36 \times 10^{11}}{1.3 \times 10^8}$ ← **Write in scientific notation.**

= 4.36 [EE] 11 [÷] 1.3 [EE] 8 [ENTER]

= 3353.846154

Each subscriber made an average of 3354 calls in 1993.

12. Try This The closest star to Earth (other than the sun) is Alpha Centauri, 4.35 light-years from Earth. How many miles from Earth is Alpha Centauri? (*Hint:* See Question 5(a).)

Exercises ON YOUR OWN

Order each set of numbers from least to greatest.

1. $10^5, 10^{-3}, 10^0, 10^{-1}, 10^1$
2. $6.2 \times 10^7, 5.1 \times 10^7, 8 \times 10^7, 1.02 \times 10^7$
3. $4.02 \times 10^5, 4.1 \times 10^4, 4.1 \times 10^5, 4 \times 10^5$
4. $5.1 \times 10^{-3}, 4.8 \times 10^{-1}, 5.2 \times 10^{-3}, 5.6 \times 10^{-2}$

Determine whether each number is in scientific notation. If it is not, write it in scientific notation.

5. 23×10^7
6. 385×10^{-6}
7. 0.0027×10^{-4}
8. 9.37×10^{-8}
9. 25.79×10^{-5}

Write each number in scientific notation.

10. 0.00325
11. 9,040,000,000
12. 13,030,000
13. 0.00092
14. 0.001 002
15. 370 billion
16. 9.3 million
17. 41.8 billion
18. 60.7×10^{22}
19. 62.9×10^{15}
20. 2 thousandths
21. 33 billionths
22. 950 millionths
23. 83.5×10^{-6}
24. 350×10^{-9}
25. lightest blue whale: 418,000 lb
26. thinnest glass: 0.00098 in.
27. lightest bird egg: 0.0128 oz
28. diameter of thinnest copper wire: 0.000 5 in.
29. diameter of smallest bacteria cells: 4 millionths in.
30. closest star (other than the Sun): 25.6 trillion mi

31. **Writing** Explain how to convert numbers like 350 billion, 7.2 trillion, or 48 millionths quickly to scientific notation.

Write each number in standard notation.

32. 7.042×10^9
33. 4.69×10^{-6}
34. 1.7×10^{-13}
35. 5×10^{10}
36. 1.097×10^8

Mental Math **Calculate each product or quotient. Give your answers in scientific notation.**

37. $8 \times (7 \times 10^{-3})$
38. $8 \times (3 \times 10^{14})$
39. $2 \times (3 \times 10^2)$
40. $(28 \times 10^5) \div 7$
41. $(8 \times 10^{-8}) \div 4$
42. $(8 \times 10^{12}) \div 4$

43. **Probability** In 1990, there were approximately 249 million residents of the United States. The census counted 37,306 centenarians (age 100 or greater). What is the probability that a randomly selected U.S. resident is a centenarian? Give your answer in scientific notation.

44. **Precious Metals** Earth's crust contains approximately 120 trillion metric tons of gold. One metric ton of gold is worth about \$11.5 million. What is the approximate value of the gold in Earth's crust?

45. **Astronomy** Light travels through space at a constant speed of about 3×10^5 km/s. Earth is about 1.5×10^8 km from the Sun. How long does it take for light from the sun to reach Earth?

Marie Rinne, 101, is a retired teacher. Ezekiel Gibbs, 102, is a folk artist.

FOX TROT by Bill Amend

46. **a.** Write 500 trillion in scientific notation.

b. Since the 10-second length of the movie is off by a factor of 500 trillion, what time span does the movie actually represent?

c. *Open-ended* Find out the length of one of your favorite movies. Calculate how many frames it has, and express the number of frames in scientific notation.

Mental Math **Double each number. Give your answers in scientific notation.**

47. 3.5×10^{-3} **48.** \$75 million **49.** 450×10^{-1}

50. 3550 **51.** 250×10^{5} **52.** 790

53. *Health Care* The total amount spent for health care in the United States in 1993 was \$884.2 billion. The U.S. population in 1993 was 258.1 million. What was the average amount spent per person on health care?

Chapter Project — Find Out by Graphing

Make a scatter plot of the growth data. Compare your graph with graphs made by other students in your group. Do the data plots look exponential? Are there differences that seem to be related to where and how long the dish was exposed?

Exercises MIXED REVIEW

Find each sum or difference.

54. $\begin{bmatrix} 2 & 9 & 5 \\ 3 & 6 & 1 \end{bmatrix} + \begin{bmatrix} 5 & 2 & 9 \\ 3 & 4 & 7 \end{bmatrix}$

55. $\begin{bmatrix} 2.6 & 4 \\ 8.1 & 6.7 \end{bmatrix} - \begin{bmatrix} 5.8 & 1.6 \\ 4 & 7.9 \end{bmatrix}$

56. *Sports* In the hockey statistics, the FOR column tells the number of goals made by each team. The OPP column tells the number of goals made by a team's opponents. The DIF column reports the difference. Find the errors in the DIF column.

Hockey Standings Central Division

Goals	FOR	OPP	DIF
Detroit	356	275	+81
Toronto	280	243	−37
Dallas	286	265	+21
St. Louis	270	283	−13
Chicago	254	240	−14
Winnipeg	245	344	+99

Getting Ready for Lesson 8-6

Rewrite each expression using exponents.

57. $t \cdot t \cdot t \cdot t \cdot t \cdot t \cdot t$ **58.** $(6 - m)(6 - m)(6 - m)$ **59.** $5 \cdot 5 \cdot 5 \cdot s \cdot s \cdot s$

Math ToolboX

Skills Review

Significant Digits

After Lesson 8-5

Significant digits tell scientists how precise a measurement is. The more significant digits there are, the more precise the measurement is. Scientists consider all the significant digits in a measurement to be exact except for the final digit, which is considered to be rounded.

Example 1

Express the length of the computer chip in centimeters to (a) one significant digit and (b) two significant digits.

a. The length of the chip is 5 cm.
b. The length of the chip is 5.2 cm.

Example 2

The moon can come within 221,463 mi of Earth. Express this distance in scientific notation to three significant digits.

$221{,}463 = 2.21463 \times 10^5$ ← Write in scientific notation.

$\approx 2.21 \times 10^5$ ← Round 2.21463 to the hundredths' place.

To three significant digits, the distance is 2.21×10^5 mi.

Tell how many significant digits are in each measurement.

1. Mercury's period of revolution: 87.9686 da

2. largest known galaxy: 3.3×10^{19} mi in diameter

3. tallest sand castle: 19.5 ft high

Express each number in scientific notation to three significant digits.

4. the surface area of Earth: 196,949,970 mi^2

5. smallest diamond: 0.000 102 2 carat

6. thinnest commercial glass: 0.000 984 in.

7. the farthest the moon can be from Earth: 252,710 mi

8. average weight of the smallest bone in the inner ear: 0.010 853 75 oz

9. 1991 U.S. deaths from heart disease: 725,010

10. *Writing* When would it be important to measure something to three or more significant digits? Explain.

8-6 A Multiplication Property of Exponents

What You'll Learn

- Multiplying powers with the same base

...And Why

To solve problems that involve the multiplication of numbers in scientific notation

What You'll Need

- calculator

WORK TOGETHER

To evaluate $5^3 \cdot 5^5$, you could multiply the value of 5^3 by the value of 5^5. But is there a shortcut for finding the value of expressions like this? Work in your group to find one.

1. *Calculator* Find the value of each expression.
   a. $5^3 \cdot 5^5$ **b.** $5^6 \cdot 5^2$ **c.** $5^1 \cdot 5^7$ **d.** $5^4 \cdot 5^4$
2. *Patterns* What pattern do you notice in your answers to Question 1?
3. Write each expression from Question 1 in the form shown below.
   $$5^3 \cdot 5^5 = (5 \cdot 5 \cdot 5) \cdot (5 \cdot 5 \cdot 5 \cdot 5 \cdot 5) = 5^8$$
4. Look for a pattern in the expressions you wrote in Question 3. Write a shortcut for finding the value of expressions such as $5^3 \cdot 5^5$.
5. Use your shortcut to find the missing value in each expression. **Verify** your answers by using a calculator.
   a. $5^3 \cdot 5^4 = 5^{■}$ **b.** $3^2 \cdot 3^5 = 3^{■}$
   c. $1.2^3 \cdot 1.2^3 = 1.2^{■}$ **d.** $7^3 \cdot 7^2 = 7^{■}$

CALCULATOR HINT

Use the y^x or ^ key to evaluate expressions with exponents.

THINK AND DISCUSS

Multiplying Powers

Any expression in the form a^n, such as 5^4, is called a **power.** In the Work Together, you discovered a shortcut for multiplying powers with the same base. This shortcut works because the factors of a power such as 8^6 can be combined in different ways. Here are two examples:

$$8^6 = \underbrace{8 \cdot 8 \cdot 8 \cdot 8}_{8^4} \cdot \underbrace{8 \cdot 8}_{8^2} \qquad 8^6 = \underbrace{8 \cdot 8 \cdot 8}_{8^3} \cdot \underbrace{8 \cdot 8 \cdot 8}_{8^3}$$

$$= 8^4 \cdot 8^2 \qquad = 8^3 \cdot 8^3$$

QUICK REVIEW

Read 5^4 as "5 to the 4th power."

Notice that $8^4 \cdot 8^2 = 8^3 \cdot 8^3 = 8^6$. When you multiply powers with the same base, you add the exponents.

Multiplying Powers with the Same Base

For any nonzero number a and any integers m and n, $a^m \cdot a^n = a^{m+n}$.

Example: $3^5 \cdot 3^4 = 3^{5+4} = 3^9$

6. Write 5^7 as a product of powers in three different ways.

7. Does $3^2 \cdot 3^5 \cdot 3^1 = 3^{2+5+1} = 3^8$? Explain.

8. Does $3^4 \cdot 2^2 = 6^{4+2}$? Explain.

QUICK REVIEW

The coefficient in $3x^8$ is the numerical factor 3.

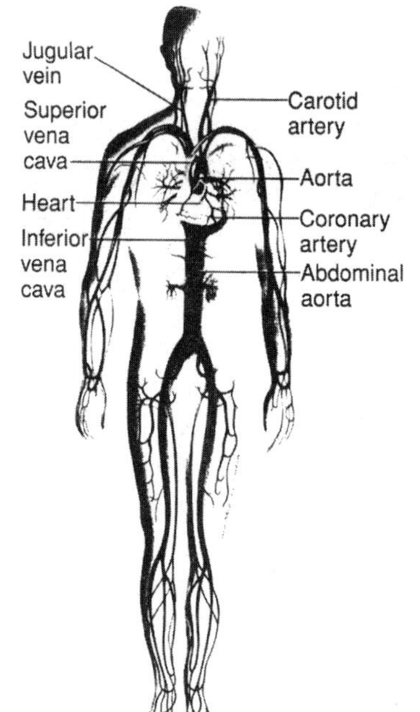

Example 1

Simplify each expression.

a. $c^4 \cdot d^3 \cdot c^2$

$= c^4 \cdot c^2 \cdot d^3$ ← Rearrange factors.

$= c^{4+2} \cdot d^3$ ← Add exponents of powers with the same base.

$= c^6 d^3$

b. $5x \cdot 2y^4 \cdot 3x^8$

$= (5 \cdot 2 \cdot 3)(x \cdot x^8)(y^4)$ ← Rearrange factors.

$= (30)(x^1 \cdot x^8)(y^4)$ ← Multiply coefficients.

$= (30)(x^{1+8})(y^4)$ ← Add exponents of powers with the same base.

$= 30x^9y^4$

9. **Try This** Simplify each expression.

a. $a \cdot b^2 \cdot a^5$ **b.** $6x^2 \cdot 3y^3 \cdot 2y^4$ **c.** $m^2 \cdot n^2 \cdot 7m$

Working with Scientific Notation

Example 2 **Relating to the Real World** 

Biology A human body contains about 3.2×10^4 µL (microliters) of blood for each pound of body weight. Each microliter of blood contains about 5×10^6 red blood cells. Find the approximate number of red blood cells in the body of a 125-lb person.

$\text{pounds} \cdot \frac{\text{microliters}}{\text{pound}} \cdot \frac{\text{cells}}{\text{microliter}} = \text{cells}$ ← Use dimensional analysis.

$125 \text{ lb} \cdot (3.2 \times 10^4)\frac{\mu L}{\text{lb}} \cdot (5 \times 10^6)\frac{\text{cells}}{\mu L}$

$= (125 \cdot 3.2 \cdot 5) \cdot (10^4 \cdot 10^6)$ ← Rearrange factors.

$= (125 \cdot 3.2 \cdot 5) \cdot 10^{10}$ ← Add exponents.

$= 2000 \cdot 10^{10}$ ← Simplify.

$= 2 \times 10^3 \cdot 10^{10}$ ← Write 2000 as 2×10^3.

$= 2 \times 10^{13}$ ← Use scientific notation.

There are about 2×10^{13} (20 trillion!) red blood cells in a 125-lb person.

10. **Try This** About how many red blood cells are in your body?

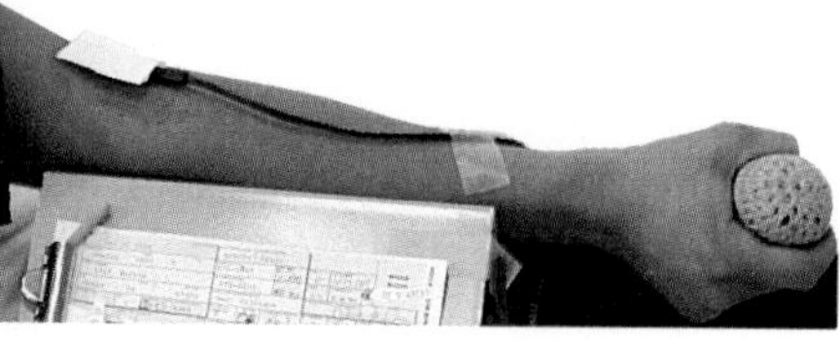

The average blood donation is 1 pint, which contains about 2.4×10^{12} red blood cells.

The property of multiplying powers with the same base works with negative exponents, also.

Example 3

Simplify $(0.2 \times 10^5)(4 \times 10^{-12})$. Give the answer in scientific notation.

$(0.2 \times 10^5)(4 \times 10^{-12})$

$= (0.2 \times 4)(10^5 \times 10^{-12})$ ← Rearrange factors.

$= 0.8 \times 10^{5+(-12)}$ ← Multiply.

$= 0.8 \times 10^{-7}$ ← Add exponents.

$= 8 \times 10^{-1} \times 10^{-7}$ ← Write 0.8 as 8×10^{-1}.

$= 8 \times 10^{-8}$ ← Add exponents.

11. Try This Simplify each expression. Give your answers in scientific notation.

a. $(0.5 \times 10^{13})(0.3 \times 10^{-4})$ **b.** $(0.7 \times 10^{-9})(0.03 \times 10^8)$

12. **Verify** that $2^5 \cdot 2^{-2} = 2^3$ by writing 2^5 as an integer and 2^{-2} as a fraction, then multiplying.

Exercises ON YOUR OWN

Write each expression as a product of powers, then simplify.

1. $(x \cdot x \cdot x \cdot x)(x \cdot x \cdot x)$

2. $(x \cdot x)\left(\frac{1}{x \cdot x \cdot x}\right)$

3. $\left(\frac{1}{x \cdot x}\right)\left(\frac{1}{x \cdot x \cdot x \cdot x \cdot x}\right)$

Complete each equation.

4. $5^2 \cdot 5^{■} = 5^{11}$

5. $5^7 \cdot 5^{■} = 5^3$

6. $a^{12} \cdot a^{■} = a^{12}$

7. $a \cdot a \cdot a^3 = a^{■}$

8. $2^{■} \cdot 2^4 = 2^1$

9. $a^{■} \cdot a^4 = 1$

10. $c^{-5} \cdot c^{■} = c^6$

11. $x^3y^{■} \cdot x^{■} = y^2$

Multiply. Give your answers in scientific notation.

12. $(9 \times 10^7)(3 \times 10^{-16})$

13. $(8 \times 10^{-3})(0.1 \times 10^9)$

14. $(0.7 \times 10^{-12})(0.3 \times 10^8)$

15. $(2 \times 10^6)(3 \times 10^3)$

16. $1 \times 10^3 \cdot 10^{-8}$

17. $(4 \times 10^6) \times 10^{-3}$

18. Standardized Test Prep Simplify $p^8 \cdot 9q^2 \cdot q^4 \cdot p^3 \cdot 2q$.

A. $-11p^{11}q^7$ **B.** $11p^{14}q^8$ **C.** $18p^{11}q^6$ **D.** $18p^{11}q^7$ **E.** $18pq^{17}$

19. **a.** Open-ended Write y^8 in four different ways as the product of two powers with the same base. Use only positive exponents.

b. Write y^8 in four different ways as the product of two powers with the same base, using negative or zero exponents in each.

c. How many ways are there to write y^8 as the product of two powers? **Summarize** your reasoning.

Simplify each expression. Use only positive exponents.

20. $(0.99^2)(0.99^4)$
21. $(1.025)^3(1.025)^{-3}$
22. $c^{-2}c^7$
23. $3r \cdot r^4$
24. $5t^{-2} \cdot 2t^{-5}$
25. $(a^2b^3)(a^6)$
26. $(x^5y^2)(x^{-6}y)$
27. $3x^2 \cdot x^2$
28. $(1.03^8)(1.03^4)$
29. $-(0.99^3)(0.99^0)$
30. $a \cdot a^{-7}$
31. $b^{-2} \cdot b^4 \cdot b$
32. $10^{-13} \cdot 10^5$
33. $(-2m^3)(3.5m^{-3})$
34. $(7x^5)(8x)$
35. $(15a^3)(-3a)$
36. $(-2.4n^4)(2n^{-1})$
37. $bc^{-6} \cdot b$
38. $(5x^5)(3y^6)(3x^2)$
39. $(4c^4)(ac^3)(3a^5c)$
40. $x^6 \cdot y^2 \cdot x^4$
41. $a^6b^3 \cdot a^2b^{-2}$
42. $\frac{1}{x^2 \cdot x^{-5}}$
43. $\frac{1}{a^3 \cdot a^{-2}}$
44. $\frac{5}{c \cdot c^{-4}}$
45. $2a^2(3a + 5)$
46. $8m^3(m^2 + 7)$
47. $-4x^3(2x^2 - 9x)$

48. **Chemistry** The term *mole* is used in chemistry to refer to a specific number of atoms or molecules. One mole is equal to 6.02×10^{23}. The mass of a single hydrogen atom is approximately 1.67×10^{-24} gram. What is the mass of 1 mole of hydrogen atoms?

49. **a.** Jerome wrote $a^3b^2b^4 = (a \cdot a \cdot a)(b \cdot b)(b \cdot b \cdot b \cdot b)$. Jeremy wrote $a^3b^2b^4 = ab^9$. Whose work is correct? Explain.
b. Use the correct work to simplify $a^3b^2b^4$.

50. **Writing** Explain why $x^3 \cdot y^5$ cannot be simplified.

Geometry **Find the area of each figure.**

51.
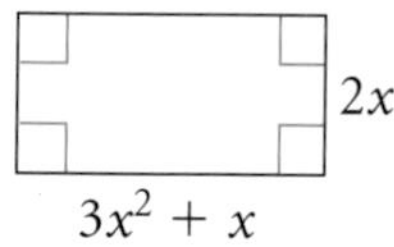

52.
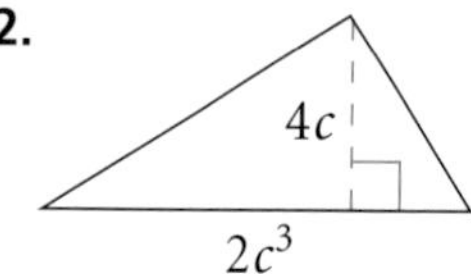

53.
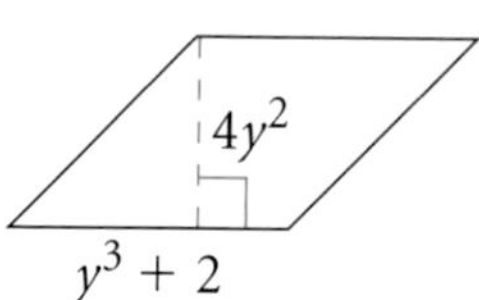

54.
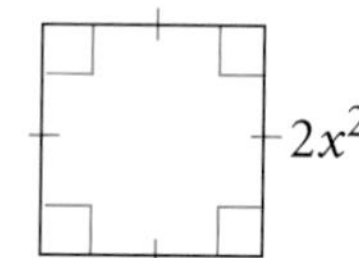

Critical Thinking **Find and correct the errors in Exercises 55–57.**

55. $(3x^2)(-2x^4) = 3(-2)x^{2 \cdot 4}$
$= -6x^8$

56. $4a^2 \cdot 3a^5 = (4 + 3)a^{2+5}$
$= 7a^7$

57. $x^6 \cdot x \cdot x^3 = x^{6+3}$
$= x^9$

58. **Technology** A CD-ROM stores about 600 megabytes (6×10^8 bytes) of information along a spiral track. Each byte uses about 9 micrometers (9×10^{-6} m) of space along the track. Find the length of the track.

59. **Medicine** Medical X-rays, with a wavelength of about 10^{-10} m, can penetrate the flesh (but not the bones) of your body.
a. Ultraviolet rays, which cause sunburn by penetrating only the top layers of skin, have a wavelength about 1000 times as long as X-rays. Find the wavelength of ultraviolet rays.
b. **Critical Thinking** The wavelengths of visible light are between 4×10^{-7}m and 7.5×10^{-7}m. Are these wavelengths longer or shorter than those of ultraviolet rays?

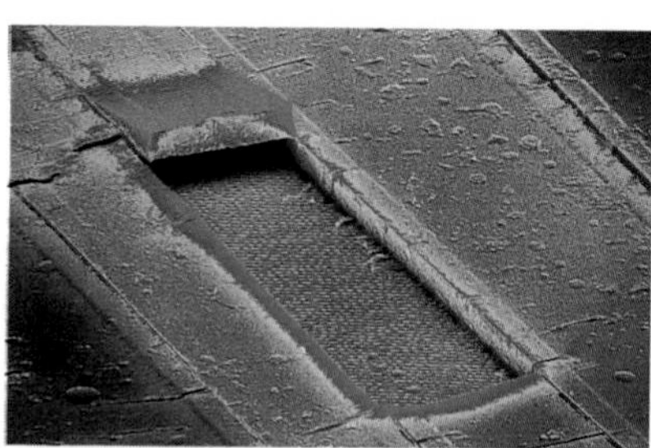

The music on a compact disc comes from a series of notches that can be read by a laser. The disc is enclosed in two layers of plastic. The plastic surface of this CD is cracked to show the notched layer underneath.

Chapter Project — Find Out by Analyzing

- Starting with the first day you see at least one square of mold, find the percent of growth from each day to the next.
- Use the average of these percents as an estimate for the base of an exponential function.
- Write an exponential function to fit the data. Graph it on your data plot.

Exercises — MIXED REVIEW

Identify each square root as *rational* or *irrational*. Simplify if possible.

60. $\sqrt{121}$ **61.** $\sqrt{67}$ **62.** $-\sqrt{49}$ **63.** $\sqrt{\frac{1}{4}}$ **64.** $-\sqrt{13}$ **65.** $\sqrt{\frac{9}{16}}$

66. Sports In 1989, United States sales of in-line skates were \$21 million. In 1994, sales were \$369 million. Find the percent of increase.

Getting Ready for Lesson 8-7

Rewrite each expression with one exponent.

67. $3^2 \cdot 3^2 \cdot 3^2$ **68.** $2^3 \cdot 2^3 \cdot 2^3 \cdot 2^3$ **69.** $5^7 \cdot 5^7 \cdot 5^7 \cdot 5^7$ **70.** $7 \cdot 7 \cdot 7$

Exercises — CHECKPOINT

Write each expression as an integer or simple fraction.

1. $(-7.3)^0$ **2.** 3^{-2} **3.** -8^{-1} **4.** $\left(\frac{1}{5}\right)^{-3}$ **5.** -4^2 **6.** $(-2)^{-3}$

Simplify each expression. Use only positive exponents.

7. $s^{-2} \cdot s^4 \cdot s$ **8.** $a^7b^2 \cdot 21a^{-6}$ **9.** $(2a^3)(-3a^{-3})(\frac{1}{6}a^0)$ **10.** g^3h^{-4} **11.** $\frac{x^{-5}}{y^2y^{-8}}$

Mental Math **Simplify. Give your answers in scientific notation.**

12. $(5 \times 10^6) \times 3$ **13.** $0.4 \times (2 \times 10^{-7})$ **14.** $(9 \times 10^{11}) \div 3$ **15.** $6 \times (4 \times 10^3)$

16. a. Biology Georg Frey collected beetles. When he died, his collection contained 3 million beetles of 90,000 different species. Write each number in scientific notation.

b. About how many beetles fit into each of his 6500 packing cases?

17. Writing LaWanda wrote $a^5 + a^5 = 2a^5$. Amanda wrote $a^5 + a^5 = a^{10}$. Whose work is correct? Explain.

Graph each function over the domain $\{-3 \leq x \leq 3\}$.

18. $f(x) = 0.8 \cdot 2^x$ **19.** $y = 0.5 \cdot 1.5^x$ **20.** $g(x) = 2 \cdot 3^x$

8-7 More Multiplication Properties of Exponents

What You'll Learn

- Using two more multiplication properties of exponents

...And Why

To solve problems that involve raising numbers in scientific notation to a power

What You'll Need

- calculator

THINK AND DISCUSS

Raising a Power to a Power

In Lesson 8-6, you used patterns to discover how to multiply powers with the same base. You can use what you discovered there to find a shortcut for simplifying expressions such as $(8^6)^3$.

1. Copy and complete each statement.
   a. $(a^3)^2 = a^3 \cdot a^3 = a^{\blacksquare + \blacksquare} = a^{3 \cdot \blacksquare} = a^{\blacksquare}$
   b. $(4^5)^3 = 4^5 \cdot 4^5 \cdot 4^5 = 4^{\blacksquare + \blacksquare + \blacksquare} = 4^{5 \cdot \blacksquare} = 4^{\blacksquare}$
   c. $(2^7)^4 = 2^7 \cdot 2^7 \cdot 2^7 \cdot 2^7 = 2^{7 \cdot \blacksquare} = 2^{\blacksquare}$
   d. $(8^6)^2 = 8^6 \cdot 8^6 = 8^{6 \cdot \blacksquare} = 8^{\blacksquare}$
   e. $(g^4)^3 = g^4 \cdot g^4 \cdot g^4 = g^{4 \cdot \blacksquare} = g^{\blacksquare}$
2. **Patterns** Look for a pattern in your answers to Question 1. Write a shortcut for simplifying an expression such as $(8^6)^3$.

You can use the property below to simplify some exponential expressions.

> **Raising a Power to a Power**
>
> For any nonzero number a and any integers m and n, $(a^m)^n = a^{mn}$.
>
> **Example:** $(5^4)^2 = 5^{4 \cdot 2} = 5^8$

3. The work you did in Question 1 involves repeated multiplication. Simplify each expression below by using repeated multiplication. Then check your work by using the property.
   a. $(2^3)^2$ b. $(h^2)^4$ c. $(3^3)^4$
4. Simplify each expression. What do you notice?
   a. $(5^2)^4 = 25^4 = \blacksquare$ b. $(5^2)^4 = 5^8 = \blacksquare$
5. Use the property to find each missing value. Then use a calculator to evaluate each expression and verify your answers.
   a. $(3^{\blacksquare})^4 = 9^4$ b. $(5^2)^{\blacksquare} = 5^8$ c. $(2^{\blacksquare})^{\blacksquare} = 4^2$
   d. $(3^4)^2 = 3^{\blacksquare}$ e. $(1.1^5)^7 = 1.1^{\blacksquare}$ f. $(123^0)^{87} = 123^{\blacksquare}$

CALCULATOR HINT

When evaluating an expression such as $(3^4)^2$, you do not need to use parentheses because the calculator evaluates powers from left to right. Pressing 3 ^ 4 ^ 2 ENTER will give you 6561.

Example 1

Simplify each expression.

a. $(x^3)^6 = x^{3 \cdot 6}$ ← Multiply exponents when raising a power to a power.
   $= x^{18}$ ← Simplify.

b. $c^5(c^3)^2 = c^5 \cdot c^{3 \cdot 2}$ ← Multiply exponents in $(c^3)^2$.
$= c^5 \cdot c^6$ ← Simplify.
$= c^{5+6}$ ← Add exponents when multiplying powers with the same base.
$= c^{11}$

6. Try This Simplify $(a^4)^2 \cdot (a^2)^5$.

Raising a Product to a Power

You can use repeated multiplication to simplify expressions like $(5y)^3$.

$$\begin{aligned}(5y)^3 &= 5y \cdot 5y \cdot 5y \\ &= 5 \cdot 5 \cdot 5 \cdot y \cdot y \cdot y \\ &= 5^3 \cdot y^3 \\ &= 125y^3\end{aligned}$$

Notice from the steps above that $(5y)^3 = 5^3y^3$. This illustrates another property of exponents.

Raising a Product to a Power

For any nonzero numbers a and b and any integer n, $(ab)^n = a^nb^n$.

Example: $(3x)^4 = 3^4x^4 = 81x^4$

7. Calculator **Verify** each equation for two values of the variable (other than 0 and 1).

a. $(5y)^3 = 125y^3$ **b.** $(3x)^4 = 3^4x^4$ **c.** $(7c)^2 = 49c^2$

Example 2

Simplify each expression.

a. $(2x^2)^4 = 2^4(x^2)^4$ ← Raise each factor to the 4th power.
$= 2^4x^8$ ← Multiply exponents.
$= 16x^8$ ← Simplify.

b. $(x^{-2})^2(3xy^2)^4 = (x^{-2})^2 \cdot 3^4x^4(y^2)^4$ ← Raise three factors to the 4th power.
$= x^{-4} \cdot 3^4x^4y^8$ ← Multiply exponents.
$= 3^4 \cdot x^{-4} \cdot x^4 \cdot y^8$ ← Rearrange factors.
$= 3^4x^0y^8$ ← Add exponents.
$= 81y^8$ ← Simplify.

8. Try This Simplify each expression.

a. $(15z)^3$ **b.** $(4g^5)^2$ **c.** $(6mn)^3(5m^{-3})^4$

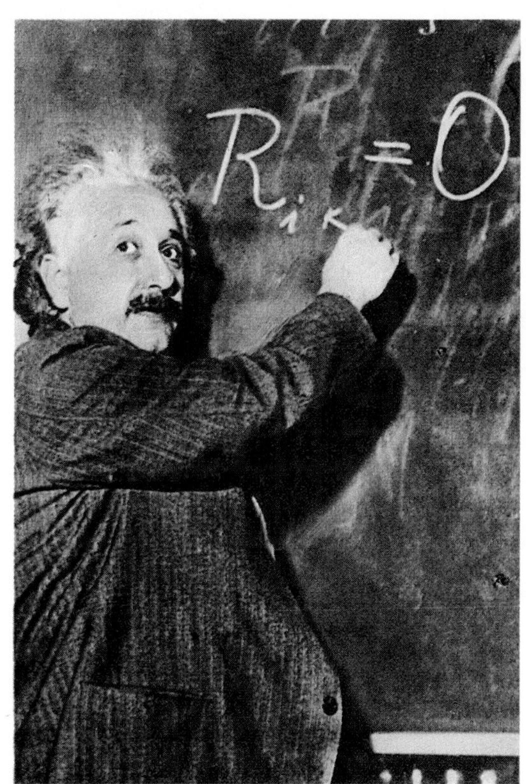

Who? Albert Einstein is famous for discovering the relationship $e = mc^2$, where *e* is energy (in joules), *m* is mass (in kg), and *c* is the speed of light (about 3×10^8 meters per second).

You can use the properties of exponents to solve real-world problems.

Example 3 **Relating to the Real World** 

Physical Science All objects, even resting ones, contain energy. The expression $10^{-3} \cdot (3 \times 10^8)^2$ describes the amount of resting energy a raisin contains, where 10^{-3} kg is the mass of the raisin. Simplify the expression.

$10^{-3} \cdot (3 \times 10^8)^2$

$= 10^{-3} \cdot 3^2 \cdot (10^8)^2$ ← Raise two factors to the 2nd power.

$= 10^{-3} \cdot 3^2 \cdot 10^{16}$ ← Multiply exponents.

$= 3^2 \cdot 10^{-3} \cdot 10^{16}$ ← Rearrange factors.

$= 3^2 \cdot 10^{-3+16}$ ← Add exponents.

$= 9 \times 10^{13}$ ← Simplify.

One raisin contains about 9×10^{13} joules of resting energy.

9. Multiply. Give your answers in scientific notation.
   a. $(4 \times 10^5)^2$
   b. $(2 \times 10^{-10})^3$
   c. $(10^3)^4(4.3 \times 10^{-8})$

10. **Energy** An hour of television use consumes 1.45×10^{-1} kWh of electricity. Each kilowatt-hour (kWh) of electric use is equivalent to 3.6×10^6 joules of energy.
    a. How many joules does a television use in 1 h? (Hint: Use a proportion.)
    b. Suppose you could release the resting energy in a raisin. About how many hours of television use could be powered by that energy?

Exercises ON YOUR OWN

Simplify each expression. Use positive exponents.

1. $(xy)^9$
2. $(c^5)^2$
3. $(a^2b^4)^3$
4. $(3m^3)^4$
5. $(g^{10})^{-4}$
6. $g^{10} \cdot g^{-4}$
7. $(x^3y)^4$
8. $(x^{-2})^3x^{-12}$
9. $(0.5^2)^{-2}$
10. $(2xy)^3x^2$
11. $(g \cdot g^4)^2$
12. $(c^2)^{-2}(c^3)^4$
13. $s^3(s^2)^4$
14. $(mg^4)^{-1}$
15. $m(g^4)^{-1}$
16. $(7cd^4)^2$
17. $(2p^6)^0$
18. $(5ac^3)^{-2}$
19. $(4a^2b)^3(ab)^3$
20. $(4xy^2)^4(2y)^{-3}$
21. $3^7 \cdot \left(\frac{1}{3}\right)^7$
22. $(5x)^2+5x^2$
23. $2^4 \cdot 5^4$
24. $(64.1^{-3})^0$
25. $(b^n)^3b^2$
26. $15^2 \cdot (0.2)^2$
27. $(4.1)^5 \cdot (4.1)^{-5}$
28. $3^2 \cdot (3x)^3$

29. a. **Geography** Earth has a radius of about 6.4×10^6 m. Approximate the surface area of Earth by using the formula for the surface area of a sphere, $S = 4\pi r^2$.

b. Earth's surface is about 70% water, almost all of it in oceans. About how many square meters of Earth's surface are covered with water?

c. The oceans have an average depth of 3795 m. What is the approximate volume of water on Earth?

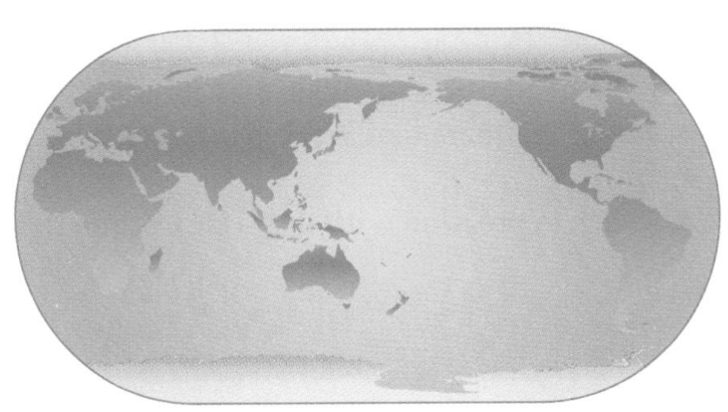

Multiply. Give your answers in scientific notation.

30. $(3 \times 10^5)^2$ **31.** $(2 \times 10^{-3})^3$ **32.** $(7 \times 10^4)^2$

33. $(6 \times 10^{12})^2$ **34.** $(3 \times 10^{-4})^3$ **35.** $(4 \times 10^8)^{-2}$

36. Which expression or expressions do *not* equal 64?
A. $2^5 \cdot 2$ **B.** 2^6 **C.** $2^2 \cdot 2^3$ **D.** $(2^3)^2$ **E.** $(2^2)(2^2)^2$

37. **Writing** Explain how the properties of exponents help you simplify algebraic expressions.

38. a. **Geometry** Write an expression for the surface area of each cube.

b. How many times greater than the surface area of the small cube is the surface area of the large cube?

c. Write an expression for the volume of each cube.

d. How many times greater than the volume of the small cube is the volume of the large cube?

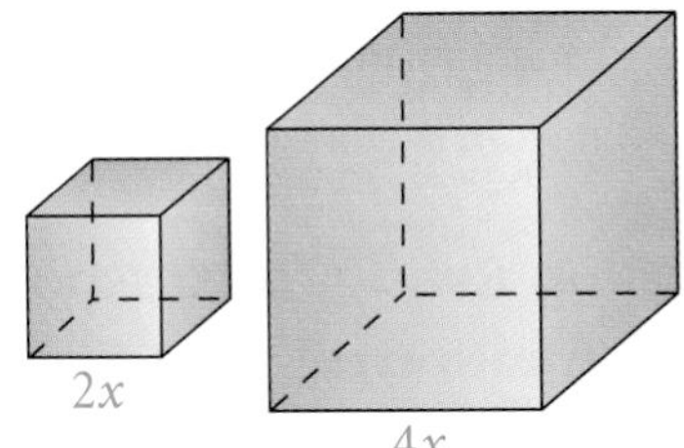

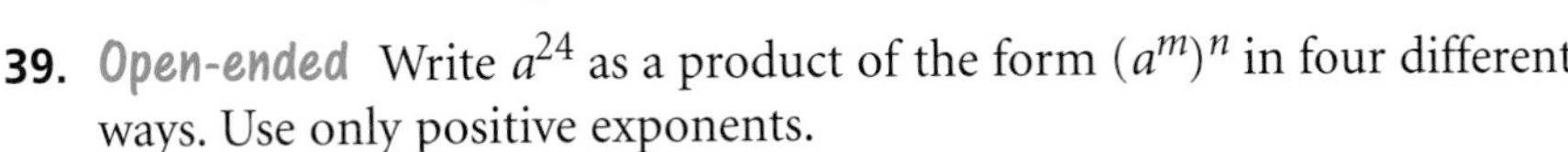

39. **Open-ended** Write a^{24} as a product of the form $(a^m)^n$ in four different ways. Use only positive exponents.

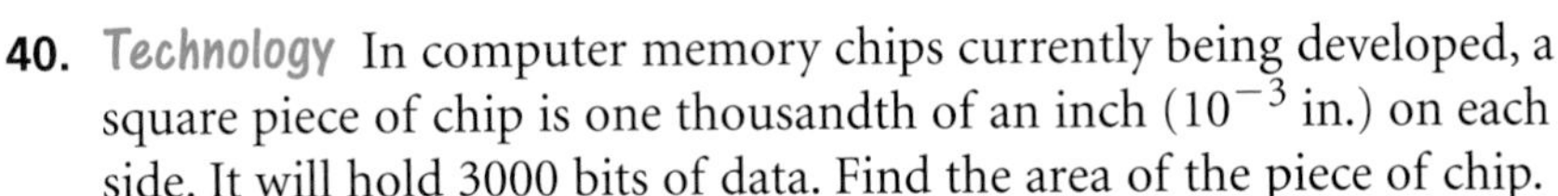

40. **Technology** In computer memory chips currently being developed, a square piece of chip is one thousandth of an inch (10^{-3} in.) on each side. It will hold 3000 bits of data. Find the area of the piece of chip.

Complete each equation.

41. $(x^2)^{\blacksquare} = x^6$ **42.** $(x^{\blacksquare})^3 = x^{-12}$ **43.** $(ab^2)^{\blacksquare} = a^4b^8$

44. $(5x^{\blacksquare})^2 = 25x^4$ **45.** $(3x^3y^{\blacksquare})^3 = 27x^6$ **46.** $(m^2n^3)^{\blacksquare} = \frac{1}{m^6n^9}$

Solve each equation. Use the sample below.

Sample:

$25^3 = 5^x$

$(5^2)^3 = 5^x$ ← Write 25 as a power of 5.

$5^6 = 5^x$ ← Multiply exponents.

$x = 6$

The solution is 6.

47. $8^2 = 2^x$ **48.** $3^x = 27^4$ **49.** $4^x = 2^6$ **50.** $5^6 = 25^x$

51. **Biology** There are an estimated 200 million insects for each person on Earth. The world population is about 5.5 billion. About how many insects are there on Earth?

Write each expression with only one exponent. Use parentheses.

52. $m^4 \cdot n^4$

53. $(a^5)(b^5)(a^0)$

54. $49x^2y^2z^2$

55. $\frac{12x^{-2}}{3y^2}$

Chapter Project *Find Out by Interpreting*

Use your exponential function to predict the growth of your mold at two weeks. Compare your predictions to the actual growth of the mold. Discuss any factors that may influence the accuracy of your exponential model.

Exercises MIXED REVIEW

56. Solve $3x^2 - 5x - 2 = 0$.

57. Solve $x^2 + 2x + 1 = 0$.

58. **Textiles** To make felt, thin layers of cotton are built up $\frac{1}{32}$ in. at a time. How many layers does it take to make felt $\frac{1}{4}$ in. thick?

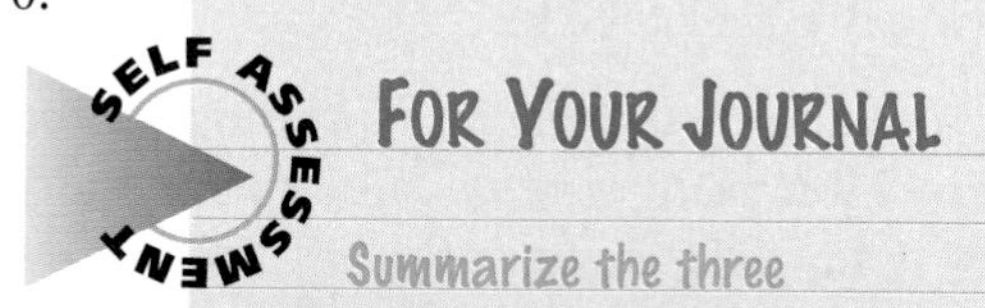

SELF ASSESSMENT — FOR YOUR JOURNAL

Summarize the three multiplication properties of exponents that you have learned in the last two lessons. Give an example of each.

Getting Ready for Lesson 8-8

Simplify each expression.

59. $x^2 \cdot x^{-3}$

60. $u^8 \cdot u^{-4}$

61. $t^{-6} \cdot t$

62. $h^{-3} \cdot h^0$

A Point in Time

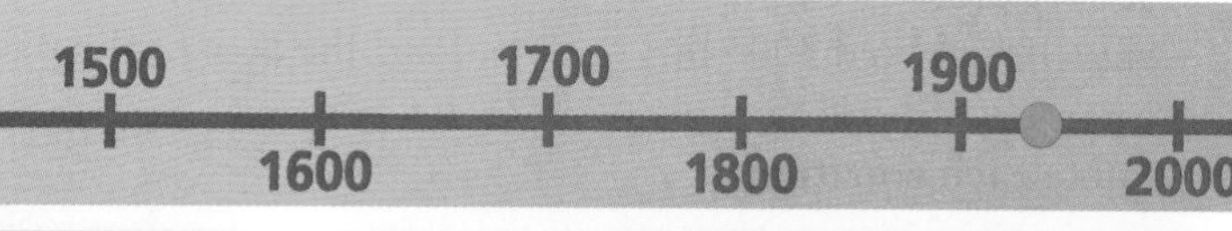

Dr. Jewel Plummer Cobb

Dr. Jewel Plummer Cobb was born in 1924 and obtained her master's and doctorate degrees in cell physiology from New York University. Dr. Cobb has concentrated on the study of normal and malignant skin cells and has published nearly fifty books, articles, and reports.

Because the number of cancer cells grows exponentially, cell biologists often write cancer cell data in scientific notation.

What You'll Learn

- Applying division properties of exponents

...And Why

To solve problems that involve dividing numbers in scientific notation

What You'll Need

- calculator

8-8 Division Properties of Exponents

THINK AND DISCUSS

Dividing Powers with the Same Base

In Lessons 8-6 and 8-7 you studied patterns that occur when you multiply powers with the same base. You can see a similar pattern when you divide powers with the same base.

You can use repeated multiplication to simplify fractions. Expand the numerator and denominator using repeated multiplication. Then cancel like terms.

$$\frac{5^6}{5^2} = \frac{\cancel{5} \cdot \cancel{5} \cdot 5 \cdot 5 \cdot 5 \cdot 5}{\cancel{5} \cdot \cancel{5}} = 5^4$$

1. Simplify each expression by expanding the numerator and the denominator and then canceling. Describe any patterns you see.

a. $\frac{5^7}{5^3}$ **b.** $\frac{5^{12}}{5^8}$ **c.** $\frac{5^8}{5^4}$ **d.** $\frac{5^5}{5^1}$ **e.** $\frac{5^5}{5^8}$

Dividing Powers with the Same Base

For any nonzero number a and any integers m and n, $\frac{a^m}{a^n} = a^{m-n}$.

Example: $\frac{3^7}{3^2} = 3^{7-2} = 3^5$

2. Calculator Find each missing value. Use a calculator to check.

a. $\frac{5^9}{5^2} = 5^{\blacksquare}$ **b.** $\frac{2^4}{2^3} = 2^{\blacksquare}$ **c.** $\frac{3^2}{3^5} = 3^{\blacksquare}$ **d.** $\frac{5^3}{5^2} = 5^{\blacksquare}$

Example 1

Simplify each expression. Use only positive exponents.

a. $\frac{a^6}{a^{14}} = a^{6-14}$ ← Subtract exponents when dividing powers with the same base.

$= a^{-8}$

$= \frac{1}{a^8}$ ← Rewrite using positive exponents.

b. $\frac{c^{-1}d^3}{c^5d^{-4}} = c^{-1-5} \cdot d^{3-(-4)}$ ← Subtract exponents.

$= c^{-6}d^7$

$= \frac{d^7}{c^6}$ ← Use positive exponents.

3. Try This Simplify each expression. Use positive exponents.

a. $\frac{b^4}{b^9}$ **b.** $\frac{z^{10}}{z^5}$ **c.** $\frac{a^2b}{a^4b^3}$ **d.** $\frac{m^{-1}n^2}{m^3n}$ **e.** $\frac{x^2yz^4}{xy^4z^{-3}}$

Example 2 Relating to the Real World 

Environment In 1993 the total amount of waste paper and cardboard recycled in the United States was 77.8 million tons. The population in 1993 was 258.1 million. How much paper was recycled per person?

$$\frac{77.8 \text{ million tons}}{258.1 \text{ million people}} = \frac{77.8 \times 10^{7} \text{ tons}}{2.581 \times 10^{8} \text{ people}}$$ ← Write in scientific notation.

$$= \frac{7.78}{2.581} \times 10^{7-8}$$ ← Subtract exponents when dividing powers with the same base.

$$= \frac{7.78}{2.581} \times 10^{-1}$$

$$\approx 3.01 \times 10^{-1}$$ ← Simplify.

$$\approx 0.3$$

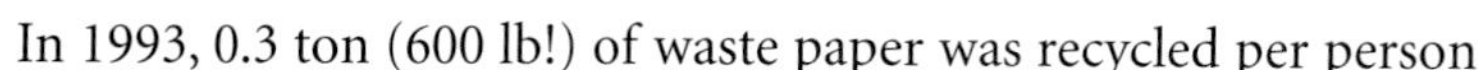

In 1993, 0.3 ton (600 lb!) of waste paper was recycled per person.

4. Only 34% of the waste paper generated in 1993 was recycled. How many pounds of waste paper were generated per person in 1993?

5. **Try This** Find each quotient. Give your answer in scientific notation.

a. $\frac{2 \times 10^{3}}{8 \times 10^{8}}$ **b.** $\frac{7.5 \times 10^{12}}{2.5 \times 10^{-4}}$ **c.** $\frac{4.2 \times 10^{5}}{12.6 \times 10^{2}}$

Raising a Quotient to a Power

You can use repeated multiplication to simplify the expression $\left(\frac{x}{y}\right)^{3}$.

$$\left(\frac{x}{y}\right)^{3} = \frac{x}{y} \cdot \frac{x}{y} \cdot \frac{x}{y}$$

$$= \frac{x \cdot x \cdot x}{y \cdot y \cdot y}$$

$$= \frac{x^{3}}{y^{3}}$$

6. **Calculator** **Verify** that $\left(\frac{x}{y}\right)^{3} = \frac{x^{3}}{y^{3}}$ for three values of x and y.

Raising a Quotient to a Power

For any nonzero numbers a and b, and any integer n, $\left(\frac{a}{b}\right)^{n} = \frac{a^{n}}{b^{n}}$.

Example: $\left(\frac{4}{5}\right)^{3} = \frac{4^{3}}{5^{3}} = \frac{64}{125}$

Example 3

Simplify each expression.

a. $\left(\frac{4}{x^2}\right)^3 = \frac{4^3}{(x^2)^3}$ ← Raise the numerator and denominator to the 3rd power.

$= \frac{4^3}{x^6}$ ← Multiply exponents.

$= \frac{64}{x^6}$ ← Simplify.

b. $\left(-\frac{3}{5}\right)^{-2} = \left(\frac{-3}{5}\right)^{-2}$ ← Write the fraction with a negative numerator.

$= \frac{(-3)^{-2}}{5^{-2}}$ ← Raise the numerator and denominator to the −2 power.

$= \frac{5^2}{(-3)^2}$ ← Apply the definition of negative exponents.

$= \frac{25}{9}$ ← Simplify.

7. In Example 3, part (b), the first step could have been to rewrite the fraction as $\left(\frac{3}{-5}\right)^{-2}$. Explain how this step would affect the rest of your work.

8. *Open-ended* Suppose you wanted to simplify $\left(\frac{5}{3}\right)^3$. What would be your first step?

When you have reduced an expression as far as possible, and when all your exponents are positive, the expression is in **simplest form.**

9. Is each expression in simplest form? If not, simplify it.

a. $\frac{(x^3)^2}{y^7}$ b. $x^{-3}y^2$ c. $\frac{a^5}{ab}$ d. $\frac{(2x)^2}{2x^2}$

Sometimes you can combine steps to shorten your work.

10. Copy and complete each statement.

a. $\left(\frac{4a^3}{b}\right)^2 = \frac{\blacksquare a^{\blacksquare}}{b^{\blacksquare}}$ ← Raising products, quotients, and powers to a power.

b. $\frac{x^{-3}x^8}{x^2} = x^{\blacksquare + \blacksquare - \blacksquare} = x^{\blacksquare}$ ← Multiplying and dividing powers with the same base.

11. **Try This** Simplify each expression.

a. $\left(\frac{2m^5}{m^2}\right)^4$ b. $\left(\frac{2n^3t}{t^2}\right)^2$ c. $\left(\frac{5x^7y^4}{x^{-2}}\right)^2$

Exercises ON YOUR OWN

Simplify each expression. Use only positive exponents.

1. $\frac{2^5}{2^7}$
2. $\left(\frac{2^2}{5}\right)^2$
3. $\left(\frac{3}{4}\right)^2$
4. $\left(\frac{2}{3}\right)^{-2}$
5. $\left(\frac{3^3}{3^4}\right)^2$
6. $\frac{c^{12}}{c^{15}}$
7. $\frac{x^{13}y^2}{x^{13}y}$
8. $\frac{m^{-2}}{m^{-5}}$
9. $\frac{(2a^7)(3a^2)}{6a^3}$
10. $\left(\frac{3b^2}{5}\right)^0$
11. $\left(\frac{-2}{3}\right)^{-3}$
12. $\frac{3^2 \cdot 5^0}{2^3}$

Explain why each expression is *not* in simplest form.

13. 5^3m^3 **14.** x^5y^{-2} **15.** $(2c)^4$ **16.** $\frac{d^7}{d}$ **17.** x^0y **18.** $(3z^2)^3$

Choose **Use a calculator, paper and pencil, or mental math to simplify each quotient. Give your answers in scientific notation.**

19. $\frac{6.5 \times 10^{15}}{1.3 \times 10^8}$ **20.** $\frac{2.7 \times 10^8}{0.9 \times 10^3}$ **21.** $\frac{2.7 \times 10^8}{3 \times 10^5}$ **22.** $\frac{8.4 \times 10^{-5}}{2 \times 10^{-8}}$ **23.** $\frac{4.7 \times 10^{-4}}{3.1 \times 10^2}$

24. a. **Writing** While simplifying the expression $\frac{c^4}{c^6}$, Kneale said, "I've found a property of exponents that's not in my algebra book!" Write an explanation of why Kneale's method works.

b. **Open-ended** Apply Kneale's method to an example you create.

Kneale

$\frac{c^4}{c^6} = \frac{1}{c^{6-4}} = \frac{1}{c^2}$

25. a. **Television** In 1999 people in the United States will watch television a total of 450 billion hours, according to industry projections. The population will be about 274 million people. Find the number of hours of TV viewing per person for 1999.

b. According to these projections, about how many hours per day will people watch television in 1999?

26. Lena and Jared used different methods to simplify $\left(\frac{b^7}{b^3}\right)^2$. Are both methods correct? Explain.

Lena

$\left(\frac{b^7}{b^3}\right)^2 = \frac{b^{14}}{b^6}$

$= b^8$

Jared

$\left(\frac{b^7}{b^3}\right)^2 = (b^4)^2$

$= b^8$

Simplify each expression. Use only positive exponents.

27. $\frac{2^7}{2^5}$ **28.** $2^5 \cdot 2^{-7}$ **29.** $\left(\frac{3^5}{3^2}\right)^2$ **30.** $\frac{a^7}{a^9}$ **31.** $\frac{6c^7}{3c}$ **32.** $\frac{5x^5}{15x^3}$

33. $\frac{a^7b^3c^2}{a^2b^6c^2}$ **34.** $\frac{a^{-21}a^{15}}{a^3}$ **35.** $\frac{c^3d^7}{c^8d^{-1}}$ **36.** $\frac{p^7qr^{-1}}{pq^{-2}r^5}$ **37.** $\frac{5x^3}{(5x)^3}$ **38.** $\left(\frac{5x^3}{20x}\right)^3$

39. $\left(\frac{c^5}{c^9}\right)^3$ **40.** $\left(\frac{7a}{b^3}\right)^2$ **41.** $\left(\frac{3b^0}{5}\right)^2$ **42.** $\frac{(3a^3)^2}{10a^{-1}}$ **43.** $\left(\frac{5m^3n}{m^5}\right)^3$ **44.** $\left(\frac{x^4x}{x^{-2}}\right)^{-4}$

Write each expression with only one exponent. You may need to use parentheses.

45. $\frac{3^5}{5^5}$ **46.** $\frac{m^7}{n^7}$ **47.** $\frac{d^8}{d^5}$ **48.** $\frac{10^7 \cdot 10^0}{10^{-3}}$ **49.** $\frac{27x^3}{8y^3}$ **50.** $\frac{4m^2}{169m^4}$

51. a. **Finance** In 1980, the U.S. Government owed $909 billion to its creditors. The population of the United States was 226.5 million people. How much did the government owe per person in 1980?

b. In 1994 the debt had grown to $4.64 trillion, with a population of 260 million. How much did the government owe per person?

c. What was the percent of increase in the amount owed per person from 1980 to 1994?

PROBLEM SOLVING HINT

Use a proportion.

Which property(ies) of exponents would you use to simplify each expression?

52. 2^{-3} **53.** $\frac{2^2}{2^5}$ **54.** $\left(\frac{1}{2}\right)^3$ **55.** $\frac{1}{2^{-4} \cdot 2^7}$ **56.** $\frac{(2^4)^3}{2^{15}}$

57. **Astronomy** The ratio of a planet's maximum to minimum distance from the Sun is a measure of how circular its orbit is.

a. Copy and complete the table below.

b. Which planet has the least circular orbit? the most circular orbit? Explain your reasoning.

Distances from the Sun (km)

Planet	Maximum	Minimum	Maximum : Minimum
Mercury	6.97×10^7	4.59×10^7	■ : ■ $= \frac{6.97 \times 10^7}{4.59 \times 10^7} = \frac{6.97}{4.59} \approx 1.52$
Venus	1.089×10^8	1.075×10^8	1.089×10^8 : ■ ≈ ■
Earth	1.521×10^8	1.471×10^8	■ : 1.471×10^8 ≈ ■
Mars	2.491×10^8	2.067×10^8	■ : ■ ≈ ■
Jupiter	8.157×10^8	7.409×10^8	■ : ■ ≈ ■
Saturn	1.507×10^9	1.347×10^9	■ : ■ ≈ ■
Uranus	3.004×10^9	2.735×10^9	■ : ■ ≈ ■
Neptune	4.537×10^9	4.457×10^9	■ : ■ ≈ ■
Pluto	7.375×10^9	4.425×10^9	■ : ■ ≈ ■

58. **Medicine** If you donate blood regularly, the American Red Cross recommends a 56-day waiting period between donations. One pint of blood contains about 2.4×10^{12} red blood cells. Your body normally produces about 2×10^6 red blood cells per second.

a. At its normal rate, in how many seconds will your body replace the red blood cells lost by giving one pint of blood?

b. Convert your answer from part (a) to days.

Exercises MIXED REVIEW

Solve each equation.

59. $x^2 = 0.36$ **60.** $t^2 - 13 = 0$ **61.** $m + 4 = -2$

Graph each inequality.

62. $y \leq 3x - 4$ **63.** $y > -2x$ **64.** $y \geq -x + 1$

65. The Folsom Dam in California holds 1 million acre-feet of water in a reservoir. An acre-foot of water is the amount of water that covers an acre to the depth of one foot, or 326,000 gal. How many gallons are in the reservoir?

SELF ASSESSMENT

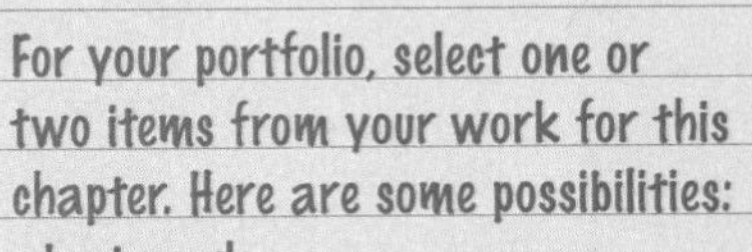

PORTFOLIO

For your portfolio, select one or two items from your work for this chapter. Here are some possibilities:
- best work
- work you found challenging
- part of your project

Explain why you have included each selection that you make.

CHAPTER PROJECT

Finishing the Chapter Project

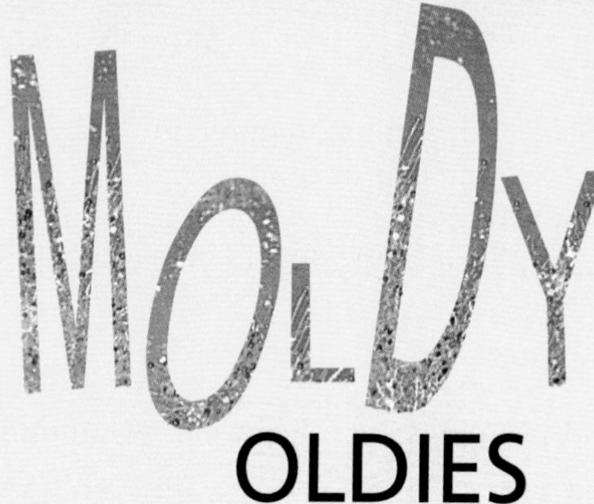

OLDIES

Questions on pages 366, 372, 389, 395, and 400 should help you to complete your project. Record all your information for the project in a notebook. Be sure to include your data and calculations. Include a picture or illustration of the mold as it appeared when it began to grow and at the end of your experiment. Add any additional information you feel is necessary.

Reflect and Revise

Share your notebook with others in your group. Check that your presentation is clear and accurate. Make any changes necessary in your work.

Follow Up

What difference in the rate of growth of the mold might have occurred if you had placed the cheese in a cooler environment? in a drier environment? Investigate other sources of mold and fungus in the natural environment.

For More Information

Dashevsky, H. Steve. *Microbiology: 49 Science Fair Projects.* Blue Ridge Summit, Pennsylvania: TAB Books, 1994.

Hershey, David R. *Plant Biology Science Projects.* New York: John Wiley & Sons, 1995.

VanCleave, Janice Pratt. *Janice VanCleave's A+ Projects in Biology: Winning Experiments for Science Fairs and Extra Credit.* New York: John Wiley & Sons, 1993.

CHAPTER 8

Wrap Up

Key Terms

compound interest (p. 369)
decay factor (p. 373)
exponential decay (p. 373)
exponential function (p. 363)
exponential growth (p. 368)
growth factor (p. 368)
interest period (p. 369)
power (p. 391)
power of ten (p. 386)
scientific notation (p. 385)
simplest form (p. 403)

How am I doing?

- State three ideas from this chapter that you think are important. Explain your choices.
- Describe several rules that you can use to simplify expressions with exponents.

Exploring Exponential Functions — 8-1

You can use exponents to show repeated multiplication. An **exponential function** repeatedly multiplies an amount by the same positive number.

Evaluate each function for the given values.

1. $f(x) = 3 \cdot 2^x$ for the domain $\{1, 2, 3, 4\}$

2. $y = 10 \cdot (0.75)^x$ for the domain $\{1, 2, 3\}$

3. a. One kind of bacterium in a laboratory culture triples in number every 30 minutes. Suppose a culture is started with 30 bacteria cells. How many bacteria will there be after 2 hours?

b. After how many minutes will there be more than 20,000 bacteria?

Exponential Growth and Decay — 8-2, 8-3

The general form of an exponential function is $y = a \cdot b^x$.

When $b > 1$, the function increases, and the function shows **exponential growth.** The base, b, of the exponent is called the **growth factor.** An example of exponential growth is **compound interest.**

When $0 < b < 1$, the function decreases, and the function shows **exponential decay.** Then b is called the **decay factor.** An example of exponential decay is half-life.

Identify each exponential function as *exponential growth* or *exponential decay.* Then identify the growth or decay factor.

4. $y = 5.2 \cdot 3^x$

5. $y = 0.15 \cdot \left(\frac{3}{2}\right)^x$

6. $y = 7 \cdot 0.32^x$

7. $y = 1.3 \cdot \left(\frac{1}{4}\right)^x$

Graph each function.

8. $f(x) = 2.5^x$

9. $y = 0.5 \cdot (0.5)^x$

10. $f(x) = \left(\frac{1}{2}\right) \cdot 3^x$

11. $y = 0.1^x$

What percent increase or decrease is modeled in each function?

12. $y = 100 \cdot 1.025^x$

13. $y = 32 \cdot 0.75^x$

14. $y = 0.4 \cdot 2^x$

15. $y = 1.01 \cdot 0.9^x$

16. The population of a city is 100,000 and is growing 7% each year.
   a. Write an equation to model the population of the city after any number of years.
   b. Use your equation to find the population after 25 years.

17. a. *Finance* Suppose you earned \$1200 last summer and you put it into a savings account that pays 5.5% interest compounded quarterly. Find the balance after 9 months and after 12 months.
   b. *Writing* Would you rather have an account that pays 5.5% interest compounded quarterly or 6% interest compounded annually? Explain.

18. *Chemistry* The half-life of radioactive carbon-11 is 20 min. You start an experiment with 160 mCi of carbon-11. After 2 h, how much radioactivity remains?

Zero and Negative Exponents 8-4

You can use zero and negative numbers as exponents. For any nonzero number a, $a^0 = 1$. For any nonzero number a and any integer n, $a^{-n} = \frac{1}{a^n}$.

Write each expression so that all exponents are positive.

19. $b^{-4}c^0d^6$ 20. $\frac{x^{-2}}{y^{-8}}$ 21. $7k^{-8}h^3$ 22. $\frac{1}{p^2q^{-4}r^0}$ 23. $\left(\frac{2}{3}\right)^{-4}$

24. *Critical Thinking* Is $(-3b)^4 = -12b^4$? Why or why not?

25. *Standardized Test Prep* If $a = 4$, $b = -3$, and $c = 0$, which expression has the greatest value?
   A. a^b B. b^c C. $\frac{1}{b^{-a}}$ D. $\frac{a^c}{b^c}$ E. $\frac{c}{a^{-b}}$

Scientific Notation 8-5

You can use **scientific notation** to express very large or very small numbers. A number is in scientific notation if it is in the form $a \times 10^n$, where $1 \leq |a| < 10$ and n is an integer.

Determine whether each number is in scientific notation. If it is not, write it in scientific notation.

26. 950×10^5 27. 72.35×10^8 28. 1.6×10^{-6} 29. 84×10^{-5} 30. 0.26×10^{-3}

Write each number in scientific notation.

31. The space probe *Voyager 2* traveled 2,793,000 miles.

32. There are 189 million passenger cars and trucks in use in the United States.

Double each number. Give your answers in scientific notation.

33. 8.03×10^7 34. 2.3×10^{-9} 35. 7.084×10^6 36. 5×10^{-13}

Multiplication Properties of Exponents 8-6, 8-7

To multiply powers with the same base, add the exponents.

$a^m \cdot a^n = a^{m+n}$

To raise a power to a power, multiply the exponents.

$(a^m)^n = a^{mn}$

To raise a product to a power, raise each factor in the product to the power.

$(ab)^n = a^n b^n$

Simplify each expression. Use only positive exponents.

37. $2d^2d^3$ **38.** $(q^3r)^4$ **39.** $(5c^{-4})(-4m^2c^8)$ **40.** $(1.34^2)^5(1.34)^{-8}$ **41.** $(12x^2y^{-2})^5(4xy^{-3})^{-8}$

42. Estimation Each square inch of your body has about 6.5×10^2 pores. The back of your hand has area about 0.12×10^2 in.^{2}. About how many pores are on the back of one hand?

43. Open-ended Write and solve a problem that involves multiplying exponents.

Division Properties of Exponents 8-8

To divide powers with the same base, subtract the exponents. $\frac{a^m}{a^n} = a^{m-n}$

To raise a quotient to a power, raise the dividend and the divisor to the power. $\left(\frac{a}{b}\right)^n = \frac{a^n}{b^n}$

Determine whether each expression is in simplest form. If it is not, simplify it.

44. $\frac{w^2}{w^5}$ **45.** $(8^3) \cdot 8^{-5}$ **46.** $\left(\frac{21x^3}{5y^2}\right)$ **47.** $\left(\frac{n^5}{v^3}\right)^7$ **48.** $\frac{e^{-6}c^3}{e^5}$ **49.** $\left(\frac{x^9}{s^{-3}}\right)^5$

Find each quotient. Give your answer in scientific notation.

50. $\frac{4.2 \times 10^8}{2.1 \times 10^{11}}$ **51.** $\frac{3.1 \times 10^4}{12.4 \times 10^2}$ **52.** $\frac{4.5 \times 10^3}{9 \times 10^7}$ **53.** $\frac{5.1 \times 10^5}{1.7 \times 10^2}$

54. Writing List the steps that you would follow to simplify $\left(\frac{5a^8}{10a^6}\right)^{-3}$.

Getting Ready for........ CHAPTER 9

Find the distance between the numbers on a number line.

55. 5 and 3 **56.** –7 and 4 **57.** –5 and –11

Simplify each expression.

58. $7r(11 + 4x)$ **59.** $8m(3 - 2t)$ **60.** $b(8 + 2b)$

61. $8p + 6d - 3p$ **62.** $-5n - 4n + 10n$ **63.** $5^2 + 6^2$

64. $9^2 - 4^2$ **65.** $(3t)^2 + (2t)^2$ **66.** $20y^2 - (4y)^2$

Find the range and mean of each set of data.

67. \$40, \$58, \$44, \$47, \$39, \$58, \$56

68. 4 kg, 3 kg, 6 kg, 3 kg, 5 kg, 8 kg, 4 kg, 3 kg

69. 1.3 min, 1.4 min, 1.1 min, 1.0 min, 1.4 min

CHAPTER 8

Assessment

Evaluate each function for $x = 1, 2,$ and 3.

1. $y = 3 \cdot 5^x$
2. $f(x) = \frac{1}{2} \cdot 4^x$
3. $f(x) = 4 \cdot (0.95)^x$
4. $g(x) = 5 \cdot \left(\frac{3}{4}\right)^x$
5. The function $y = 10 \cdot 1.08^x$ models the cost of annual tuition (in thousands of dollars) at a local college in the years since 1987.
   a. Graph the function.
   b. What is the annual percent increase?
   c. How much was tuition in 1987? in 1992?
   d. How much will tuition be the year you plan to graduate from high school?
6. The function $y = 1.3 \cdot (1.07)^n$ models a city's annual electrical consumption for the n years since 1965, where y is billions of kilowatt-hours.
   a. Determine whether the function models exponential growth or decay, and find the growth or decay factor.
   b. What value of n should be substituted to find the value of y now? Use this value for n to find y.
   c. What will be the annual electrical usage in 10 years?
   d. What was the annual electrical usage 10 years ago?
7. **Open-ended** Write and solve a problem involving exponential decay.
8. **Writing** Explain when the function $y = a \cdot b^x$ shows exponential growth and when it shows exponential decay.
9. **Standardized Test Prep** If $a = -3$, which expression has the least value?
   A. a^2a^0 B. a^a C. a^8a^{-5}
   D. $-a^aa^{-4}$ E. $(a^3a^{-4})^2$

Graph each function.

10. $y = \frac{1}{2} \cdot 2^x$
11. $y = 2 \cdot \left(\frac{1}{2}\right)^x$
12. $f(x) = 3^x$
13. **Critical Thinking** Is there a solution to the equation $3^x = 5^x$? Explain.

Write each number in scientific notation.

14. There were 44,909,000 votes cast for Bill Clinton in the 1992 presidential election.
15. More than 450,000 households in the United States have reptiles as pets.

Determine whether each number is in scientific notation. If it is not, write it in scientific notation.

16. 76×10^{-9}
17. 7.3×10^5
18. $4.05 \times 10 \times 10^{-8}$
19. 32.5×10^{13}

Simplify each expression. Use positive exponents.

20. $\frac{r^3t^{-7}}{t^5}$
21. $\left(\frac{a^3}{m}\right)^{-4}$
22. $\frac{t^{-8}m^2}{m^{-3}}$
23. $c^3v^9c^{-1}c^0$
24. $h^2k^{-5}d^3k^2$
25. $9y^4j^2y^{-9}$
26. $(w^2k^0p^{-5})^{-7}$
27. $2y^{-9}h^2(2y^0h^{-4})^{-6}$
28. $(1.2)^5(1.2)^{-2}$
29. $(-3q^{-1})^3q^2$
30. a. **Astronomy** The speed of light in a vacuum is 186,300 mi/s. Use scientific notation to express how far light travels in one hour.
    b. How long does light take to travel to Saturn, about 2.3×10^9 mi away from Earth?
31. **Banking** A customer deposits $1000 in a savings account that pays 4% interest compounded quarterly. How much money will the customer have in the account after 2 years? after 5 years?
32. **Automobiles** Suppose a new car is worth $14,000. Its value decreases by one fifth each year. The function $y = 14{,}000(0.8)^x$ models the car's value after x years.
    a. Find the value of the car after one year.
    b. Find the value of the car after four years.

CHAPTER 8

Cumulative Review

For Exercises 1–14, choose the correct letter.

1. If a is positive and b is negative, which of the following is negative?
   A. $|ab|$ B. $a + |b|$ C. $a|b|$
   D. $|a|b$ E. $|a| - b$

2. What is the value of the function $f(x) = 2x^2 + x + 3$ when $x = -3$?
   A. 42 B. -18 C. 24 D. 36 E. 18

3. Which equation does *not* have the solution -1.5?
   A. $\frac{9}{w} = -6$ B. $-10w = 15$
   C. $4 - 3w = 8.5$ D. $-1 - 2w = -4$
   E. $w^2 = 2.25$

4. Your test scores are 88, 78, 81, 83, and 90. What score do you need on your next test to raise your median to 85?
   A. 90 B. 87 C. 85 D. 86 E. 92

5. Use the quadratic formula to find the solutions of $2x^2 + 5x + 3 = 0$.
   A. $\frac{-3}{2}, -1$ B. $\frac{3}{2}, -1$ C. $\frac{3}{2}, 1$
   D. $-3, -1$ E. $-3, -2$

6. Identify the function.
   A. $2y + x = 2$
   B. $y + 2x = -2$
   C. $2y - x = 1$
   D. $y + 2x = 1$
   E. $y - 2x = 1$

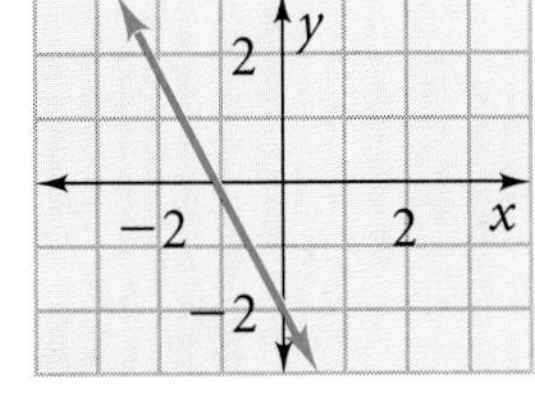

7. Which value of x is *not* a solution of the inequality $5 - 6x < -x + 2$?
   A. -1 B. 5 C. 1 D. $\frac{3}{4}$ E. 3

8. Find the solution of the system of equations.
   $\frac{1}{3}x - y = 4$ $x + 3y = 0$
   A. $(9, -1)$ B. $(-6, 2)$ C. $(6, -2)$
   D. $(-3, 1)$ E. $(-9, 1)$

9. You earn a commission of 6% on your first \$500 of sales and 10% on all sales above \$500. If you earn \$130 in commissions, what are your total sales?
   A. \$800 B. \$1000 C. \$1300
   D. \$1500 E. \$2000

10. You flip a coin and roll a number cube. Find the probability of getting a head and a multiple of 3.
    A. $\frac{1}{4}$ B. $\frac{1}{6}$ C. $\frac{1}{12}$ D. $\frac{3}{2}$ E. $\frac{5}{6}$

11. Find the minimum value of the function $f(x) = x^2 + x + 4$.
    A. $\frac{15}{4}$ B. 4 C. $\frac{17}{4}$ D. -2 E. -1

12. Which number has the least value?
    A. $2.8 \cdot 10^{-5}$ B. $5.3 \cdot 10^{-4}$
    C. $8.3 \cdot 10^{-7}$ D. $1.6 \cdot 10^{-8}$
    E. $7.04 \cdot 10^{-8}$

Compare the boxed quantity in Column A with the boxed quantity in Column B. Choose the best answer.

A. The quantity in Column A is greater.
B. The quantity in Column B is greater.
C. The two quantities are equal.
D. The relationship cannot be determined on the basis of the information supplied.

Find each answer.

	Column A	Column B
13.	$x^2 + x - 20 = 0$	
	the value of the discriminant of the equation	the sum of the solutions of the equation
14.	the growth factor of an exponential function	the decay factor of an exponential function

15. Graph $y = -2x^2 + 3x + 8$.

16. **Open-ended** Describe a situation that you could model using the equation $17 - 3x = 5$.

17. **Writing** The slopes of four lines are
    a: $\frac{3}{5}$ b: $-\frac{10}{6}$ c: $-\frac{5}{3}$ d: $\frac{9}{15}$
    Do these lines determine a rectangle? Explain why or why not.

CHAPTER 9

Right Triangles and Radical Expressions

Relating to the Real World

Right triangles have been important in surveying and construction since early civilization. Since then, special relationships in right triangles have led to improved navigation for ships and planes, to formulas for a pendulum and for distance, and to other areas of mathematics that use radical expressions.

On a CLEAR Day...

Suppose it's a clear day and you have a view with no obstructions — maybe not as clear as from an air traffic control tower, but fairly clear. How far would you be able to see to the horizon? You can use the Pythagorean theorem and other concepts in this chapter to find this distance.

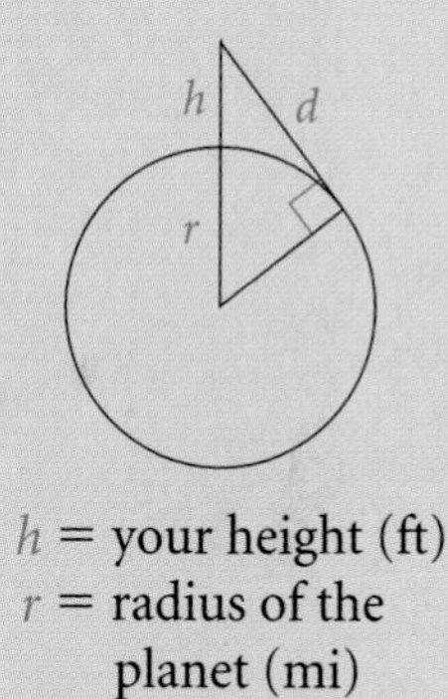

h = your height (ft)
r = radius of the planet (mi)
d = distance you can see (mi)

As you work through the chapter, you will determine and compare the distances you would be able to see to the horizon if you could stand on any planet, including Earth. Your project should include diagrams of the planets, formulas for the distances visible, and graphs of these formulas.

To help you complete the project:

- **p. 418** *Find Out by Writing*
- **p. 424** *Find Out by Calculating*
- **p. 429** *Find Out by Researching*
- **p. 444** *Find Out by Communicating*
- **p. 449** *Find Out by Organizing*
- **p. 456** *Finishing the Project*

Solving Radical Equations 9-6

Graphing Square Root Functions 9-7

Analyzing Data Using Standard Deviation 9-8

9-1 The Pythagorean Theorem

What You'll Learn

- Finding lengths of sides of a right triangle
- Deciding if a triangle is a right triangle

...And Why

To calculate distances that cannot be measured directly

What You'll Need

- rectangular objects
- ruler
- graph paper

WORK TOGETHER

Work with a partner.

1. Measure the length l and width w of the cover of your mathematics textbook. Be as precise in your measurements as you can.

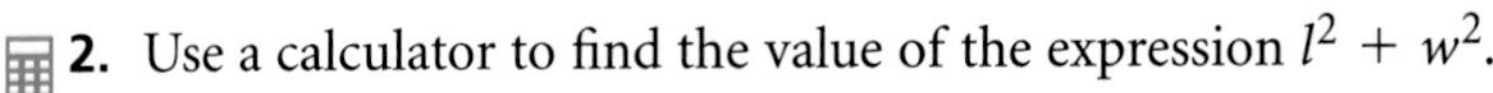

2. Use a calculator to find the value of the expression $l^2 + w^2$.
3. Measure the length d of one of the diagonals of the cover of your book. Calculate the value of d^2.
4. What can you say about the values of $l^2 + w^2$ and d^2?
5. Choose rectangular objects or draw rectangles on graph paper. Repeat the same steps. What can you say about the length of a diagonal?

THINK AND DISCUSS

Solving Equations Using the Pythagorean Theorem

When you draw a diagonal of a rectangle, you separate the rectangle into two right triangles. In a right triangle, the side opposite the right angle is the longest. It is called the **hypotenuse.** The other two sides are called **legs.** There is a relationship among the lengths of the sides of a right triangle.

QUICK REVIEW

A *right triangle* is a triangle with one right angle.

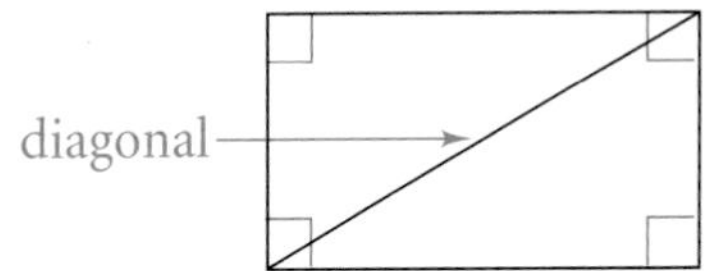

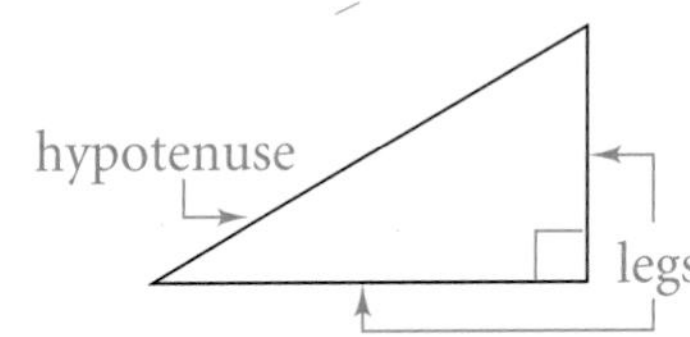

The Pythagorean Theorem

In a right triangle, the sum of the squares of the lengths of the legs is equal to the square of the length of the hypotenuse.

$a^2 + b^2 = c^2$

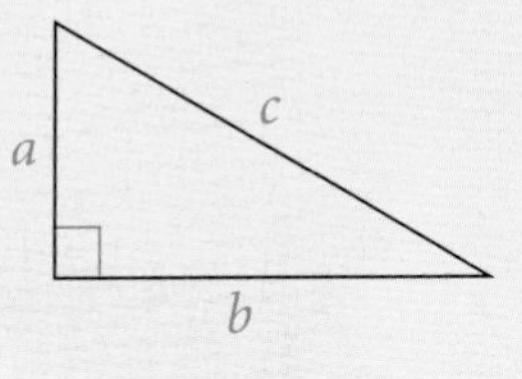

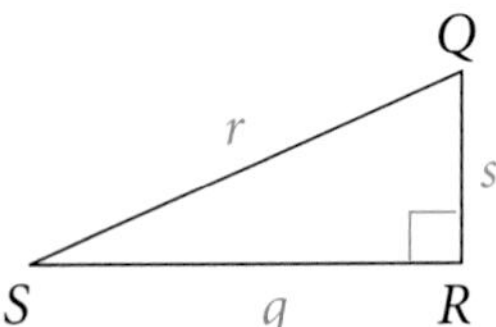

6. Restate the Pythagorean theorem for $\triangle QRS$ to the left.
7. A right triangle has legs of length 5 in. and 12 in. The length of the hypotenuse is 13 in. **Verify** that the Pythagorean theorem is true for this triangle.

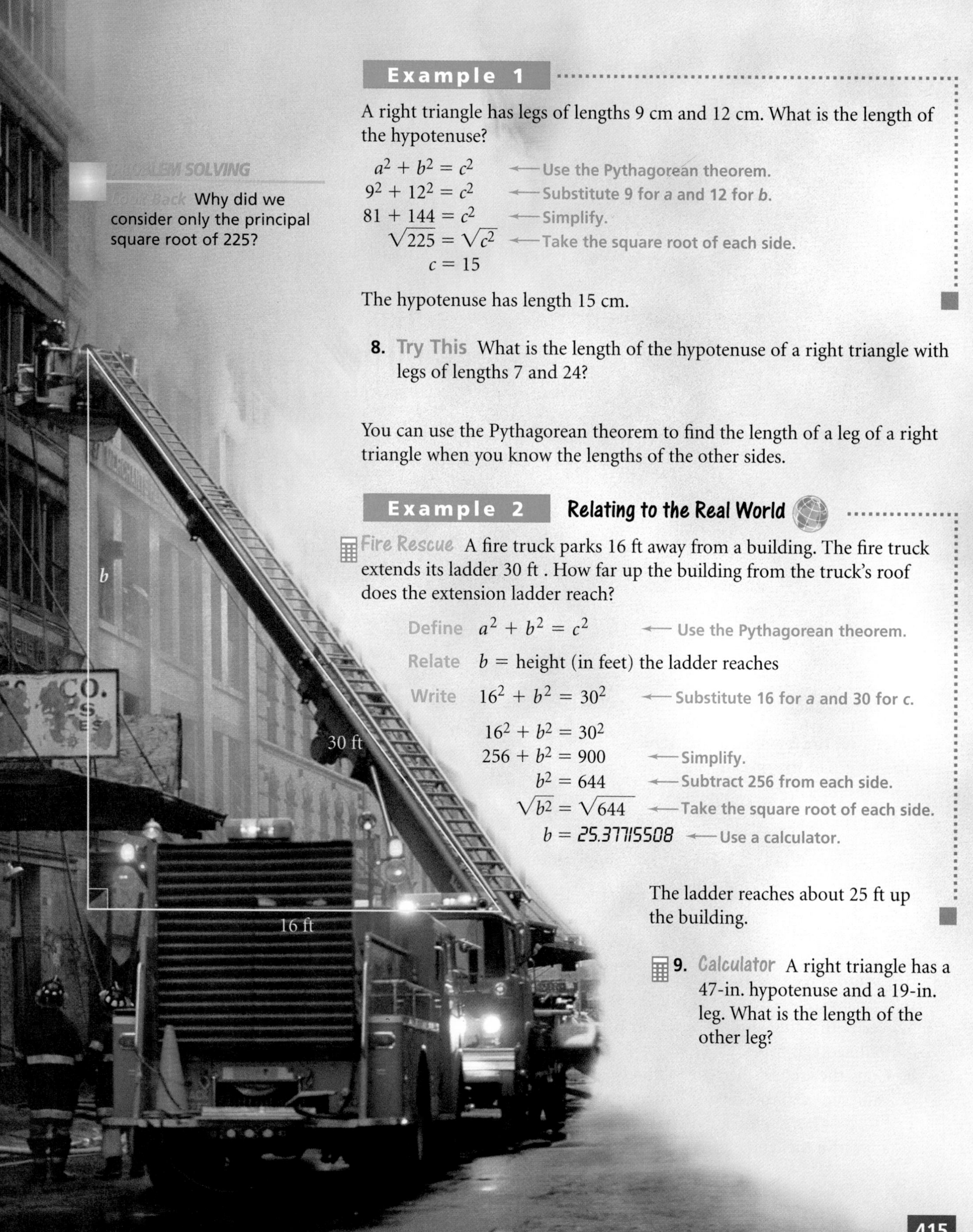

Example 1

A right triangle has legs of lengths 9 cm and 12 cm. What is the length of the hypotenuse?

$a^2 + b^2 = c^2$ ← Use the Pythagorean theorem.
$9^2 + 12^2 = c^2$ ← Substitute 9 for *a* and 12 for *b*.
$81 + 144 = c^2$ ← Simplify.
$\sqrt{225} = \sqrt{c^2}$ ← Take the square root of each side.
$c = 15$

The hypotenuse has length 15 cm.

PROBLEM SOLVING

Look Back Why did we consider only the principal square root of 225?

8. **Try This** What is the length of the hypotenuse of a right triangle with legs of lengths 7 and 24?

You can use the Pythagorean theorem to find the length of a leg of a right triangle when you know the lengths of the other sides.

Example 2 *Relating to the Real World*

Fire Rescue A fire truck parks 16 ft away from a building. The fire truck extends its ladder 30 ft . How far up the building from the truck's roof does the extension ladder reach?

Define $a^2 + b^2 = c^2$ ← Use the Pythagorean theorem.

Relate b = height (in feet) the ladder reaches

Write $16^2 + b^2 = 30^2$ ← Substitute 16 for *a* and 30 for *c*.

$16^2 + b^2 = 30^2$
$256 + b^2 = 900$ ← Simplify.
$b^2 = 644$ ← Subtract 256 from each side.
$\sqrt{b^2} = \sqrt{644}$ ← Take the square root of each side.
$b = 25.37715508$ ← Use a calculator.

The ladder reaches about 25 ft up the building.

9. **Calculator** A right triangle has a 47-in. hypotenuse and a 19-in. leg. What is the length of the other leg?

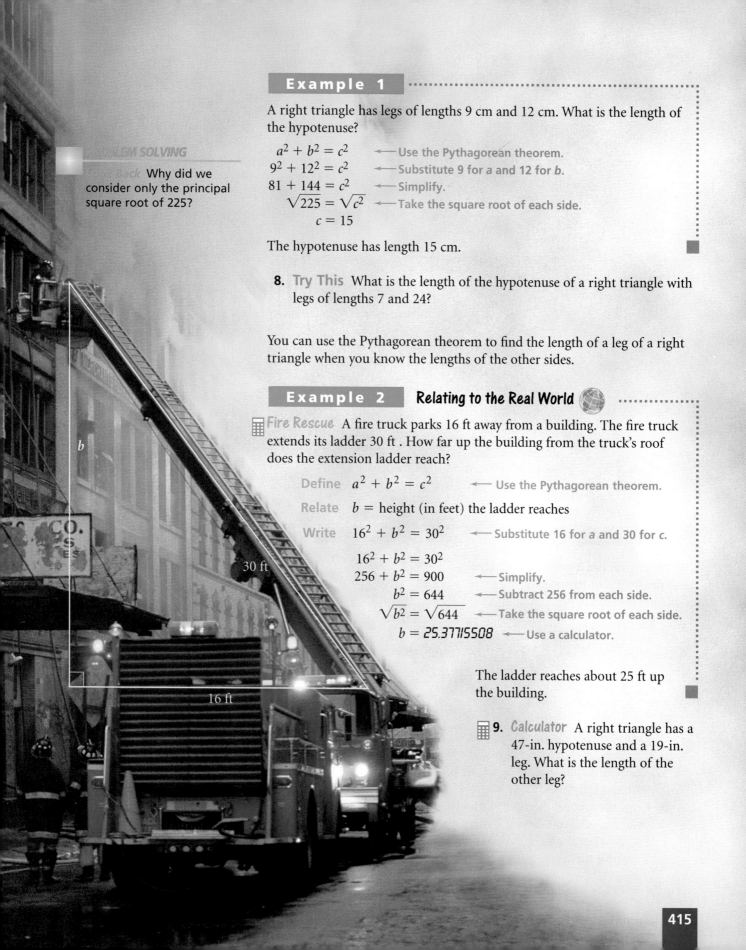

Using the Converse

You can find out whether a triangle is a right triangle by using the converse of the Pythagorean theorem.

The Converse of the Pythagorean Theorem

If a triangle has sides of lengths a, b, and c, and $a^2 + b^2 = c^2$, then the triangle is a right triangle with hypotenuse of length c.

Example 3

A triangle has sides of lengths 7, 9, and 12. Is it a right triangle?

Apply the converse of the Pythagorean theorem.

$a^2 + b^2 \stackrel{?}{=} c^2$

$7^2 + 9^2 \stackrel{?}{=} 12^2$ ← Substitute 12 for c, since 12 is the length of the longest side. Substitute 7 and 9 for a and b.

$49 + 81 \stackrel{?}{=} 144$

$130 \neq 144$

The triangle is not a right triangle. ■

10. Try This A triangle has sides of lengths 10, 24, and 26. Is the triangle a right triangle? Explain.

Exercises ON YOUR OWN

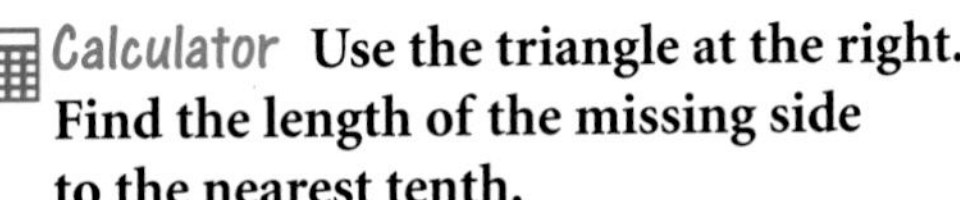

Calculator **Use the triangle at the right. Find the length of the missing side to the nearest tenth.**

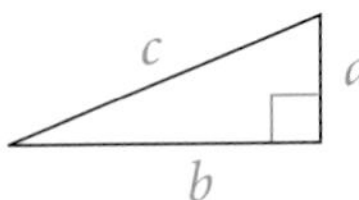

1. $a = 6, b = 8, c = ■$

2. $a = 8, b = 24, c = ■$

3. $a = 1, b = 2, c = ■$

4. $a = 3, b = ■, c = 5$

5. $a = ■, b = 7, c = 10$

6. $a = ■, b = 12, c = 13$

7. $a = 4, b = 4, c = ■$

8. $a = 13, b = 2, c = ■$

9. $a = 15, b = ■, c = 25$

10. $a = ■, b = 10, c = 15$

11. $a = 75, b = ■, c = 100$

12. $a = ■, b = 12, c = 18$

13. Any set of three positive integers that satisfies the relationship $a^2 + b^2 = c^2$ is called a *Pythagorean triple.*

a. Verify that the numbers 6, 8, and 10 form a Pythagorean triple.

b. Copy the table at the right. Complete the table so that the values in each row form a Pythagorean triple.

c. Group Activity Find a Pythagorean triple that does not appear in the table.

a	b	c
3	4	■
5	■	13
■	24	25
9	40	■

Find the missing length to the nearest tenth.

14. 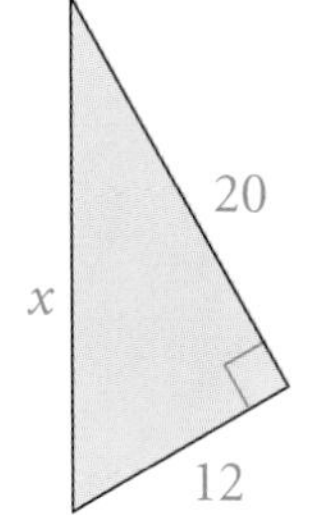

15. 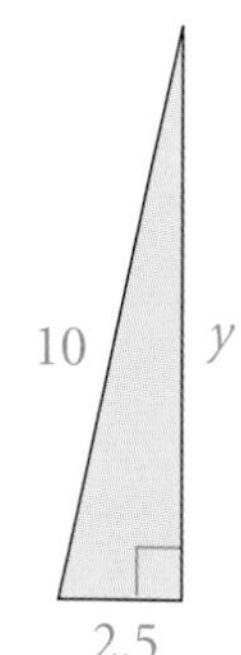

16. 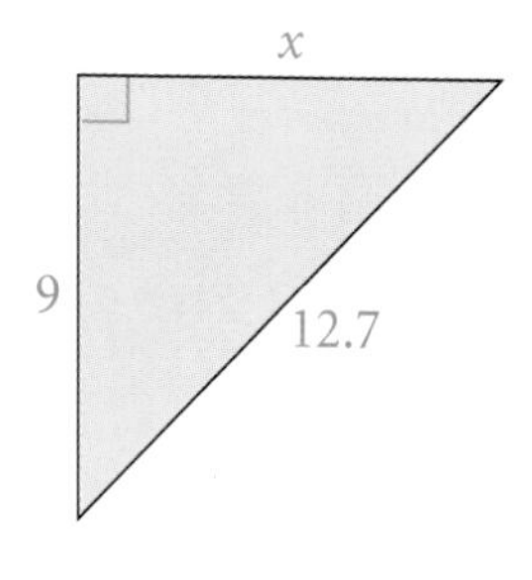

17. 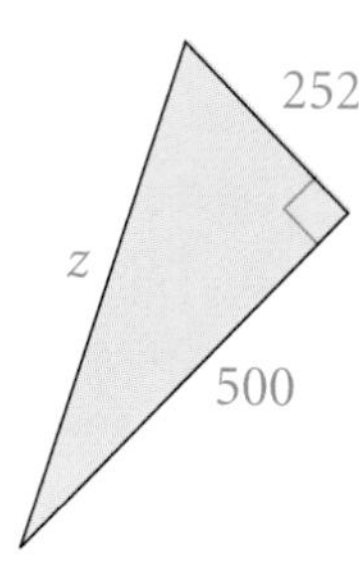

18. Birds A pigeon leaves its nest and flies 5 km due east. The pigeon then flies 3 km due north. How far is the pigeon from its nest?

19. You know that two sides of a right triangle measure 10 in. and 8 in.

a. Writing Why is this not enough information to be sure of finding the length of the third side?

b. Give two different possible values for the length of the third side. Explain how you found your answers.

20. Geometry The yellow, green, and blue figures are squares. Use the Pythagorean theorem and your knowledge of lengths to find the length of one side of the blue square.

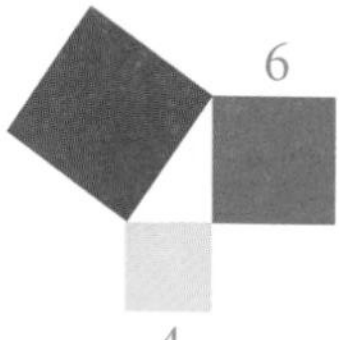

Can each set of three numbers represent the lengths of the sides of a right triangle? Explain your answers.

21. 9, 12, 15

22. 1, 2, 3

23. 2, 4, 5

24. 34, 16, 30

25. 4, 4, 8

26. 5000, 4000, 3000

27. 1.25, 3, 3.25

28. 19, 21, 23

29. 14, 48, 50

30. $\frac{1}{3}, \frac{1}{4}, \frac{1}{5}$

31. 2, 1.5, 1

32. 10, 24, 26

33. 4, 5, 6

34. 15, 20, 25

35. 18, 80, 82

36. $\frac{3}{4}, 1, 1\frac{1}{4}$

37. a. Sightseeing A gondola travels between two elevations along a cable. What is the distance the gondola travels from the bottom of the hill to the top?

b. The gondola travels from the bottom of the hill to the top of the hill in 20 min. What is the average speed of the gondola in feet per minute? in miles per hour?

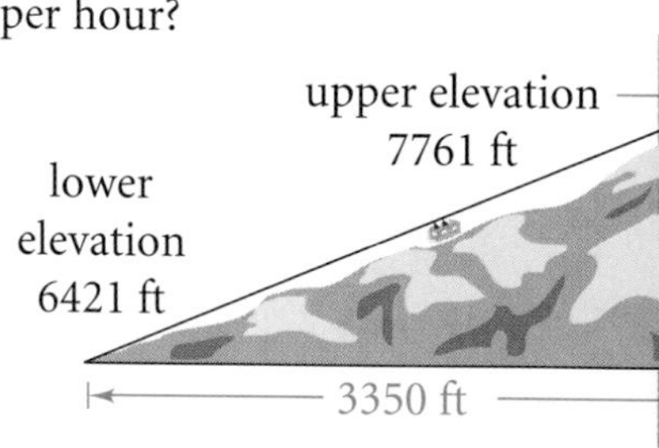

38. *Solar Heating Technician* Find the length of the glass insert for the solar heating panel shown. Round your answer to the nearest inch.

39. What is the diameter of the smallest circular opening that the rectangular rod shown will fit through? Round your answer to the nearest tenth.

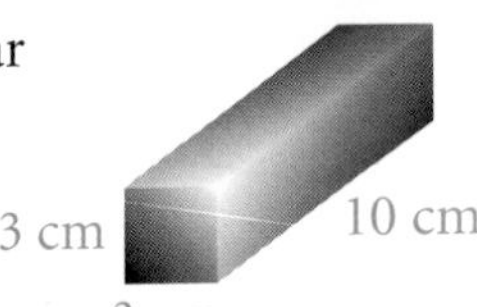

Chapter Project — *Find Out by Writing*

- How many feet are in a mile?
- How would you convert 15 ft into miles?
- How would you represent the quantity h feet in miles?
- In the diagram on page 413, replace h with the expression that represents h feet in miles. Use the Pythagorean theorem to write an equation relating r, d, and h. Do not simplify the equation.

Exercises MIXED REVIEW

Solve each system of equations by substitution.

40. $y = 3x + 5,\ x + y = 4$

41. $y = -3x + 2,\ x - y = 0$

42. *Architecture* A model of a house is $\frac{1}{25}$ of its actual size. One side of the model house is 48 in. long. How long is the corresponding side in the actual house?

Getting Ready for Lesson 9-2

Let $c = \sqrt{a^2 + b^2}$. For each set of values, calculate c to the nearest tenth.

43. $a = 3,\ b = 4$

44. $a = -2,\ b = 5$

45. $a = -3,\ b = 8$

46. $a = 7,\ b = -5$

Math ToolboX

Technology

Testing for a Right Triangle

After Lesson 9-1

With a graphing calculator, you can create a program and save it to use in the future. This program tests three numbers to see if they can be the lengths of the sides of a right triangle.

To input the program, choose PRGM, then *NEW*. To name the program, press 1, type PYTHAG, and then press ENTER.

To enter the program you will find commands in the PRGM feature under *CTL* and *I/O*. After each line press ENTER to go to the next line.

To type the variables *A*, *B*, and *C*, use ALPHA before typing each letter. You can use *A-LOCK* to type a string of letters such as the information in quotes. The equal sign is in the TEST feature.

After entering your program, press 2nd QUIT. To run your program, press PRGM, select PYTHAG, and choose *EXEC*.

```
PROGRAM:PYTHAG
:Prompt A,B,C
:If A²+B²=C²
:Goto 1
:Disp "NOT A RIGHT
TRIANGLE"
:Goto 2
:Lbl 1
:Disp "RIGHT TRIANGLE"
:Lbl 2
```

Use the program to tell if each set of numbers can represent the sides of a right triangle. Always input the longest side as *c*.

1. {3, 4, 5}
2. {7, 9, 12}
3. {9, 12, 15}
4. {10, 11, 12}
5. {8, 15, 17}
6. {17, 17, 17}
7. {1.4, 4.8, 5}
8. {6, 8, 10}
9. {3, 7, 8}
10. {7, 24, 25 }
11. {20, 21, 29}
12. {12, 13, 20}

Use the program to see if each triangle is a right triangle.

13.
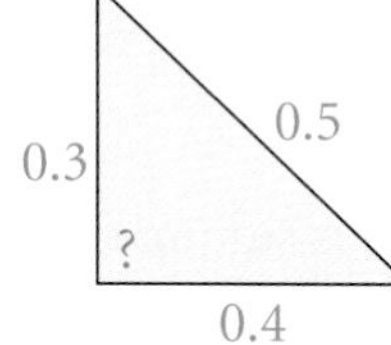

14.
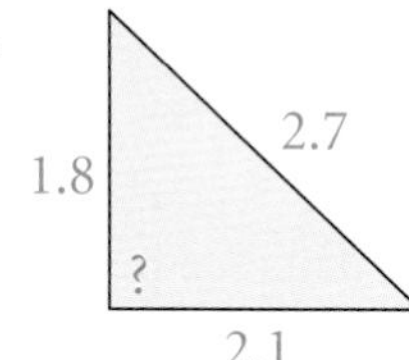

15.
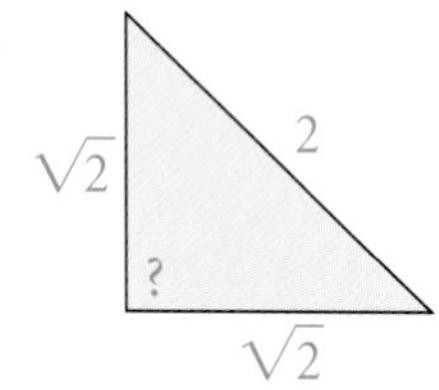

16. Any three integers *a*, *b*, and *c* form a Pythagorean triple if $a^2 + b^2 = c^2$. The following formulas generate Pythagorean triples using positive integers *x* and *y* where $x > y$.

$$a = x^2 - y^2$$
$$b = 2xy$$
$$c = x^2 + y^2$$

a. Find the Pythagorean triple that is generated by the values $x = 3$ and $y = 2$.

b. Find the values of *x* and *y* that generate the set {9, 40, 41}.

17. *Writing* The set {–3, –4, 5} could not represent the sides of a right triangle because the sides of triangles cannot have negative lengths. Explain why the calculator display indicates a right triangle when you input the values –3, –4, and 5.

```
prgmPYTHAG
A=?-3
B=?-4
C=?5
RIGHT TRIANGLE
                Done
```

9-2 The Distance Formula

What You'll Learn

- Finding the distance between two points in a coordinate plane
- Finding the coordinates of the midpoint of two points

...And Why

To find the distance between two groups of hikers

What You'll Need

- graph paper
- ruler

QUICK REVIEW

AB is the distance between points *A* and *B* and the length of $\overline{AB}$.

WORK TOGETHER

Work with a partner as you apply the Pythagorean theorem to find the distance between two points.

1. On graph paper, graph points $A(-3, 4)$, $B(1, 1)$, and $C(-3, 1)$. Then connect the points.
2. Find *AC* and *BC*.
3. $\triangle ABC$ is a right triangle. Use the Pythagorean theorem to write an equation relating *AC*, *BC*, and *AB*.
4. Substitute values for *AC* and *BC* in the equation you wrote in Question 3. Solve the equation to find *AB*.

THINK AND DISCUSS

Finding the Distance

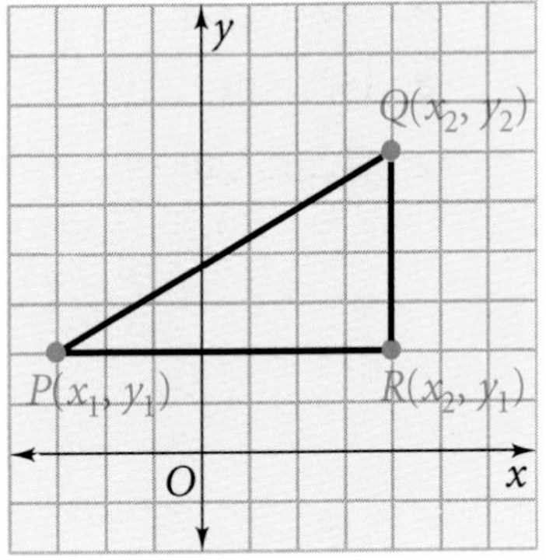

In the Work Together activity, you found the distance between two particular points. If you have any two points $P(x_1, y_1)$ and $Q(x_2, y_2)$, you can graph them and form a right triangle as shown in the diagram. You can then use the Pythagorean theorem to find the distance between the points.

$(PQ)^2 = (PR)^2 + (RQ)^2$ ← Use the Pythagorean theorem.

$(PQ)^2 = (x_2 - x_1)^2 + (y_2 - y_1)^2$ ← Substitute the lengths you know.

$PQ = \sqrt{(x_2 - x_1)^2 + (y_2 - y_1)^2}$ ← Take the principal square root of each side.

This method for finding the distance between two points is summarized in the *distance formula.*

The Distance Formula

The distance *d* between any two points (x_1, y_1) and (x_2, y_2) is

$$d = \sqrt{(x_2 - x_1)^2 + (y_2 - y_1)^2}.$$

Example 1 Relating to the Real World 

Hiking The Gato and Wilson families are staying at a campground. The Gatos leave camp and hike 2 km west and 5 km south. The Wilsons leave camp and hike 1 km east and 4 km north. How far apart are the families?

Let the campground be (0, 0). Then the Gato family's location is (−2, −5) and the Wilson family's location is (1, 4).

$d = \sqrt{(x_2 - x_1)^2 + (y_2 - y_1)^2}$ ← Use the distance formula.

$d = \sqrt{(1 - (-2))^2 + (4 - (-5))^2}$ ← Substitute (1, 4) for (x_2, y_2) and (−2, −5) for (x_1, y_1).

$d = \sqrt{3^2 + 9^2}$ ← Simplify.

$d = \sqrt{90}$

$d = 9.486832981$ ← Use a calculator.

The two families are about 9.5 km apart.

PROBLEM SOLVING

Look Back Would the result in Example 1 be different if you used (1, 4) for (x_1, y_1) and (−2, −5) for (x_2, y_2)? Explain your answer.

5. **Try This** One hiker is 4 mi west and 3 mi north of the campground. Another is 6 mi east and 3 mi south of the campground. How far apart are the hikers?

You can also use the distance formula to determine if lengths of opposite sides in a figure are equal.

Example 2

Geometry Quadrilateral $ORST$ is shown here in a coordinate plane. Use the distance formula to show that $\overline{OR}$ and $\overline{ST}$ are equal in length.

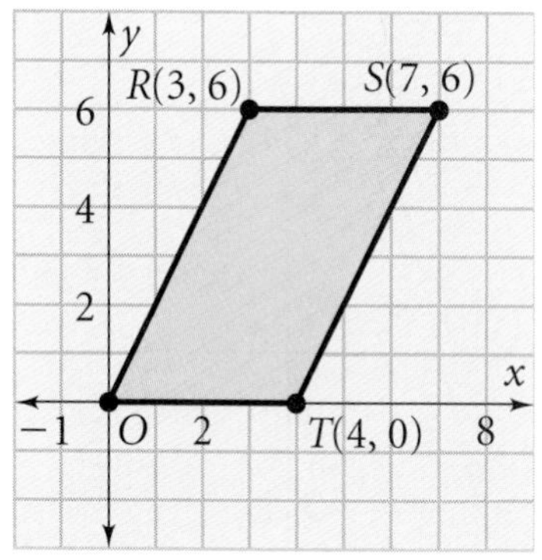

$OR = \sqrt{(3 - 0)^2 + (6 - 0)^2}$	$ST = \sqrt{(7 - 4)^2 + (6 - 0)^2}$
$OR = \sqrt{3^2 + 6^2}$	$ST = \sqrt{3^2 + 6^2}$
$OR = \sqrt{45}$	$ST = \sqrt{45}$

$OR = ST$. So, $\overline{OR}$ and $\overline{ST}$ are equal in length.

6. Use slopes to show that $\overline{OR}$ and $\overline{ST}$ are parallel.

7. a. Try This Quadrilateral *KLMN* has vertices with coordinates *K*(–3, –2), *L*(–5, 6), *M*(2, 6), and *N*(4, –2). Show that $LK = MN$.

b. Use slopes to show that $\overline{LK}$ and $\overline{MN}$ are parallel.

c. Critical Thinking Describe quadrilateral *KLMN* in as much detail as you can. **Justify** your descriptions and conclusions.

Using the Midpoint Formula

The **midpoint** of a segment $\overline{AB}$ is the point *M* halfway between *A* and *B* where $AM = MB$. The coordinates of the midpoint of a line segment are the averages of the coordinates of the endpoints.

The Midpoint Formula

The midpoint *M* of a line segment with endpoints $A(x_1, y_1)$ and $B(x_2, y_2)$ is $\left(\frac{x_1 + x_2}{2}, \frac{y_1 + y_2}{2}\right)$.

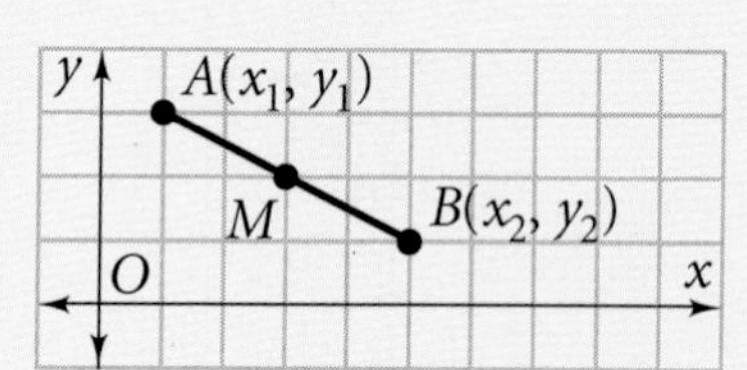

Example 3

Geometry Find the midpoint of the segment from *A*(–1, 6) to *B*(5, 0).

$$\left(\frac{x_1 + x_2}{2}, \frac{y_1 + y_2}{2}\right) = \left(\frac{-1 + 5}{2}, \frac{6 + 0}{2}\right)$$
$$= \left(\frac{4}{2}, \frac{6}{2}\right)$$
$$= (2, 3)$$

The midpoint of $\overline{AB}$ is *M*(2, 3).

8. In Example 3, use the distance formula to **verify** that $AM = MB$.

9. Try This Find the coordinates of the midpoint of the line segment with endpoints *X*(–7.2, 2) and *Y*(4.5, 7.5).

Exercises ON YOUR OWN

Calculator **Approximate *AB* to the nearest tenth of a unit.**

1.

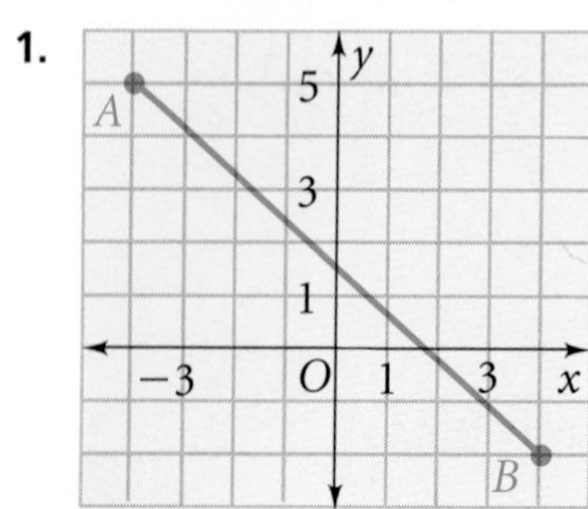

2.

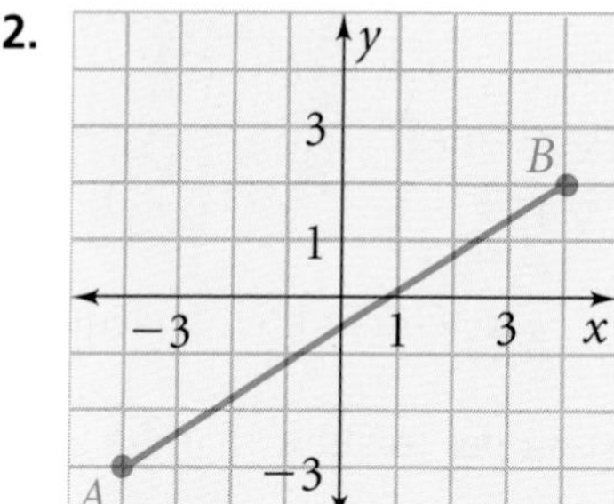

3.

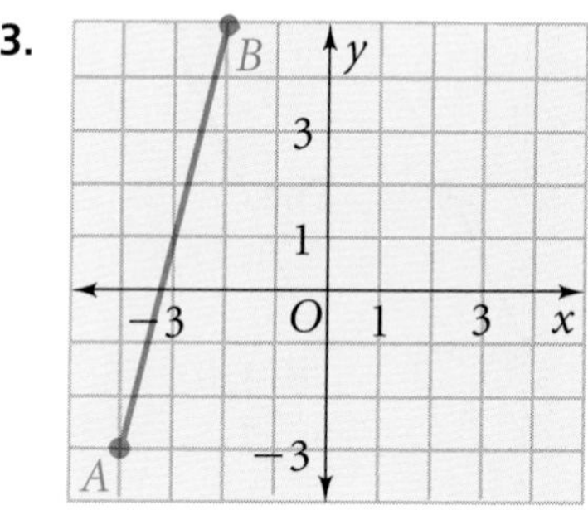

Find the distance between each pair of points to the nearest tenth.

4. $(3, -2), (-1, 5)$

5. $(-4, -4), (4, 4)$

6. $(0, 3), (13, -6)$

7. $(4, 0), (2, -1)$

8. $(7, -2), (-8, -2)$

9. $(5, 9), (10, -1)$

10. $(0, 0), (6, -9)$

11. $(-3, 7), (-11, 9)$

12. $(11, 0), (-3, -7)$

13. $(-2, 7), (-2, -7)$

14. $(9, 10), (11, 12)$

15. $(-3.5, 4.5), (-4.5, 5.5)$

16. a. **News Coverage** Two news helicopters are on their way to a political rally, flying at the same altitude. One helicopter is 20 mi due west of the rally. The other is 15 mi south and 15 mi east of the rally. How far apart are they?

b. How far from the rally are they?

c. Each helicopter is flying at 80 mi/h. How many minutes will it take each of them to arrive at the scene?

17. a. **Electrical Line Technician** Graph Mr. Tanaka's and Ms. Elisa's locations on a coordinate grid with the substation at the origin.

b. What are the coordinates of the point where they will meet?

c. Describe their meeting point in miles north/south and east/west of the substation.

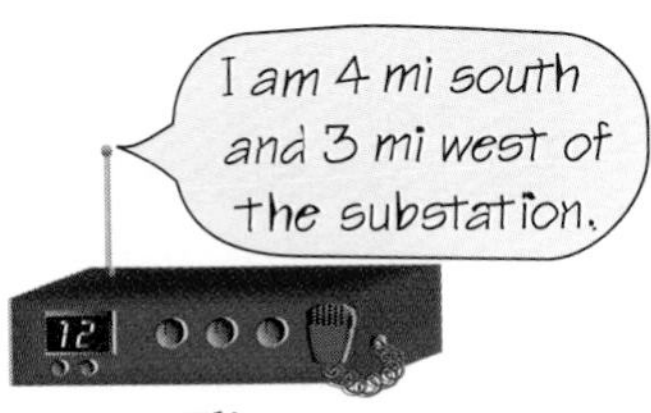

I am 4 mi south
and 3 mi west of
the substation.
12

Ms. Elisa

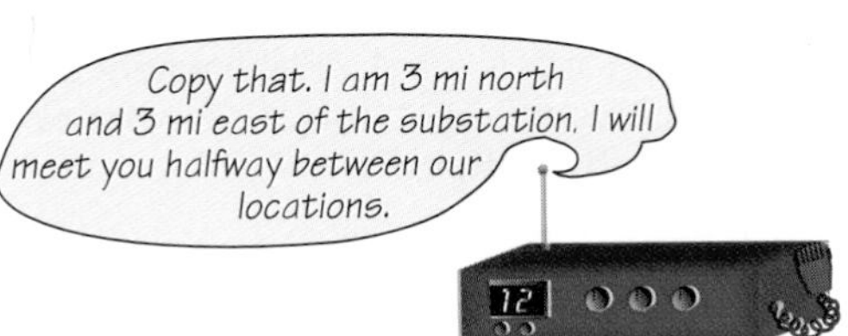

Copy that. I am 3 mi north
and 3 mi east of the substation. I will
meet you halfway between our
locations.
12

Mr. Tanaka

Find the midpoint of $\overline{XY}$.

18. $X(2, 5)$ and $Y(0, 7)$

19. $X(-3, 14)$ and $Y(6, 1)$

20. $X(8, -5)$ and $Y(-4, 5.5)$

21. $X(4, 3)$ and $Y(-9, 3)$

22. $X(0, 6)$ and $Y(-5, -8)$

23. $X(-1, 8)$ and $Y(-7, 0)$

24. $X(4, 1)$ and $Y(1, 4)$

25. $X(5, -11)$ and $Y(12, -7)$

26. $X(2, 9)$ and $Y(-2, -9)$

27. $X(3, 11)$ and $Y(11, 3)$

28. $X\left(4\frac{1}{2}, -2\right)$ and $Y\left(-1\frac{1}{2}, 5\right)$

29. $X(9, 7)$ and $Y(-9, -7)$

30. a. **Transportation** On the map, each unit represents one mile. A van breaks down on its way to a factory. The driver calls a garage for a tow truck. There is a bridge halfway between the garage and the van. How far is the bridge from the van?

b. The van is towed to the factory and then to the garage. How many miles does the tow truck tow the van?

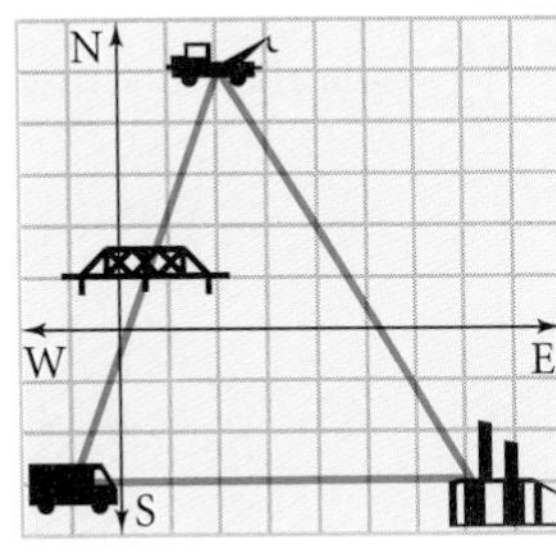

Geometry **Find the perimeter of each figure to the nearest tenth.**

31. 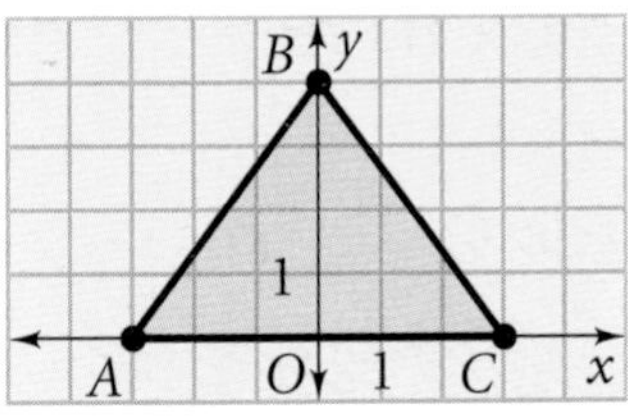

32. 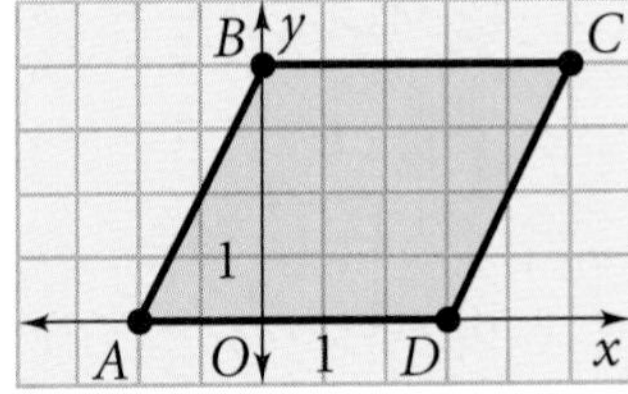

33. 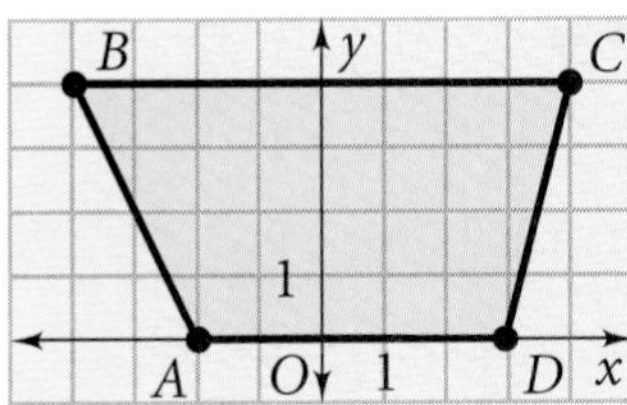

34. a. **Open-ended** Suppose the distance between two points on a coordinate plane is between 10 and 13 units. Identify two points A and B not directly above or across from one another that meet this requirement.

b. Plot your points on graph paper.

c. **Verify** that your points satisfy the requirement by finding AB.

35. **Critical Thinking** If the midpoint of a line segment is the origin, what must be true of the coordinates of the endpoints of the segment?

36. **Writing** **Summarize** the distance formula and the midpoint formula. Use examples of your own to show the use of each formula.

Chapter Project ***Find Out by Calculating***

The radius of Earth is about 3960 mi. The formula for the distance you can see to the horizon on Earth is $d = 1.225\sqrt{h}$ where d is the distance visible in miles and h is your height in feet. How far can you see on a clear day with no obstructions?

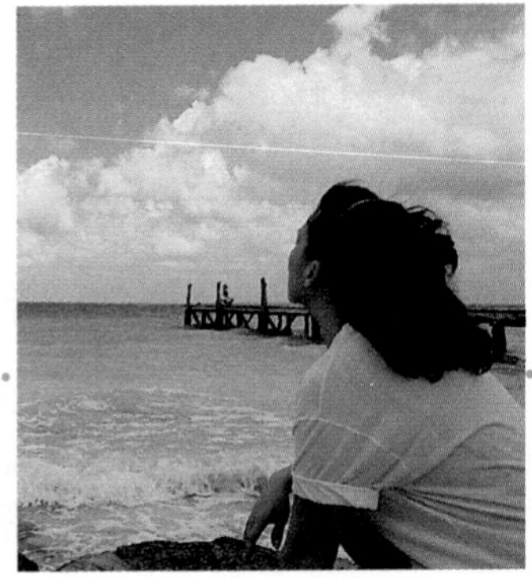

Exercises MIXED REVIEW

Solve each equation for the given variable.

37. $2x + 7y = 4; x$

38. $3x - 5y = 7; y$

39. $V = \pi r^2 h; h$

40. $S = 2\pi rh; r$

41. **Finance** You deposit $3000 into a bank account paying 6% simple interest annually. How much interest will you receive after 4 years?

Getting Ready for Lesson 9-3

Let $c = \frac{A}{H}$, $s = \frac{O}{H}$, $t = \frac{O}{A}$. Calculate c, s, and t for each of the following.

42. $A = 3, O = 4, H = 5$

43. $A = 5, O = 12, H = 13$

Solve each equation.

44. $\frac{15}{x} = 0.75$

45. $\frac{x}{20} = 0.34$

46. $0.82x = 25$

47. $\frac{x}{0.52} = 14$

What You'll Learn

- Exploring and calculating trigonometric ratios
- Using sine, cosine, and tangent to solve problems

...And Why

To find distances indirectly

What You'll Need

- graph paper
- ruler

9-3 Trigonometric Ratios

WORK TOGETHER

Work with a partner.

1. On graph paper, draw a right triangle like the one at the left. Extend sides $\overline{AB}$ and $\overline{AC}$ to form a second triangle similar to the first triangle. One example is shown at the left.

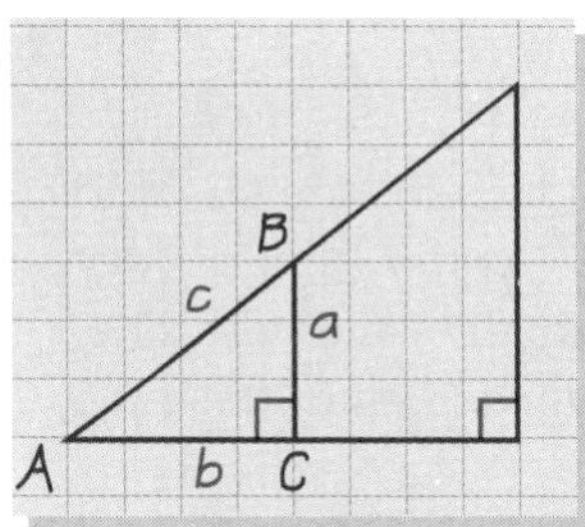

2. a. Copy the table below. Measure and record the lengths of the legs of each triangle.

Triangle	a	b	c	$\frac{a}{b}$	$\frac{a}{c}$	$\frac{b}{c}$
first	■	■	■	■	■	■
second	■	■	■	■	■	■

   b. Calculate and record c, the length of each hypotenuse.

   c. Calculate and record the ratios $\frac{a}{b}$, $\frac{a}{c}$, and $\frac{b}{c}$ for each triangle.

3. How do corresponding ratios in the two triangles compare?

THINK AND DISCUSS

Finding Trigonometric Ratios

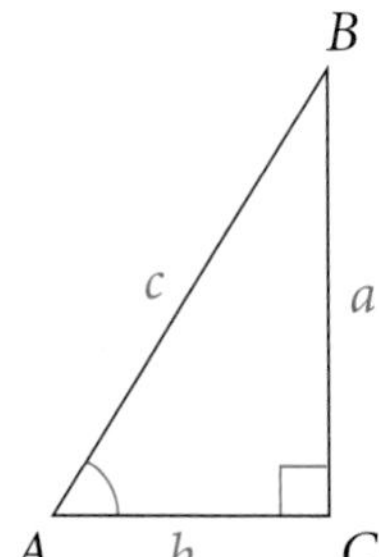

The ratios you explored in the Work Together are called **trigonometric ratios,** meaning triangle measurement ratios. In $\triangle ABC$, $\overline{BC}$ is the leg opposite $\angle A$ and $\overline{AC}$ is the leg adjacent to $\angle A$. The hypotenuse is $\overline{AB}$.

You can use these relationships to express trigonometric ratios.

sine of $\angle A = \dfrac{\text{length of leg opposite } \angle A}{\text{length of hypotenuse}}$ or $\textbf{sin } A = \frac{a}{c}$

cosine of $\angle A = \dfrac{\text{length of leg adjacent to } \angle A}{\text{length of hypotenuse}}$ or $\textbf{cos } A = \frac{b}{c}$

tangent of $\angle A = \dfrac{\text{length of leg opposite } \angle A}{\text{length of leg adjacent to } \angle A}$ or $\textbf{tan } A = \frac{a}{b}$

Example 1

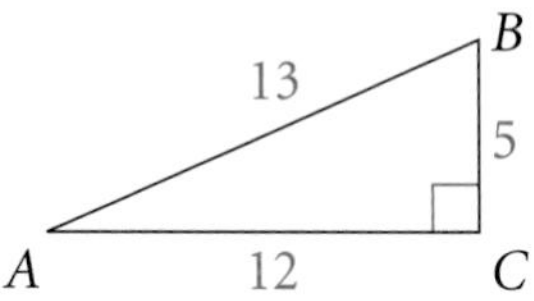

Use the diagram at the left. Find sin A, cos A, and tan A.

$\sin A = \frac{5}{13}$ $\cos A = \frac{12}{13}$ $\tan A = \frac{5}{12}$

4. **Try This** Use the diagram to find sin B, cos B, and tan B.

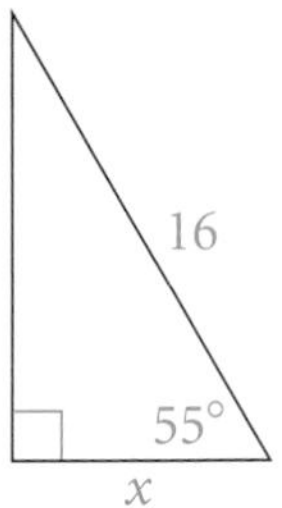

You can use trigonometry to find missing lengths in a triangle.

Example 2

Find the value of x in the triangle at the left.

First, decide which trigonometric ratio to use. You know the angle and hypotenuse and are trying to find the adjacent side. So use cosine.

$$\cos 55^\circ = \frac{\text{side adjacent}}{\text{hypotenuse}} \quad \leftarrow \text{This is a short form of the definition.}$$

$$\cos 55^\circ = \frac{x}{16}$$

$$0.573576436 = \frac{x}{16} \quad \leftarrow \text{Use a calculator.}$$

$$16(0.573576436) = x \quad \leftarrow \text{Cross multiply.}$$

$$9.177222982 = x \quad \leftarrow \text{Use a calculator.}$$

The value of x is about 9.2.

CALCULATOR HINT

Use degree mode when finding trigonometric ratios. Use the key sequence COS 55 ENTER.

5. You know the lengths of two sides of the triangle in Example 2. You can use different methods to find the length of the third side.

a. Use the Pythagorean theorem to find the length of the third side.

b. Use either the sine or tangent ratio to find the length of the third side.

c. Compare your answers to parts (a) and (b).

Solving Problems Using Trigonometric Ratios

You can use trigonometric ratios to measure distances indirectly when you know an angle of elevation. An **angle of elevation** is an angle from the horizontal up to a line of sight.

96 ft

35°

x

Example 3 Relating to the Real World 

Navigation Suppose that an angle of elevation from a rowboat to a lighthouse is 35°. You know that the lighthouse is 96 ft tall. How far from the lighthouse is the rowboat?

Make a diagram.

Define x = the distance from the lighthouse to the boat

Relate You know the angle and the opposite side and you are trying to find the adjacent side. So use tangent.

Write $\tan A = \frac{\text{side opposite}}{\text{side adjacent}}$

$\tan 35° = \frac{96}{x}$ ← Substitute for the angle and sides.

$x(\tan 35°) = 96$ ← Cross multiply.

$x = \frac{96}{\tan 35°}$ ← Divide to put in calculator-ready form.

$x = 137.1022086$ ← Use a calculator.

$x \approx 137$

The rowboat is about 137 ft from the lighthouse.

6. Could you use the sine or cosine to solve Example 3? Explain.

Exercises ON YOUR OWN

1. **Language Arts** Write a nonmathematical sentence using the word *adjacent.*

Use $\triangle RST$ to evaluate each expression.

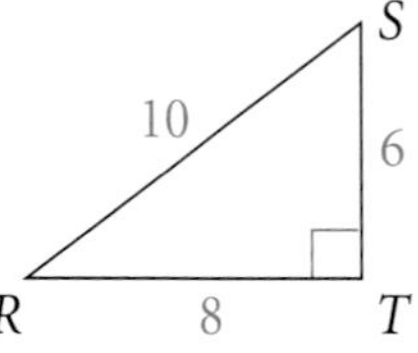

2. $\sin R$ **3.** $\cos R$

4. $\tan R$ **5.** $\sin S$

6. $\cos S$ **7.** $\tan S$

Calculator **Evaluate each expression. Round to four decimal places.**

8. $\sin 32°$ **9.** $\cos 40°$ **10.** $\tan 52°$ **11.** $\sin 85°$ **12.** $\tan 7°$

For each figure, find $\sin A$, $\cos A$, and $\tan A$.

13.

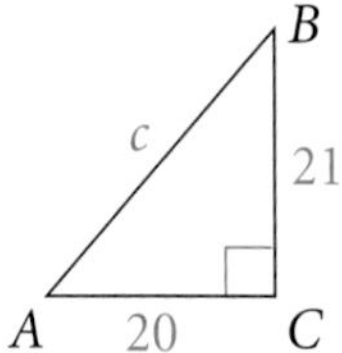

14.

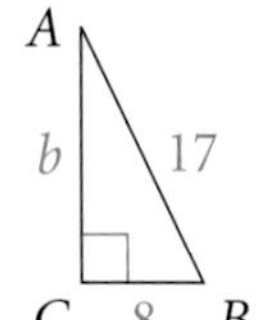

15.

A

26

10

C

a

B

Find the value of x to the nearest tenth.

16. 

17. 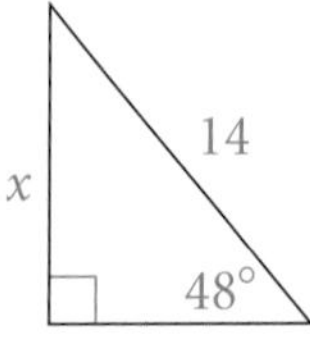

18. 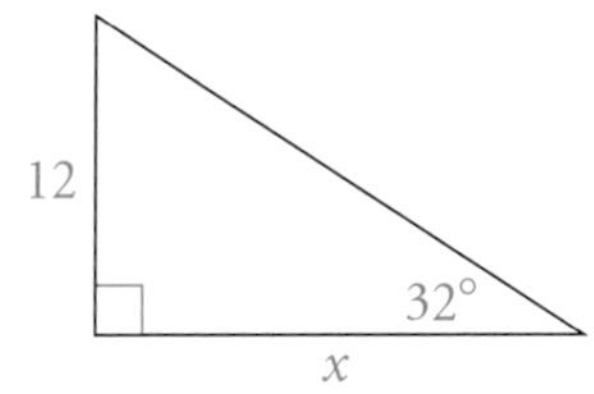

19. **Nature** Suppose you look up from a cabin on the floor of a canyon to a cliff at the top of a vertical wall of rock. The angle of elevation from your location to the cliff is 32°. The cabin is 400 ft from the base of the canyon wall. How high is the canyon wall?

20. **Recreation** A Ferris wheel is shown at the right. Find the distance x that the seat is above the horizontal line through the center of the wheel. Then find the seat's height above the ground.

21. **Aviation** Suppose you live about 5 mi from a tower. From your home, you see a plane directly above the tower. Your angle of elevation to the plane is 21°. What is the plane's altitude?

22. **Writing** Suppose you know that a right triangle has a 30° angle and you know the length of the leg adjacent to the 30° angle. Describe how you would find the length of the leg opposite the 30° angle.

Find the indicated length to the nearest tenth.

23. 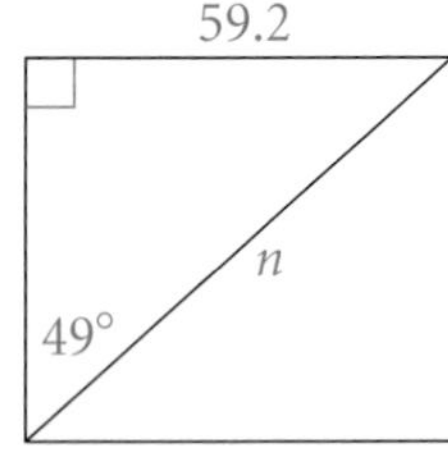

24. 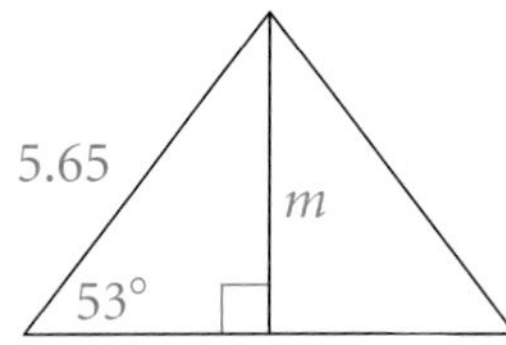

25. 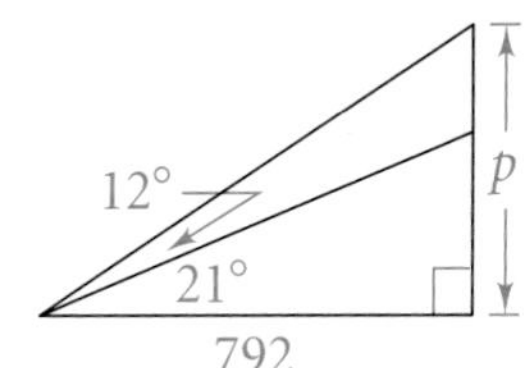

26. **Standardized Test Prep** $\triangle KLM$ is a right triangle with a right angle at M. Which of the following is false?

A. $\sin K = \frac{LM}{KL}$ **B.** $\cos K = \frac{KL}{KM}$ **C.** $\tan K = \frac{LM}{KM}$ **D.** $\cos L = \frac{LM}{KL}$ **E.** $\sin L = \frac{KM}{KL}$

27. **Open-ended** Name some ways you might use a trigonometric ratio to calculate a distance instead of measuring it directly.

28. **Nature** Suppose you are lying on the ground looking up at a California redwood tree. Your angle of elevation to the top of the tree is 42°. You are 280 ft from the base of the tree.
   a. How tall is the tree?
   b. How far would a bird have to fly to get from the top of the tree to your location?

Chapter Project *Find Out by Researching*

Do research to find the radii of all the planets in our solar system. Express your answers in miles.

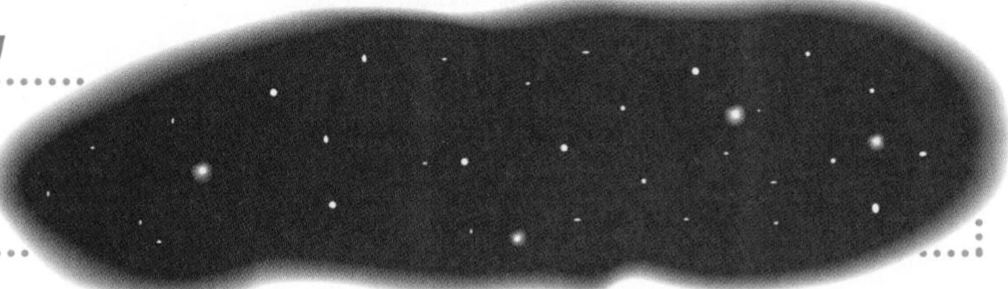

Exercises MIXED REVIEW

Graph each equation.

29. $y = x + 2$

30. $y = |x| + 2$

31. $y = x^2 + 2$

32. $y = 2^x$

33. Transportation A car is traveling at a constant speed. After 3 h, the car has gone 150 mi. How many miles will the car have gone after 5 h?

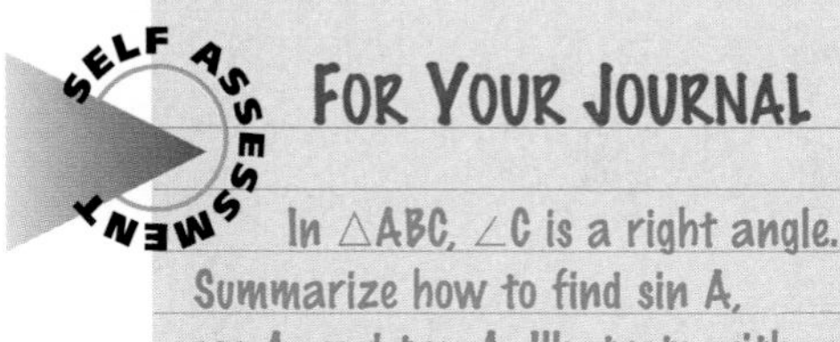

FOR YOUR JOURNAL

In $\triangle ABC$, $\angle C$ is a right angle. Summarize how to find sin A, cos A, and tan A. Illustrate with diagrams.

Getting Ready for Lesson 9-4

Find each value.

34. $\sqrt{4}$

35. $\sqrt{169}$

36. $3\sqrt{25}$

37. $-2\sqrt{9}$

38. $-3\sqrt{49}$

Exercises CHECKPOINT

A right triangle has legs of lengths *a* and *b* and hypotenuse of length *c*. Find the missing value.

1. $a = 2, b = 4$

2. $a = 3, b = 5$

3. $a = 1, b = 7$

4. $a = 4, b = 3$

5. $a = 10, c = 26$

6. $b = 3, c = 9$

7. $a = 8, c = 12$

8. $b = 20, c = 25$

9. Writing Describe how to find the distance between points (x_1, y_1) and (x_2, y_2). Include examples.

10. The angle of elevation from a point on the ground 300 ft from a tower is 42°. How tall is the tower?

Approximate *AB* to the nearest tenth.

11. $A(1, 4), B(2, 7)$

12. $A(-2, -1), B(4, 2)$

13. $A(-3, 5), B(6, 1)$

14. $A(2, 3), B(5, 4)$

15. Open-ended Write the coordinates of a pair of points *A* and *B*. Then find the midpoint of $\overline{AB}$.

In $\triangle ABC$, $\angle C$ is a right angle. Find the length of the indicated side.

16. $m\angle B = 43°, AB = 4, AC = ■$

17. $m\angle A = 33°, AC = 7, BC = ■$

What You'll Learn

- Simplifying radicals involving products and quotients
- Solving problems involving radicals

...And Why

To solve distance problems

9-4 Simplifying Radicals

THINK AND DISCUSS

Multiplication with Radicals

A radical expression is in **simplest form** when *all three* statements are true.

- The expression under the radical sign has no perfect square factors other than 1.
- The expression under the radical sign does not contain a fraction.
- The denominator does not contain a radical expression.

1. Explain why each expression *is* or *is not* in simplest form.

a. $\sqrt{20}$ **b.** $4\sqrt{5}$ **c.** $\frac{1}{\sqrt{3}}$ **d.** $\sqrt{\frac{2}{5}}$

Multiplication Property of Square Roots

For any numbers $a \geq 0$ and $b \geq 0$, $\sqrt{ab} = \sqrt{a} \cdot \sqrt{b}$.

Example: $\sqrt{54} = \sqrt{9} \cdot \sqrt{6} = 3 \cdot \sqrt{6} = 3\sqrt{6}$

You can simplify radical expressions that contain numbers and variables. Assume that all variables under radicals represent positive numbers.

Example 1

Simplify each radical expression.

a. $\sqrt{192} = \sqrt{64 \cdot 3}$ ← 64 is a perfect square and a factor of 192.
$= \sqrt{64} \cdot \sqrt{3}$ ← Use the multiplication property.
$= 8\sqrt{3}$ ← Simplify $\sqrt{64}$.

b. $\sqrt{16a^3} = \sqrt{16} \cdot \sqrt{a^2} \cdot \sqrt{a}$ ← Use the multiplication property.
$= 4a\sqrt{a}$ ← Simplify.

Example 2

Simplify the radical expression $\sqrt{6} \cdot \sqrt{15}$.

$\sqrt{6} \cdot \sqrt{15} = \sqrt{90}$ ← Combine factors under one radical.
$= \sqrt{9 \cdot 10}$ ← 9 is a perfect square and a factor of 90.
$= \sqrt{9} \cdot \sqrt{10}$ ← Use the multiplication property.
$= 3\sqrt{10}$ ← Simplify $\sqrt{9}$.

2. Try This Simplify each expression.

a. $5\sqrt{300}$ **b.** $\sqrt{13} \cdot \sqrt{52}$ **c.** $\sqrt{x^2y^5}$ **d.** $(3\sqrt{5})^2$

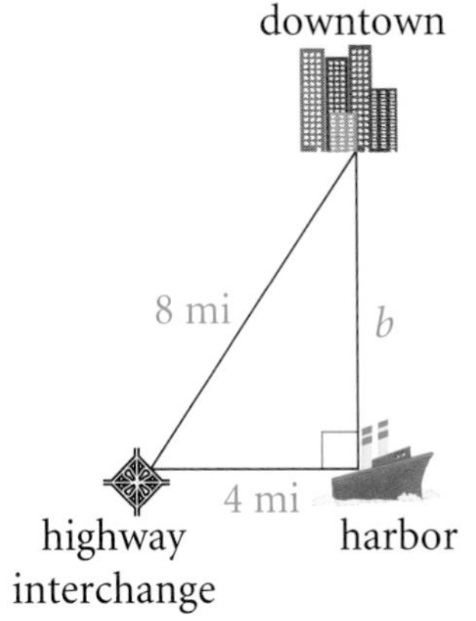

When you use radical expressions to solve real-world problems, you need to evaluate any radicals to get a numerical answer.

Example 3 **Relating to the Real World** 

Commuting Use the figure at the left. About how many miles is it from downtown to the harbor? Round to the nearest tenth of a mile.

$$a^2 + b^2 = c^2$$ ← Use the Pythagorean theorem.

$$4^2 + b^2 = 8^2$$ ← Substitute. Remember that the hypotenuse is the longest side.

$$b^2 = 8^2 - 4^2$$

$$b = \sqrt{8^2 - 4^2}$$ ← Solve for b.

$$= \sqrt{48}$$ ← Use a calculator.

$$= 6.92820323$$

It is about 6.9 miles from downtown to the harbor.

PROBLEM SOLVING

Look Back Explain how you can use $\sqrt{49}$ to check the reasonableness of the answer in Example 3.

3. **Calculator** Suppose a classmate did Example 3 and got the answer $4\sqrt{3}$. Use a calculator to check if this answer is correct.

Division with Radicals

You can use the division property of square roots to simplify expressions.

Division Property of Square Roots

For any numbers $a \geq 0$ and $b > 0$, $\sqrt{\frac{a}{b}} = \frac{\sqrt{a}}{\sqrt{b}}$.

Example: $\sqrt{\frac{4}{9}} = \frac{\sqrt{4}}{\sqrt{9}} = \frac{2}{3}$

4. Explain why there are the restrictions $a \geq 0$ and $b > 0$ in the properties of square roots.

When you simplify a radical expression involving division, sometimes it is easier to simplify the numerator and denominator separately.

Example 4

Simplify each radical expression.

a. $\sqrt{\frac{11}{49}} = \frac{\sqrt{11}}{\sqrt{49}}$ ← Use the division property.

$= \frac{\sqrt{11}}{7}$ ← Simplify $\sqrt{49}$.

b. $\sqrt{\frac{25}{b^4}} = \frac{\sqrt{25}}{\sqrt{b^4}}$ ← Use the division property.

$= \frac{5}{b^2}$ ← Simplify $\sqrt{25}$ and $\sqrt{b^4}$.

When you simplify a radical expression involving division, sometimes it is easier to divide first and then simplify the radical expression.

Example 5

Simplify the radical expression $\frac{\sqrt{96}}{\sqrt{12}}$.

$\frac{\sqrt{96}}{\sqrt{12}} = \sqrt{\frac{96}{12}}$ ← Use the division property.

$= \sqrt{8}$ ← Divide.

$= \sqrt{4 \cdot 2}$ ← 4 is a perfect square and a factor of 8.

$= \sqrt{4} \cdot \sqrt{2}$ ← Use the multiplication property.

$= 2\sqrt{2}$ ← Simplify $\sqrt{4}$.

5. Try This Simplify each expression.

a. $\sqrt{\frac{144}{9}}$ **b.** $\frac{\sqrt{24}}{\sqrt{8}}$ **c.** $\sqrt{\frac{25c^3}{b^2}}$

When you have a square root in a denominator that is not a perfect square, you should **rationalize** the denominator. To do this, make the denominator a rational number without changing the value of the expression.

Example 6

Simplify $\frac{2}{\sqrt{5}}$.

$\frac{2}{\sqrt{5}} = \frac{2}{\sqrt{5}} \cdot \frac{\sqrt{5}}{\sqrt{5}}$ ← Multiply by $\frac{\sqrt{5}}{\sqrt{5}} = 1$.

$= \frac{2\sqrt{5}}{\sqrt{25}}$ ← Use the multiplication property.

$= \frac{2\sqrt{5}}{5}$ ← Simplify.

PROBLEM SOLVING

Look Back Why did you choose to multiply by $\frac{\sqrt{5}}{\sqrt{5}}$ to rationalize the expression?

6. Try This Simplify each expression by rationalizing the denominator.

a. $\frac{3}{\sqrt{3}}$ **b.** $\frac{14}{\sqrt{7}}$ **c.** $\frac{9}{\sqrt{10}}$

Exercises ON YOUR OWN

Tell whether each expression is in simplest form.

1. $\frac{13}{\sqrt{4}}$
2. $2\sqrt{12}$
3. $\frac{3}{\sqrt{13}}$
4. $5\sqrt{30}$
5. $\sqrt{\frac{2}{5}}$

Simplify each radical expression.

6. $\sqrt{25} \cdot \sqrt{100}$
7. $\sqrt{8} \cdot \sqrt{32}$
8. $3\sqrt{81} \cdot \sqrt{81}$
9. $\sqrt{10} \cdot \sqrt{40}$
10. $\sqrt{10^4}$
11. $\sqrt{200}$
12. $5\sqrt{320}$
13. $(5\sqrt{7})^3$
14. $\sqrt{96}$
15. $(2\sqrt{18})^2$
16. $\sqrt{12} \cdot \sqrt{75}$
17. $\sqrt{3} \cdot \sqrt{51}$
18. $\sqrt{26 \cdot 2}$
19. $2\sqrt{6 \cdot 4}$
20. $\sqrt{8} \cdot \sqrt{26}$

Use the Pythagorean theorem to find *s*. Express *s* as a radical in simplest form.

21.
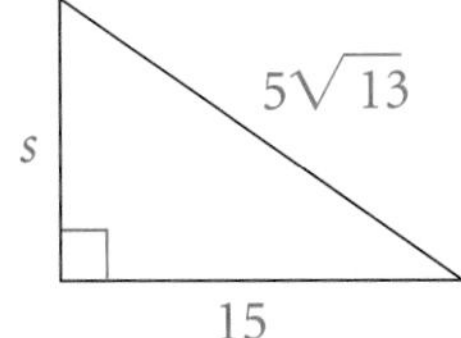

22.
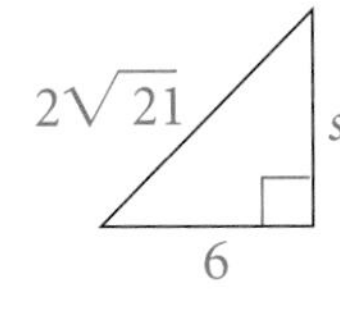

23.
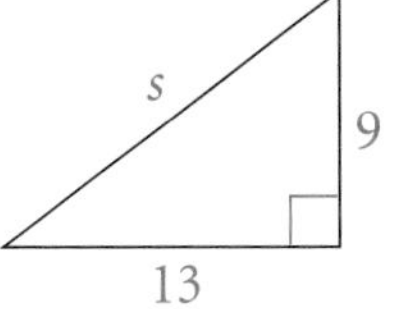

24. **Diving** Suppose you are standing at the top of a diving platform h feet tall. Looking down, you can see a raft on the water 8 feet from the bottom of the diving platform.
    a. Find the distance d from you to the raft if $h = 6$ ft.
    b. Find the distance d from you to the raft if $h = 12$ ft.
    c. Suppose you know the distance d from you to the raft is 16 ft. About how tall is the diving platform?
    d. **Critical Thinking** Could the distance d from you to the raft be 7 ft? Why or why not?

Simplify each radical expression.

25. $3\sqrt{\frac{1}{4}}$
26. $\sqrt{\frac{21}{49}}$
27. $\sqrt{\frac{625}{100}}$
28. $\frac{\sqrt{96}}{\sqrt{9}}$
29. $\sqrt{\frac{120}{121}}$
30. $\frac{\sqrt{15}}{\sqrt{5}}$
31. $\frac{\sqrt{72}}{\sqrt{64}}$
32. $\sqrt{\frac{48}{24}}$
33. $\frac{\sqrt{169}}{\sqrt{144}}$
34. $\frac{\sqrt{400}}{\sqrt{121}}$

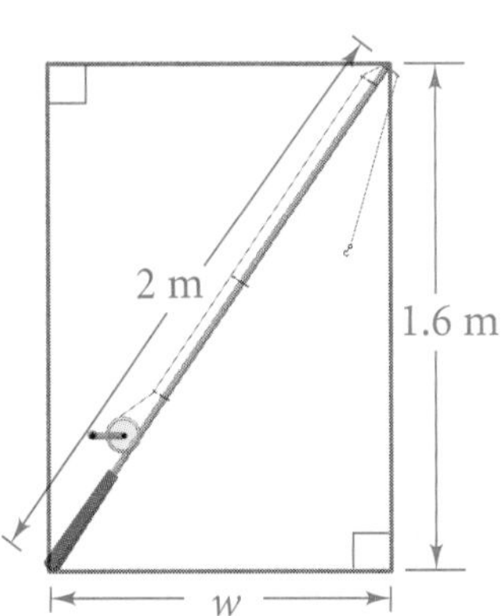

35. **Packaging** Use the diagram at right. Find the width w that the box needs to be to fit the fishing rod.

36. **Writing** How do you know when to rationalize a radical expression?

37. Suppose a and b are positive integers.
    a. **Verify** that if $a = 18$ and $b = 10$, then $\sqrt{a} \cdot \sqrt{b} = 6\sqrt{5}$.
    b. **Open-ended** Find several other pairs of positive integers a and b such that $\sqrt{a} \cdot \sqrt{b} = 6\sqrt{5}$.

38. *Sailing* The diagram at the right shows a sailboat.
   a. Use the Pythagorean theorem to find the height of the sail in simplest radical form.
   b. Use the result of part (a) and the formula for the area of a triangle to find the area of the sail. Round your answer to the nearest tenth.

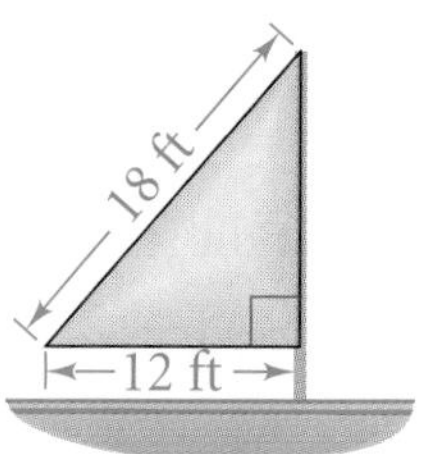

39. *Standardized Test Prep* Suppose that x and y are positive numbers. Which of the following is *not* equivalent to $\sqrt{24x^2y}$?
   A. $2x\sqrt{6y}$ B. $\sqrt{24x}\sqrt{xy}$ C. $\sqrt{4xy}\sqrt{6x}$
   D. $2x^2\sqrt{6y}$ E. $x\sqrt{24y}$

Simplify each radical expression. Assume that all variables represent positive numbers.

40. $\sqrt{v^6}$ 41. $\frac{2}{\sqrt{a^3}}$ 42. $\sqrt{20a^2b^3}$ 43. $\sqrt{a^3b^5c^3}$

44. $\sqrt{12x^3y^2}$ 45. $\sqrt{4y^4}$ 46. $\frac{\sqrt{x^2}}{\sqrt{y^3}}$ 47. $\sqrt{\frac{18x}{81}}$

Simplify each expression by rationalizing the denominator.

48. $\frac{3}{\sqrt{7}}$ 49. $\frac{12}{\sqrt{12}}$ 50. $\frac{2\sqrt{2}}{\sqrt{5}}$ 51. $\frac{9}{\sqrt{8}}$

52. $\frac{3\sqrt{2}}{\sqrt{6}}$ 53. $\frac{25}{\sqrt{5}}$ 54. $\frac{2\sqrt{5}}{\sqrt{12}}$ 55. $\frac{16}{\sqrt{6}}$

56. *Hobbies* Use the Pythagorean theorem to find the missing dimensions a, b, and c of each triangle in the quilt square.

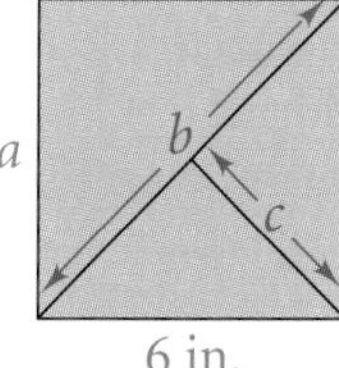

Exercises MIXED REVIEW

Find the x- and y-intercepts of each equation.

57. $2x + 3y = 6$ 58. $4x + 2y = 8$ 59. $-3x + 5y = 15$ 60. $-2x - 4y = 12$

61. *Consumer* You are shopping for food to serve for a lunch party. Crab sandwiches cost \$5 per serving and turkey sandwiches cost \$3 per serving. You have \$30.00 total to spend on sandwiches. Write an inequality to model the situation. How many of each kind can you buy?

Getting Ready for Lesson 9-5

Simplify each square root. Then add or subtract.

62. $\sqrt{16} + \sqrt{36}$ 63. $\sqrt{49} - \sqrt{64}$ 64. $\sqrt{121} + \sqrt{81}$ 65. $\sqrt{400} - \sqrt{100}$

What You'll Learn

- Simplifying radicals involving addition and subtraction
- Solving problems involving sums and differences of radicals

...And Why

To solve geometric problems involving art

9-5 Adding and Subtracting Radicals

WORK TOGETHER

Work in pairs.

1. Copy and complete the table.

a	b	$\sqrt{a}$	$\sqrt{b}$	$\sqrt{a}+\sqrt{b}$	$\sqrt{a+b}$	$\sqrt{a}-\sqrt{b}$	$\sqrt{a-b}$
9	16	■	■	■	■	■	■
25	100	■	■	■	■	■	■
64	36	■	■	■	■	■	■
4	121	■	■	■	■	■	■
49	1	■	■	■	■	■	■

2. a. Compare the values in the addition columns. What do you notice?
b. In general, does $\sqrt{a} + \sqrt{b} = \sqrt{a + b}$? Explain.

3. a. Compare the values in the subtraction columns. What do you notice?
b. Does $\sqrt{a} - \sqrt{b} = \sqrt{a - b}$? Explain.

4. Is there a rule for adding and subtracting radicals? **Justify** your reasoning.

THINK AND DISCUSS

Simplifying Sums and Differences

You can simplify radical expressions by combining like terms. Like terms have the same radical part.

like terms	unlike terms
$4\sqrt{7}$ and $-12\sqrt{7}$	$3\sqrt{11}$ and $2\sqrt{5}$

5. Identify each pair of expressions as like or unlike terms. **Justify** your answers.
a. $\sqrt{8}$ and $2\sqrt{8}$ **b.** $2\sqrt{3}$ and $3\sqrt{2}$ **c.** $2\sqrt{7}$ and $-3\sqrt{7}$

Example 1

Simplify the expression $\sqrt{2} + 3\sqrt{2}$.

$\sqrt{2} + 3\sqrt{2} = 1\sqrt{2} + 3\sqrt{2}$ ← Both $1\sqrt{2}$ and $3\sqrt{2}$ have $\sqrt{2}$.

$= 4\sqrt{2}$ ← Combine like terms.

Example 2

Simplify the expression $4\sqrt{3} - \sqrt{12}$.

$$\begin{aligned} 4\sqrt{3} - \sqrt{12} &= 4\sqrt{3} - \sqrt{4 \cdot 3} && \leftarrow \text{4 is a perfect square and a factor of 12.} \\ &= 4\sqrt{3} - \sqrt{4} \cdot \sqrt{3} && \leftarrow \text{Use the multiplication property.} \\ &= 4\sqrt{3} - 2\sqrt{3} && \leftarrow \text{Simplify } \sqrt{4}. \\ &= 2\sqrt{3} && \leftarrow \text{Combine like terms.} \end{aligned}$$

6. Try This Simplify each expression.

a. $2\sqrt{5} + \sqrt{5}$ **b.** $3\sqrt{45} + 2\sqrt{5}$ **c.** $3\sqrt{3} - 2\sqrt{12}$

Simplifying Products, Sums, and Differences

QUICK REVIEW

The distributive property says $a(b + c) = ab + ac$.

Sometimes you need to use the distributive property and what you have learned in lessons 9-4 and 9-5 to simplify expressions.

Example 3 Relating to the Real World 

Art The ratio length : width of this painting by Mondrian is approximately equal to the *golden ratio* $(1 + \sqrt{5}) : 2$. The width of the painting is 50 in. Find the length of the painting. Express your answer in simplest radical form. Then estimate the length in inches.

Define 50 = width of painting
x = length of painting

Relate $(1 + \sqrt{5}) : 2 =$ length : width

Write

$$\begin{aligned} \frac{1 + \sqrt{5}}{2} &= \frac{x}{50} \\ 50(1 + \sqrt{5}) &= 2x && \leftarrow \text{Cross multiply.} \\ \frac{50(1 + \sqrt{5})}{2} &= x && \leftarrow \text{Solve for } x. \\ 25(1 + \sqrt{5}) &= x \\ 25 + 25\sqrt{5} &= x && \leftarrow \text{Use the distributive property.} \\ 80.90169944 &= x && \leftarrow \text{Use a calculator.} \\ 81 &\approx x \end{aligned}$$

The length of Mondrian's painting is about 81 in.

7. a. Calculator Write the golden ratio as a decimal to the nearest hundredth.

b. Calculator Write $\frac{25 + 25\sqrt{5}}{50}$ as a decimal to the nearest hundredth.

c. Compare your answers to parts (a) and (b). What do you notice about the two values?

Example 4

Simplify $\sqrt{2}(5 - \sqrt{8})$.

$$\begin{aligned}\sqrt{2}(5 - \sqrt{8}) &= \sqrt{2}(5) - \sqrt{2}(\sqrt{8}) && \leftarrow \text{Use the distributive property.}\\ &= 5\sqrt{2} - \sqrt{2 \cdot 8} && \leftarrow \text{Use the multiplication property.}\\ &= 5\sqrt{2} - \sqrt{16} && \leftarrow \text{Multiply.}\\ &= 5\sqrt{2} - 4 && \leftarrow \text{Simplify.}\end{aligned}$$

8. **Try This** Simplify each expression.
   a. $2(2 + \sqrt{3})$
   b. $\sqrt{2}(1 - 2\sqrt{10})$
   c. $\sqrt{3}(5\sqrt{2} - 2\sqrt{6})$
9. Simplify $3\sqrt{2}(\sqrt{24} + 2\sqrt{6})$ by first simplifying $\sqrt{24}$.

Exercises ON YOUR OWN

Simplify each expression.

1. $15\sqrt{9} - \sqrt{9}$
2. $3(\sqrt{27} + 1)$
3. $\sqrt{18} + \sqrt{3}$
4. $2\sqrt{12} - 7\sqrt{3}$
5. $2\sqrt{3}(\sqrt{3} - 1)$
6. $\sqrt{8} + 2\sqrt{2}$
7. $\sqrt{27} - \sqrt{18}$
8. $-3\sqrt{6} + 8\sqrt{6}$
9. $3\sqrt{7} - \sqrt{28}$
10. $16\sqrt{10} + 2\sqrt{10}$
11. $\sqrt{3}(\sqrt{15} + \sqrt{4})$
12. $\sqrt{5} - 3\sqrt{5}$
13. $\sqrt{12} + \sqrt{24} - \sqrt{36}$
14. $\sqrt{3}(\sqrt{2} + 2\sqrt{3})$
15. $\sqrt{2}(\sqrt{8} - 4)$
16. **Recreation** You can make a box kite in the shape of a rectangular solid. The opening at each end of the kite is a square.
   a. Suppose the sides of the square are 2 ft long. How long are the diagonal struts used for bracing?
   b. Suppose each side of the square has length s. Find the length of the diagonal struts in terms of s. Write your answer in simplest form.

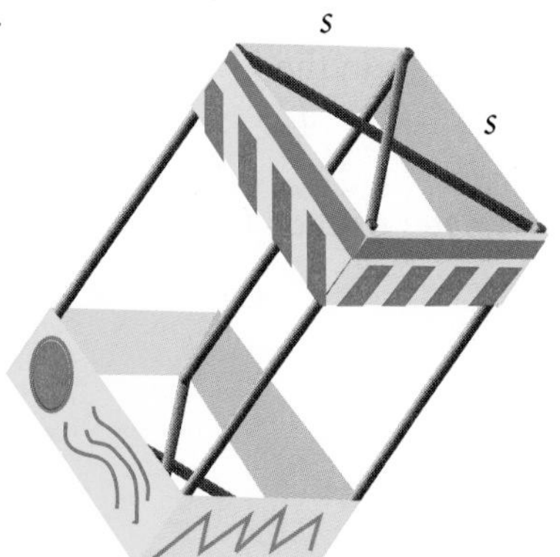

Calculator **Use a calculator to evaluate each expression. Round your answers to the nearest tenth.**

17. $\sqrt{2} + \sqrt{3}$
18. $4\sqrt{5} + \sqrt{10}$
19. $\sqrt{40} + \sqrt{90}$
20. $6\sqrt{8} - 8\sqrt{6}$
21. $\sqrt{3}(\sqrt{6} + 1)$
22. $\sqrt{18} + \sqrt{2}$
23. $5\sqrt{5} - \sqrt{7}$
24. $\sqrt{13} - 2\sqrt{2}$
25. $3\sqrt{2} - 3\sqrt{3}$

Simplify each expression.

26. $3\sqrt{3}(4\sqrt{27} - \sqrt{3})$

27. $\sqrt{12} + \sqrt{32}$

28. $\sqrt{5} + 2\sqrt{50}$

29. $2\sqrt{2}(-2\sqrt{32} + \sqrt{8})$

30. $3\sqrt{10}(\sqrt{10} + 4\sqrt{5})$

31. $3\sqrt{2}(2 + \sqrt{6})$

32. $\sqrt{18} - 2\sqrt{2}$

33. $\sqrt{68} + 17$

34. $-\sqrt{6}(\sqrt{6} - 5)$

35. **Open-ended** Make up three sums that are less than or equal to 50. Use the square roots of 2, 3, 5, or 7 and the whole numbers less than 10. For example, $8\sqrt{5} + 9\sqrt{7} \leq 50$.

36. **Choose** Use a calculator, paper and pencil, or estimation to find the value of the numerical expression in the cartoon.

from the cartoon *Bound & Gagged*

37. Bill wrote $\sqrt{24} + \sqrt{48} = 3\sqrt{24} = 6\sqrt{6}$.

a. Simplify $\sqrt{24} + \sqrt{48}$.

b. **Critical Thinking** What error did Bill make? Explain.

38. **Writing** Explain the errors in the work below.

a. $\sqrt{5} + \sqrt{11} = \sqrt{16} = 4$

b. $\sqrt{41} = \sqrt{16 + 25} = \sqrt{16} + \sqrt{25} = 9$

Geometry **Find the perimeter of each figure below.**

39.

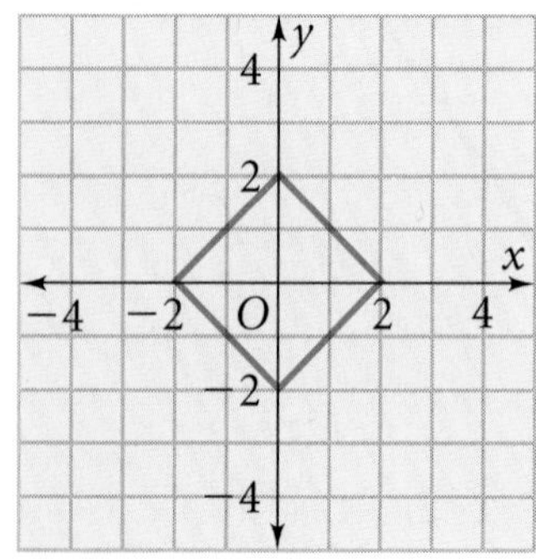

40.

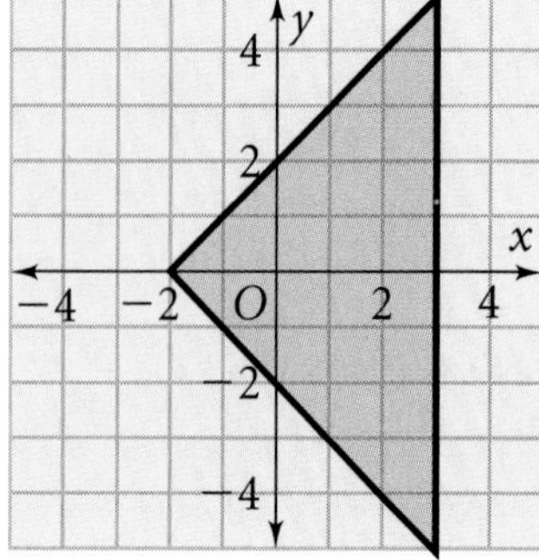

41.

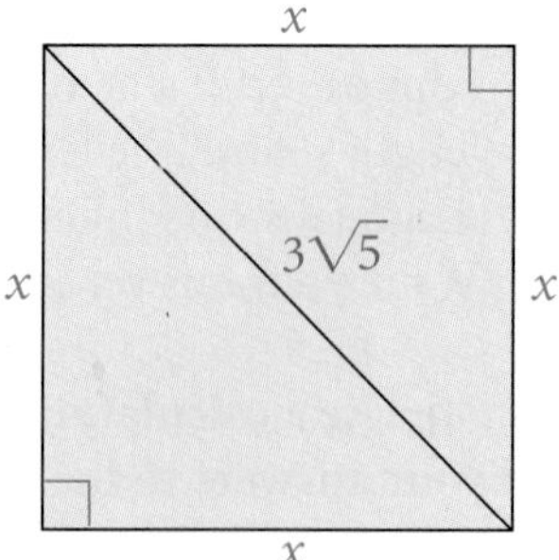

42. **Architecture** The ratio width : height of the front face of a building is equal to the *golden ratio* $(1 + \sqrt{5}) : 2$. The height of the front face of the building is 24 ft. Find the width of the building. Express your answer in simplest radical form. Then estimate in feet.

43. Standardized Test Prep Simplify $\frac{\sqrt{50} + \sqrt{32}}{\sqrt{2}}$.

A. $\sqrt{41}$ B. $5 + 4\sqrt{2}$ C. $4 + 5\sqrt{2}$ D. $9\sqrt{2}$ E. 9

Exercises MIXED REVIEW

44. a. Travel Aruba is changing $\frac{1}{4}$ of its 75 mi^2 into protected parkland. How many square miles will the protected area be?

b. The island has 88,000 residents. What is its population density (people/mi^2) for the whole island?

c. What is the population density excluding the protected parkland?

Aruba

Solve using the quadratic formula. Tell whether each solution is *rational* or *irrational*.

45. $x^2 - 2x - 15 = 0$

46. $x^2 + 6x + 2 = 0$

Getting Ready for Lesson 9-6

Evaluate each expression for the given value.

47. $\sqrt{x} - 3$ for $x = 16$

48. $\sqrt{x + 7}$ for $x = 9$

49. $2\sqrt{x + 3} - 4$ for $x = 1$

Algebra at Work

Auto Mechanic

An auto mechanic's job is to see that car engines get the most out of every gallon of gas. Formulas used by mechanics often involve radicals. For example, a car gets its power when gas and air in each cylinder are compressed and ignited by a spark plug. An engine's efficiency (e) is given by the formula $e = \frac{c - \sqrt{c}}{c}$, where c is the compression ratio.

Because of the complexity of such formulas and of modern high-performance engines, today's auto mechanic must be a highly trained and educated professional who understands algebra, graph reading, and the operation of computerized equipment.

Mini Project: Evaluate the formula to find the engine efficiency for even-numbered compression ratios from 2 to 20.

What You'll Learn

- Solving equations that contain radicals
- Identifying extraneous solutions

...And Why

To design amusement park rides

9-6 Solving Radical Equations

THINK AND DISCUSS

Solving a Radical Equation

An equation that has a variable under a radical is a **radical equation.** You can often solve a radical equation by squaring both sides. To do this, first get the radical by itself on one side of the equation. Remember that the expression under the radical must be positive.

$$\text{When } x \geq 0, (\sqrt{x})^2 = x.$$

Example 1

Solve $\sqrt{x} - 3 = 4$. Check your solution.

$\sqrt{x} - 3 = 4$

$\sqrt{x} - 3 + 3 = 4 + 3$ ← Add 3 to both sides.

$\sqrt{x} = 7$ ← Simplify.

$(\sqrt{x})^2 = 7^2$ ← Square both sides.

$x = 49$

Check $\sqrt{x} - 3 = 4$

$\sqrt{49} - 3 \stackrel{?}{=} 4$ ← Substitute 49 for x.

$7 - 3 = 4$ ✓

The solution of $\sqrt{x} - 3 = 4$ is 49.

1. a. Find the values of $\sqrt{36} - 3$ and $\sqrt{64} - 3$.
   b. *Critical Thinking* Do the results in part (a) suggest that $x = 49$ is a reasonable solution to $\sqrt{x} - 3 = 4$? Explain.
   c. Explain how parts (a) and (b) are a form of estimation.
2. **Try This** Solve and check.
   a. $\sqrt{x} + 5 = 12$ b. $2\sqrt{x} + 7 = 19$ c. $\sqrt{x} + 3 = 5$
3. a. Solve $x^2 - 3 = 4$.
   b. Compare and contrast how you solved the equation in part (a) with how you solved $\sqrt{x} - 3 = 4$.
4. a. *Graphing Calculator* Graph $y = \sqrt{x} - 3$ and $y = 4$ together. Use the range shown on the screen at the left.
   b. How many intersection points are there?
   c. What are the coordinates of the intersection point(s)?
   d. *Critical Thinking* How does your answer to part (c) confirm the solution of $\sqrt{x} - 3 = 4$ in Example 1?

WINDOW FORMAT
Xmin=0
Xmax=64
Xscl=1
Ymin=–10
Ymax=10
Yscl=1

Example 2 Relating to the Real World 

Amusement Parks On a roller coaster ride, your speed in a loop depends on the height of the hill you have just come down and the radius of the loop in feet. The equation $v = 8\sqrt{h - 2r}$ gives the velocity v in feet per second of a car at the top of the loop. Suppose the loop has a radius of 18 ft. You want the car to have a velocity of 30 ft/s at the top of the loop. How high should the hill be?

Solve $v = 8\sqrt{h - 2r}$ for $v = 30$ and $r = 18$.

$$30 = 8\sqrt{h - 2(18)} \quad \leftarrow \text{Substitute for } r \text{ and } v.$$

$$\frac{30}{8} = \sqrt{h - 2(18)} \quad \leftarrow \text{Divide each side by 8 to get the radical alone.}$$

$$3.75 = \sqrt{h - 36}$$

$$(3.75)^2 = (\sqrt{h - 36})^2 \quad \leftarrow \text{Square both sides.}$$

$$14.0625 = h - 36$$

$$50.0625 = h$$

The hill should be about 50 ft high.

5. **Try This** Find the height of the hill when the velocity at the top of the loop is 35 ft/s and radius of the loop is 24 ft.
6. **Try This** Find the radius of the loop when the hill is 150 ft high and the velocity of the car is 30 ft/s.
7. About how many miles per hour is 30 ft/s? (*Hint:* 1 mi = 5280 ft)
8. **Critical Thinking** Would you expect the velocity of the car to increase or decrease in each situation? Explain your reasoning.
   - **a.** as the radius of the loop increases
   - **b.** as the height of the hill decreases

Squaring both sides of an equation also works when each side of the equation is a radical expression.

Example 3

Solve $\sqrt{3x-2} = \sqrt{x+6}$.

$$(\sqrt{3x-2})^2 = (\sqrt{x+6})^2 \quad \leftarrow \text{Square both sides.}$$
$$3x - 2 = x + 6$$
$$3x = x + 8$$
$$2x = 8$$
$$x = 4$$

The solution is 4.

PROBLEM SOLVING

Look Back Show how to check that 4 is the solution of $\sqrt{3x-2} = \sqrt{x+6}$.

9. *Graphing Calculator* Graph the equations $y = \sqrt{3x - 2}$ and $y = \sqrt{x + 6}$ together. How does the display confirm the solution of Example 3?

10. **Try This** Solve $\sqrt{5x - 6} = \sqrt{3x + 5}$. Check your solution.

Solving Equations with Extraneous Solutions

When you solve equations by squaring both sides, you sometimes find two possible solutions. You need to determine which solution actually satisfies the original equation.

Example 4

Solve $x = \sqrt{x + 6}$.

$$(x)^2 = (\sqrt{x+6})^2 \quad \leftarrow \text{Square both sides.}$$
$$x^2 = x + 6$$
$$x^2 - x - 6 = 0 \quad \leftarrow \text{Subtract } x \text{ and 6 from both sides.}$$
$$x = \frac{-(-1) \pm \sqrt{(-1)^2 - 4(1)(-6)}}{2(1)} \quad \leftarrow \text{Use the quadratic formula to solve for } x.$$
$$x = \frac{1 \pm \sqrt{1 - (-24)}}{2}$$
$$x = \frac{1 \pm \sqrt{25}}{2}$$
$$x = \frac{1 \pm 5}{2} \quad \leftarrow \text{Simplify } \sqrt{25}.$$
$$x = \frac{1+5}{2} \text{ or } x = \frac{1-5}{2}$$
$$x = 3 \text{ or } x = -2$$

Check $x = \sqrt{x+6}$

$3 \stackrel{?}{=} \sqrt{3+6}$ $\qquad -2 \stackrel{?}{=} \sqrt{-2+6} \quad \leftarrow \sqrt{4} = 2$

$3 = 3$ ✔ $\qquad -2 \neq 2$

The only solution is 3.

QUICK REVIEW

The quadratic formula states that for an equation of the form $ax^2 + bx + c = 0$, if $a \neq 0$, then $x = \frac{-b \pm \sqrt{b^2 - 4ac}}{2a}$.

The value -2 is called an **extraneous solution** of Example 4. It is a solution of the derived equation ($x^2 = x + 6$), but not of the original equation ($x = \sqrt{x + 6}$).

11. How could you have determined that -2 was not a solution of $x = \sqrt{x + 6}$ without going through all the steps of the check?

Exercises ON YOUR OWN

Solve each radical equation. Check your solutions.

1. $\sqrt{5x + 10} = 5$ **2.** $7 = \sqrt{x + 5}$ **3.** $6 - \sqrt{3x} = -3$

4. $\sqrt{n} = \frac{7}{8}$ **5.** $20 = \sqrt{x} - 5$ **6.** $\sqrt{x} - 10 = 1$

7. **Geometry** In the right triangle $\triangle ABC$, the altitude $\overline{CD}$ is at a right angle to the hypotenuse. You can use $CD = \sqrt{(AD)(DB)}$ to find certain lengths.

a. Find AD if $CD = 10$ and $DB = 4$.

b. Find DB if $AD = 20$ and $CD = 15$.

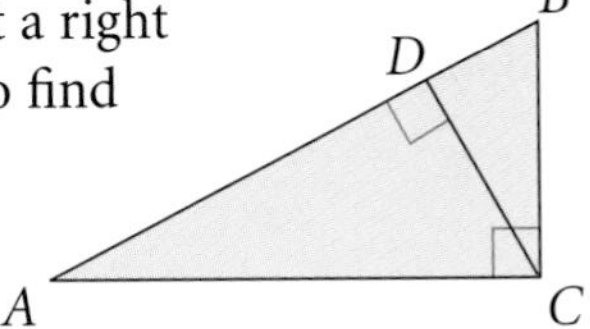

8. **Physics** The equation $T = \sqrt{\frac{2\pi^2 r}{F}}$ gives the time T in seconds it takes a body with mass 0.5 kg to complete one orbit of radius r meters. The force F in newtons pulls the body toward the center of the orbit.

a. It takes 2 s for an object to make one revolution with a force of 10 N (newtons). Find the radius of the orbit.

b. Find the radius of the orbit if the force is 160 N and $T = 2$.

Solve each radical equation. Check your solutions.

9. $\sqrt{3x + 1} = \sqrt{x}$ **10.** $\sqrt{x + 5} = \sqrt{3x + 6}$ **11.** $\sqrt{3x + 10} = \sqrt{9 - x}$

12. $\sqrt{7x + 5} = \sqrt{x - 3}$ **13.** $\frac{x}{2} = \sqrt{3x}$ **14.** $\sqrt{x + 12} = 3\sqrt{x}$

15. $\sqrt{5x - 4} = \sqrt{3x + 10}$ **16.** $\sqrt{2x} = \sqrt{9 - x}$ **17.** $x = \sqrt{2x + 3}$

18. **Standardized Test Prep** Which of the following radical equations has no *real* solution?

A. $-\sqrt{x} = -25x$ **B.** $\sqrt{2x + 1} = \sqrt{3x - 5}$ **C.** $-3\sqrt{3x} = -5$

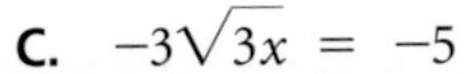

D. $\sqrt{3x + 1} = -10$ **E.** $\frac{x}{2} = \sqrt{x} - 1$

19. **Packaging** The volume V in cubic units of a cylindrical can is given by the formula $V = \pi r^2 h$, where r is the radius of the can and h is its height. The radius of a can is 2.5 in. and the height of the can is 5 in. Find the can's volume in cubic inches.

20. **Writing** Tell how you would solve the equation $\sqrt{2x} + \sqrt{x + 2} = 0$.

Storage tanks in Knoxville, Tennessee

Solve each radical equation. Check your solutions.

21. $x = \sqrt{x + 2}$ **22.** $2x = \sqrt{10x + 6}$ **23.** $\frac{x}{3} = \sqrt{x - 2}$

24. $\sqrt{x + 5} = 2x$ **25.** $2x = 2\sqrt{x - 5}$ **26.** $\sqrt{2x - 15} = \frac{x}{4}$

27. $\sqrt{x + 12} = x$ **28.** $\sqrt{2x - 1} = \frac{x + 8}{2}$ **29.** $x = \sqrt{7x - 6}$

30. **Writing** Explain in your own words what an extraneous solution is.

31. The diagram shows a piece of cardboard that makes a box when sections of it are folded and taped. The ends of the box are x in. long and the box is 10 in. long.

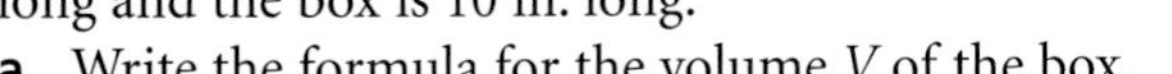

a. Write the formula for the volume V of the box.

b. Solve the equation in part (a) for x.

c. **Open-ended** Find some integer values of x that make the box have a volume between 40 in.^{3} and 490 in.^{3}.

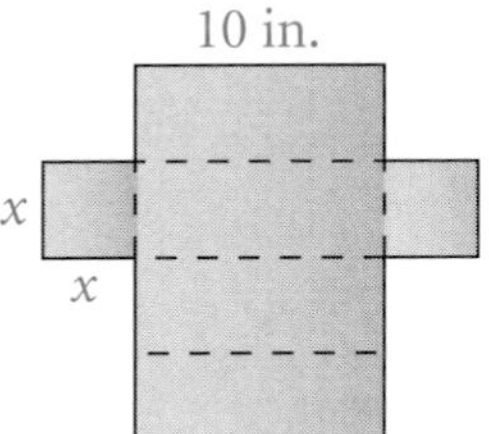

Tell which solution(s), if any, are extraneous for the given equation.

32. $-x = \sqrt{-x + 6};\ x = -3, x = 2$ **33.** $\sqrt{12 - x} = x;\ x = -4, x = 3$

34. $x = \sqrt{2x};\ x = 0, x = 2$ **35.** $2x = \sqrt{4x + 3};\ x = \frac{3}{2}, x = -\frac{1}{2}$

36. $x = \sqrt{28 - 3x};\ x = 4, x = -7$ **37.** $-x = \sqrt{-6x - 5};\ x = -5, x = -1$

Chapter Project *Find Out by Communicating*

- Solve the formula $d = 1.225\sqrt{h}$ for h where d is in miles and h is in feet. (*Hint:* See page 424.)
- How tall would a person on Earth have to be to see 7 mi to the horizon?
- Could a person possibly see such a distance? Why or why not?

Exercises MIXED REVIEW

Simplify each expression. Assume that no denominator is equal to zero.

38. $\frac{x^2y^7}{x^4y^5}$ **39.** $\frac{a^2b^5}{a^7b^{10}}$ **40.** $\frac{15x^4y^5}{45x^2y^3}$ **41.** $\frac{14x^2y^3}{7x^3y^5}$

42. **Business** A salesperson earns \$750 per month plus 8% commission on the amount she sells. Write an equation to show how her monthly income relates to her sales in dollars.

Getting Ready for Lesson 9-7

Find the value of y for the given value of x.

43. $y = \sqrt{x + 7} - 3$ for $x = 2$ **44.** $y = 3\sqrt{x} + 2$ for $x = 9$ **45.** $y = -2\sqrt{x - 1} + 2$ for $x = 1$

What You'll Learn

- Graphing and exploring square root functions
- Solving real-world problems using square root functions

...And Why

To solve problems involving firefighting

What You'll Need

- graphing calculator

9-7 Graphing Square Root Functions

THINK AND DISCUSS

Firefighters When firefighters are trying to put out a fire, the rate at which they can spray water on the fire is very important to them. For a hose with a 2 in. nozzle diameter, the flow rate, f, in gal/min is given by this formula.

$$f = 120\sqrt{p}, \text{ where } p \text{ is the nozzle pressure in lb/in.}^2$$

The flow-rate function is an example of a square root function. The simplest **square root function** is $y = \sqrt{x}$.

x	y
0	0
1	1
4	2
9	3
16	4

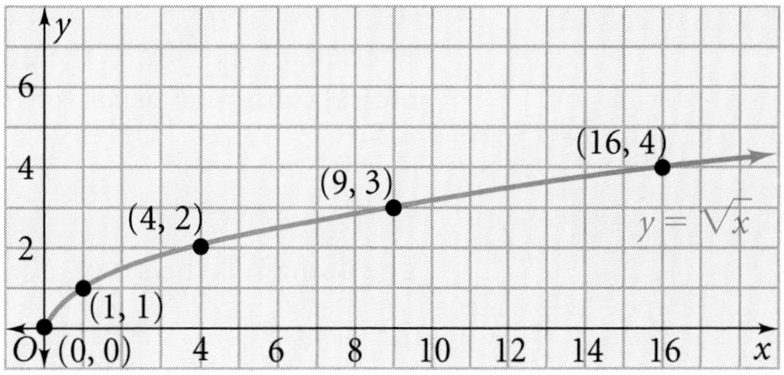

1. Why do you think the x-values in the table were chosen?
2. Find an approximate value of $\sqrt{3}$ and see if it seems to fit the graph.
3. Why is the graph not continued to the left of the y-axis?

Example 1

Compare the graph of $y = \sqrt{x} - 1$ to the graph of $y = \sqrt{x}$.

Method 1 Use a table.

x	$\sqrt{x}$	$\sqrt{x} - 1$
0	$\sqrt{0} = 0$	$\sqrt{0} - 1 = -1$
1	$\sqrt{1} = 1$	$\sqrt{1} - 1 = 0$
4	$\sqrt{4} = 2$	$\sqrt{4} - 1 = 1$
9	$\sqrt{9} = 3$	$\sqrt{9} - 1 = 2$
16	$\sqrt{16} = 4$	$\sqrt{16} - 1 = 3$

Method 2 Use a graphing calculator.

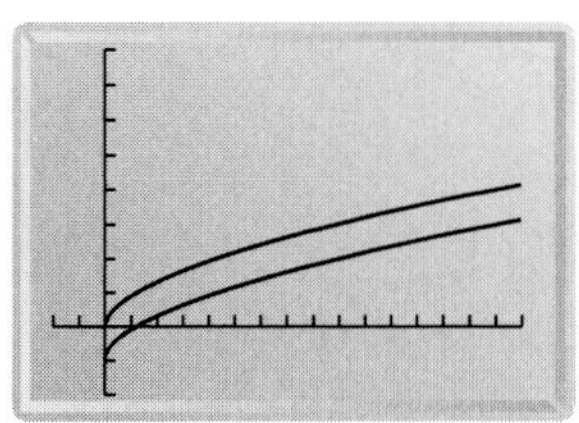

Xmin=–2 Ymin=–2
Xmax=16 Ymax=8
Xscl=1 Yscl=1

For each value of x, the value of $\sqrt{x} - 1$ is one less than the value of $\sqrt{x}$. The graph of $y = \sqrt{x} - 1$ is one unit lower than the graph of $y = \sqrt{x}$.

4. Try This **Analyze** the graph of $y = \sqrt{x} + 1$ by comparing it to the graph of $y = \sqrt{x}$.

5. a. **Predict** how the graph of $y = \sqrt{x} + k$ will compare to the graph of $y = \sqrt{x}$ when k is a negative number.
   b. *Graphing Calculator* Confirm your prediction by graphing $y = \sqrt{x} - 3$ and $y = \sqrt{x}$.

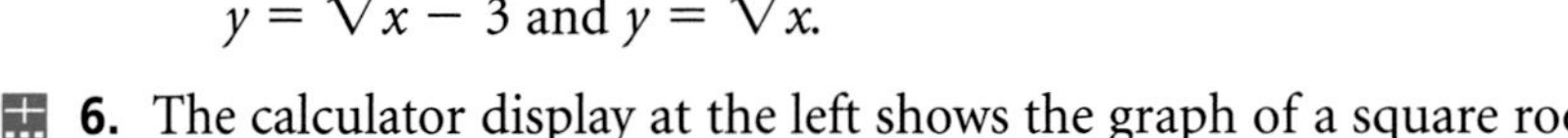

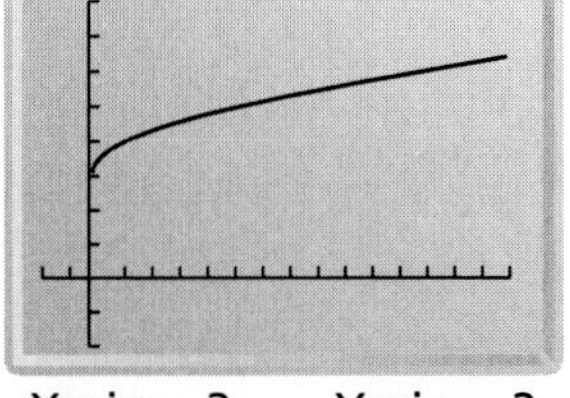

Xmin=–2 Ymin=–2
Xmax=15 Ymax=8
Xscl=1 Yscl=1

6. The calculator display at the left shows the graph of a square root function of the form $y = \sqrt{x} + k$. What is the value of k?

You can solve an inequality to find the domain of a square root function.

Example 2

Find the domain of $y = \sqrt{x + 3}$. Then graph the function.

The square root limits the domain because the expression under the radical cannot be negative. To find the domain, solve $x + 3 \geq 0$.

$$x + 3 \geq 0$$
$$x \geq -3$$

The domain is the set of all real numbers greater than or equal to –3.

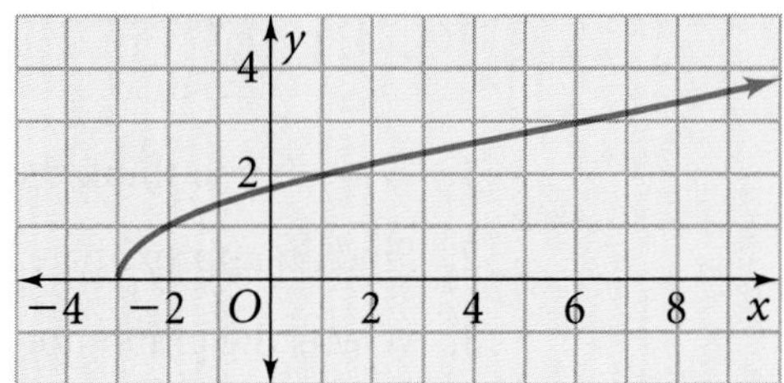

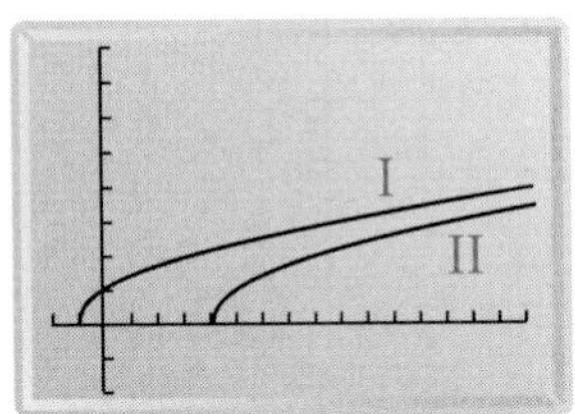

Xmin=–2 Ymin=–2
Xmax=16 Ymax=8
Xscl=1 Yscl=1

7. Compare the graph in Example 2 to the graph of $y = \sqrt{x}$.

8. Try This Find the domain of $y = \sqrt{x - 3}$. Then graph the function.

9. a. The diagram at the left shows the graphs of two functions of the form $y = \sqrt{x + k}$. Describe the domain of each function.
b. Which graph is the graph of $y = \sqrt{x + 1}$? **Justify** your response.

10. **Summarize** how the graph of $y = \sqrt{x + k}$ compares to the graph of $y = \sqrt{x}$.

You can use square root functions to describe real-life situations.

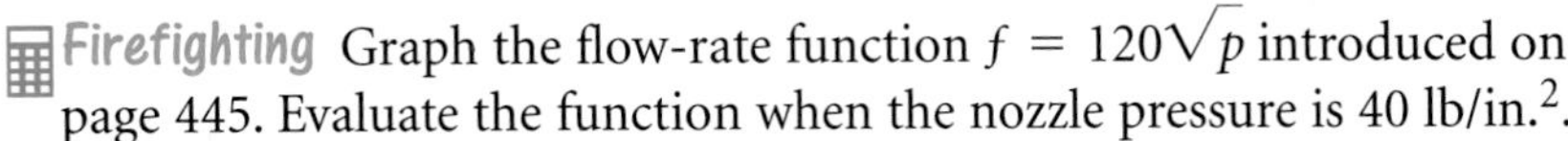

Firefighting Graph the flow-rate function $f = 120\sqrt{p}$ introduced on page 445. Evaluate the function when the nozzle pressure is 40 lb/in.^{2}.

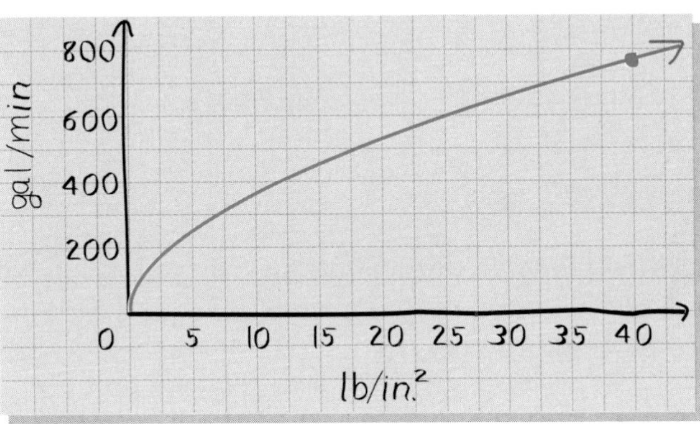

$f = 120\sqrt{40}$ ← Substitute 40 for p.
$= 758.9466384$ ← Use a calculator.

The flow rate is about 759 gal/min when the nozzle pressure is 40 lb/in.^{2}.

11. In Example 3, why are there different scales on the axes?

12. Compare the graph in Example 3 to the graph of $y = \sqrt{x}$.

13. **Summarize** how the graph of $y = k\sqrt{x}$ compares to the graph of $y = \sqrt{x}$.

Exercises ON YOUR OWN

Find the domain of each function.

1. $y = \sqrt{x - 2}$
2. $f(x) = \sqrt{4x + 3}$
3. $y = \sqrt{1.5x}$
4. $y = \sqrt{3x + 5}$
5. $y = \sqrt{7 + x}$
6. $f(x) = \sqrt{2 + x}$
7. $f(x) = \sqrt{3 + x}$
8. $y = \sqrt{x + 3} - 1$
9. $y = \sqrt{x - 5} + 1$

10. **Business** Last year a store had an advertising campaign. Sales figures for disposable cameras are shown. The function $n = 27\sqrt{5t} + 53$ models sales volume n of the cameras as a function of time t, the number of months after the start of the campaign.

   a. Evaluate the function to find how many disposable cameras the store sold in the seventh month.

   b. Solve an equation to find the month in which the number of disposable cameras sold was about 175.

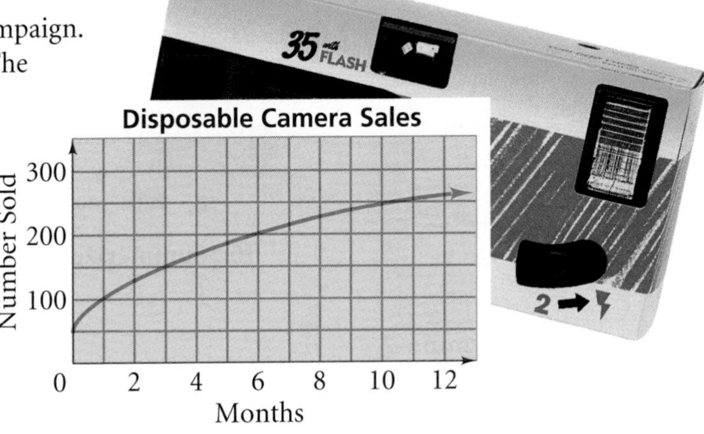

Match each function with its graph.

11. $y = \sqrt{x + 4}$

12. $y = \sqrt{x} - 2$

13. $y = 3\sqrt{x}$

A. 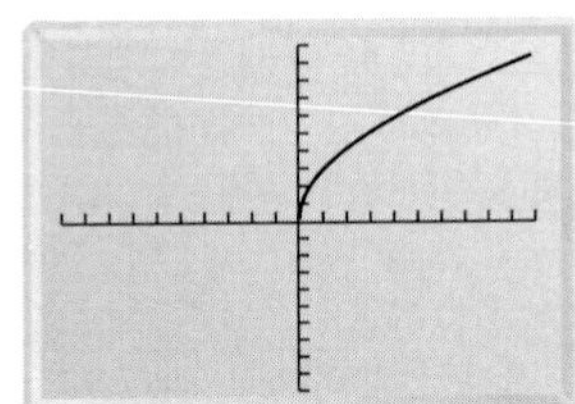

B. 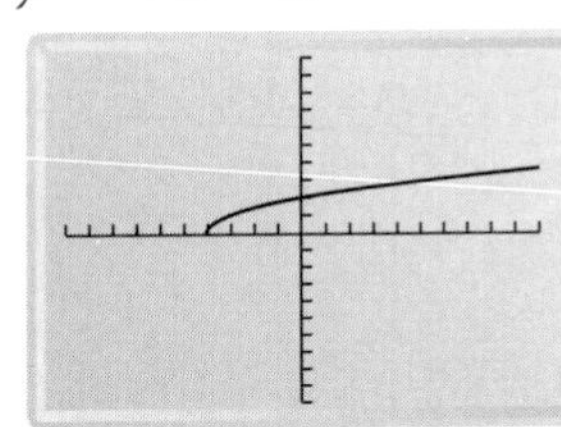

C. 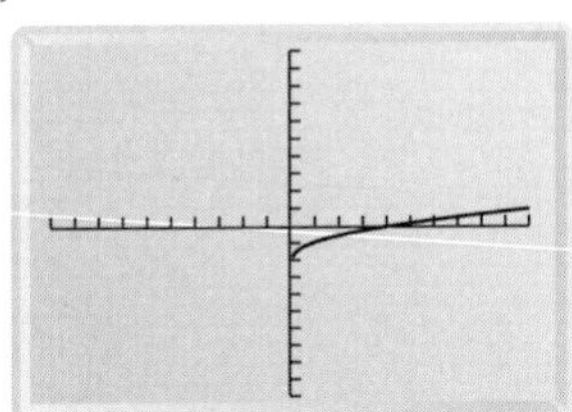

14. **Standardized Test Prep** In which of the following quadrants will your calculator display the graph of $y = \sqrt{x} + 7$?

   A. I, II, and III B. I and IV C. I D. IV E. I and II

Graph each function.

15. $y = \sqrt{x + 2}$

16. $y = \sqrt{x - 2.5}$

17. $f(x) = \sqrt{x} - 5$

18. $y = 4\sqrt{x}$

19. $f(x) = \sqrt{x} + 2$

20. $y = \sqrt{x + 3}$

21. $y = \sqrt{x - 6}$

22. $f(x) = 5\sqrt{x}$

23. $y = \sqrt{x - 2} + 3$

24. $f(x) = \sqrt{x - 3} - 1$

25. $y = \sqrt{x + 5} + 2$

26. $f(x) = \sqrt{x + 2} - 4$

Writing Using words like "shift up," "shift down," "shift left," and "shift right," describe to a friend how to use the graph of $y = \sqrt{x}$ to obtain the graph of each function.

27. $f(x) = \sqrt{x + 8}$

28. $y = \sqrt{x} - 10$

29. $y = \sqrt{x} + 12$

30. $f(x) = \sqrt{x - 9}$

31. a. **Open-ended** Give an example of a square root function in each form. Assume $k > 0$.

   $y = \sqrt{x} + k,$
   $y = \sqrt{x + k},$
   $y = k\sqrt{x}$

   b. Graph each function on the same coordinate grid.

Chapter Project — Find Out by Organizing

- The formula for the distance you can see on any planet is $d = \sqrt{\frac{rh}{2640}}$, where h is your height in feet and r is the radius of the planet in miles. Use the planet radii you researched on page 429 to write a separate formula for each planet.
- Graph each formula.

Exercises MIXED REVIEW

Solve each system of equations by graphing.

32. $x + y = 5$
$2x - 3y = -5$

33. $3x - y = 4$
$4x + 2y = 2$

34. *Finance* You deposit $1000 into a bank account that pays 6% compounded annually. How much will be in the bank account at the end of 3 years?

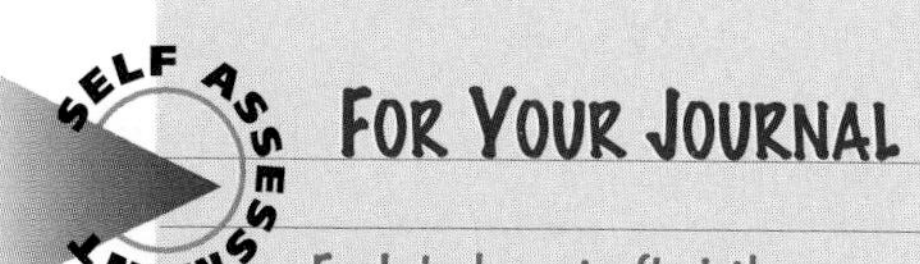

FOR YOUR JOURNAL

Explain how to find the domain of a square root function. Include an example.

Getting Ready for Lesson 9-8

Find the mean of each set of data.

35. 4, 6, 8, 10, 11 **36.** 3, 4, 5, 7, 9 **37.** −8, −6, 0, 2, 3 **38.** −3, −2, 0, 2, 9

Exercises CHECKPOINT

Simplify each radical expression.

1. $\sqrt{3} \cdot \sqrt{27}$ **2.** $\sqrt{7 \cdot 28}$ **3.** $\sqrt{64b^5}$ **4.** $\sqrt{18} - \sqrt{8}$

5. $\sqrt{3}(\sqrt{3} + 4)$ **6.** $\frac{\sqrt{24}}{\sqrt{3}}$ **7.** $\sqrt{\frac{x^3}{4}}$ **8.** $\frac{6}{\sqrt{3}}$

Solve each radical equation. Check your solutions.

9. $8 = \sqrt{x - 4}$ **10.** $\sqrt{x} = \sqrt{3x - 12}$ **11.** $\sqrt{2x - 5} = \sqrt{11}$ **12.** $7 - \sqrt{2x} = 1$

Graph each function.

13. $y = \sqrt{x} + 4$ **14.** $f(x) = \sqrt{x - 5}$ **15.** $f(x) = 2\sqrt{x}$ **16.** $y = \sqrt{x} - 3$

17. *Writing* How is combining like terms with radicals similar to combining like terms with variables?

18. *Standardized Test Prep* What is the perimeter of the figure?

A. $2\sqrt{7} + \sqrt{5}$ **B.** $\sqrt{5} + \sqrt{7}$ **C.** $\sqrt{35}$
D. $2\sqrt{7} + 2\sqrt{5}$ **E.** none of the above

(Figure: rectangle with sides $\sqrt{5}$ and $\sqrt{7}$)

Math ToolboX

Skills Review

Box-and-Whisker Plots

Before Lesson 9-8

To show how data items are spread out, you can arrange a set of data in order from least to greatest. The maximum, minimum, and median give you some information about the data. You can better describe the data by dividing it into fourths. The **lower quartile** is the median of the lower half of the data. The **upper quartile** is the median of the upper half of the data.

The data below describes the highway gas mileage (mi/gal) for several brands of cars.

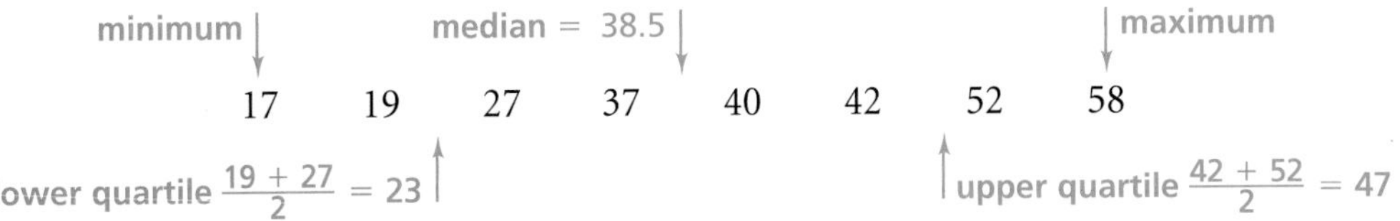

A **box-and-whisker plot** is a visual representation of data. The box-and-whisker plot at the right displays the gas mileage information. The box represents the data from the lower quartile to the upper quartile. The vertical line segment represents the median. Horizontal line segments called whiskers show the spread of the data to the minimum and to the maximum.

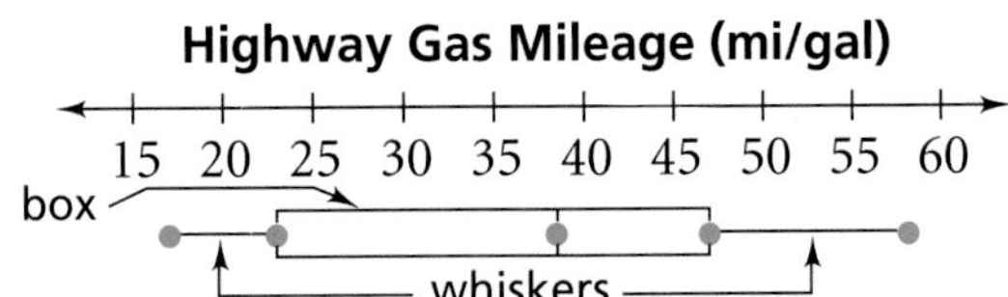

Create a box-and-whisker plot for each data set.

1. {3, 2, 3, 4, 6, 6, 7}
2. {1, 1.5, 1.7, 2, 6.1, 6.2, 7}
3. {1, 2, 5, 6, 9, 12, 7, 10}
4. {65, 66, 59, 61, 67, 70, 67, 66, 69, 70, 63}
5. {29, 32, 40, 31, 33, 39, 27, 42}
6. {3, 3, 5, 7, 1, 10, 10, 4, 4, 7, 9, 8, 6}
7. {1, 1.2, 1.3, 4, 4.1, 4.2, 7}
8. {1, 3.8, 3.9, 4, 4.3, 4.4, 7, 5}

9. *Jobs* Below are the number of hours a student worked each week at her summer job. When she applied for the job, she was told the typical work week was 29 hours.

   29, 23, 21, 20, 17, 16, 15, 33, 33, 32, 15

   a. Make a box-and-whisker plot for the data.

   b. How many weeks are above the upper quartile? What are the number of hours worked?

   c. What is the median number of hours she worked? What is the mean? Compare these to the typical work week.

10. *Writing* In what ways are histograms and box-and-whisker plots alike and in what ways are they different?

What You'll Learn

- Exploring standard deviation
- Calculating and using standard deviation

...And Why

To analyze job opportunities

9-8 Analyzing Data Using Standard Deviation

WORK TOGETHER

Jobs Work with a partner.

Four students had summer jobs at a camp last year. Four other students had jobs at a nursing home. Their weekly pay is listed below.

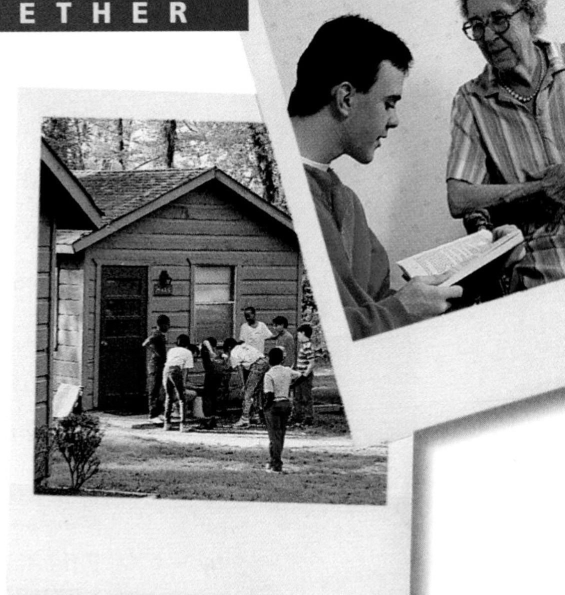

Salaries

Camp	Nursing Home
$150	$140
$160	$190
$220	$210
$270	$260

1. a. Calculate the mean for the pay in each location.
   b. What does the mean represent?

QUICK REVIEW

The *range* of a set of data is the difference between the greatest number and the least number in the set.

2. a What is the range of weekly pay for each location?
   b. Use the ranges to describe how the pay varies at the two locations.
3. Copy the table below.

Salary	Mean	Deviation from Mean	Square of Deviation
$150	$200	−50	2500
$160	$200	■	■
$220	$200	■	■
$270	$200	70	■
sum of the squares of the deviations →			■

4. You find deviation from the mean by subtracting the mean from each salary value. Fill in the missing values in column 3.
5. Complete column 4 by squaring each value in column 3.
6. Complete a table like the one above for the nursing home workers.
7. a. Compare the deviations from the mean at the two locations. At which location does the pay vary more from the mean?
   b. Compare the sum of the squares of the deviations for the two locations. How does this support your answer to part (a)?

THINK AND DISCUSS

A way to show how a set of data is spread out is the **standard deviation.** It reflects how all the data points in a set vary from the mean. The symbol for standard deviation is σ, pronounced "sigma."

small standard deviation ⟶ data cluster around the mean
large standard deviation ⟶ data spread out from the mean

You can calculate the standard deviation by following these six steps.

- Find the mean of the data set. The expression $\bar{x}$ represents the mean.
- Find the difference of each data value from the mean.
- Calculate the square of each difference.
- Find the sum of the squares of the differences.
- Divide the sum by the number of data values.
- Take the square root of the quotient just calculated.

Example 1

Find the standard deviation of the two data sets below.

a. Data Set 1 {83, 88, 75, 69, 70} **b.** Data Set 2 {69, 75, 76, 77, 88}

a. Find the mean.

$$\text{mean} = \frac{83 + 88 + 75 + 69 + 70}{5} = \frac{385}{5} = 77$$

Calculate the standard deviation.

x	$\bar{x}$	$x - \bar{x}$	$(x - \bar{x})^2$
83	77	6	36
88	77	11	121
75	77	−2	4
70	77	−7	49
69	77	−8	64
		Sum:	274

$$\text{sum of squares} = 274$$

$$\frac{\text{sum of squares}}{5} = \frac{274}{5} = 54.8$$

$$\sqrt{54.8} = 7.402702209$$

The standard deviation is about 7.4.

b. Find the mean.

$$\text{mean} = \frac{69 + 75 + 76 + 77 + 88}{5} = \frac{385}{5} = 77$$

Calculate the standard deviation.

x	$\bar{x}$	$x - \bar{x}$	$(x - \bar{x})^2$
69	77	−8	64
75	77	−2	4
76	77	−1	1
77	77	0	0
88	77	11	121
		Sum:	190

$$\text{sum of squares} = 190$$

$$\frac{\text{sum of squares}}{5} = \frac{190}{5} = 38$$

$$\sqrt{38} = 6.164414003$$

The standard deviation is about 6.2.

8. In which data set do the values cluster closer to the mean?

You can use a calculator to find the standard deviation of a set of data.

Example 2 **Relating to the Real World** 

Golf Three friends play golf. Their scores on six holes of golf are below. Calculate the mean and standard deviation for Player 1's scores.

Player 1	5	4	2	4	10	5
Player 2	5	5	5	5	5	5
Player 3	3	10	4	4	7	2

You can use a calculator to calculate the mean and standard deviation.

- Choose STAT and *EDIT* to enter your data.
- Choose STAT, *CALC*, and *1-VAR STATS* to calculate.
- The screen displays information about your data including the mean, $\overline{x}$, the standard deviation, σx, and the number of entries, n.

The mean of Player 1's scores is 5. The standard deviation is about 2.4.

9. a. Predict whether the standard deviations of Player 2's and Player 3's scores will be greater or less than the standard deviation of Player 1's scores.

b. Explain how you made your predictions in part (a).

10. a. Try This Use a calculator to find the mean and standard deviation for Player 2's and Player 3's golf scores.

b. What does a standard deviation of zero mean?

c. Estimation Suppose a friend got the answer 27.5 when using a calculator to find the standard deviation of Player 3's golf scores. How do you know that your friend made an error?

◀ **At age 20, Tiger Woods was a three-time United States Amateur champion.**

Exercises ON YOUR OWN

Calculator **Make a table like the one in Example 1 to find the standard deviation for each data set. Use a calculator to find the square root.**

1. $\{5, 3, 2, 5, 10\}$
2. $\{10, 9, 10, 12, 11, 14\}$
3. $\{3.5, 4.5, 6.0, 4.0, 2.5, 2.5, 5.0\}$
4. $\{11, 11, 17, 17, 10, 11, 12, 19\}$

5. Tell what you know about the following data sets.
   a. Data Set 1: The mean is 25 and the standard deviation is 100.
   b. Data Set 2: The mean is 25 and the standard deviation is 2.

6. The table at the right records the outdoor temperatures (°F) reported to a local meteorologist by twelve weather watchers near Denver, Colorado, in January. Find the standard deviation of the temperature data.

January Temperatures (°F)	
15.8°	16.3°
16.5°	17.0°
15.9°	16.1°
16.5°	16.2°
16.0°	16.4°
16.1°	16.6°

7. **Writing** Explain the effects of a very large or very small data value on the mean and standard deviation of a data set.

8. **Open-ended** Create data sets with at least 6 entries as follows.
   a. The mean is 12 and the standard deviation is 0.
   b. The mean is 7 and the range is 12.

9. **Jobs** When Lyman interviewed for a summer job, he asked about the average salary of summer employees. He was excited that the average weekly wage was \$400. When his employer offered him a job at \$265 a week, he was confused. His employer stated: "Of my 20 summer employees, 17 make \$265 per week."
   a. During the job interview, what other statistics should Lyman have asked about in order to find out more information about salaries? Explain your choice(s).
   b. The three highly-paid summer employees each earn the same amount. How much do they earn?
   c. **Estimate** Do you expect the standard deviation for the company's summer salaries to be large or small? Why?
   d. **Verify** your prediction by calculating the standard deviation.

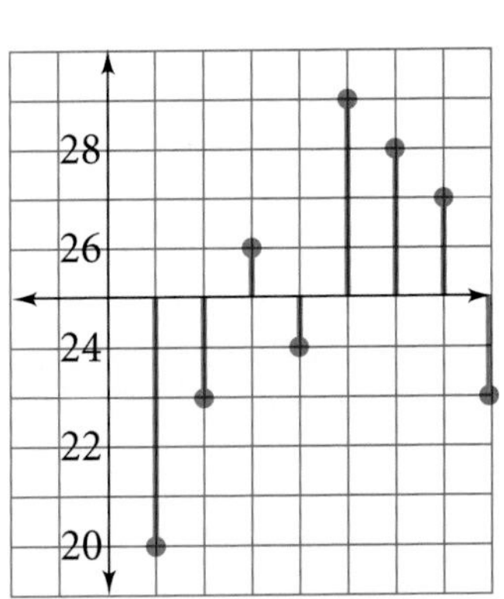

10. The graph at the right shows the differences from the mean in a set of data containing eight data values.
    a. Find the square of each difference from the mean.
    b. Find the sum of the squares calculated in part (a).
    c. Use the result of part (b) to find the standard deviation of the data set.

Graphing Calculator **Use a calculator to find the standard deviation of each set of data.**

11. {11.4, 10.1, 9.5, 9.9, 10.1, 11.2, 12.0, 12.3}

12. {102.4, 100.8, 99.5, 103.4, 105.6, 111.5, 120.5}

13. {13, 19, 23, 50, 43, 44, 50, 52, 74, 83, 88, 90}

14. {–3.2, 0, 1.3, –2.0, –3.5, 0, 3.2, 2.3, 1.1, 0.3}

15. **Math in the Media** You are writing a magazine article on ski resorts in the Sierras. The information at the right is part of your research.

a. What is the range for the price of a lift ticket?

b. Find the standard deviation of the ticket prices.

c. To give your readers a feel for the variability of ticket prices, you include the following sentence in your article. Fill in the blanks.

Lift ticket prices vary about $ ■ around an average of $ ■ for an all-day adult ticket.

d. **Writing** Explain why your sentence in part (c) is more helpful than simply telling your readers the range, as in "The prices vary from $26 to $46."

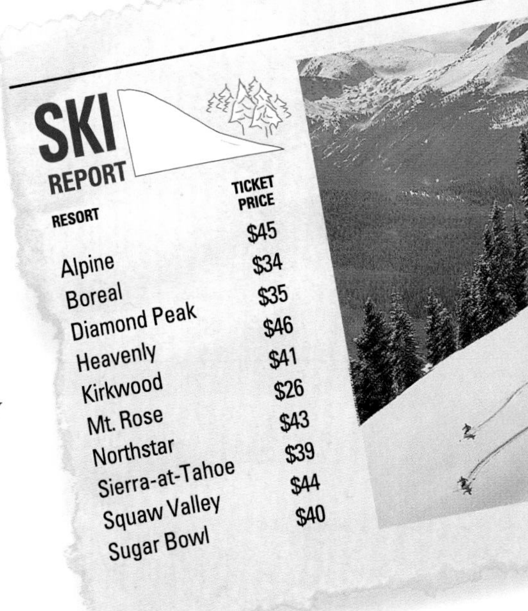

SKI REPORT

RESORT	TICKET PRICE
Alpine	$45
Boreal	$34
Diamond Peak	$35
Heavenly	$46
Kirkwood	$41
Mt. Rose	$26
Northstar	$43
Sierra-at-Tahoe	$39
Squaw Valley	$44
Sugar Bowl	$40

16. **Research** Collect data on a topic of interest such as classmates' batting averages or students' curfew times. Gather at least 15 measurements and calculate the mean and standard deviation. Write a paragraph describing your data.

Exercises MIXED REVIEW

Write each number in scientific notation.

17. 0.00347

18. 3,112,200

19. 0.000825

20. 50,147,235

Solve each system of equations.

21. $3x + 2y = 7$
$2x + 3y = 8$

22. $5x - 2y = 3$
$4x + 2y = 6$

23. $x + y = 7$
$2x - y = 8$

24. $3x - 4y = 5$
$3x + 2y = 11$

Find the domain of each function.

25. $y = \sqrt{x - 5}$

26. $f(x) = 5 + \sqrt{6 + 3x}$

27. **Automobiles** A new car costs $20,000. It loses value at a rate of 7% per year. How much is the car worth in four years?

SELF ASSESSMENT

PORTFOLIO

For your portfolio, select one or two items from your work for this chapter. Here are possibilities:

- corrected work
- diagrams, graphs, or charts
- a journal entry

Explain why you have included each selection you make.

CHAPTER PROJECT

Finishing the Chapter Project

On a CLEAR *Day...*

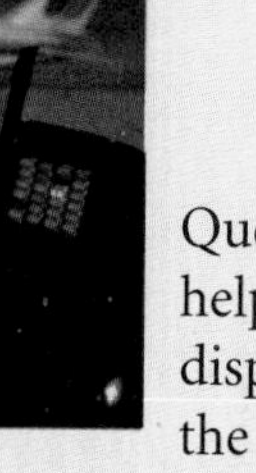

Questions on pages 418, 424, 429, 444, and 449 should help you to complete your project. Prepare a visual display and a report of your results. You should include the formula and graph for each planet and the formula for height on Earth when sight distance is known.

Reflect and Revise

Your notebook should present a comparison of sight distances and graphs for each planet. Check that your formulas and graphs are clearly labeled and easy to understand. Be sure that you have included a separate category with your display for Earth giving the formula for height on Earth when sight distance is known.

Follow Up

Suppose you were in an airplane at 30,000 ft above your town. How far could you see? Write a description of what you would see. Include any points of interest, cities or towns, and geological features like rivers or mountains.

For More Information

Adler, David. *Hyperspace! Facts and Fun from All Over the Universe.* New York: Viking Children's Books, 1982.

"Living and Working in Space: The Countdown Has Begun." PBS Video, 1320 Braddock Place, Alexandria, Virginia 22314. (800) 344-3337.

Free videotapes, slides, books, pamphlets: National Aeronautics and Space Administration, Education Programs Officer, NASA Headquarters, Code XEE, Washington, D.C. 20546. (202) 453-8396.

CHAPTER

9 Wrap Up

Key Terms

angle of elevation (p. 426)
box-and-whisker plot (p. 450)
converse of the Pythagorean theorem (p. 416)
cosine (p. 425)
distance formula (p. 420)
division property of square roots (p. 431)
extraneous solution (p. 443)
hypotenuse (p. 414)
legs (p. 414)
like terms (p. 435)
lower quartile (p. 450)
midpoint (p. 422)
midpoint formula (p. 422)
multiplication property of square roots (p. 430)
Pythagorean theorem (p. 414)
radical equation (p. 440)
rationalize (p. 432)
simplest form (p. 430)
sine (p. 425)
square root function (p. 445)
standard deviation (p. 452)
tangent (p. 425)
trigonometric ratios (p. 425)
unlike terms (p. 435)
upper quartile (p. 450)

How am I doing?

- State three ideas from this chapter that you think are important. Explain your choices.
- Describe the method for finding the distance between two points A and B.

The Pythagorean Theorem 9-1

For a right triangle with **legs** a and b and **hypotenuse** c, the **Pythagorean theorem** states that $a^2 + b^2 = c^2$. The **converse of the Pythagorean theorem** states that if a triangle has sides of lengths a, b, and c, and if $a^2 + b^2 = c^2$, then it is a right triangle with hypotenuse of length c.

A rectangle has sides with lengths a and b. Find the length of the diagonal to the nearest hundredth.

1. $a = 3, b = 5$ **2.** $a = 11, b = 14$ **3.** $a = 7, b = 13$ **4.** $a = 4, b = 9$

5. **Writing** The hypotenuse of a right triangle is 26 cm. The length of one leg is 10 cm. Describe how to find the length of the other leg.

The Distance Formula 9-2

The **distance formula** $d = \sqrt{(x_2 - x_1)^2 + (y_2 - y_1)^2}$ gives the distance between two points (x_1, y_1) and (x_2, y_2). The **midpoint formula** $M = \left(\frac{x_1 + x_2}{2}, \frac{y_1 + y_2}{2}\right)$ gives the coordinates of their midpoint.

Find the midpoint of $\overline{AB}$.

6. $A(3, 7), B(-2, 4)$ **7.** $A(5, -2), B(6, 14)$ **8.** $A(3, -9), B(14, 16)$ **9.** $A(12, 17), B(-7, 9)$

10. **Open-ended** Find two points with integer coordinates $\sqrt{74}$ units apart.

Trigonometric Ratios 9-3

Trigonometric ratios are triangle measurement ratios. For a right triangle of a given shape, they do not change no matter how large or small the triangle is. Three trigonometric ratios are **sine** (sin), **cosine** (cos), and **tangent** (tan), shown at the right.

$$\sin A = \frac{\text{length of side of opposite } \angle A}{\text{length of hypotenuse}}$$

$$\cos A = \frac{\text{length of side of adjacent to } \angle A}{\text{length of hypotenuse}}$$

$$\tan A = \frac{\text{length of side opposite } \angle A}{\text{length of side adjacent to } \angle A}$$

You can use trigonometric ratios to measure distances indirectly. You can use an **angle of elevation** to measure heights indirectly.

In $\triangle ABC$, $\angle C$ is a right angle. Find the lengths of the missing sides.

11. $AB = 12, m\angle A = 34°$ **12.** $BC = 9, m\angle B = 72°$ **13.** $AC = 8, m\angle B = 52°$

14. ***Standardized Test Prep*** In $\triangle ABC$, $\angle C$ is a right angle. Which of the following is (are) true?

I. $\cos B = \frac{AC}{AB}$ **II.** $\tan B = \frac{BC}{AC}$ **III.** $\sin A = \frac{BC}{AB}$

A. I only **B.** II only **C.** III only **D.** I and II **E.** II and III

Simplifying Radicals 9-4

You can simplify some radical expressions by using products or quotients. The **multiplication property of square roots** states that for any two nonnegative numbers $\sqrt{ab} = \sqrt{a} \cdot \sqrt{b}$. The **division property of square roots** is at the right.

$$\sqrt{\frac{a}{b}} = \frac{\sqrt{a}}{\sqrt{b}}$$

$a \geq 0, b > 0$
division property

Simplify each radical expression.

15. $\sqrt{32} \cdot \sqrt{144}$ **16.** $\frac{\sqrt{84}}{\sqrt{121}}$ **17.** $\sqrt{96} \cdot \sqrt{25}$ **18.** $\sqrt{\frac{100}{169}}$

19. A rectangle is 7 times as long as it is wide. Its area is 1400 cm^2. Find the dimensions of the rectangle in simplified form.

Adding and Subtracting Radicals 9-5

You can use the distributive property to simplify expressions with sums and differences of radicals. First, simplify the radicals to have like terms.

Simplify each radical expression.

20. $6\sqrt{7} - 2\sqrt{28}$ **21.** $5(\sqrt{20} + \sqrt{80})$ **22.** $\sqrt{54} - 2\sqrt{6}$ **23.** $\sqrt{125} - 3\sqrt{5}$

24. $\sqrt{10}(\sqrt{10} - \sqrt{20})$ **25.** $7\sqrt{90} + \sqrt{160}$ **26.** $\sqrt{72} + 3\sqrt{32}$ **27.** $\sqrt{28} + 5\sqrt{63}$

28. A box is 2 in. long, 3 in. wide, and 4 in. tall. What is the length of the longest distance between corners of the box? Express your answer in simplified form.

Solving Radical Equations 9-6

A **radical equation** has a variable under a radical. You can often solve a radical equation by solving for the square root, then squaring both sides of the equation. Squaring each side of an equation also works when both sides are square roots. When you square both sides of a radical equation, you may produce an **extraneous solution**. It is not a solution of the original equation.

Solve each radical equation.

29. $\sqrt{x + 7} = 3$ **30.** $\sqrt{x} + 3\sqrt{x} = 16$ **31.** $\sqrt{x + 7} = \sqrt{2x - 1}$ **32.** $\sqrt{x} - 5 = 4$

33. The volume V of a cylinder is given by $V = \pi r^2 h$, where r is the radius of the cylinder and h is its height. If the volume of a cylinder is 54 in.^{2}, and its height is 2 in., what is its radius to the nearest 0.01 in.?

Graphing Square Root Functions 9-7

The simplest **square root function** is $y = \sqrt{x}$. To find the domain of a square root function, solve the inequality where the expression under the radical is greater than or equal to zero.

Find the domain of each function. Then graph the function.

34. $y = \sqrt{x} + 5$ **35.** $y = \sqrt{x} - 2$ **36.** $y = \sqrt{x + 1}$ **37.** $y = 2\sqrt{x}$

Analyzing Data Using Standard Deviation 9-8

The **standard deviation** shows how spread out a set of data is from the mean. You can calculate the standard deviation by following these six steps. Find the mean, $\bar{x}$, of the data set. Find the difference of each data value from the mean. Square each difference. Find the sum of the squares of the differences. Divide the sum by the number of data values. The square root of the quotient just calculated is the standard deviation.

Find the standard deviation of each set of data.

38. 2, 7, 9, 15, 17 **39.** 5, 8, 11, 12, 19 **40.** 4, 10, 12, 13, 23 **41.** 7, 15, 20, 23, 29

Getting Ready for... CHAPTER 10

Use the quadratic formula to solve these equations to the nearest hundredth. If the equation has no real solution, write *no solution*.

42. $2x^2 + 5x - 4 = 0$ **43.** $3x^2 - 2x - 7 = 0$ **44.** $x^2 - 3x - 8 = 0$

45. $2x^2 - 5x + 15 = 0$ **46.** $5x^2 - 4x - 12 = 0$ **47.** $7x^2 + 2x - 18 = 0$

CHAPTER

9 Assessment

Find whether the following sets of numbers determine a right triangle.

1. 6, 8, 10 **2.** 6, 7, 9

3. 4, 5, 11 **4.** 10, 24, 26

Approximate AB to the nearest hundredth.

5. $A(1, -2)$, $B(5, 7)$ **6.** $A(3, 5)$, $B(7, 4)$

7. $A(4, 7)$, $B(-11, -6)$ **8.** $A(0, -5)$, $B(3, 2)$

Find the coordinates of the midpoint of $\overline{AB}$.

9. $A(4, 9)$, $B(1, -5)$ **10.** $A(-2, -7)$, $B(3, 0)$

11. $A(3, -10)$, $B(-4, 6)$ **12.** $A(0, 8)$, $B(-1, 1)$

Find the lengths to the nearest hundredth.

13. AB

14. AC

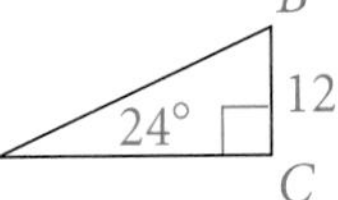

15. The distance between consecutive bases in a baseball diamond is 90 ft. How far is it from first base to third base?

16. One house is 12 mi east of a school. Another house is 9 mi north of the school. How far apart from each other are the houses?

Simplify each radical expression.

17. $\sqrt{\frac{128}{64}}$ **18.** $\frac{\sqrt{27}}{\sqrt{75}}$

19. $\sqrt{48}$ **20.** $\sqrt{12} \cdot \sqrt{8}$

21. $3\sqrt{32} + 5\sqrt{2}$ **22.** $2\sqrt{27} + 5\sqrt{3}$

23. $7\sqrt{125} - 3\sqrt{175}$ **24.** $\sqrt{128} - \sqrt{192}$

25. *Standardized Test Prep* If x and y are positive, which expression(s) is (are) equivalent to $\sqrt{24x^2y^3}$?

I. $2xy\sqrt{12xy^2}$ **II.** $2xy\sqrt{6y}$ **III.** $xy\sqrt{24y}$

A. I only **B.** II only **C.** III only

D. I and II **E.** II and III

26. *Open-ended* Write a problem involving addition of two like terms with radical expressions. Simplify the sum.

Solve each radical equation.

27. $3\sqrt{x} + 2\sqrt{x} = 10$ **28.** $8 = \sqrt{5x - 1}$

29. $5\sqrt{x} = \sqrt{15x + 60}$

30. $\sqrt{x} = \sqrt{2x - 7}$

31. $3\sqrt{x + 3} = 2\sqrt{x + 9}$

32. A rectangle is 5 times as long as it is wide. The area of the rectangle is 100 ft^2. How wide is the rectangle? Express your answer in simplified form.

Find the domain of each function. Then graph the function.

33. $y = 3\sqrt{x}$ **34.** $y = \sqrt{x} + 4$

35. $y = \sqrt{x - 4}$ **36.** $y = \sqrt{x + 9}$

37. A cube has 3-in. sides. Find the longest distance between a pair of corners. Express your answer in simplified form.

Find the standard deviation of each set of data.

38. 5, 7, 9, 11, 12 **39.** 2, 4, 7, 11, 15

40. 4, 12, 13, 15, 17 **41.** 1, 2, 4, 6, 7

42. *Writing* Explain how these two data sets differ based on the following information.
Set A: mean 20; range 10; standard deviation 4
Set B: mean 20; range 20; standard deviation 2

43. *Geometry* The formula for the volume V of a cylinder of height h and radius r is $V = \pi r^2 h$. Solve the formula for r in terms of V and h.

44. From the ground you can see a satellite dish on the roof of a building 60 feet high. The angle of elevation is 62°. How far away is the building from you?

CHAPTER 9

Preparing for Standardized Tests

For Exercises 1–13, choose the correct letter.

1. At a supermarket, salad costs $.40 per ounce. Which rule represents the cost in dollars of buying x ounces of salad?
   A. $y = -0.4x$ **B.** $y = 0.4x$
   C. $y = 0.4$ **D.** $y = x + 0.4$
   E. $y = x - 0.4$

2. Which function is modeled by the table?

x	-1	1	3	5
y	-5	-1	3	7

   A. $y = 2x$ **B.** $y = 2x + 3$
   C. $y = \frac{1}{2}x$ **D.** $y = \frac{1}{2}x + 3$
   E. $y = 2x - 3$

3. Find the value of n if $3n - 5 = 7$.
   A. 3 **B.** 4 **C.** 5 **D.** 6 **E.** 7

4. The sum of four consecutive integers is 190. What is the third integer?
   A. 44 **B.** 45 **C.** 46 **D.** 47 **E.** 48

5. Which are solutions of $3(x - 4) \leq 18$ and $2(x - 1) \geq 6$?
   I. 9 **II.** 12 **III.** 15
   A. I only **B.** II only **C.** III only
   D. I and III **E.** II and III

6. What is the slope of a line perpendicular to $3x + 2y = 7$?
   A. $-\frac{3}{2}$ **B.** $-\frac{2}{3}$ **C.** $\frac{2}{3}$ **D.** $\frac{3}{2}$ **E.** 7

7. How many solutions are there to the quadratic equation $2x^2 + 5x + 1 = 0$?
   A. 0 **B.** 1 **C.** 2 **D.** 3 **E.** 4

8. Which of the functions is quadratic?
   I. $y = 2x^2 - 7$ **II.** $y = 2x + 3$
   III. $y = 3x^2 + 2x$
   A. I only **B.** II only **C.** III only
   D. I and III **E.** I, II, and III

9. If $y - x > 0$, what equals $|x - y|$?
   I. $y - x$ **II.** $|y - x|$ **III.** $x - y$
   A. I and II **B.** II and III **C.** I and III
   D. II only **E.** I, II, and III

10. What is the probability of *not* rolling a 1 or 2 on a number cube?
    A. $\frac{1}{6}$ **B.** $\frac{1}{3}$ **C.** $\frac{1}{2}$ **D.** $\frac{2}{3}$ **E.** $\frac{5}{6}$

11. A box is 2 cm wide, 5 cm long, and 4 cm high. What is the distance in centimeters between the most distant pair of corners?
    A. 11 **B.** $3\sqrt{5}$ **C.** $\sqrt{41}$ **D.** $\sqrt{29}$ **E.** $2\sqrt{5}$

Compare the boxed quantity in Column A with the boxed quantity in Column B. Choose the best answer.

A. The quantity in Column A is greater.
B. The quantity in Column B is greater.
C. The two quantities are equal.
D. The relationship cannot be determined on the basis of the information supplied.

	Column A	Column B
12.	$5\sqrt{3} + 1$	$6\sqrt{3} - 1$
13.	$-x - 1$	$x + 1$

Find each answer.

14. **Open-ended** Find two points with integer coordinates that are $\sqrt{41}$ units apart.

15. The test scores of one student are 79, 80, 85, 87, and 94. Find the mean and standard deviation of these scores.

16. **Geometry** In $\triangle ABC$, $\angle C$ is a right angle, $AB = 7$, and $m\angle B = 28°$. What are the lengths of $\overline{BC}$ and $\overline{AC}$ to the nearest hundredth?

17. **Art** In 1996, the National Gallery in Washington, DC, exhibited 21 paintings by Johannes Vermeer. This is about $\frac{2}{3}$ of his paintings that are known to exist. How many of his paintings do we know of today?

18. **Geometry** What is the length of the diagonal of a rectangle with sides 6 cm and 10 cm?

CHAPTER

10 Polynomials

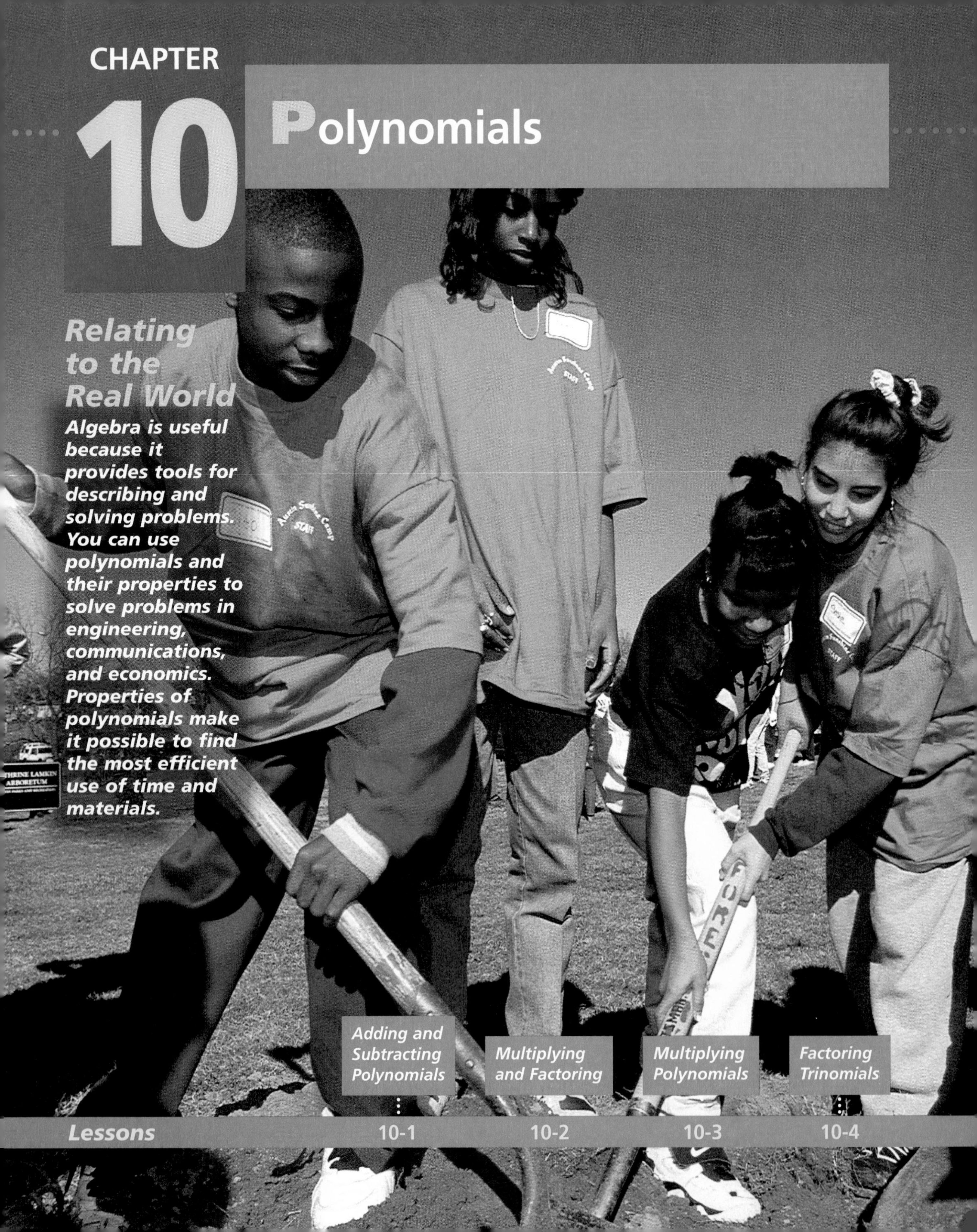

Relating to the Real World

Algebra is useful because it provides tools for describing and solving problems. You can use polynomials and their properties to solve problems in engineering, communications, and economics. Properties of polynomials make it possible to find the most efficient use of time and materials.

Lessons	10-1	10-2	10-3	10-4
	Adding and Subtracting Polynomials	*Multiplying and Factoring*	*Multiplying Polynomials*	*Factoring Trinomials*

CHAPTER PROJECT

Trees are us.

Rings indicate age.

Wood splits as it dries.

Scar shows fire damage.

Many schools celebrate Arbor Day by planting young trees to replenish our ecosystem. Trees use the carbon dioxide that humans and animals exhale to make oxygen. Trees anchor the soil and prevent erosion. They also produce fruit. Wood from trees is used for the construction of everything from pencils to houses.

As you work through the chapter, you will learn more about the uses of trees. You will use formulas to analyze data and predict the production of wood and fruit. Then you will decide how to organize and display your results.

To help you complete the project:

- **p. 474** *Find Out by Researching*
- **p. 479** *Find Out by Calculating*
- **p. 485** *Find Out by Calculating*
- **p. 495** *Find Out by Graphing*
- **p. 502** *Finishing the Project*

Connections Business . . . and more

10-1 Adding and Subtracting Polynomials

What You'll Learn

- Describing polynomials
- Adding and subtracting polynomials

...And Why

To use polynomials in real-world situations, such as working in a store

What You'll Need

- tiles

WORK TOGETHER

Business Work in groups. Suppose you work at a pet store. The spreadsheet shows the contents of several customers' orders.

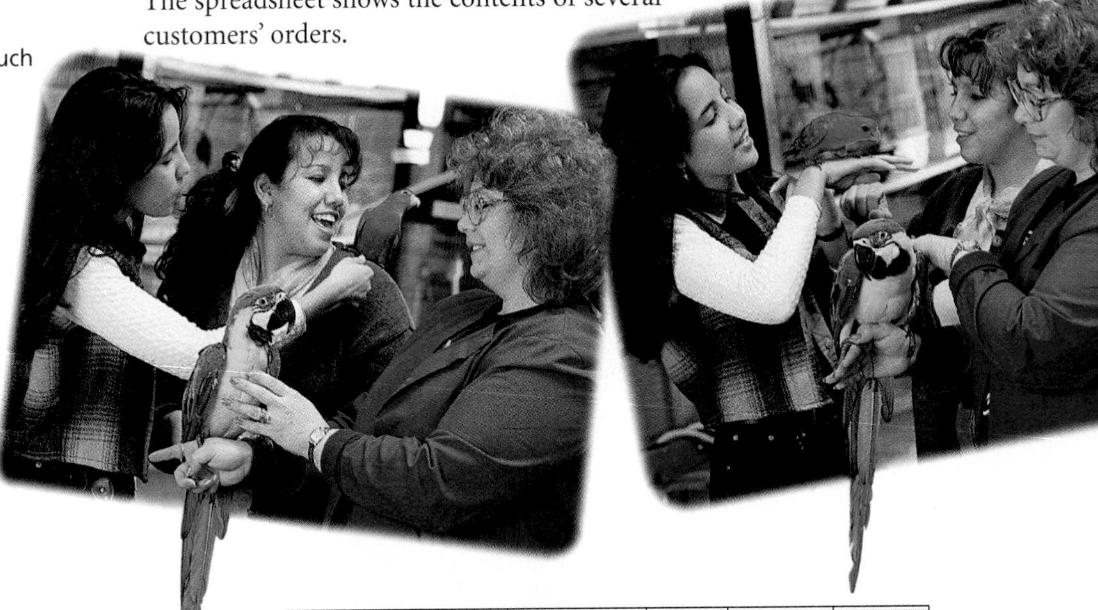

	A	B	C	D	E	F
1	Customer	Seed	Cuttlebone	Millet	G. Paper	Perches
2	Davis			✔		
3	Brooks	✔	✔			
4	Casic	✔		✔		
5	Martino	✔			✔	✔

ROCKY'S FRIENDS
Bird Supplies
• bird seed (5 lb) $3.99
• cuttlebone (2 ct) 2.00
• spray millet (5 lb) 24.00
• gravel paper (1 pkg) 2.29
• perches (2 ct) 1.89
Tidbits

The variables represent the number of each item ordered.
s = bags of birdseed m = bags of millet p = packages of perches
c = packages of cuttlebone g = packages of gravel paper

1. Which expression represents the cost of Casic's order?
   A. $27.99(s + m)$ **B.** $3.99s + 24m$ **C.** $27.99sm$
2. Write expressions to represent each of the other customers' orders.
3. Martino buys 10 bags of birdseed, 4 packages of gravel paper, and 2 packages of perches. What is the total cost of his order?
4. *Open-ended* Make up several orders and write expressions for these orders. Have other members of your group find the cost of your orders. Check each other's work.

THINK AND DISCUSS

Describing Polynomials

QUICK REVIEW

A *term* is a number or the product or quotient of a number and a variable.

A **polynomial** is one term or the sum or difference of two or more terms. A polynomial has no variables in a denominator. For a term that has only one variable, the **degree of a term** is the exponent of the variable.

$$x^3 - 4x + 5x^2 + 7$$

The degree of a constant is 0.

degree → 3 1 2 0

QUICK REVIEW

$x = x^1$

The **degree of a polynomial** is the same as the degree of the term with the highest degree. You can name a polynomial by its degree or by the number of its terms.

Polynomial	Degree	Name Using Degree	Number of Terms	Name Using Number of Terms
$7x + 4$	1	linear	2	**binomial**
$3x^2 + 2x + 1$	2	quadratic	3	**trinomial**
$4x^3$	3	cubic	1	**monomial**
5	0	constant	1	monomial

The polynomials in the chart are in **standard form,** which means the terms decrease in degree from left to right and no terms have the same degree.

Example 1

Write each polynomial in standard form. Then name each polynomial by its degree and the number of its terms.

a. $5 - 2x$
$-2x + 5$
linear binomial

b. $3x^4 - 4 + 2x^2$
$3x^4 + 2x^2 - 4$
fourth degree trinomial

c. $-2x + 5 - 4x^2 + x^3$
$x^3 - 4x^2 - 2x + 5$
cubic polynomial with four terms

5. Try This Write each polynomial in standard form. Then name each polynomial by its degree and the number of its terms.

a. $6x^2 + 7 - 9x^4$ **b.** $3y - 9 - y^3$ **c.** $9 + 7v$

Adding Polynomials

You can use tiles to add and subtract polynomials.

Opposite terms form zero pairs. → x^2, $-x^2$ $= 0$ x, $-x$ $= 0$ 1, -1 $= 0$

6. What polynomial is shown using each set of tiles?

a. 

b. 

Example 2

Find $(2x^2 - 3x + 4) + (3x^2 + 2x - 3)$.

Method 1 Add using tiles.

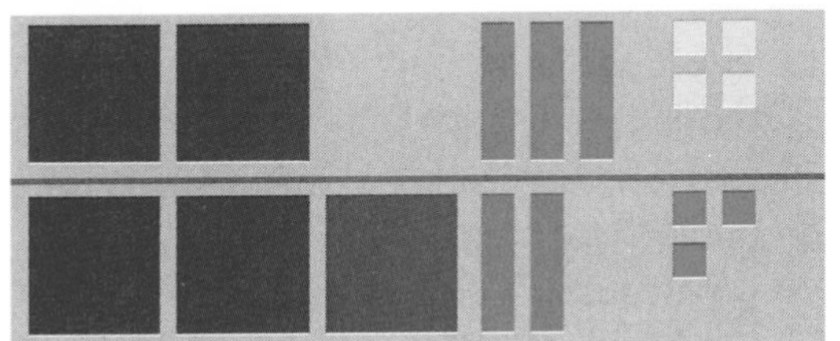

$2x^2 - 3x + 4$

$3x^2 + 2x - 3$

Group like tiles together. Remove zero pairs. Write an expression for the remaining tiles.

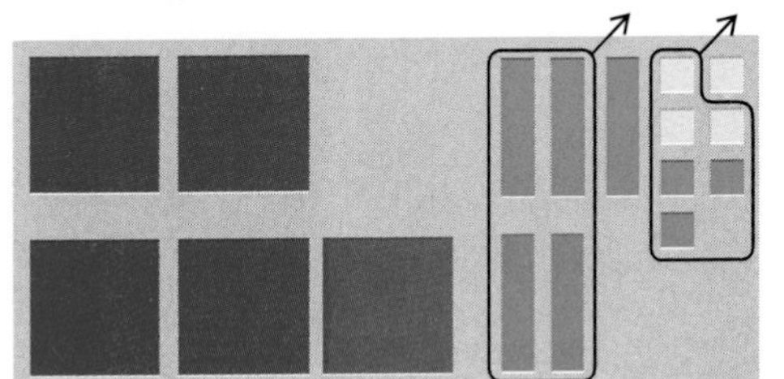

$5x^2 - x + 1$

Quick Review

Like terms have the same variable and the same number of variable factors, or the same degree.

Method 2 Add vertically.

Line up like terms.
Then add the coefficients.

$$\begin{array}{r} 2x^2 - 3x + 4 \\ \underline{3x^2 + 2x - 3} \\ 5x^2 - x + 1 \end{array}$$

The sum is $5x^2 - x + 1$.

Method 3 Add horizontally.

Group like terms. Then add the coefficients.

$(2x^2 - 3x + 4) + (3x^2 + 2x - 3)$
$= (2x^2 + 3x^2) + (-3x + 2x) + (4 - 3)$
$= 5x^2 - x + 1$

7. a. **Try This** Find $(5x^2 + 4x - 7) + (-4x^2 + 8x - 1)$ using any method you choose.
   b. Why did you choose the method you used?

Subtracting Polynomials

In Chapter 1, you learned that subtraction means to add the opposite. So when you subtract a polynomial, change each of its terms to the opposite. Then add the coefficients.

Example 3

Find $(7x^3 - 3x + 1) - (x^3 + 4x^2 - 2)$.

Method 1 Subtract vertically.

Line up like terms.

$$\begin{array}{rrrr} 7x^3 & & -\ 3x & +\ 1 \\ -(x^3 & +\ 4x^2 & & -\ 2) \\ \hline \end{array}$$

Add the opposite.

$$\begin{array}{rrrr} 7x^3 & & -\ 3x & +\ 1 \\ -x^3 & -\ 4x^2 & & +\ 2 \\ \hline 6x^3 & -\ 4x^2 & -\ 3x & +\ 3 \end{array}$$

Method 2 Subtract horizontally.

Write the opposite of each term in the polynomial being subtracted. Group like terms. Then add the coefficients of like terms.

$(7x^3 - 3x + 1) - (x^3 + 4x^2 - 2)$

$= 7x^3 - 3x + 1 - x^3 - 4x^2 + 2$

$= (7x^3 - x^3) - 4x^2 - 3x + (1 + 2)$ ← The coefficients of $7x^3$ and $-x^3$ are 7 and -1. $7x^3 - 1x^3 = 6x^3$.

$= 6x^3 - 4x^2 - 3x + 3$

The difference is $6x^3 - 4x^2 - 3x + 3$.

Check Substitute a value for x to check. Here 2 is substituted for x.

$$(7x^3 - 3x + 1) - (x^3 + 4x^2 - 2) \stackrel{?}{=} 6x^3 - 4x^2 - 3x + 3$$

$$7(2^3) - 3(2) + 1 - [2^3 + 4(2^2) - 2] \stackrel{?}{=} 6(2^3) - 4(2^2) - 3(2) + 3$$

$$(56 - 6 + 1) - (8 + 16 - 2) \stackrel{?}{=} 48 - 16 - 6 + 3$$

$$51 - 22 \stackrel{?}{=} 29$$

$$29 = 29 ✓$$

8. **Try This** Subtract $(3x^2 + 4x - 1) - (x^2 - x - 2)$.

9. **Critical Thinking** How are subtracting vertically and subtracting horizontally alike?

Exercises ON YOUR OWN

Match each expression with its name.

1. $5x^2 - 2x + 3$

2. $\frac{3}{4}z + 5$

3. $7a^3 + 4a - 12$

4. $\frac{3}{x} + 5$

5. -15

A. constant monomial

B. *not* a polynomial

C. quadratic trinomial

D. linear binomial

E. cubic trinomial

Write each polynomial in standard form. Then name each polynomial by its degree and number of terms.

6. $4x - 3x^2$

7. $4x + 9$

8. $6 - 3x - 7x^2$

9. $9z^2 - 11z^3 + 5z - 5$

10. $y - 7y^3 + 15y^8$

11. $c^2 - 2 + 4c$

12. $7 + 5b^2$

13. $-10 + 4q^4 - 8q + 3q^2$

Find the sum of the two sets of tiles.

14. 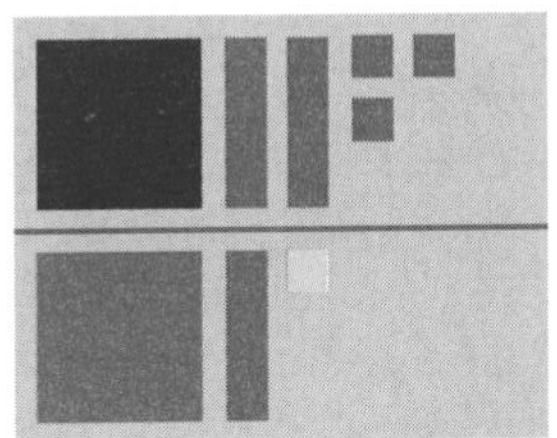

15. 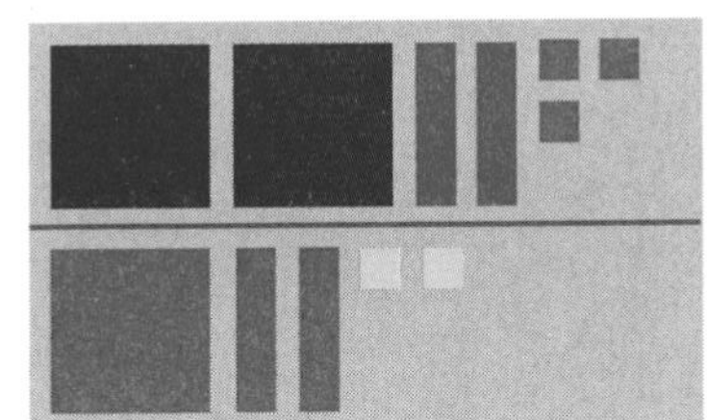

Find each sum or difference.

16. $(7y^2 - 3y + 4y) + (8y^2 + 3y^2 + 4y)$

17. $(2x^3 - 5x^2 + 3x - 1) - (8x^3 - 8x^2 + 4x + 3)$

18. $(-7z^3 + 3z - 1) - (-6z^2 + z + 4)$

19. $(7a^3 + 3a^2 - a + 2) + (8a^2 - 3a - 4)$

20. $(5y^3 + 7y) - (3y^3 + 9y^2) + (7y^3 + 2y)$

21. $(2x^2 - 4) + (3x^2 - 6) - (-x^2 + 2)$

22. **Critical Thinking** Kwan rewrote $(5x^2 - 3x + 1) - (2x^2 - 4x - 2)$ as $5x^2 - 3x + 1 - 2x^2 - 4x - 2$. What mistake did he make?

Language Arts **Use a dictionary if necessary.**

23. **Writing** Write the definition of each word.

a. monogram **b.** binocular **c.** tricuspid **d.** polyglot

24. **a.** **Open-ended** Find other words that begin with *mono*, *bi*, *tri*, or *poly*.

b. Do these prefixes have meanings similar to those in mathematics?

Geometry **Find the perimeter of each figure.**

25. 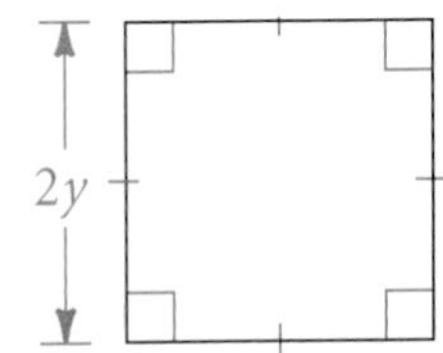

26. 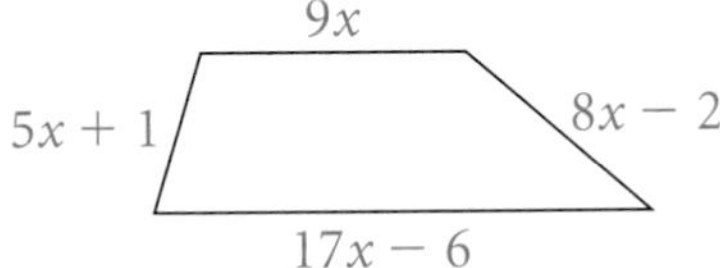

27. 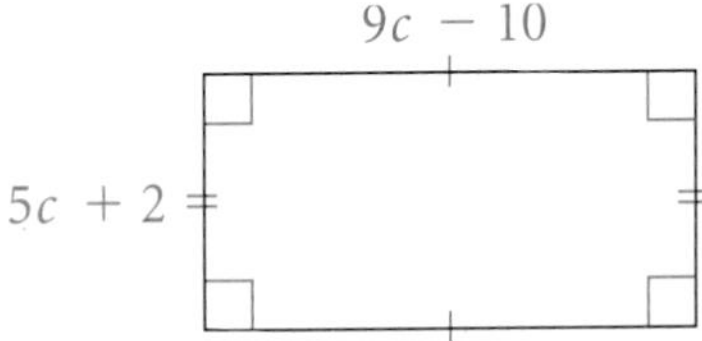

28.

29. ***Open-ended*** In his will, Mr. McAdoo is leaving equal shares of the land shown at the right to his two brothers. Write a polynomial expression for the land that each brother should inherit.

30. ***Critical Thinking*** Is it possible to write a binomial with degree 0? Explain.

Geometry **Find each missing length.**

31. Perimeter $= 25x + 8$

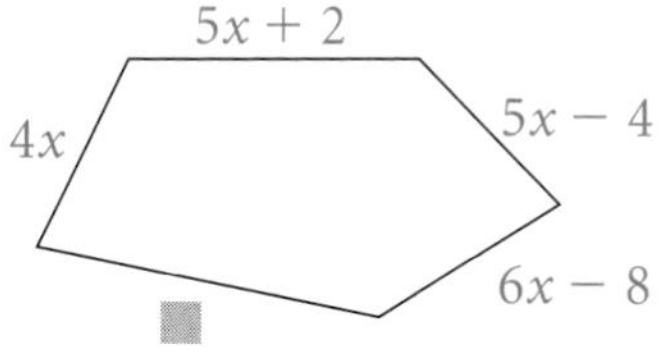

32. Perimeter $= 23a - 7$

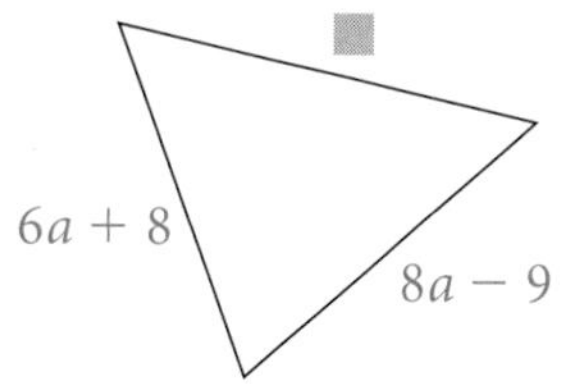

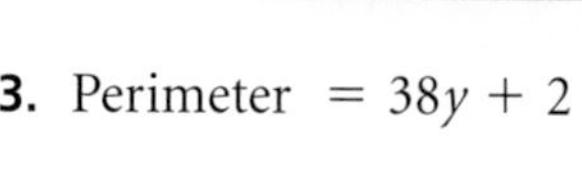

33. Perimeter $= 38y + 2$

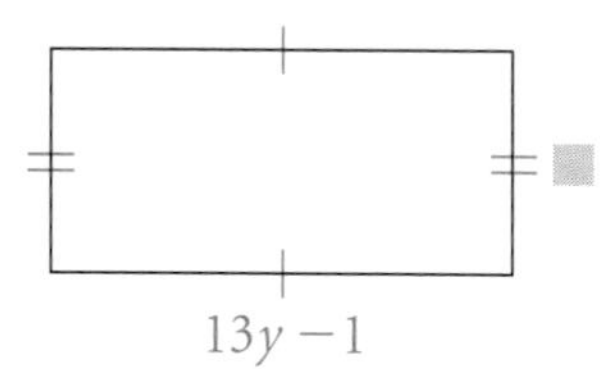

Simplify. Write each answer in standard form.

34. $(3 - 2x + 3x^2) + (7 + 6x - 2x^2)$

35. $(4x^3 - 2x^2 - 13) + (-4x^3 + 2 - 7x)$

36. $(3x^3 - 3x^2 - x - 1) - (3x^2 - 6x)$

37. $(-2r^2 + r - 6) - (1 + 2r - 4r^2)$

38. $(9c^3 - c + 8 + 6c^2) - (3c^3 + 3c - 4)$

39. $(b^4 - 6 + 5b) + (8b^4 + 2b - 3b^2)$

40. ***Critical Thinking*** Why is $3x^2$ a monomial and $3x^{-2}$ *not* a monomial?

Exercises MIXED REVIEW

Use exponential notation to write each expression.

41. $4 \cdot 4 \cdot 4 \cdot 4$

42. $(0.5)(0.5)(0.5)$

43. $\left(\frac{2}{3}\right)\left(\frac{2}{3}\right)\left(\frac{2}{3}\right)\left(\frac{2}{3}\right)$

44. $28 \cdot 28 \cdot 28$

Find the standard deviation of each set of numbers to the nearest tenth.

45. 10, 12, 16, 5, 2

46. 11, 7, 10, 12

47. 5, 3, 7, 8, 3, 4

48. ***Science*** The surface area of a sphere is found using the formula $S = 4\pi r^2$. The approximate radius of Jupiter is 4.4×10^4 mi. Find the approximate surface area of Jupiter.

Getting Ready for Lesson 10-2

Multiply.

49. $2(x - 3)$

50. $-6(3x - 2)$

51. $(-3)(-5a + 7)$

52. $(-7)(c^2 - 8c)$

Connections Building Models . . . and more

10-2 Multiplying and Factoring

What You'll Learn

- Multiplying a polynomial by a monomial
- Factoring a monomial from a polynomial

...And Why

To explore formulas for area

What You'll Need

- tiles

THINK AND DISCUSS

Multiplying by a Monomial

You can use the distributive property to multiply polynomials. You can also use tiles to multiply polynomials.

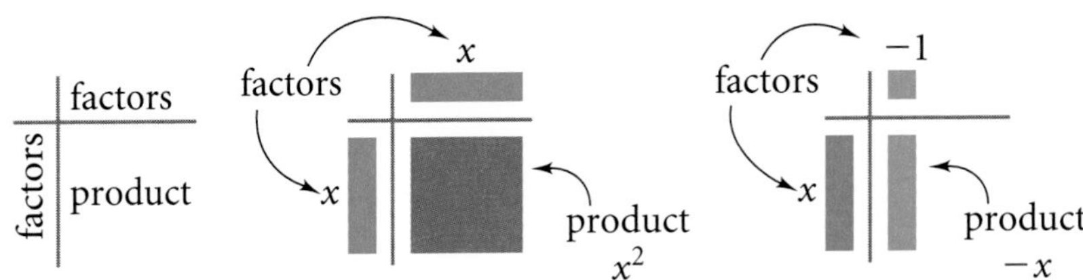

Example 1

Multiply $3x$ and $(2x + 1)$.

Method 1 Use tiles.

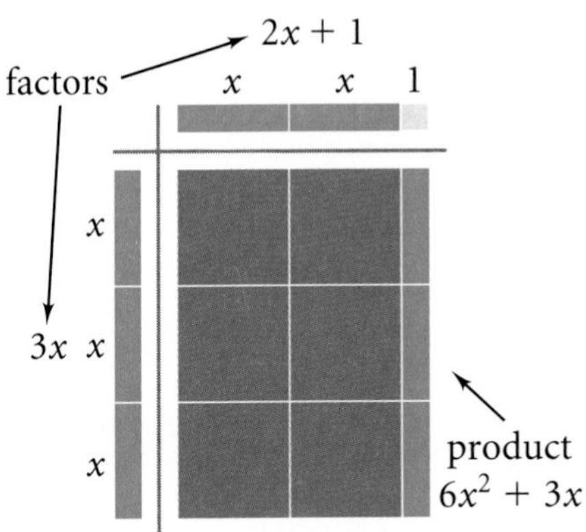

Method 2 Use the distributive property.

$$3x(2x + 1) = 3x(2x) + 3x(1)$$
$$= 6x^2 + 3x$$

1. **Try This** Use the distributive property to multiply $2x(x - 2)$. Then check your work by using tiles.
2. **a.** Use tiles to find each product: $2x(4x - 3)$ and $(4x - 3)(2x)$.
   b. Do both models represent the same area? Explain.
3. **a.** **Critical Thinking** Kevin said that $-2x(4x - 3) = -8x^2 - 6x$. Karla said that $-2x(4x - 3) = -8x^2 + 6x$. Who is correct?
   b. Explain the error that Kevin or Karla made.

Factoring Out a Monomial

Factoring a polynomial reverses the multiplication process. You can use tiles to make a rectangle to find the factors of a polynomial.

Example 2

Factor $2x^2 - 10x$.

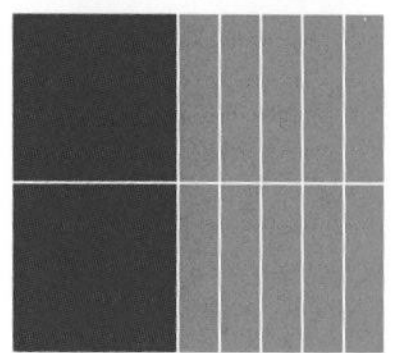

Make a rectangle that is as close to square as possible.

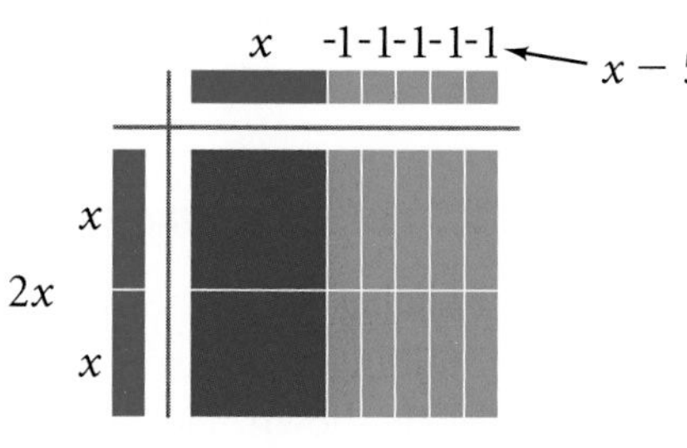

$2x^2 - 10x = 2x(x - 5)$

4. Try This Use tiles to factor each polynomial.

a. $x^2 + 8x$ **b.** $3x^2 - 12x$ **c.** $-3x^2 + 6x$

QUICK REVIEW

The *greatest common factor* (GCF) is the greatest factor that divides evenly into each term.

For practice with greatest common factors, see Skills Handbook page 574.

To factor out a monomial using the distributive property, it is helpful to find the greatest common factor (GCF).

Example 3

Find the GCF of the terms of the polynomial $4x^3 + 12x^2 - 8x$.

List the factors of each term. Identify the factors common to all terms.

$$4x^3 = 2 \cdot 2 \cdot x \cdot x \cdot x$$
$$12x^2 = 2 \cdot 2 \cdot 3 \cdot x \cdot x$$
$$8x = 2 \cdot 2 \cdot 2 \cdot x$$

The GCF is $2 \cdot 2 \cdot x$ or $4x$.

5. Try This Find the GCF of the terms of each polynomial.

a. $4x^3 - 2x^2 - 6x$ **b.** $5x^5 + 10x^3$ **c.** $3x^2 - 18$

Example 4

Factor $3x^3 - 9x^2 + 15x$.

Step 1 Find the GCF.

$$3x^3 = 3 \cdot x \cdot x \cdot x$$
$$9x^2 = 3 \cdot 3 \cdot x \cdot x$$
$$15x = 3 \cdot 5 \cdot x$$

The GCF is $3 \cdot x$ or $3x$.

Step 2 Factor out the GCF.

$$3x^3 - 9x^2 + 15x$$
$$= 3x(x^2) - 3x(3x) + 3x(5)$$
$$= 3x(x^2 - 3x + 5)$$

6. Use the distributive property to check the factoring in Example 4.

7. **Try This** Use the GCF to factor each polynomial.

a. $8x^2 - 12x$ **b.** $5x^3 + 10x$ **c.** $6x^3 - 12x^2 - 24x$

Example 5 Relating to the Real World

Building Models Suppose you are building a model of the square castle shown. The moat of the model castle is made of silver paper. Find the area of the moat.

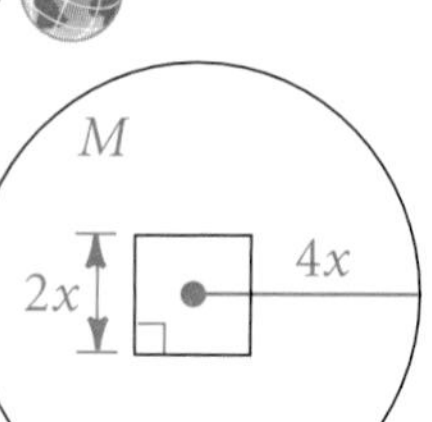

Define M = area of the moat
$2x$ = length of the side of the castle
$4x$ = radius of the moat
$A = \pi r^2$ ⟵ formula for the area of a circle

Relate	area of moat	is	area of circle	minus	area of square
Write	M	$=$	$\pi(4x)^2$	$-$	$(2x)^2$

$$M = 16\pi x^2 - 4x^2 \quad \longleftarrow \text{Simplify } (4x)^2 \text{ and } (2x)^2.$$
$$= 4x^2(4\pi - 1) \quad \longleftarrow \text{The GCF is } 4x^2.$$

The area of the moat is $4x^2(4\pi - 1)$.

8. **Try This** Use the GCF to factor each polynomial.

a. $2g^2 - 4$

b. $2x^3 - 4x^2 + 6x$

c. $6x^3 + 24x^2 + 6x$

Exercises ON YOUR OWN

Use tiles to find each product.

1. $3(x + 4)$
2. $x(x - 3)$
3. $2x(2x + 1)$
4. $4x(5x - 8)$
5. $4x(2x + 3)$

For each set of tiles, find the missing factors or product. Then write the factors and product as variable expressions.

6. 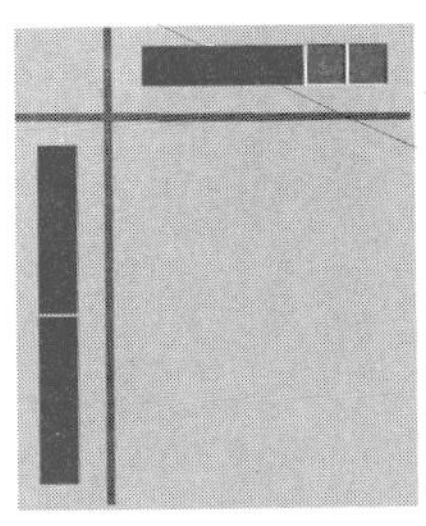

7. 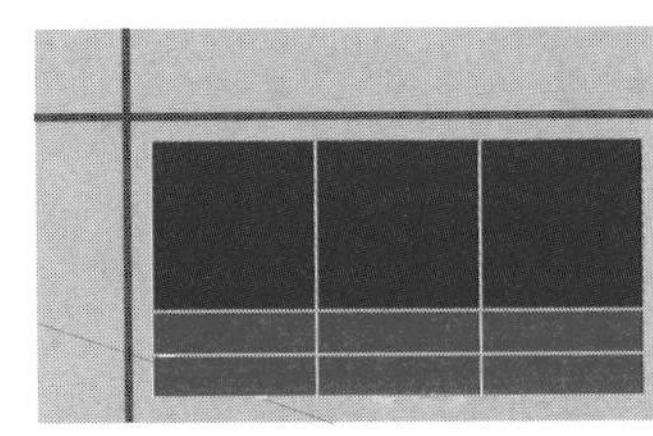

8. 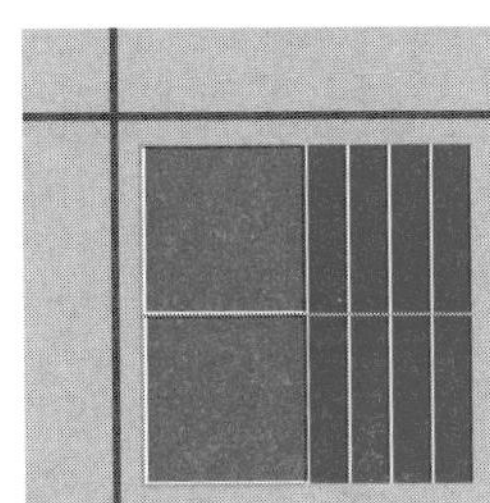

Find each product.

9. $4(2x + 7)$
10. $t(5t^2 + 6t)$
11. $6x(-9x^3 + 6x - 8)$
12. $2g^2(g^2 + 6g + 5)$
13. $-3a(4a^2 - 5a + 9)$
14. $7x^2(5x^2 - 3)$
15. $-3p^2(-2p^3 + 5p)$
16. $4n^2(2n^2 + 4n)$
17. $x(x + 3) - 5x(x - 2)$
18. $12c(-5c^2 + 3c - 4)$
19. $x^2(x + 1) - x(x^2 - 1)$
20. $-4j(3j^2 - 4j + 3)$

Find the greatest common factor (GCF) for each polynomial.

21. $15x + 21$
22. $6a^2 - 8a$
23. $36s + 24$
24. $x^3 + 7x^2 - 5x$
25. $5b^3 - 30$
26. $w^4 - 9w^2$
27. $9x^3 - 6x^2 + 12x$
28. $5r^5 - 3r^2 + 4r$
29. $25s^2 + 5s - 15s^3$
30. $8p^3 - 24p^2 + 16p$
31. $56x^4 - 32x^3 - 72x^2$
32. $2x + 3x^2$

33. a. **Open-ended** Draw two different tile diagrams to represent $6x^2 + 12x$ as a product. Place the x^2 tiles in the upper left area.
    b. Write the factored form of $6x^2 + 12x$ for each diagram in part (a).

34. a. Factor $n^2 - n$.
    b. **Writing** Suppose n is an integer. Is $n^2 - n$ *always, sometimes,* or *never* even? **Justify** your answer.

35. **Manufacturing** The diagram shows a solid block of metal with a cylinder cut out of it. The formula for the volume of a cylinder is $V = \pi r^2 h$, where r is the radius and h is the height.
    a. Write a formula for the volume of the cube in terms of s.
    b. Write a formula for the volume of the cylinder in terms of s.
    c. Write a formula in terms of s for the volume of the metal left after the cylinder has been removed.
    d. Factor your formula from part (c).
    e. What is the volume of the block of metal after the cylinder has been removed if $s = 15$ in?

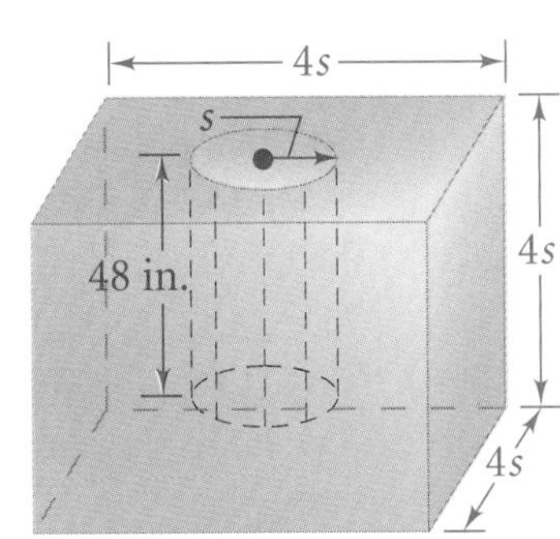

Factor each expression.

36. $6x - 4$

37. $s^4 + 4s^3 - 2s$

38. $10r^2 - 25r + 20$

39. $2x^2 - 4x^4$

40. $12p^3 + 4p^2 - 2p$

41. $7k^3 - 35k^2 + 70k$

42. $15n^3 + 3n^2 - 12n$

43. $9x + 12x^2$

44. $24n^3 - 12n^2 + 12n$

45. $6m^6 - 24m^4 + 6m^2$

46. $15k^3 + 3k^2 - 12k$

47. $5m^3 - 7m^2$

Factor by grouping like terms.

Sample $2x^3 + 2x + 3x^2 + 3$ ← Group the terms with common factors together.

$2x(x^2 + 1) + 3(x^2 + 1)$ ← Factor the GCF from each group.

$(2x + 3)(x^2 + 1)$ ← Factor out the common polynomial.

48. $3v^3 + 18v^2 - 4v - 24$

49. $2x^3 + x^2 - 14x - 7$

50. $2x^3 + 3x^2 + 4x + 6$

51. a. *Geometry* How many sides does the polygon at the right have? How many diagonals does it have from one vertex?
   b. Suppose a polygon, like the one at the right, has n sides. How many diagonals will it have from one vertex?
   c. The number of diagonals that can be drawn from all the vertices is $\frac{n}{2}(n - 3)$. Multiply the two factors.

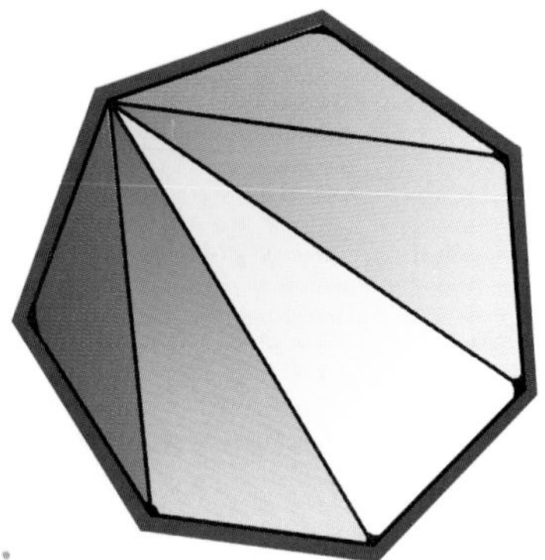

Chapter Project *Find Out by Researching*

A board foot is a linear measure of lumber equal to a square foot of wood 1 in. thick. What can you make from 10 board feet? 100 board feet? 1000 board feet? How is the size of a house related to the amount of wood used to build it? What different types of wood are needed for cabinets, floors, and roofs? What tools do carpenters use to make these items?

Exercises MIXED REVIEW

Use $\triangle ABC$ to find each trigonometric ratio.

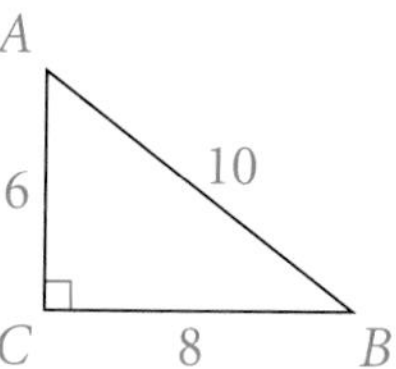

52. $\sin A$ 53. $\cos B$ 54. $\tan A$ 55. $\sin B$ 56. $\cos A$ 57. $\tan B$

58. *Geography* Two buses are on their way to the same bus terminal. One bus is 1.5 mi due north of the terminal. The other bus is 2.0 mi due east of the terminal. How far from each other are the buses?

Getting Ready for Lesson 10-3

Simplify and write in standard form.

59. $(4x)(32) - (4x)(12x) + (4x)(7x^2)$

60. $(3y)(7) - (3y)(2y) + (3)(5y^2) - (7y)(6) - (7y)(8y)$

What You'll Learn

- Multiplying two binomials
- Multiplying a trinomial and a binomial

...And Why

To investigate real-world situations, such as savings accounts

What You'll Need

- tiles
- graphing calculator

10-3 Multiplying Polynomials

THINK AND DISCUSS

Multiplying Two Binomials

You can use tiles or the distributive property to multiply two binomials.

Example 1

Find the product $(2x + 1)(x - 5)$.

Method 1 Use tiles.

Step 1 Show the factors.

$(x - 5)$

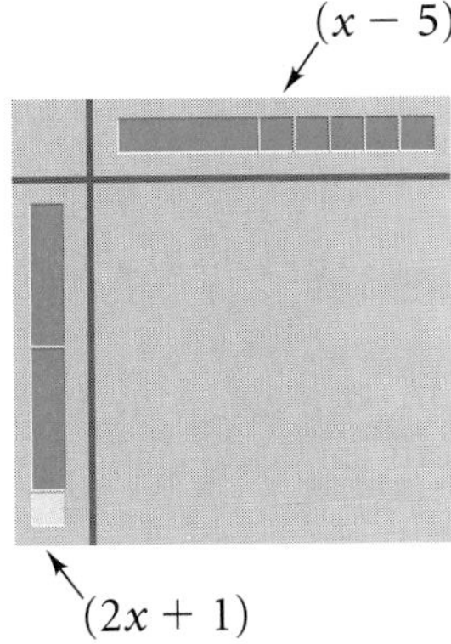

$(2x + 1)$

Step 2 Find the product.

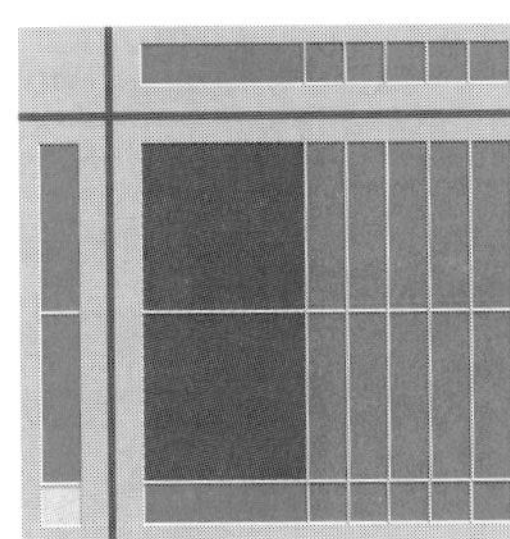

$2x^2 - 10x + x - 5$ ← Add coefficients of like terms.

$2x^2 - 9x - 5$

Method 2 Use the distributive property.

$$(2x + 1)(x - 5) = 2x(x) + 2x(-5) + 1(x) + 1(-5)$$
$$= 2x^2 - 10x + x - 5$$
$$= 2x^2 - 9x - 5$$

The product is $2x^2 - 9x - 5$.

1. Rework Example 1 using tiles. Put $2x + 1$ on the horizontal line and $x - 5$ on the vertical line. Do you get the same result as in Example 1?
2. **Try This** Find the product $(3x + 1)(2x + 3)$ using tiles.
3. **Try This** Find the product $(6x - 7)(3x + 5)$ using the distributive property.

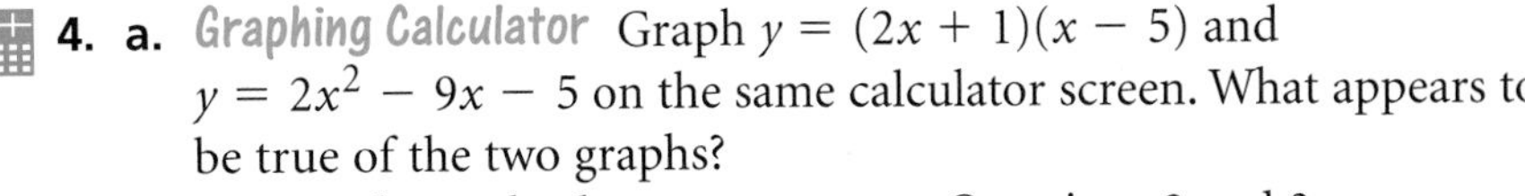

4. a. **Graphing Calculator** Graph $y = (2x + 1)(x - 5)$ and $y = 2x^2 - 9x - 5$ on the same calculator screen. What appears to be true of the two graphs?
   b. Use graphs to check your answers to Questions 2 and 3.

Multiplying Using FOIL

One way to organize how you multiply two binomials is to use *FOIL*, which stands for "First, Outer, Inner, Last." The term FOIL is a memory device for applying the distributive property.

Example 2

Find the product $(3x - 5)(2x + 7)$.

$$\begin{aligned}(3x - 5)(2x + 7) &= \underset{\text{First}}{(3x)(2x)} + \underset{\text{Outer}}{(3x)(7)} - \underset{\text{Inner}}{(5)(2x)} - \underset{\text{Last}}{(5)(7)} \\ &= 6x^2 + 21x - 10x - 35 \\ &= 6x^2 + 11x - 35\end{aligned}$$

First, Last, Inner, Outer

$11x$ ← middle term

The product is $6x^2 + 11x - 35$.

5. **Mental Math** What is the middle term of each product?
   - **a.** $(2x + 3)(x + 1)$
   - **b.** $(2x - 3)(x + 1)$
   - **c.** $(2x + 3)(x - 1)$
   - **d.** $(2x - 3)(x - 1)$
6. **Try This** Find each product.
   - **a.** $(3x + 4)(2x + 5)$
   - **b.** $(3x - 4)(2x + 5)$
   - **c.** $(3x + 4)(2x - 5)$
   - **d.** $(3x - 4)(2x - 5)$
7. **Graphing Calculator** Use a graphing calculator to check your answers in Question 6.

Example 3 **Relating to the Real World** 

Savings Many students and their families start saving money early to pay for college. Suppose you deposit \$500 at the beginning of each of two consecutive years. If your bank pays interest annually at the rate r, you can use the expression $(1 + r)(2 + r)500$ to find the amount in your account at the end of the two years. Write the expression in standard form.

$$\begin{aligned}&(1 + r)(2 + r)500 \\ &= (1 + r)(2 + r)500 && \leftarrow \text{Use FOIL to simplify } (1 + r)(2 + r). \\ &= (2 + r + 2r + r^2)(500) \\ &= (2 + 3r + r^2)(500) && \leftarrow \text{Add like terms.} \\ &= 1000 + 1500r + 500r^2 && \leftarrow \text{Use the distributive property.} \\ &= 500r^2 + 1500r + 1000 && \leftarrow \text{Write in standard form.}\end{aligned}$$

8. How much money is in your account if the interest rate in Example 3 is 4%? (*Hint*: Write the interest rate as a decimal.)

Multiplying a Trinomial and a Binomial

FOIL works when you multiply two binomials, but it is not helpful when multiplying a trinomial and a binomial. You can use the vertical method or the horizontal method to distribute each term in a factor.

Example 4

Find the product $(3x^2 + x - 6)(2x - 3)$.

Method 1 Multiply vertically.

$$\begin{array}{rl} 3x^2 + x - 6 & \\ 2x - 3 & \\ \hline -9x^2 - 3x + 18 & \leftarrow \text{Multiply by } -3. \\ 6x^3 + 2x^2 - 12x \quad\quad & \leftarrow \text{Multiply by } 2x. \\ \hline 6x^3 - 7x^2 - 15x + 18 & \leftarrow \text{Add like terms.} \end{array}$$

Method 2 Multiply horizontally.

$$(2x - 3)(3x^2 + x - 6)$$

$$= 2x(3x^2) + 2x(x) + 2x(-6) - 3(3x^2) - 3(x) - 3(-6)$$

$$= 6x^3 + 2x^2 - 12x - 9x^2 - 3x + 18$$

$$= 6x^3 - 7x^2 - 15x + 18 \quad \leftarrow \text{Add like terms.}$$

The product is $6x^3 - 7x^2 - 15x + 18$.

9. a. **Try This** Find the product $(3a + 4)(5a^2 + 2a - 3)$ using both methods shown in Example 4.
   b. Do you prefer the vertical or the horizontal method? Why?

Exercises ON YOUR OWN

What are the factors shown with the tiles? What will be the product?

1. 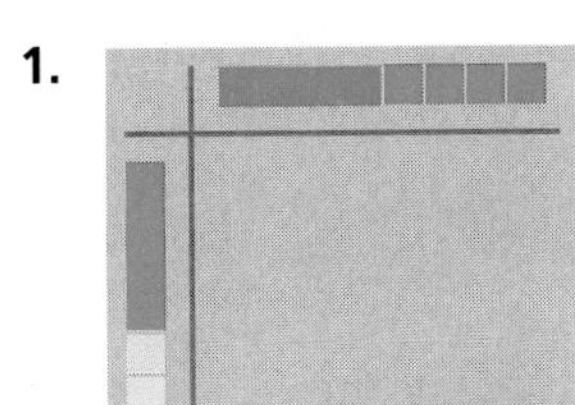

2. 

3. 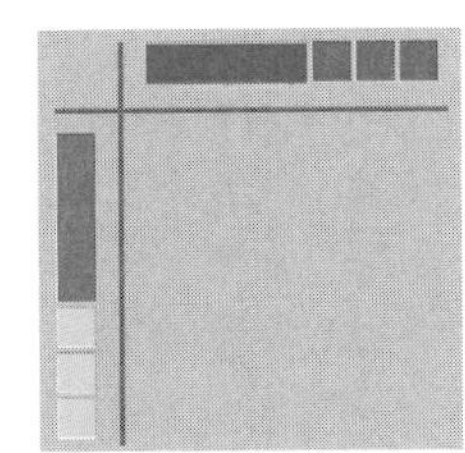

Use tiles to find each product.

4. $(x + 2)(x + 5)$

5. $(x - 5)(x + 4)$

6. $(2x - 1)(x + 2)$

Copy and fill in each blank.

7. $(5a + 2)(6a - 1) = \blacksquare a^2 + 7a - 2$

8. $(3c - 7)(2c - 5) = 6c^2 - 29c + \blacksquare$

9. $(z - 4)(2z + 1) = 2z^2 - \blacksquare z - 4$

10. $(2x + 9)(x + 2) = 2x^2 + \blacksquare x + 18$

Choose **Use any method you choose to find each product.**

11. $(x + 7)(x - 6)$

12. $(a - 8)(a - 9)$

13. $(2y + 5)(y - 3)$

14. $(r + 6)(r - 4)$

15. $(y + 4)(5y - 8)$

16. $(x + 9)(x^2 - 4x + 1)$

17. $(a - 4)(a^2 - 2a + 1)$

18. $(x - 3)(2x^2 + 3x + 3)$

19. $(2t^2 - 6t + 3)(2t - 5)$

20. **Geometry** Use the formula $V = lwh$ to write a polynomial in standard form for the volume of the box shown at the right.

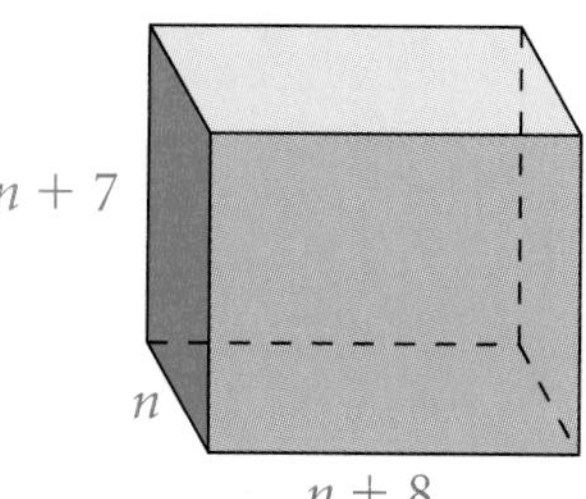

21. **Open-ended** Write a binomial and a trinomial. Find their product.

22. **Construction** You are planning a rectangular garden. Its length is 4 ft more than twice its width. You want a walkway 2 ft wide around the garden. Write an expression for the area of the garden and walk. (*Hint:* Draw a diagram.)

Find each product using FOIL.

23. $(x + 3)(x + 5)$

24. $(2y + 1)(3y + 4)$

25. $(a - 1)(a - 7)$

26. $(4x + 3)(4x - 3)$

27. $(5a - 2)(a + 3)$

28. $(6x + 1)(2x - 3)$

29. $(3y - 7)(-2y + 2)$

30. $(8 - 6x)(5 + 2x)$

31. **Writing** Which method do you prefer for multiplying two binomials? Why?

32. **Financial Planning** Suppose you deposit \$2000 in a savings account for college that has an annual interest rate r. At the end of three years, the value of your account will be $2000(1 + r)^3$ dollars.
   a. Simplify $2000(1 + r)^3$ by finding the product of $2000(1 + r)(1 + r)(1 + r)$. Write your answer in standard form.
   b. Find the amount of money in the account if the interest rate is 3%.

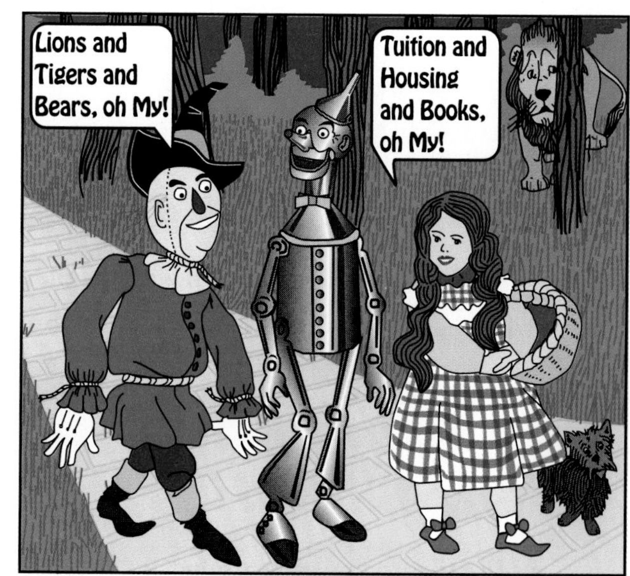

Find each product. Is the product *rational* or *irrational?*

33. $(\sqrt{3} + \sqrt{2})(\sqrt{3} - \sqrt{2})$

34. $(\sqrt{3} + 2)^2(\sqrt{3} - 2)^2$

35. $(\sqrt{5} + 3)(\sqrt{5} + 7)$

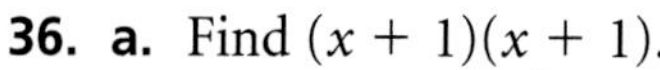

36. a. Find $(x + 1)(x + 1)$.
   b. Find $(x + 1)(x^2 + x + 1)$.
   c. Find $(x + 1)(x^3 + x^2 + x + 1)$.
   d. **Patterns** Use the pattern you see in parts (a) – (c) to **predict** the product of $(x + 1)(x^7 + x^6 + x^5 + x^4 + x^3 + x^2 + x + 1)$.

Chapter Project *Find Out by Calculating*

You can use the expression $0.0655\ell(1 - p)(d - s)^2$ to find the number of usable board feet in a log.

- Estimate the usable board feet in a 35-ft log if its diameter is 20 in. Assume the log loses 10% (0.10) of its volume from the saw cuts and a total of 2 in. is trimmed off the log.
- The diameter of a log is 25 in. A total of 2 in. will be trimmed off the log. The estimated volume loss due to saw cuts is 10%. How long must the log be to yield 600 board feet of lumber?

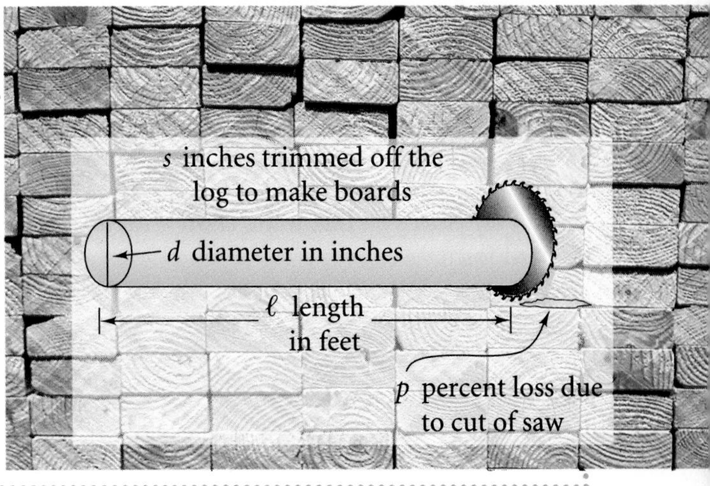

Exercises MIXED REVIEW

Solve each equation.

37. $6x^2 = 24$ **38.** $8x - 23 = 41$ **39.** $-x^2 + x + 2 = 0$

40. *Language* The *Oxford English Dictionary* defines 616,500 words. Write this number in scientific notation.

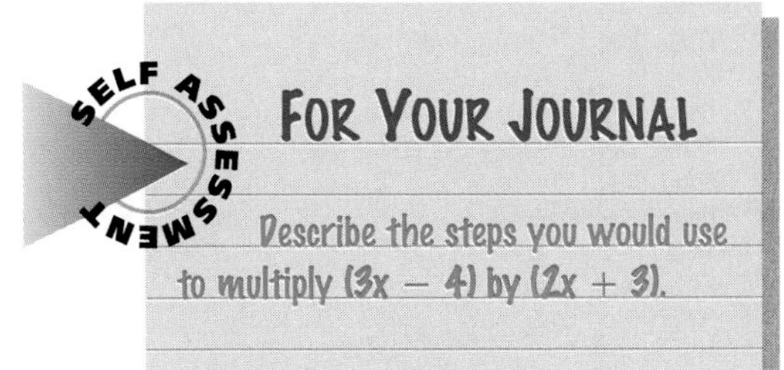

SELF ASSESSMENT
FOR YOUR JOURNAL
Describe the steps you would use to multiply (3x − 4) by (2x + 3).

Getting Ready for Lesson 10-4

Factor by grouping.

41. $2x(3x + 5) + 4(3x + 5)$ **42.** $5x(2x - 7) + 3(2x - 7)$ **43.** $-3x(4x + 1) + 5(4x + 1)$

Exercises CHECKPOINT

Simplify.

1. $(x^2 + x - 3) + (2x^2 + 4x - 1)$ **2.** $(3a^3 + 2a^2 - 5) - (a^3 + a^2 + 2)$

3. $(m^2 - m + 7) - (3m^2 + 4m - 1)$ **4.** $(6x^2 - 2x - 5) + (3x^2 + x - 3)$

Find each product.

5. $(-w + 3)(w + 3)$ **6.** $2t(-3t^2 - 2t + 6)$ **7.** $(m + 4)(m - 3)$ **8.** $(b - 6)(b - 3)$

Factor each expression.

9. $-3c^3 + 15c^2 - 3c$ **10.** $10a^3 + 5a^2 + 5a$ **11.** $8p^3 - 20p^2 - 24p$ **12.** $x^3 + 4x^2 + 7x$

13. a. *Open-ended* Write two binomials using the variable z.
b. Find the sum and product of the two binomials.

14. *Writing* How is distributing a number similar to distributing a term with a variable? Include examples.

Math ToolboX

Technology

Exploring Factors and Products

After Lesson 10-3

You can often write a quadratic expression using factored form as well as standard form.

Factored Form	Standard Form
$(2x - 5)(x + 4)$	$2x^2 + 3x - 20$

The product of the linear expressions $2x - 5$ and $x + 4$ is the quadratic expression $2x^2 + 3x - 20$. You can explore the linear factors and their quadratic product using a graphing calculator. The related function of the expression $2x - 5$ is $y = 2x - 5$.

Graphing Calculator **Graph the functions in each exercise on the same calculator screen. Make sketches of each display.**

1. $y = 2x - 5$
$y = x + 4$
$y = 2x^2 + 3x - 20$

2. $y = 2x - 5$
$y = 2x + 3$
$y = 4x^2 - 4x - 15$

3. $y = -x + 1$
$y = x - 5$
$y = -x^2 + 6x - 5$

4. $y = -\frac{1}{2}x + 3$
$y = x + 2$
$y = -\frac{1}{2}x^2 + 2x + 6$

5. $y = x + 3$
$y = x - 3$
$y = x^2 - 9$

6. $y = x + 3$
$y = -2x - 1$
$y = -2x^2 - 7x - 3$

7. Use your graphs in Exercises 1–6. How are the x-intercepts of the linear functions related to the x-intercepts of the quadratic function?

8. **a.** Write equations in slope-intercept form of the lines at the right.
b. What linear expressions are related to the equations in part (a)?
c. Write the product of the linear expressions. Use standard form.
d. Check your work by graphing the linear equations in part (a) and the quadratic function related to the expression in part (c).

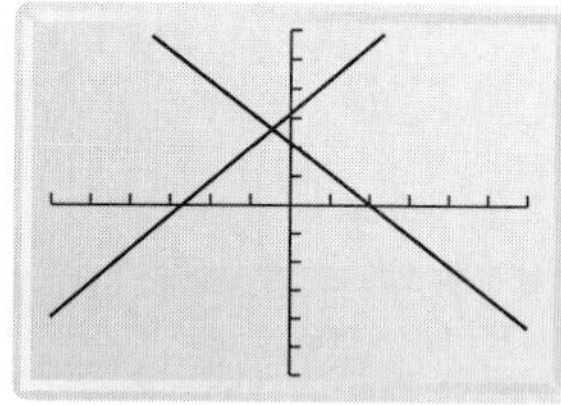

Xmin=–6 Ymin=–6
Xmax=6 Ymax=6
Xscl=1 Yscl=1

Write the expressions related to each linear graph. Then write the quadratic product of the expressions in standard form.

9. 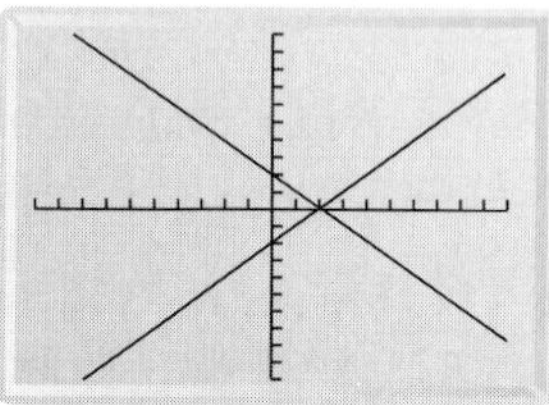

10. 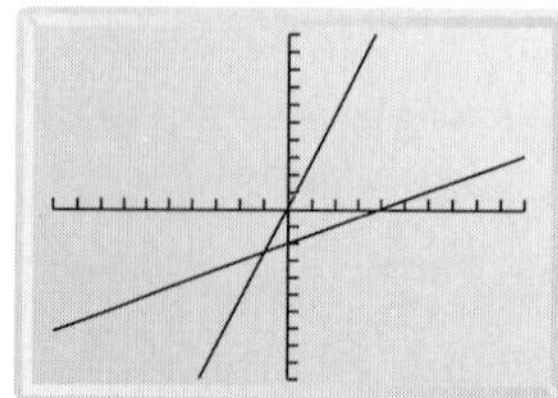

11. 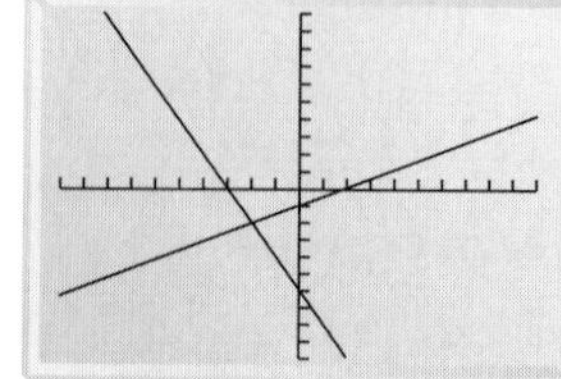

12. *Writing* **Summarize** the relationship between a quadratic expression and its linear factors. Include an example.

10-4 Factoring Trinomials

What You'll Learn

- Factoring quadratic expressions
- Identifying quadratic expressions that cannot be factored

...And Why

To solve civil engineering and landscaping problems

What You'll Need

- tiles
- graph paper

WORK TOGETHER

Construction A contractor has agreed to pour the concrete for the floor of a garage. He knows the area of the floor is 221 ft^2 but cannot remember its dimensions. He does remember that the dimensions are prime numbers.

Work with a partner to find the dimensions of the garage floor.

1. Explain how you know that 221 is not the product of two 1-digit numbers.
2. Explain how you could decide if 221 has a factor greater than 20 other than itself.
3. Use graph paper. Cut out several 10×10 squares, some 1×10 rectangles, and some 1×1 squares. Use these pieces to make a rectangle representing the garage floor. What are its dimensions?
4. Repeat this process to find a pair of prime numbers with each product.
   a. 133 **b.** 161 **c.** 209

THINK AND DISCUSS

Using Tiles

Some quadratic trinomials are the product of two **binomial factors.**

quadratic trinomial		binomial factors
$x^2 + 10x + 16$	$\longrightarrow$	$(x + 2)(x + 8)$

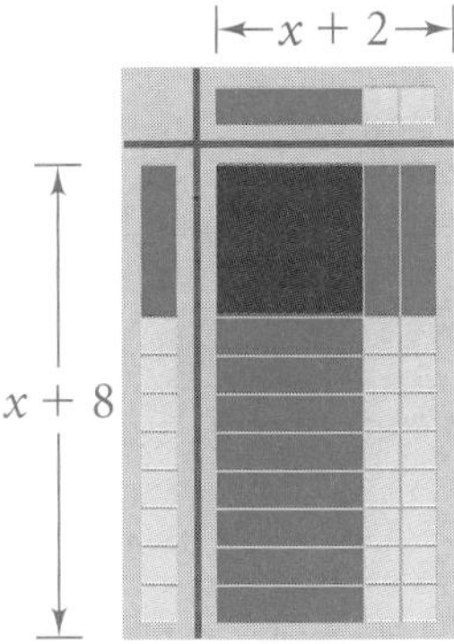

The diagram at the left shows how $x^2 + 10x + 16$ can be displayed as a rectangle with sides of length $x + 2$ and $x + 8$.

You can use tiles to factor quadratic trinomials.

Example 1

Use tiles to factor $x^2 + 7x + 12$.

Choose one x^2-tile, seven x-tiles and twelve 1-tiles. Use the strategy *Guess and Test* to form a rectangle using all the tiles.

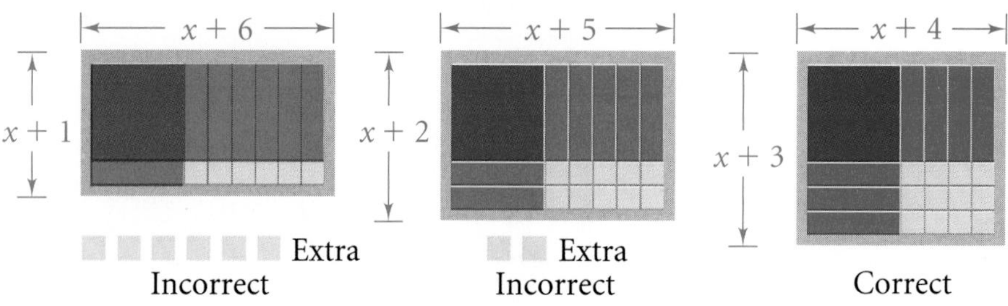

Write the correct factors as a product.

$x^2 + 7x + 12 = (x + 3)(x + 4)$

5. **Try This** Use tiles to factor these trinomials. **Verify** your answers using FOIL.
   a. $x^2 + 6x + 8$ **b.** $x^2 + 11x + 10$

Testing Possible Factors

To factor trinomials of the form $x^2 + bx + c$, you can use FOIL with the strategy *Guess and Test.*

The sum of the numbers you use here must equal *b*.

$$x^2 + bx + c = (x + \square)(x + \square)$$

The product of the numbers you use here must equal *c*.

Example 2

Factor $x^2 - 9x + 20$.

Choose numbers that are factors of 20. Look for a pair with sum -9.

Factors of 20	Sum of Factors
-1 and -20	$-1 + (-20) = -21$
-2 and -10	$-2 + (-10) = -12$
-4 and -5	$-4 + (-5) = -9$

List only negative factors because you are looking for a sum of -9. Two positive numbers cannot have a negative sum.

The numbers -4 and -5 have a product of 20 and a sum of -9.
The correct factors are $(x - 4)$ and $(x - 5)$.
So, $x^2 - 9x + 20 = (x - 4)(x - 5)$.

Check $x^2 - 9x + 20 \stackrel{?}{=} (x - 4)(x - 5)$ ← Find the product of the right side.

$x^2 - 9x + 20 \stackrel{?}{=} x^2 - 5x - 4x + 20$

$x^2 - 9x + 20 = x^2 - 9x + 20$ ✔

6. **Critical Thinking** Is $x^2 - 6x - 16 = (x - 8)(x + 2)$ factored correctly? Explain.

Example 3

Factor $x^2 - 2x - 8$.

Choose numbers that are factors of -8. Look for a pair with sum -2.

Factors of -8	Sum of Factors
-1 and 8	$-1 + 8 = 7$
-8 and 1	$-8 + 1 = -7$
-2 and 4	$-2 + 4 = 2$
-4 and 2	$-4 + 2 = -2$

← -4 and 2 have a sum of -2.

$x^2 - 2x - 8 = (x - 4)(x + 2)$

7. **Try This** Factor $x^2 - 4x - 12$.

Factoring $ax^2 + bx + c$

To factor quadratic trinomials where $a \neq 1$, list factors of a and c. Use these factors to write binomials. Test for the correct value for b.

Example 4

Factor $3x^2 - 7x - 6$.

List factors of 3: 1 and 3; -1 and -3.

List factors of -6: 1 and -6; -1 and 6; 2 and -3; -2 and 3.

Use the factors to write binomials. Look for -7 as the middle term.

$(\boxed{1}x + \boxed{1})(\boxed{3}x + \boxed{-6})$ $\quad -6x + 3x = -3x$

$(\boxed{1}x + \boxed{-6})(\boxed{3}x + \boxed{1})$ $\quad 1x - 18x = -17x$

$(\boxed{1}x + \boxed{-1})(\boxed{3}x + \boxed{6})$ $\quad 6x - 3x = 3x$

$(\boxed{1}x + \boxed{6})(\boxed{3}x + \boxed{-1})$ $\quad -1x + 18x = 17x$

$(\boxed{1}x + \boxed{2})(\boxed{3}x + \boxed{-3})$ $\quad -3x + 6x = 3x$

$(\boxed{1}x + \boxed{-3})(\boxed{3}x + \boxed{2})$ $\quad 2x - 9x = -7x$ Correct!

$3x^2 - 7x - 6 = (x - 3)(3x + 2)$.

8. **Try This** Factor $2x^2 - 3x - 5$.

Exercises ON YOUR OWN

Write the length and width of each rectangle as a binomial. Then write an expression for the area of each rectangle.

1. 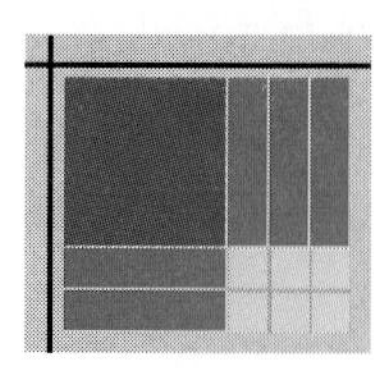

2. 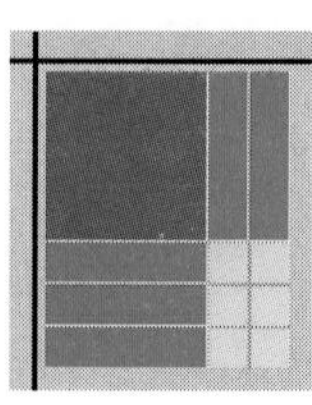

3. 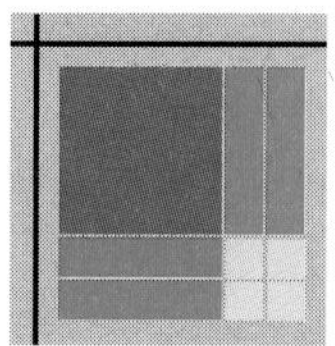

Can you form a rectangle using all the pieces in each set? Explain.

4. one x^2-tile, two x-tiles, and one 1-tile
5. one x^2-tile, five x-tiles, and eight 1-tiles
6. one x^2-tile, six x-tiles, and six 1-tiles
7. one x^2-tile, nine x-tiles, and eight 1-tiles

Use tiles or make drawings to represent each expression as a rectangle. Then write the area as the product of two binomials.

8. $x^2 + 4x + 3$
9. $x^2 - 3x + 2$
10. $x^2 + 3x - 4$
11. $x^2 - 2x - 8$
12. $x^2 + 5x + 6$
13. $x^2 - 3x - 4$
14. $x^2 + x - 6$
15. $x^2 - 2x + 1$

Complete.

16. $x^2 - 6x - 7 = (x + 1)(x + \blacksquare)$
17. $k^2 - 4k - 12 = (k - 6)(k + \blacksquare)$
18. $t^2 + 7t + 10 = (t + 2)(t + \blacksquare)$
19. $c^2 + c - 2 = (c + 2)(c + \blacksquare)$
20. $y^2 - 13y + 36 = (y - 4)(y + \blacksquare)$
21. $x^2 + 3x - 18 = (x + 6)(x + \blacksquare)$

22. **Writing** Suppose you can factor $x^2 + bx + c$ into the product of two binomials.
    a. Explain what you know about the factors if $c > 0$.
    b. Explain what you know about the factors if $c < 0$.

23. **Community Gardening** The diagram at the right shows 72 plots in a community garden.
    a. Write a quadratic expression that represents the area of the garden.
    b. Write the factors of the expression you wrote in part (a).

Factor each quadratic trinomial.

24. $x^2 + 6x + 8$
25. $a^2 - 5a + 6$
26. $d^2 - 7d + 12$
27. $k^2 + 9k + 8$
28. $y^2 - 4y - 45$
29. $r^2 - 10r - 11$
30. $c^2 + 2c + 1$
31. $x^2 + 2x - 15$
32. $t^2 + 7t - 18$
33. $x^2 + 12x + 35$
34. $y^2 - 10y + 16$
35. $a^2 - 9a + 14$
36. $r^2 + 6r - 16$
37. $y^2 + 13y - 48$
38. $x^2 + 10x + 25$
39. $w^2 - 2w - 24$

Open-ended **Find three different values to complete each expression so that it can be factored into the product of two binomials. Show each factorization.**

40. $x^2 - 3x - ■$ **41.** $x^2 + x - ■$ **42.** $x^2 + ■x + 12$

Factor each expression.

43. $2x^2 - 15x + 7$ **44.** $5x^2 - 2x - 7$ **45.** $2x^2 - x - 3$

46. $8x^2 - 14x + 3$ **47.** $2x^2 - 11x - 21$ **48.** $3x^2 + 13x - 10$

49. $2x^2 - 7x + 3$ **50.** $6t^2 + 13t - 5$ **51.** $7x^2 - 20x - 3$

52. $2x^2 + x - 3$ **53.** $3x^2 + 17x + 20$ **54.** $2x^2 + 3x - 20$

Chapter Project — *Find Out by Calculating*

20 ft

With aerial photography, you can study a forest of ponderosa pines without ever walking through it.

To find the diameter in inches of trees in the forest, use this expression:

$3.76 + (1.35 \times 10^{-2})hv - (2.45 \times 10^{-6})hv^2 + (2.44 \times 10^{-10})hv^3$

The variable h is the height of the tree in feet, and v is the crown diameter visible in feet (from a photograph).

- Determine the diameter of 100-ft trees that have a visible crown diameter of 20 ft.

Exercises MIXED REVIEW

Find the distance between the given points.

55. (3, 5); (6, 1) **56.** (−2, 8); (4, −1)

57. (−7, −2); (−3, −9) **58.** (8, 0); (−3, −4)

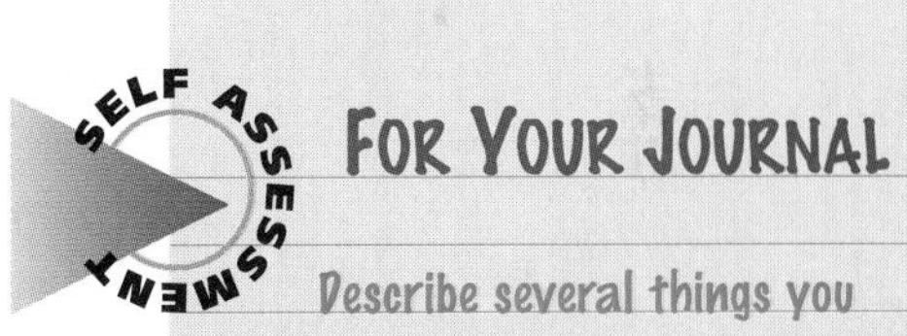

FOR YOUR JOURNAL

Describe several things you like and/or do not like about using tiles.

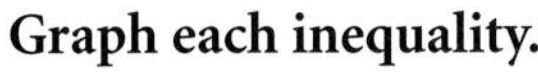

Graph each inequality.

59. $y \leq 4x - 9$ **60.** $y > x^2 + 3x + 1$

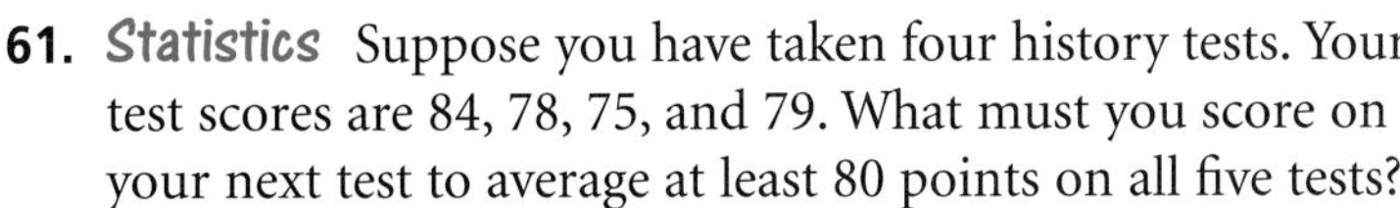

61. **Statistics** Suppose you have taken four history tests. Your test scores are 84, 78, 75, and 79. What must you score on your next test to average at least 80 points on all five tests?

Getting Ready for Lesson 10-5

Find each product.

62. $(x + 9)^2$ **63.** $(2x + 3)^2$ **64.** $(5x - 4)^2$ **65.** $(x + 8)(x - 8)$

66. $(x + 4)(x - 4)$ **67.** $(2x + 7)(2x - 7)$ **68.** $(3x + 5)(3x - 5)$ **69.** $(2x - 1)^2$

10-5 Factoring Special Cases

What You'll Learn

- Factoring the difference of two squares
- Factoring perfect square trinomials

...And Why

To solve problems related to geometry and construction

What You'll Need

- tiles
- graphing calculator

WORK TOGETHER

Work with a partner. Answer each question for Groups A, B, and C.

Group A	Group B	Group C
$(x + 7)(x - 7)$	$(x + 7)(x + 7)$	$(x - 7)(x - 7)$
$(k + 3)(k - 3)$	$(k + 3)(k + 3)$	$(k - 3)(k - 3)$
$(w + 5)(w - 5)$	$(w + 5)(w + 5)$	$(w - 5)(w - 5)$
$(3x + 1)(3x - 1)$	$(3x + 1)(3x + 1)$	$(3x - 1)(3x - 1)$

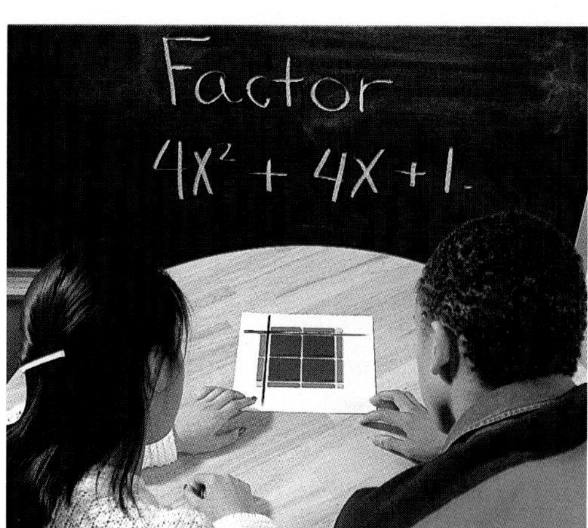

1. Describe the pattern in each of the pairs of factors.
2. Find each product.
3. How can you use mental math to quickly multiply binomials like those in each group? Explain using examples.

THINK AND DISCUSS

Factoring a Difference of Two Squares

As you saw in the Work Together activity, sometimes when you multiply two binomials, the *middle* term in the product is 0.

4. What polynomial is modeled by each set of tiles ? What are the factors of each polynomial?

a. 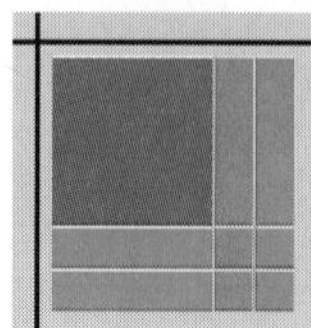

b. 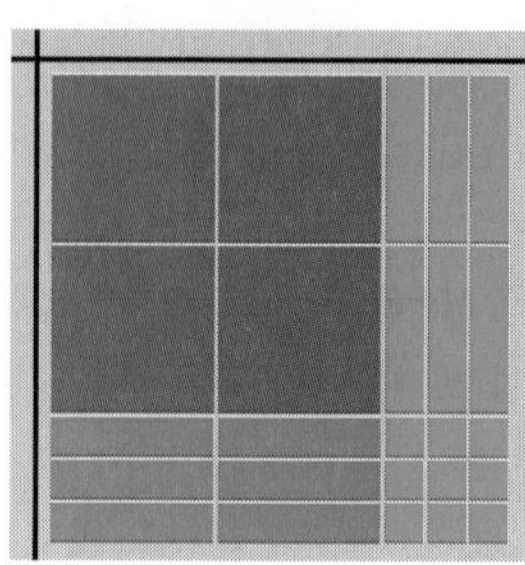

When you factor a difference of two squares, the result is two binomial factors that are the same except for the signs between the terms.

Difference of Two Squares

For all real numbers a and b, $a^2 - b^2 = (a + b)(a - b)$.

Example: $x^2 - 16 = (x + 4)(x - 4)$

Example 1

Factor $x^2 - 64$.

$x^2 - 64 = x^2 - 8^2$ ← Rewrite 64 as 8^2.

$= (x + 8)(x - 8)$ ← Factor.

Check Use FOIL to multiply.

$(x + 8)(x - 8)$

$x^2 - 8x + 8x - 64$

$x^2 - 64$ ✓

5. Mental Math Factor $x^2 - 36$.

Example 2

Factor $4x^2 - 121$.

$4x^2 - 121 = 4x^2 - 11^2$ ← Rewrite 121 as 11^2.

$= (2x)^2 - (11)^2$ ← Rewrite $4x^2$ as $(2x)^2$.

$= (2x + 11)(2x - 11)$ ← Factor.

QUICK REVIEW

For $a \neq 0$ and $b \neq 0$ and all integers n, $(ab)^n = a^n b^n$.

6. Critical Thinking Suppose a classmate factored $4x^2 - 121$ and got $(4x + 11)(4x - 11)$. What mistake did this classmate make?

7. Mental Math Factor $9x^2 - 25$.

Factoring a Perfect Square Trinomial

In the Work Together activity you multiplied a binomial by itself. This is called squaring a binomial. The result is a **perfect square trinomial.** When you factor a perfect square trinomial, the two binomial factors are the same.

Perfect Square Trinomial

For all real numbers a and b:

$$a^2 + 2ab + b^2 = (a + b)(a + b) = (a + b)^2$$
$$a^2 - 2ab + b^2 = (a - b)(a - b) = (a - b)^2$$

Examples: $x^2 + 10x + 25 = (x + 5)(x + 5) = (x + 5)^2$

$x^2 - 10x + 25 = (x - 5)(x - 5) = (x - 5)^2$

Example 3

Factor $x^2 - 8x + 16$.

$x^2 - 8x + 16 = x^2 - 8x + 4^2$ ← Rewrite 16 as 4^2.

$= x^2 - 2(x)(4) + 4^2$ ← Does the middle term equal $2ab$? $8x = 2(x)(4)$ ✔

$= (x - 4)^2$ ← Factor as a squared binomial.

So, $x^2 - 8x + 16 = (x - 4)^2$.

8. a. *Graphing Calculator* Graph $y = x^2 - 8x + 16$.

b. Find the x-intercept(s) of the graph.

c. *Critical Thinking* What information about the factorization does the x-intercept(s) give you?

9. The expression $(3x + 4)^2$ equals $9x^2 +$ ■ $+ 16$. What is the middle term?

Example 4

Factor $9x^2 + 12x + 4$

$9x^2 + 12x + 4$

$= (3x)^2 + 12x + 2^2$ ← Rewrite $9x^2$ as $(3x)^2$ and 4 as 2^2.

$= (3x)^2 + 2(3x)(2) + 2^2$ ← Does the middle term equal $2ab$? $12x = 2(3x)(2)$ ✔

$= (3x+ 2)^2$ ← Factor as a squared binomial.

So, $9x^2 + 12x + 4 = (3x+ 2)^2$

PROBLEM SOLVING

Look Back Multiply the factors to check the factorization.

10. **Try This** Factor each trinomial.

a. $x^2 - 14x + 49$ **b.** $x^2 + 18x + 81$ **c.** $4x^2 - 12x + 9$

11. a. *Open-ended* Write a quadratic expression of your own that is a perfect square trinomial.

b. Explain how you know your trinomial is a perfect square trinomial.

Sometimes a quadratic expression looks like it can't be factored when actually it can. Take out any common factors. Then see if you can factor further.

Example 5

Factor $10x^2 - 40$.

$10x^2 - 40 = 10(x^2 - 4)$ ← Factor out the GCF: 10.

$= 10(x - 2)(x + 2)$ ← Factor $(x^2 - 4)$.

So, $10x^2 - 40 = 10(x - 2)(x + 2)$.

12. **Try This** Factor $8x^2 - 50$.

Exercises ON YOUR OWN

What polynomial is modeled by each set of tiles and what are the factors of each polynomial?

1. 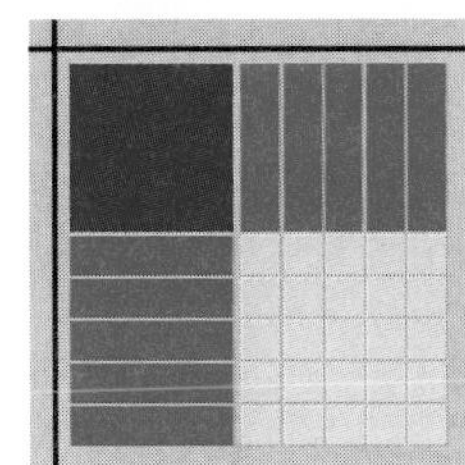

2. 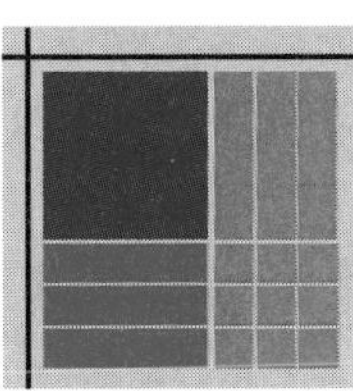

3. 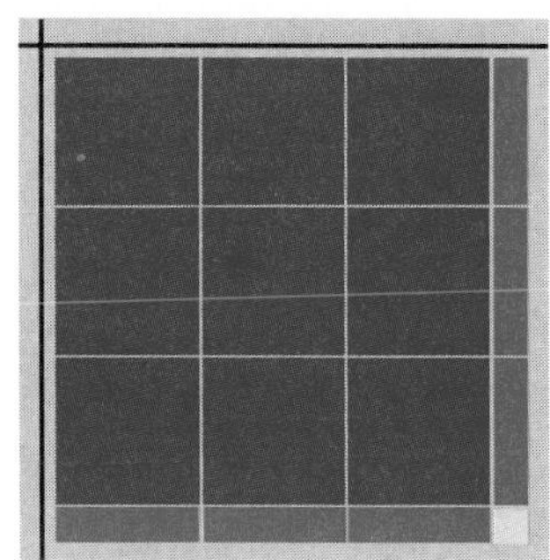

4. a. *Open-ended* Use a minimum of three x^2-tiles, one x-tile, and one 1-tile. Draw the model of the difference of two squares and a model of a perfect square trinomial.
   b. Represent each model from part (a) as a polynomial in both factored and unfactored form.

Factor each expression.

5. $x^2 + 2x + 1$
6. $t^2 - 144$
7. $x^2 - 18x + 81$
8. $15t^2 - 15$
9. $3x^2 - 6x + 3$
10. $9w^2 - 16$
11. $6x^2 - 150$
12. $k^2 - 6k + 9$
13. $x^2 - 49$
14. $a^2 + 12a + 36$
15. $4x^2 - 4x + 1$
16. $16n^2 - 56n + 49$
17. $9x^2 + 6x + 1$
18. $2g^2 + 24g + 72$
19. $x^2 - 400$
20. $2x^3 - 18x$

21. *Writing* **Summarize** the procedure for factoring a perfect square trinomial. Give at least two examples.

22. *Math in the Media* Use the brochure below.
    a. Show by factoring that this inequality is true.
    $(\pi d - \sqrt{15w})(\pi d + \sqrt{15w}) \geq 0$
    b. Show that $d \geq \frac{\sqrt{15w}}{\pi}$.
    c. *Calculator* Is a cable 3 in. in diameter sufficient to lift an object weighing 5 tons? **Justify** your response.

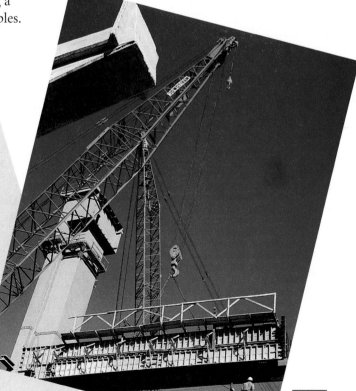

Load Requirements For Crane Operators

The weight of a load is limited by the diameter of the fiber cable. As the load gets heavier, the diameter of the cable must increase. To raise a load weighing w tons, a fiber cable having diameter d in inches must satisfy the inequality $(\pi d)^2 - (\sqrt{15w})^2 \geq 0$.

23. a. *Geometry* Write two expressions in terms of n and m for the area of the solid region at the right. One expression should be in factored form.
b. Use either form of your answer to part (a). Find the area of the solid region if $n = 10$ in. and $m = 3$ in.

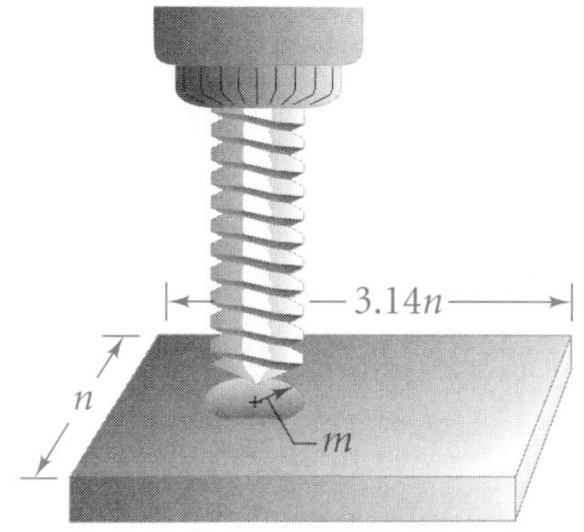

24. *Standardized Test Prep* Which of the following expressions is the factorization of $100x^2 + 220x + 121$?
A. $(10x + 1)(10x - 1)$
B. $(10x - 11)(10x - 11)$
C. $(10x + 11)(10x + 11)$
D. $(10x - 10)(11x + 11)$

Mental Math Find each product using the difference of two squares.

Sample: $(17)(23) = (20 - 3)(20 + 3)$ ⟵ Write the factors in the form $(a - b)(a + b)$.
$= 400 - 9$ ⟵ Multiply.
$= 391$ ⟵ Subtract.

25. $(27)(33)$
26. $(19)(21)$
27. $(43)(37)$
28. $(29)(31)$
29. $(16)(24)$
30. $(51)(49)$
31. $(18)(22)$
32. $(98)(102)$

Factor each expression using rational numbers in your factors.

33. $\frac{1}{4}m^2 - \frac{1}{9}$
34. $\frac{1}{4}p^2 - 2p + 4$
35. $\frac{1}{9}n^2 - \frac{1}{25}$
36. $\frac{1}{25}k^2 + \frac{6}{5}k + 9$

37. a. *Critical Thinking* The expression $(t - 3)^2 - 16$ is a difference of two squares. Using the expression $a^2 - b^2$, identify a and b.
b. Factor $(t - 3)^2 - 16$.

38. a. *Graphing Calculator* Graph $y = 4x^2 - 12x + 9$.
b. Use the x-intercept(s) of the graph to write $4x^2 - 12x + 9$ in factored form.

Exercises MIXED REVIEW

Simplify each expression.

39. $\sqrt{25} + \sqrt{72}$
40. $8^2 - (4 + \sqrt{8})$
41. $\sqrt{5^2 + 4^2}$
42. $\sqrt{100} - \sqrt{4}$

43. *Sales* Suppose you buy a watch for \$35 that regularly sells for \$50. Find the percent of decrease in the price of the watch.

Getting Ready for Lesson 10-6

Solve each equation.

44. $2x + 3 = 0$
45. $-3x - 4 = 0$
46. $8x - 9 = 0$
47. $-3x + 5 = 0$

10-6 Solving Equations by Factoring

What You'll Learn

- Solving quadratic equations by factoring

...And Why

To find the dimensions of a box that can be manufactured from a given amount of material

What You'll Need

- graphing calculator

THINK AND DISCUSS

When you solve a quadratic equation by factoring, you use the zero-product property.

Zero-Product Property

For all real numbers a and b, if $ab = 0$, then $a = 0$ or $b = 0$.

Example: If $(x + 3)(x + 2) = 0$, then $x + 3 = 0$ or $x + 2 = 0$.

Example 1

Solve $(x + 5)(x + 6) = 0$.

$(x + 5)(x + 6) = 0$
$x + 5 = 0$ or $x + 6 = 0$ ← Use the zero-product property.
$x = -5$ or $x = -6$ ← Solve for x.

The solutions are -5 and -6.

Check Substitute -5 for x.
$(-5 + 5)(-5 + 6) \stackrel{?}{=} 0$
$(0)(1) = 0$ ✓

Substitute -6 for x.
$(-6 + 5)(-6 + 6) \stackrel{?}{=} 0$
$(-1)(0) = 0$ ✓

PROBLEM SOLVING

Look Back How could you solve $(x + 5)(x + 6) = 0$ by graphing?

1. Try This Solve each equation.
a. $(x + 7)(x - 4) = 0$
b. $(3y - 5)(y - 2) = 0$

You can sometimes solve a quadratic equation by factoring. Write the equation in standard form. Factor the quadratic expression. Then use the zero-product property.

Example 2

Solve $2x^2 - 5x = 88$ by factoring.

$2x^2 - 5x = 88$
$2x^2 - 5x - 88 = 0$ ← Subtract 88 from each side.
$(2x + 11)(x - 8) = 0$ ← Factor $2x^2 - 5x - 88$.

$2x + 11 = 0$ or $x - 8 = 0$ ← Use the zero-product property.
$x = -5.5$ or $x = 8$ ← Solve for x.

The solutions are -5.5 and 8.

2. a. **Graphing Calculator** Graph $y = 2x^2 - 5x - 88$.
   b. In the CALC feature, use *ROOT* to find the x-intercepts of the graph.
   c. Explain how your answers to part (b) are related to the solutions found in Example 2.

3. a. Solve $x^2 - 12x + 36 = 0$ by factoring.
   b. **Critical Thinking** Why does the equation in part (a) have only one solution?

You can solve some real-world problems by factoring and using the zero-product property.

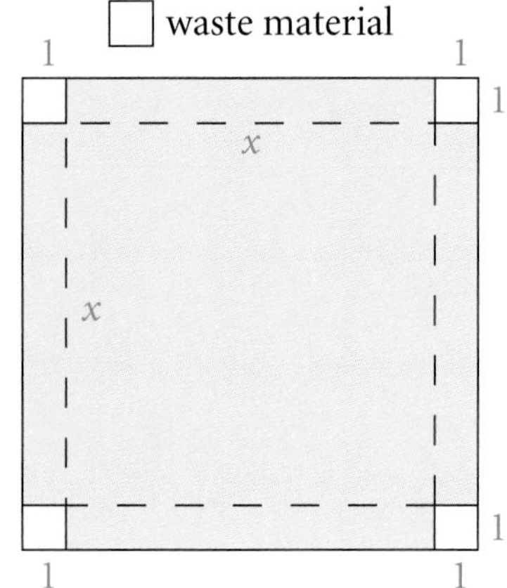

Example 3 **Relating to the Real World** 

Manufacturing The diagram shows a pattern for an open-top box. The total area of the sheet of material used to manufacture the box is 144 in.^{2}. The height of the box is 1 in. Therefore 1 in. $\times$ 1 in. squares are cut from each corner. Find the dimensions of the box.

Define width $= x + 1 + 1 = x + 2$
length $= x + 1 + 1 = x + 2$

Relate length $\times$ width $=$ area

Write $(x + 2)(x + 2) = 144$

$(x + 2)(x + 2) = 144$

$x^2 + 4x + 4 = 144$ ← Find the product $(x + 2)(x + 2)$.

$x^2 + 4x - 140 = 0$ ← Subtract 144 from each side.

$(x + 14)(x - 10) = 0$ ← Factor $x^2 + 4x - 140$.

$x + 14 = 0$ or $x - 10 = 0$ ← Use the zero-product property.

$x = -14$ or $x = 10$

Since the length must be positive, the solution is 10. The dimensions of the box are 10 in. $\times$ 10 in. $\times$ 1 in.

4. Suppose that a box with a square base has height 2 in. It is cut from a square sheet of material with area 121 in.^{2}. Find the dimensions of the box.

Exercises ON YOUR OWN

Mental Math **Use mental math to solve each equation.**

1. $(x - 3)(x - 7) = 0$

2. $(x + 4)(2x - 9) = 0$

3. $(7x + 2)(5x + 4) = 0$

Solve each equation by factoring.

4. $b^2 + 3b - 4 = 0$

5. $m^2 - 5m - 14 = 0$

6. $w^2 - 8w = 0$

7. $x^2 - 16x + 55 = 0$

8. $x^2 - 3x - 10 = 0$

9. $n^2 + n - 12 = 0$

10. $2x^2 - 7x + 5 = 0$

11. $x^2 - 10x = 0$

12. $4x^2 - 25 = 0$

13. $5q^2 + 18q = 8$

14. $z^2 - 5z = -6$

15. $10 = x^2 - 9x$

16. Writing **Summarize** the procedure for solving a quadratic equation by factoring. Include an example.

17. Geometry The sides of a square are each increased by 3 cm. The area of the new square is 64 cm^2. Find the length of a side of the original square.

Simplify each equation and write it in standard form. Then solve each equation.

18. $3a^2 + 4a = 2a^2 - 2a - 9$

19. $4x^2 + 20 = 10x + 3x^2 - 4$

20. $6y^2 + 12y + 13 = 2y^2 + 4$

21. $2q^2 + 22q = -60$

22. $3t^2 + 8t = t^2 - 3t - 12$

23. $4 = -5n + 6n^2$

24. $3x^2 = 9x + 30$

25. $20p^2 - 74 = 6$

26. $2x^2 + 5x^2 = 3x$

27. $7n^2 = 3n^2 + 100$

28. $12x^2 + 8x = -4x^2 + 8x$

29. $9c^2 = 36$

30. Standardized Test Prep If $a^2 + b^2 = 9$ and $ab = 6$, what does $(a + b)^2$ equal?

A. 3 **B.** 15 **C.** 21 **D.** 30 **E.** 36

31. Geometry A rectangular box has volume 280 in.^3. Its dimensions are 4 in. $\times$ $(x + 2)$ in. $\times$ $(x + 5)$ in. Find x. Use the formula $V = lwh$.

32. Baseball Suppose you throw a baseball into the air from a starting height s. You toss the ball with an upward starting velocity of v ft/s. You can use the equation $h = -16t^2 + vt + s$ to find the ball's height h in feet t seconds after it is thrown.

a. Suppose you toss a baseball directly upward with an starting velocity of 46 ft/s from a starting height of 6 ft. When will the ball hit the ground?

b. Graphing Calculator Graph the related function for the equation you wrote in part (a). Use your graph to estimate how high the ball is tossed.

33. **Sailing** The height of a right-triangular sail on a boat is 2 ft greater than twice the base of the sail. Suppose the area of the sail is 110 ft^2.
   a. Find the dimensions of the sail.
   b. Find the approximate length of the hypotenuse of the sail. (*Hint:* Use the Pythagorean theorem ($c^2 = a^2 + b^2$).)

34. **Construction** You are building a rectangular wading pool. You want the area of the bottom to be 90 ft^2. You want the length of the pool to be 3 ft longer than twice its width. What will be the dimensions of the pool?

Solve each cubic equation.

Sample: $x^3 + 7x^2 + 12x = 0$ ← The highest degree of a term is three. This is a cubic equation.

$x^3 + 7x^2 + 12x = 0$

$x(x^2 + 7x + 12) = 0$ ← Factor out the GCF.

$x(x + 3)(x + 4) = 0$ ← Factor the quadratic trinomial.

$x = 0,\ x + 3 = 0,\ \text{or}\ x + 4 = 0$ ← Use the zero-product property.

$x = 0,\quad x = -3,\quad \text{or}\quad x = -4$ ← Solve for x.

The solutions are 0, −3, and −4.

35. $x^3 - 10x^2 + 24x = 0$
36. $x^3 - 5x^2 + 4x = 0$
37. $3x^3 - 9x^2 = 0$
38. $x^3 + 3x^2 - 70x = 0$
39. $3x^3 - 30x^2 + 27x = 0$
40. $2x^3 = -2x^2 + 40x$

In each diagram, you are given a right triangle that has special characteristics. Use the Pythagorean theorem ($c^2 = a^2 + b^2$) to find possible lengths of the sides of each right triangle.

41. three consecutive integers

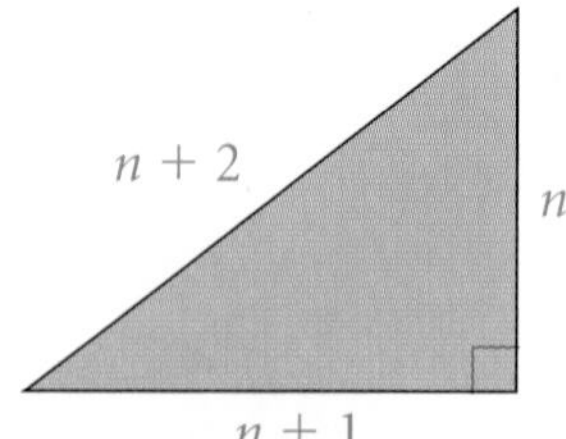

42. three consecutive even integers

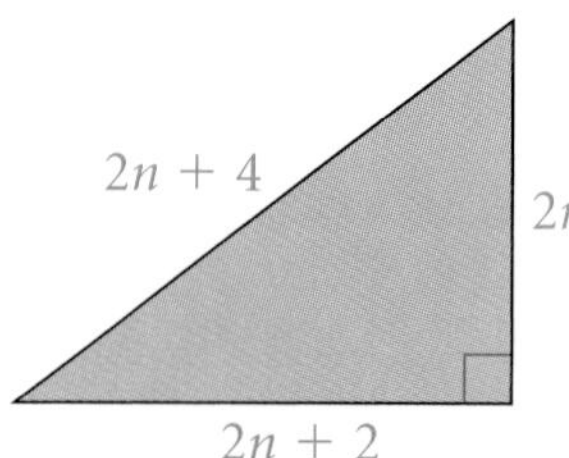

43. **Critical Thinking** A number plus its square equals zero. For which two numbers is this true?

44. **Open-ended** In the diagram at the right, x is a positive integer and a and b are integers. List several possible values for x, a, and b so that the large rectangle will have an area of 56 square units.

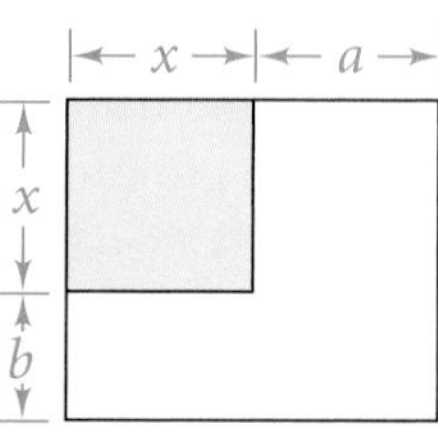

45. **Manufacturing** An open box with height 1 in. has a length that is 2 in. greater than its width. The box was made with minimum waste from an 80 $in.^2$ rectangular sheet of material. What were the dimensions of the sheet of material? (*Hint:* Draw a diagram.)

Chapter Project — Find Out by Graphing

You can use the function $b = -0.01t^2 + 0.8t$ to find the number of bushels b of walnuts produced on an acre of land. The variable t represents the number of trees per acre.

- Graph this function. What number of trees per acre gives the greatest yield?
- How many walnut trees would you advise a farmer to plant on 5 acres of land? Explain your reasoning.

Exercises MIXED REVIEW

Simplify.

46. $(x^2)^4$ **47.** $(3y^3)^{-1}$ **48.** $4(n^3)^0$ **49.** $(x^3)(x^{-3})$

Solve each equation.

50. $\sqrt{a} = 5$ **51.** $\sqrt{3a} = 5$ **52.** $3\sqrt{a} = \sqrt{a} + 18$

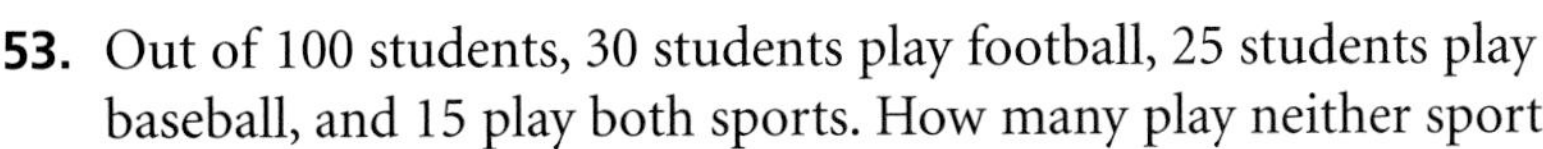

53. Out of 100 students, 30 students play football, 25 students play baseball, and 15 play both sports. How many play neither sport?

FOR YOUR JOURNAL

Suppose you are to solve $2x^2 - 11x + 5 = 0$. Would you use the quadratic formula or factoring? Explain why.

Getting Ready for Lesson 10-7

Use the quadratic formula to solve each equation. If there is no real solution, write *no real solution*.

54. $x^2 + x - 12 = 0$ **55.** $10x^2 + 13x - 3 = 0$ **56.** $4x^2 + 4x + 3 = 0$

Exercises CHECKPOINT

Factor.

1. $x^2 - 5x + 6$ **2.** $n^2 - 6n + 9$ **3.** $g^2 - 8g - 20$ **4.** $9x^2 - 49$

Mental Math **Use mental math to solve each equation.**

5. $(a + 3)(3a - 2) = 0$ **6.** $(m - 6)(2m + 3) = 0$ **7.** $(x + 7)(x + 2) = 0$

Solve each equation.

8. $25x^2 - 100 = 0$ **9.** $9x^2 + 24x = -16$ **10.** $10x^2 - 11x - 6 = 0$

11. **Standardized Test Prep** If $x^2 + 4x = -4$, what is the value of x^3?

A. -8 **B.** 0 **C.** 8 **D.** 16

E. It cannot be determined from the information given.

Math ToolboX

Skills Review

Completing the Square

After Lesson 10-6

In Chapter 7, you solved quadratic equations by taking the square root of each side of an equation. In Lesson 10-5 you factored perfect square trinomials. Completing the square allows you to combine these skills to solve any quadratic equation that has real solutions.

What is the value of *c* needed to create a perfect square trinomial?

1. $y^2 + 4y + c$ **2.** $a^2 - 10a + c$ **3.** $n^2 + 14n + c$ **4.** $x^2 - 20x + c$

5. Explain the steps you used to find c in Questions 1–4.

To solve an equation using completing the square, you create a perfect square trinomial on one side of the equation so that you can take the square root of both sides.

Example

Solve by completing the square: $x^2 + 6x + 4 = 0$.

$x^2 + 6x + 4 = 0$

$x^2 + 6x = -4$ ← Subtract 4 from each side.

$x^2 + 6x + 3^2 = -4 + 3^2$ ← Find half of 6. Square it, and add the result to both sides.

$x^2 + 6x + 9 = 5$ ← Simplify.

$(x + 3)^2 = 5$ ← Write the left side in factored form.

$\sqrt{(x + 3)^2} = \pm\sqrt{5}$ ← Take the square root of each side.

$x + 3 = \pm\sqrt{5}$ ← Simplify.

$x = -3 + \sqrt{5}$ or $x = -3 - \sqrt{5}$ ← Solve for x.

The solutions are $-3 \pm \sqrt{5}$.

Solve each equation by completing the square.

6. $x^2 - 2x - 3 = 0$ **7.** $x^2 + 8x + 12 = 0$ **8.** $x^2 + 2x = 8$ **9.** $x^2 + 6x = 16$

10. $x^2 + 10x = 16$ **11.** $x^2 + 4x = 12$ **12.** $x^2 - 4x = 3$ **13.** $x^2 - 4x - 45 = 0$

14. $x^2 - 12x = 4$ **15.** $x^2 + 10x = 10$ **16.** $x^2 - 6x = 10$ **17.** $x^2 + 8x + 3 = 0$

18. **Writing** Solve one of the equations in Exercises 6–17 using the quadratic formula. Which method do you prefer, completing the square or the quadratic formula? Why?

10-7 Choosing an Appropriate Method for Solving

What You'll Learn

- Choosing the best way to solve a quadratic equation

...And Why

To choose efficient ways to solve construction problems

What You'll Need

- graphing calculator

THINK AND DISCUSS

In this chapter and in Chapter 7, you learned many methods for solving quadratic equations. You can always use the quadratic formula to solve a quadratic equation, but sometimes another method may be easier. Other methods include graphing and factoring.

Methods for Solving Quadratic Equations

Example: $2x^2 - 4x - 6 = 0$

Graphing

Graph the related function.

$y = 2x^2 - 4x - 6$

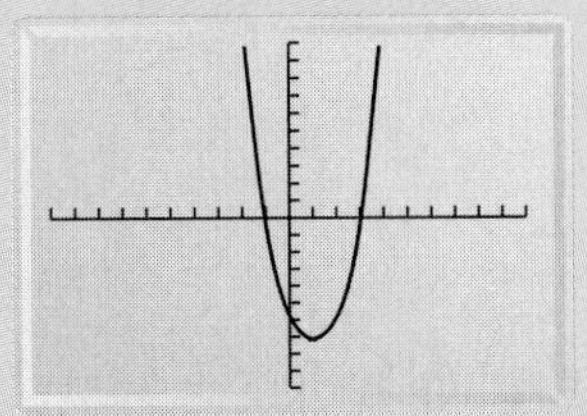

The x-intercepts are –1 and 3.

Quadratic Formula

If $ax^2 + bx + c = 0$ and $a \neq 0$,

$$x = \frac{-b \pm \sqrt{b^2 - 4ac}}{2a}.$$

$$x = \frac{-(-4) \pm \sqrt{(-4)^2 - (4)(2)(-6)}}{2(2)}$$

$$= \frac{4 \pm \sqrt{64}}{4}$$

$$= \frac{12}{4} \text{ or } \frac{-4}{4}$$

$$= 3 \text{ or } -1$$

Factoring

Factor the equation. Use the zero-product property.

$$2x^2 - 4x - 6 = 0$$

$$(2x - 6)(x + 1) = 0$$

$$2x - 6 = 0 \quad \text{or} \quad x + 1 = 0$$

$$2x = 6$$

$$x = 3 \quad \text{or} \quad x = -1$$

When you have an equation to solve, first write it in standard form. Then decide which method to use.

Method	When to Use
Graphing	Use if you have a graphing calculator handy.
Square Roots	Use if the equation has only an x^2 term and a constant term.
Factoring	Use if you can factor the equation easily.
Quadratic Formula	Use if you cannot factor the equation or if you are using a scientific calculator.

1. *Open-ended* Which method(s) would you choose to solve each equation? **Justify** your reasoning.
   - **a.** $2x^2 - 6 = 0$
   - **b.** $9x^2 + 24x + 16 = 0$
   - **c.** $25x^2 - 36 = 0$
   - **d.** $6x^2 + 5x - 6 = 0$
   - **e.** $2x^2 + 7x - 15 = 0$
   - **f.** $16t^2 - 96t + 135 = 0$

PROBLEM SOLVING HINT

Draw a diagram.

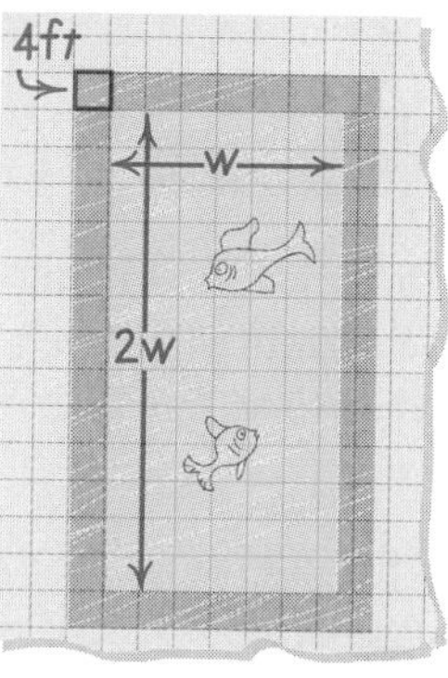

Example 1 Relating to the Real World 

City Parks A fountain has dimensions w and $2w$. The concrete walkway around it is 4 ft wide. Together, the fountain and walkway cover 1500 ft^2 of land. Find the dimensions of the fountain.

Define $w =$ width of fountain $\qquad 2w =$ length of fountain

$w + 2(4) = w + 8 =$ width of fountain and walkway

$2w + 2(4) = 2w + 8 =$ length of fountain and walkway

Relate	width of fountain and walkway	times	length of fountain and walkway	=	area of fountain and walkway
Write	$(w + 8)$	$\cdot$	$(2w + 8)$	=	1500

$$(w + 8)(2w + 8) = 1500$$

$$2w^2 + 24w + 64 = 1500 \quad \longleftarrow \text{Expand the product.}$$

$$2w^2 + 24w - 1436 = 0 \quad \longleftarrow \text{Write in standard form.}$$

$$w = \frac{-24 \pm \sqrt{24^2 - 4(2)(-1436)}}{2(2)} \quad \longleftarrow \text{Use the quadratic formula.}$$

$$w = \frac{-24 + 109.8}{4} \quad \longleftarrow \text{Take the positive square root.}$$

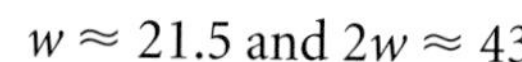

$$w \approx 21.5 \text{ and } 2w \approx 43$$

The fountain is about 21.5 ft wide and about 43 ft long.

2. *Critical Thinking* Why would using the negative square root have led to an unreasonable solution of Example 1?

3. Which of the methods for solving quadratic equations would *not* be appropriate for solving Example 1? Explain.

Example 2

Solve $7x^2 - 175 = 0$.

Because this equation has only an x^2 term and a constant, try taking the square root of both sides or factoring a difference of two squares.

QUICK REVIEW

Zero-Product Property

For all real numbers a and b, if $ab = 0$, then $a = 0$ or $b = 0$.

Method 1 Square roots

$$7x^2 - 175 = 0$$
$$7x^2 = 175$$
$$x^2 = 25$$
$$x = \pm 5$$
$$x = 5 \text{ or } x = -5$$

Method 2 Factoring

$$7x^2 - 175 = 0$$
$$7(x^2 - 25) = 0$$
$$7(x - 5)(x + 5) = 0$$
$$x - 5 = 0 \text{ or } x + 5 = 0$$
$$x = 5 \text{ or } x = -5$$

Both methods give the same solutions.

4. **Try This** Solve each equation.
   a. $4x^2 = 256$ b. $y^2 - 12 = 0$ c. $3t^2 - 192 = 0$

Example 3

Solve $-x^2 - 6x - 14 = 0$.

The equation cannot be easily factored, so you can use a graphing calculator.

Graph the related quadratic function $y = -x^2 - 6x - 14$. The related function has no x-intercepts. Therefore, the equation $-x^2 - 6x - 14 = 0$ has no real solutions.

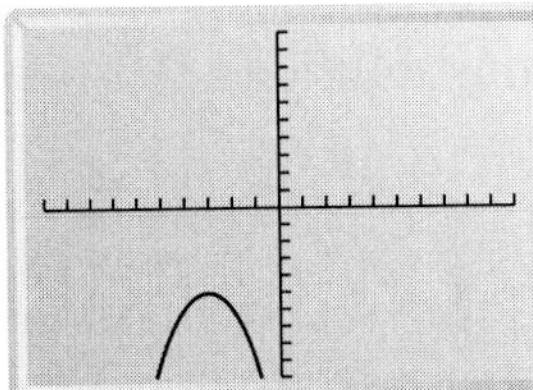

QUICK REVIEW

For a quadratic equation in standard form, the discriminant is $b^2 - 4ac$.

If $b^2 - 4ac < 0$, then there are no real number solutions.

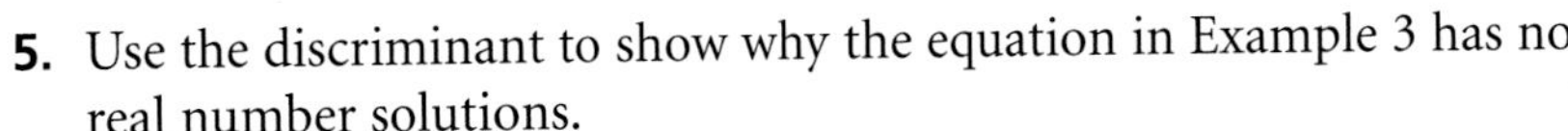

5. Use the discriminant to show why the equation in Example 3 has no real number solutions.

6. **Try This** Solve each equation by graphing.
   a. $x^2 - 4x - 11 = 0$ b. $2x^2 + 7x - 15 = 0$

You can also use the discriminant to check if an equation can be factored. If the discriminant is a perfect square, then there are two rational solutions, and the equation can be factored.

Example 4

Solve $2x^2 - 7x - 4 = 0$.

First, find the discriminant to determine if the equation can be factored.

$$\begin{aligned} b^2 - 4ac &= (-7)^2 - (4)(2)(-4) \\ &= 49 - (-32) \\ &= 81 \end{aligned}$$

Since the discriminant is a perfect square, you can factor.

$(x - 4)(2x + 1) = 0$ ← Use guess and test to factor.

$x - 4 = 0$ or $2x + 1 = 0$ ← Use the zero-product property.

$x = 4$ or $x = -0.5$ ← Solve for x.

PROBLEM SOLVING

Look Back Check the solutions of Example 4.

7. **Critical Thinking** Explain why you should substitute your solutions in the original equation and not in the factored equation to check Example 4.

8. **Try This** Use the discriminant to check if each can be factored. If so, solve each by factoring. Otherwise, use the quadratic formula.
   a. $5x^2 + 14x - 3 = 0$ b. $3c^2 - 6c + 1 = 0$
   c. $2d^2 - d + 1 = 0$ d. $6y^2 - 5y - 4 = 0$

Exercises ON YOUR OWN

Calculator **Use the quadratic formula to solve each equation. Round solutions to the nearest hundredth.**

1. $13x^2 + 170x + 13 = 0$
2. $2.5w^2 + 10w - 2 = 0$
3. $12n^2 + n = 20$
4. $49x^2 - 64x = 25$
5. $6x^2 - 2x + 4 = 0$
6. $-x^2 - 5x + 9 = 0$

Solve each equation using square roots and then using factoring. Compare your solutions.

7. $9d^2 - 81 = 0$
8. $36e^2 = 121$
9. $2n^2 - 8 = 0$
10. $98 = 128x^2$

11. a. Find the x-intercepts of the parabola at the right.
    b. Use the graph to find the solutions of the equation $2x^2 - 5x - 3 = 0$.
    c. **Verify** your answer to part (b) by solving the equation using factoring.

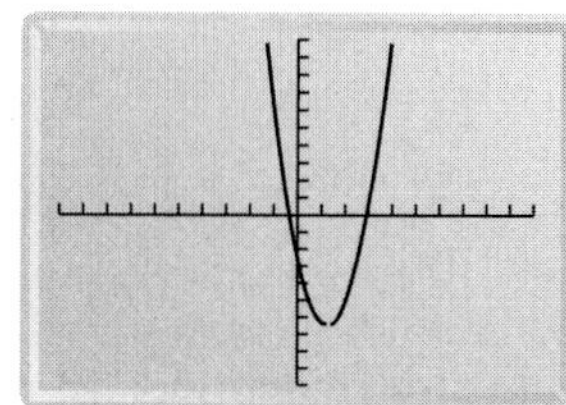

12. **Writing** Explain how to solve $x^2 + 8 = 7x$ by graphing.

Graphing Calculator **Solve each quadratic equation by graphing the related quadratic function and finding the x-intercepts. If there are no real solutions, write *no real solutions.***

13. $x^2 + 2x - 8 = 0$
14. $2x^2 + 3x = 6$
15. $x^2 - 2x + 5 = 0$
16. $8x^2 - 4x - 16 = 0$
17. $0.5x^2 + x = -2$
18. $x^2 = 2x$

Choose **Select a method to solve each quadratic equation. Explain why you chose each method. Then solve. If the equation has no real solutions, write *no real solutions.***

19. $2k^2 = 16k - 32$
20. $4t^2 + 8t + 8 = 0$
21. $8n = 10n^2$
22. $-y^2 + y = -3$
23. $3k^2 - 9k - 27 = 0$
24. $36g^2 = 121$
25. $16k^2 - 56k + 49 = 0$
26. $1.5r^2 + 2r - 2.5 = 0$
27. $169 = 49b^2$
28. $5a^2 + 7a = 7a^2 + 5a - 2$

29. **Standardized Test Prep** Which quadratic equation has 2 and -7 as its solutions?
    A. $x^2 + 5x + 14 = 0$
    B. $x^2 + 5x - 14 = 0$
    C. $x^2 - 5x + 14 = 0$
    D. $x^2 - 5x - 14 = 0$

30. Refer to the cartoon. Suppose the man's initial velocity v is 5 ft/s. Use $0 = -16t^2 + vt + s$, where s is the initial height. Find the number of seconds t before he hits the water.

CLOSE TO HOME by John McPherson

There are times when being a whiz at physics can be a definite drawback.

31. **Surveying** To find the distance across a marsh, a surveyor marked off a right triangle and measured two sides. Solve the equation $d^2 = 150^2 + 75^2$ to find this distance. Explain what solution method you used and why.

32. **Geometry** Find all values of x such that rectangle $ACDG$ at the right has an area of 70 square units *and* rectangle $ABEF$ has an area of 72 square units.

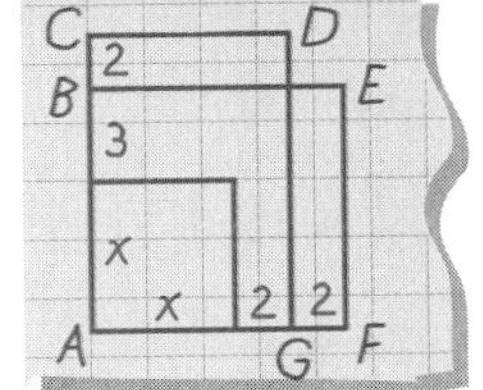

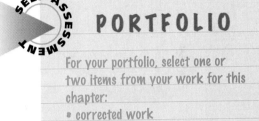

33. **Open-ended** Create an area situation and a question you can answer by solving a quadratic equation. Illustrate and solve your problem.

Exercises MIXED REVIEW

Find the minimum and maximum of each equation.

34. $x \geq 0, y \geq 0$
$x \leq 5$
$y \leq 4$
$C = x + 2y$

35. $x + y \leq 10$
$x \geq 2$
$y \geq 3$
$C = 2x + 3y$

36. $2x + y \leq 7$
$x \geq 0$
$y \geq 0$
$C = 4x + y$

37. Describe the graph of $y = x^2 - 4x + 3$. Where is the axis of symmetry? What is the y-intercept? What are the roots?

38. Find the product of $3x$ and $4x^2 - 2x + 5$.

PORTFOLIO

For your portfolio, select one or two items from your work for this chapter:

- corrected work
- diagrams, graphs, or charts
- a journal entry

Explain why you have included each selection that you make.

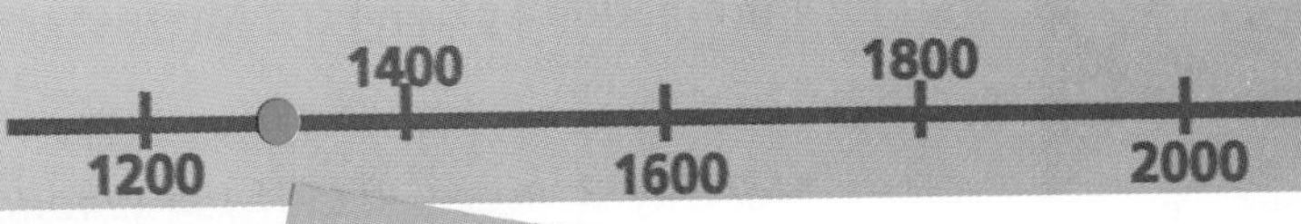

Chu Shih-Chieh

Very little is known about the life of Chu Shih-Chieh, the Chinese mathematician and teacher who had many pupils during the last two decades of the 1200s. In 1303 Chu wrote *Ssu-yüan-yü-chien,* "The Precious Mirror of the Four Elements." He described what is now known as Pascal's Triangle and how it could be used to solve polynomial equations. He also invented "the method of the celestial element" to write and solve polynomial equations and linear systems with up to four variables.

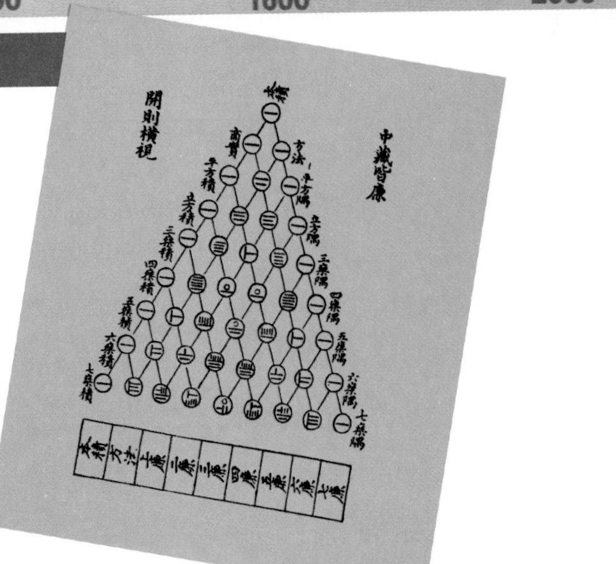

CHAPTER PROJECT

Finishing the Chapter Project

Trees are us.

Questions on pages 474, 479, 485, and 495 should help you to complete your project. Assemble all the parts of your project in a notebook. Add a summary telling what you have learned about the uses of trees.

Reflect and Revise

Ask a classmate to review your project notebook with you. Together, check that your graphs are clearly labeled and accurate. Check that you have used formulas correctly and that your calculations are accurate. Make any revisions necessary to improve your work.

Follow Up

Trees have many uses that you could investigate. You can do more research by contacting the United States Department of Agriculture Forest Service or a local, state, or national park. You can also get more information by using the Internet or one of the resources listed below.

For More Information

Hoadley, R. Bruce. *Identifying Wood: Accurate Results with Simple Tools.* Newtown, Connecticut: Taunton Press, 1990.

Miller, Cameron. *Woodlore.* New York: Ticknor & Fields Books for Young Readers, 1995.

The Encyclopedia of Wood. Alexandria, Virginia: Time-Life Books, 1993.

Warren, Jean. *Exploring Wood and the Forest.* Everett, Washington: Warren Publishing House, 1993.

CHAPTER

10 Wrap Up

Key Terms

binomial (p. 465)
binomial factors (p. 481)
degree of a polynomial (p. 465)
degree of a term (p. 465)
difference of two squares (p. 487)
monomial (p. 465)
perfect square trinomial (p. 487)
polynomial (p. 465)
standard form (p. 465)
trinomial (p. 465)
zero-product property (p. 491)

How am I doing?

SELF ASSESSMENT

- State three ideas from this chapter that you think are important. Explain your choices.
- Explain the different methods you can use to factor $2x^2 + 7x - 15$.

Adding and Subtracting Polynomials 10-1

The **degree of a term** with one variable is the exponent of the variable. A **polynomial** is one term or the sum or difference of two or more terms. The **degree of a polynomial** is the same as the degree of the term with the highest degree. A polynomial can be named by its degree or by the number of its terms. You can simplify polynomials by adding the coefficients of like terms.

Find each sum or difference.

1. $(3x^3 + 8x^2 + 2x + 9) - (-4x^3 + 5x - 3)$

2. $(3g^4 + 5g^2 + 5) + (5g^4 - 10g^2 + 11g)$

3. $(-4b^5 + 3b^3 - b + 10) + (3b^5 - b^3 + b - 4)$

4. $(2t^3 - 4t^2 + 9t - 7) - (t^3 + t^2 - 3t + 1)$

5. ***Open-ended*** Write a polynomial using the variable z. What is the degree of your polynomial?

Multiplying and Factoring 10-2

You can use the distributive property or tiles to multiply polynomials. You can factor a polynomial by finding the greatest common factor (GCF) of the terms of the polynomial, or by using tiles.

Find each product. Write it in standard form.

6. $8x(2 - 5x)$

7. $5g(3g + 7g^2 - 9)$

8. $8t^2(3t - 4 - 5t^2)$

9. $5m(3m + m^2)$

10. $-2w^2(4w - 10 + 3w^2)$

11. $b(10 + 5b - 3b^2)$

Find the greatest common factor (GCF) of the terms of each polynomial. Then factor the polynomial.

12. $9x^4 + 12x^3 + 6x$

13. $4t^5 - 12t^3 + 8t^2$

14. $40n^5 + 70n^4 - 30n^3$

Multiplying Polynomials 10-3

You can use tiles or the distributive property to multiply polynomials. You can use the FOIL method (First, Outer, Inner, Last) to multiply two binomials.

Find each product.

15. $(x + 3)(x + 5)$ **16.** $(5x + 2)(3x - 7)$ **17.** $(2x + 5)(3x - 2)$ **18.** $(x - 1)(-x + 4)$

19. $(x + 2)(x^2 + x + 1)$ **20.** $(4x - 1)(x - 5)$ **21.** $(x - 4)(x^2 - 5x - 2)$ **22.** $(3x + 4)(x + 2)$

23. *Geometry* A rectangle has dimensions $2x + 1$ and $x + 4$. Write an expression for the area of the rectangle as a product and as a polynomial in standard form.

Factoring Trinomials 10-4

Some quadratic trinomials are the product of two **binomial factors.** You can factor trinomials using tiles or by using FOIL with the strategy *Guess and Test.*

Factor each quadratic trinomial.

24. $x^2 + 3x + 2$ **25.** $y^2 - 9y + 14$ **26.** $x^2 - 2x - 15$ **27.** $2w^2 - w - 3$

28. $-b^2 + 7b - 12$ **29.** $2t^2 + 3t - 2$ **30.** $x^2 + 5x - 6$ **31.** $6x^2 + 10x + 4$

32. *Standardized Test Prep* What is $21x^2 - 22x - 8$ in factored form?

A. $(7x + 2)(3x - 4)$ **B.** $(21x + 8)(x - 1)$ **C.** $(3x + 2)(7x - 4)$

D. $(3x - 2)(7x + 4)$ **E.** $(x - 8)(21x + 1)$

Factoring Special Cases 10-5

When you factor a **difference of two squares,** the two binomial factors are the sum and difference of two terms.

$$a^2 - b^2 = (a + b)(a - b)$$

When you factor a **perfect square trinomial,** the two binomial factors are the same.

$$a^2 + 2ab + b^2 = (a + b)^2 \qquad a^2 - 2ab + b^2 = (a - b)^2$$

Factor each polynomial.

33. $q^2 + 2q + 1$ **34.** $b^2 - 16$ **35.** $x^2 - 4x + 4$ **36.** $4t^2 - 121$

37. $4d^2 - 20d + 25$ **38.** $9c^2 + 6c + 1$ **39.** $9k^2 - 25$ **40.** $x^2 + 6x + 9$

41. *Critical Thinking* Suppose you are using tiles to factor a quadratic trinomial. What do you know about the factors of the trinomial if the tiles form a square?

Solving Equations by Factoring — 10-6

You can solve a quadratic equation by factoring and using the **zero-product property.** For all real numbers a and b, if $ab = 0$, then $a = 0$ or $b = 0$.

Simplify each equation if necessary. Then solve by factoring.

42. $x^2 + 7x + 12 = 0$

43. $5x^2 - 10x = 0$

44. $2x^2 - 9x = x^2 - 20$

45. $2x^2 + 5x = 3$

46. $3x^2 - 5x = -3x^2 + 6$

47. $x^2 - 5x + 4 = 0$

48. *Gardening* Alice is planting a garden. Its length is 3 feet less than twice its width. Its area is 170 ft^2. Find the dimensions of the garden.

Choosing an Appropriate Method for Solving — 10-7

You can solve a quadratic equation four different ways. You can graph the related function and find the x-intercepts. For $x^2 = c$, you can take the square root of each side of the equation. You can factor the equation and use the zero-product property. You can use the quadratic formula.

If the discriminant is a perfect square, there are two rational solutions, and the equation can be factored.

Writing **Solve each quadratic equation. Explain why you chose the method you used.**

49. $5x^2 - 10 = x^2 + 90$

50. $9x^2 + 30x - 29 = 0$

51. $8x^2 - 6x = 4x^2 + 6x - 2$

52. A square pool has length p. The border of the pool is 1 ft wide. The combined area of the border and the pool is 400 ft^2. Find the area of the pool.

Getting Ready for... CHAPTER 11

Rewrite each decimal as an improper fraction.

53. 5.7 **54.** −8.25 **55.** 3.14 **56.** 10.4 **57.** −1.849 **58.** 7.67

Evaluate each expression.

59. $\frac{3}{2x + 1}$ for $x = 4$

60. $\frac{3x^2}{5x + 2}$ for $x = -2$

61. $\frac{-3}{y^2 + 3}$ for $y = 2$

62. $\frac{2x}{3x - 2}$ for $x = 5$

Solve each proportion.

63. $\frac{x}{3} = \frac{10}{4}$

64. $\frac{1}{y} = \frac{3}{7}$

65. $\frac{11}{3} = \frac{2r}{5}$

66. $\frac{6}{13} = \frac{12}{d}$

67. *Probability* Make a tree diagram to show all the possible outcomes of rolling two number cubes.

CHAPTER 10

Assessment

Simplify. Write each answer in standard form.

1. $(4x^2 + 2x + 5) + (7x^2 - 5x + 2)$
2. $(9a^2 - 4 - 5a) - (12a - 6a^2 + 3)$
3. $(-4m^2 + m - 10) + (3m + 12 - 7m^2)$
4. $(3c - 4c^2 + c^3) - (5c^2 + 8c^3 - 6c)$
5. **Open-ended** Write a trinomial with degree 6.

Write each product in standard form.

6. $8b(3b + 7 - b^2)$
7. $-t(5t^2 + t)$
8. $3q(4 - q + 3q^3)$
9. $2c(c^5 + 4c^3)$
10. $(x + 6)(x + 1)$
11. $(x + 4)(x - 3)$
12. $(2x - 1)(x - 4)$
13. $(2x + 5)(3x - 7)$
14. $(x + 2)(2x^2 - 5x + 4)$
15. $(x - 4)(6x^2 + 10x - 3)$
16. **Writing** Explain how to use the distributive property to multiply polynomials. Include an example.

Find the greatest common factor of the terms of each polynomial.

17. $21x^4 + 18x^2 + 36x^3$
18. $3t^2 - 5t - 2t^4$
19. $-3a^{10} + 9a^5 - 6a^{15}$
20. $9m^3 - 7m^4 + 8m^2$

Write an expression for each situation as a product and in standard form.

21. A plot of land has width x meters. The length of the plot of land is 5 m more than 3 times its width. What is the area of the land?
22. The height of a box is 2 in. less than its width w. The length of a box is 3 in. more than 4 times its width. What is the volume of the box in terms of w?

Factor each expression.

23. $x^2 - 5x - 14$
24. $x^2 + 10x + 25$
25. $9x^2 + 24x + 16$
26. $x^2 - 100$
27. $x^2 - 4x + 4$
28. $4x^2 - 49$
29. **Standardized Test Prep** Which of the following are perfect square trinomials?
    I. $x^2 + 14x + 49$
    II. $16x^2 + 25$
    III. $9x^2 - 30x + 25$
    IV. $4x^2 - 81$

    A. I only
    B. II only
    C. I and III
    D. I, III, and IV
    E. I, II, III, and IV

Write each equation in standard form. Then solve the equation.

30. $4x^2 - 5x = -2x^2 + 2x + 3$
31. $2x^2 + 3x = x^2 + 28$
32. $3x^2 - 4 = x^2 - 5x + 12$
33. $x^2 - 5 = -x^2 + 9x$
34. **Geometry** The base of a triangle is 8 ft more than twice its height. The area of the triangle is 45 ft^2. Find the dimensions of the triangle.

Use the quadratic formula to solve each equation to the nearest hundredth. If there are no real solutions, write *no real solutions.*

35. $4x^2 + 4x + 9 = 0$
36. $x^2 + 10x + 11 = 0$
37. $-2x^2 - x + 8 = 0$
38. $x^2 - 7x + 10 = 0$
39. **Writing** Explain when you would use the different methods of solving quadratic equations. Give examples.

CHAPTER 10

Cumulative Review

For Exercises 1–12, choose the correct letter.

1. A parachutist opens her parachute at 800 ft. Her rate of change in altitude is -30 ft/s. Which expression represents her altitude in feet t seconds after she opens her parachute?
   A. $30t$ **B.** $-30t$ **C.** 800
   D. $800 - 30t$ **E.** $800 + 30t$

2. What is the standard form of the product $(3x - 1)(5x + 3)$?
   A. $15x^2 + 2x - 3$ **B.** $15x^2 + 2x + 3$
   C. $15x^2 + 4x + 3$ **D.** $15x^2 - 4x - 3$
   E. $15x^2 + 4x - 3$

3. Which relations are functions?

I.

x	1	−1	2	1
y	3	4	5	7

II.

x	1	2	3	4
y	1	1	3	5

III.

x	0	1	2	3
y	0	1	3	2

   A. I **B.** II **C.** III
   D. II and III **E.** I, II, and III

4. A rectangle has a perimeter of 72 in. The length is 3 in. more than twice the width. What is the length of the rectangle?
   A. 11 **B.** 22 **C.** 25 **D.** 36 **E.** 50

5. A and B are independent events. If $P(A) = \frac{5}{6}$ and $P(A \text{ and } B) = \frac{1}{8}$, what is $P(B)$?
   A. $\frac{1}{10}$ **B.** $\frac{3}{20}$ **C.** $\frac{1}{5}$ **D.** $\frac{1}{4}$ **E.** $\frac{3}{10}$

6. One leg of a right isosceles triangle is 8 cm long. What is the length of the hypotenuse?
   A. 16 **B.** $16\sqrt{3}$ **C.** $8\sqrt{3}$ **D.** $4\sqrt{3}$ **E.** $8\sqrt{2}$

7. A truck traveling 45 mi/h and a car traveling 55 mi/h cover the same distance. The truck travels 4 h longer than the car. How far did they travel?
   A. 880 **B.** 940 **C.** 960 **D.** 990 **E.** 900

8. Which compound inequality could the graph represent?

   −3 −2 −1 0 1 2 3

   A. $-1 \le x \le 2$ **B.** $x \le -2$ or $x \ge 1$
   C. $-2 < x$ and $x \ge 1$ **D.** $-2 \le x \le 1$
   E. $x \le -2$ and $x \ge 1$

9. Suppose you toss three coins. What is the probability of getting 2 heads and 1 tail?
   A. $\frac{1}{8}$ **B.** $\frac{1}{4}$ **C.** $\frac{3}{8}$
   D. $\frac{1}{2}$ **E.** $\frac{5}{8}$

10. Which of the following is a monomial?
    I. $5x^2$ **II.** $17x^{-2}$ **III.** $\frac{1}{x}$
    A. I **B.** II **C.** III
    D. I and III **E.** II and III

Compare the boxed quantity in Column A with the boxed quantity in Column B. Choose the best answer.

- **A.** The quantity in Column A is greater.
- **B.** The quantity in Column B is greater.
- **C.** The two quantities are equal.
- **D.** The relationship cannot be determined on the basis of the information supplied.

	Column A	Column B
	$0 < x < 1$	
11.	x^2	x^4
12.	$a^2 - b^2$	$a^2 + b^2$

Find each answer.

13. The product of two positive integers is 45. The first is 4 less than the second. Find the integers.

14. **Open-ended** Write a quadratic function for a graph that opens downward with vertex (–2, 3).

15. The length of a rectangular garden is 3 m less than twice its width. The area of the garden is 35 m^2. Find the dimensions of the garden.

11 Rational Expressions and Functions

Relating to the Real World

Sixty dollars will buy you six $10 pizzas or four $15 pizzas. This simple relationship leads to fractions with variables in the denominators, called rational expressions. Rational expressions give social scientists and others who use statistics flexibility in applying formulas to their work.

CHAPTER PROJECT

GOOD VIBRATIONS

Sounds are caused by vibrations—for example, a string vibrating on a violin. When the string is shortened it vibrates faster, and a higher pitch results. Pitch is also affected by tension (an example is your vocal cords).

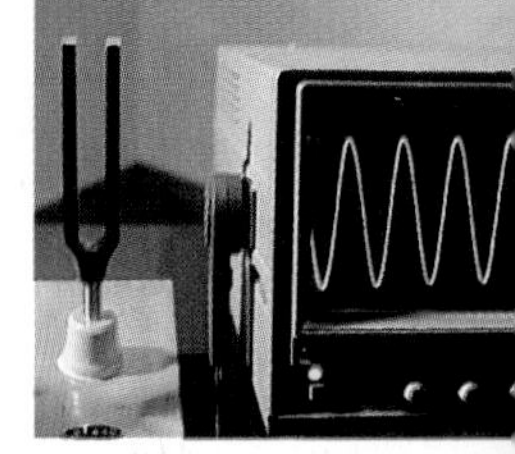

As you work through the chapter, you will investigate a variety of musical pitches. You will use inverse variation to find pitch. You will create simple musical instruments to compare ratios of lengths to different pitches. Finally, you will choose a musical instrument and explain how it produces sounds at different pitches.

To help you complete the project:

- **p. 514** *Find Out by Calculating*
- **p. 526** *Find Out by Analyzing*
- **p. 531** *Find Out by Creating*
- **p. 536** *Find Out by Interviewing*
- **p. 547** *Find Out by Communicating*
- **p. 548** *Finishing the Project*

Solving Rational Equations 11-5

Counting Outcomes and Permutations 11-6

Combinations 11-7

11-1 Inverse Variation

What You'll Learn

- Solving inverse variations
- Comparing direct and inverse variation

...And Why

To investigate real-world situations, such as those relating time and rate of work

WORK TOGETHER

Construction Suppose you are part of a volunteer crew constructing low-cost housing. Building a house requires a total of 160 workdays. For example, a crew of 20 people can complete a house in 8 days.

1. How long should it take a crew of 40 people?

2. Copy and complete the table.

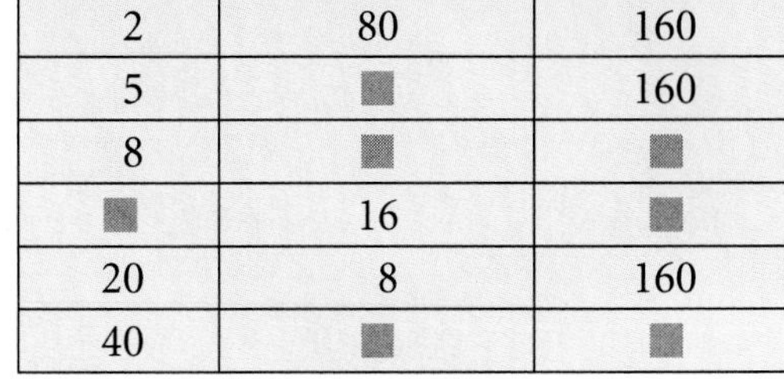

Crew Size (x)	Construction Days (y)	Total Workdays
2	80	160
5	■	160
8	■	■
■	16	■
20	8	160
40	■	■

Who? Using volunteers, Habitat for Humanity has helped build thousands of homes for low-income families around the world.

Source: Habitat for Humanity

3. Graph the (x, y) data from the table.

4. Describe what happens to construction time as the crew size increases.

THINK AND DISCUSS

Solving Inverse Variations

When the product of two quantities remains constant, they form an **inverse variation.** As one quantity increases, the other decreases. The product of the quantities is called the **constant of variation** k. An inverse variation can be written $xy = k$, or $y = \frac{k}{x}$.

5. a. In the Work Together, what two quantities vary?
b. What is the constant of variation?
c. Write an equation that models this variation.

6. a. Complete the table for the inverse variation $xy = 100$.

x	1	2	4	5	10	20	50	100
y	100	■	■	■	■	■	■	■

b. Describe how the values of y change as the values of x increase.

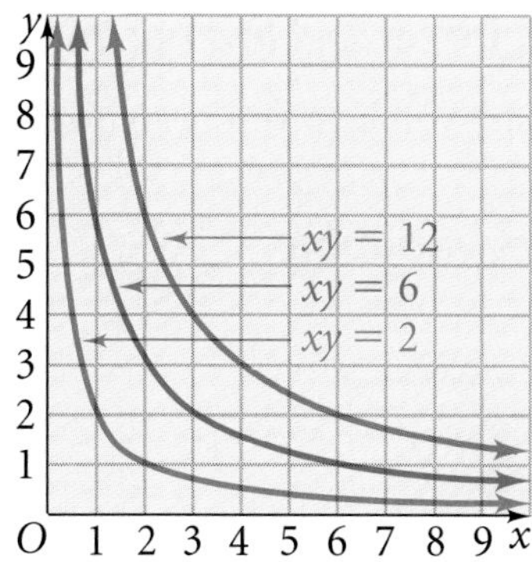

Inverse variations have graphs with the same general shape.

7. **a.** Name the constant of variation k for each graph shown above.
b. **Open-ended** Name three points that lie on the graph of each inverse variation.

Suppose (x_1, y_1) and (x_2, y_2) are two ordered pairs in an inverse variation. Since each ordered pair has the same product, you can write the *product* equation $x_1 \cdot y_1 = x_2 \cdot y_2$. You can use this equation to solve problems involving inverse variation.

Example 1 **Relating to the Real World** 

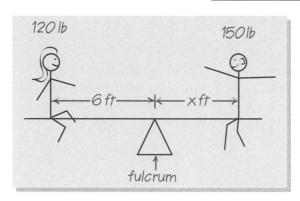

120 lb
150 lb
6 ft
x ft
fulcrum

Physics The weight needed to balance a lever varies inversely with the distance from the fulcrum to the weight. Where should Julio sit to balance the lever?

Relate A weight of 120 lb is 6 ft from the fulcrum. A weight of 150 lb is x ft from the fulcrum. Weight and distance vary inversely.

Define $\text{weight}_1 = 120$ lb
$\text{weight}_2 = 150$ lb
$\text{distance}_1 = 6$ ft
$\text{distance}_2 = x$ ft

Write $\text{weight}_1 \cdot \text{distance}_1 = \text{weight}_2 \cdot \text{distance}_2$ ← **Use a product equation.**

$$120 \cdot 6 = 150 \cdot x$$ ← **Substitute.**

$$720 = 150x$$

$$x = \frac{720}{150}$$

$$x = 4.8$$

Julio should sit 4.8 feet from the fulcrum to balance the lever.

8. **Try This** Solve each inverse variation.
a. When $x = 75$, $y = 0.2$. Find x when $y = 3$.
b. What weight placed on a lever 6 ft from the fulcrum will balance 80 lb placed 9 ft from the fulcrum?
c. A trip takes 3 h at 50 mi/h. Find the time when the rate is 60 mi/h.

Comparing Direct and Inverse Variation

This summary will help you recognize and use direct and inverse variations.

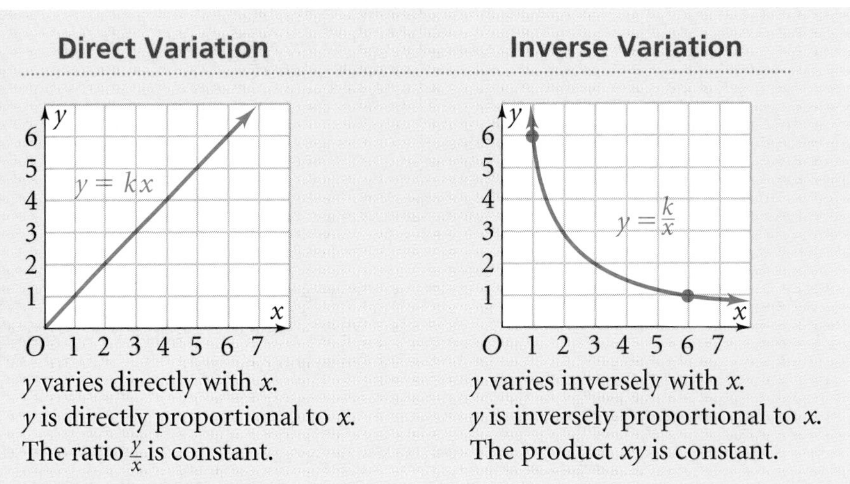

Direct Variation	Inverse Variation
y varies directly with x.	y varies inversely with x.
y is directly proportional to x.	y is inversely proportional to x.
The ratio $\frac{y}{x}$ is constant.	The product xy is constant.

Example 2

Do the data in each table represent a *direct variation* or an *inverse variation?* For each table, write an equation to model the data.

a.

x	2	4	10
y	5	10	25

The values of y seem to vary directly with the values of x. Check the ratio $\frac{y}{x}$.

$\frac{y}{x} = \frac{5}{2} = 2.5$

$\frac{10}{4} = 2.5$

$\frac{25}{10} = 2.5$

The ratio $\frac{y}{x}$ is the same for each pair of data. So, this is a direct variation and $k = 2.5$. The equation is $y = 2.5x$.

b.

x	5	10	25
y	20	10	4

The values of y seem to vary inversely with the values of x. Check the product xy.

$xy = 5(20) = 100$

$10(10) = 100$

$25(4) = 100$

The product xy is the same for each pair of data. So, this is an inverse variation and $k = 100$. The equation is $xy = 100$.

9. Match each situation with the equation that models it. Is the relationship between the data *direct* or *inverse*?

a. The cost of \$20 worth of gasoline is split among several people.

b. You buy several markers for 20¢ each.

c. You walk 5 miles each day. Your pace (speed) and time vary from day to day.

d. Several people buy souvenirs for \$5 apiece.

I. $y = 5x$

II. $xy = 5$

III. $y = \frac{20}{x}$

IV. $y = 20x$

Exercises ON YOUR OWN

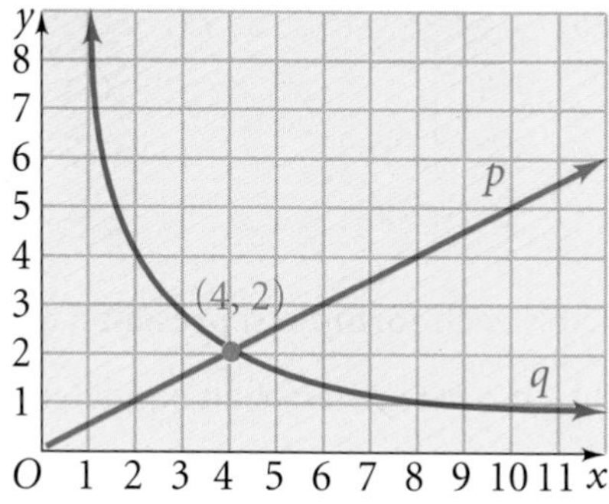

1. **a.** Suppose you want to earn \$80. How long will it take you if you are paid \$5/h; \$8/h; \$10/h; \$20/h?
   b. What are the two variable quantities in part (a)?
   c. Write an equation to represent this situation.

2. **Critical Thinking** The graphs p and q represent a direct variation and an inverse variation. Write the equation for each graph.

Each pair of points is from an inverse variation. Find the missing value.

3. $(6, 12)$ and $(9, y)$
4. $(3, 5)$ and $(1, n)$
5. $(x, 55)$ and $(5, 77)$
6. $(9.4, b)$ and $(6, 4.7)$
7. $(24, 1.6)$ and $(c, 0.4)$
8. $(\frac{1}{2}, 24)$ and $(6, y)$
9. $(x, \frac{1}{2})$ and $(\frac{1}{3}, \frac{1}{4})$
10. $(500, 25)$ and $(4, n)$
11. $(\frac{1}{2}, 5)$ and $(b, \frac{1}{8})$
12. $(x, 11)$ and $(1, 66)$
13. $(50, 13)$ and $(t, 5)$
14. $(4, 3.6)$ and $(1.2, g)$

15. **Standardized Test Prep** Which proportion represents an inverse variation?

    A. $\frac{x_2}{y_2} = \frac{y_1}{x_1}$ **B.** $\frac{x_1}{y_2} = \frac{y_1}{x_2}$ **C.** $\frac{x_2}{y_2} = \frac{x_1}{y_1}$ **D.** $\frac{x_1}{x_2} = \frac{y_2}{y_1}$ **E.** $\frac{x_1}{y_1} = \frac{x_2}{y_2}$

Find the constant of variation *k* for each inverse variation.

16. $y = 8$ when $x = 4$
17. $r = 3.3$ when $t = \frac{1}{3}$
18. $a = 25$ when $b = 0.04$
19. $x = \frac{1}{2}$ when $y = 5$
20. $p = 10.4$ when $q = 1.5$
21. $x = 5$ when $y = 75$

22. According to the First Law of Air Travel, will the distance to your gate be *greater* or *less* for this trip than for your last trip?
    a. You have more luggage.
    b. You have less time to make your flight.
    c. You have less luggage.

CLOSE TO HOME by John McPherson

The First Law of Air Travel: The distance to your connecting gate is directly proportional to the amount of luggage you are carrying and inversely proportional to the amount of time you have.

23. **Travel** The time to travel a certain distance is inversely proportional to your speed. Suppose it takes you $2\frac{1}{2}$ h to drive from your house to the lake at a rate of 48 mi/h.
    a. What is the constant of variation? What does it represent?
    b. How long will your return trip take at 40 mi/h?

Solve each inverse variation.

24. **Surveying** Two rectangular building lots are each one-quarter acre in size. One plot measures 99 ft by 110 ft. Find the length of the other plot if its width is 90 ft.

25. **Construction** If 4 people can paint a house working 3 days each, how long will it take a crew of 5 people?

Do the data in each table represent a *direct* or an *inverse* variation? Write an equation to model the data. Then complete the table.

26.

x	y
5	6
2	15
10	■

27.

x	y
0.4	28
1.2	84
■	63

28.

x	y
10	4
20	■
8	3.2

29.

x	y
1.6	30
4.8	10
■	96

30.

x	y
3	1
1	3
9	■

Does each formula represent a *direct* or an *inverse* variation? Explain.

31. the perimeter of an equilateral triangle: $P = 3s$

32. a rectangle with area 24 square units: $lw = 24$

33. the time t to travel 150 mi at r mi/h: $t = \frac{150}{r}$

34. the circumference of a circle with radius r: $C = 2\pi r$

35. **Writing** Explain how the variable y changes in each situation.

 a. y varies directly with x. The value of x is doubled.

 b. y varies inversely with x. The value of x is doubled.

36. **Open-ended** Write and graph a direct variation and an inverse variation that use the same constant of variation.

Chapter Project ***Find Out by Calculating***

Under equal tension, the frequency of a vibrating string varies inversely with the string length. Violins and guitars use this principle to produce the different pitches of a musical scale. Find the string lengths for a C-Major scale.

C-Major Scale

Pitch	C	D	E	F	G	A	B	C
Frequency (cycles/s)	523	587	659	698	784	880	988	1046
String length (mm)	420	■	■	■	■	■	■	■

Exercises MIXED REVIEW

Factor each polynomial.

37. $x^2 + 10x + 25$ **38.** $4t^2 - 9m^2$ **39.** $x^2 - 6x + 9$

40. **Education** The number of high school students taking advanced placement exams increased from 177,406 in 1984 to 459,000 in 1994. What percent increase is this?

SELF ASSESSMENT

FOR YOUR JOURNAL

Describe differences and similarities between direct variation and inverse variation. Include equations and graphs.

Getting Ready for Lesson 11-2

Find the reciprocal of each number.

41. 5 **42.** -4 **43.** $\frac{8}{3}$ **44.** $3\frac{1}{7}$ **45.** -1 **46.** $\frac{3}{4}$

Math ToolboX

Technology

Graphing Rational Functions

Before Lesson 11-2

When you use a graphing calculator to graph a rational function, sometimes false connections appear on the screen. When this happens, you need to make adjustments to see the true shape of the graph.

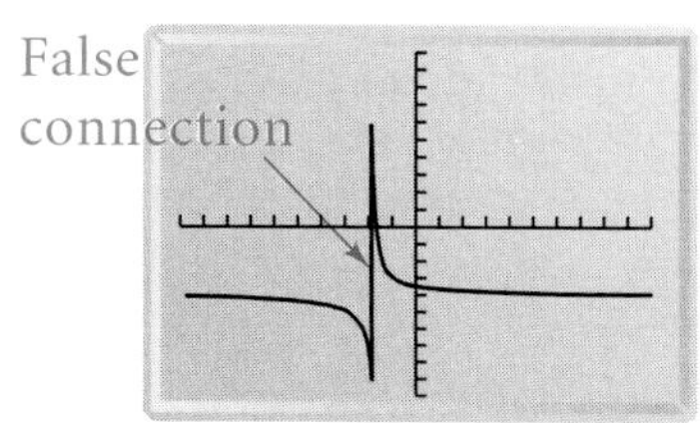

For example, on your graphing calculator the graph of the function $y = \frac{1}{x + 2} - 4$ may look like the graph at the right. The highest point and lowest point on the graph are not supposed to connect. If you trace the graph, no point on the graph lies on this connecting line. So, this is a false connection.

Here's how you can graph a rational function and avoid false connections.

First press the MODE key. Then scroll down and right to highlight the word "Dot." Then press ENTER.

```
Normal Sci Eng
Float 0123456789
Radian Degree
Func Par Pol Seq
Connected Dot
Sequential Simul
Full Screen Split
```

Graph again. Now the false connection is gone!

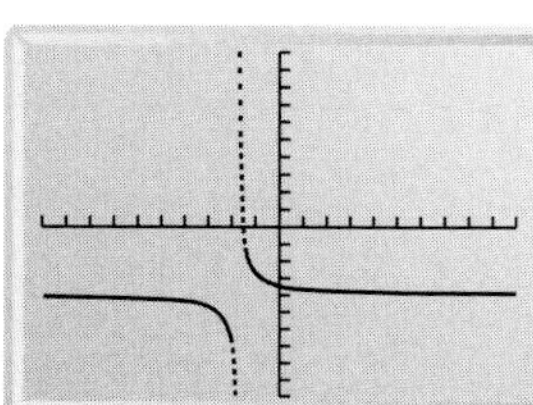

Use the TRACE key or TABLE key to find points on the graph. Sketch the graph.

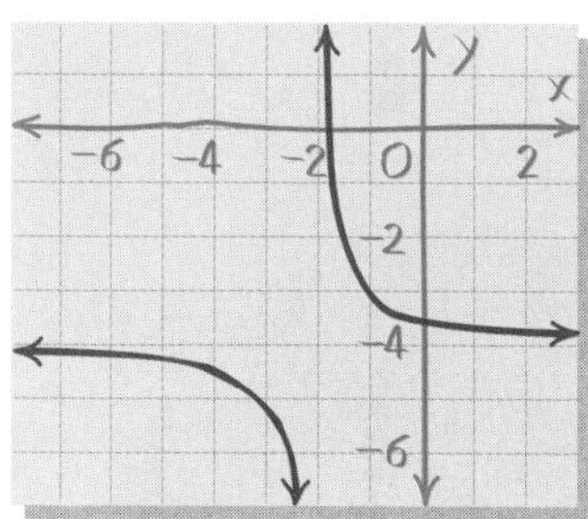

Graphing Calculator **Use a graphing calculator to graph each function. Then sketch the graph. (*Hint*: Use parentheses to enter binomials.)**

1. $y = \frac{1}{x - 3}$

2. $y = \frac{1}{x} + 3$

3. $y = \frac{5}{3x + 2}$

4. $y = \frac{4}{3x + 6}$

5. $y = \frac{x + 3}{x - 2}$

6. $y = \frac{1}{x - 2} + 1$

7. $y = \frac{6}{x^2 - x - 6}$

8. $y = \frac{1}{x - 4} + 2$

9. $y = \frac{8}{x}$

10. $y = \frac{4}{x + 1} - 3$

11. $y = \frac{3x}{x + 3}$

12. $y = \frac{2x + 1}{x - 4}$

13. a. Graphing Calculator Graph $y = \frac{1}{x}$, $y = \frac{1}{x - 3}$, and $y = \frac{1}{x + 4}$. What do you notice?

b. Graphing Calculator Graph $y = \frac{1}{x}$, $y = \frac{1}{x} - 3$, and $y = \frac{1}{x} + 4$. What do you notice?

14. Writing Graph $y = \frac{1}{x}$.

a. Examine both negative and positive values of x. Describe what happens to the y-values when x is near zero.

b. Describe what happens to the y-values as $|x|$ increases.

Connections — Photography . . . and more

11-2 Rational Functions

What You'll Learn

- Evaluating rational functions
- Graphing rational functions

...And Why

To solve problems using rational functions, such as those involving light intensity

What You'll Need

- graph paper
- graphing calculator
- index cards

QUICK REVIEW

Two numbers are *reciprocals* of each other if their product is 1.

THINK AND DISCUSS

Exploring Rational Functions

Photography Automatic cameras calculate shutter speed based on the amount of available light. The relationship between shutter speed and the amount of light can be modeled with a rational function. A **rational function** is a function that can be written in the form $f(x) = \frac{\text{polynomial}}{\text{polynomial}}$.

1. Evaluate each rational function for $x = 3$.
   a. $f(x) = \frac{1}{x - 4}$ **b.** $y = \frac{2}{x^2}$ **c.** $g(x) = \frac{x^2 - 3x + 2}{x + 2}$

The function $y = \frac{1}{x}$ is an example of a rational function. You can use the graph of $y = \frac{1}{x}$ to show the relationship between reciprocals.

Table

Number (x)	-1	$-\frac{1}{3}$	1	1.5	3
Reciprocal (y)	-1	-3	1	$\frac{2}{3}$	$\frac{1}{3}$

Graph

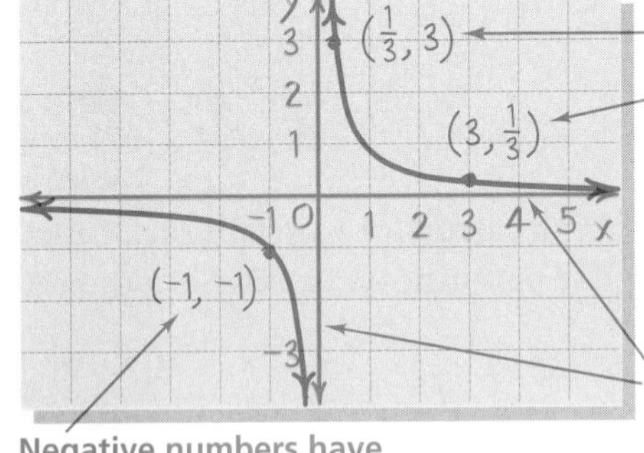
y
3
2
1
$(\frac{1}{3}, 3)$
$(3, \frac{1}{3})$
-1 0 1 2 3 4 5 x
$(-1, -1)$
-3
Since 3 and $\frac{1}{3}$ are reciprocals of each other, both $(3, \frac{1}{3})$ and $(\frac{1}{3}, 3)$ are on the graph.
For $x = 0$ and $y = 0$ the function is undefined. So the graph never intersects either axis.
Negative numbers have negative reciprocals.

2. Does each point lie on the graph of $y = \frac{1}{x}$? Why or why not?
   a. $(-100, -0.01)$ **b.** $(-5, 0.2)$ **c.** $(1{,}000{,}000, 0)$ **d.** $(0.04, 25)$

A line is an **asymptote** of a graph if the graph of the function gets closer and closer to the line, but does not cross it.

3. The y-axis is a vertical asymptote of the function $y = \frac{1}{x}$. Is there a horizontal asymptote of the graph? Explain.

Graphing Rational Functions

When you evaluate a rational function, some values of x may lead to division by zero. For the function $y = \frac{1}{x - 3}$, the denominator is zero for $x = 3$. So, the function is undefined when $x = 3$, and the vertical line $x = 3$ is an asymptote of the graph of $y = \frac{1}{x - 3}$.

Example 1

Graph $y = \frac{4}{x + 3}$.

Step 1 Find the vertical asymptote.

$$x + 3 = 0$$
$$x = -3 \leftarrow \text{vertical asymptote}$$

Step 2 Make a table using values of x near -3.

x	y
−6	$-\frac{4}{3}$
−5	−2
−4	−4
−2	4
−1	2
0	$\frac{4}{3}$

Step 3 Draw the graph.

Use a dashed line for the asymptote $x = -3$.

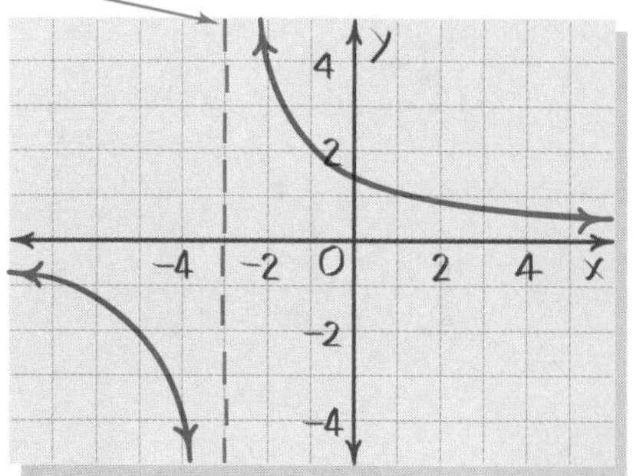

PROBLEM SOLVING

Look Back How does the graph of a rational function compare with the graph of an exponential function?

4. a. Copy the graph above and add the graph of the line $y = -x - 3$.

b. *Critical Thinking* Fold the graph along the line you drew. What is true about the two parts of the graph of $y = \frac{4}{x + 3}$?

5. a. Evaluate $y = \frac{4}{x + 3}$ for $x = 1000$ and $x = -1000$.

b. Is there a horizontal asymptote for the graph? Explain.

The graphs of many rational functions are related to each other.

$y = \frac{1}{x}$

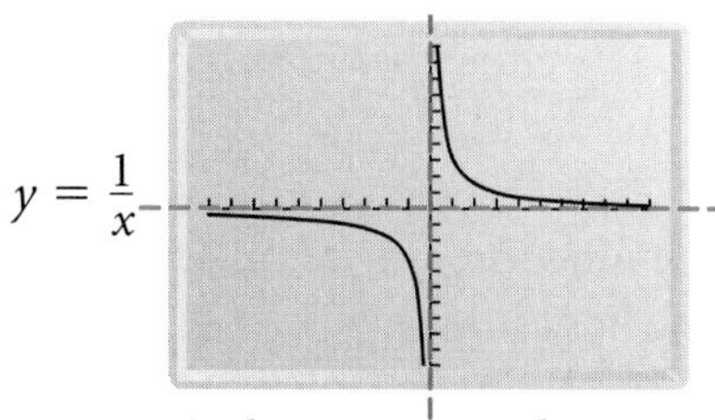

vertical asymptote when $x = 0$
horizontal asymptote along the x-axis

$y = \frac{1}{x - 2}$

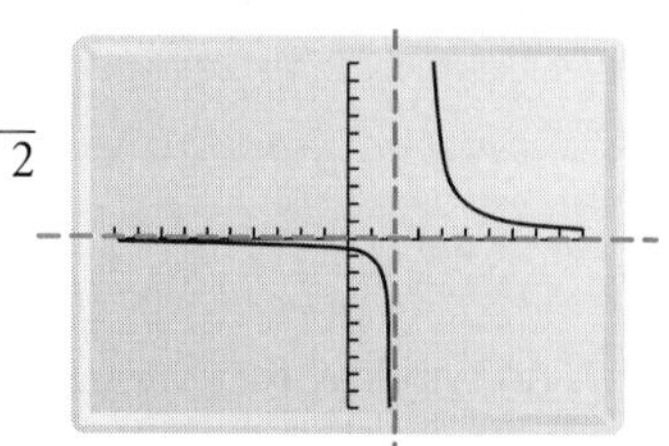

vertical asymptote when $x = 2$
horizontal asymptote along the x-axis

The graphs are identical in shape, but the second graph is shifted two units to the right.

6. Where is the vertical asymptote of the graph of each function?

a. $y = \frac{6}{x}$ b. $y = \frac{6}{x - 3}$ c. $y = \frac{6}{x + 1}$

7. **Try This** Graph each function in Question 6.

8. **Critical Thinking** Graph the functions $y = \frac{3}{x}$ and $y = \frac{3}{x} + 2$. Are the graphs identical in shape? What shift occurs?

You can use rational functions to describe relationships in the real world.

Example 2 Relating to the Real World 

Photography The output from the photographer's lighting system is 72,000 lumens. To get a good photo, the intensity of light at the circus performers must be at least 600 lumens. The light intensity y is related to their distance x in feet from the light by the function $y = \frac{72{,}000}{x^2}$. How far can the circus performers be from the light?

Relate light intensity at performers is at least 600 lumens

Write $\frac{72{,}000}{x^2} \geq 600$

Use a graphing calculator. Enter $y = \frac{72{,}000}{x^2}$ and $y = 600$. Find the point of intersection.

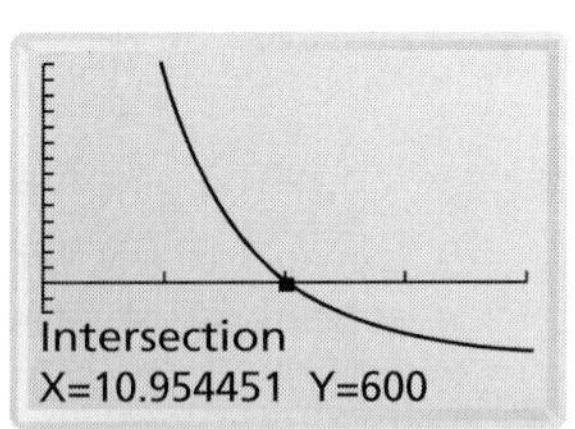

Xmin=0 Ymin=0
Xmax=20 Ymax=2000
Xscl=5 Yscl=100

The curved graph shows that the light intensity y decreases as the distance x increases.

The light intensity is about 600 lumens when $x \approx 11$. The circus performers should be within about 11 ft of the light.

GRAPHING CALCULATOR HINT

Use a viewing window for Quadrant I, since distance and lumens are positive.

9. a. Use the function in Example 2 to find the light intensity at each distance in the table.
b. Describe how the light intensity changes when the distance doubles.

Distance (x)	Intensity (y)
3 ft	■
6 ft	■
12 ft	■

10. *Graphing Calculator* Graph $y = \frac{1}{x}$ and $y = \frac{1}{x^2}$.

a. What is the vertical asymptote of the graph of each function?

b. *Critical Thinking* What is the range of $y = \frac{1}{x}$? of $y = \frac{1}{x^2}$?

WORK TOGETHER

You have studied six families of functions this year. Their properties and graphs are shown in this summary.

Families of Functions

Linear function

$y = mx + b$

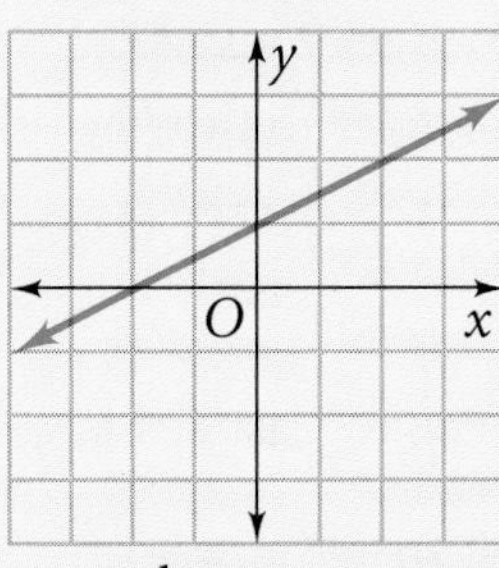

slope $= m$
y-intercept $= b$

Absolute value function

$y = |x - b|$

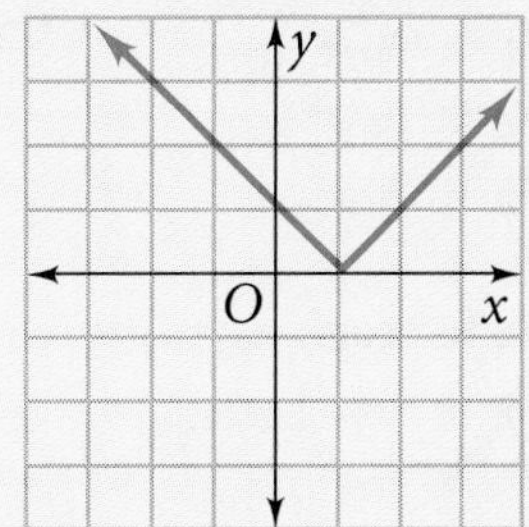

V-shape with vertex at $(b, 0)$

Quadratic function

$y = ax^2 + bx + c$

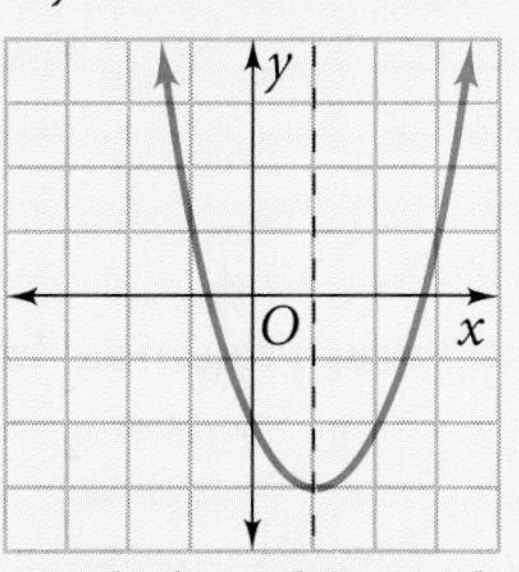

parabola with axis of symmetry at $x = -\frac{b}{2a}$

Exponential function

$y = ab^x$

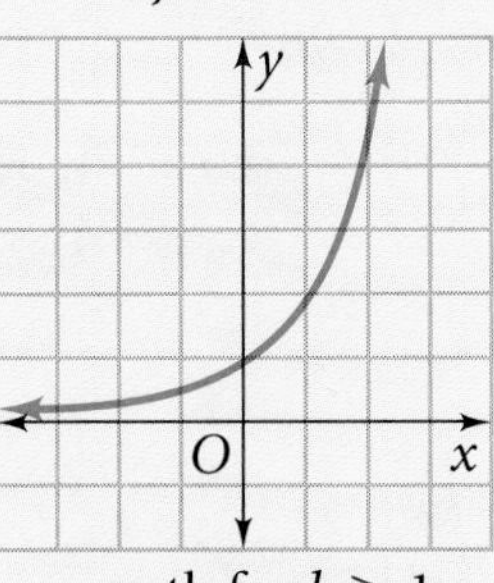

growth for $b > 1$
decay for $0 < b < 1$

Radical function

$y = \sqrt{x - b} + c$

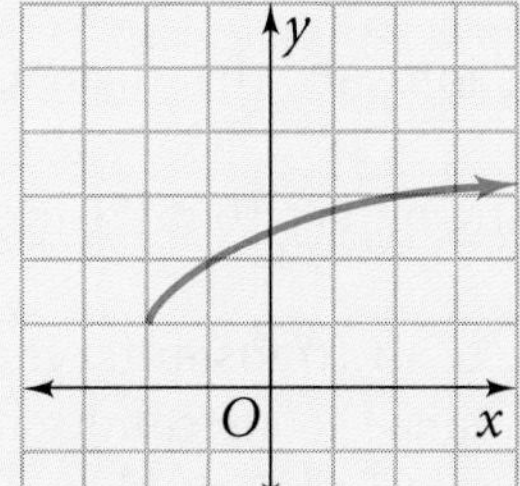

shift horizontally b units
shift vertically c units

Rational function

$y = \frac{k}{x - b} + c$

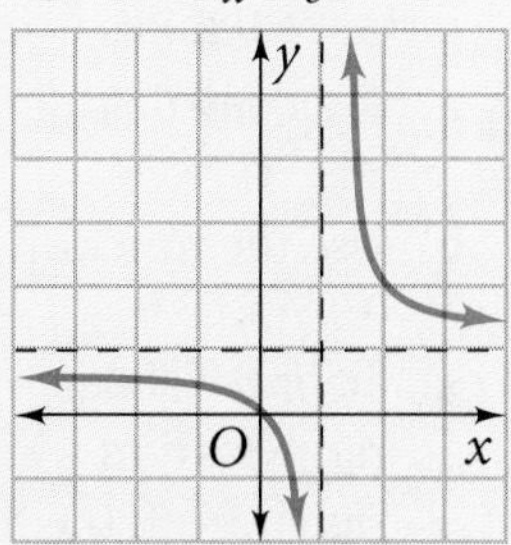

vertical asymptote at $x = b$

11. Work with a partner to prepare a note card for each family of functions. Include this information:

- one or more examples for that family
- a graph for each example
- notes about each function you have graphed (for instance, how to find the slope, the axis of symmetry, or an asymptote)

12. Make duplicate cards so that you and your partner each have a full set.

Exercises ON YOUR OWN

Evaluate each function for $x = -1$, $x = 2$, and $x = 4$.

1. $y = \frac{x - 2}{x}$
2. $f(x) = \frac{3}{x - 1}$
3. $y = \frac{2x}{x - 3}$
4. $g(x) = \frac{12}{x^2}$

What value of x makes the denominator of each function equal zero?

5. $f(x) = \frac{3}{x}$
6. $y = \frac{1}{x - 2}$
7. $y = \frac{x}{x + 2}$
8. $h(x) = \frac{3}{2x - 4}$

Describe the asymptotes in each graph.

9.
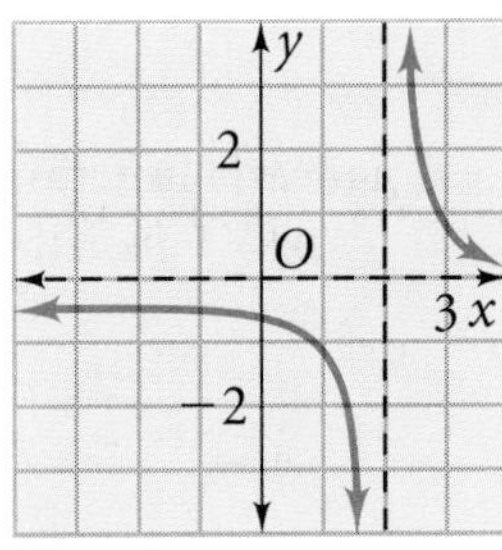

10.
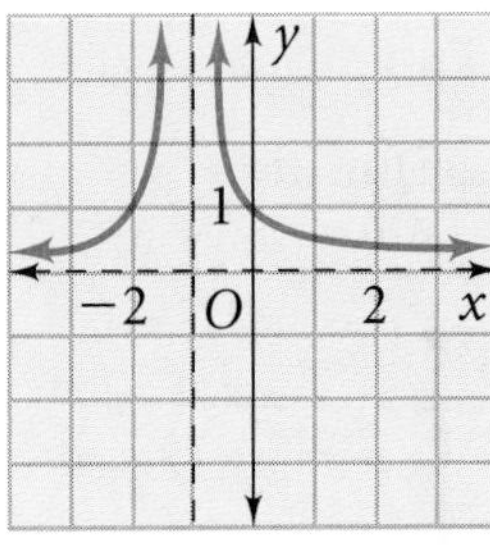

11.
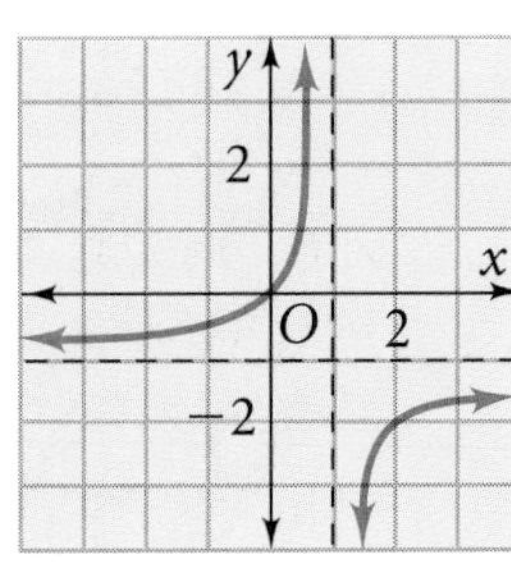

12.
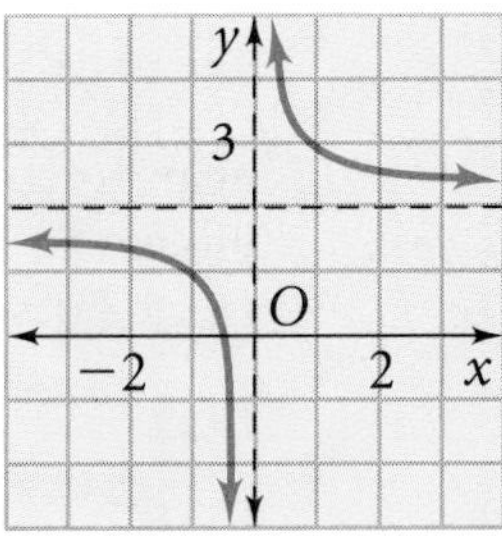

Graph each function. Include a dashed line for each asymptote.

13. $y = \frac{4}{x}$
14. $f(x) = \frac{4}{x - 5}$
15. $y = \frac{4}{x + 4}$
16. $g(x) = \frac{4}{x} + 2$
17. $g(x) = \frac{12}{x}$
18. $y = \frac{12}{x + 2}$
19. $f(x) = \frac{12}{x} - 3$
20. $h(x) = \frac{12}{x + 2} - 3$
21. $f(x) = \frac{-1}{x}$
22. $y = \frac{-4}{x}$
23. $g(x) = \frac{4}{x - 2} + 1$
24. $y = \frac{x + 2}{x - 2}$

25. **Physics** As radio signals move away from a transmitter, they become weaker. The function $s = \frac{1600}{d^2}$ relates the strength s of a signal at a distance d miles from the transmitter.

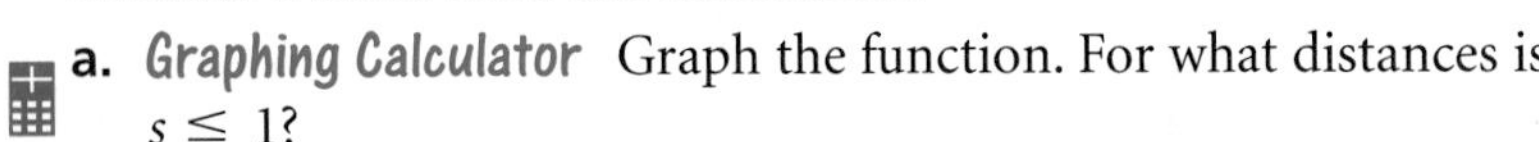

   a. **Graphing Calculator** Graph the function. For what distances is $s \leq 1$?

   b. Use the function to find the signal strength at 10 mi, 1 mi, and 0.1 mi.

   c. **Critical Thinking** Suppose you drive by the transmitter for one radio station while your car radio is tuned to a second station. The signal from the first station can interfere and come through your radio. Use your results from part (b) to explain why.

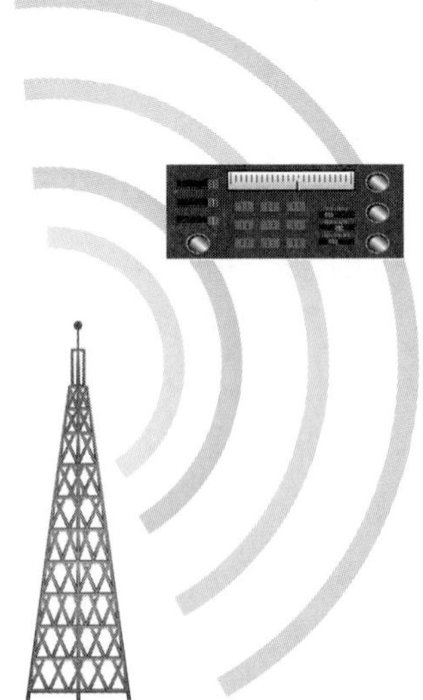

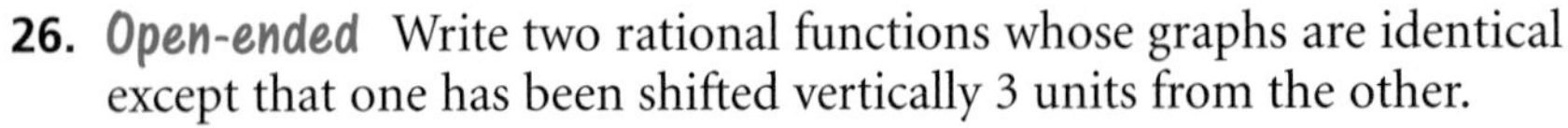

26. **Open-ended** Write two rational functions whose graphs are identical except that one has been shifted vertically 3 units from the other.

27. **Writing** Suppose a friend missed class. How would you explain how to graph $y = \frac{5}{x - 1} + 2$?

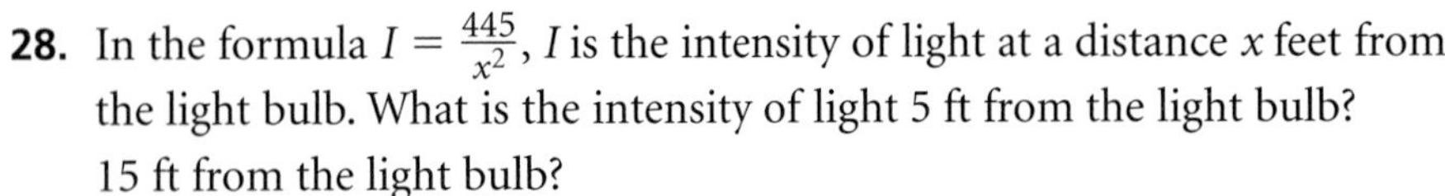

28. In the formula $I = \frac{445}{x^2}$, I is the intensity of light at a distance x feet from the light bulb. What is the intensity of light 5 ft from the light bulb? 15 ft from the light bulb?

Graphing Calculator **Graph each function on a graphing calculator. Then sketch the graph. Include a dashed line for each asymptote.**

29. $y = \frac{x + 4}{x}$ **30.** $y = \frac{x + 1}{x + 3}$ **31.** $y = \frac{4}{x^2 - 1}$ **32.** $y = \frac{6}{x^2 - x - 2}$

Graph each function.

33. $y = x^2 + 3$ **34.** $y = \sqrt{x + 3}$ **35.** $y = x + 3$ **36.** $y = |x - 3|$

37. $y = 3x$ **38.** $y = 3^x$ **39.** $y = \frac{3}{x}$ **40.** $y = \frac{1}{x + 3} + 3$

41. $y = x^2 + 3x + 2$ **42.** $y = \left(\frac{1}{3}\right)^x$ **43.** $y = \frac{3}{x - 3}$ **44.** $y = \frac{3}{x} + 3$

Exercises MIXED REVIEW

Factor.

45. $g^2 - 12g + 35$ **46.** $9h^2 + 24h + 16$ **47.** $a^2 + 6a - 7$ **48.** $25x^2 - 4$

49. **Delivery Services** During the blizzard of 1996, a pizza delivery driver in Alexandria, Virginia, got tips that were 1000% of the usual $1 for each delivery. How much did the delivery driver receive in tips for a delivery during the blizzard?

Getting Ready for Lesson 11-3

Find the value(s) of *x* that makes each expression equal zero.

50. $10 - x$ **51.** $x^2 - 3x$ **52.** $x + 4$ **53.** $x^2 - 16$

Exercises CHECKPOINT

Each pair of points is from an inverse variation. Find the missing value.

1. $(9, 2)$ and $(x, 6)$ **2.** $(8.2, 3)$ and $(12.3, y)$ **3.** $(0.5, 7.2)$ and $(0.9, y)$

Graph each function.

4. $y = \frac{5}{x}$ **5.** $y = \frac{8}{x - 4}$ **6.** $y = \frac{6}{x^2}$ **7.** $y = \frac{1}{x} + 4$

8. **Writing** Describe the similarities and differences between the graphs of $y = \frac{3}{x}$ and $y = \frac{-3}{x}$.

9. **Physics** What weight placed on a lever 9 ft from the fulcrum will balance 126 lb placed 6.5 ft from the fulcrum?

10. The graphs of a direct variation and an inverse variation both pass through the point $(3, 5)$. Write an equation for each graph.

Connections Baking . . . and more

What You'll Learn

- Simplifying rational expressions
- Multiplying and dividing rational expressions

...And Why

To solve real-world problems that involve ratios of unknown quantities

11-3 Rational Expressions

WORK TOGETHER

Work in groups to review how to simplify, multiply, and divide rational numbers.

1. a. Simplify each expression.

$\frac{8}{2}$ $\qquad -\frac{15}{24}$ $\qquad \frac{25}{35}$

b. Consider the steps you took to simplify each expression in part (a). Write the steps you use to simplify rational numbers.

2. a. Express each product in simplest form.

$-\frac{8}{21} \cdot \frac{7}{4}$ $\qquad \frac{3}{5} \cdot \frac{2}{7}$ $\qquad -\frac{3}{4} \cdot (-2)$

b. Consider the steps you took to find each product in part (a). Write the steps you use to multiply rational numbers.

3. a. Express each quotient in simplest form.

$6 \div \frac{3}{8}$ $\qquad \frac{2}{3} \div \left(-\frac{4}{5}\right)$ $\qquad \frac{3}{4} \div 2$

b. Consider the steps you took to find each quotient in part (a). Write the steps you use to divide rational numbers.

QUICK REVIEW

Rational numbers are numbers that can be represented as the ratio of two integers.

THINK AND DISCUSS

Simplifying Rational Expressions

A **rational expression** is an expression that can be written in the form $\frac{\text{polynomial}}{\text{polynomial}}$, where a variable is in the denominator.

4. Evaluate each rational expression for $x = 2$. What do you notice?

a. $\frac{1}{x - 2}$ $\qquad$ **b.** $\frac{3}{x^2 - 4}$ $\qquad$ **c.** $\frac{2}{x^2 + x - 6}$

The **domain** of a rational expression is all real numbers excluding the values for which the denominator is zero. The values that are excluded are restricted from the domain. For the expression $\frac{1}{x - 2}$, 2 is restricted from the domain.

5. What other values are restricted from the domain in parts (b) and (c) of Question 4? (*Hint:* Solve an equation to find the values for which the denominator equals zero.)

A rational expression is in *simplest form* if the numerator and denominator have no common factors except 1.

Example 1

Simplify $\frac{6x + 12}{x + 2}$ and state any values restricted from the domain.

$x + 2 = 0, x = -2$ ← Find the values restricted from the domain.

$\frac{6x + 12}{x + 2} = \frac{6(x + 2)}{x + 2}$ ← Factor the numerator. The denominator cannot be factored.

$= \frac{6}{1} \cdot \frac{x + 2}{x + 2}$ ← Rewrite to show a fraction equal to 1.

$= 6$ ← Simplify.

The solution is 6. The domain does not include $x = -2$.

6. **Try This** Simplify each expression and state any restrictions on the domain of the variable.
   a. $\frac{15b}{25b^2}$ b. $\frac{12c^2}{3c + 6}$ c. $\frac{x + 3}{x^2 - 9}$

Example 2 — Relating to the Real World

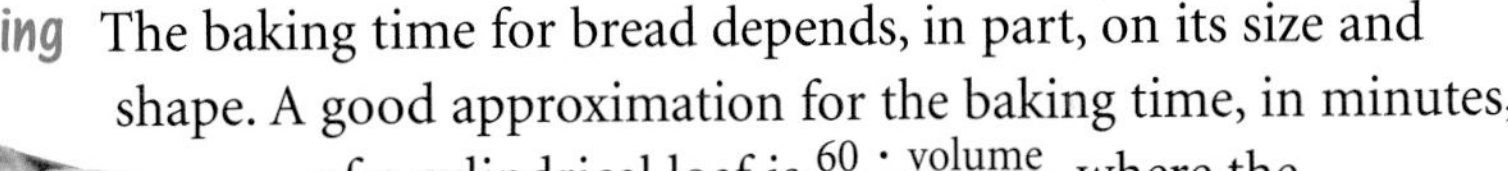

Baking The baking time for bread depends, in part, on its size and shape. A good approximation for the baking time, in minutes, of a cylindrical loaf is $\frac{60 \cdot \text{volume}}{\text{surface area}}$, where the radius r and height h of the baked loaf are in inches. Rewrite this expression in terms of r and h.

$\frac{60 \cdot \text{volume}}{\text{surface area}} = \frac{60\pi r^2 h}{2\pi r^2 + 2\pi rh}$ ← Use formulas for the volume and surface area of a cylinder.

$= \frac{(2)(30)\pi rrh}{2\pi r(r + h)}$ ← Factor the numerator and denominator.

$= \frac{2\pi r}{2\pi r} \cdot \frac{30rh}{r + h}$ ← Rewrite to show a fraction equal to 1.

$= \frac{30rh}{r + h}$ ← Simplify.

You can approximate the baking time using the expression $\frac{30rh}{r + h}$.

7. Check the answer to Example 2 by substituting values for r and h in both the original expression and the simplified expression.

8. **Critical Thinking** What values of r and h make sense in this situation? Would any values you would reasonably choose for r and h be restricted from the domain? Explain.

Multiplying and Dividing Rational Expressions

To multiply the rational expressions $\frac{a}{b}$ and $\frac{c}{d}$, where $b \neq 0$ and $d \neq 0$, you multiply the numerators and multiply the denominators. Then write the product in simplest form.

$$\frac{a}{b} \cdot \frac{c}{d} = \frac{ac}{bd}$$

Example 3

Multiply $\frac{2x+1}{3} \cdot \frac{6x}{4x^2-1}$.

$= \frac{2x+1}{3} \cdot \frac{6x}{(2x+1)(2x-1)}$ ← Factor the denominator.

$= \frac{\cancel{2x+1}^{1}}{\cancel{3}_{1}} \cdot \frac{\cancel{6x}^{2}}{\cancel{(2x+1)}_{1}(2x-1)}$ ← Divide out the common factors 3 and $(2x + 1)$.

$= \frac{2x}{2x-1}$ ← Simplify.

9. What values are restricted from the domain in Example 3?

10. Check the solution to Example 3 by substituting a value for x in the original expression and the simplified expression.

11. Robin's first step in finding the product $\frac{2}{w} \cdot w^5$ was to rewrite the expression as $\frac{2}{w} \cdot \frac{w^5}{1}$. Why do you think Robin did this?

To divide the rational expression $\frac{a}{b}$ by $\frac{c}{d}$, where $b \neq 0$, $c \neq 0$, and $d \neq 0$, you multiply by the reciprocal of $\frac{c}{d}$.

$$\frac{a}{b} \div \frac{c}{d} = \frac{a}{b} \cdot \frac{d}{c}$$

12. Find the reciprocal of each expression.

a. $\frac{-6d^2}{5}$ **b.** $x^2 - 1$ **c.** $\frac{1}{s+4}$

Example 4

Divide $\frac{3x^3}{2}$ by $(-15x^5)$.

$\frac{3x^3}{2} \div (-15x^5) = \frac{3x^3}{2} \cdot \frac{1}{-15x^5}$ ← Multiply by the reciprocal of $-15x^5$.

$= \frac{\cancel{3x^3}^{1}}{2} \cdot \frac{1}{\cancel{-15x^5}_{-5x^2}}$ ← Divide out the common factor $3x^3$.

$= -\frac{1}{10x^2}$ ← Simplify.

13. Try This Find each product or quotient.

a. $\frac{8y^3}{3} \cdot \frac{9}{y^4}$ **b.** $\frac{m-2}{3m+9} \cdot (2m + 6)$ **c.** $\frac{y+3}{y+2} \div (y + 2)$

Exercises ON YOUR OWN

Simplify each expression and state any values restricted from the domain.

1. $\frac{5a^2}{20a}$
2. $\frac{3c}{12c^3}$
3. $\frac{4x-8}{4x+8}$
4. $\frac{24y+18}{36}$
5. $\frac{6a+9}{12}$
6. $\frac{5c-15}{c-3}$
7. $\frac{4x^3}{28x^4}$
8. $\frac{5-2m}{15-6m}$
9. $\frac{24-2p}{48-4p}$
10. $\frac{b-4}{b^2-16}$
11. $\frac{2x^2+2x}{3x^2+3x}$
12. $\frac{2s^2+s}{s^3}$
13. $\frac{3x^2-9x}{x-3}$
14. $\frac{3x+6}{3x^2}$
15. $\frac{w^2+7w}{w^2-49}$
16. $\frac{a^2+2a+1}{a+1}$
17. **Critical Thinking** Explain why $\frac{x^2-9}{x+3}$ is not the same as $x-3$.
18. **Baking** Use the expression $\frac{30rh}{r+h}$, where r is the radius and h is the height, to estimate the baking times in minutes for each type of bread shown.

a.

biscuit:
$r = 1$ **in.,** $h = 0.75$ **in.**

b.

pita:
$r = 3.5$ **in.,** $h = 0.5$ **in.**

c.

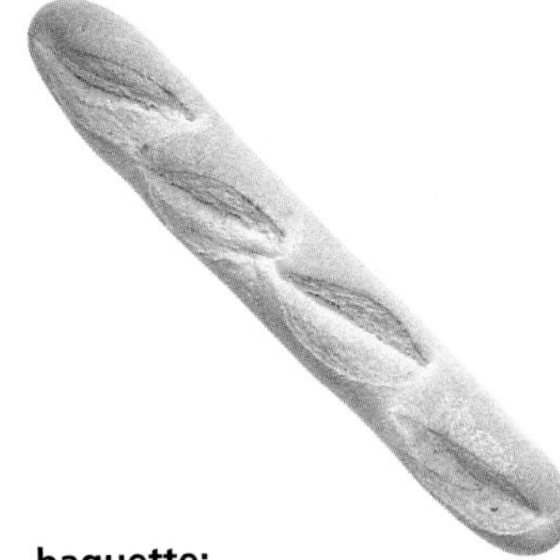

baguette:
$r = 1.25$ **in.,** $h = 26$ **in.**

19. **Writing** Explain why the simplified form of $\frac{7-x}{x-7}$ is -1 when $x \neq 7$.

Find each product or quotient.

20. $\frac{7}{3} \cdot \frac{6}{21}$
21. $\frac{25}{4} \div \left(-\frac{4}{5}\right)$
22. $\frac{7b^2}{10} \div \frac{14b^3}{15}$
23. $\frac{6x^2}{5} \cdot \frac{10}{x^3}$
24. $15x^2 \div \frac{5x^4}{6}$
25. $\frac{-x^3}{8} \div \frac{-x^2}{16}$
26. $\frac{3}{a^2} \div 6a^4$
27. $\frac{5x^3}{x^2} \cdot \frac{3x^4}{10x}$
28. $\frac{x}{x+4} \div \frac{x+3}{x+4}$
29. $\frac{3t+12}{5t} \div \frac{t+4}{10t}$
30. $\frac{3x+9}{x} \div (x+3)$
31. $\frac{y-4}{10} \div \frac{4-y}{5}$
32. $\frac{4x^2+x}{5x} \cdot \frac{15}{2x-2}$
33. $\frac{11k+121}{7k-15} \div (k+11)$
34. **Open-ended** Write an expression that has 2 and -3 restricted from the domain.
35. **Geometry** Write and simplify the ratio for the $\frac{\text{volume of sphere}}{\text{surface area of sphere}}$. The formula for the volume of a sphere is $\frac{4}{3}\pi r^3$, and the formula for the surface area of a sphere is $4\pi r^2$, where r is the radius of the sphere.

36. *Standardized Test Prep* Compare the quantities in Column A and Column B. Assume $x \neq -1, 0$.

Column A	Column B
$\frac{-(5x + 5)}{x + 1}$	$-10x \cdot \frac{2x}{4x^2}$

A. The quantity in Column A is greater.
B. The quantity in Column B is greater.
C. The quantities are equal.
D. The relationship cannot be determined from the information given.

Geometry **Write an expression in simplest form for $\frac{\text{area of shaded figure}}{\text{area of larger figure}}$.**

37.

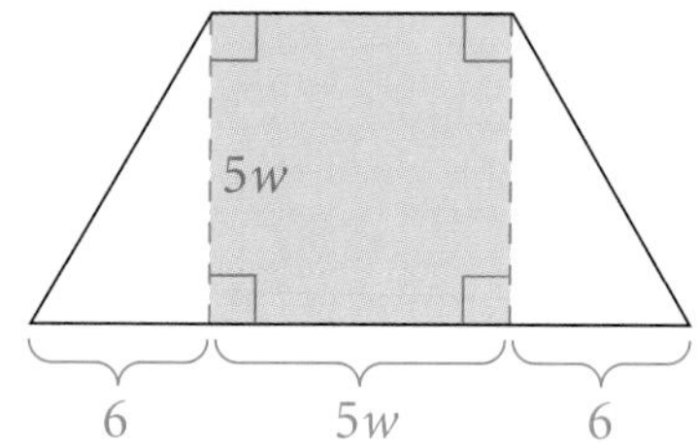

38.

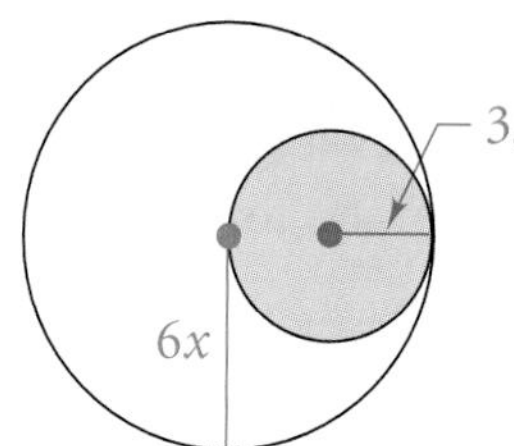

39.

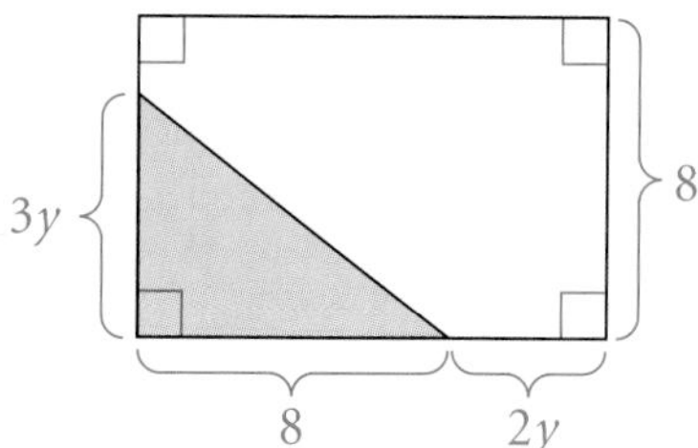

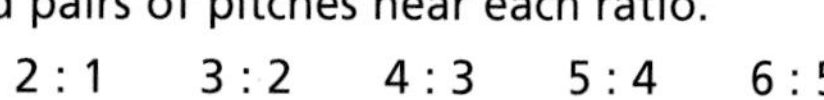

Chapter Project *Find Out by Analyzing*

Pythagoras (540 B.C.) discovered that simple ratios of length produce pleasing combinations of musical pitches.

- Use the lengths you calculated in the Find Out question on page 514 to find pairs of pitches near each ratio.

  2 : 1 3 : 2 4 : 3 5 : 4 6 : 5

- A C-major chord consists of the pitches C, E, G, and C. What ratios are between the pitches of this chord?

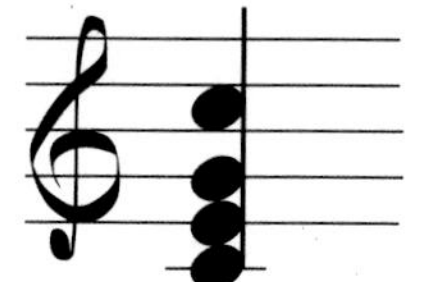

Exercises MIXED REVIEW

Find each product.

40. $y^2(5 - y)$ **41.** $3^x \cdot 3^5$ **42.** $4x^7z^2 \cdot 9xz^{-6}$ **43.** $-6m(2m^3 + 3)$

44. *Writing* Explain why a vertical line cannot be the graph of a function.

Getting Ready for Lesson 11-4

Express each sum or difference in simplest form.

45. $\frac{1}{3} + \frac{1}{3}$ **46.** $\frac{1}{2} - \frac{2}{3}$ **47.** $\frac{4}{5} - \frac{1}{5}$ **48.** $\frac{4}{9} + \frac{1}{6}$

11-4 Operations with Rational Expressions

What You'll Learn

- Adding and subtracting rational expressions
- Finding the LCD of two rational expressions

...And Why

To investigate real-world situations, such as groundspeed for air travel

WORK TOGETHER

Work with a partner to complete the following.

1. Add.
   a. $\frac{4}{9} + \frac{2}{9}$ b. $\frac{4x}{9} + \frac{2x}{9}$ c. $\frac{4}{9x} + \frac{2}{9x}$
2. Subtract.
   a. $\frac{7}{12} - \frac{1}{12}$ b. $\frac{7x}{12} - \frac{x}{12}$ c. $\frac{7}{12x} - \frac{1}{12x}$
3. If $\frac{a}{b}$ and $\frac{c}{b}$ are rational expressions, where $b \neq 0$, write rules for adding and subtracting the two expressions.

THINK AND DISCUSS

In the Work Together activity, you added and subtracted rational expressions with the same monomial denominator. You use the same method when you have a denominator that is a polynomial.

Example 1

Simplify $\frac{2}{x+3} + \frac{5}{x+3}$.

$\frac{2}{x+3} + \frac{5}{x+3} = \frac{2+5}{x+3}$ ← Add the numerators.

$= \frac{7}{x+3}$ ← Simplify the numerator.

4. **Try This** Simplify each expression.
   a. $\frac{3}{x+2} - \frac{2}{x+2}$ b. $\frac{y}{y-5} + \frac{3y}{y-5}$ c. $\frac{5}{n+1} - \frac{2}{n+1}$

To add or subtract rational expressions with different denominators, you must write the expressions with a common denominator. Your work will be simpler if you find the least common denominator (LCD), which is the least common multiple of the denominators.

5. Look at the table below. How is finding the LCD of $\frac{3}{4}$ and $\frac{1}{6}$ like finding the LCD of $\frac{3}{4x}$ and $\frac{1}{6x^2}$?

LCD of Numbers	*LCD of Variable Expressions*
$4 = 2 \cdot 2$	$4x = 2 \cdot 2 \cdot x$
$6 = 2 \cdot 3$	$6x^2 = 2 \cdot 3 \cdot x \cdot x$
$\text{LCD} = 2 \cdot 2 \cdot 3 = 12$	$\text{LCD} = 2 \cdot 2 \cdot 3 \cdot x \cdot x = 12x^2$

Example 2

Simplify $\frac{2}{3x} + \frac{1}{6}$.

Step 1: Find the LCD of $\frac{2}{3x}$ and $\frac{1}{6}$.

$3x = 3 \cdot x$ and $6 = 2 \cdot 3$ ← Factor each denominator.

The LCD is $3 \cdot x \cdot 2$ or $6x$.

PROBLEM SOLVING

Look Back Why is multiplying both the numerator and the denominator of a fraction by $2x$ equivalent to multiplying the fraction by 1?

Step 2: Rewrite the original expression and add.

$\frac{2}{3x} = \frac{2 \cdot 2}{3x \cdot 2} = \frac{4}{6x}$ ← Multiply numerator and denominator by 2.

$\frac{1}{6} = \frac{1 \cdot x}{6 \cdot x} = \frac{x}{6x}$ ← Multiply numerator and denominator by x.

Step 3: Rewrite the original expression and add.

$\frac{2}{3x} + \frac{1}{6} = \frac{4}{6x} + \frac{x}{6x}$ ← Replace each expression with its equivalent.

$= \frac{4 + x}{6x}$ ← Add the numerators.

6. Try This Simplify.

a. $\frac{5}{12b} + \frac{1}{36b^2}$ b. $\frac{3}{7y^4} + \frac{2}{3y^2}$ c. $\frac{4}{25x} - \frac{49}{100}$

You can factor to find the LCD when the denominators are polynomials.

Example 3

Simplify $\frac{1}{y^2 + 5y + 4} - \frac{3}{5y + 5}$.

Step 1: Find the LCD.

$y^2 + 5y + 4 = (y + 1)(y + 4)$ and $5y + 5 = 5(y + 1)$ ← Factor each denominator.

The LCD is $5(y + 1)(y + 4)$.

Step 2: Write equivalent expressions with denominator $5(y + 1)(y + 4)$.

$\frac{1}{(y + 1)(y + 4)} = \frac{5}{5(y + 1)(y + 4)}$ ← Multiply numerator and denominator by 5.

$\frac{3}{5(y + 1)} = \frac{3(y + 4)}{5(y + 1)(y + 4)}$ ← Multiply numerator and denominator by $(y + 4)$.

Step 3: Subtract.

$$\frac{5}{5(y + 1)(y + 4)} - \frac{3(y + 4)}{5(y + 1)(y + 4)} = \frac{5 - 3(y + 4)}{5(y + 1)(y + 4)}$$
$$= \frac{5 - 3y - 12}{5(y + 1)(y + 4)}$$
$$= \frac{-7 - 3y}{5(y + 1)(y + 4)}$$

7. Explain why the LCD in Example 3 is not $5(y + 1)(y + 1)(y + 4)$.

You can combine rational expressions to investigate real-world situations.

Example 4 Relating to the Real World 

Air Travel The groundspeed for jet traffic from Los Angeles to New York City is about 15% faster than the groundspeed from New York City to Los Angeles. This difference is due to a strong westerly wind at high altitudes. If r is a jet's groundspeed from New York to Los Angeles, write an expression for the round-trip air time. The two cities are about 2500 mi apart.

QUICK REVIEW

15% more than a number is 115% of the number.
115% = 1.15.

NYC to LA time: $\frac{2500}{r}$ ← time = $\frac{\text{distance}}{\text{rate}}$

LA to NYC time: $\frac{2500}{1.15r}$ ← time = $\frac{\text{distance}}{\text{rate}}$

Write an expression for the total time.

$$\frac{2500}{r} + \frac{2500}{1.15r} = \frac{2875}{1.15r} + \frac{2500}{1.15r}$$ ← Rewrite using the LCD.

$$= \frac{5375}{1.15r}$$ ← Add.

$$\approx \frac{4674}{r}$$ ← Simplify.

The expression $\frac{4674}{r}$ approximates the total time for the trip, where r is the speed of the jet.

8. Suppose a jet flies from Los Angeles to New York City at 420 mi/h. How long will the round-trip take?

Exercises ON YOUR OWN

Simplify the following expressions.

1. $\frac{4}{5} + \frac{3}{5}$
2. $\frac{6}{x} + \frac{1}{x}$
3. $-\frac{2}{3b} - \frac{4}{3b}$
4. $\frac{5}{h} - \frac{3}{h}$
5. $\frac{7}{11g} - \frac{3}{11g}$
6. $\frac{3x}{7} + \frac{6x}{7}$
7. $\frac{5}{6d} + \frac{7}{6d}$
8. $\frac{5x}{9} - \frac{x}{9}$
9. $\frac{3n}{7} + \frac{2n}{7}$
10. $\frac{6}{17p} - \frac{9}{17p}$
11. $\frac{12r}{5} + \frac{14r}{5}$
12. $-\frac{8}{7k} - \frac{9}{7k}$

Find the LCD.

13. $\frac{1}{2x}; \frac{1}{4x^2}$
14. $\frac{b}{6}; \frac{2b}{9}$
15. $\frac{6}{2m^2}; \frac{1}{m}$
16. $\frac{1}{z}; \frac{3}{7z}$
17. $\frac{-5}{6t^5}; \frac{3}{2t^2}$
18. $\frac{3}{7s^5}; \frac{-4}{5s^2}$
19. $\frac{24}{23d^3}; \frac{25}{2d^4}$
20. $-\frac{3y^2}{15}; \frac{11y^5}{6}$
21. $\frac{6a}{5}; \frac{-5}{a}$
22. $\frac{7}{2k^4}; \frac{7}{9k^{11}}$
23. $\frac{8}{5b}; \frac{12}{7b^3}$
24. $\frac{6}{h^7}; \frac{1}{k^3}$

Simplify.

25. $\frac{7}{3a} + \frac{2}{5a^4}$
26. $\frac{4}{x} - \frac{2}{3x^5}$
27. $\frac{6}{5x^8} + \frac{4}{3x^6}$
28. $\frac{12}{k} - \frac{5}{k^2}$
29. $\frac{3}{6b} - \frac{4}{2b^4}$
30. $\frac{2}{y} + \frac{3}{5y}$
31. $\frac{3}{8m^3} + \frac{1}{12m^2}$
32. $\frac{1}{5x^3} + \frac{3}{20x^2}$
33. $-\frac{5}{4k} - \frac{8}{9k}$
34. $\frac{27}{n^3} - \frac{9}{7n^2}$
35. $\frac{9}{4x^2} + \frac{9}{5}$
36. $\frac{5}{12m^3} + \frac{7}{6m^8}$

37. a. **Exercise** Suppose Jane walks one mile from her house to her grandparents' house. Then she returns home walking with her grandfather. Her return rate is 70% of her normal walking rate. Let r represent her normal walking rate. Write an expression for the amount of time Jane spends walking.
    b. Suppose Jane's normal walking rate is 3 mi/h. How much time does she spend walking?

Simplify.

38. $\frac{10}{x-1} - \frac{5}{x-1}$
39. $\frac{7}{m+1} + \frac{3}{m+1}$
40. $\frac{4}{6m-1} + \frac{3}{6m-1}$
41. $\frac{m}{m+3} + \frac{2}{m+3}$
42. $\frac{3n}{n+4} - \frac{n-8}{n+4}$
43. $\frac{5}{t^2+1} - \frac{3}{t^2+1}$
44. $\frac{y}{y-1} - \frac{1}{y-1}$
45. $\frac{s}{4s^2+2} + \frac{2}{4s^2+2}$
46. $\frac{1}{2-b} - \frac{4}{2-b}$
47. $\frac{1}{m+2} + \frac{1}{m^2+3m+2}$
48. $\frac{4}{x-5} - \frac{3}{x+5}$
49. $\frac{5}{y+2} + \frac{4}{y^2-y-6}$

50. **Writing** When adding or subtracting rational expressions, will the answer be in simplest form if you use the LCD? Explain.

51. **Open-ended** Write two rational expressions with different denominators. Find the LCD and add the two expressions.

Chapter Project

Find Out by Creating

How does a flute or a pipe organ create different pitches? Get two cardboard tubes used to hold wrapping paper or to mail posters. Cut one tube into two lengths A and B whose ratio is 2:1. Hold your hand tightly over the longer piece (A) and blow over the open end until you get a pitch. Now try the shorter piece. What do you hear?

Cut two more pieces from the other tube by measuring them against piece A. Make one $\frac{2}{3}$ of A and the other $\frac{4}{5}$ of A. (You should have a small piece left over.) Get some friends together and play the first phrase of "The Star Spangled Banner."

Exercises MIXED REVIEW

Find the hypotenuse of a right triangle with the given legs.

52. $a = 9, b = 12$ **53.** $a = 10, b = 7$ **54.** $a = 12, b = 5$ **55.** $a = 6, b = 9$

56. Population Surveys The 1990 census may have missed 4 million people out of about 250 million people living in the United States. What percent of the people may have been missed?

Getting Ready for Lesson 11-5

Mental Math **Find the value of each variable.**

57. $\frac{1}{2} + \frac{1}{m} = \frac{3}{4}$ **58.** $\frac{3}{x} + \frac{1}{x} = 1$ **59.** $\frac{2}{n} + \frac{1}{n} = \frac{1}{2}$ **60.** $\frac{4}{3} - \frac{2}{x} = \frac{2}{3}$

Algebra at Work

Electrician

More than half a million men and women make their livings as electricians. All are highly skilled technicians licensed by the states in which they work. Electricians use formulas containing rational expressions. For example, when a circuit connected "in parallel" contains two resistors with resistances r_1 and r_2 ohms, the total resistance R (in ohms) of the circuit can be found using the formula $\frac{1}{R} = \frac{1}{r_1} + \frac{1}{r_2}$.

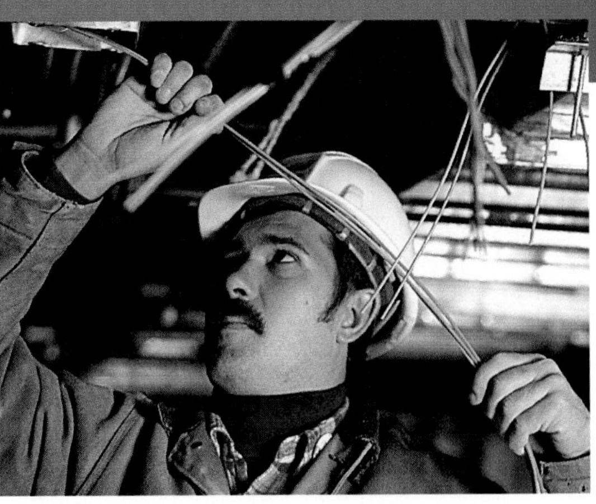

Mini Project: Research the difference between circuits connected *in parallel* and *in series*. Write a brief report of your findings. Include diagrams with your report.

Connections · Business . . . and more

What You'll Learn

- Solving equations involving rational expressions

...And Why

To solve real-world situations, such as those involving mail processors

11-5 Solving Rational Equations

THINK AND DISCUSS

A **rational equation** contains rational expressions. A method for solving rational equations is similar to the method you learned in Chapter 3 for solving equations with rational numbers.

Solving Equations with Rational Numbers

$\frac{1}{2}x + \frac{3}{4} = \frac{1}{5}$ ← The denominators are 2, 4, and 5. The LCD is 20.

$20\left(\frac{1}{2}x + \frac{3}{4}\right) = 20\left(\frac{1}{5}\right)$ ← Multiply each side by 20.

$\overset{10}{\cancel{20}}\left(\frac{1}{\underset{1}{\cancel{2}}}x\right) + \overset{5}{\cancel{20}}\left(\frac{3}{\underset{1}{\cancel{4}}}\right) = \overset{4}{\cancel{20}}\left(\frac{1}{\underset{1}{\cancel{5}}}\right)$ ← Use the distributive property.

$10x + 15 = 4$ ← No fractions! This equation is much easier to solve.

Solving Equations with Rational Expressions

$\frac{1}{2x} + \frac{3}{4} = \frac{1}{5x}$ ← The denominators are $2x$, 4, and $5x$. The LCD is $20x$.

$20x\left(\frac{1}{2x} + \frac{3}{4}\right) = 20x\left(\frac{1}{5x}\right)$ ← Multiply each side by $20x$.

$\overset{10}{\cancel{20x}}\left(\frac{1}{\underset{1}{\cancel{2x}}}\right) + \overset{5}{\cancel{20}}x\left(\frac{3}{\underset{1}{\cancel{4}}}\right) = \overset{4}{\cancel{20x}}\left(\frac{1}{\underset{1}{\cancel{5x}}}\right)$ ← Use the distributive property.

$10 + 15x = 4$ ← No rational expressions! Now you can solve.

1. Find the LCD of each equation.

a. $\frac{3}{4n} - \frac{1}{2} = \frac{2}{n}$ **b.** $\frac{1}{3x} + \frac{2}{5} = \frac{4}{3x}$ **c.** $\frac{1}{8y} = \frac{5}{6} - \frac{1}{y}$

There are often values that are excluded from the domain of a rational expression. When you solve rational equations, check your solutions to be sure that your answer satisfies the original equation.

Example 1

Solve $\frac{5}{x^2} = \frac{6}{x} - 1$.

$x^2\left(\frac{5}{x^2}\right) = x^2\left(\frac{6}{x} - 1\right)$ ← Multiply each side by the LCD, x^2.

$\overset{1}{\cancel{x^2}}\left(\frac{5}{\underset{1}{\cancel{x^2}}}\right) = \overset{x}{\cancel{x^2}}\left(\frac{6}{\underset{1}{\cancel{x}}}\right) - x^2(1)$ ← Use the distributive property.

$5 = 6x - x^2$ ← Simplify.

$x^2 - 6x + 5 = 0$ ← Collect terms on one side.

$(x - 5)(x - 1) = 0$ ← Factor the quadratic expression.

$(x - 5) = 0$ or $(x - 1) = 0$ ← Use the zero-product property.

$x = 5$ $\quad x = 1$ ← Solve.

Check $\frac{5}{5^2} \stackrel{?}{=} \frac{6}{5} - 1$ $\qquad \frac{5}{1^2} \stackrel{?}{=} \frac{6}{1} - 1$

$\frac{1}{5} = \frac{1}{5}$ ✔ $\qquad 5 = 5$ ✔

Since 5 and 1 check in the original equation, they are the solutions.

Example 2 Relating to the Real World 

Business The Fresia Company owns two electronic mail processors. The newer machine works three times as fast as the older one. Together the two machines process 1000 pieces of mail in 25 min. How long does it take each machine, working alone, to process 1000 pieces of mail?

Define

	Time to process 1000 pieces (min)	Processing rate (pieces/min)
New machine	n	$\frac{1000}{n}$
Old machine	$3n$	$\frac{1000}{3n}$
Both machines	25	$\frac{1000}{25} = 40$

Relate Processing rate of new machine + Processing rate of old machine = Processing rate of both machines

Write $\frac{1000}{n} + \frac{1000}{3n} = 40$

$3n\left(\frac{1000}{n} + \frac{1000}{3n}\right) = 3n(40)$ ← Multiply each side by the LCD, $3n$.

$\overset{3}{3n}\left(\frac{1000}{\cancel{n}_1}\right) + \overset{1}{\cancel{3n}}\left(\frac{1000}{\cancel{3n}_1}\right) = 3n(40)$ ← Use the distributive property.

$3000 + 1000 = 120n$ ← Simplify.

$4000 = 120n$

$33.3 \approx n$ ← Divide each side by 120.

The new machine can process 1000 pieces of mail in about 33 min. The old machine takes $3 \cdot 33.3$, or 100 min, to process 1000 pieces of mail.

2. **Try This** Solve each equation.

a. $\frac{1}{3} + \frac{1}{3x} = \frac{1}{7}$

b. $\frac{2}{3x} = \frac{1}{5} - \frac{3}{x}$

The process of multiplying by the LCD can sometimes lead to a solution that does not check in the original equation.

Example 3

Solve $\frac{-1}{x-2} = \frac{x-4}{2(x-2)} + \frac{1}{3}$.

The LCD is $6(x-2)$. Multiply each side by the LCD, then solve.

$$6(x-2)\left(\frac{-1}{x-2}\right) = 6(x-2)\left(\frac{x-4}{2(x-2)} + \frac{1}{3}\right)$$

$$6(x-2)\left(\frac{-1}{x-2}\right) = 6(x-2)\left(\frac{x-4}{2(x-2)}\right) + 6(x-2)\left(\frac{1}{3}\right)$$

$$-6 = 3(x-4) + 2(x-2) \quad \longleftarrow \text{Simplify.}$$

$$-6 = 3x - 12 + 2x - 4 \quad \longleftarrow \text{distributive property}$$

$$-6 = 5x - 16 \quad \longleftarrow \text{Combine like terms.}$$

$$10 = 5x \quad \longleftarrow \text{Add 16 to each side.}$$

$$2 = x \quad \longleftarrow \text{Divide each side by 5.}$$

Check

$$\frac{-1}{2-2} \stackrel{?}{=} \frac{2-4}{2(2-2)} + \frac{1}{3}$$

$$\frac{-1}{0} = \frac{-2}{0} + \frac{1}{3} \quad \longleftarrow \text{Undefined!}$$

The equation has *no* solution because 2 makes a denominator equal 0.

3. **Try This** Solve each equation. Be sure to check your answers!

a. $\frac{2}{x} - \frac{8}{x^2} = -1$

b. $\frac{1}{w+1} = 1 - \frac{1}{w(w+1)}$

Exercises ON YOUR OWN

1. Carlos studied the problem at the right and said, "I'll start by finding the LCD." Ingrid studied the problem and said, "I'll start by cross-multiplying."

   Solve $\frac{40}{x} = \frac{15}{x-20}$.

   a. Solve the equation using Carlos's method, and then using Ingrid's method.

   b. **Writing** Which method do you prefer? Why?

   c. **Critical Thinking** Will Ingrid's method work for all rational equations? Explain.

Solve each equation. Be sure to check your answers!

2. $\frac{1}{2} + \frac{2}{x} = \frac{1}{x}$

3. $\frac{1}{20} + \frac{1}{30} = \frac{1}{x}$

4. $5 + \frac{2}{p} = \frac{17}{p}$

5. $\frac{3}{a} - \frac{5}{a} = 2$

6. $\frac{5}{n} - \frac{1}{2} = 2$

7. $\frac{1}{x+2} = \frac{1}{2x}$

8. $y - \frac{6}{y} = 5$

9. $\frac{30}{x + 3} = \frac{30}{x - 3}$

10. $\frac{4}{a + 1} = \frac{8}{2 - a}$

11. $\frac{5}{y} + \frac{3}{2} = \frac{1}{3y}$

12. $\frac{2}{3b} - \frac{3}{4} = \frac{1}{6b}$

13. $\frac{5}{2s} + \frac{3}{4} = \frac{9}{4s}$

14. **Business** The PRX Company owns one scanning machine that scans 10,000 documents in 25 min. The company then buys a newer scanner, and together, the two machines scan 10,000 documents in 10 min. How long would it take the newer machine, working alone, to scan 10,000 documents?

15. **Plumbing** You can fill a 30-gallon tub in 15 min with both faucets running. If the cold water faucet runs twice as fast as the hot water faucet, how long will it take to fill the tub with only cold water?

16. **Graphing Calculator** Write two functions using the expressions on each side of the equation $\frac{6}{x^2} + 1 = \frac{(x + 7)^2}{6}$. Graph the functions. Find the coordinates of the points of intersection. Are the x-values solutions to the equation? Explain.

Geometry **Find each value of x if the area of each shaded region is 64 square units. Assume that each quadrilateral shown is a rectangle.**

17.

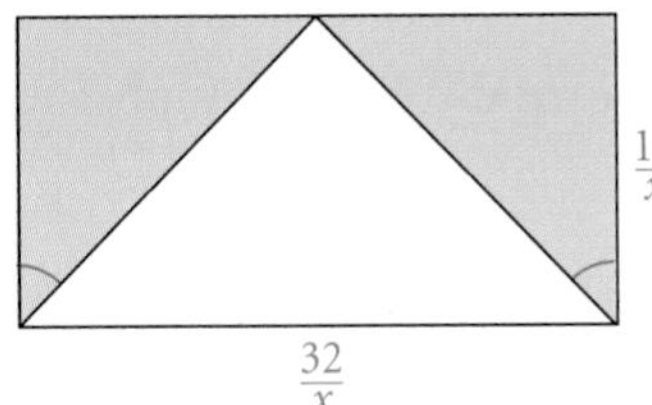

18.

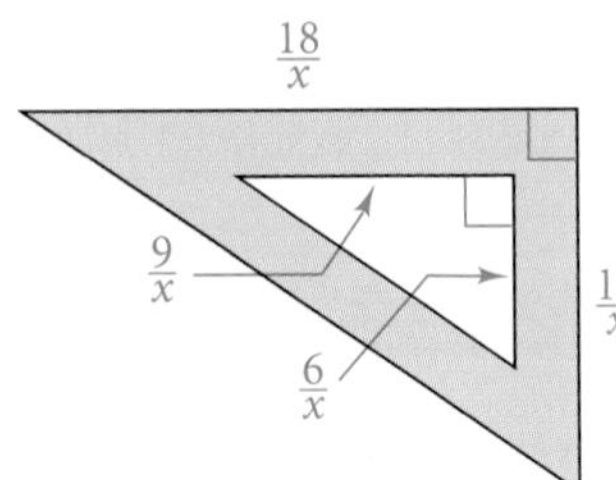

19.

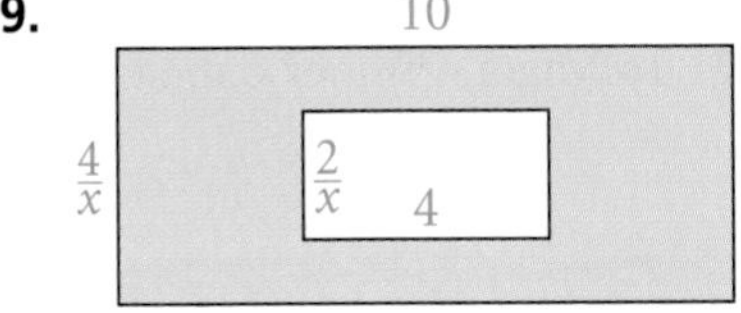

Solve each equation. Be sure to check your answers!

20. $\frac{1}{2} = -\frac{1}{3(x - 3)}$

21. $\frac{1}{t - 2} = \frac{t}{8}$

22. $\frac{x - 11}{3x} = \frac{x - 19}{5x}$

23. $\frac{4}{3(c + 4)} + 1 = \frac{2c}{c + 4}$

24. $\frac{8}{x + 3} = \frac{1}{x} + 1$

25. $\frac{x + 2}{x + 4} = \frac{x - 2}{x - 1}$

26. $\frac{2}{c - 2} = 2 - \frac{4}{c}$

27. $\frac{5}{3p} + \frac{2}{3} = \frac{5 + p}{2p}$

28. $\frac{3}{s - 1} + 1 = \frac{12}{s^2 - 1}$

29. **Standardized Test Prep** Which inequality contains both of the solutions of the equation $5x = \frac{7}{2} + \frac{6}{x}$?

   A. $-1 < x < 3$
   B. $0 < x < \frac{3}{2}$
   C. $-2 \leq x < 0$
   D. $-3 \leq x \leq -1$
   E. none of the above

30. A plane flies 450 mi/h. It can travel 980 mi with a wind in the same amount of time as it travels 820 mi against the wind. Solve the equation $\frac{980}{450 + s} = \frac{820}{450 - s}$ to find the speed s of the wind.

31. Find the value of each variable. $\begin{bmatrix} \frac{5a}{3} & \frac{7}{3b} \\ \frac{2c-15}{35c} & \frac{5}{2d}+\frac{3}{4} \end{bmatrix} = \begin{bmatrix} 2+\frac{7a}{6} & 9 \\ \frac{1}{5c} & \frac{9}{4d} \end{bmatrix}$

Chapter Project ***Find Out by Interviewing***

The pitch produced by a vibrating string is affected by how tightly it is stretched, or its tension. Find out how a violin, guitar, or other stringed instrument is tuned by talking with someone who plays it.

Exercises MIXED REVIEW

Solve each equation. Round to the nearest hundredth, where necessary.

32. $x^2 = 3x + 8$ 33. $x^2 - 4 = 0$ 34. $2x^2 + 6 = 4x$ 35. $7x = 5x - 11$

36. **Open-ended** Give an example of two quantities that vary inversely. Write an equation to go with your example.

Getting Ready for Lesson 11-6

List the possible outcomes of each action.

37. rolling a number cube once 38. tossing a coin twice 39. tossing a coin and rolling a number cube

Exercises CHECKPOINT

Simplify each expresssion and state any restrictions on the variable.

1. $\frac{8m^2}{2m^3}$ 2. $\frac{6x^2 - 24}{x + 2}$ 3. $\frac{3c + 9}{3c - 9}$ 4. $\frac{3z^2 + 12z}{z^4}$

5. **Open-ended** Write an expression where the variable cannot equal 3.

Solve each equation.

6. $\frac{9}{t} + \frac{3}{2} = 12$ 7. $\frac{10}{z + 4} = \frac{30}{2z + 3}$ 8. $\frac{1}{m - 2} = \frac{5}{m}$ 9. $c - \frac{8}{c} = 10$

Find each sum or difference.

10. $\frac{5}{c} + \frac{4}{c}$ 11. $\frac{9}{x - 3} - \frac{4}{x - 3}$ 12. $\frac{8}{m + 2} - \frac{6}{3 - m}$ 13. $\frac{6}{t} + \frac{3}{t^2}$

14. **Standardized Test Prep** What is the LCD of $\frac{8}{n}, \frac{5}{3 - n}$, and $\frac{1}{n^2}$?

A. $n^2 + 3n$ B. $3n^2 - n^3$ C. $n^2 + 3$ D. $3n^3 - n^4$ E. $n^3 - 3n^2$

Math ToolboX

Problem Solving

Algebraic Reasoning

After Lesson 11-5

You can use the properties you have studied and the three below to prove algebraic relationships and to justify steps in the solution of an equation.

Properties of Equality

For all real numbers a, b, and c:

Reflexive Property: $a = a$ Example: $5x = 5x$

Symmetric Property: If $a = b$, then $b = a$. Example: If $15 = 3t$, then $3t = 15$.

Transitive Property: If $a = b$ and $b = c$, then $a = c$. Example: If $d = 3y$ and $3y = 6$, then $d = 6$.

Example 1

Prove that if $a = b$, then $ac = bc$.

Statements	Reasons
$a = b$	← Given
$ac = ac$	← Reflexive prop.
$ac = bc$	← Substitute b for a.

Example 2

Solve $-32 = 4(y - 3)$. Justify each step.

Steps	Reasons
$-32 = 4(y - 3)$	← Given
$-32 = 4y - 12$	← Distributive prop.
$-20 = 4y$	← Addition prop. of equality
$-5 = y$	← Division prop. of equality
$y = -5$	← Symmetric prop. of equality

Name the property that each exercise illustrates.

1. If $3.8 = z$, then $z = 3.8$.
2. If $x = \frac{1}{2}y$, and $\frac{1}{2}y = -2$, then $x = -2$.
3. $-4r = -4r$

Supply the missing reasons.

4. Solve $-5 = 1 + 3d$. Justify each step.

Steps	Reasons
$-5 = 1 + 3d$	← Given
$-6 = 3d$	← **a.** ?
$-2 = d$	← **b.** ?
$d = -2$	← **c.** ?

5. Prove that if $ax^2 + bx = 0$, then $x = 0$ or $-\frac{b}{a}$.

Statements	Reasons
$ax^2 + bx = 0$	← Given
$x^2 + \frac{b}{a}x = 0$	← **a.** ?
$x(x + \frac{b}{a}) = 0$	← **b.** ?
$x = 0$ or $x + \frac{b}{a} = 0$	← Zero-product prop.
$x = 0$ or $x = -\frac{b}{a}$	← **c.** ?

6. *Writing* If Cal is Mia's cousin, then Mia is Cal's cousin. This relationship is symmetric. Describe a relationship that is transitive.

What You'll Learn

- Using the multiplication counting principle to count outcomes
- Using permutations to count outcomes
- Finding probability

...And Why

To investigate the number of arrangements in situations such as the arrangement of players on a team

What You'll Need

- calculator

11-6 Counting Outcomes and Permutations

WORK TOGETHER

Entertainment Suppose you play the following CDs:

- *cracked rear view* by Hootie and the Blowfish
- *Design of a Decade* by Janet Jackson
- *Destiny* by Gloria Estefan

1. In how many different orders can you play the CDs?
2. Describe how you determined the number of different ways to order the CDs.
3. What is the probability that the CDs will be played in alphabetical order?

THINK AND DISCUSS

Using the Multiplication Counting Principle

One way you could find outcomes is to make an organized list or a tree diagram. Both help you to see if you have thought of all possibilities.

Suppose you have three shirts and two pair of pants that coordinate well together. You can use a tree diagram to find the number of possible outfits you have.

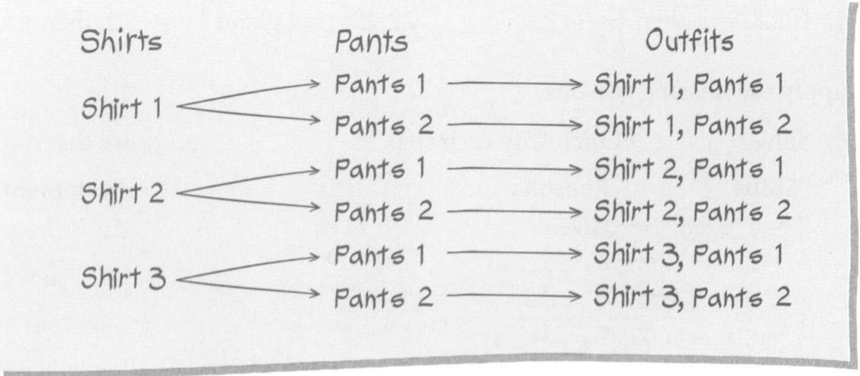

There are six possible outfits.

4. Would you want to use a tree diagram to find the number of outfits for five shirts and eight pairs of pants? Explain.

QUICK REVIEW

When one event does not affect the result of a second event, they are *independent events*.

When events are independent, you can find the number of outcomes by using the multiplication counting principle.

Multiplication Counting Principle

If there are m ways to make a first selection and n ways to make a second selection, there are $m \times n$ ways to make the two selections.

Example: For 3 shirts and 2 pairs of pants, the number of possible outfits is $3 \cdot 2 = 6$.

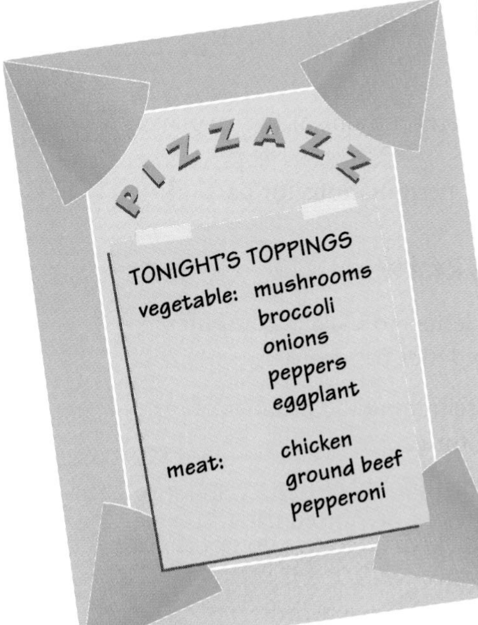

Example 1 **Relating to the Real World** 

Travel Suppose there are two routes you can choose to get from Austin, Texas, to Dallas, Texas, and four routes from Dallas to Tulsa, Oklahoma. How many routes are there from Austin to Tulsa through Dallas?

$2 \cdot 4 = 8$ ← routes from Austin to Tulsa through Dallas

(2: routes from Austin to Dallas; 4: routes from Dallas to Tulsa)

There are eight possible routes from Austin to Tulsa.

5. **Try This** At the neighborhood pizza shop, there are five vegetable toppings and three meat toppings for a pizza. How many possible pizzas can you order with one meat and one vegetable topping?

Finding Permutations

ABC	ACB
BAC	BCA
CAB	CBA

A common kind of counting problem is to find the number of arrangements of a set of objects. The list at the left shows the possible arrangements for the letters A, B, and C without repeating any letters in an arrangement.

Each of the arrangements is called a permutation. A **permutation** is an arrangement of some or all of a set of objects in a specific order.

Example 2 **Relating to the Real World** 

Sports In how many ways can nine baseball players be listed for batting order?

There are 9 choices for the first batter, 8 for the second, 7 for the third, and so on.

$9 \cdot 8 \cdot 7 \cdot 6 \cdot 5 \cdot 4 \cdot 3 \cdot 2 \cdot 1 = 362880$ ← Use a calculator.

There are 362,880 possible arrangements of the batters.

CALCULATOR HINT

The notation 9!, read as *nine factorial*, means the product of the integers from 9 to 1. Use this sequence to find 9!:

 MATH PRB! 

6. **Critical Thinking** Why are there only 8 choices for the second batter and 7 choices for the third batter?

CALCULATOR HINT

You can use the following calculator steps to find $_8P_3$:

8 MATH **PRB $_NP_R$** 3 

In how many ways can you select a right, center, and left fielder from eight people? This means finding the number of permutations of 8 objects (players) arranged 3 at a time. You can use $_nP_r$ to express the number of permutations where n equals the number of objects and r equals the number of selections to make. Eight players arranged three at a time is $_8P_3$.

You can use the multiplication counting principle to evaluate permutations.

$_8P_3 = 8 \cdot 7 \cdot 6$, or 336 arrangements of 8 players arranged 3 at a time.

$_nP_r = n(n-1)(n-2)\ldots$ Stop when you have r factors.

first factor (points to n); number of factors (points to r)

7. a. Use $_nP_r$ to express the number of permutations of twelve players for five positions on a baseball team.

b. *Calculator* Evaluate the number of permutations for part (a).

Example 3 Relating to the Real World 

Computers Suppose you use six different letters to make a computer password. Find the number of possible six-letter passwords.

There are 26 letters in the alphabet. You are finding the number of permutations of 26 letters arranged 6 at a time.

$_{26}P_6 = 26 \cdot 25 \cdot 24 \cdot 23 \cdot 22 \cdot 21 = 165{,}765{,}600$ ← Use a calculator.

There are 165,765,600 six-letter passwords in which letters do not repeat.

8. What would $_{26}P_8$ mean if you were making a password?

9. a. *Probability* Lena wants a password that uses the four letters of her name. How many permutations are possible using each letter in her name only once?

b. Suppose a four-letter password with no repeated letters is assigned randomly. What is the probability that it uses the letters L, E, N, and A?

c. *Critical Thinking* Is creating a password based on your name a good idea? Explain.

Exercises ON YOUR OWN

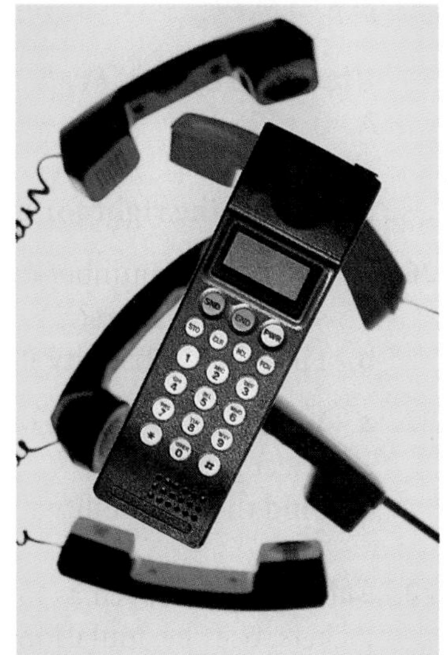

1. **Jobs** James must wear a shirt and tie for a job interview. He has two dress shirts and five ties. How many shirt-tie choices does he have?

2. **Telephones** A seven-digit telephone number can begin with any digit except 0 and 1.
   a. How many possible choices are there for the first digit? the second digit? the third digit? the seventh digit?
   b. How many different seven-digit telephone numbers are possible?

3. On a bookshelf there are five novels, two volumes of short stories, and three biographies. In how many ways can you select one of each?

4. A student council has 24 members. A 3-person committee is to arrange a car wash. Each person on the committee will have a task: One person will find a location, another will organize publicity, and the third will schedule workers. In how many different ways can three students be selected and assigned a job?

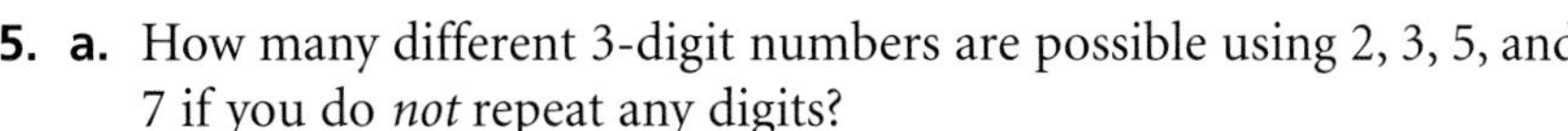

5. a. How many different 3-digit numbers are possible using 2, 3, 5, and 7 if you do *not* repeat any digits?
   b. **Critical Thinking** How many of the 3-digit numbers are even?
   c. **Writing** Explain how you found how many numbers are even in part (b).
   d. What is the probability that a number selected at random is even?

Calculator **Use a calculator to evaluate.**

6. $_8P_3$	7. $_7P_3$	8. $_6P_3$	9. $_5P_3$	10. $_4P_3$	11. $_3P_3$
12. $_7P_7$	13. $_7P_6$	14. $_7P_5$	15. $_7P_4$	16. $_7P_2$	17. $_7P_1$

18. **School Paper** For an article in the school newspaper, Cora took a poll in which she asked students to rank the top four basketball players on the high school team. There are fifteen members on the team. How many possible outcomes are there?

19. **Writing** Write a problem for which $_{24}P_3$ would be the solution.

20. a. **Open-ended** Use the letters of your last name. If any letters are repeated, use only one of them. For example, for the last name Bell, use the letters BEL. In how many ways can the resulting letters be arranged?
    b. In how many ways can two different letters be selected and arranged from your last name?

21. **Sports** In ice skating competitions, the order in which competitors skate is determined by a draw. If there are eight skaters in the finals, how many different orders are possible for the final program?

Calculator **Which is greater?**

22. ${}_8P_6$ or ${}_6P_2$

23. ${}_9P_7$ or ${}_9P_2$

24. ${}_{10}P_3$ or ${}_8P_4$

25. *Standardized Test Prep* For $r = 3$ and ${}_nP_r = 210$, find n.
   A. 3 B. 6 C. 7 D. 8 E. 70

Use the tiles at the right for Exercises 26 and 27.

26. a. What is the number of possible arrangements in which you can select four letters?
    b. Find the probability that you select C, A, R, and then E.

27. a. What is the number of possible arrangements in which you can select five letters?
    b. Find the probability that you select B, R, A, I, and then N.

28. *Safety* A lock, such as the ones used on many bikes and school lockers, uses permutations. This is because the order of the numbers *is* important. Suppose you have a lock with the digits 0–9. A three-digit sequence opens the lock, and no numbers are repeated.
    a. How many different sequences are possible?
    b. How many sequences use a 7 as the first digit?
    c. What is the probability that the sequence of numbers that opens your lock uses a 7 as the first digit?
    d. *Critical Thinking* What is the probability that the sequence of numbers that opens your lock includes a 7?

Exercises MIXED REVIEW

Graph each function.

29. $y = 6x$

30. $y = \sqrt{x}$

31. $y = \frac{5}{x}$

32. $y = |x| + 3$

33. *Camping* Your family is planning a camping trip. The state park has two camping plans available. The first costs $95 for four nights at a campsite with family trail passes for three days. The second costs $70 for three nights at a campsite with family trail passes for two days. There is one daily charge for the campsite and one daily charge for the trail pass. Find each daily charge.

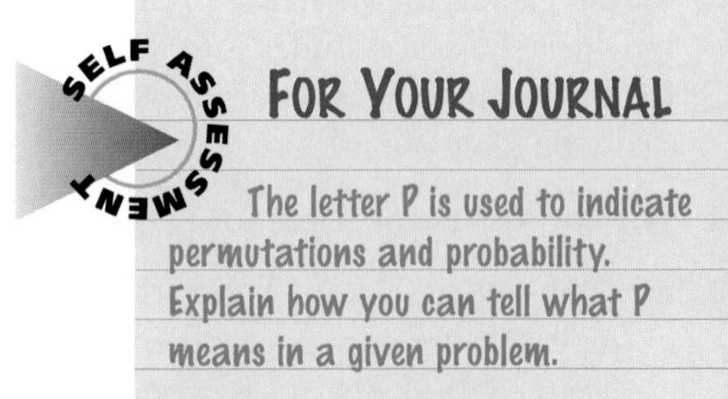

SELF ASSESSMENT
FOR YOUR JOURNAL
The letter P is used to indicate permutations and probability. Explain how you can tell what P means in a given problem.

Getting Ready for Lesson 11-7

***A* and *B* are independent events. Find *P*(*A* and *B*) for the given probabilities.**

34. $P(A) = \frac{1}{3}, P(B) = \frac{3}{4}$

35. $P(A) = \frac{1}{8}, P(B) = \frac{5}{9}$

36. $P(A) = \frac{9}{10}, P(B) = \frac{5}{6}$

11-7 Combinations

What You'll Learn

- Finding combinations
- Solving probability problems involving combinations

...And Why

To investigate situations like selecting a jury

What You'll Need

- calculator

THINK AND DISCUSS

Food Suppose you are making a sandwich with three of these ingredients: turkey, cheese, tomato, and lettuce. Below are the permutations of the four ingredients taken three at a time.

- turkey, cheese, tomato
- turkey, tomato, cheese
- cheese, tomato, turkey
- cheese, turkey, tomato
- tomato, turkey, cheese
- tomato, cheese, turkey

- turkey, tomato, lettuce
- turkey, lettuce, tomato
- tomato, lettuce, turkey
- tomato, turkey, lettuce
- lettuce, turkey, tomato
- lettuce, tomato, turkey

- cheese, tomato, lettuce
- cheese, lettuce, tomato
- tomato, lettuce, cheese
- tomato, cheese, lettuce
- lettuce, cheese, tomato
- lettuce, tomato, cheese

For sandwiches the *order* of the ingredients does not matter. So there are only four types of sandwiches. Each sandwich type is a **combination,** a collection of objects without regard to order.

The number of combinations of sandwiches equals the number of permutations divided by the number of times each type of sandwich is repeated.

$$\text{number of combinations} = \frac{\text{total number of permutations}}{\text{number of times the objects in each group are repeated}}$$

You can use the notation ${}_nC_r$ to write the number of combinations of n objects chosen r at time. The number of times each group of objects is repeated depends on r.

$$ {}_4C_3 = \frac{4P3}{3P3} = \frac{4 \cdot 3 \cdot 2}{3 \cdot 2 \cdot 1} \quad \begin{matrix} \leftarrow \text{4 factors chosen 3 at a time} \\ \leftarrow \text{3 factors chosen 3 at a time} \end{matrix}$$

$$ {}_nC_r = \frac{nP_r}{rP_r} = \frac{n(n-1)(n-2)\ldots}{r(r-1)(r-2)\ldots} \quad \begin{matrix} \leftarrow r \text{ factors starting with } n \\ \leftarrow r \text{ factors starting with } r \end{matrix}$$

CALCULATOR HINT

You can use the following calculator steps to find ${}_4C_3$:

 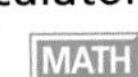 PRB $_NC_R$  ENTER

1. **Calculator** Evaluate each expression.
   a. ${}_4C_2$ b. ${}_8C_5$ c. ${}_7C_3$ d. ${}_{10}C_4$
2. a. **Try This** For your history report, you can choose to write about two of five Presidents of the United States. Use ${}_nC_r$ notation to write the number of combinations possible for your report.
   b. Calculate the number of combinations of presidents on whom you could report.

Example 1 Relating to the Real World 

Juries Twenty people report for jury duty. How many different twelve-person juries can be chosen?

The order in which jury members are listed does not distinguish one jury from another. You need the number of combinations of 20 objects chosen 12 at a time.

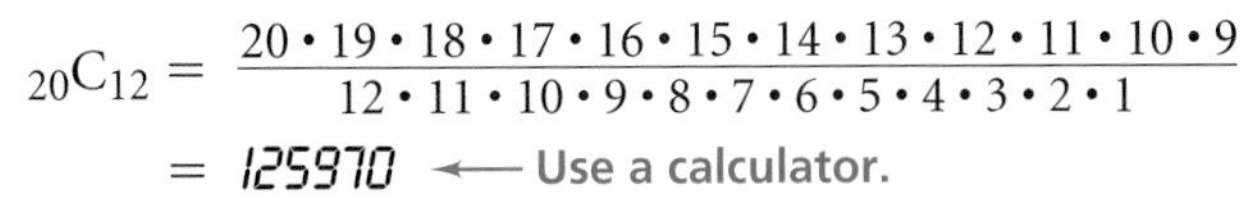

$${}_{20}C_{12} = \frac{20 \cdot 19 \cdot 18 \cdot 17 \cdot 16 \cdot 15 \cdot 14 \cdot 13 \cdot 12 \cdot 11 \cdot 10 \cdot 9}{12 \cdot 11 \cdot 10 \cdot 9 \cdot 8 \cdot 7 \cdot 6 \cdot 5 \cdot 4 \cdot 3 \cdot 2 \cdot 1}$$

$$= 125970 \quad \leftarrow \text{Use a calculator.}$$

There are 125,970 different twelve-person juries possible.

3. For some civil cases, at least nine of twelve jurors must agree on a verdict. How many combinations of nine jurors are possible on a twelve-person jury?

You can use combinations to solve probability problems. When finding the number of favorable outcomes, use the total number of objects that may give you a favorable outcome as the n value in ${}_nC_r$.

Example 2 Relating to the Real World 

Restaurants You and four friends visit a Thai restaurant. There are twelve different items on the menu. Seven are mild and the rest are spicy. You each order a different item at random. What is the probability that your group orders only mild items?

number of favorable outcomes $= {}_7C_5$ ← number of ways to choose 5 mild items from 7 mild items

number of possible outcomes $= {}_{12}C_5$ ← number of ways to choose 5 items from 12 items

$$P(5\text{ mild menu items}) = \frac{\text{number of favorable outcomes}}{\text{total number of outcomes}}$$

$$= \frac{{}_7C_5}{{}_{12}C_5}$$

$$= \frac{7}{264}$$

The probability your group orders only mild items is $\frac{7}{264}$, or about 3%.

4. Suppose you and your friends like spicy food. What is the probability that you choose five different spicy items at random?

Exercises ON YOUR OWN

1. a. *Spelling Bee* Every spring the National Spelling Bee Championships are held in Washington, D.C. Prizes are awarded to the top three spellers. In 1995, 247 students competed. How many different arrangements of winners were possible?
   b. Many students in the competition hoped to make it to the final round of 10 students. How many combinations of 10 students were possible?

2. *Sports* A basketball team has 11 players. Five players are on the court at a time. Your little brother doesn't know much about basketball and randomly names 5 players on the team. What is the probability that your brother's line-up lists the same 5 players as the coach's line-up for the next game?

3. *Writing* Explain the difference between a permutation and a combination.

Calculator **Use a calculator to evaluate.**

4. ${}_6C_6$	5. ${}_6C_5$	6. ${}_6C_4$	7. ${}_6C_3$	8. ${}_6C_2$	9. ${}_6C_1$
10. ${}_{15}C_{11}$	11. ${}_{15}C_4$	12. ${}_8C_5$	13. ${}_8C_3$	14. ${}_7C_4$	15. ${}_7C_3$

16. a. Describe any patterns you see in the answers to Exercises 4–15.
    b. *Critical Thinking* Explain why the pattern you described is true.
    c. *Open-ended* Write two more combinations that have the pattern you described in part (a).

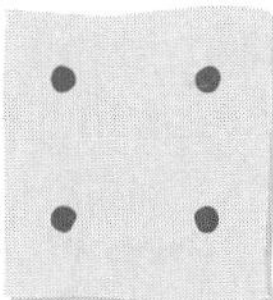
Figure 1

17. a. *Geometry* Draw four points on your paper like those in Figure 1. Draw line segments so that every point is joined with every other point.
    b. How many segments did you draw?
    c. Now find the number of segments you need for the drawing using combinations. You are joining four points, taking two at a time.
    d. How many segments would you need to join each point to all the others in Figure 2?

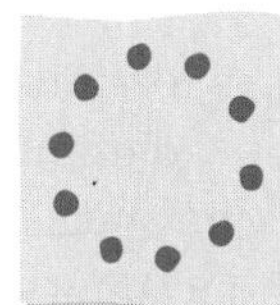
Figure 2

18. A famous problem, known as the Handshake Problem asks, "If ten people in a room shake hands with everyone else in the room, how many different handshakes occur?"
    a. Karen thinks that the Handshake Problem is a permutation problem while Tashia thinks it is a combination problem. What do you think? **Justify** your answer.
    b. Solve the problem.
    c. *Critical Thinking* Is the Handshake Problem similar to the problem in Exercise 17 (d)? Explain.

14

HEALTH NOTES

The U.S. Department of Health and Human Services and the Department of Agriculture guidelines recommend that daily food intake should include at least 3–5 servings of vegetables, at least 2–4 servings of fruit, 6–11 servings of grains, 2–3 servings of milk or cheese, and 2–3 servings of meat or poultry.

19. *Math in the Media* Suppose you want to have the highest number of recommended daily servings of fruit without repeating a fruit. Find how many different combinations of these products you can have.

One Serving of Fruit

apple	1
apple juice	1 cup
banana	1
cherries	10
grapefruit	$\frac{1}{2}$
orange	1
orange juice	1 cup
raisins	1 cup
strawberries	1 cup

Classify each of the following as a permutation or a combination problem. Explain your choice.

20. A locker contains eight books. You select three books at random. How many different sets of books could you select?

21. You rent three videos to watch during spring vacation. In how many different orders can you view the three videos?

22. The security guard at an auto plant must visit 10 different sections of the building each night. He varies his route each evening. How many different routes are possible?

23. A committee of four people needs to be formed from your homeroom of 25 students. How many four-person committees are possible?

24. *Standardized Test Prep* Compare the quantities in Columns A and B.

Column A	Column B
${}_{10}C_7$	${}_{7}P_4$

A. The quantity in Column A is greater.
B. The quantity in Column B is greater.
C. The quantities are equal.
D. The relationship cannot be determined from the given information.

Find the number of combinations of letters taken three at a time from each set of letters.

25. A B C D E

26. P Q R

27. E F G H I J K

28. M N O P

29. *Open-ended* Write and solve two problems: one that can be solved using permutations and one that can be solved using combinations.

30. For your birthday you received a gift certificate from a local music store for three CDs. There are eight that you would like to have. In how many different ways can you select your CDs?

31. **Manufacturing** Twelve computer screens are stored in a warehouse. The warehouse manager knows that three of the screens are defective, but the report telling him which ones are defective is missing. He selects five screens to begin testing.
   a. How many different choices of five screens does the manager have?
   b. In how many ways could he select five screens that include the defective ones?
   c. What is the probability that he finds the three defective screens when he tests the first five screens?

32. a. A committee of three people is to be selected from three boys and five girls. How many different committees are possible?
   b. How many committees could have all boys?
   c. What is the probability that a committee will have all boys?
   d. **Critical Thinking** What is the probability that the committee will have no boys?

33. The letters A, B, C, D, E, F, G, H, I, and J are written on slips of paper and placed in a hat. Two letters are drawn from the hat.
   a. What is the number of possible combinations of letters?
   b. How many combinations consist only of the vowels A, E, or I?
   c. What is the probability the letters chosen consist only of vowels?
   d. What is the probability the letters chosen consist only of B, C, D or F?

34. **Research** Find the number of members in your state legislature. Find how many ways a committee of ten people may be formed from the members of the legislature.

Chapter Project **Find Out by Communicating**

Every musical instrument has a part that vibrates to make different pitches. Choose an instrument and find out how it works. Make a poster that describes what vibrates and how different pitches are produced.

Exercises MIXED REVIEW

Evaluate.

35. $_4P_2$
36. $_8P_3$
37. $_7P_6$
38. $_8P_6$
39. $_9P_1$
40. $_7P_4$

Express each sum or difference in simplest form.

41. $\frac{4x^2}{3x} + \frac{5}{3x}$
42. $\frac{5c}{8m} - \frac{7m}{c}$
43. $\frac{9x}{x^2 - 4} + \frac{4}{x + 2}$
44. $\frac{9}{z} + \frac{10}{3z}$
45. $\frac{12}{5n} - \frac{15}{4n}$
46. $\frac{8w^2}{3 - w} - \frac{5w}{18 - 2w^2}$

47. a. **Weather** After a heavy snowfall, a homeowner had to clear about four tons of snow off a 20 ft by 20 ft driveway. A full shovel of snow weighs about 7 lb. How many times would the homeowner have to fill his shovel to clear the driveway?
   b. How many tons of snow would be on a 20 ft by 30 ft driveway?

PORTFOLIO

Select one or two items from your work for this chapter. Consider:
- corrected work
- diagrams, graphs, or charts
- a journal entry

Explain why you have included each selection you make.

CHAPTER PROJECT

Finishing the Chapter Project

GOOD VIBRATIONS

Questions on pages 514, 526, 531, 536, and 547 should help you to complete your project. Plan a presentation of what you have learned for your classmates. Include graphs, charts, illustrations, and demonstrations on homemade or professional instruments.

Reflect and Revise

Share your presentation with a small group of your classmates. Were your explanations clear and accurate? How does your musical instrument sound? Were you able to describe its pitch? If necessary, make any changes in your work.

Follow Up

In Western culture, C and C# are consecutive pitches in the chromatic scale. The ratio of their frequencies is about 1:1.06. Find out about the scales used in Asian cultures. How might their scales affect the design of their instruments?

For More Information

Haak, Sheila. "Using the Monochord: A Classroom Demonstration on the Mathematics of Musical Scales." *Applications of Secondary School Mathematics.* Reston, Virginia: National Council of Teachers of Mathematics, 1991.

Macaulay, David. *The Way Things Work*. Boston: Houghton Mifflin, 1988. Software Version: Dorling Kindersley Multimedia, 1994.

Wilkinson, Scott R. *Tuning In: Microtonality in Electronic Music: A Basic Guide to Alternate Scales, Temperaments, and Microtuning Using Synthesizers*. Milwaukee, Wisconsin: H. Leonard Books, 1988.

CHAPTER

11 Wrap Up

Key Terms

asymptote (p. 516)
combination (p. 543)
constant of variation (p. 510)
domain (p. 522)
inverse variation (p. 510)
multiplication counting principle (p. 539)
${}_nC_r$ (p. 543)
${}_nP_r$ (p. 540)
permutation (p. 539)
rational equation (p. 532)
rational expression (p. 522)
rational function (p. 516)

How am I doing?

- State three ideas from this chapter that you think are important. Explain your choices.
- Explain the importance of restrictions on the variable in rational expressions.

Inverse Variation 11-1

When two quantities are related so that their product is constant, they form an **inverse variation.** An inverse variation can be written $xy = k$, where k is the **constant of variation.**

Find the constant of variation for each inverse variation.

1. $m = 6$ when $n = 1$

2. $g = 90$ when $h = 0.1$

3. $s = 88$ when $t = 0.05$

For each table, tell whether it represents an inverse variation. If so, write an equation to model the data.

4.

x	1	1.4	3	7
y	4	5.6	12	28

5.

x	4	1	2	2.5
y	2.65	10.6	5.3	4.24

Rational Functions 11-2

A **rational function** can be written in the form $f(x) = \frac{\text{polynomial}}{\text{polynomial}}$. The graph of a rational function may have asymptotes. An **asymptote** is a line that a graph approaches, but does not cross.

Graph each function. Use a dashed line for each asymptote.

6. $y = \frac{8}{x}$

7. $y = \frac{20}{x}$

8. $y = \frac{6}{x - 5}$

9. $y = \frac{3}{x} + 2$

10. **Open-ended** Write the equation of a rational function with a graph that is in three quadrants only.

11. **Writing** Explain why the function $f(x) = \frac{5}{x + 3}$ has asymptotes.

Rational Expressions 11-3

A **rational expression** can be written in the form $\frac{\text{polynomial}}{\text{polynomial}}$ where a variable is in the denominator. The **domain** of a variable is all real numbers excluding the values for which the denominator is zero. A rational expression is in simplest form when the numerator and denominator have no common factors other than 1.

You can multiply and divide rational expressions.

$\frac{a}{b} \cdot \frac{c}{d} = \frac{ac}{bd}$, where b and d are nonzero

$\frac{a}{b} \div \frac{c}{d} = \frac{a}{b} \cdot \frac{d}{c}$, where b, c, and d are nonzero

Simplify each expression and state any restrictions on the variable.

12. $\frac{x^2 - 4}{x + 2}$ **13.** $\frac{5x}{20x + 15}$ **14.** $\frac{-3t}{t^3 - t^2}$ **15.** $\frac{z + 2}{2z^2 + z - 6}$

Find each product or quotient.

16. $\frac{8}{m - 3} \cdot \frac{3m}{m + 1}$ **17.** $\frac{2e + 1}{8e - 4} \div \frac{4e^2 + 4e + 1}{4e - 2}$ **18.** $\frac{5c + 3}{c^2 - 1} \cdot \frac{c + 1}{2c}$ **19.** $\frac{4n + 8}{3n} \div \frac{4}{9n}$

Operations with Rational Expressions 11-4

You can add and subtract rational expressions. Restate each expression with the LCD as the denominator, then add or subtract the numerators.

Add or subtract.

20. $\frac{5}{k} + \frac{3}{k}$ **21.** $\frac{8x}{x - 7} - \frac{4}{x - 7}$ **22.** $\frac{9}{3x - 1} + \frac{5x}{2x + 3}$ **23.** $\frac{7m}{(m + 1)(m - 1)} - \frac{10}{m + 1}$

24. *Standardized Test Prep* What is the LCD of $\frac{1}{4}$, $\frac{2}{x}$, $\frac{5x}{3x - 2}$, and $\frac{3}{8x}$?

A. $96x^3 - 64x^2$ **B.** $12x + 2$ **C.** $24x^2 - 16x$ **D.** $27x^2 - 6x - 8$ **E.** $6x + 2$

Solving Rational Equations 11-5

You can use the least common denominator (LCD) to solve **rational equations.** Check possible solutions in the original equation to make sure that they do not make the denominator equal to zero.

Solve each equation.

25. $\frac{1}{2} + \frac{3}{t} = \frac{5}{8}$ **26.** $\frac{3}{m - 4} + \frac{1}{3(m - 4)} = \frac{6}{m}$ **27.** $\frac{2c}{c - 4} - 2 = \frac{4}{c + 5}$

28. *Business* A new photocopier can make 72 copies in 2 min. When an older photocopier is working, the two photocopiers can make 72 copies in 1.5 min. How long does it take the older photocopier working alone to make 72 copies?

Counting Outcomes and Permutations 11-6

You can find a number of different outcomes using the **multiplication counting principle.** If there are m ways to make a first selection and n ways to make a second selection, there are $m \times n$ ways to make the two selections.

A **permutation** is an arrangement of objects in a definite order. To calculate ${}_nP_r$, the number of permutations of n objects taken r at a time, use the formula

${}_nP_r = n(n - 1)(n - 2)\ldots$ ← *r factors starting with n*

Evaluate.

29. ${}_5P_3$ **30.** ${}_8P_4$ **31.** ${}_6P_4$ **32.** ${}_5P_2$ **33.** ${}_9P_4$ **34.** ${}_7P_2$

35. a. *Telephones* Before 1995, three-digit area codes could begin with any number except 0 or 1. The middle number was either 0 or 1, and the last number could be any digit. How many possible area codes were there?

b. Beginning in 1995, area codes were not limited to having 0 or 1 as the middle number. How many new area codes became available?

Combinations 11-7

A **combination** is an arrangement of objects without regard to order. The

$$\text{number of combinations} = \frac{\text{number of permutations}}{\text{number of times the objects in each group are repeated}}.$$

To find ${}_nC_r$, the combinations of n objects taken r at a time, use the formula

$${}_nC_r = \frac{{}_nP_r}{{}_rP_r} = \frac{n(n-1)(n-2)\ldots}{r(r-1)(r-2)\ldots}$$

← *r factors starting with n* (numerator)
← *r factors starting with r* (denominator)

Evaluate.

36. ${}_6C_5$ **37.** ${}_{10}C_4$ **38.** ${}_9C_2$ **39.** ${}_{11}C_3$ **40.** ${}_5C_4$ **41.** ${}_6C_4$

42. *Nutrition* You want to have three servings of dairy products without repeating a food. Milk, yogurt, cottage cheese, and cheddar cheese are in the refrigerator. How many different combinations can you have?

43. Ten friends go to an amusement park. A roller-coaster car holds eight people. Find how many different groups from the ten friends can ride in one car.

44. You subscribe to eight monthly magazines. Two are news magazines, three are on sports, two are on health and fitness, and one is about gardening. What is the probability that the next two magazines you receive in the mail are sports magazines?

CHAPTER 11

Assessment

Find the constant of variation for each inverse variation.

1. $y = 5$ when $x = 6$
2. $y = 2.4$ when $x = 10$
3. $y = 78$ when $x = 0.1$
4. $y = 5.3$ when $x = 9.1$

5. *Standardized Test Prep* Which point is *not* on the same graph of an inverse variation as the others?
   A. (3, 12) B. (9, 4) C. (6, 6)
   D. (16, 2) E. (2, 18)

6. It took you 1.5 h to drive to a concert at 40 mi/h. How long will it take you to drive back driving at 50 mi/h?

Graph each function. Include a dashed line for each asymptote.

7. $y = \frac{6}{x}$
8. $y = \frac{15}{x}$
9. $y = \frac{1}{x} + 3$
10. $y = \frac{4}{x} + 3$

11. *Writing* Explain how direct variations and inverse variations are similar and different. Include an example of each.

Find each product or quotient.

12. $\frac{3}{x - 2} \cdot \frac{x^2 - 4}{12}$
13. $\frac{5x}{x^2 + 2x} \div \frac{30x^2}{x + 2}$
14. $\frac{4w}{3w - 5} \cdot \frac{7}{2w}$
15. $\frac{6c - 2}{c + 5} \div \frac{3c - 9}{c}$

16. *Open-ended* Write a rational expression for which 6 and 3 are restricted from the domain.

Solve each equation.

17. $\frac{v}{3} + \frac{v}{v + 5} = \frac{4}{v + 5}$
18. $\frac{16}{x + 10} = \frac{8}{2x - 1}$
19. $\frac{2}{3} + \frac{t + 6}{t - 3} = \frac{18}{2(t - 3)}$

20. If three people can clean an apartment working two hours each, how long will it take a crew of four people?

Simplify.

21. $\frac{5}{t} + \frac{t}{t + 1}$
22. $\frac{9}{n} - \frac{8}{n + 1}$
23. $\frac{2y}{y^2 - 9} - \frac{1}{y - 3}$
24. $\frac{4b - 2}{3b} + \frac{b}{b + 2}$

Classify each of the following as a combination or permutation problem. Explain your choice. Then solve the problem.

25. The 30-member debate club needs a president and treasurer. How many different pairs of officers are possible?
26. How many different ways can you choose two books from the six books on your shelf?
27. You have enough money for two extra pizza toppings. If there are six possible toppings, how many different pairs of toppings can you choose?

Find the number of combinations of letters taken four at a time from each set.

28. A E I O U Y
29. E Q U A T I O N
30. L E A R N

Evaluate.

31. ${}_4C_3$
32. ${}_8P_6$
33. ${}_{10}P_7$
34. ${}_5C_2$

35. You have 5 kinds of wrapping paper and 4 different colored bows. How many different combinations of paper and bows can you have?
36. There are 15 books on your summer reading list. Three of them are plays, one is poetry, and the rest are novels. What is the probability that you will choose three novels if you choose the books at random?

CHAPTER 11

Preparing for Standardized Tests

For Exercises 1–11, choose the correct letter.

1. Subtract $(3x^2 - 7x - 2) - (8x - 3)$.
A. $3x^2 + x - 5$ **B.** $-5x^3 + 1$
C. $3x^2 - 5x - 5$ **D.** $3x^2 - 15x + 1$
E. none of the above

2. The value of x varies inversely with y, and $x = 2$ when $y = 5$. What is x when $y = 10$?
A. 0 **B.** 4 **C.** 5 **D.** 7 **E.** 1

3. Multiply $(2x - 3)(5x + 4)$.
A. $10x + 1$
B. $10x^2 - 12$
C. $10x^2 - 7x - 12$
D. $10x^2 + 23x - 12$
E. $10x^2 - 7x + 12$

4. Factor $x^2 + 3x - 10$.
A. $(x - 2)(x + 5)$
B. $(x + 2)(x - 5)$
C. $(x - 2)(x - 5)$
D. $-(x + 2)(x + 5)$
E. $(x - 10)(x + 1)$

5. Which expression is equal to $8x^3 - 12x^2 + 4x$?
A. x^6
B. $2x(4x^2 + 6x + 2)$
C. $x(8x^3 - 12x + 4)$
D. $4x(2x^2 - 3x + 1)$
E. $4x(4x^2 - 3x + 1)$

6. Solve $4x^2 - 4x - 3 \leq 0$.
A. $x \leq \frac{1}{2}$ or $x \geq \frac{3}{2}$
B. $x \leq -\frac{1}{2}$ or $x \geq \frac{3}{2}$
C. $-\frac{1}{2} \leq x \leq \frac{3}{2}$
D. $-\frac{1}{2} \geq x \geq \frac{3}{2}$
E. $x = -\frac{1}{2}$ and $x = \frac{3}{2}$

7. Simplify $\frac{3x - 9}{x^2 - 6x + 9}$.
A. $\frac{1}{3}x - \frac{1}{3}$ **B.** $\frac{3}{x - 3}$
C. $\frac{1}{x + 3}$ **D.** $x^2 + \frac{1}{3}x - \frac{1}{3}$
E. cannot be simplified

8. Find the restriction on the variable in $\frac{x - 8}{x - 10}$.
A. $x \neq 7$ **B.** $x \neq 8$ **C.** $x \neq 9$
D. $x \neq 10$ **E.** $x \neq 11$

9. Divide $\frac{x - 4}{x^2 + 2x} \div \frac{x^2 - 16}{x^2 - x}$.
A. $\frac{x - 1}{x^2 + 6x + 8}$ **B.** $\frac{1}{x^2 + x - 4}$
C. 1 **D.** $\frac{x^2 - 6^x + 4}{x^2 + x - 4}$
E. $\frac{x^2 + 6x + 8}{x^2 - 1}$

Compare the boxed quantity in Column A with the boxed quantity in Column B. Choose the best answer.

A. The quantity in Column A is greater.
B. The quantity in Column B is greater.
C. The two quantities are equal.
D. The relationship cannot be determined on the basis of the information supplied.

	Column A	Column B
10.	the degree of $4x^3 - 8x^2 - 7x$	the GCF of $6x^3, 9x^2, 12$
11.	the solution of $x^2 - 8x + 16 = 0$	the solution of $\frac{x - 4}{2} = \frac{x - 2}{4}$

Find each answer.

12. Simplify $\frac{4x + 10}{2x^2 + 7x + 5}$.

13. Factor $4x^2 - 12x + 9$.

14. One baker can shape 24 bagels in 15 min. When the baker works with an apprentice, they can shape 24 bagels in 10 min. How long does it take the apprentice to shape 24 bagels working alone?

15. Find the asymptotes, the x-intercept, and the y-intercept of the graph of $y = \frac{5}{x - 2} + 1$.

16. Find the values of ${}_{10}P_3$ and ${}_8C_4$.

CHAPTER 11

Cumulative Review

For Exercises 1–21, choose the correct letter.

1. Evaluate $2y + 7$ for $y = 4$.
   A. 31 **B.** 12 **C.** 11
   D. 22 **E.** 15

2. Suppose you buy 2 items costing d dollars each and you give the cashier \$10. Which expression models the change you should receive?
   A. $10 + 2d$ **B.** $2d - 10$ **C.** $10 - 2d$
   D. $2d$ **E.** $\frac{10}{2d}$

3. A manufacturing company spends \$1200 each day on plant costs plus \$7 per item for labor and materials. The items sell for \$23 each. How many items must the company sell in one day to equal its daily costs?
   A. 160 **B.** 52 **C.** 200
   D. 150 **E.** 75

4. Which compound inequality represents the set of numbers shown on the number line?

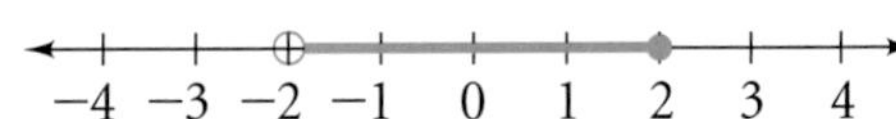

   A. $3 \leq x < 2$ **B.** $-2 < x \leq 2$
   C. $3 \geq x$ and $x < 2$ **D.** $2 \geq x$ or $x < -2$
   E. $-2 \leq x \leq 2$

5. Find the greatest common factor (GCF) of the terms of the polynomial $12x^5 + 4x^3 - 16x^2$.
   A. $4x^2$ **B.** $-2x$ **C.** x^3 **D.** $4x^3$ **E.** $16x^2$

6. Find the product of $(w - 5)(w + 7)$.
   A. $w^2 + 12w - 35$ **B.** $w^2 + 2w - 2$
   C. $w^2 - 2w - 2$ **D.** $w^2 - 35$
   E. $w^2 + 2w - 35$

7. If $x^2 = 36$ and $y^2 = 16$, choose the least possible value for $y - x$.
   A. 2 **B.** -2 **C.** 10 **D.** -10 **E.** 0

8. Which of the following points is *not* a solution of $y \leq 2x^2 - 5x + 3$?
   A. $(3, 6)$ **B.** $(0, -2)$ **C.** $(-1, 4)$
   D. $(2, 18)$ **E.** $(-2, -5)$

9. Which of the following is an equation of a line passing through (5, 1) and (3, −3)?
   A. $y = \frac{1}{2}x - \frac{3}{2}$ **B.** $y = \frac{3}{2}x - 2$
   C. $y = 2x - \frac{3}{2}$ **D.** $y = 2x - 9$
   E. $y = 2x + 9$

10. The function $y = |2x + 6|$ belongs to which family of functions?
    A. polynomial function
    B. quadratic function
    C. linear function
    D. rational function
    E. absolute value function

11. Which of the following describes the shaded region of the graph?

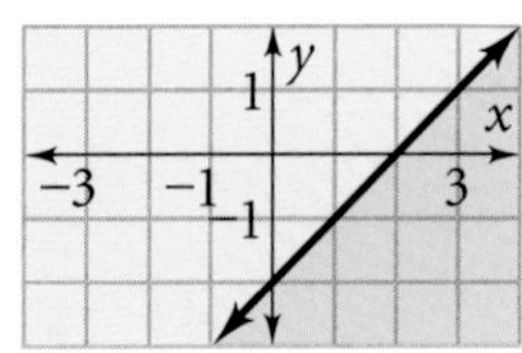

    A. $y \leq x - 2$ **B.** $y \geq x - 2$
    C. $y = x - 2$ **D.** $y < x - 2$
    E. $y > x - 2$

12. Evaluate $a^2b^3c^{-1}$ for $a = 2$, $b = -1$, and $c = -2$.
    A. 2 **B.** -2 **C.** 8 **D.** -10 **E.** 4

13. Suppose you deposit \$1000 in an account paying 5.5% interest, compounded annually. Which expression represents the value of the investment after 10 years?
    A. $1000 \cdot 1.55^{10}$ **B.** $1000 \cdot 1.055^{10}$
    C. $1000 \cdot 0.055^{10}$ **D.** $1000 \cdot 10^{1.055}$
    E. $1000^{10} \cdot 0.055$

14. Potassium-42 has a half-life of 12.5 h. How many half-lives are in 75 h?
    A. 150 **B.** 6 **C.** 25 **D.** 4 **E.** 8

15. Simplify $(2.5 \times 10^4)(3.0 \times 10^{-15})$.
    A. 7.5×10^{19} **B.** 7.5×10^{-19}
    C. 7.5×10^{11} **D.** 7.5×10^{-11}
    E. 7.5×10

16. Simplify $-3a^8 \cdot cb^{-3} \cdot b^{12} \cdot 9c^5$.

A. $6a^9b^5c^6$ B. $-27a^8b^9c^5$

C. $-27a^8b^9c^6$ D. $-3abc$

E. $-27a^8b^{15}c^6$

17. A support wire from the top of a tower is 100 ft long. It is anchored at a spot 60 ft from the base of the tower. Find the height of the tower.

A. 80 ft B. 40 ft C. 160 ft

D. 20 ft E. $4\sqrt{10}$ ft

18. Triangle *DEF* is a right triangle with a right angle at *F*. Which of the following is *false*?

A. $\sin D = \frac{EF}{DE}$ B. $\tan D = \frac{EF}{DF}$

C. $\cos D = \frac{DE}{DF}$ D. $\cos E = \frac{EF}{DE}$

E. $\sin E = \frac{DF}{DE}$

Compare the boxed quantity in Column A with the boxed quantity in Column B. Choose the best answer.

A. The quantity in Column A is greater.
B. The quantity in Column B is greater.
C. The two quantities are equal.
D. The relationship cannot be determined on the basis of the information supplied.

	Column A	Column B
19.	$f(4)$ when $f(x) = 2x^2 - 23$	$f(3)$ when $f(x) = x^2 + 5$

Use the equation $y = -12x + 2$.

	Column A	Column B
20.	the slope	the y-intercept

Use $2x - y = 3$ and $0.5(4x - 2y) = 3$.

	Column A	Column B
21.	x	y

Find each answer.

22. **Open-ended** Write two quadratic trinomials that cannot be factored.

23. a. Find the x-intercepts of the function $y = 4x^2 - 9x + 2$.
b. Make a sketch of the function.

24. Solve the system using elimination:
$x + y = 34$
$x - y = 16$

25. Graph the system: $y > x^2 - 3x + 5$
$y \leq 3x + 2$

26. A bag contains 5 green cubes and 7 yellow cubes. You pick two cubes without replacing the first one.
a. What is the probability of choosing a yellow cube and then choosing a green cube?
b. What is the probability of choosing two yellow cubes?

27. **Writing** Explain how you can use slope to determine the equation of a line perpendicular to a given line.

28. What is the perimeter of a right triangle with legs measuring 8 ft and 15 ft?

29. Solve $\frac{-2}{x - 3} = \frac{x + 4}{2(x - 3)} + \frac{1}{4}$.

30. **Open-ended** Describe a situation that you can model with a two-step equation. Define what the variable represents, then solve the equation.

31. Russell wanted to purchase a computer that costs \$1575. With a different disk drive, the cost of the computer rose 8%. How much will the upgraded computer cost?

32. **Writing** Explain how to use the distributive property to multiply binomials.

33. Workers at a local charity worked the following numbers of hours: 3, 5, 9, 5, 8, 4, 2, 10, 7, 3, 4, 6.
a. Find the mean.
b. Find the range of the data.
c. Find the standard deviation.

Extra Practice

Find the mean, median, and mode for each set of data. ■ Lesson 1-1

1. 36, 42, 35, 40, 35, 51, 41, 35 **2.** 1.2, 0.9, 0.7, 1.1, 0.8, 1.3, 0.6 **3.** 5, 8, 6, 8, 3, 5, 8, 6, 5, 9

4. A student surveyed the members of the drama club. She included a question about age. Her results are at the right.
   a. Make a line plot for the data.
   b. What is the median age of the drama club members?

Ages of Drama Club Members								
14	18	16	15	17	14	15	18	15
13	14	15	18	14	17	16	14	16

■ Lesson 1-2

5. Write an equation to model each situation.
   a. The length of three cars is 24 feet.
   b. The weight of two books equals 39 pens.

6. a. Write a sentence and an equation to describe the relationship between the number of notebooks and the price.
   b. If you have $5, can you buy a notebook for each of your classes? Explain.

Notebooks	Price
1	$.99
2	$1.98
3	$2.97

Simplify each expression. ■ Lessons 1-3 to 1-6

7. $4 + 3 \cdot 8$ **8.** $2 \cdot 3^2 - 7$ **9.** $6 \cdot (5 - 2) - 9$ **10.** $2 - 12 \div 3$

11. $\left(\frac{1}{3}\right)^2 + 8 \div 2$ **12.** $\frac{1}{2} \div \frac{4}{3}$ **13.** $-6 \cdot 4.2 - 5 \div 2$ **14.** $9 - (3 + 1)^2$

15. $\frac{1}{3} - \frac{5}{6}$ **16.** $-4 + 9 \div 3 - 2$ **17.** $(8 - 1.5) \cdot -4$ **18.** $\frac{3}{4} \cdot 6 - \frac{1}{2}$

Evaluate each expression for $a = 8$, $b = -3$, and $c = \frac{1}{2}$.

19. $a - b - c$ **20.** $c - a^2$ **21.** $8c + ab$ **22.** $c(a - 2c)$

23. $9b - 4a$ **24.** $\frac{1}{2}b - ac$ **25.** $(2b)^2 - 2b^2$ **26.** $\frac{1}{a} + \frac{1}{c}$

The results of rolling a number cube 54 times are at the right. Use the results to find each experimental probability. ■ Lesson 1-7

6 3 4 5 1 1 5 5 3 6 3 2 1 3 3 3 2 1
2 3 6 3 3 4 5 1 2 2 6 3 3 6 5 4 5 3
2 5 1 4 5 2 6 2 5 2 1 2 5 3 2 4 6 3

27. $P(3)$ **28.** $P(4)$ **29.** $P(\text{not } 5)$

30. $P(7)$ **31.** $P(\text{even number})$ **32.** $P(\text{not } 1)$

Find the sum or difference. ■ Lesson 1-8

33. $\begin{bmatrix} -3 & 0 \\ 11 & -5 \end{bmatrix} + \begin{bmatrix} -4 & 6 \\ -8 & 13 \end{bmatrix}$ **34.** $\begin{bmatrix} 6 & 12 \\ -9 & 7 \end{bmatrix} - \begin{bmatrix} 8 & -6 \\ 15 & 0 \end{bmatrix}$ **35.** $\begin{bmatrix} 4.2 & 0.6 \\ 1.7 & 9.5 \end{bmatrix} - \begin{bmatrix} 5.8 & -3.5 \\ 0.2 & 4.9 \end{bmatrix}$

■ Lesson 1-9

36. You can find the surface area of a cube using the formula $A = 6s^2$, where s is the length of a side.
   a. Write a spreadsheet formula for cell B2.
   b. Find the values for cells B2, C2, and D2.
   c. Write a spreadsheet formula to find the sum of the surface areas of the three cubes.

	A	B	C	D
1	Side Length	3	5.2	9
2	Surface Area	■	■	■

Extra Practice

Use the table for Exercise 1. ■ Lesson 2-1

Cover Price and Number of Pages of Some Magazines

Cover Price	\$2.25	\$2.50	\$3.75	\$3.00	\$4.95	\$1.95	\$2.95	\$2.50
Number of Pages	208	68	122	124	234	72	90	90

1. a. Draw a scatter plot of the data.
   b. Draw a trend line on the scatter plot. What is the relationship between the cover price and the number of pages in a magazine?
   c. How many pages would you expect a \$2.00 magazine to have? Explain.

Sketch a graph to describe each situation. Explain the activity in each section of the graph. ■ Lesson 2-2

2. the amount of milk in your bowl as you eat cereal
3. the energy you use in a 24-h period
4. your distance from home plate after your home run
5. the number of apples on a tree over one year

Graph the data. Then write a function rule for each table of values. ■ Lessons 2-3, 2-5, 2-6

6.

x	$f(x)$
–3	–1
–1	1
1	3
3	5

7.

x	$f(x)$
0	0
3	6
6	12
9	18

8.

x	$f(x)$
21	14
25	18
29	22
33	26

9.

x	$f(x)$
–8	–4
–6	–3
–4	–2
–2	–1

Find the range of each function when the domain is {–4, –1, 0, 3, 8}. Each equation belongs to what family of functions? ■ Lessons 2-4, 2-7

10. $y = 6x - 5$
11. $y = |x| - 2$
12. $y = x^2 + 3x + 1$
13. $y = \frac{1}{2}x + 8$
14. $y = -x^2 - x$
15. $y = \frac{2}{3}x$
16. $y = |x - 2|$
17. $y = 2x^2 - 5x$
18. $y = |4 - x|$
19. $y = x + 5$
20. $y = \frac{4}{9}x^2$
21. $y = |\frac{3}{5}x|$

Find each theoretical probability for one roll of a number cube. ■ Lesson 2-8

22. P(an odd number)
23. P(a negative number)
24. P(an integer)
25. P(a factor of 6)

At the Sock Hop, socks are sold in three sizes and six colors. The sizes are small, medium, and large. The color selection consists of white, gray, blue, red, black, and purple. Find the probability of choosing each kind of sock randomly.

26. P(large and gray)
27. P(blue or red)
28. P(small and purple)
29. P(medium)
30. Make a tree diagram to show all the kinds of socks.

CHAPTER 3

Extra Practice

Solve each equation. ■ Lesson 3-1 to 3-5

1. $h - 4 = 10$ **2.** $8p - 3 = 13$ **3.** $8j - 5 + j = 67$ **4.** $6t = -42$

5. $-n + 8.5 = 14.2$ **6.** $6(t + 5) = -36$ **7.** $m + 9 = 11$ **8.** $\frac{1}{2}(s + 5) = 7.5$

9. $\frac{s}{3} = 8$ **10.** $7h + 2h - 3 = 15$ **11.** $\frac{7}{12}x = \frac{3}{14}$ **12.** $3r - 8 = -32$

13. $8g - 10g = 4$ **14.** $-3(5 - t) = 18$ **15.** $3(c - 4) = -9$ **16.** $\frac{3}{8}z = 9$

17. $0.1(h + 20) = 3$ **18.** $\frac{3m}{5} = 6$ **19.** $4 - y = 10$ **20.** $8q + 2q = -7.4$

Write an equation to solve each problem.

21. *School* Your test scores for the semester are 87, 84, and 85. Can you raise your test average to 90 with your next test?

22. You spend $\frac{1}{2}$ of your allowance each week on school lunches. Each lunch costs $1.25. How much is your weekly allowance?

You pick two balls from a jar. The jar has five blue, three yellow, six green, and two purple balls. Find each probability. ■ Lesson 3-6

23. *P*(purple and blue), with replacement **24.** *P*(yellow and purple), without replacement

25. *P*(green and yellow), with replacement **26.** *P*(green and blue), without replacement

27. *P*(purple and green), without replacement **28.** *P*(green and blue), with replacement

29. *P*(blue and yellow), without replacement **30.** *P*(blue and purple), with replacement

Write and solve an equation to answer each question. ■ Lesson 3-7

31. What is 10% of 94? **32.** What percent of 10 is 4? **33.** 147 is 14% of what?

34. What percent of 1.2 is 6? **35.** 13.2 is 55% of what? **36.** What is 0.4% of 800?

37. What is 75% of 68? **38.** 5 is 200% of what? **39.** What percent of 54 is 28?

40. 114 is 95% of what? **41.** What percent of 20 is 31? **42.** What is 35% of 15?

Find each percent of change. Describe each as a percent of increase or decrease. Round to the nearest percent. ■ Lesson 3-8

43. $4.50 to $5.00 **44.** 56 in. to 57 in. **45.** 18 oz to 12 oz **46.** 1 s to 3 s

47. 8 lb to 5 lb **48.** 6 km to 6.5 km **49.** 39 h to 40 h **50.** 7 ft to 2 ft

51. 0.2 mL to 0.45 mL **52.** $\frac{1}{2}$ tsp to $\frac{1}{8}$ tsp **53.** 18 kg to 20 kg **54.** 55 min to 50 min

55. In 1988, the average resident of the United States ate about 2.4 lb of bagels per year. In 1993, bagel consumption had increased to about 3.5 lb annually. What percent increase is this?

Extra Practice

Solve each proportion. ■ Lesson 4-1

1. $\frac{3}{4} = \frac{-6}{m}$ 2. $\frac{t}{7} = \frac{3}{21}$ 3. $\frac{9}{j} = \frac{3}{16}$ 4. $\frac{2}{5} = \frac{w}{65}$ 5. $\frac{s}{15} = \frac{4}{45}$ 6. $\frac{9}{4} = \frac{x}{10}$
7. $\frac{10}{q} = \frac{8}{62}$ 8. $\frac{3}{2} = \frac{18}{y}$ 9. $\frac{5}{9} = \frac{t}{3}$ 10. $\frac{6}{m} = \frac{3}{5}$ 11. $\frac{c}{8} = \frac{13.5}{36}$ 12. $\frac{7}{9} = \frac{35}{x}$

13. Architecture A blueprint scale is 1 in. : 4 ft. On the plan, the garage is 2 in. by 3 in. What are the actual dimensions of the garage?

Solve and check. If the equation is an identity or if it has no solution, write *identity* or *no solution*. ■ Lessons 4-2, 4-3

14. $|t| = 6$ 15. $5m + 3 = 9m - 1$ 16. $8d = 4d - 18$ 17. $4h + 5 = 9h$
18. $|k| - 4 = -7$ 19. $7t = 80 + 9t$ 20. $|w - 9| = 4$ 21. $|m + 3| = 12$
22. $-b + 4b = 8b - b$ 23. $8 - |p| = 3$ 24. $|h + 17| = -8$ 25. $6p + 1 = 3p$
26. $10z - 5 + 3z = 8 - z$ 27. $3(g - 1) + 7 = 3g + 4$ 28. $17 - 20q = -13 - 5q$

29. Transportation A bus traveling 40 mi/h and a car traveling 50 mi/h cover the same distance. The bus travels 1 h more than the car. How many hours did each travel?

Solve each equation for the given variable. ■ Lesson 4-4

30. $A = lw; w$ 31. $c = \frac{w + t}{v}, t$ 32. $h = \frac{r}{t}(p - m); r$ 33. $P = 2l + 2w; l$
34. $v = \pi r^2 h; h$ 35. $m = \frac{t}{b - a}; t$ 36. $y = bt - c; b$ 37. $g = 1.9\frac{m}{r^2}; m$

Solve each inequality and graph the solutions on a number line. ■ Lessons 4-5 to 4-8

38. $-8w < 24$ 39. $9 + p \leq 17$ 40. $\frac{r}{4} > -1$ 41. $7y + 2 \leq -8$
42. $t - 5 \geq -13$ 43. $9h > -108$ 44. $|8w + 7| > 5$ 45. $\frac{s}{6} \leq 3$
46. $\frac{6c}{5} \geq -12$ 47. $-8l + 3.7 \leq 31.7$ 48. $9 - t \leq 4$ 49. $|m + 4| \geq 8$
50. $y + 3 < 16$ 51. $|n - 6| \leq 8.5$ 52. $12b - 5 > -29$ 53. $4 - a > 15$
54. $6m - 15 \leq 9$ or $10m > 84$ 55. $9j - 5j \geq 20$ and $8j > -36$ 56. $37 < 3c + 7 < 43$

57. The booster club raised \$102 in their car wash. They want to buy \$18 soccer balls for the soccer team. How many can they buy?

Solve and graph each inequality. The replacement set is the positive integers. ■ Lesson 4-9

58. $t - 5 \leq -3$ 59. $-6m + 2 > -19$ 60. $|3c + 1| \geq 7$ 61. $8 - w < 8$
62. $2b + 3 < 7$ 63. $-c - 5 \leq 6$ 64. $|n| + 4 \leq 5$ 65. $\frac{3}{5}t > 6$

66. You are solving a problem involving weight. Find the replacement set.

Extra Practice

Find the slope of the line passing through each pair of points. Then write the equation of the line. ■ Lessons 5-1, 5-5

1. (2, 5) and (4, 8) **2.** (1, 6) and (7, 3) **3.** (–2, 4) and (3, 9) **4.** (1, 6) and (9, –4)

5. (–5, –7) and (–1, 3) **6.** (7, 0) and (3, –4) **7.** (0, 0) and (–7, 1) **8.** (10, –5) and (–2, 7)

Write an equation for a line through the given point with the given slope. Then graph the line.

9. (4, 6); $m = -5$ **10.** (3, –1); $m = 1$ **11.** (8, 5); $m = \frac{1}{2}$ **12.** (0, –6); $m = \frac{4}{3}$

13. (–2, 7); $m = 2$ **14.** (–5, –9); $m = -3.5$ **15.** (4, 0); $m = 7$ **16.** (6, –4); $m = -\frac{1}{5}$

Find the rate of change for each situation. ■ Lesson 5-2

17. growing from 1.4 m to 1.6 m in one year **18.** bicycling 3 mi in 15 min and 7 mi in 55 min

19. walking 3 blocks in 10 min and 12 blocks in 55 min **20.** reading 8 pages in 9 min and 22 pages in 30 min

Draw the graph of a direct variation that includes the given point. Write the equation of the line. ■ Lesson 5-3

21. (5, 4) **22.** (7, 7) **23.** (–3, –10) **24.** (4, –8) **25.** (–2, 9) **26.** (11, 1)

27. (8, –2) **28.** (–5, 9) **29.** (6, 8) **30.** (1, –4) **31.** (–3, 3) **32.** (1, 12)

Find the slope and *y*-intercept. Then graph each equation. ■ Lessons 5-4, 5-7

33. $y = 6x + 8$ **34.** $3x + 4y = -24$ **35.** $-2y = 5x - 12$ **36.** $6x + y = 12$

37. $y = \frac{-3}{4}x - 8$ **38.** $2y = 8$ **39.** $y = \frac{1}{2}x + 3$ **40.** $y = -7x$

41. **a.** Graph the ages and grade levels of some students in a school below. ■ Lesson 5-6
b. Draw a trend line.
c. Find the equation of the line of best fit.

(10, 6), (16, 10), (15, 10), (18,12), (17, 11), (17, 12), (19, 12), (16, 11), (11, 7), (15, 9), (13, 8)

Write an equation that satisfies the given conditions. ■ Lesson 5-8

42. parallel to $y = 4x + 1$, through (–3, 5) **43.** perpendicular to $y = -x - 3$, through (0, 0)

44. perpendicular to $3x + 4y = 12$, through (7, 1) **45.** parallel to $2x - y = 6$, through (–6, –9)

46. perpendicular to $y = -2x + 5$, through (4, –10) **47.** parallel to $2y = 5x + 12$, through (2, –1)

Solve each equation by graphing. ■ Lesson 5-9

48. $x + 5 = 3x - 7$ **49.** $-4x + 1 = 2x - 5$ **50.** $9x - 2 = 7x + 4$ **51.** $6x + 1 = 3x - 5$

52. $8x - 2 = 7x + 9$ **53.** $12x + 4 = x - 29$ **54.** $-x - 4 = x + 18$ **55.** $5x = 6x - 19$

Extra Practice

Choose your own method to solve each system.

■ Lessons 6-1 to 6-3

1. $x - y = 7$
$3x + 2y = 6$

2. $x + 4y = 1$
$3x - 2y = -25$

3. $4x - 5y = 9$
$-2x - y = -29$

4. $x - y = 13$
$y - x = -13$

5. $3x - y = 4$
$x + 5y = -4$

6. $x + y = 4$
$y = 7x + 4$

7. $x + y = 19$
$x - y = -7$

8. $-3x + 4y = 29$
$3x + 2y = -17$

9. $4x - 9y = 61$
$10x + 3y = 25$

10. $6x + y = 13$
$y - x = -8$

11. $3x + y = 3$
$-3x + 2y = -30$

12. $4x - y = 105$
$x + 7y = -10$

Write a system of equations to solve each problem.

■ Lesson 6-4

13. Suppose you have 12 coins that total \$.32. Some of the coins are nickels and the rest are pennies. How many of each coin do you have?

14. Your school drama club will put on a play you wrote. Royalties are \$50 plus \$.25 for each ticket sold. The cost for props and costumes is \$85. The tickets for the play will be \$2 each.

a. Write an equation for the expenses.

b. Write an equation for the income. What is the break-even point?

c. How much will the club earn if 200 tickets are sold?

Graph each linear inequality.

■ Lesson 6-5

15. $y \geq 4x - 3$

16. $y < x - 4$

17. $y > -6x + 5$

18. $y \leq 14 - x$

19. $x < -8$

20. $2x + 3y \leq 6$

21. $y \leq 12$

22. $y > -3x + 1$

Graph each system.

■ Lessons 6-6, 6-8

23. $y \leq 5x + 1$
$y > x - 3$

24. $y > 4x + 3$
$y \geq -2x - 1$

25. $y = |2x| - 3$
$y = x + 4$

26. $y < -2x + 1$
$y > -2x - 3$

27. $y = |6x| - 2$
$y = x^2 - 2$

28. $y = 4x^2 - 5$
$y = x$

29. $y \leq 8$
$y \geq |-x| + 1$

30. $y \leq 5x - 2$
$y > 3$

31. $y = -2x - 7$
$y = |x + 3|$

32. $y > -3x - 9$
$y < 5x + 7$

33. $y = x^2 + 2$
$y = \left|\frac{1}{2}x\right| + 4$

34. $y \geq x$
$y \leq x + 1$

Graph each system of restrictions. Find the coordinates of each vertex. Evaluate the equation to find the maximum and minimum values of *B*.

■ Lesson 6-7

35. $x \geq 0$
$y \geq 0$
$x \leq 5$
$y \leq 4$
$B = 2x + 5y$

36. $x \geq 2$
$x \leq 6$
$y \geq 1$
$y \leq 4$
$B = x + 3y$

37. $x \geq 2$
$y \geq 1$
$x + y \leq 10$
$B = 3x + 2y$

38. $x \geq 0$
$y \geq 0$
$y \leq -2x + 10$
$y \leq 4x + 2$
$B = x + y$

Extra Practice

Lessons 7-1 to 7-3

Without graphing, describe how each graph differs from the graph of $y = x^2$.

1. $y = 3x^2$ **2.** $y = -4x^2$ **3.** $y = -0.5x^2$ **4.** $y = 0.2x^2$

5. $y = x^2 - 4$ **6.** $y = x^2 + 1$ **7.** $y = 2x^2 + 5$ **8.** $y = -0.3x^2 - 7$

Graph each quadratic function. Label the axis of symmetry, the vertex, and the y-intercept.

9. $y = 3x^2$ **10.** $y = -2x^2 + 1$ **11.** $y = 0.5x^2 - 3$

12. $y = -x^2 + 2x + 1$ **13.** $y = 3x^2 + 5x$ **14.** $y = \frac{3}{4}x^2$

15. $y = 2x^2 - 9$ **16.** $y = -5x^2 + x + 4$ **17.** $y = x^2 - 7x$

18. $y = x^2 - 3x + 8$ **19.** $y = -x^2 + x + 12$ **20.** $y = -\frac{1}{2}x^2 + x - 3$

Graph each quadratic inequality.

21. $y > x^2 - 4$ **22.** $y \geq -x^2 + 3x + 10$ **23.** $y < 2x^2 + x$

24. $y \leq 2x^2 + 5$ **25.** $y > -\frac{1}{2}x^2 - 3x$ **26.** $y \leq x^2 + x - 2$

Lesson 7-4

Find the square roots of each number.

27. 25 **28.** $\frac{4}{9}$ **29.** 64 **30.** $\frac{25}{36}$ **31.** 0.81 **32.** 900

33. 2.25 **34.** 16 **35.** $\frac{1}{25}$ **36.** 169 **37.** $\frac{4}{36}$ **38.** 289

Lessons 7-5, 7-6

Solve each equation. Round solutions to the nearest hundredth when necessary. If the equation has no real solution, write *no real solution*.

39. $x^2 = 36$ **40.** $x^2 + x - 2 = 0$ **41.** $c^2 - 100 = 0$

42. $9d^2 = 25$ **43.** $(x - 4)^2 = 100$ **44.** $3x^2 = 27$

45. $2x^2 - 54 = 284$ **46.** $7n^2 = 63$ **47.** $h^2 + 4 = 0$

48. $x^2 + 6x - 2 = 0$ **49.** $x^2 - 5x = 7$ **50.** $x^2 - 10x + 3 = 0$

51. $2x^2 - 4x + 1 = 0$ **52.** $3x^2 + x + 5 = 0$ **53.** $\frac{1}{2}x^2 - 8 = 3x$

54. $x^2 + 8x - 5 = -9$ **55.** $2x^2 - 5x = x^2 - 3x + 6$ **56.** $-3x^2 + x - 2 = 5$

Lesson 7-7

Evaluate the discriminant. Determine the number of real solutions of each equation.

57. $x^2 - x + 5 = 0$ **58.** $3x^2 + 4x = -3 - 2x$ **59.** $-2x^2 - x + 7 = 0$

60. $3x^2 + 8x = 9$ **61.** $3x^2 + 5 = 6x$ **62.** $6x^2 + 11x - 4 = 0$

63. $-x^2 + x - 4 = 3$ **64.** $6x - x^2 = 4$ **65.** $x^2 = 5x - 1$

Extra Practice

Lessons 8-1 to 8-3

Graph each function. Label each graph as *exponential growth* or *exponential decay*.

1. $y = 3^x$ **2.** $y = \left(\frac{3}{4}\right)^x$ **3.** $y = 1.5^x$ **4.** $y = \frac{1}{2} \cdot 3^x$

5. $y = 3 \cdot 7^x$ **6.** $y = 4^x$ **7.** $y = 3 \cdot \left(\frac{1}{5}\right)^x$ **8.** $y = 2^x$

9. $y = 2 \cdot 3^x$ **10.** $y = (0.8)^x$ **11.** $y = 2.5^x$ **12.** $y = 4 \cdot (0.2)^x$

Identify the growth factor or decay factor for each exponential function.

13. $y = 8^x$ **14.** $y = \frac{3}{4} \cdot 2^x$ **15.** $y = 9 \cdot \left(\frac{1}{2}\right)^x$ **16.** $y = 4 \cdot 9^x$

17. $y = 0.65^x$ **18.** $y = 3 \cdot 1.5^x$ **19.** $y = \frac{2}{5} \cdot \left(\frac{1}{4}\right)^x$ **20.** $y = 0.1 \cdot 0.9^x$

Write an exponential function to model each situation. Find each amount after the specified time.

21. \$200 principal
4% compounded annually
5 years

22. \$1000 principal
3.6% compounded monthly
10 years

23. \$3000 investment
8% loss each year
3 years

Lessons 8-4, 8-6 to 8-8

Simplify each expression. Use only positive exponents.

24. $(2t)^{-6}$ **25.** $5m^5m^{-8}$ **26.** $(4.5)^4(4.5)^{-2}$ **27.** $(m^7t^{-5})^2$

28. $(x^2n^4)(n^{-8})$ **29.** $(w^{-2}j^{-4})^{-3}(j^7j^3)$ **30.** $(t^6)^3(m^2)$ **31.** $(3n^4)^2$

32. $\frac{r^5}{g^3}$ **33.** $\frac{1}{a^{-4}}$ **34.** $\frac{w^7}{w^{-6}}$ **35.** $\frac{6}{t^{-4}}$

36. $\frac{a^2b^{-7}c^4}{a^5b^3c^{-2}}$ **37.** $\frac{(2r^5)^3}{4t^8t^{-1}}$ **38.** $\left(\frac{a^6}{a^7}\right)^{-3}$ **39.** $\left(\frac{c^5c^{-3}}{c^{-4}}\right)^{-2}$

Evaluate each expression for $m = 2$, $t = -3$, $w = 4$, and $z = 0$.

40. t^m **41.** t^{-m} **42.** $(w \cdot t)^m$ **43.** $w^m \cdot t^m$

44. $(w^z)^m$ **45.** w^mw^z **46.** $z^t(m^t)^z$ **47.** $w^{-t} \cdot t^t$

Lesson 8-5

Write each number in scientific notation.

48. 34,000,000 **49.** 0.000 63 **50.** 1500 **51.** 0.0002

52. 360,000 **53.** 6,200,000,000 **54.** 0.05 **55.** 0.000 000 000 891

56. 910,000,000,000 **57.** 0.38 **58.** 0.000 000 07 **59.** 5,070,000,000,000

Write each number in standard notation.

60. 8.05×10^6 **61.** 3.2×10^{-7} **62.** 9.0×10^8 **63.** 4.25×10^{-4}

Extra Practice

Could each set of three numbers represent the lengths of the sides of a right triangle? Explain your answers.

■ Lesson 9-1

1. 4, 5, 7
2. 6, 8, 10
3. 6, 9, 13
4. 10, 13, 17
5. 15, 36, 39
6. 3, 7, 10
7. 8, 15, 17
8. 9, 12, 15

Find the length of the diagonal of a rectangle with sides of the given lengths *a* and *b*. Round to the nearest tenth.

9. $a = 6, b = 8$
10. $a = 5, b = 9$
11. $a = 4, b = 10$
12. $a = 9, b = 1$

Find the distance between the endpoints of each segment. Round your answers to the nearest tenth. Then find the midpoint of each segment.

■ Lesson 9-2

13. $A(1, 3), B(2, 8)$
14. $R(6, -2), S(-7, -10)$
15. $G(4, 0), H(5, -1)$
16. $A(-4, 1), B(3, 5)$
17. $G(11, 7), H(-7, -11)$
18. $R(1, -6), S(4, -2)$
19. $R(-8, -4), S(5, 7)$
20. $A(0, 6), B(-2, 9)$
21. $G(5, 10), H(0, 0)$

Use $\triangle ABC$ to evaluate each expression.

■ Lesson 9-3

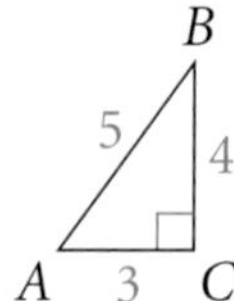

22. $\sin A$
23. $\cos A$
24. $\tan A$
25. $\sin B$
26. $\cos B$
27. $\tan B$

Simplify each radical expression.

■ Lessons 9-4, 9-5

28. $\frac{\sqrt{27}}{\sqrt{81}}$
29. $\sqrt{\frac{25}{4}}$
30. $\sqrt{\frac{50}{9}}$
31. $\frac{\sqrt{72}}{\sqrt{50}}$
32. $\sqrt{75} - 4\sqrt{75}$
33. $\sqrt{5}(\sqrt{20} - \sqrt{80})$
34. $\sqrt{25} \cdot \sqrt{4}$
35. $\sqrt{6}(\sqrt{6} - 3)$
36. $3\sqrt{300} + 2\sqrt{27}$
37. $5\sqrt{2} \cdot 3\sqrt{50}$
38. $\sqrt{8} - 4\sqrt{2}$
39. $\sqrt{27} \cdot \sqrt{3}$

Solve each radical equation. Check your solutions.

■ Lesson 9-6

40. $\sqrt{3x + 4} = 1$
41. $6 = \sqrt{8x - 4}$
42. $2x = \sqrt{14x - 6}$
43. $\sqrt{2x + 5} = \sqrt{3x + 1}$
44. $2x = \sqrt{6x + 4}$
45. $\sqrt{5x + 11} = \sqrt{7x - 1}$

Find the domain of each function. Then graph the function.

■ Lesson 9-7

46. $y = \sqrt{x + 5}$
47. $y = \sqrt{x} - 2$
48. $y = \sqrt{x + 1}$
49. $y = \sqrt{x} - 4$
50. $y = \sqrt{x - 3}$
51. $y = \sqrt{x} + 6$

Find the standard deviation of each set of data to the nearest tenth.

■ Lesson 9-8

52. 11, 14, 10, 13, 15
53. 2, 4, 3, 5, 3, 7
54. 21, 20, 26, 18, 30
55. 15, 13, 10, 20, 17
56. 32, 33, 30, 37
57. 7, 10, 4, 8, 2, 11

Extra Practice

Find each sum or difference. Write in standard form. Lesson 10-1

1. $(5x^3 + 3x^2 - 7x + 10) - (3x^3 - x^2 + 4x - 1)$
2. $(x^2 + 3x - 2) + (4x^2 - 5x + 2)$
3. $(4m^3 + 7m - 4) + (2m^3 - 6m + 8)$
4. $(8t^2 + t + 10) - (9t^2 - 9t - 1)$
5. $(-7c^3 + c^2 - 8c - 11) - (3c^3 + 2c^2 + c - 4)$
6. $(6v + 3v^2 - 9v^3) + (7v - 4v^2 - 10v^3)$
7. $(s^4 - s^3 - 5s^2 + 3s) - (5s^4 + s^3 - 7s^2 - s)$
8. $(9w - 4w^2 + 10) + (8w^2 + 7 + 5w)$

Find each product. Lessons 10-2, 10-3

9. $4b(b^2 + 3)$
10. $(5c + 3)(-c + 2)$
11. $(3t - 1)(2t + 1)$
12. $9c(c^2 - 3c + 5)$
13. $8m(4m - 5)$
14. $(w - 1)(w^2 + w + 1)$
15. $5k(k^2 + 8k)$
16. $(3t + 5)(t + 1)$
17. $(2n - 3)(2n + 4)$
18. $5r^2(r^2 + 4r - 2)$
19. $(b + 3)(b + 7)$
20. $2m^2(m^3 + m - 2)$
21. **Geometry** A rectangle has dimensions $3x - 1$ and $2x + 5$. Write an expression for its area as a product and in standard form.

Find the greatest common factor of each expression.

22. $t^6 + t^4 - t^5 + t^2$
23. $3m^2 - 6 + 9m$
24. $16c^2 - 4c^3 + 12c^5$
25. $8v^6 + 2v^5 - 10v^9$
26. $6n^2 - 3n^3 + 2n^4$
27. $5r + 20r^3 + 15r^2$
28. $9x^6 + 5x^5 + 4x^7$
29. $4d^8 - 2d^{10} + 7d^4$
30. $5t^2 + 3t - 8t^4$
31. $4m^2 + 16m - 20$
32. $7n + 14n^2 + 21n^3$
33. $5w - 8w^2 + 2w^3$

Factor each polynomial. Lessons 10-4, 10-5

34. $x^2 + 6x + 9$
35. $x^2 - 25$
36. $4t^2 + t - 3$
37. $9c^2 - 169$
38. $2c^2 - 5c - 3$
39. $t^2 - 6t + 9$
40. $x^2 - 8x + 16$
41. $4d^2 - 12d + 9$
42. $4m^2 - 121$
43. $3v^2 + 10v - 8$
44. $4g^2 + 4g + 1$
45. $w^2 + 3w - 4$
46. $9t^2 + 12t + 4$
47. $12m^2 - 5m - 2$
48. $36s^2 - 1$
49. $c^2 - 10c + 25$

Solve each quadratic equation. Round answers to the nearest hundredth, if necessary. Lessons 10-6, 10-7

50. $x^2 + 5x + 6 = 0$
51. $d^2 - 144 = 0$
52. $c^2 + 6 = 2 - 4c$
53. $x^2 + 4x = 2x^2 - x + 6$
54. $3x^2 + 2x - 12 = x^2$
55. $r^2 + 4r + 1 = r$
56. $d^2 + 2d + 10 = 2d + 100$
57. $3c^2 + c - 10 = c^2 - 5$
58. $t^2 - 3t - 10 = 0$
59. $4x^2 - 5x - 5 = 2x^2 + 4x$
60. $4m^2 + 6m + 1 = 6m + 82$
61. $d^2 - 5d = 3d^2 + 1$
62. **Agriculture** You are planting a rectangular vegetable garden. It is 5 feet longer than 3 times its width. The area of the garden is 250 ft^2. Find the dimensions of the garden.

CHAPTER 11

Extra Practice

Find the constant of variation for each inverse variation. ■ Lesson 11-1

1. $y = 10$ when $x = 7$
2. $y = 8$ when $x = 12$
3. $y = 0.2$ when $x = 4$
4. $y = 4$ when $x = 5$
5. $y = 0.1$ when $x = 6$
6. $y = 3$ when $x = 7$

Each pair of points is from an inverse variation. Find the missing value.

7. $(5.4, 3)$ and $(2, y)$
8. $(x, 4)$ and $(5, 6)$
9. $(3, 6)$ and $(9, y)$
10. $(100, 2)$ and $(x, 25)$
11. $(6, 1)$ and $(x, 2)$
12. $(8, y)$ and $(2, 4)$
13. $(7, 35)$, and $(49, y)$
14. $(x, 32)$ and $(16, 1)$

Graph each function. Include a dashed line for each asymptote. ■ Lesson 11-2

15. $y = \frac{6}{x}$
16. $y = \frac{8}{x + 2}$
17. $y = \frac{4}{x} - 3$
18. $y = \frac{5}{x + 1} + 3$
19. $y = \frac{-1}{x}$
20. $y = \frac{5}{x} - 1$
21. $y = \frac{-2}{x - 3}$
22. $y = \frac{2}{x - 1}$
23. $y = \frac{3}{x} + 4$
24. $y = \frac{5}{x}$
25. $y = \frac{2}{x + 1} - 1$
26. $y = \frac{x - 3}{x + 3}$

Simplify each expression and state any values restricted from the domain. ■ Lessons 11-3, 11-4

27. $\frac{4t^2}{16t}$
28. $\frac{c - 5}{c^2 - 25}$
29. $\frac{4m - 12}{m - 3}$
30. $\frac{a^2 + 2a - 3}{a + 3}$
31. $\frac{4}{x} - \frac{3}{x}$
32. $\frac{6t}{5} + \frac{4t}{5}$
33. $\frac{6}{c} + \frac{4}{c^2}$
34. $\frac{6}{3d} - \frac{4}{3d}$
35. $\frac{5s^4}{10s^3}$
36. $\frac{4n^2}{7} \cdot \frac{14}{2n^3}$
37. $\frac{8b^2 - 4b}{3b} \div \frac{2b - 1}{9b^2}$
38. $\frac{v^5}{v^3} \cdot \frac{4v^{-1}}{v^2}$
39. $\frac{5}{t + 4} + \frac{3}{t - 4}$
40. $\frac{8}{m^2 + 6m + 5} + \frac{4}{m + 1}$
41. $\frac{3y}{4y - 8} \div \frac{9y}{2y^2 - 4y}$
42. $\frac{4}{d^2} - \frac{3}{d^3}$

Solve each equation. Check your answers. ■ Lesson 11-5

43. $\frac{1}{4} + \frac{1}{x} = \frac{3}{8}$
44. $\frac{4}{m} - 3 = \frac{2}{m}$
45. $\frac{1}{b - 3} = \frac{1}{4b}$
46. $\frac{4}{x - 1} = \frac{3}{x}$
47. $\frac{4}{n} + \frac{5}{9} = 1$
48. $\frac{x}{x + 2} = \frac{x - 3}{x + 1}$
49. $t - \frac{8}{t} = \frac{17}{t}$
50. $\frac{x + 2}{x + 5} = \frac{x - 4}{x + 4}$
51. $\frac{4}{c + 1} - \frac{2}{c - 1} = \frac{3c + 6}{c^2 - 1}$
52. $\frac{4}{m + 3} = \frac{6}{m - 3}$
53. $\frac{4}{t + 5} + 1 = \frac{15}{t^2 - 25}$

Evaluate. ■ Lessons 11-6, 11-7

54. ${}_6C_4$
55. ${}_7P_2$
56. ${}_{10}C_5$
57. ${}_8C_7$
58. ${}_{12}P_6$
59. ${}_9C_7$
60. ${}_6P_4$
61. ${}_9C_3$
62. ${}_5P_2$
63. ${}_{12}P_3$
64. ${}_8C_3$
65. ${}_7P_6$

66. You are choosing a personal identification number using the digits 1, 3, 5, and 6 exactly once each. How many different numbers can you choose from?

67. The 18 members of the debate team need to form a committee of five people. How many different five-person committees are possible?

Problem Solving Strategies

You may find one or more of these strategies helpful in solving a word problem.

STRATEGY	WHEN TO USE IT
Draw a Diagram	The problem describes a picture or diagram.
Guess and Test	The needed information seems to be missing.
Look for a Pattern	The problem describes a relationship.
Make a Table	The problem has data that need to be organized.
Solve a Simpler Problem	The problem is complex or has numbers that are too cumbersome to use at first.
Use Logical Reasoning	You need to reach a conclusion using given information.
Work Backward	You need to find the number that led to the result in the problem.

Problem Solving: Draw a Diagram

Example **Two cars started from the same point. One traveled east at 45 mi/h, the other west at 50 mi/h. How far apart were the cars after 5 hours?**

Draw a diagram: West ← 50 mi/h • 5 — Start — 45 mi/h • 5 → East

The first car traveled: $45 \cdot 5$ or 225 mi. The second car traveled: $50 \cdot 5$ or 250 mi.

The diagram shows that the two distances should be added:
$225 + 250 = 475$ mi

After 5 hours, the cars were 475 mi apart.

EXERCISES

1. Jason, Lee, Melba, and Bonnie want to play each of the others in tennis. How many games will be played?
2. A playground, a zoo, a picnic area, and a flower garden will be in four corners of a new park. Straight paths will connect each of these areas to all the other areas. How many pathways will be built?
3. Pedro wants to tack 4 posters on a bulletin board. He will tack the four corners of each poster, overlapping the sides of each poster a little. What is the least number of tacks that Pedro can use?

Problem Solving: Guess and Test

When you are not sure how to start, guess an answer and then test it. In the process of testing a guess, you may see a way to revise your guess to get closer to the answer or to get the answer.

Example **Maria bought books and CDs as gifts. Altogether she bought 12 gifts and spent $84. The books cost $6 each and the CDs cost $9 each. How many of each gift did she buy?**

Guess: 6 books, 6 CDs

Test: $6 \cdot \$6 = \$36$; $6 \cdot \$9 = +\$54$; total $\$90$

Revise your guess. You need fewer CDs to bring the total cost down.

Guess: 7 books, 5 CDs

Test: $7 \cdot \$6 = \$42$; $5 \cdot \$9 = +\$45$; total $\$87$

The cost is still too high.

Guess: 8 books, 4 CDs

Test: $8 \cdot \$6 = \$48$; $4 \cdot \$9 = +\$36$; total $\$84$

Maria bought 8 books and 4 CDs.

EXERCISES

1. Find two consecutive odd integers whose product is 323.
2. Mika bought 9 rolls of film to take 180 pictures on a field trip. Some rolls had 36 exposures and the rest had 12 exposures. How many of each type did Mika buy?
3. Tanya is 18 years old. Her brother Shawn is 16 years younger. How old will Tanya be when she is 3 times as old as Shawn is then?
4. Steven has 100 ft of fencing and wants to build a fence in the shape of a rectangle to enclose the largest possible area. What should be the dimensions of the rectangle?
5. The combined ages of a mother, her son, and her daughter are 61 years. The mother is 22 years older than her son and 31 years older than her daughter. How old is each person?
6. Kenji traveled 40 mi in a two-day bicycle race. He biked 8 mi farther on the first day than he did on the second day. How many miles did Kenji travel each day?

Problem Solving: Look for a Pattern and Make a Table

Some problems describe relationships that involve regular sequences of numbers or other things. To solve the problem you need to be able to recognize and describe the *pattern* that gives the relationship for the numbers or things. One way to organize the information given is to *make a table.*

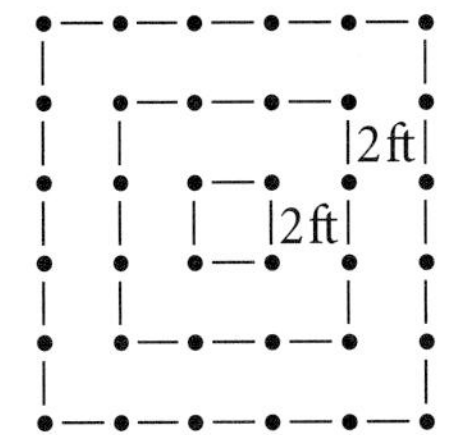

Example **A tree farm is planted as shown at the right. The dots represent trees. The lot will be enlarged by larger squares. How many trees will be in the fifth square?**

Make a table to help find a pattern.

Square position	1st	2nd	3rd	4th	5th
Number of trees	4	12	20	■	■

Pattern: 8 more trees are planted in each larger square.

The fourth square will have 28 trees. The fifth square will have 36 trees.

EXERCISES

1. Kareem made a display of books at a book fair. One book was in the first row and the other rows each had two more books than the row before it. How many books does Kareem have if he has nine rows?
2. Chris is using green and white tiles to cover her floor. If she uses tiles in the pattern, G, W, G, G, W, G, G, W, G, G, what will be the color of the twentieth tile?
3. Jay read one story the first week of summer vacation, 3 the second week, 6 the third week, and 10 the fourth week. He kept to this pattern for eight weeks. How many stories did he read the eighth week?
4. Jan has 6 coins, none of which is a half dollar. The coins have a value of $.85. What coins does she have?
5. Sam is covering a wall with rows of red, white, and blue siding. The red siding is cut in 1.8-m strips, the white in 2.4-m strips, and the blue in 1.2-m strips. What is the shortest length that Sam can cover by uncut strips to form equal length rows of each color?
6. A train leaves a station at 8:00 A.M. and averages 40 mi/h. Another train leaves the same station one hour later and averages 50 mi/h traveling in the same direction. At what time will the second train catch up with the first train? How many miles would each train have traveled by that time?
7. The soccer team held a car wash and earned $200. They charged $7 per truck and $5 per car. In how many different ways could the team have earned the $200?

Problem Solving: Solve a Simpler Problem

By solving one or more simpler problems you can often find a pattern that will help solve a more complicated problem.

Example **How many different rectangles are in a strip with 10 squares?**

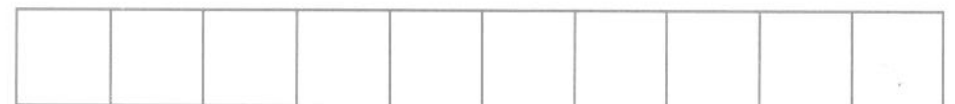

Begin with one square, then add one square at a time. Find out whether there is a pattern.

Squares in the strip:	1	2	3	4	5
Number of rectangles:	1	3	6	10	15
Pattern:		1 + 2 = 3	3 + 3 = 6	6 + 4 = 10	10 + 5 = 15

Now continue the pattern.

Squares in the strip:	6	7	8	9	10
Number of rectangles:	21	28	36	45	55
Pattern:	15 + 6 = 21	21 + 7 = 28	28 + 8 = 36	36 + 9 = 45	45 + 10 = 55

There are 55 rectangles in a strip with 10 squares.

EXERCISES

1. Lockers in the east wing of Hastings High School are numbered 1–120. How many contain the digit 8?
2. What is the sum of all of the numbers from 1 to 100? (*Hint:* What is 1 + 100? What is 2 + 99?)
3. Suppose your heart beats 70 times per minute. At this rate, how many times had it beaten by the time you were 10?
4. For a community project you have to create the numbers 1 through 148 using large glittered digits, which you have to make by hand. How many glittered digits do you have to make?
5. There are 63 teams competing in the state soccer championship. If a team loses a game it is eliminated. How many games have to be played in order to get a single champion team?
6. You work in a supermarket. Your boss asks you to arrange oranges in a pyramid for a display. The pyramid's base should be a square with 25 oranges. How many layers of oranges will be in your pyramid? How many oranges will you need?
7. Kesi has her math book open. The product of the two page numbers on the facing pages is 1056. What are the two page numbers?

Problem Solving: Use Logical Reasoning

Some problems can be solved without the use of numbers. They can be solved by the use of logical reasoning, given some information.

Example **Joe, Melissa, Liz, and Greg each play a different sport. Their sports are running, basketball, baseball, and tennis. Liz's sport does not use a ball. Joe hit a home run in his sport. Melissa is the sister of the tennis player. Which sport does each person play?**

Make a table to organize what you know.

	Running	Basketball	Baseball	Tennis
Joe	✗	✗	✓	✗
Melissa				✗
Liz	✓	✗	✗	✗
Greg				

← A home run means Joe plays baseball.

← Melissa cannot be the tennis player.

← Liz must run, since running does not involve a ball.

Use logical reasoning to complete the table.

	Running	Basketball	Baseball	Tennis
Joe	✗	✗	✓	✗
Melissa	✗	✓	✗	✗
Liz	✓	✗	✗	✗
Greg	✗	✗	✗	✓

← The only option for Greg is tennis.

Greg plays tennis, Melissa plays basketball, Liz runs, and Joe plays baseball.

EXERCISES

1. Juan has a dog, a horse, a bird, and a cat. Their names are Bo, Cricket, K.C., and Tuffy. Tuffy and K.C. cannot fly or be ridden. The bird talks to Bo. Tuffy runs from the dog. What is each pet's name?

2. A math class has 25 students. There are 13 students who are only in the band, 4 who are only on the swimming team, and 5 who do both activities. How many students are not in either activity?

3. Annette is taller than Heather but shorter than Garo. Tanya's height is between Garo's and Annette's. Karin would be the shortest if it weren't for Alexa. List the names in order from shortest to tallest.

4. The Colts, Cubs, and Bears played each other two games of basketball. The Colts won 3 of their games. The Bears won 2 of their games. How many games did each team win and lose?

5. The girls' basketball league has a calling chain when it needs to cancel its games. The leader takes 1 min to call 2 players. These 2 players take 1 min to call 2 more players, and so on. How many players will be called in 6 min?

Problem Solving: Work Backward

To solve some problems you need to start with the end result and work backward to the beginning.

Example **On Monday, Rita withdrew $150 from her savings account. On Wednesday, she deposited $400 into her account. She now has $1000. How much was in her account on Monday before she withdrew the money?**

Money in account now: $1000

Undo the deposit: − $400
$600

Undo the withdrawal: + $150
$750

Rita had $750 in her account on Monday before the withdrawal.

EXERCISES

1. Ned gave the following puzzle to Connie: I am thinking of a number. I doubled it, then tripled the result. The final result was 36. What is my number?

2. Fernando gave the following puzzle to Maria: I am thinking of a number. I divided it by 3. Then I divided the result by 5. The final result was 8. What is my number?

3. This week Sandy withdrew $350 from her savings account. She made a deposit of $125, wrote a check for $275, and made a deposit of $150. She now has $225 in her account. How much did she have in her account at the beginning of the week?

4. Jeff paid $12.50 for a taxi fare from his home to the airport including a $1.60 tip. City Cab charges $1.90 for the first mile plus $.15 for each additional $\frac{1}{6}$ mile. How many miles is Jeff's home from the airport?

5. Ben sold $\frac{1}{4}$ as many tickets to the fund-raiser as Charles. Charles sold 3 times as many as Susan. Susan sold 4 fewer than Tom. If Tom sold 12 tickets, how many did Ben sell?

6. Two cars start traveling towards each other. One car is averaging 30 mi/h and the other 40 mi/h. After 4 h the cars are 10 mi apart. How far apart were the cars when they started?

7. Nina has a dentist appointment at 8:45 A.M. She wants to arrive 10 min early. Nina needs to allow 25 min to travel to the appointment and 45 min to dress and have breakfast. What is the latest time Nina could get up?

Prime Numbers and Composite Numbers

A *prime number* is a whole number greater than 1 that has exactly two factors, the number 1 and itself.

Prime number:	2	5	17	29
Factors:	1, 2	1, 5	1, 17	1, 29

A *composite number* is a number that has more than two factors. The number 1 is neither prime nor composite.

Composite number:	6	15	26	48
Factors:	1, 2, 3, 6	1, 3, 5, 15	1, 2, 13, 26	1, 2, 3, 4 , 6, 8, 12, 16, 24, 48

Example 1 **Is 51 prime or composite?**

$51 = 3 \cdot 17$ ← Try to find factors other than 1 and 51.

51 is a composite number.

Every composite number can be factored into prime factors using a factor tree. When all the factors are prime numbers, it is called the *prime factorization* of the number.

Example 2 **Use a factor tree to write the prime factorization of 28.**

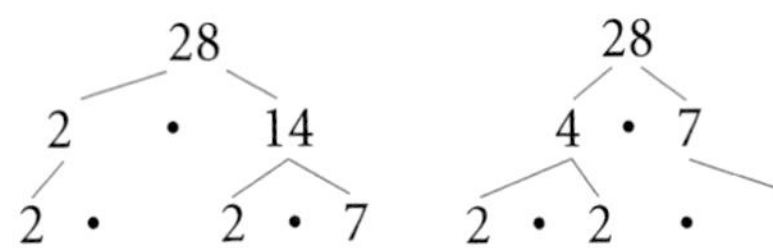

The order of listing the factors may be different, but the end result is the same.

The prime factorization of 28 is $2 \cdot 2 \cdot 7$.

EXERCISES

Is each number prime or composite?

1. 9 **2.** 16 **3.** 34 **4.** 61 **5.** 7 **6.** 13

7. 12 **8.** 40 **9.** 57 **10.** 64 **11.** 120 **12.** 700

13. 39 **14.** 23 **15.** 63 **16.** 19 **17.** 522 **18.** 101

List all the factors of each number.

19. 46 **20.** 32 **21.** 11 **22.** 65 **23.** 27 **24.** 29

Use a factor tree to write the prime factorization of each number.

25. 18 **26.** 20 **27.** 27 **28.** 54 **29.** 64 **30.** 96

31. 100 **32.** 125 **33.** 84 **34.** 150 **35.** 121 **36.** 226

Factors and Multiples

A common factor is a number that is a factor of two or more numbers. The *greatest common factor* (GCF) is the greatest number that is a common factor of two or more numbers.

Example 1 **Find the GCF of 14 and 42.**

Factors of 24: 1, 2, 3, 4, 6, 8, 12, 24 — Find the common factors: 1, 2, 4, 8
Factors of 64: 1, 2, 4, 8, 16, 32, 64 ← The greatest common factor is 8.
GCF (24, 64) = 8

Another way to find the GCF is to first find the prime factors of the numbers.

$24 = 2 \cdot 2 \cdot 2 \cdot 3$ ← Multiply the common prime factors.
$64 = 2 \cdot 2 \cdot 2 \cdot 2 \cdot 2 \cdot 2$
$GCF = 2 \cdot 2 \cdot 2 = 8$ ← Use the factor the number of times it appears as a common factor.

A common multiple is a number that is a multiple of two or more numbers. The *least common multiple* (LCM) is the least number that is a common multiple of two or more numbers.

Example 2 **Find the LCM of 12 and 18.**

Multiples of 12: 12, 24, 36,. . . — List a number of multiples until you find the first common multiple.
Multiples of 18: 18, 36,. . .
LCM = (12, 18) = 36

Another way to find the LCM is to first find the prime factors of the numbers.
$12 = 2 \cdot 2 \cdot 3$
$18 = 2 \cdot 3 \cdot 3$
$LCM = 2 \cdot 2 \cdot 3 \cdot 3 = 36$ ← Use each prime factor the greatest number of times it appears in either number.

EXERCISES

Find the GCF of each set of numbers.

1. 12 and 22 **2.** 7 and 21 **3.** 24 and 48 **4.** 17 and 51
5. 9 and 12 **6.** 10 and 25 **7.** 21 and 49 **8.** 27 and 36
9. 14 and 42 **10.** 20 and 30 **11.** 27 and 15 **12.** 12 and 28
13. 10, 30, and 25 **14.** 56, 84, and 140 **15.** 42, 63, and 105 **16.** 20, 28, and 40

Find the LCM of each set of numbers.

17. 16 and 20 **18.** 14 and 21 **19.** 11 and 33 **20.** 8 and 9
21. 5 and 12 **22.** 54 and 84 **23.** 48 and 80 **24.** 25 and 36
25. 54 and 80 **26.** 75 and 175 **27.** 10 and 25 **28.** 24 and 28
29. 10, 15, and 25 **30.** 6, 7, and 12 **31.** 5, 8, and 20 **32.** 18, 21, and 36

Simplifying Fractions

A *fraction* can name a part of a group or region. This region is divided into 10 equal parts and 6 of the equal parts are shaded.

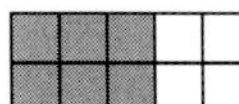

$\frac{6}{10}$ ← Numerator, ← Denominator Read: *six tenths*

A fraction can have many names. Different names for the same fraction are called *equivalent fractions.* You can find an equivalent fraction for any given fraction by multiplying the numerator and denominator of the given fraction by the same number.

Example 1 **Write five equivalent fractions for $\frac{3}{5}$.**

$\frac{3}{5} = \frac{3 \cdot 2}{5 \cdot 2} = \frac{6}{10}$ $\frac{3}{5} = \frac{3 \cdot 3}{5 \cdot 3} = \frac{9}{15}$ $\frac{3}{5} = \frac{3 \cdot 4}{5 \cdot 4} = \frac{12}{16}$ $\frac{3}{5} = \frac{3 \cdot 5}{5 \cdot 5} = \frac{15}{25}$ $\frac{3}{5} = \frac{3 \cdot 6}{5 \cdot 6} = \frac{18}{30}$

The fraction $\frac{3}{5}$ is in *simplest form* because its numerator and denominator are *relatively prime,* that is, their only common factor is the number 1. To write a fraction in simplest form, divide its numerator and denominator by their greatest common factor (GCF).

Example 2 **Write $\frac{6}{24}$ in simplest form.**

First find the GCF of 6 and 24.

$6 = 2 \cdot 3$ ← Multiply the common prime factors.

$24 = 2 \cdot 2 \cdot 2 \cdot 3$ ← GCF $= 2 \cdot 3 = 6$

Then divide the numerator and denominator of $\frac{6}{24}$ by the GCF, 6.

$\frac{6}{24} = \frac{6 \div 6}{24 \div 6} = \frac{1}{4}$ ← simplest form

EXERCISES

Complete.

1. $\frac{3}{7} = \frac{\blacksquare}{21}$ **2.** $\frac{5}{8} = \frac{20}{\blacksquare}$ **3.** $\frac{11}{12} = \frac{44}{\blacksquare}$ **4.** $\frac{12}{16} = \frac{\blacksquare}{4}$ **5.** $\frac{50}{100} = \frac{1}{\blacksquare}$

6. $\frac{5}{9} = \frac{\blacksquare}{27}$ **7.** $\frac{3}{8} = \frac{\blacksquare}{24}$ **8.** $\frac{5}{6} = \frac{20}{\blacksquare}$ **9.** $\frac{12}{20} = \frac{\blacksquare}{5}$ **10.** $\frac{75}{150} = \frac{1}{\blacksquare}$

Which fractions are in simplest form?

11. $\frac{4}{12}$ **12.** $\frac{3}{16}$ **13.** $\frac{5}{30}$ **14.** $\frac{9}{72}$ **15.** $\frac{11}{22}$ **16.** $\frac{24}{25}$

Write in simplest form.

17. $\frac{8}{16}$ **18.** $\frac{7}{14}$ **19.** $\frac{6}{9}$ **20.** $\frac{20}{30}$ **21.** $\frac{8}{20}$ **22.** $\frac{12}{40}$

23. $\frac{15}{45}$ **24.** $\frac{14}{56}$ **25.** $\frac{10}{25}$ **26.** $\frac{9}{72}$ **27.** $\frac{45}{60}$ **28.** $\frac{20}{35}$

29. $\frac{27}{33}$ **30.** $\frac{18}{72}$ **31.** $\frac{45}{85}$ **32.** $\frac{63}{126}$ **33.** $\frac{125}{150}$ **34.** $\frac{256}{320}$

Fractions, Decimals, and Mixed Numbers

Fractions can be written as decimals.

Example 1 **Write $\frac{3}{5}$ as a decimal.**

$$\begin{array}{r} 0.6 \\ 5\overline{)3.0} \\ -\underline{3.0} \end{array}$$

Divide the denominator into the numerator.

The decimal for $\frac{3}{5}$ is 0.6.

Decimals can be written as fractions.

Example 2 **Write 0.38 as a fraction.**

$0.38 = 38 \text{ hundredths} = \frac{38}{100} = \frac{19}{50}$

A fraction for 0.38 is $\frac{38}{100}$ or $\frac{19}{50}$.

An *improper fraction* is a fraction in which the numerator is greater than or equal to the denominator. An improper fraction can be written as a *mixed number*, that is as a whole number and a fraction.

Example 3 **Write $\frac{13}{5}$ as a mixed number.**

Divide the denominator into the numerator and write the remainder over the denominator.

$$\frac{13}{5} = \begin{array}{r} 2\text{r}3 \\ 5\overline{)13} \\ -\underline{10} \\ 3 \end{array} = 2\frac{3}{5}$$

← remainder
← denominator

A mixed number can be written as an improper fraction.

Example 4 **Write $5\frac{3}{4}$ as an improper fraction.**

$5\frac{3}{4} = \frac{23}{4}$

First multiply the denominator by the whole number: $4 \cdot 5 = 20$.
Next add the numerator of the fraction to the answer: $3 + 20 = 23$.
Then write the result over the denominator: $\frac{23}{4}$.

EXERCISES

Write as a decimal.

1. $\frac{3}{10}$ **2.** $\frac{1}{5}$ **3.** $\frac{4}{20}$ **4.** $\frac{25}{75}$ **5.** $\frac{2}{3}$ **6.** $\frac{1}{6}$

Write as a fraction.

7. 0.3 **8.** 0.25 **9.** 0.37 **10.** 0.13 **11.** 0.07 **12.** 0.875

Write as a mixed number.

13. $\frac{12}{7}$ **14.** $\frac{23}{9}$ **15.** $\frac{21}{10}$ **16.** $\frac{30}{21}$ **17.** $\frac{22}{5}$ **18.** $\frac{27}{13}$

Write as an improper fraction.

19. $2\frac{1}{2}$ **20.** $3\frac{1}{4}$ **21.** $5\frac{1}{6}$ **22.** $3\frac{4}{5}$ **23.** $4\frac{1}{7}$ **24.** $6\frac{3}{8}$

25. Celia answered $\frac{7}{8}$ of the decimal test correctly. Write this fraction as a decimal.

Adding and Subtracting Fractions

You can add and subtract fractions when they have the same denominator. Fractions with the same denominator are called *like fractions.*

Example 1 **Add $\frac{4}{5} + \frac{3}{5}$.**

$\frac{4}{5} + \frac{3}{5} = \frac{4 + 3}{5} = \frac{7}{5} = 1\frac{2}{5}$ ← Add the numerators and keep the same denominator.

Example 2 **Subtract $\frac{5}{9} - \frac{2}{9}$.**

$\frac{5}{9} - \frac{2}{9} = \frac{5 - 2}{9} = \frac{3}{9} = \frac{1}{3}$ ← Subtract the numerators and keep the same denominator.

Fractions with unlike denominators are called *unlike fractions.* To add or subtract fractions with unlike denominators, find the least common denominator (LCD) and write equivalent fractions with the same denominator. Then add or subtract the like fractions.

Example 3 **Add $\frac{3}{4} + \frac{5}{6}$.**

$\frac{3}{4} + \frac{5}{6} =$ ← Find the LCD. The LCD is the same as the least common multiple (LCM). The LCD(4, 6) is 12.

$\frac{9}{12} + \frac{10}{12} = \frac{9 + 10}{12} = \frac{19}{12}$ or $1\frac{7}{12}$ ← Write equivalent fractions with the same denominator.

Example 4 **Subtract $\frac{5}{12} - \frac{2}{9}$.**

$\frac{5}{12} - \frac{2}{9} =$ ← Find the LCD. The LCD (12, 9) is 36.

$\frac{15}{36} - \frac{8}{36} = \frac{15 - 8}{36} = \frac{7}{36}$ ← Write equivalent fractions with the same denominator.

To add or subtract mixed numbers, add or subtract the fractions. Then add or subtract the whole numbers. Sometimes when subtracting mixed numbers you may have to regroup.

Example 5 **Subtract $5\frac{1}{4} - 3\frac{2}{3}$.**

$5\frac{1}{4} - 3\frac{2}{3}$ ← Write equivalent fractions with the same denominator.

$5\frac{3}{12} - 3\frac{8}{12} =$ ← Write $5\frac{3}{12}$ as $4\frac{15}{12}$ so you can subtract the fractions.

$4\frac{15}{12} - 3\frac{8}{12} = 1\frac{7}{12}$ ← Subtract the fractions. Then subtract the whole numbers.

EXERCISES

Add. Write each answer in simplest terms.

1. $\frac{2}{7} + \frac{3}{7}$
2. $\frac{3}{8} + \frac{7}{8}$
3. $\frac{6}{5} + \frac{9}{5}$
4. $\frac{4}{9} + \frac{8}{9}$
5. $6\frac{2}{3} + 3\frac{4}{5}$
6. $1\frac{4}{7} + 2\frac{3}{14}$
7. $4\frac{5}{6} + 1\frac{7}{18}$
8. $2\frac{4}{5} + 3\frac{6}{7}$
9. $4\frac{2}{3} + 1\frac{6}{11}$
10. $3\frac{7}{9} + 5\frac{5}{27}$

Subtract. Write each answer in simplest terms.

11. $\frac{7}{8} - \frac{3}{8}$
12. $\frac{9}{10} - \frac{3}{10}$
13. $\frac{17}{5} - \frac{2}{5}$
14. $\frac{11}{7} - \frac{2}{7}$
15. $\frac{5}{11} - \frac{4}{11}$
16. $8\frac{5}{8} - 6\frac{1}{4}$
17. $3\frac{2}{3} - 1\frac{8}{9}$
18. $8\frac{5}{6} - 5\frac{1}{2}$
19. $12\frac{3}{4} - 4\frac{5}{6}$
20. $17\frac{2}{7} - 8\frac{2}{9}$

Multiplying and Dividing Fractions

To multiply two or more fractions, multiply the numerators, multiply the denominators, and simplify the product, if necessary.

Example 1 **Multiply $\frac{3}{7} \cdot \frac{5}{6}$.**

$$\frac{3}{7} \cdot \frac{5}{6} = \frac{3 \cdot 5}{7 \cdot 6} = \frac{15}{42} = \frac{15 \div 3}{42 \div 3} = \frac{5}{14}$$

Sometimes you can simplify before multiplying.

$$\frac{{}^{1}\cancel{3}}{7} \cdot \frac{5}{\cancel{6}_{2}} = \frac{5}{14}$$ ← Divide a numerator and a denominator by a common factor.

To multiply mixed numbers, change the mixed numbers to improper fractions and multiply the fractions. Write the product as a mixed number.

Example 2 **Multiply $2\frac{4}{5} \cdot 1\frac{2}{3}$.**

$$2\frac{4}{5} \cdot 1\frac{2}{3} = \frac{14}{{}_{1}\cancel{5}} \cdot \frac{\cancel{5}^{1}}{3} = \frac{14}{3} = 4\frac{2}{3}$$

To divide fractions, change the division problem to a multiplication problem. Remember that $8 \div \frac{1}{4}$ is the same as $8 \cdot 4$.

Example 3 **Divide $\frac{4}{5} \div \frac{3}{7}$.**

$$\frac{4}{5} \div \frac{3}{7} = \frac{4}{5} \cdot \frac{7}{3}$$ ← Multiply by the reciprocal of the divisor. Simplify the answer.

$$= \frac{4}{5} \cdot \frac{7}{3} = \frac{28}{15} = 1\frac{13}{15}$$

To divide mixed numbers, change the mixed numbers to improper fractions and divide the fractions.

Example 4 **Divide $4\frac{2}{3} \div 7\frac{3}{5}$.**

$$4\frac{2}{3} \div 7\frac{3}{5} = \frac{14}{3} \div \frac{38}{5} = \frac{14}{3} \cdot \frac{5}{38} = \frac{70}{114} = \frac{35}{57}$$

EXERCISES

Multiply. Write your answers in simplest form.

1. $\frac{2}{5} \cdot \frac{3}{4}$ **2.** $\frac{3}{7} \cdot \frac{4}{3}$ **3.** $\frac{5}{4} \cdot \frac{3}{8}$ **4.** $\frac{6}{7} \cdot \frac{9}{2}$ **5.** $\frac{7}{3} \cdot \frac{4}{7}$

6. $2\frac{3}{4} \cdot \frac{5}{8}$ **7.** $1\frac{1}{2} \cdot 5\frac{3}{4}$ **8.** $3\frac{4}{5} \cdot 10$ **9.** $12 \cdot 1\frac{2}{3}$ **10.** $5\frac{1}{4} \cdot \frac{2}{3}$

Divide. Write your answers in simplest form.

11. $\frac{3}{5} \div \frac{1}{2}$ **12.** $\frac{4}{5} \div \frac{9}{10}$ **13.** $\frac{4}{7} \div \frac{2}{3}$ **14.** $\frac{5}{8} \div \frac{7}{3}$ **15.** $\frac{4}{7} \div \frac{4}{3}$

16. $1\frac{4}{5} \div 2\frac{1}{2}$ **17.** $2\frac{1}{2} \div 3\frac{1}{2}$ **18.** $3\frac{1}{6} \div 1\frac{3}{4}$ **19.** $9\frac{1}{2} \div 4\frac{1}{4}$ **20.** $6\frac{3}{5} \div 2\frac{3}{5}$

Fractions, Decimals, and Percents

Percent means *per hundred.* 50% means 50 per hundred. $50\% = \frac{50}{100} = 0.50$

You can use a shortcut to write a decimal as a percent and a percent as a decimal.

Example 1 **Write each number as a percent.**

a. 0.47 **b.** 0.8 **c.** 2.475

Move the decimal point two places to the right and write a percent sign.

a. $0.47 = 47\%$ **b.** $0.80 = 80\%$ **c.** $2.475 = 247.5\%$

Example 2 **Write each number as a decimal.**

a. 25% **b.** 3% **c.** 360%

Move the decimal point two places to the left and drop the percent sign.

a. $25\% = 0.25$ **b.** $03\% = 0.03$ **c.** $360\% = 3.6$

You can write fractions as percents by writing the fraction as a decimal first. Then move the decimal point two places to the right and write a percent sign.

Example 3 **Write each number as a percent.** **a.** $\frac{3}{5}$ **b.** $\frac{7}{20}$ **c.** $\frac{2}{3}$

a. $\frac{3}{5} = 0.6 = 60\%$ **b.** $\frac{7}{20} = 0.35 = 35\%$ **c.** $\frac{2}{3} = 0.66\overline{6} = 66.\overline{6}\%$ or 66.7% (rounded to the nearest tenth of a percent)

You can write a percent as a fraction by writing the percent as a fraction with a denominator of 100 and simplifying if possible.

Example 4 **Write each number as a fraction or mixed number.**

a. $43\% = \frac{43}{100}$ **b.** $\frac{1}{2}\% = \frac{\frac{1}{2}}{100} = \frac{1}{2} \div 100 = \frac{1}{2} \cdot \frac{1}{100} = \frac{1}{200}$ **c.** $180\% = \frac{180}{100} = \frac{9}{5} = 1\frac{4}{5}$

EXERCISES

Write each number as a percent.

1. 0.56 **2.** 0.09 **3.** 6.02 **4.** 5.245 **5.** 8.2 **6.** 0.14

7. $\frac{1}{5}$ **8.** $\frac{9}{20}$ **9.** $\frac{1}{9}$ **10.** $\frac{5}{6}$ **11.** $\frac{3}{4}$ **12.** $\frac{7}{8}$

Write each number as a decimal.

13. 7% **14.** 8.5% **15.** 0.9% **16.** 250% **17.** 83% **18.** 110%

Write each number as a fraction or mixed number in simplest form.

19. 19% **20.** $\frac{3}{4}\%$ **21.** 450% **22.** $\frac{4}{5}\%$ **23.** 64% **24.** $\frac{2}{3}\%$

Exponents

You can express $2 \cdot 2 \cdot 2 \cdot 2 \cdot 2$ as 2^5. The raised number, 5, shows the number of times 2 is used as a factor. The number 2 is the *base.* The number 5 is the *exponent.*

2^5 ← exponent
↑ base

Factored Form		Exponential Form		Standard Form
$2 \cdot 2 \cdot 2 \cdot 2 \cdot 2$	=	2^5	=	32

A number with an exponent of 1 is the number itself: $8^1 = 8$.
Any number, except 0, with an exponent of 0 is 1: $5^0 = 1$.

Example 1 **Write using exponents.**

a. $8 \cdot 8 \cdot 8 \cdot 8 \cdot 8$ b. $2 \cdot 9 \cdot 9 \cdot 9 \cdot 9 \cdot 9 \cdot 9$ c. $6 \cdot 6 \cdot 10 \cdot 10 \cdot 10 \cdot 6 \cdot 6$

Count the number of times the number is used as a factor.

a. 8^5 b. $2 \cdot 9^6$ c. $6^4 \cdot 10^3$

Example 2 **Write each product.**

a. 2^3 b. $8^2 \cdot 3^4$ c. $10^3 \cdot 5^2$

Write in factored form and multiply.

a. $2 \cdot 2 \cdot 2 = 8$ b. $8 \cdot 8 \cdot 3 \cdot 3 \cdot 3 \cdot 3 = 5184$ c. $10 \cdot 10 \cdot 10 \cdot 5 \cdot 5 = 25{,}000$

In powers of 10, the exponent tells how many zeros are in the standard form.

$10^1 = 10$
$10^2 = 10 \cdot 10 = 100$
$10^3 = 10 \cdot 10 \cdot 10 = 1000$
$10^4 = 10 \cdot 10 \cdot 10 \cdot 10 = 10{,}000$
$10^5 = 10 \cdot 10 \cdot 10 \cdot 10 \cdot 10 = 100{,}000$

You can use exponents to write numbers in *expanded form.*

Example 3 **Write 739 in expanded form using exponents.**

$739 = 700 + 30 + 9 = (7 \cdot 100) + (3 \cdot 10) + (9 \cdot 1) = (7 \cdot 10^2) + (3 \cdot 10^1) + (9 \cdot 10^0)$

EXERCISES

Write using exponents.

1. $6 \cdot 6 \cdot 6 \cdot 6$ **2.** $7 \cdot 7 \cdot 7 \cdot 7 \cdot 7$ **3.** $5 \cdot 2 \cdot 2 \cdot 2 \cdot 2$ **4.** $3 \cdot 3 \cdot 3 \cdot 3 \cdot 3 \cdot 14 \cdot 14$

Write in standard form.

5. 4^3 **6.** 9^4 **7.** 12^2 **8.** $6^2 \cdot 7^1$ **9.** $11^2 \cdot 3^3$

Write in expanded form using exponents.

10. 658 **11.** 1254 **12.** 7125 **13.** 83,401 **14.** 294,863

Angles

An *angle* is a geometric figure formed by two rays with a common endpoint. The rays are *sides* of the angle and the endpoint is the *vertex* of the angle. An angle is measured in degrees. The symbol for an angle is ∠.

The angle pictured at the right can be named in three different ways: ∠A, ∠BAC, or ∠CAB.

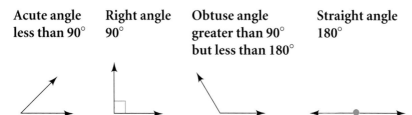

Angles can be classified by their measures.

Acute angle	**Right angle**	**Obtuse angle**	**Straight angle**
less than 90°	**90°**	**greater than 90° but less than 180°**	**180°**

Example **Measure the angle and tell if it is *acute, right, obtuse,* or *straight.***

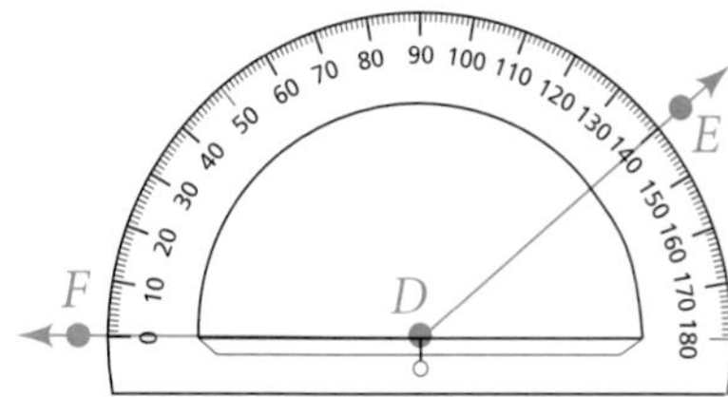

Line up side DF through 0° with the vertex at the center of the protractor. Read the scale number through which side DE passes.

The measure of the angle is 140°. The angle is obtuse.

EXERCISES

Measure each angle and tell whether it is *acute, right, obtuse,* or *straight.*

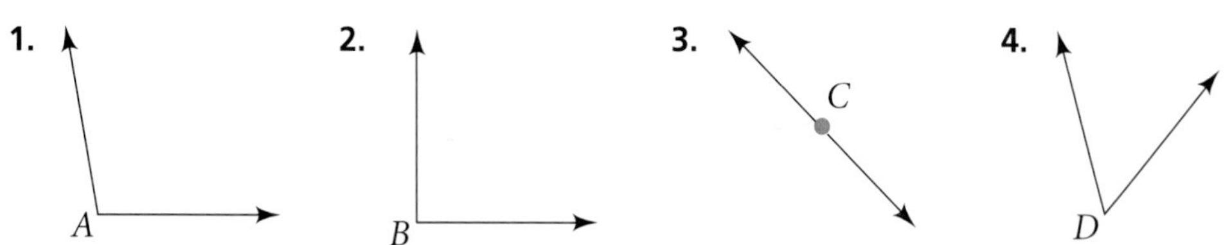

Draw an angle with the given measure.

5. 45°

6. 95°

7. 120°

8. 170°

9. **Open-ended** Draw a triangle. Use a protractor to find the measure of each angle of your triangle.

Perimeter, Area, and Volume

The *perimeter* of a figure is the distance around the figure. The *area* of a figure is the number of square units contained in the figure. The *volume* of a space figure is the number of cubic units contained in the space figure.

Example 1 **Find the perimeter of each figure.**

a.

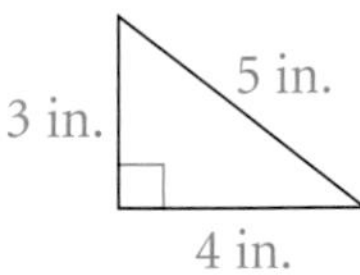

Add the measures of the sides.
$3 + 4 + 5 = 12$
The perimeter is 12 in.

b.

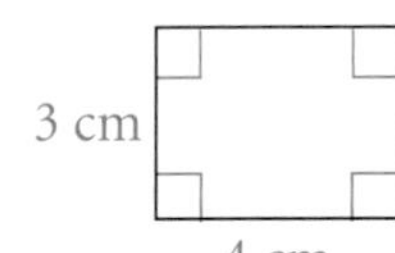

Use the formula $p = 2\ell + 2w$.
$p = 2(3) + 2(4)$
$= 6 + 8 = 14$
The perimeter is 14 cm.

Example 2 **Find the area of each figure.**

a.

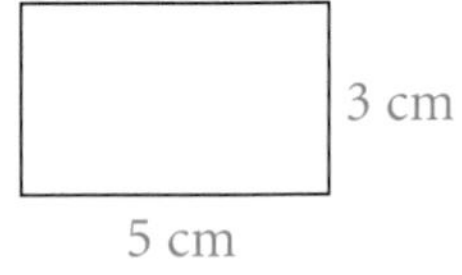

Use the formula $A = lw$.

$A = 3 \cdot 5 = 15 \text{ cm}^2$

b.

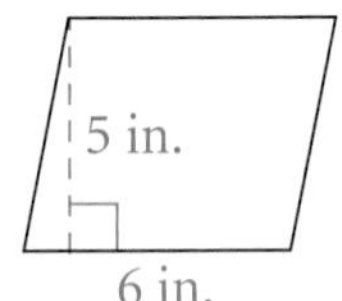

Use the formula $A = bh$.

$A = 6 \cdot 5 = 30 \text{ in.}^2$

c.

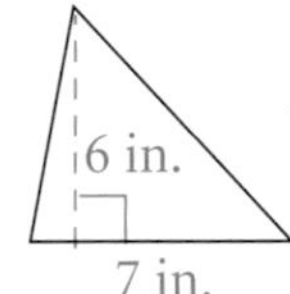

Use the formula $A = \frac{1}{2}(bh)$.

$A = \frac{1}{2}(7 \cdot 6) = 21 \text{ in.}^2$

Example 3 **Find the volume of each figure.**

a.

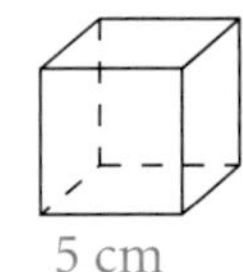

$V = e^3$
$V = 5^3 = 125 \text{ cm}^3$

b.

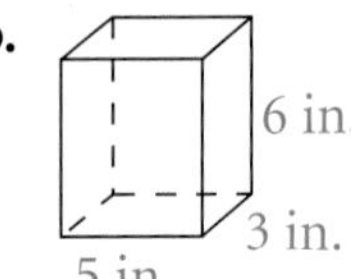

$V = Bh$ (B = area of the base)
$V = 3 \cdot 5 \cdot 6 = 90 \text{ in.}^3$

c.

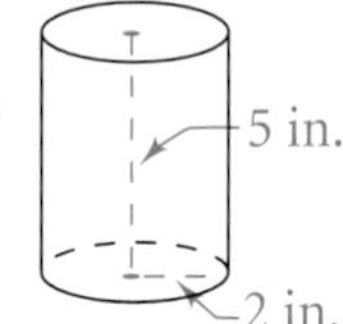

$V = \pi r^2 h$
$V = 3.14 \cdot 2^2 \cdot 5$
$= 3.14 \cdot 4 \cdot 5 = 62.8 \text{ in.}^3$

EXERCISES

Find the perimeter of each figure.

1.

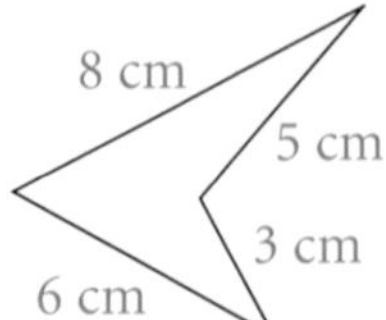

2.

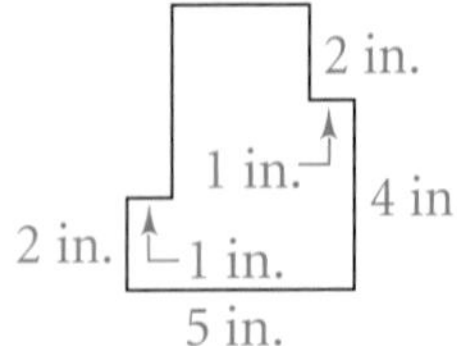

Find the area of each figure.

3.

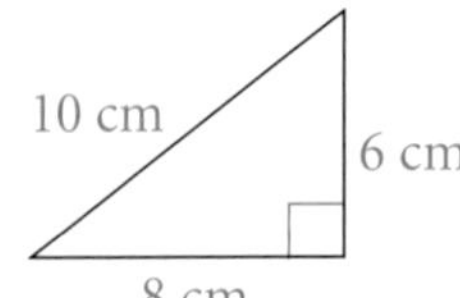

4.

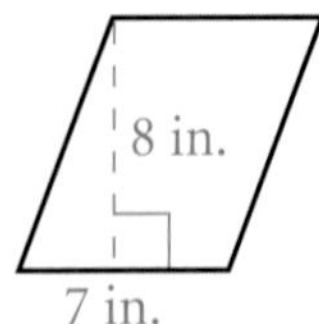

Find the volume of each figure.

5.

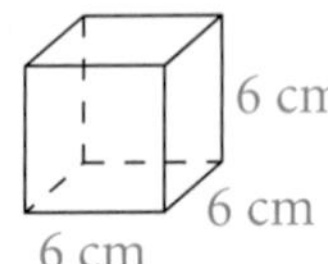

6.

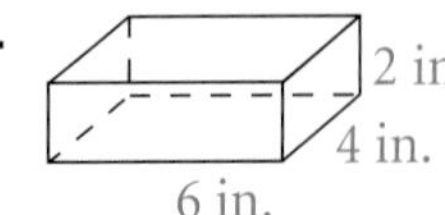

7.

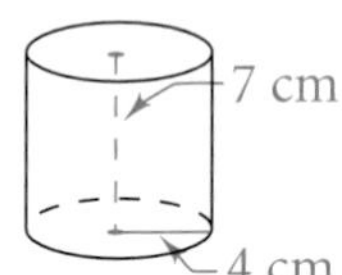

Measures

United States Customary	Metric
Length	
12 inches (in.) = 1 foot (ft)	10 millimeters (mm) = 1 centimeter (cm)
36 in. = 1 yard (yd)	100 cm = 1 meter (m)
3 ft = 1 yard	1000 mm = 1 meter
5280 ft = 1 mile (mi)	1000 m = 1 kilometer (km)
1760 yd = 1 mile	
Area	
144 square inches (in.^{2}) = 1 square foot (ft^2)	100 square millimeters (mm^2) = 1 square centimeter (cm^2)
9 ft^2 = 1 square yard (yd^2)	10,000 cm^2 = 1 square meter (m^2)
43,560 ft^2 = 1 acre (a)	10,000 m^2 = 1 hectare (ha)
4840 yd^2 = 1 acre	
Volume	
1728 cubic inches (in.^{3}) = 1 cubic foot (ft^3)	1000 cubic millimeters (mm^3) = 1 cubic centimeter (cm^3)
27 ft^3 = 1 cubic yard (yd^3)	1,000,000 cm^3 = 1 cubic meter (m^3)
Liquid Capacity	
8 fluid ounces (fl oz) = 1 cup (c)	1000 milliliters (mL) = 1 liter (L)
2 c = 1 pint (pt)	1000 L = 1 kiloliter (kL)
2 pt = 1 quart (qt)	
4 qt = 1 gallon (gal)	
Mass	
16 ounces (oz) = 1 pound (lb)	1000 milligrams (mg) = 1 gram (g)
2000 pounds = 1 ton (t)	1000 g = 1 kilogram (kg)
	1000 kg = 1 metric ton (t)
Temperature	
32°F = freezing point of water	0°C = freezing point of water
98.6°F = normal body temperature	37°C = normal body temperature
212°F = boiling point of water	100°C = boiling point of water

Time	
60 seconds (s) = 1 minute (min)	365 days = 1 year (yr)
60 minutes = 1 hour (h)	52 weeks (approx.) = 1 year
24 hours = 1 day (da)	12 months = 1 year
7 days = 1 week (wk)	10 years = 1 decade
4 weeks (approx.) = 1 month (mo)	100 years = 1 century

Symbols

$=$	equals	p. 5
$\approx$	is approximately equal to	p. 5
$\cdot$	multiplication sign, times ($\times$)	p. 5
$(\ )$	parentheses for grouping	p. 15
a^n	*n*th power of *a*	p. 15
$[\ ]$	brackets for grouping	p. 17
$\ldots$	and so on	p. 19
$\lvert a \rvert$	absolute value of *a*	p. 20
$-a$	opposite of *a*	p. 22
$^\circ$	degree(s)	p. 23
$<$	is less than	p. 28
$>$	is greater than	p. 28
π	pi, an irrational number, approximately equal to 3.14	p. 30
$\frac{1}{a}$	reciprocal of *a*	p. 32
P(event)	probability of the event	p. 36
$\begin{bmatrix} 1 & 2 \\ 3 & 4 \end{bmatrix}$	matrix	p. 40
^	raised to a power (in a spreadsheet formula)	p. 46
*	multiply (in a spreadsheet formula)	p. 46
/	divide (in a spreadsheet formula)	p. 46
(x, y)	ordered pair	p. 58
$f(x)$	*f* of *x*; the function value at *x*	p. 79
x_1, x_2, etc.	specific values of the variable *x*	p. 89
y_1, y_2, etc.	specific values of the variable *y*	p. 89
$\stackrel{?}{=}$	is the statement true?	p. 109
$\angle A$	angle *A*	p. 111
%	percent	p. 139
$a : b$	ratio of *a* to *b*	p. 158
$\neq$	is not equal to	p. 159
$\triangle ABC$	triangle *ABC*	p. 159
AB	length of $\overline{AB}$; distance between points *A* and *B*	p. 159
$\leq$	is less than or equal to	p. 179
$\geq$	is greater than or equal to	p. 179
$\{\ \}$	set braces	p. 202
$\overleftrightarrow{AB}$	line through points *A* and *B*	p. 218
m	slope of a linear function	p. 231
b	*y*-intercept of a linear function	p. 231
$\sqrt{x}$	nonnegative square root of *x*	p. 332
$\pm$	plus or minus	p. 332
a^{-n}	$\frac{1}{a^n}, a \neq 0$	p. 380
$\overline{AB}$	segment with endpoints *A* and *B*	p. 420
$\sin A$	sine of $\angle A$	p. 425
$\cos A$	cosine of $\angle A$	p. 425
$\tan A$	tangent of $\angle A$	p. 425
$m\angle A$	measure of angle *A*	p. 429
$\overline{x}$	mean of data values of *x*	p. 452
$n!$	*n* factorial	p. 539
${}_nP_r$	permutations of *n* things taken *r* at a time	p. 540
${}_nC_r$	combinations of *n* things taken *r* at a time	p. 543

Properties and Formulas of Algebra

CHAPTER 1

Order of Operations

1. Perform any operation(s) inside grouping symbols.
2. Simplify any terms with exponents.
3. Multiply and divide in order from left to right.
4. Add and subtract in order from left to right.

The Identity Property

For every real number a:

$$a + 0 = a \quad \text{and} \quad 0 + a = a$$
$$a \cdot 1 = a \quad \text{and} \quad 1 \cdot a = a$$

The Commutative Property

For all real numbers a and b:

$$a + b = b + a \qquad a \cdot b = b \cdot a$$

The Associative Property

For all real numbers a, b, and c:

$$(a + b) + c = a + (b + c)$$
$$(a \cdot b) \cdot c = a \cdot (b \cdot c)$$

Property of Opposites

The sum of a number and its **opposite,** or **additive inverse,** is zero. $a + (-a) = 0$

Property of Reciprocals

The **reciprocal**, or **multiplicative inverse**, of a rational number $\frac{a}{b}$ is $\frac{b}{a}$. $a \cdot \frac{1}{a} = 1$

CHAPTER 2

The Probability Formula

$$P(\text{event}) = \frac{\text{number of favorable outcomes}}{\text{number of possible outcomes}}$$

CHAPTER 3

Properties of Equality

For all real numbers a, b, and c:

Addition: If $a = b$, then $a + c = b + c$.

Subtraction: If $a = b$, then $a - c = b - c$.

Multiplication: If $a = b$, then $a \cdot c = b \cdot c$.

Division: If $a = b$, and $c \neq 0$, then $\frac{a}{c} = \frac{b}{c}$.

Probability of Two Events

If A and B are independent events, then

$$P(A \text{ and } B) = P(A) \cdot P(B).$$

If A and B are dependent events, then

$$P(A \text{ and } B) = P(A) \cdot P(B \text{ after } A).$$

The Distributive Property

For all real numbers a, b, and c,

$$a(b + c) = ab + ac \qquad (b + c)a = ba + ca$$
$$a(b - c) = ab - ac \qquad (b - c)a = ba - ca$$

CHAPTER 4

Properties of Inequality

For all real numbers a, b, and c:

Addition: If $a > b$, then $a + c > b + c$.
If $a < b$, then $a + c < b + c$.

Subtraction: If $a > b$, then $a - c > b - c$.
If $a < b$, then $a - c < b - c$.

Multiplication: $c > 0$: If $a > b$, then $ac > bc$.
If $a < b$, then $ac < bc$.

$c < 0$: If $a > b$, then $ac < bc$.
If $a < b$, then $ac > bc$.

Division: $c > 0$: If $a < b$, then $\frac{a}{c} < \frac{b}{c}$.
If $a > b$, then $\frac{a}{c} > \frac{b}{c}$.

$c < 0$: If $a < b$, then $\frac{a}{c} > \frac{b}{c}$.
If $a > b$, then $\frac{a}{c} < \frac{b}{c}$.

CHAPTER 5

Slope-Intercept Form of a Linear Equation

The slope-intercept form of a linear equation is $y = mx + b$, where m is the slope and b is the y-intercept.

CHAPTER 7

Quadratic Formula

If $ax^2 + bx + c = 0$ and $a \neq 0$, then

$$x = \frac{-b \pm \sqrt{b^2 - 4ac}}{2a}.$$

Tables

Property of the Discriminant

For the quadratic equation $ax^2 + bx + c = 0$, where $a \neq 0$, the value of the discriminant $b^2 - 4ac$ tells you the number of solutions.

$b^2 - 4ac > 0$	two solutions
$b^2 - 4ac = 0$	one solution
$b^2 - 4ac < 0$	no solution

CHAPTER 8

Zero as an Exponent

For any nonzero number a, $a^0 = 1$.

Negative Exponents

For any nonzero number a and any integer n:

$$a^{-n} = \frac{1}{a^n}$$

Multiplying or Dividing Powers

For any nonzero number a and any integers m and n:

$$a^m \cdot a^n = a^{m+n}$$

$$\frac{a^m}{a^n} = a^{m-n}$$

Raising a Power to a Power

For any nonzero number a and any integers m and n:

$$(a^m)^n = a^{mn}$$

Raising a Product or a Quotient to a Power

For any nonzero numbers a and b and any integer n:

$$(ab)^n = a^n b^n$$

$$\left(\frac{a}{b}\right)^n = \frac{a^n}{b^n}$$

CHAPTER 9

Properties of Square Roots

For any numbers $a \geq 0$ and $b \geq 0$,

$$\sqrt{ab} = \sqrt{a} \cdot \sqrt{b}.$$

For any numbers $a \geq 0$ and $b > 0$, $\sqrt{\frac{a}{b}} = \frac{\sqrt{a}}{\sqrt{b}}$.

The Pythagorean Theorem

In a right triangle, the sum of the squares of the lengths of the legs is equal to the square of the length of the hypotenuse.

$$a^2 + b^2 = c^2$$

The Converse of the Pythagorean Theorem

If a triangle has sides of lengths a, b, and c, and $a^2 + b^2 = c^2$, then the triangle is a right triangle with hypotenuse of length c.

The Distance Formula

The distance d between any two points (x_1, y_1) and (x_2, y_2) is

$$d = \sqrt{(x_2 - x_1)^2 + (y_2 - y_1)^2}.$$

The Midpoint Formula

The midpoint M of a line segment with endpoints $A(x_1, y_1)$ and $B(x_2, y_2)$ is

$$\left(\frac{x_1 + x_2}{2}, \frac{y_1 + y_2}{2}\right).$$

Trigonometric Ratios

sine of $\angle A = \dfrac{\text{length of side opposite } \angle A}{\text{length of hypotenuse}}$

cosine of $\angle A = \dfrac{\text{length of side adjacent to } \angle A}{\text{length of hypotenuse}}$

tangent of $\angle A = \dfrac{\text{length of side opposite } \angle A}{\text{length of side adjacent to } \angle A}$

CHAPTER 10

Factoring Special Cases

For all real numbers a and b:

$a^2 - b^2 = (a + b)(a - b)$

$a^2 + 2ab + b^2 = (a + b)(a + b) = (a + b)^2$

$a^2 - 2ab + b^2 = (a - b)(a - b) = (a - b)^2$

Zero-Product Property

For all real numbers a and b, if $ab = 0$, then $a = 0$ *or* $b = 0$.

CHAPTER 11

Multiplication Counting Principle

If there are m ways to make a first selection and n ways to make a second selection, there are $m \cdot n$ ways to make the two selections.

Properties of Equality

For all real numbers a, b, and c:

Reflexive Property: $a = a$

Symmetric Property: If $a = b$, then $b = a$.

Transitive Property: If $a = b$ and $b = c$, then $a = c$.

Formulas from Geometry

You will use a number of geometric formulas as you work through your algebra book. Here are some perimeter, area, and volume formulas.

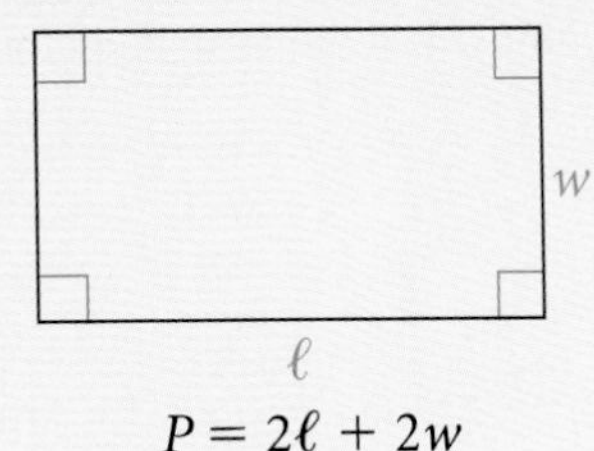

$P = 2\ell + 2w$
$A = \ell w$

Rectangle

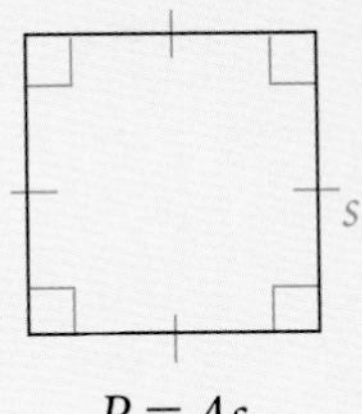

$P = 4s$
$A = s^2$

Square

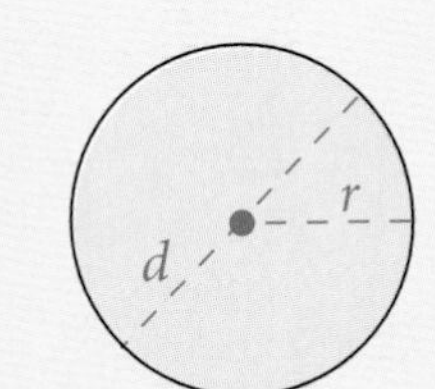

$C = 2\pi r$ or $C = \pi d$
$A = \pi r^2$

Circle

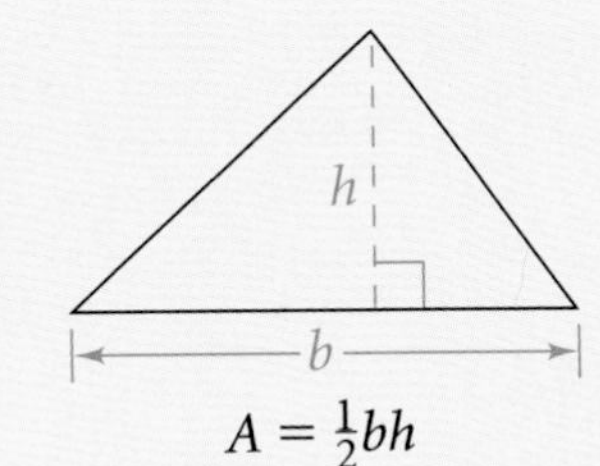

$A = \frac{1}{2}bh$

Triangle

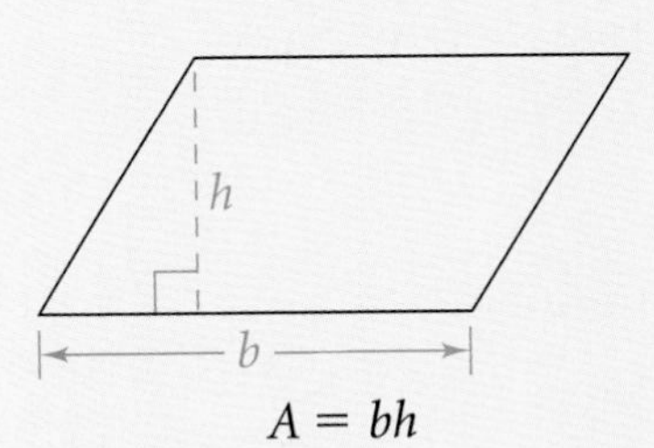

$A = bh$

Parallelogram

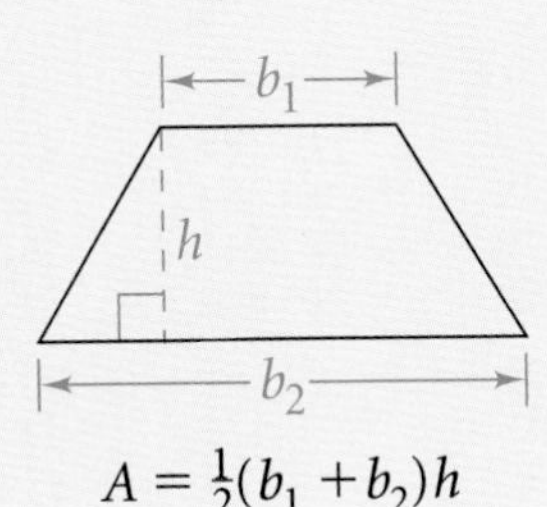

$A = \frac{1}{2}(b_1 + b_2)h$

Trapezoid

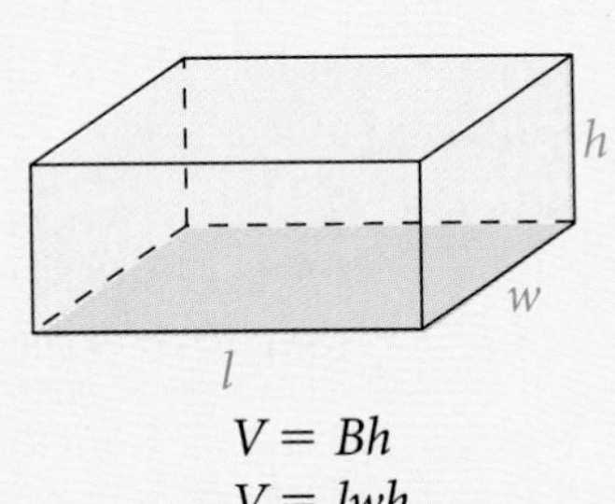

$V = Bh$
$V = lwh$

Rectangular Prism

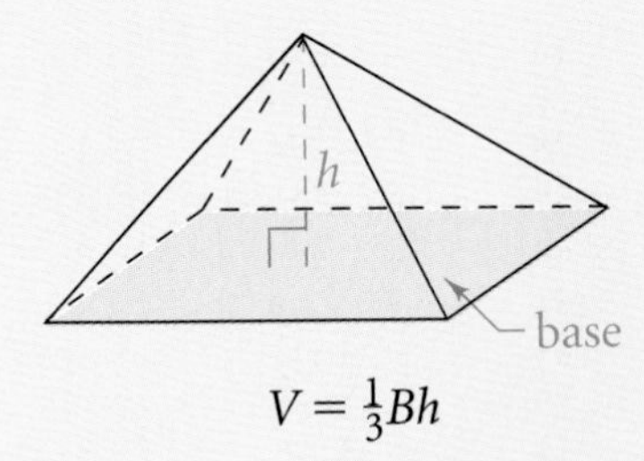

$V = \frac{1}{3}Bh$

Pyramid

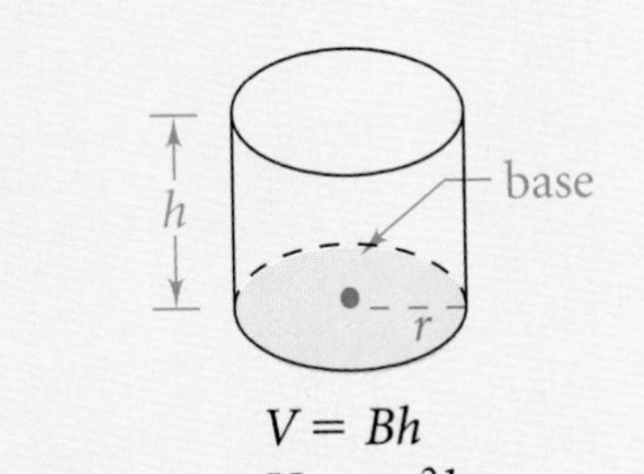

$V = Bh$
$V = \pi r^2 h$

Cylinder

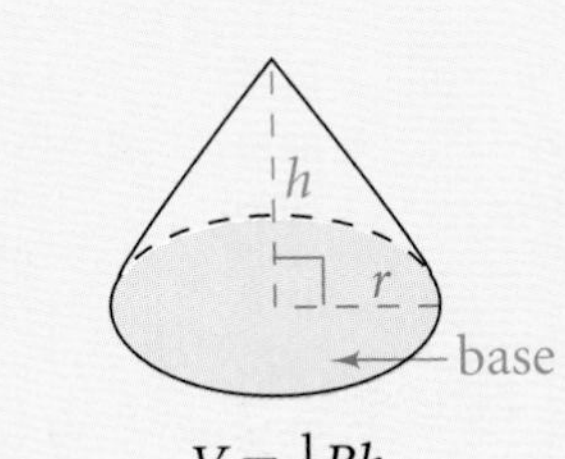

$V = \frac{1}{3}Bh$
$V = \frac{1}{3}\pi r^2 h$

Cone

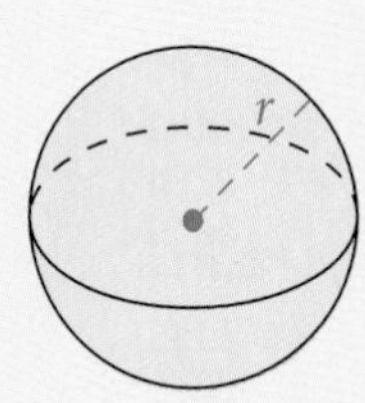

$V = \frac{4}{3}\pi r^3$

Sphere

Tables

Squares and Square Roots

Number n	Square n^2	Positive Square Root $\sqrt{n}$	Number n	Square n^2	Positive Square Root $\sqrt{n}$	Number n	Square n^2	Positive Square Root $\sqrt{n}$
1	1	1.000	51	2601	7.141	101	10,201	10.050
2	4	1.414	52	2704	7.211	102	10,404	10.100
3	9	1.732	53	2809	7.280	103	10,609	10.149
4	16	2.000	54	2916	7.348	104	10,816	10.198
5	25	2.236	55	3025	7.416	105	11,025	10.247
6	36	2.449	56	3136	7.483	106	11,236	10.296
7	49	2.646	57	3249	7.550	107	11,449	10.344
8	64	2.828	58	3364	7.616	108	11,664	10.392
9	81	3.000	59	3481	7.681	109	11,881	10.440
10	100	3.162	60	3600	7.746	110	12,100	10.488
11	121	3.317	61	3721	7.810	111	12,321	10.536
12	144	3.464	62	3844	7.874	112	12,544	10.583
13	169	3.606	63	3969	7.937	113	12,769	10.630
14	196	3.742	64	4096	8.000	114	12,996	10.677
15	225	3.873	65	4225	8.062	115	13,225	10.724
16	256	4.000	66	4356	8.124	116	13,456	10.770
17	289	4.123	67	4489	8.185	117	13,689	10.817
18	324	4.243	68	4624	8.246	118	13,924	10.863
19	361	4.359	69	4761	8.307	119	14,161	10.909
20	400	4.472	70	4900	8.367	120	14,400	10.954
21	441	4.583	71	5041	8.426	121	14,641	11.000
22	484	4.690	72	5184	8.485	122	14,884	11.045
23	529	4.796	73	5329	8.544	123	15,129	11.091
24	576	4.899	74	5476	8.602	124	15,376	11.136
25	625	5.000	75	5625	8.660	125	15,625	11.180
26	676	5.099	76	5776	8.718	126	15,876	11.225
27	729	5.196	77	5929	8.775	127	16,129	11.269
28	784	5.292	78	6084	8.832	128	16,384	11.314
29	841	5.385	79	6241	8.888	129	16,641	11.358
30	900	5.477	80	6400	8.944	130	16,900	11.402
31	961	5.568	81	6561	9.000	131	17,161	11.446
32	1024	5.657	82	6724	9.055	132	17,424	11.489
33	1089	5.745	83	6889	9.110	133	17,689	11.533
34	1156	5.831	84	7056	9.165	134	17,956	11.576
35	1225	5.916	85	7225	9.220	135	18,225	11.619
36	1296	6.000	86	7396	9.274	136	18,496	11.662
37	1369	6.083	87	7569	9.327	137	18,769	11.705
38	1444	6.164	88	7744	9.381	138	19,044	11.747
39	1521	6.245	89	7921	9.434	139	19,321	11.790
40	1600	6.325	90	8100	9.487	140	19,600	11.832
41	1681	6.403	91	8281	9.539	141	19,881	11.874
42	1764	6.481	92	8464	9.592	142	20,164	11.916
43	1849	6.557	93	8649	9.644	143	20,449	11.958
44	1936	6.633	94	8836	9.695	144	20,736	12.000
45	2025	6.708	95	9025	9.747	145	21,025	12.042
46	2116	6.782	96	9216	9.798	146	21,316	12.083
47	2209	6.856	97	9409	9.849	147	21,609	12.124
48	2304	6.928	98	9604	9.899	148	21,904	12.166
49	2401	7.000	99	9801	9.950	149	22,201	12.207
50	2500	7.071	100	10,000	10.000	150	22,500	12.247

Trigonometric Ratios

Angle	Sine	Cosine	Tangent	Angle	Sine	Cosine	Tangent
1°	0.0175	0.9998	0.0175	**46°**	0.7193	0.6947	1.0355
2°	0.0349	0.9994	0.0349	**47°**	0.7314	0.6820	1.0724
3°	0.0523	0.9986	0.0524	**48°**	0.7431	0.6691	1.1106
4°	0.0698	0.9976	0.0699	**49°**	0.7547	0.6561	1.1504
5°	0.0872	0.9962	0.0875	**50°**	0.7660	0.6428	1.1918
6°	0.1045	0.9945	0.1051	**51°**	0.7771	0.6293	1.2349
7°	0.1219	0.9925	0.1228	**52°**	0.7880	0.6157	1.2799
8°	0.1392	0.9903	0.1405	**53°**	0.7986	0.6018	1.3270
9°	0.1564	0.9877	0.1584	**54°**	0.8090	0.5878	1.3764
10°	0.1736	0.9848	0.1763	**55°**	0.8192	0.5736	1.4281
11°	0.1908	0.9816	0.1944	**56°**	0.8290	0.5592	1.4826
12°	0.2079	0.9781	0.2126	**57°**	0.8387	0.5446	1.5399
13°	0.2250	0.9744	0.2309	**58°**	0.8480	0.5299	1.6003
14°	0.2419	0.9703	0.2493	**59°**	0.8572	0.5150	1.6643
15°	0.2588	0.9659	0.2679	**60°**	0.8660	0.5000	1.7321
16°	0.2756	0.9613	0.2867	**61°**	0.8746	0.4848	1.8040
17°	0.2924	0.9563	0.3057	**62°**	0.8829	0.4695	1.8807
18°	0.3090	0.9511	0.3249	**63°**	0.8910	0.4540	1.9626
19°	0.3256	0.9455	0.3443	**64°**	0.8988	0.4384	2.0503
20°	0.3420	0.9397	0.3640	**65°**	0.9063	0.4226	2.1445
21°	0.3584	0.9336	0.3839	**66°**	0.9135	0.4067	2.2460
22°	0.3746	0.9272	0.4040	**67°**	0.9205	0.3907	2.3559
23°	0.3907	0.9205	0.4245	**68°**	0.9272	0.3746	2.4751
24°	0.4067	0.9135	0.4452	**69°**	0.9336	0.3584	2.6051
25°	0.4226	0.9063	0.4663	**70°**	0.9397	0.3420	2.7475
26°	0.4384	0.8988	0.4877	**71°**	0.9455	0.3256	2.9042
27°	0.4540	0.8910	0.5095	**72°**	0.9511	0.3090	3.0777
28°	0.4695	0.8829	0.5317	**73°**	0.9563	0.2924	3.2709
29°	0.4848	0.8746	0.5543	**74°**	0.9613	0.2756	3.4874
30°	0.5000	0.8660	0.5774	**75°**	0.9659	0.2588	3.7321
31°	0.5150	0.8572	0.6009	**76°**	0.9703	0.2419	4.0108
32°	0.5299	0.8480	0.6249	**77°**	0.9744	0.2250	4.3315
33°	0.5446	0.8387	0.6494	**78°**	0.9781	0.2079	4.7046
34°	0.5592	0.8290	0.6745	**79°**	0.9816	0.1908	5.1446
35°	0.5736	0.8192	0.7002	**80°**	0.9848	0.1736	5.6713
36°	0.5878	0.8090	0.7265	**81°**	0.9877	0.1564	6.3138
37°	0.6018	0.7986	0.7536	**82°**	0.9903	0.1392	7.1154
38°	0.6157	0.7880	0.7813	**83°**	0.9925	0.1219	8.1443
39°	0.6293	0.7771	0.8098	**84°**	0.9945	0.1045	9.5144
40°	0.6428	0.7660	0.8391	**85°**	0.9962	0.0872	11.4301
41°	0.6561	0.7547	0.8693	**86°**	0.9976	0.0698	14.3007
42°	0.6691	0.7431	0.9004	**87°**	0.9986	0.0523	19.0811
43°	0.6820	0.7314	0.9325	**88°**	0.9994	0.0349	28.6363
44°	0.6947	0.7193	0.9657	**89°**	0.9998	0.0175	57.2900
45°	0.7071	0.7071	1.0000	**90°**	1.0000	0.0000	

A

Examples

Absolute value (p. 20) The distance that a number is from zero on a number line.

-7 is 7 units from 0, so $|-7| = 7$.

Absolute value function (p. 92) Function whose graph forms a "V" that opens up or down.

$y = |x - 3|$

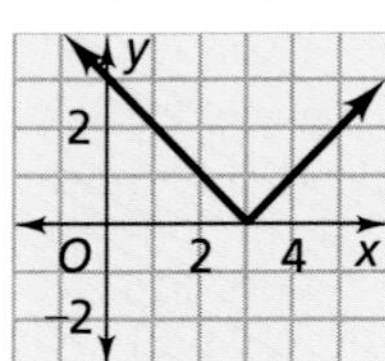

Addition Property of Inequality (p. 180) For all real numbers a, b, and c: if $a > b$, then $a + c > b + c$ and if $a < b$, then $a + c < b + c$.

$4 > -2$, so $4 + 3 > -2 + 3$.
$5 < 9$, so $5 + 2 < 9 + 2$.

Additive inverses (p. 20) A number and its opposite. Additive inverses have a sum of 0.

5 and -5 are additive inverses because $5 + -5 = 0$.

Angle of elevation (p. 426) Used to measure heights indirectly. An angle from the horizontal up to a line of sight.

Associative Properties of Addition and Multiplication (p. 35) Changing the grouping of the addends or factors does not change the sum or product.
$(a + b) + c = a + (b + c)$ and $(a \cdot b) \cdot c = a \cdot (b \cdot c)$

$(9 + 2) + 3 = 9 + (2 + 3)$.
$(5 \cdot 8) \cdot 2 = 5 \cdot (8 \cdot 2)$.

Asymptote (p. 516) A line the graph of a function gets closer and closer to, but does not cross.

Example: The y-axis is a vertical asymptote for $y = \frac{1}{x}$. The x-axis is a horizontal asymptote for $y = \frac{1}{x}$.

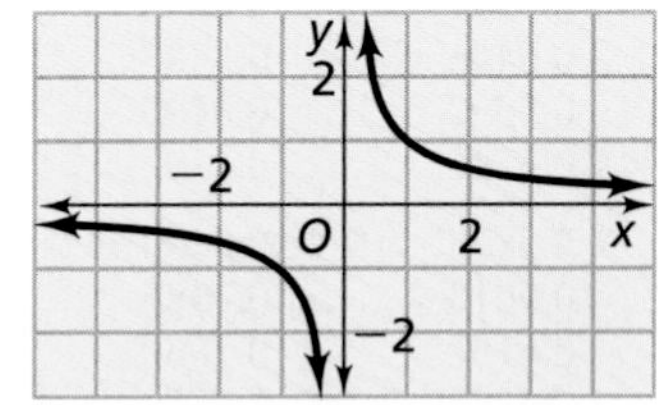

Axis of symmetry (p. 318) The line about which you can reflect a parabola onto itself.

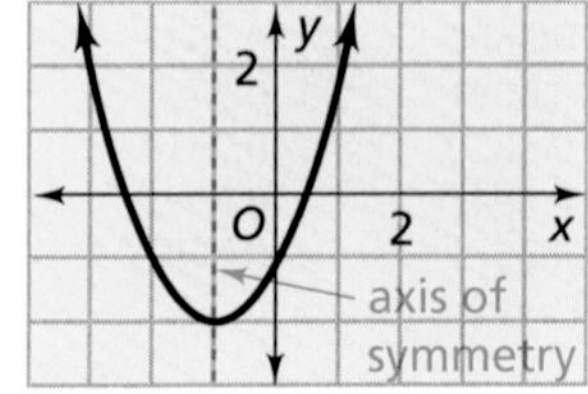

B

Examples

Bar graph (p. 6) A bar graph is used to compare amounts.

Example: The bar graph compares the number of students for grades 9, 10, and 11 over a three-year period.

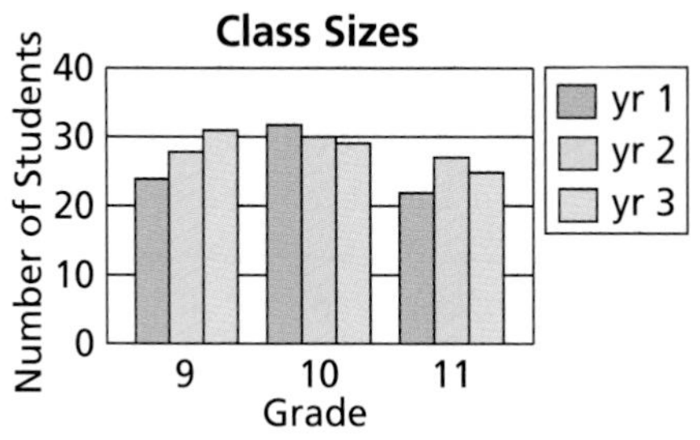

Base (p. 15) The number that is multiplied repeatedly.

$4^5 = 4 \cdot 4 \cdot 4 \cdot 4 \cdot 4$. The base 4 is used as a factor 5 times.

Binomial factors (p. 481) Some quadratic trinomials are the products of two binomial factors.

$(x + 2)(x + 1) = x^2 + 3x + 2$

binomial factors ↑ ↑ — quadratic trinomial ↑

C

Cell (p. 45) A cell is a box where a row and a column meet in a spreadsheet.

	A	B	C	D	E
1	0.50	0.70	0.60	0.50	2.30
2	1.50	0.50	2.75	2.50	7.25

A2 is the cell where row 2 and column A meet. The entry 1.50 is in cell A2.

Certain event (p. 96) A certain event always happens, and has a probability of 1.

Rolling an integer less than 7 on a number cube is a certain event.

Coefficient (p. 119) The numerical factor when a term has a variable.

In the expression $2x + 3y + 16$, 2 and 3 are coefficients.

Combination (p. 543) An arrangement of some or all of a set of objects without regard to order. The number of combinations

$$= \frac{\text{total number of permutations}}{\text{number of times the objects in each group are repeated}}$$

You can use the notation ${}_nC_r$ to write the number of combinations of n objects chosen r at a time.

The number of combinations of 10 things taken 4 at a time is:

$${}_{10}C_4 = \frac{{}_{10}P_4}{{}_4P_4} = \frac{10 \cdot 9 \cdot 8 \cdot 7}{4 \cdot 3 \cdot 2 \cdot 1} = 210$$

Common factors (p. 471) Numbers, variables, and any products formed from the prime factors that appear in all the terms of an expression.

x, 2, and $2x$ are common factors of $2x^2 + 4x$.

Examples

Commutative Properties of Addition and Multiplication (p. 35) Changing the order of the addends or factors does not change the sum or product. For all real numbers a and b: $a + b = b + a$ and $a \cdot b = b \cdot a$.

$5 + 7 = 7 + 5$ and $9 \cdot 3 = 3 \cdot 9$.

Complement of an event (p. 96) All possible outcomes that are not in the event.
$P(\text{complement of event}) = 1 - P(\text{event})$

The complement of rolling a 1 or a 2 on a number cube is rolling a 3, 4, 5, or 6.

Compound inequalities (p. 195) Two inequalities that are joined by *and* or *or*.

$5 < x$ and $x < 10$
$x < -14$ or $x \geq 3$

Constant of variation (p. 225) The constant k in a direct variation.

For the function $y = 24x$, 24 is the constant of variation.

Constant term (p. 119) A term that has no variable factor.

In the expression $4x + 13y + 17$, 17 is a constant term.

Continuous data (p. 65) Have measurements that change between data points, such as temperature, length, and weight.

The height of a tree changes between annual measurings.

Converse of the Pythagorean Theorem (p. 416) If a triangle has sides of lengths a, b, and c, and $a^2 + b^2 = c^2$, then the triangle is a right triangle with hypotenuse of length c.

Conversion factors (p. 219) Used to change from one unit of measure to another.

Convert 2 h to minutes.
Since 60 min $= 1$ h, $\frac{60 \text{ min}}{1 \text{ h}} = 1$.
Use $\frac{60 \text{ min}}{1 \text{ h}}$ to convert 2 h to minutes.
$\frac{2 \text{ h}}{1} \cdot \frac{60 \text{ min}}{1 \text{ h}} = 120$ min

---

Coordinate plane (p. 58) Formed when two number lines intersect at right angles. The x-axis is the horizontal axis and the y-axis is the vertical axis. The two axes meet at the origin, $O(0, 0)$.

Correlation (p. 60) A trend between two sets of data. A trend shows positive, negative, or no correlation.

Examples

Correlation coefficient (p. 242) Tells how well the equation of best fit models the data. The value r of the correlation coefficient is in the range $-1 \leq r \leq 1$.

Example: The correlation coefficient for the data points (68, 0.5), (85, 0.89), (100, 0.9), (108, 1.1) is approximately 0.94.

```
LinReg
  y=ax+b
  a=.0134039132
  b=-.3622031627
  r=.9414498267
```

Cosine (p. 425) In $\triangle ABC$ with right $\angle C$,

$$\text{cosine of } \angle A = \frac{\text{length of side adjacent to } \angle A}{\text{length of hypotenuse}}, \text{ or } \cos A = \frac{b}{c}.$$

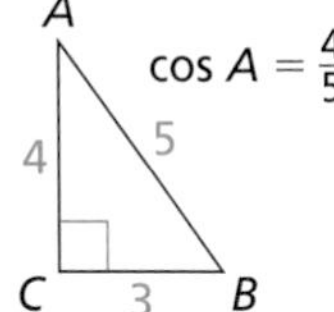

Cross products (p. 159) In a proportion, the product of the numerator of the first ratio and the denominator of the second ratio; also the product of the denominator of the first ratio and the numerator of the second ratio. These products are equal.

$\frac{3}{4} = \frac{6}{8}$
The cross products are $3 \cdot 8$ and $4 \cdot 6$.
$3 \cdot 8 = 24$ and $4 \cdot 6 = 24$

Cubic equation (p. 494) An equation in the form $ax^3 + bx^2 + cx + d = 0$, where a, b, c, and d are real numbers and $a \neq 0$.

$14x^3 + 2x^2 - 8x - 2 = 0$

Degree of a polynomial (p. 465) The highest degree of any of its terms.

The degree of $3x^2 + x - 9$ is 2.

Degree of a term (p. 465) For a term that has only one variable, the degree is the exponent of the variable. The degree of a constant is zero.

The degree of $3x^2$ is 2.

Dependent events (p. 135) When the outcome of one event affects the outcome of a second event, the events are dependent events.

If you pick a marble from a bag and pick another without replacing the first, the events are dependent events.

Dependent variable (p. 69) A variable is dependent if it relies on another variable.

In the equation $y = 3x$, the value of y depends upon the value of x.

Difference of two squares (p. 487) A quadratic binomial of the form $a^2 - b^2$.

$x^2 - 16$

Dimensional analysis (p. 219) The process of analyzing units to decide which conversion factors to use to solve a problem.

$0.5 \text{ mi} = \frac{0.5 \text{ mi}}{1} \cdot \frac{5280 \text{ ft}}{1 \text{ mi}} = 2640 \text{ ft}$

Examples

Direct variation (p. 225) A linear function that can be expressed in the form $y = kx$, where $k \neq 0$.

$y = 18x$ is a direct variation.

Discrete data (p. 65) Involves a count of data items, such as number of people or objects.

the number of books on a shelf in the library

Discriminant (p. 349) The quantity $b^2 - 4ac$ for a quadratic equation of the form $ax^2 + bx + c = 0$.

The discriminant of $2x^2 + 9x - 2 = 0$ is $9^2 - 4(2)(-2) = 97$.

Distance Formula (p. 420) The distance d between any two points (x_1, y_1) and (x_2, y_2) is

$d = \sqrt{(x_2 - x_1)^2 + (y_2 - y_1)^2}$.

The distance between $(-2, 4)$ and $(4, 5)$ is

$$d = \sqrt{(4 - (-2))^2 + (5 - 4)^2}$$
$$= \sqrt{(6)^2 + (1)^2}$$
$$= \sqrt{37}$$

Distributive Property (p. 124) For all real numbers a, b, and c:

$a(b + c) = ab + ac$ $\quad (b + c)a = ba + ca$

$a(b - c) = ab - ac$ $\quad (b - c)a = ba - ca$

$3(19 + 4) = 3(19) + 3(4)$
$(19 + 4)3 = 19(3) + 4(3)$
$7(11 - 2) = 7(11) - 7(2)$
$(11 - 2)7 = 11(7) - 2(7)$

Division Property of Inequality (p. 187) For all real numbers a and b, and for

$c > 0$: If $a < b$, then $\frac{a}{c} < \frac{b}{c}$.

If $a > b$, then $\frac{a}{c} > \frac{b}{c}$.

$c < 0$: If $a < b$, then $\frac{a}{c} > \frac{b}{c}$.

If $a > b$, then $\frac{a}{c} < \frac{b}{c}$.

$2 < 8$, so $\frac{2}{4} < \frac{8}{4}$.

$5 > 1$, so $\frac{5}{2} > \frac{1}{2}$.

$-2 < 6$, so $\frac{-2}{-3} > \frac{6}{-3}$.

$-2 > -4$, so $\frac{-2}{-5} < \frac{-4}{-5}$.

Division Property of Square Roots (p. 431) For any numbers $a \geq 0$ and $b > 0$, $\sqrt{\frac{a}{b}} = \frac{\sqrt{a}}{\sqrt{b}}$.

$\sqrt{\frac{4}{9}} = \frac{\sqrt{4}}{\sqrt{9}} = \frac{2}{3}$

Domain (p. 74) The set of all possible input values.

In the function $f(x) = x + 22$, the domain is all real numbers.

E

Elimination (p. 280) A method for solving a system of linear equations. You add or subtract the equations to eliminate a variable.

$3x - y = 19$
$2x - y = 1$
$x + 0 = 18$ ← Subtract the second equation from the first.
$x = 18$ ← Solve for x.
$2(18) - y = 1$ ← Substitute 18 for x in the second equation.
$36 - y = 1$
$y = 35$ ← Solve for y.

The solution is (18, 35).

Examples

Entry (p. 40) An item in a matrix.	2 is an entry in the matrix $\begin{bmatrix} 9 & 2 \\ 5.3 & 1 \end{bmatrix}$.
Equation (p. 11) An equation shows that two expressions are equal.	$x + 5 = 3x - 7$
Equivalent equations (p. 109) Equations that have the same solution.	$a = 3$ and $3a = 9$ are equivalent equations.
Equivalent inequalities (p. 180) Equivalent inequalities have the same set of solutions.	$n < 2$ and $n + 3 < 5$ are equivalent inequalities.
Event (p. 36) In probability, any group of outcomes.	When rolling a number cube, there are six possible outcomes. Rolling an even number is an event with three possible outcomes: 2, 4, and 6.
Experimental probability (p. 36) The ratio of the number of times an event actually happens to the number of times the experiment is done. $P(\text{event}) = \frac{\text{number of times an event happens}}{\text{number of times the experiment is done}}$	A baseball player's batting average shows how likely it is that a player will get a hit based on previous times at bat.
Exponent (p. 15) Shows repeated multiplication.	$3^4 = 3 \cdot 3 \cdot 3 \cdot 3$ The exponent 4 indicates that 3 is used as a factor four times.
Exponential decay (p. 373) For $a > 0$ and $0 < b < 1$, the function $y = ab^x$ models exponential decay. b is the decay factor.	$y = 5(0.1)^x$
Exponential function (p. 363) A function that repeatedly multiplies an initial amount by the same positive number. You can model all exponential functions using $y = ab^x$ where $b > 0$ and $b \neq 1$.	$y = 4.8(1.1)^x$
Exponential growth (p. 368) For $a > 0$ and $b > 1$, the function $y = ab^x$ models exponential growth. b is the growth factor.	$y = 100(2)^x$
Extraneous solution (p. 443) An apparent solution of an equation that does not satisfy the original equation.	$\frac{b}{b+4} = 3 - \frac{4}{b+4}$ Solving the equation by multiplying by $(b + 4)$ gives b as -4. Replacing b with -4 in the original equation makes the denominator 0, so -4 is an extraneous solution. The equation has no solution.

F

Examples

Families of functions (p. 92) Similar functions can be grouped into families of functions. Some families of functions are linear functions, quadratic functions, and absolute value functions.

$y = 3x^2$, $y = -9x^2$, and $y = \frac{3}{4}x^2$ belong to the quadratic family of functions.

Favorable outcomes (p. 95) In a probability experiment, favorable outcomes are the possible results that you want to happen.

In a board game you advance more spaces if you roll an even number on a number cube. The favorable outcomes are 2, 4, and 6.

Function (p. 73) A relation that assigns exactly one value of the dependent variable to each value of the independent variable.

Earned income is a function of the number of hours worked. If you earn \$4.50/h, then your income is expressed by the function $f(n) = 4.5n$.

Function notation (p. 79) To write a rule in function notation, you use the symbol $f(x)$ in place of y.

$f(x) = 3x - 8$ is in function notation.

Function rule (p. 74) An equation that describes a function.

$y = 4x + 1$ is a function rule.

H

Histogram (p. 4) A bar graph that shows the frequency of data. The height of the bars shows the number of items in each interval.

The histogram shows the birth months of 27 students in one math class.

Birth Months of Students

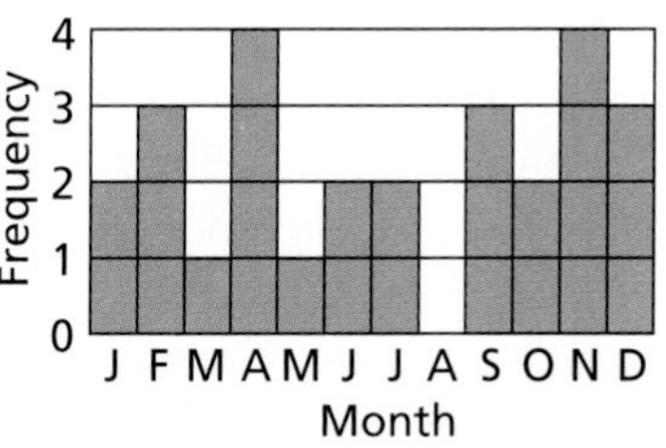

Hypotenuse (p. 414) In a right triangle, the side opposite the right angle. It is the longest side in the triangle.

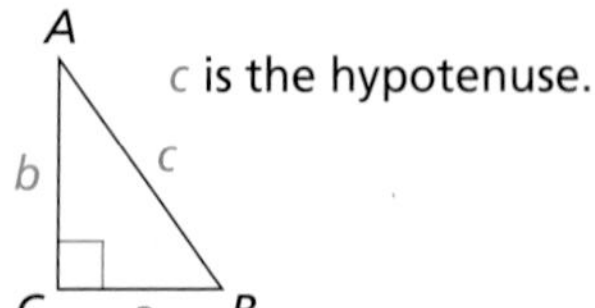

I

Identity (p. 166) An equation that is true for every value.

$5 - 14x = 5(1 - \frac{14}{5}x)$ is an identity because it is true for any value of x.

Examples

Identity Property of Addition (p. 35) The sum of any number and 0 is that number. For every real number a: $0 + a = a$.	$9 + 0 = 9, 0 + 9 = 9$
Identity Property of Multiplication (p. 35) The product of any number and 1 is that number. For every real number a: $a \cdot 1 = a, 1 \cdot a = a$.	$7 \cdot 1 = 7, 1 \cdot 7 = 7$
Impossible event (p. 96) An impossible event never happens, and has a probability of 0.	Getting a decimal when rolling a number cube is an impossible event.
Independent events (p. 134) Events are independent when the outcome of one does not affect the other.	Picking a colored marble from a bag, replacing it, and picking another are two independent events.
Independent variable (p. 69) A variable is independent if it does not depend on another variable.	In the function $y = -2x$, the value of x does not depend on the value of y.
Integers (p. 19) The whole numbers and their opposites.	$\ldots -3, -2, -1, 0, 1, 2, 3, \ldots$
Inverse operations (p. 108) Operations that undo one another are called inverse operations.	Addition and subtraction are inverse operations. Multiplication and division are inverse operations.
Inverse variation (p. 512) A function that can be written in the form $xy = k$ or $y = \frac{k}{x}$. The product of the quantities remains constant, so as one quantity increases, the other decreases.	The length x and the width y of a rectangle with a fixed area vary inversely. If the area is 40, $xy = 40$.
Irrational number (p. 30) A number that cannot be written as a ratio of two integers. Irrational numbers in decimal form are nonterminating and nonrepeating.	$\sqrt{11}$ and 3.141592653. . . are irrational numbers.

L

Legs of a right triangle (p. 414) The sides that form the right angle.	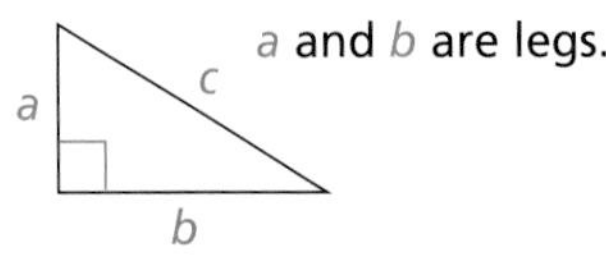 a and b are legs.
Like terms (p. 119) Terms with exactly the same variable factors in a variable expression.	$4y$ and $16y$ are like terms.

Examples

Line graph (p. 7) A graph that shows how a set of data changes over time.

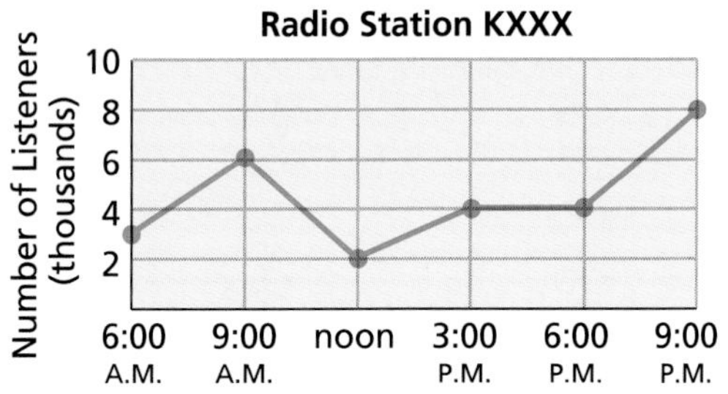

The line graph at the left shows the change in the number of listeners to station KXXX during the day.

Line of best fit (p. 242) The most accurate trend line showing the relationship between two sets of data. One way to find the line of best fit for two sets of data is to enter the data into a graphing calculator and then use the linear regression feature.

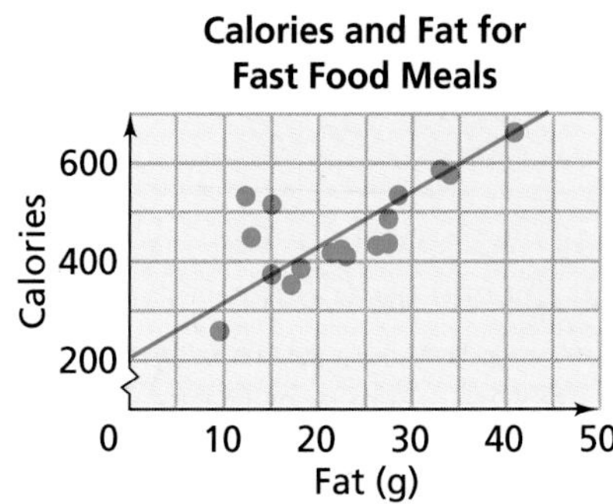

Line plot (p. 4) A graph that shows the number of times a data item appears.

Birth Month Line Plot

				X							
		X		X						X	
		X		X	X		X	X		X	
X		X	X	X	X	X	X	X		X	X
Jan	Feb	Mar	Apr	May	Jun	Jul	Aug	Sep	Oct	Nov	Dec

The line plot at the left shows the data collected on birth months for 20 people.

Linear function (pp. 92, 221) A function whose graph forms a straight line. Its rule is an equation that has 1 as the greatest power of x.

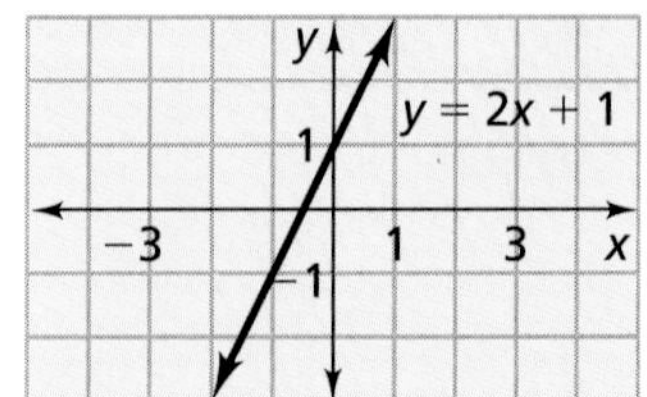

Linear inequality (p. 290) Describes a region of the coordinate plane that has a boundary line. Each point in the region is a solution of the inequality. A sign of ≤ or ≥ indicates a solid boundary line. A sign of < or > indicates a dashed boundary line.

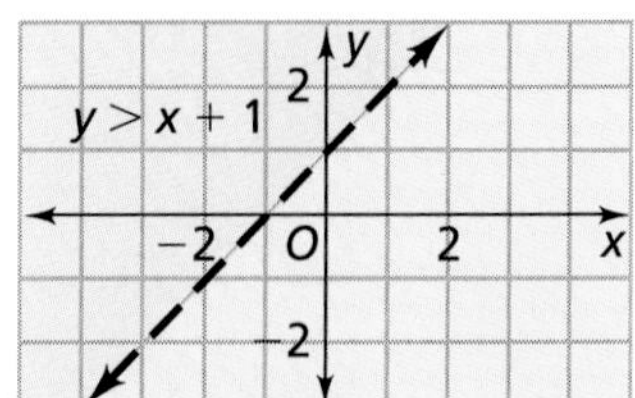

Examples

Linear programming (p. 300) A process that involves maximizing or minimizing a quantity. The quantity is expressed as the equation. Limits on the variables in the equation are called restrictions.

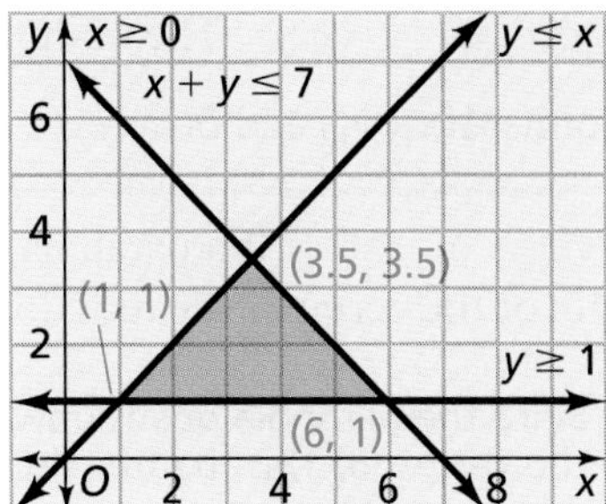

Example: Restrictions: $y \geq 1$, $x + y \leq 7$, and $y \leq x$
Equation: $B = 2x + 4y$
Graph the restrictions and find the coordinates of each vertex.
Evaluate $B = 2x + 4y$ at each vertex.
$B = 2(1) + 4(1) = 6$
$B = 2(3.5) + 4(3.5) = 21$
$B = 2(7) + 4(0) = 14$
The minimum value of B occurs at (1, 1).
The maximum value of B occurs at (3.5, 3.5).

Literal equation (p. 176) An equation involving two or more variables.

$ax + b = c$ is a literal equation.

M

Matrix (p. 40) A rectangular arrangement of numbers. The number of rows and columns of a matrix determines its size. Each item in a matrix is an entry.

$\begin{bmatrix} 2 & 5 & 6.3 \\ -8 & 0 & -1 \end{bmatrix}$ is a 2×3 matrix.

Maximum value (p. 320) If a parabola opens downward, the y-coordinate of the vertex is the function's maximum value.

Example: Since the parabola opens downward, the y-coordinate of the vertex $(0, -2)$ is the function's maximum value. The maximum value is -2.

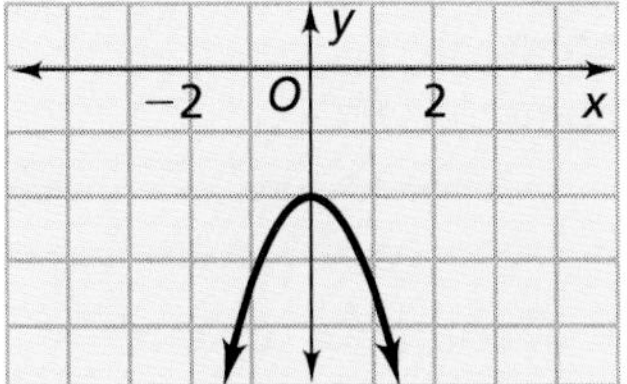

Mean (p. 5) To find the mean of a set of numbers, find the sum of the numbers and divide the sum by the number of items.

mean is $\frac{\text{sum of the data items}}{\text{number of data items}}$

In the set 12, 11, 12, 10, 13, 12, and 7, the mean is $\frac{12 + 11 + 12 + 10 + 13 + 12 + 7}{7} = 11$.

Median (p. 5) The middle value in an ordered set of numbers.

In the set 7, 10, 11, 12, 15, 19, and 27, the median is 12.

Midpoint (p. 422) The point that divides a segment into two congruent segments.

M is the midpoint of $\overline{XY}$.

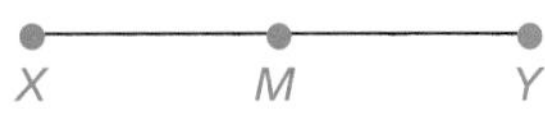

Glossary/Study Guide

Examples

Midpoint Formula (p. 422) The midpoint M of a line segment with endpoints $A(x_1, y_1)$ and $B(x_2, y_2)$ is $\left(\frac{x_1 + x_2}{2}, \frac{y_1 + y_2}{2}\right)$.

The midpoint of a segment with endpoints $A(3, 5)$ and $B(7, 1)$ is $(5, 3)$.

Minimum value (p. 320) If a parabola opens upward, the y-coordinate of the vertex is the function's minimum value.

Example: Since the parabola opens upward, the y-coordinate of the vertex $(0, 1)$ is the function's minimum value. The minimum value is 1.

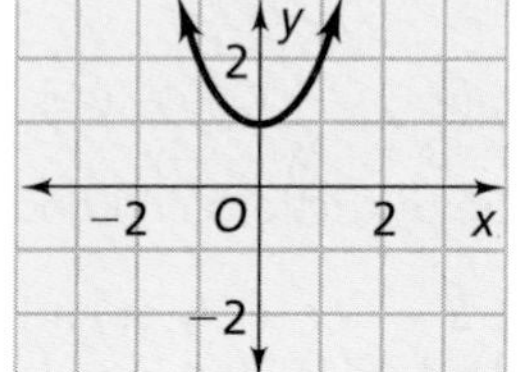

Mode (p. 4) The data item that occurs in a data set the greatest number of times. A data set may have no mode, one mode, or more than one mode.

In the data set 7, 7, 9, 10, 11, and 13, the mode is 7. The data set 5, 3, 2, 1.5, 9, 3, 6, 3, 2, 1, 4, 2 has two modes: 2 and 3.

Multiplicative inverse (p. 32) The multiplicative inverse, or reciprocal, of a rational number $\frac{a}{b}$ is $\frac{b}{a}$. The product of a nonzero number and its multiplicative inverse is 1.

$\frac{3}{4}$ is the multiplicative inverse of $\frac{4}{3}$ because $\frac{3}{4} \times \frac{4}{3} = 1$.

Multiplication Property of Inequality (p. 185) For all real numbers a and b, and for $c > 0$:
If $a > b$, then $ac > bc$.
If $a < b$, then $ac < bc$.
For all real numbers a and b, and for $c < 0$:
If $a > b$, then $ac < bc$.
If $a < b$, then $ac > bc$.

$5 > 1$, so $5(2) > 1(2)$.
$2 < 4$, so $2(3) < 4(3)$.
$-2 > -4$, so $-2(-5) < -4(-5)$.
$-2 < 6$, so $-2(-3) > 6(-3)$.

Multiplication Property of Square Roots (p. 430) For any numbers $a \geq 0$ and $b \geq 0$, $\sqrt{ab} = \sqrt{a} \cdot \sqrt{b}$.

$\sqrt{54} = \sqrt{9 \cdot 6} = \sqrt{9} \cdot \sqrt{6}$
$= 3 \cdot \sqrt{6} = 3\sqrt{6}$

N

Negative square root (p. 332) $-\sqrt{b}$ is the negative square root of b.

$-\sqrt{49} = -7$ is the negative square root of 49.

O

Opposites (p. 19) Two numbers are opposites, or additive inverses, if they are the same distance from zero on the number line. The sum of two opposites is 0.

-3 and 3 are opposites.

Examples

Order of operations (p. 15)
1. Perform any operation(s) inside grouping symbols.
2. Simplify any terms with exponents.
3. Multiply and divide in order from left to right.
4. Add and subtract in order from left to right.

$6 - (4^2 - [2 \cdot 5]) \div 3$
$= 6 - (4^2 - 10) \div 3$
$= 6 - (16 - 10) \div 3$
$= 6 - 6 \div 3$
$= 6 - 2$
$= 4$

Ordered pair (p. 58) An ordered pair of numbers identifies the location of a point.

The ordered pair $(4, -1)$ identifies the point 4 units to the right and 1 unit down from the origin.

Origin (p. 58) The axes of the coordinate plane intersect at the origin.

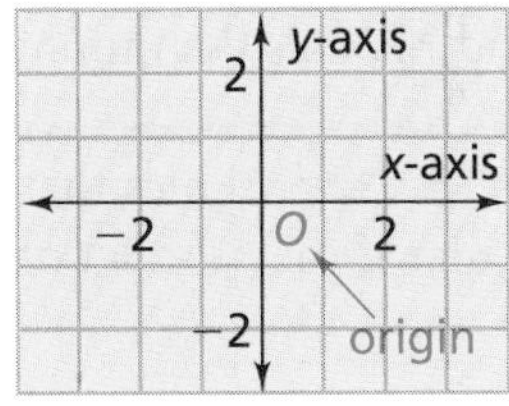

Outcomes (p. 95) The possible results of a probability experiment.

The outcomes of rolling a number cube are 1, 2, 3, 4, 5, and 6.

Parabola (p. 318) The graph of a quadratic function is a parabola.

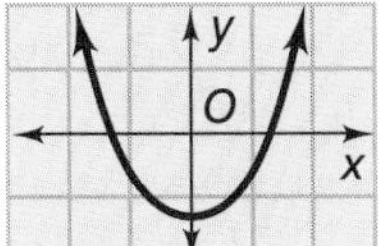

Parallel lines (p. 250) Two lines that are always the same distance apart. The lines do not intersect and have the same slope.

Example: Lines ℓ and m are parallel.

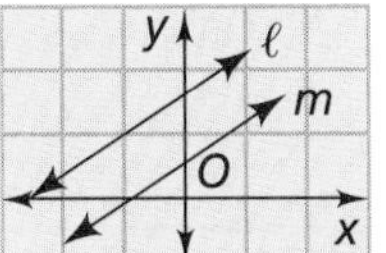

Percent of change (p. 146) The percent an amount changes from its original amount.
$\text{percent of change} = \frac{\text{amount of change}}{\text{original amount}}$

The price of a meal at a restaurant was \$7.95 last week; this week it is \$9.95.
$\text{percent of change} = \frac{9.95 - 7.95}{7.95} = \frac{2.00}{7.95}$
≈ 0.25 or 25%.

Percent of decrease (p. 147) When a value decreases from its original amount, you call the percent of change the percent of decrease.

The number of oranges in the bag decreased from 12 to 9.
$\text{percent of decrease} = \frac{3}{12} = 0.25$ or 25%

Percent of increase (p. 146) When a value increases from its original amount, you call the percent of change the percent of increase.

The average class size will increase from 30 to 33.
$\text{percent of increase} = \frac{3}{30} = 0.1$ or 10%

	Examples
Perfect square trinomial (p. 487) A quadratic expression whose factorization contains two factors that are the same.	$x^2 + 6x + 9 = (x + 3)(x + 3)$ $= (x + 3)^2$
Perfect squares (p. 333) Numbers whose square roots are integers.	The numbers 1, 4, 9, 16, 25, 36, . . . are perfect squares because they are the squares of integers.
Permutation (p. 539) An arrangement of some or all of a set of objects in a definite order. You can use the notation ${}_nP_r$ to express the number of permutations, where n equals the number of objects available and r equals the number of selections to make.	How many ways can 5 children be arranged three at a time? ${}_5P_3 = 5 \cdot 4 \cdot 3 = 60$ arrangements
Perpendicular lines (p. 251) Lines that form right angles. Two lines are perpendicular if the product of their slopes is -1.	Lines ℓ and m are perpendicular. 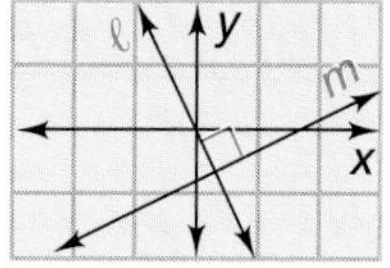
Polynomial (p. 465) A sum of monomials. A quotient with a variable in the denominator is not a polynomial.	$2x^2$, $3x + 7$, 28, and $-7x^3 - 2x^2 + 9$ are all polynomials.
Power (p. 391) Any expression in the form a^n.	5^4
Principal square root (p. 332) The expression $\sqrt{b}$ is called the principal square root of b.	$\sqrt{25} = 5$ is the principal square root of 25.
Probability of two dependent events (p. 135) If A and B are dependent events, then $P(A \text{ and } B) = P(A) \cdot P(B \text{ after } A)$.	You have 4 red marbles and 3 white marbles. The probability that you select one red marble, and then, without replacing it, randomly select another red marble is $P(\text{red and red}) = \frac{4}{7} \cdot \frac{3}{6} = \frac{2}{7}$.
Probability of two independent events (p. 134) If A and B are independent events, you multiply the probabilities of the events to find the probability of both events occurring. $P(A \text{ and } B) = P(A) \cdot P(B)$	The probability of rolling a 1 on a number cube is $\frac{1}{6}$. The probability of rolling an even number on a number cube is $\frac{1}{2}$. The probability of rolling a 1 and then an even number is $P(1 \text{ and even number}) = \frac{1}{6} \cdot \frac{1}{2} = \frac{1}{12}$.
Properties of Equality (pp. 109, 110) For all real numbers a, b, and c: Addition: If $a = b$, then $a + c = b + c$. Subtraction: If $a = b$, then $a - c = b - c$. Multiplication: If $a = b$, then $a \cdot c = b \cdot c$. Division: If $a = b$, and $c \neq 0$, then $\frac{a}{c} = \frac{b}{c}$.	Since $\frac{2}{4} = \frac{1}{2}$, then $\frac{2}{4} + 5 = \frac{1}{2} + 5$. Since $\frac{9}{3} = 3$, then $\frac{9}{3} - 6 = 3 - 6$. Since $\frac{10}{5} = 2$, then $\frac{10}{5} \cdot 15 = 2 \cdot 15$. Since $6 + 2 = 8$, then $\frac{6+2}{4} = \frac{8}{4}$.

Examples

Proportion (p. 158) A statement that two ratios are equal.

$\frac{2}{3} = \frac{10}{15}$ is a proportion.

Pythagorean Theorem (p. 414) In a right triangle, the sum of the squares of the lengths of the legs is equal to the square of the length of the hypotenuse. $a^2 + b^2 = c^2$.

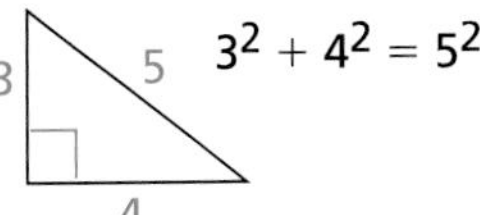

$3^2 + 4^2 = 5^2$

Quadrants (p. 58) The coordinate plane is divided by its axes into four quadrants.

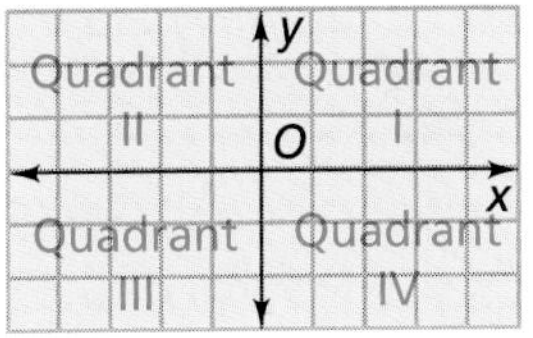

Quadratic equation (p. 337) An equation you can write in the form $ax^2 + bx + c = 0$, where a, b, and c are real numbers and $a \neq 0$.

$4x^2 + 9x - 5 = 0$

Quadratic Formula (p. 343) If $ax^2 + bx + c = 0$ and $a \neq 0$, then $x = \frac{-b \pm \sqrt{b^2 - 4ac}}{2a}$.

$2x^2 + 10x + 12 = 0$

$x = \frac{-b \pm \sqrt{b^2 - 4ac}}{2a}$

$x = \frac{-10 \pm \sqrt{10^2 - 4(2)(12)}}{2(2)}$

$x = \frac{-10 \pm \sqrt{4}}{4}$

$x = \frac{-10 + 2}{4}$ or $\frac{-10 - 2}{4}$

$x = -2$ or $x = -3$

Quadratic function (pp. 92, 319) A function with an equation of the form $y = ax^2 + bx + c$, where $a \neq 0$. The graph of a quadratic function is a parabola, which is a U-shaped curve that opens up or down.

$y = 5x^2 - 2x + 1$

Quadratic trinomial (p. 481) A quadratic trinomial is an expression of the form $ax^2 + bx + c$, where a, b, and c are nonzero real numbers.

$4x^2 + 2x + 9$

R

Radical equation (p. 440) An equation that has a variable under a radical.

$\sqrt{x} - 2 = 12$

	Examples
Range (p. 74) The set of all possible output values of a function.	In the function $f(x) = \|x\|$, the range is the set of all positive numbers and 0.
Rate of change (p. 220) Allows you to see the relationship between two quantities that are changing. The rate of change is also called slope. Rate of change $= \frac{\text{change in dependent variable}}{\text{change in independent variable}}$	Video rental for 1 day is \$1.99. Video rental for 2 days is \$2.99. rate of change $= \frac{2.99 - 1.99}{2 - 1}$ $= \frac{1.00}{1} = 1$
Ratio (p. 158) A comparison of two numbers by division.	$\frac{5}{7}$ and 7 : 3 are ratios.
Rational expression (p. 522) An expression that can be written in the form $\frac{\text{polynomial}}{\text{polynomial}}$. The value of the variable cannot make the denominator equal to 0.	$\frac{3}{x^2 - 4}$, $x \neq 2, -2$.
Rational function (p. 520) A function that can be written in the form $f(x) = \frac{\text{polynomial}}{\text{polynomial}}$. The value of the variable cannot make the denominator equal to 0.	$y = \frac{x}{x - 5}, x \neq 5$
Rational number (p. 30) A real number that can be written as a ratio of two integers. Rational numbers in decimal form are terminating or repeating.	$\frac{2}{3}$, 1.548, and 2.292929. . . are all rational numbers.
Rationalize the denominator (p. 432) Make the denominator of a fraction a rational number without changing the value of the expression.	$\frac{2}{\sqrt{5}} = \frac{2}{\sqrt{5}} \cdot \frac{\sqrt{5}}{\sqrt{5}} = \frac{2\sqrt{5}}{\sqrt{25}} = \frac{2\sqrt{5}}{5}$
Real number (p. 30) A number that is either rational or irrational.	5, –3, $\sqrt{5}$, 9.2, –0.666. . . , $5\frac{4}{11}$, 0, π, and $\frac{15}{2}$ are all real numbers.
Reciprocal (p. 32) The reciprocal, or multiplicative inverse, of a rational number $\frac{a}{b}$ is $\frac{b}{a}$. The product of a nonzero number and its reciprocal is 1. Zero does not have a reciprocal.	$\frac{2}{5}$ and $\frac{5}{2}$ are reciprocals because $\frac{2}{5} \times \frac{5}{2} = 1$.
Relation (p. 73) Any set of ordered pairs.	{(0, 0), (2, 3), (2, –7)} is a relation.
Replacement set (p. 202) The set of possible values for the variable in an inequality.	When the replacement set is all integers, the solution of the inequality $x > -2.5$ is {–2, –1, 0, 2, . . .}.
Restrictions (p. 522) Values that make the denominator of a rational expression equal to 0 are restrictions on the variable.	For $\frac{4}{x - 3}$, the restriction is $x \neq 3$.

S

Examples

Sample space (p. 97) The set of all possible outcomes of an event.

When tossing two coins one at a time, the sample space is (H,H), (T,T), (H,T), (T,H).

Scatter plot (p. 59) A graph that relates data of two different sets. The two sets of data are displayed as ordered pairs.

Example: The scatter plot displays the amounts various companies spent on advertising versus product sales.

Scientific notation (p. 385) A number expressed in the form $a \times 10^n$, where n is an integer and $1 \leq a < 10$.

3.4×10^6

Similar figures (p. 159) Figures that have the same shape, but not necessarily the same size.

$\triangle DEF$ and $\triangle GHI$ are similar.

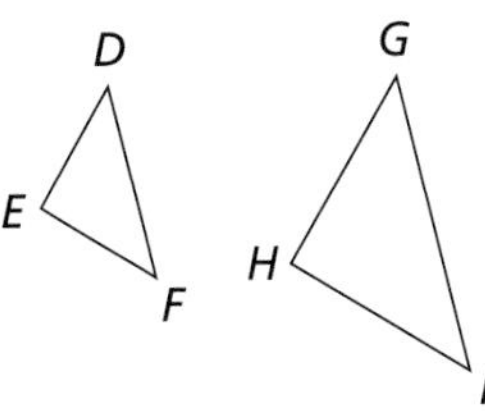

Simple interest (p. 141) Calculated using the formula $I = prt$, where p is the principal, r is the rate of interest per year, and t is the time in years.

The simple interest on $200 with an annual rate of interest of 4% for 3 years is $I = prt = 200\,(0.04)\,(3) = 24$. The simple interest is $24.

Simulation (p. 37) A simulation is a model of a real-life situation.

A random number table can be used to simulate many situations.

Sine (p. 425) In $\triangle ABC$ with right $\angle C$,

$$\text{sine of } \angle A = \frac{\text{length of side opposite } \angle A}{\text{length of hypotenuse}}, \text{ or } \sin A = \frac{a}{c}.$$

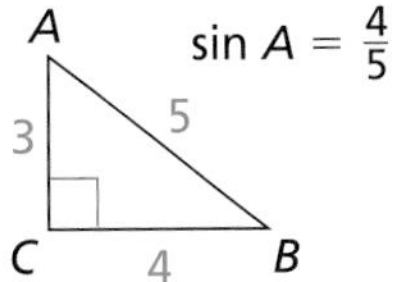

$\sin A = \frac{4}{5}$

Slope (p. 220) The measure of the steepness of a line. The ratio of the vertical change to the horizontal change.

$$\text{Slope} = \frac{\text{vertical change}}{\text{horizontal change}} = \frac{y_2 - y_1}{x_2 - x_1}, \text{ where } x_2 - x_1 \neq 0$$

The slope of the line is $\frac{2 - 0}{4 - 0} = \frac{1}{2}$.

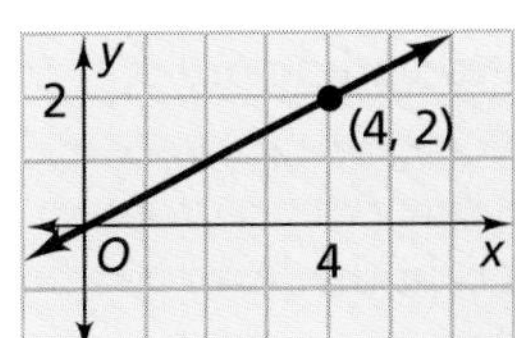

Glossary/Study Guide

Examples

Slope-intercept form (p. 231) The slope-intercept form of a linear equation is $y = mx + b$ where m is the slope and b is the y-intercept.

$y = 8x + 2$

Solution (p. 108) Any value or values that make an equation true.

For the equation $y + 22 = 11$, the solution is -11.

Solution, no (pp. 165, 192, 271) (1) An equation has no solution if no value makes the statement true.
(2) An inequality has no solution if it is false for all values of the variable.
(3) A linear system has no solution if the graphs of the equations in the system are parallel.

$2a + 3 = 2a + 5$

$4n + 1 > 4n + 7$

$y = 3x + 9$ and $y = 3x + 28$

Solution of the inequality (p. 179) Any value or values of a variable in the inequality that makes an inequality true.

The solution of the inequality $x < 9$ is all numbers less than 9.

Solutions, infinitely many (p. 271) A linear system has infinitely many solutions when the equations are equivalent.

$2y = x + 7$ and $6y = 3x + 21$

Spreadsheet (p. 45) Organizes data in rows and columns. A cell is a box where a row and column meet.

In the spreadsheet, column C and row 2 meet at the shaded box, cell C2. The value in cell C2 is 2.75.

	A	B	C	D	E
1	0.50	0.70	0.60	0.50	2.30
2	1.50	0.50	2.75	2.50	7.25

Square root (p. 332) If $a^2 = b$, then a is a square root of b. $\sqrt{b}$ is the principal square root. $-\sqrt{b}$ is the negative square root.

-3 and 3 are square roots of 9.
$\sqrt{9} = 3$; $-\sqrt{9} = -3$.

Standard deviation (p. 452) Shows how spread out a set of data is from the mean.

The standard deviation for the data set {2, 12, 6, 10, 9} is about 3.49.

Standard form of a polynomial (p. 465) When the degree of the terms in a polynomial decrease from left to right, it is in standard form, or descending order.

$15x^3 + x^2 + 3x - 9$

Standard form of a quadratic equation (p. 319) When a quadratic equation is in the form $ax^2 + bx + c = 0$.

$-x^2 + 2x + 9 = 0$

Examples

Stem-and-leaf plot (p. 10) A stem-and-leaf plot displays data items in order. A leaf is a data item's last digit on the right. A stem represents the digits to the left of the leaf.

This stem-and-leaf plot displays recorded times in a race. The stem records the whole number of seconds. The leaves represents tenths of a second. So, 27|7 represents 27.7 seconds.

stem	leaves
27	7
28	5 6 8
29	6 9
30	8

stem → 29 | 6 9 ← leaves

Subtraction Property of Inequality (p. 181) For all real numbers a, b, and c, if $a > b$, then $a - c > b - c$ and if $a < b$, then $a - c < b - c$.

$5 > 2$, so $5 - 4 > 2 - 4$.
$9 < 13$, so $9 - 3 < 13 - 3$.

System of linear equations (p. 269) Two or more linear equations using the same variables together form a system of linear equations.

$y = 5x + 7, y = \frac{1}{2}x - 3$

System of linear inequalities (p. 295) Two or more linear inequalities using the same variables together form a system of linear inequalities.

$y \leq x + 11, y < 5x$

T

Tangent (p. 425) In $\triangle ABC$ with right $\angle C$,

tangent of $\angle A = \frac{\text{length of side opposite } \angle A}{\text{length of side adjacent to } \angle A}$, or $\tan A = \frac{a}{b}$.

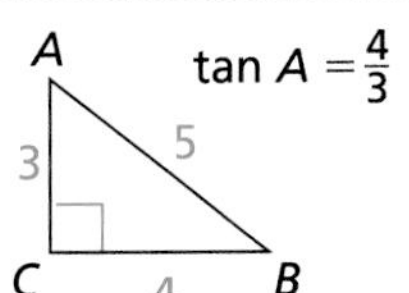

$\tan A = \frac{4}{3}$

Term (p. 11) A number, variable, or the product or quotient of a number and a variable.

The expression $5x + \frac{y}{2} - 8$ has three terms: $5x$, $\frac{y}{2}$, and -8.

Theoretical probability (p. 95) If each outcome has an equally likely chance of happening, you can find the theoretical probability of an event using the ratio of the number of favorable outcomes to the number of possible outcomes.

$$P(\text{event}) = \frac{\text{number of favorable outcomes}}{\text{number of possible outcomes}}$$

In tossing a coin the chance of getting heads or tails is equally likely. The probability of getting heads is $P(\text{heads}) = \frac{1}{2}$.

Examples

Tree diagram (p. 97) A diagram that shows all possible outcomes in a probability experiment.

Example: The tree diagram shows the 4 possible outcomes for tossing two coins one at a time: (H,H), (H,T), (T,H), (T,T).

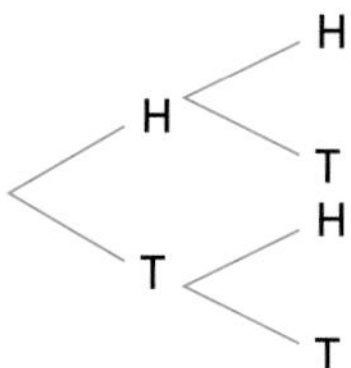

Trend line (p. 60) A line on a scatter plot that can be drawn near the points. It shows a correlation between two sets of data.

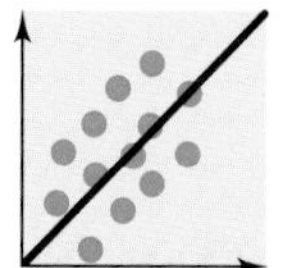
Positive

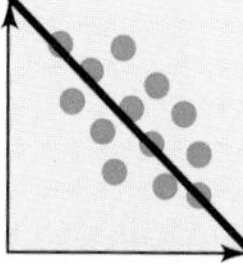
Negative

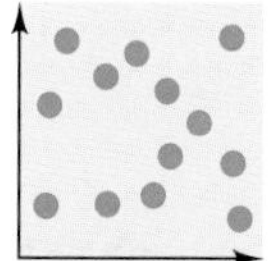
No Correlation

Trigonometric ratios (p. 425) See cosine, sine, and tangent.

Two-step equation (p. 114) An equation that has two operations.

$5x - 4 = 1$ is a two-step equation.

V

Variable (p. 11) A letter used to stand for a quantity that changes in value.

x is a variable in the expression $9 - x$.

Variable expression (p. 11) A mathematical phrase that uses numbers, variables, and operation symbols.

$7 + x$ is a variable expression.

Vertex (p. 320) The point where the axis of symmetry intersects the parabola.

The vertex of the parabola is $(-1, -1)$.

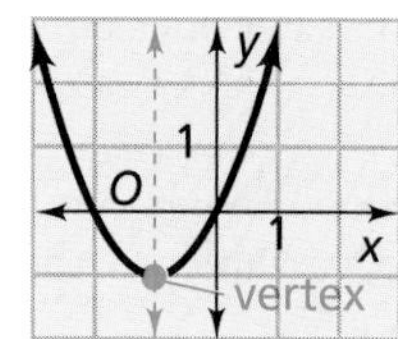

Vertical-line test (p. 75) A method used to determine if a relation is a function or not. If a vertical line passes through a graph more than once, the graph is not the graph of a function.

Vertical motion formula (p. 344) When an object is dropped or thrown straight up or down, you can use the vertical-motion formula to find the height of the object.

$h = -16t^2 + vt + s$, where h is the height of the object in feet, t is the time the object is in motion in seconds, v is the velocity in feet per second, and s is the starting height in feet.

An object is thrown straight up with a starting velocity of 36 ft/s. It is thrown from a height of 10 ft. The formula $h = -16t^2 + 36t + 10$ describes the height h of the object after t seconds.

Examples

Whole numbers (p. 19) Whole numbers are the nonnegative integers.

0, 1, 2, 3, . . .

x-axis (p. 58) The horizontal axis of the coordinate plane.

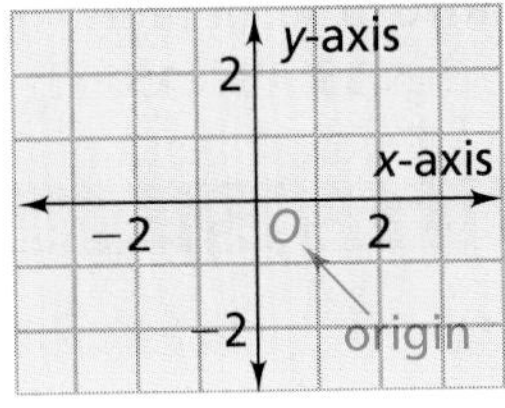

x-coordinate (p. 58) The x-coordinate of a point shows the location of a point in the coordinate plane along the x-axis.

In the ordered pair $(4, -1)$, 4 is the x-coordinate.

x-intercept (p. 246) The x-coordinate of the point where a line crosses the x-axis.

The x-intercept of $3x + 4y = 12$ is 4.

y-axis (p. 58) The vertical axis of the coordinate plane.

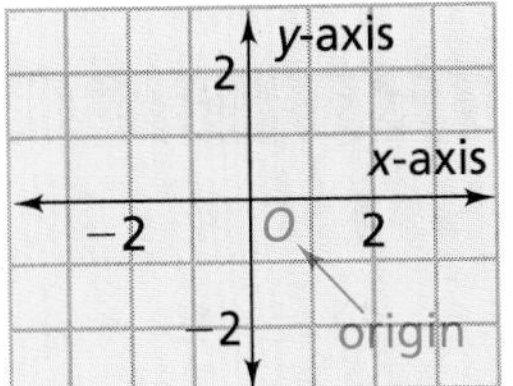

y-coordinate (p. 58) The y-coordinate of a point shows the location of a point in the coordinate plane along the y-axis.

In the ordered pair $(4, -1)$, -1 is the y-coordinate.

y-intercept (p. 230) The y-coordinate of the point where a line crosses the y-axis.

The y-intercept of $y = 5x + 2$ is 2.

Zero pairs (p. 20) ▢ ■ is a zero pair.

Zero-product property (p. 491) For all real numbers a and b, if $ab = 0$, then $a = 0$ or $b = 0$.

$x(x + 3) = 0$
$x = 0$ or $x + 3 = 0$
$x = 0$ or $x = -3$

Glossary/Study Guide

REVIEW CHAPTER

Toolbox page 2R

1. identity prop. of mult. **3.** associative prop. of mult. **5.** commutative prop. of mult. **7.** 830 **9.** 7400 **11.** $9m + 15$ **13.** 13 **15.** $72pqr$

Lesson 1-3 pages 3R–6R

ON YOUR OWN **1.** 23 **3.** 1 **5.** 64 **7.** 50.43 **9.** 75 **11.** 14 **15.** 1 **17.** 12.8 **19.** 104.58 **21.** 26 **23.** 2.4 **25.** $14 - (2 + 5) - 3 = 4$ **29.** F; simplify the power before multiplying. **31.** F; simplify within parentheses first.

MIXED REVIEW **33.** $\frac{2}{3}$ **35.** $4\frac{1}{2}$ **37.** $\frac{4}{5}$ **39.** 2 units **41.** 3 units

Preparing for Standardized Tests page 7R

1. D **3.** A **5.** D **7.** B **9.** B **11.** A **13.** 3

Lesson 1-6 pages 8R–12R

ON YOUR OWN **1.** > **3.** > **5.** > **7.** > **9.** $\frac{5}{3}$ **11.** $\frac{8}{7}$ **13.** -2 **15.** $\frac{2}{3}$ **17.** 1 **19.** $-6\frac{3}{4}$ **21.** $2\frac{1}{6}$ **23.** $-2\frac{1}{12}$ **25.** $-\frac{2}{3}, -\frac{1}{2}, \frac{1}{4}$ **27.** $-9\frac{3}{4}, -9.7, -9\frac{7}{12}$ **29a.** -44°F **29b.** -4°F **31.** $-\frac{9}{16}$ **33.** $-\frac{5}{48}$ **37.** $2\frac{3}{5}$ **39.** -4.5 **41.** $-\frac{1}{10}$ **43.** false; $-\frac{3}{4}$ **45.** true; since integers are real numbers, some real numbers are integers.

MIXED REVIEW **47.** c = change, p = purchase; $c = 10 - p$ **49.** $1,290,000

Toolbox page 13R

1. H **3.** E **5.** (4, 5) **7.** $(-5, 0)$ **13.** II **15.** IV

17a.

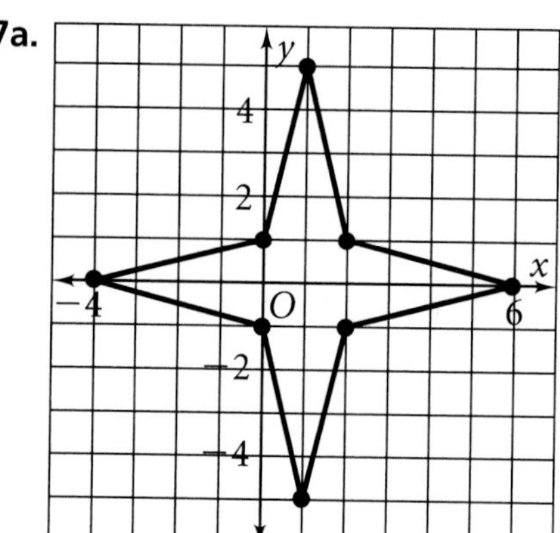

17b. It looks like a four-pointed star.

Lesson 2-6 pages 14R–18R

ON YOUR OWN

1. Sample table:

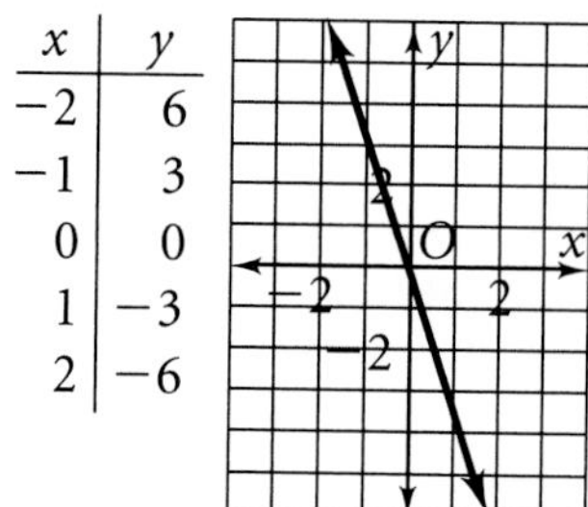

x	y
−2	6
−1	3
0	0
1	−3
2	−6

3. Sample table:

x	$f(x)$
0	−7
1	−5
2	−3
3	−1
4	1

9a. C **9b.** 9 **9c.**

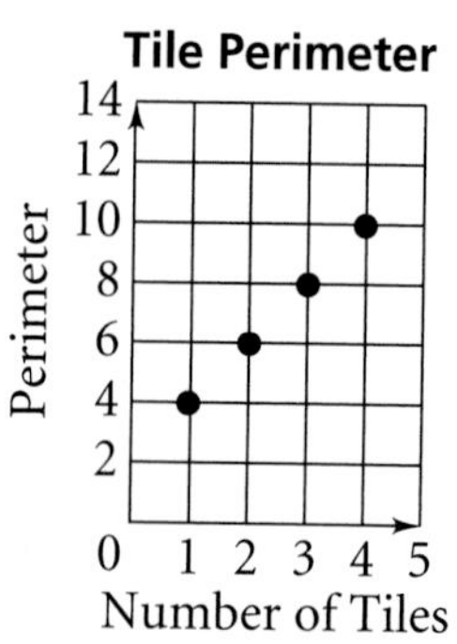

11a. $s(t) = 6t$ **11b.** $w(t) = 3t$ **11c.** 55.2 gal

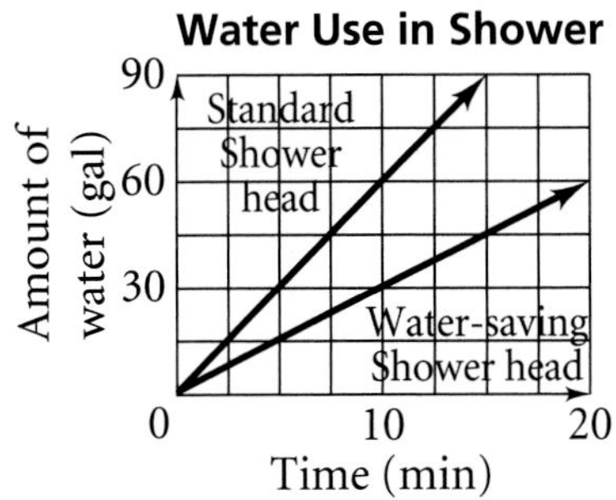

Sample: The graph shows that the difference in water use between the two shower heads grows quickly over time.

13.

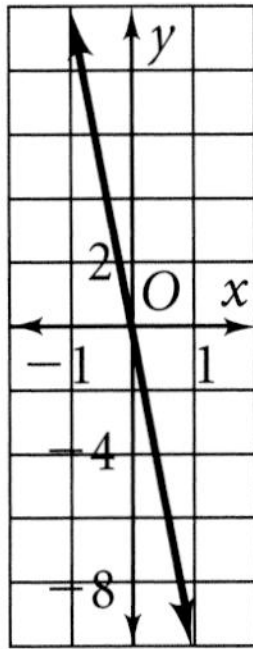

15.

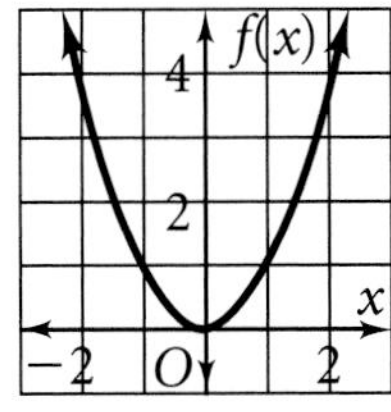

29. Sample table:

x	y
−2	2
0	2
2	2
4	2

31a. \$.71 **31b.** Sample table:

a	$C(a)$
0	\$.27
1	\$.38
2	\$.49
3	\$.60
4	\$.71
5	\$.82

31c. at most 12 min **33.** B

MIXED REVIEW **39.** {3, 7, 9, 15} **41.** {4, 2, 1, −2} **43.** −20 **45.** 4 **47.** −1

Cumulative Review page 19R

1. B **3.** D **5.** C **7.** B **9.** A **11.** {13, 7, 5}

Lesson 3-2 pages 21R–24R

ON YOUR OWN **1.** $3x + 2 = 5$ **3.** $3x + 1 = -2$ **5.** −1 **7.** −2 **9.** 1 **11.** −2 **13.** 21 **15.** 7 **17.** −6 **19.** 27 **21.** 0.382 **23.** −60 **25.** $18 + 2t = 60$; 21 min **27.** −6 **29.** 4.5 **31.** 16 **33.** 30 **35.** −6 **37.** 75 **39.** 0 **41.** −19 **43.** 2.2 **45.** 3.864 **47a.** Yes; with this estimate, the total bill is \$55, which is close to \$60. **47b.** 125 mi

49. 14 bulbs **51.** Multiplying by 100 changes all the numbers in the equation to integers and it might be easier to work with integers. **53.** $r = (2.8 - 1.34) \cdot 2$; 2.92 **55.** $n = (8 + 0.5) \div 0.05$; 170 **57.** $n = (7 - 5.3) \div (-0.8)$; −2.125 **59.** $t = (-7.06 - 3)(-2.5)$; 25.15

MIXED REVIEW **63.** 12 **65.** −9 **67.** 9 **69.** −20 **71.** 3

Preparing for Standardized Tests page 25R

1. E **3.** D **5.** A **7.** C **9.** $g(x) = x - 3$ **11.** 0 **13.** $5a - 5b + 4$

Lesson 3-4 pages 26R–30R

ON YOUR OWN **1.** $2(t - 2) = -6$; −1 **3.** $4(z + 1) = 4$; 0 **5.** No; $2a \cdot 2b = 4ab$. You cannot use the distributive property because ab is a product, not a sum. **7.** $-2n + 12$ **9.** $2b - \frac{8}{5}$ **11.** $4y + 6$ **13.** $18n - 42$ **15.** $-4.5b + 13.5$ **17.** $-36 + 16n$ **19.** 900° **21.** 3 **23.** 9 **25.** 1 **27.** −1 **29.** 8 **31.** −2 **33.** −1 **35.** 1 **37.** 380 mi; 280 mi **39.** 9 aluminum bats and 6 wooden bats **43.** \$3.96 **45.** \$29.55 **47.** \$98.97

MIXED REVIEW **49.** $-\frac{2}{3}$ **51.** −7 **53a.** B2/250 **53b.** 2.9; 0.9; 0.5 **53c.** \$504 million **55.** −17

CHECKPOINT **1.** 1 **2.** 33 **3.** 20 **4.** $2\frac{1}{2}$ **5.** 120 **6.** −2 **7.** −2 **8.** 10 **9.** $18\frac{1}{3}$ **10.** −2.7 **11.** −16 **12.** 2 **13.** 63 in. by 83 in. **14.** B

Lesson 3-5 pages 31R–34R

ON YOUR OWN **1.** 12 **3.** −10 **5.** −1 **7.** −48 **9.** In using the distributive property, the student did not multiply 1 by 8. **11.** A **13.** \$4/yd **15.** −45 **17.** −3 **19.** 15 **21.** −7 **23.** $-14\frac{1}{7}$ **25.** −10 **27.** 32 **29.** $\frac{6}{13}$ **31.** −60 **33.** 54 **35.** about 61.5 mi/h **37.** 33.7 h/wk **39.** −21 **41.** 5 **43.** −33 **45.** −1 **47.** $\frac{3}{5}$ **49.** −9 **51.** $1\frac{5}{6}$ **53.** $1\frac{1}{14}$ **55.** about \$141 million **57.** $2\frac{1}{2}$ h

MIXED REVIEW **59.** −7 **61.** $\frac{1}{2}$ **63.** 12 **65.** 1 **67.** $\frac{1}{5}$ **69.** $\frac{2}{5}$

Lesson 4-2 pages 35R–40R

ON YOUR OWN **1.** $2x + 2 = x - 8; -10$ **3.** $2x + 3 = 3x - 7; 10$ **5.** 7 **7.** 3 **9.** no solution **11.** no solution **13.** identity **15.** You should add y, not subtract, on the third line; 5.3. **17.** 0 **19.** no solution **21.** 2 **23.** no solution **25.** −41 **27.** $-\frac{1}{2}$ **29.** identity **31.** $a = -\frac{1}{4}; w = -4;$ $x = -1; y = 0$ **35.** 20 h **43.** $DF = 7, DE = 10,$ $EF = 6$ **45.** 7 **47.** −3 **49.** −0.5 **51.** 10 **53.** C

MIXED REVIEW **55.** −28 **57.** 7.7 **59.** 15 **61.** 34 **63.** 11 **65.** −19 **67.** −2

Cumulative Review page 41R

1. D **3.** C **5.** E **7.** B **9.** B **11.** $3x + 17 = 32;$ $x = 5$ **13.** 20%

Lesson 4-7 pages 42R–46R

ON YOUR OWN **1.** Subtract 5 from each side. Then divide each side by 4. **3.** Subtract 8 from each side. **5.** Subtract y from each side. Then add 5 to each side. **7.** Add s to each side. Then subtract 6 from each side. **9.** Multiply or divide each side by −1. Reverse the order of the inequality. **11.** E **13.** A **15.** C

17. $h \geq -2$
−5 −4 −3 −2 −1 0

19. $x > -2\frac{1}{2}$
−5 −4 −3 −2 −1 0

27a. 74 boxes **27b.** 5 trips **29.** $k > -\frac{1}{4}$ **31.** all numbers **33.** no solutions **35.** $k \leq -33$ **37.** $s \geq -\frac{22}{37}$ **41.** at least $7000 **43.** $15n - (490 + 45 + 65) \geq 1200$

MIXED REVIEW **45.** $m > 1850$ **47.** Absolute value; variable expression is inside the absolute value symbol. **49.** Quadratic; highest power of x is 2. **51a.** about 1.125 tons **51b.** about 10.7 million tons

53.
−6 −5 −4 −3 −2 −1

55.
−2 −1 0 1 2 3

Toolbox page 47R

1. A **3.** B **5.** $3\frac{1}{3}$ **7.** 270 **9.** about 15.83 mi/h **11.** 20,000 mi/h

Lesson 5-4 pages 48R–52R

ON YOUR OWN **1.** $-\frac{3}{4}; -5$ **3.** 3; −9 **5.** 0; 3 **7.** III **9.** II **11a.** 12 in. **11b.** $h = -\frac{2}{15}t + 12$ **11c.** 90 min

13.
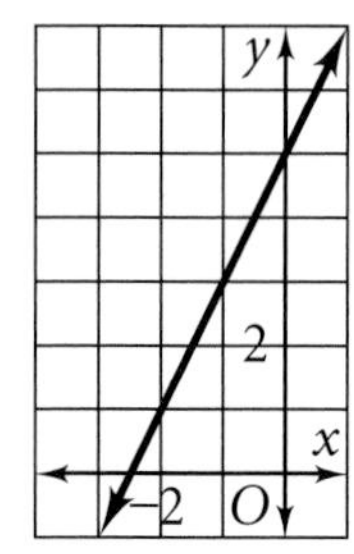

15.
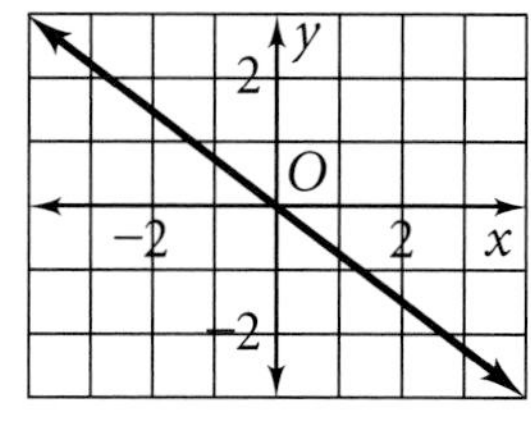

21. $-\frac{2}{3}; 2; y = -\frac{2}{3}x + 2$ **23.** 0; 1; $y = 1$ **27.** $y = \frac{2}{9}x + 3$ **29.** $y = -\frac{5}{4}x$

MIXED REVIEW **31.** $-\frac{9}{7}$ **33.** $-\frac{1}{5}$ **35.** 2 **37.** 1

CHECKPOINT **1.** yes; $\frac{y}{x} = m$ **2.** no; $\frac{y}{x} \neq m$ **3.** No; a vertical line cannot be a direct variation. **4.** yes; $\frac{y}{x} = m$ **5.** $121.75 billion/yr

Preparing for Standardized Tests page 53R

1. B **3.** B **5.** C **7.** A **9.** D **11.** B **13.** $\frac{3}{5}$ **15.** 4, 5

Lesson 5-5 pages 54R–57R

ON YOUR OWN **1.** $y = 2x - 11$ **3.** $y = \frac{4}{3}x + 3\frac{1}{3}$ **5.** $y = x + 3$ **7.** $y = 2$ **9.** $y = -\frac{1}{4}x + 3\frac{3}{4}$ **11.** $y = -\frac{3}{4}x - 3\frac{1}{2}$ **13a.** $L = 0.025M + 7.25$ **13b.** The y-intercept is the length of the spring when no mass is attached. **13c.** 9 cm **15.** $y = \frac{1}{5}x + 1\frac{3}{5}$ **17.** $y = \frac{1}{9}x + 2\frac{8}{9}$ **19.** $y = -2x + 150$ **21.** $y = -\frac{2}{5}x + 2\frac{4}{5}$ **23a.** For 86 corresponding to 1986, $r = 0.5t - 39.1$ **23b.** $15.9 billion **25.** yes; $y = -2x + 1$ **27.** yes; $y = 3x + 25$ **29a.** $c = 2.5l + 2$ **29b.** slope: cost/mi; y-intercept: initial cost of ride

MIXED REVIEW **31.** $c < 8$ **33.** $m \leq -1\frac{3}{4}$ **35.** $-1\frac{4}{7}$ **37.** 928.6% increase **39.** positive **41.** positive

Lesson 5-7 pages 58R–61R

ON YOUR OWN **1.** A **3.** C

5.

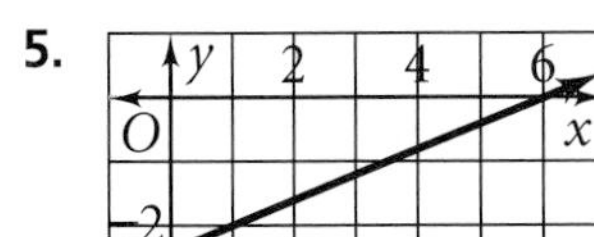

7.

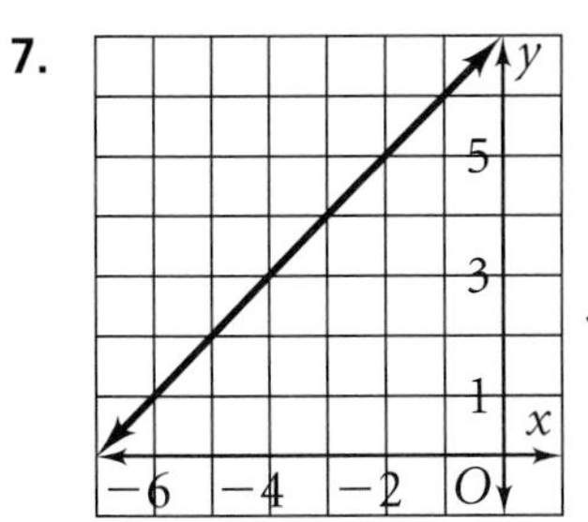

9.

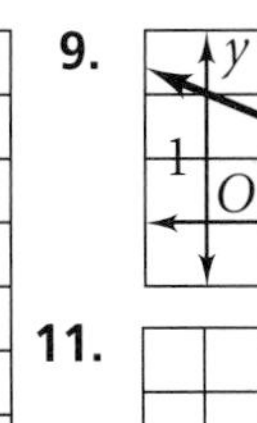

11.

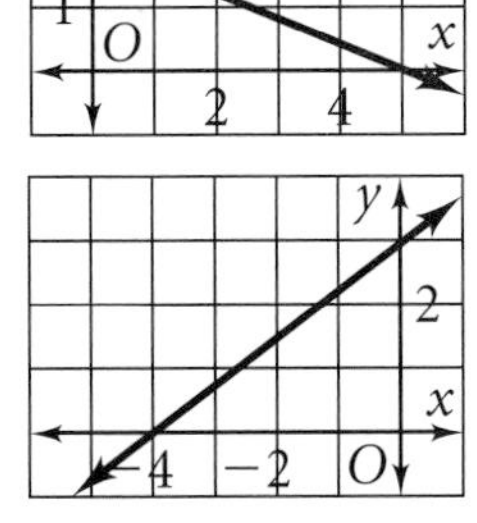

15.

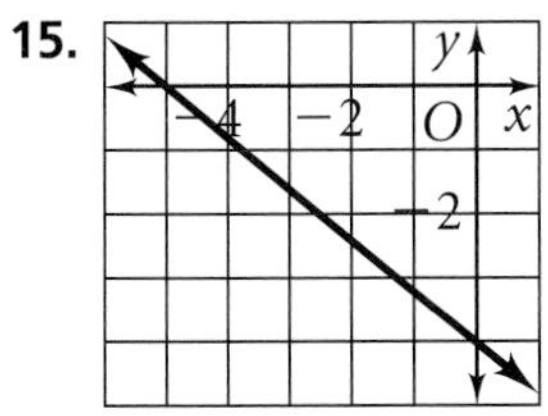

intercepts: $(0, -4)$ and $(-5, 0)$;

17.

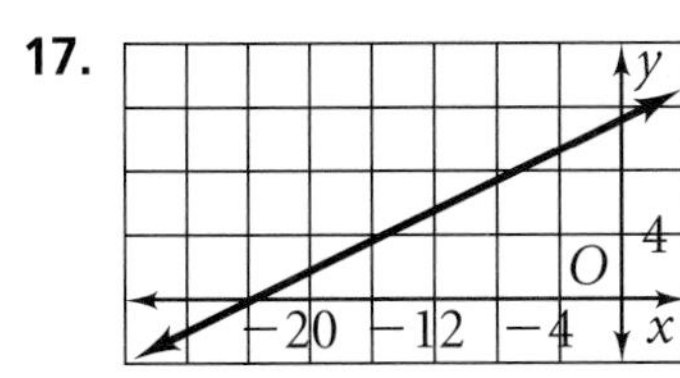

intercepts: $(0, 10\frac{10}{11})$ and $(-24, 0)$;

23. $y = \frac{A}{B}x + \frac{C}{B}$ **25.** $x + 3y = 26$ **27.** $3x + 2y = -20$ **29.** $3x + y = 7$ **31.** $x + 5y = -39$

MIXED REVIEW **33.** $\frac{1}{36}$

35.

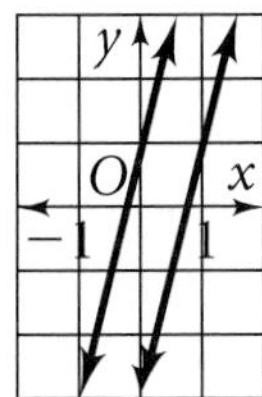

37.

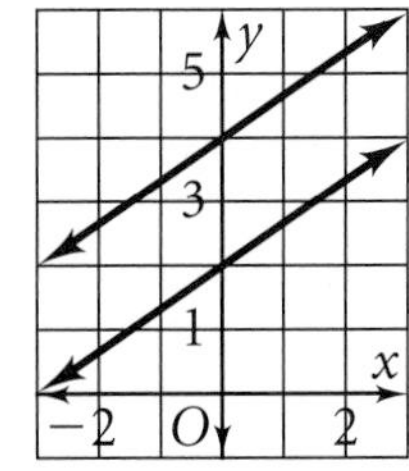

CHAPTER 6

Toolbox page 268

1. 4 and 8 **3a.** about 2:13 P.M. **3b.** about 13.5 mi

Lesson 6-1 pages 269–274

ON YOUR OWN

1. no solution;

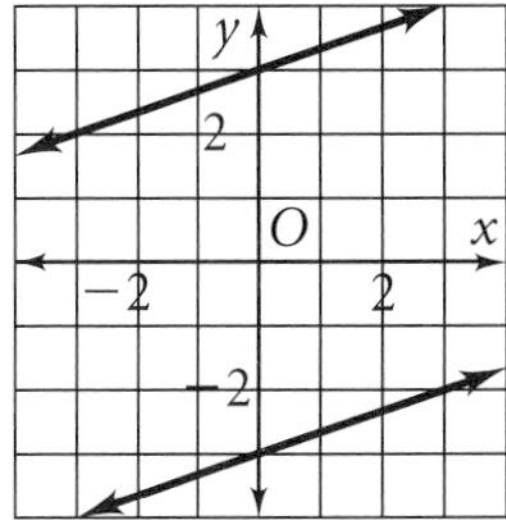

3. $(1, 1)$;

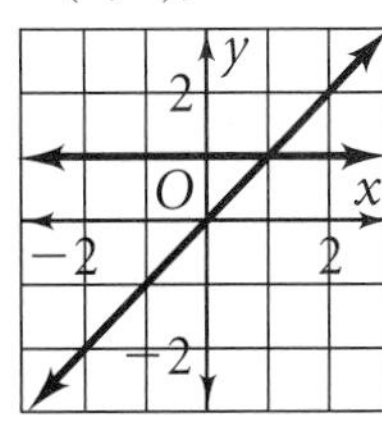

5. infinitely many solutions;

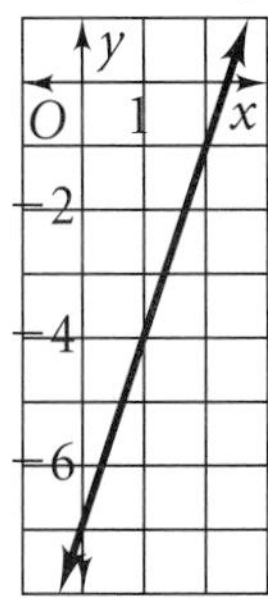

7. yes **9.** yes **11a.** No; the graphs are not straight lines. **11b.** The solution of the system is the point in time when the fear of commitment is equal to the fear of baldness. **11c.** The solution on Lily's chart shows the point in time when the level of hope of meeting Brad Pitt is equal to the level of fear of cellulite. **11d.** feelings; time

13. $(1, 3)$;

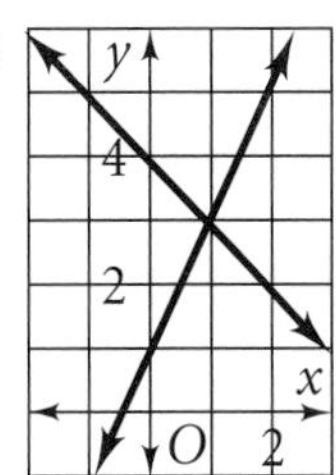

15. $(0, 0)$;

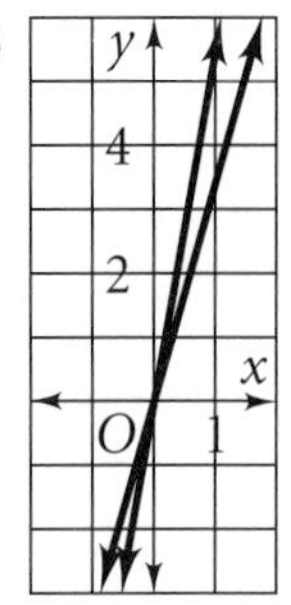

17. $(3, -4)$;

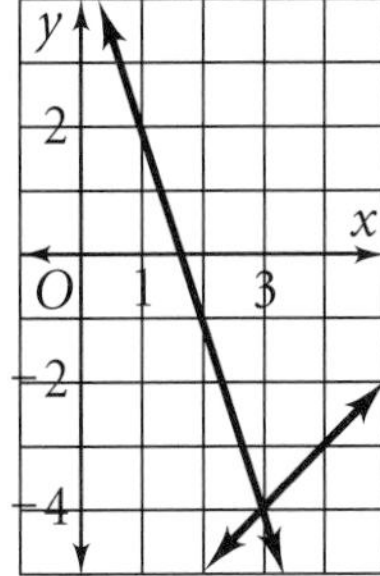

19. no solution;

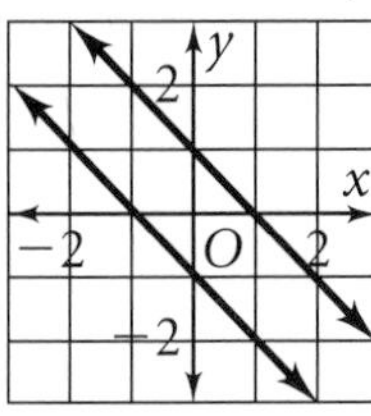

Selected Answers

21. $(0, -1)$; 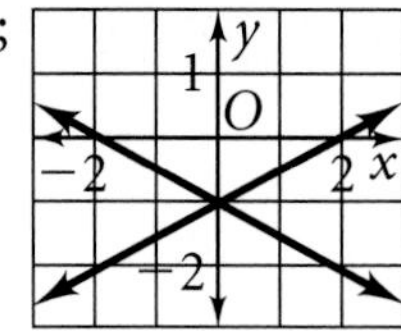

23. no solution; 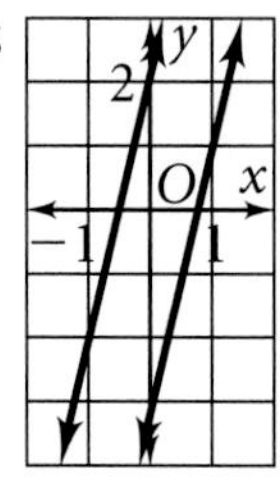

25. True; the graphs of lines can intersect once, not intersect, or be the same line. **27.** False; the system may have no solutions. **29.** parallel; no solutions **31.** intersect; one solution **33.** same line; infinitely many solutions **35.** intersect; one solution **41a.** (2, 200) **41b.** Both studios charge $200 rent for 2 h. **43.** (4.5, 6.5) **45.** $(4, -6)$

MIXED REVIEW **47.** $\frac{1}{36}$ **49.** 1 **51.** $b \leq 6$ **53a.** about 138.5 mi^2 **53b.** about 72 million **55.** $x = 8y$ **57.** $x = \frac{3}{2}y + \frac{5}{2}$

Lesson 6-2 pages 275–279

ON YOUR OWN **1.** one **3.** no solution **5.** infinitely many solutions **7.** one **9.** 12 cm by 3 cm **11.** (2, 4) **13.** $(-\frac{1}{2}, -\frac{1}{2})$ **15.** $(2, \frac{1}{2})$ **17.** $(-\frac{1}{2}, 0)$ **19.** (3, 5) **21.** infinitely many solutions

23. $(\frac{1}{2}, 1)$; 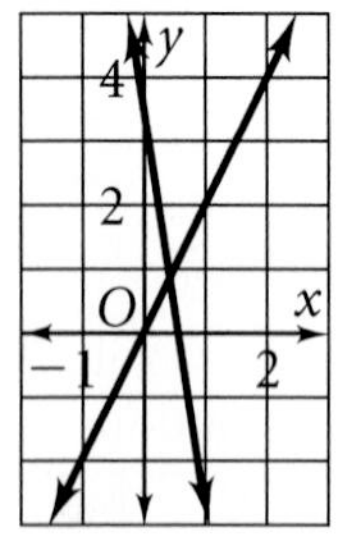

25. $(-1, 1)$; 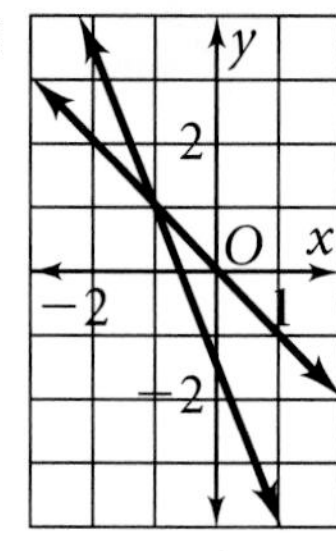

27. no solution; 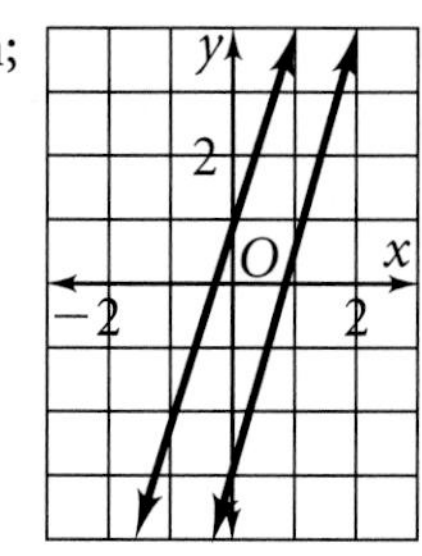

29. D **31.** C **33.** A **35.** infinitely many solutions **37.** no solution **39.** 160 acres of soybeans; 80 acres of corn **41.** $(3, -3)$ **43.** $(\frac{1}{4}, 0)$ **45.** $(12, -8)$ **47.** $(-2, -5)$

MIXED REVIEW **49.** 7; −4 **51.** 9; 0 **53.** $y = \frac{3}{2}x$ **55.** $-7x$ **57.** $15x$

Lesson 6-3 pages 280–284

ON YOUR OWN **1.** Add equations; $(5, -6)$ **3.** Multiply the first equation by 4; (5, 4) **5.** Add equations; $(2, -3)$ **7.** Subtract first equation from second; (4, 2) **9.** Brass parts cost $6; steel parts cost $3. **11.** (5, 2) **13.** (1, 3) **15.** $(-4.5, 8)$ **17.** (14, 14) **19.** $(-\frac{2}{3}, 2)$ **21.** (2, 0) **23.** infinitely many solutions **25.** $(2\frac{1}{2}, 3\frac{1}{2})$ **27.** 3 V, 1.5 V **29.** Agree; you do not need to solve an equation for *y* before substituting the values. **31.** infinitely many solutions **33.** (18, 52) **35.** (3, 4) **37.** $(1\frac{1}{2}, -\frac{1}{2})$ **39a.** (81.25, 8.125) **39b.** Room for one night costs $81.25 per person; the average cost of one meal is about $8.13.

MIXED REVIEW **41.** $x = 0$ **43.** $x = 10$ **45.** $2s + d = 6.50$ **47.** $5p + 2n = 32$

CHECKPOINT **1.** $(-1\frac{2}{9}, 3\frac{1}{9})$ **2.** $(3, -4)$ **3.** (9, 10) **4.** $(2, -5\frac{1}{3})$ **5.** Sample: $2x - y = 3$; $\frac{1}{2}x + \frac{1}{2}y = 6$ **6a.** $(p, c) = (20, 33)$

Lesson 6-4 pages 285–288

ON YOUR OWN **1.** 72.5° and 107.5° **3.** 7 dimes and 3 nickels **5.** $(\frac{1}{3}, 2\frac{1}{3})$ **7.** (5, 1) **9.** no solution **11.** (0, 0) **13a.** $m = 254 + 400 + 1.2n$ **13b.** $m = 4n + 150$ **13c.** 180 tickets **15.** 577 games **17.** C **19.** Sample: Substitution; at least one equation is solved for one of the variables. **21.** Sample: Elimination; coefficients match well for subtraction. **23.** Sample: Substitution; coefficients −1 and 1 make it easy to solve either equation for one of the variables. **25a.** $2s + t = 12$ **25b.** $s = 3t$ **25c.** $5\frac{1}{7}, 5\frac{1}{7}, 1\frac{5}{7}$

MIXED REVIEW **27.** −2 **29.** 25 or −17 **31.** \$130 billion

33.

35.

Lesson 6-5 pages 289–293

ON YOUR OWN **1.** A **3.** B **5.** 1 and 3

9.

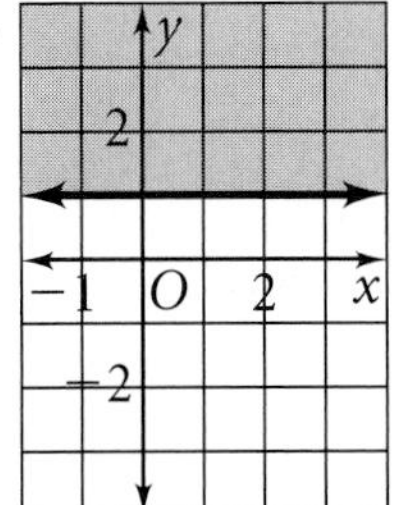

11.

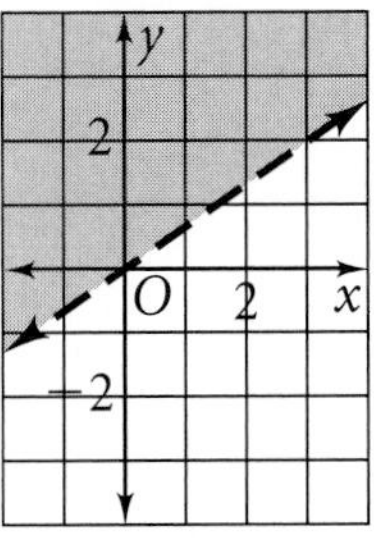

13.

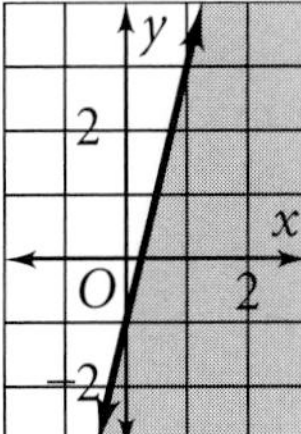

15.

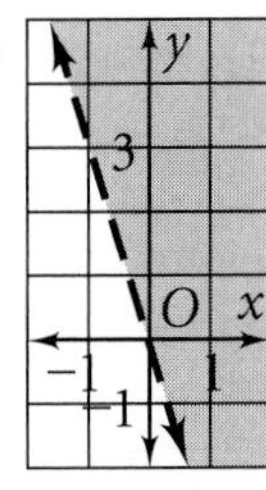

17.

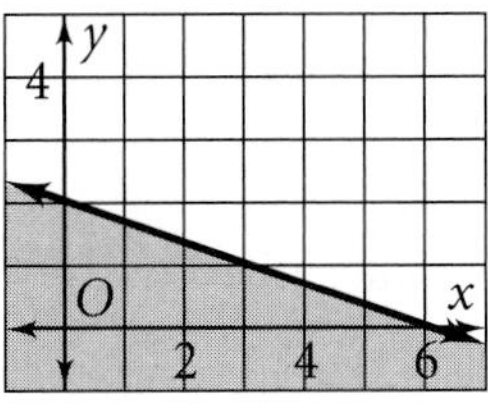

19.

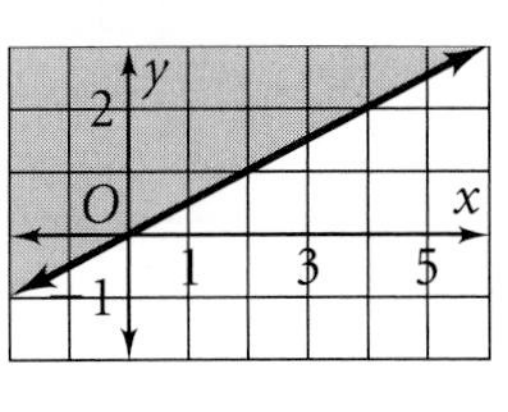

21.

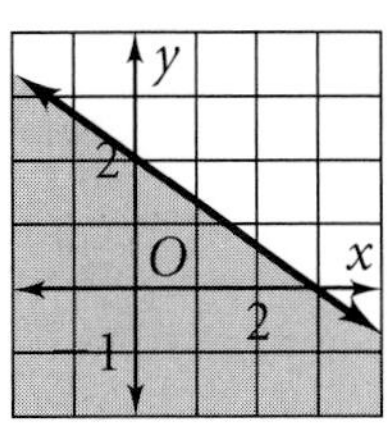

23.

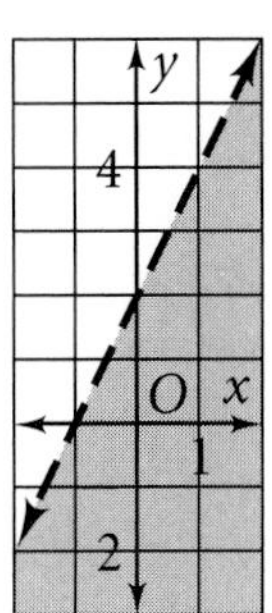

25. $y < x + 2$ **27.** $y > 2x + 1$ **29.** $y \leq \frac{1}{3}x - 2$

31. $x > 0$;

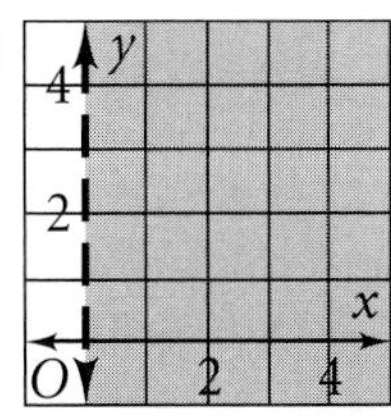

33. $y \geq 0$;

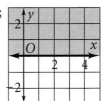

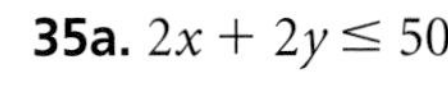

35a. $2x + 2y \leq 50$

35b.

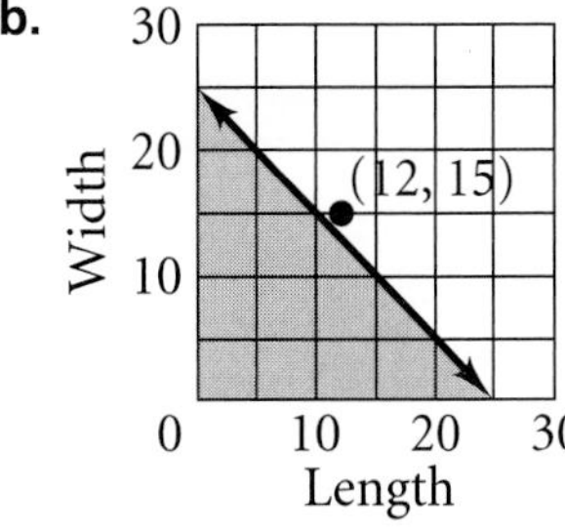

35d. No; $2(12) + 2(15) \leq 50$ is false. On the graph, (12, 15) is not in the shaded region. **37.** yes **39.** yes

MIXED REVIEW **41.** 5 **43.** $\frac{8}{3}$ **45.** 1.2 h **47.** (3, 5) **49.** $(4\frac{2}{3}, 37\frac{1}{3})$

Toolbox page 294

1.

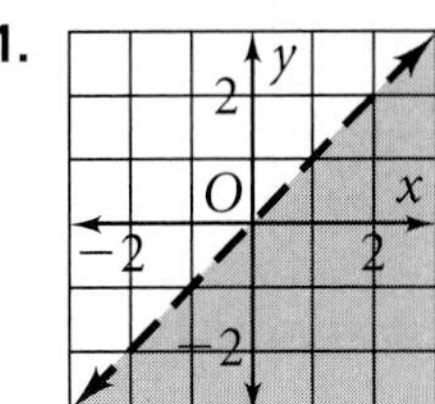

3. 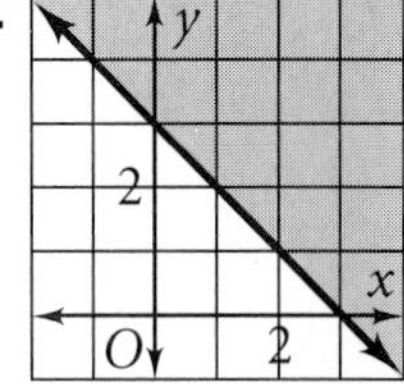

5. 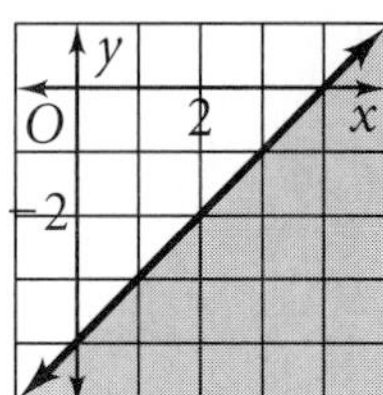

7. 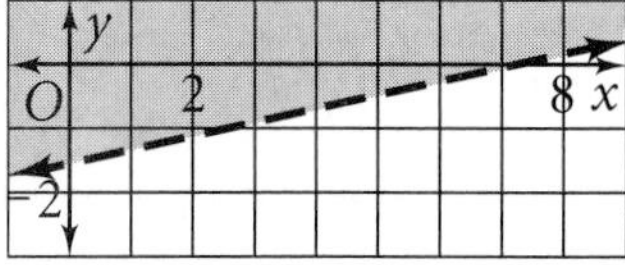

Lesson 6-6 pages 295–299

ON YOUR OWN **1.** C **3.** The point is on the boundary line of $2x + y > 2$, so it is not a solution of $2x + y > 2$.

5. 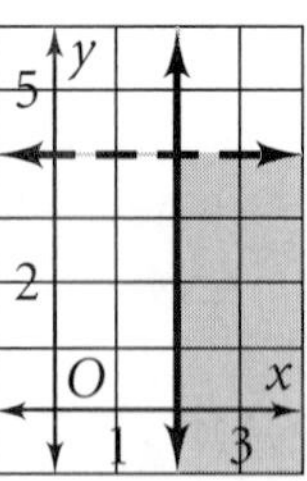

7. no solution;

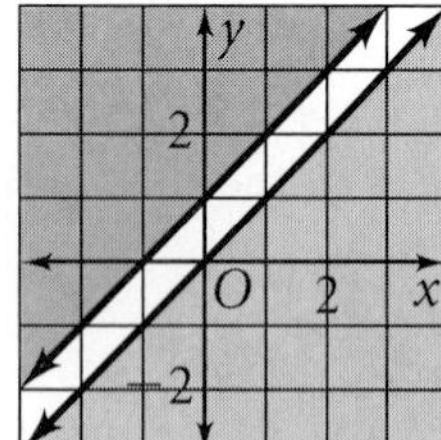

9. 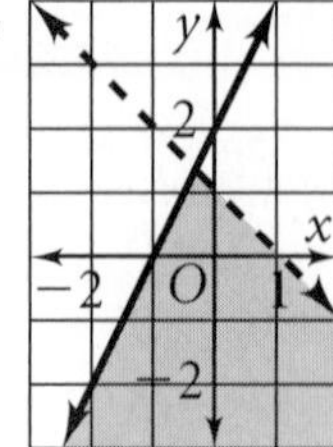

11. 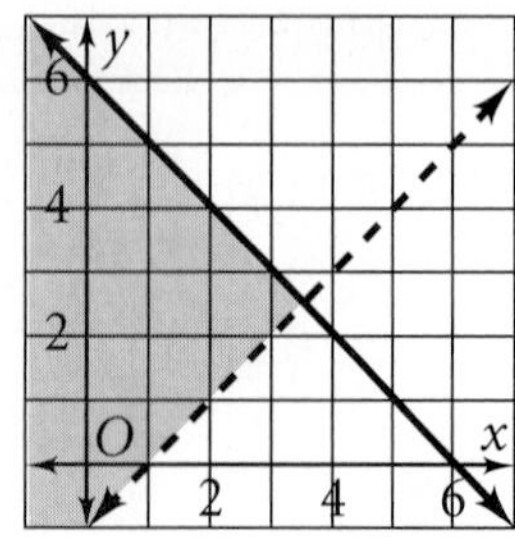

13. 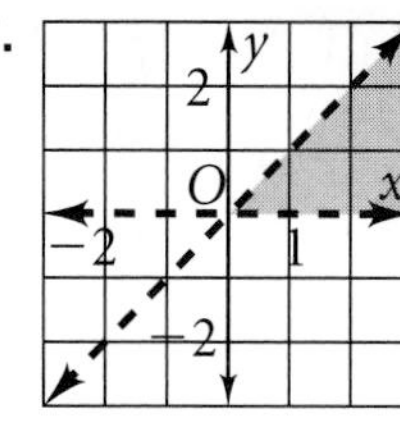

15. 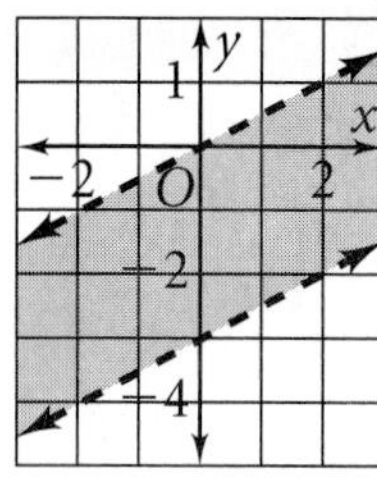

17a. $0.6f + 0.55c \leq 33$; $f \geq 9$; $c \geq 12$

17b. 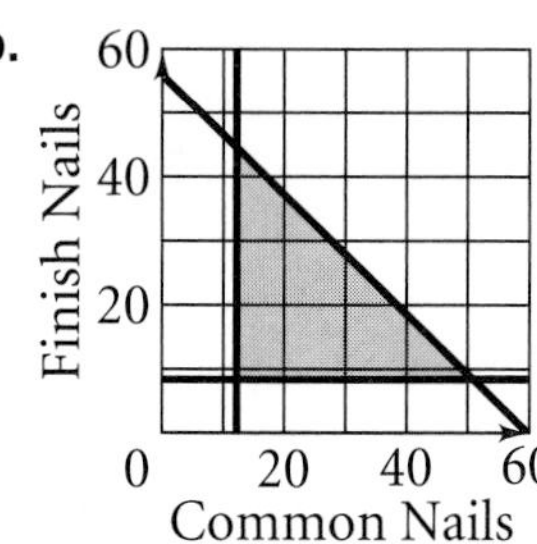

17c. Sample: (20, 20) **17d.** Sample: (40, 25)

23. 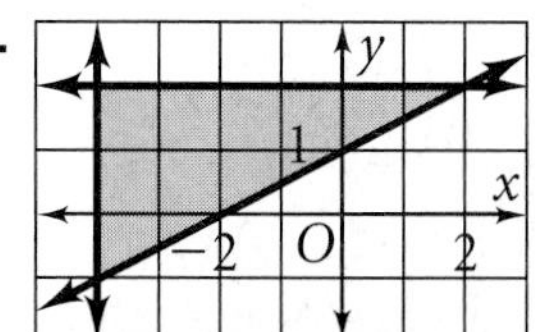

23a. triangle **23b.** $(-4, -1), (-4, 2), (2, 2)$
23c. 9 sq. units

25. 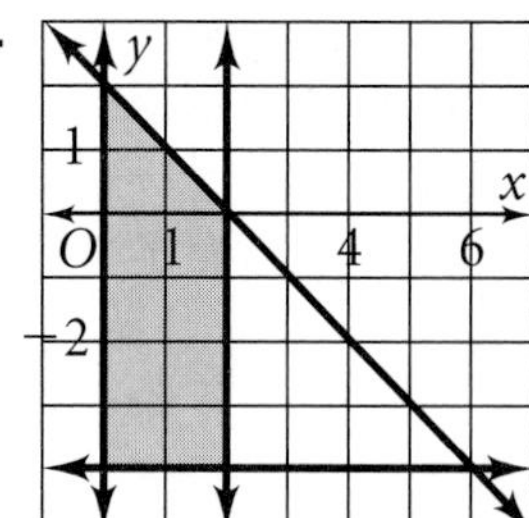

25a. trapezoid **25b.** $(0, -4)$ $(0, 2), (2, 0), (2, -4)$
25c. 10 sq. units **27a.** $5.99x + 9.99y \leq 50$; $x \geq 0$; $y \geq 1$

27b. 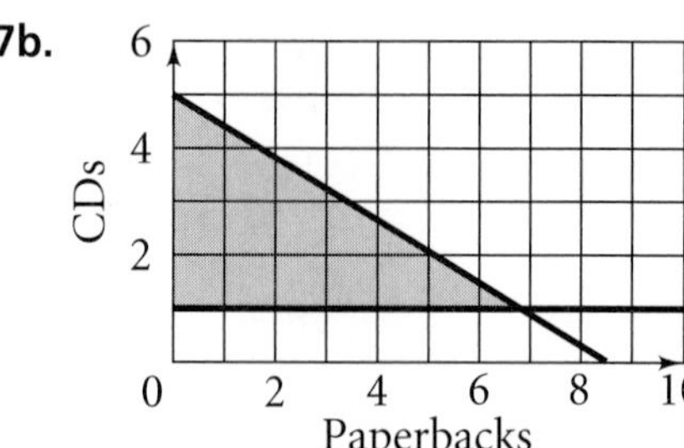

27c. 2 books and 6 CDs; (2, 6) is not a solution of the system because 2 books and 6 CDs cost $71.92.
27d. 5 CDs, no books **27e.** 8 books

MIXED REVIEW **29.** 1 **31.** 4 **33.** 4 **35.** 22 **37.** 62 **39.** 1350

CHECKPOINT

1.

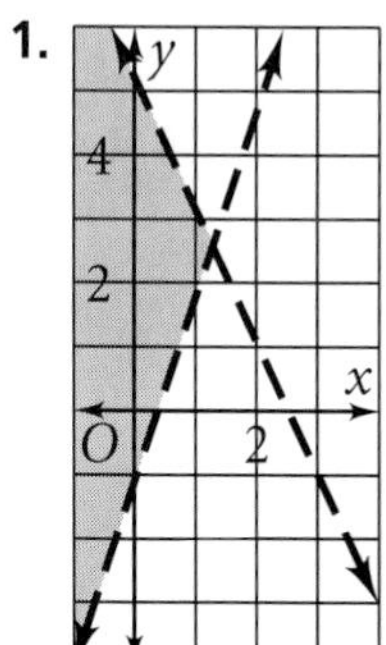

2.

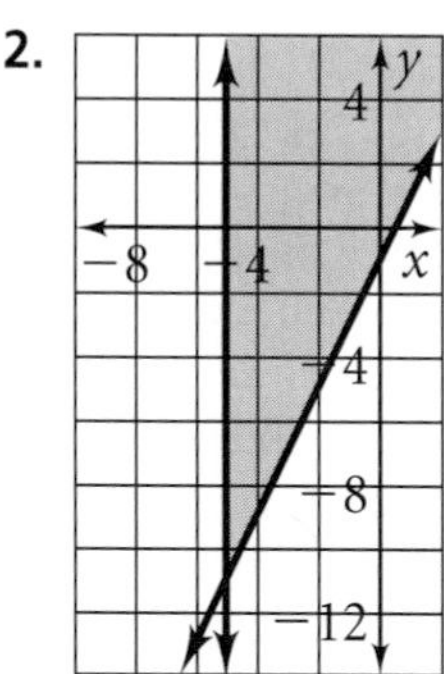

3.

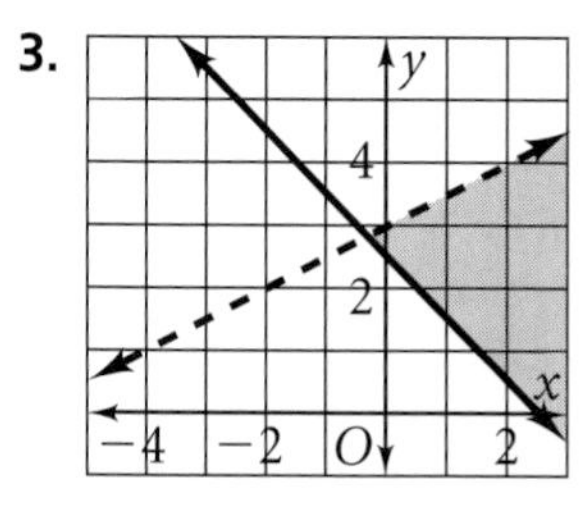

4.

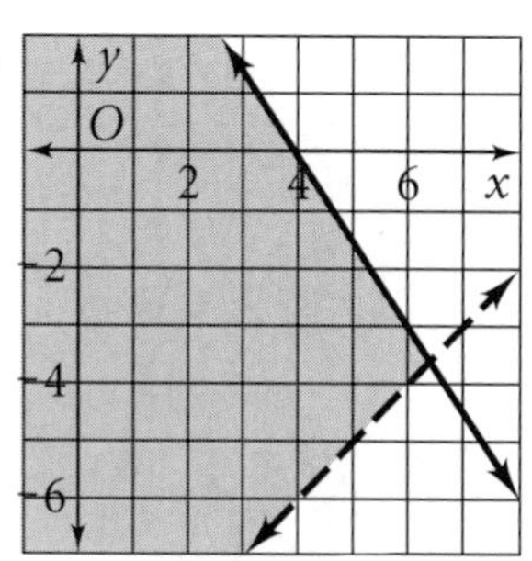

5. D **6a.** $p = 7 + 0.75t$; $p = 8 + 0.5t$ **6b.** (4, 10); a pizza with 4 toppings costs $10 in each restaurant.

Lesson 6-7 pages 300–304

ON YOUR OWN **1.** 24, 32, 34, 30; (3, 5), (8, 0) **3.** 0, 100, 400, 800; (20, 10), (0, 0) **5.** (6, 0) **7.** (4, 0) **9.** 0; 36 **11.** 1; 8 **13.** $c = 8d + 20t$
15b. $N = 30x + 40y$

15c. 400 ft^2 at Location A and 100 ft^2 at Location B

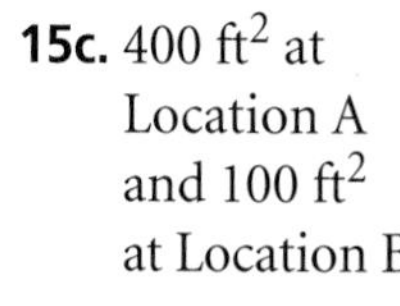

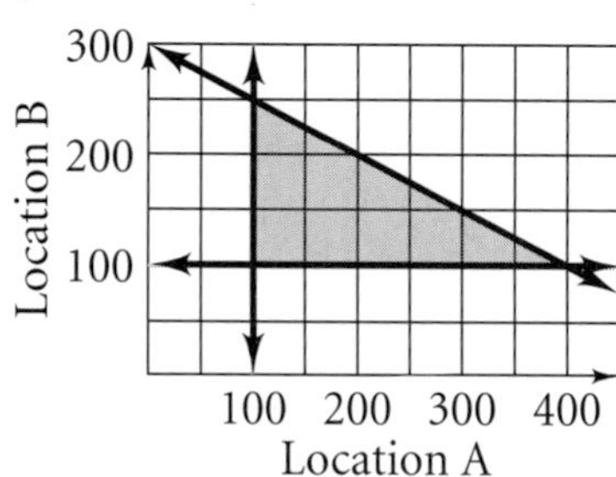

MIXED REVIEW **17.** $y = -\frac{1}{2}x + 2\frac{1}{2}$ **19.** $y = \frac{8}{3}x$
21. quadratic **23.** linear

Lesson 6-8 pages 305–309

ON YOUR OWN **1.** (0, 0), (2, 4) **3.** (0, 0) **5.** (−2, −2), (2, −2) **7.** (−2, 1), (2, 1)

9. (−1.94, 0.15), (1.94, 0.15)

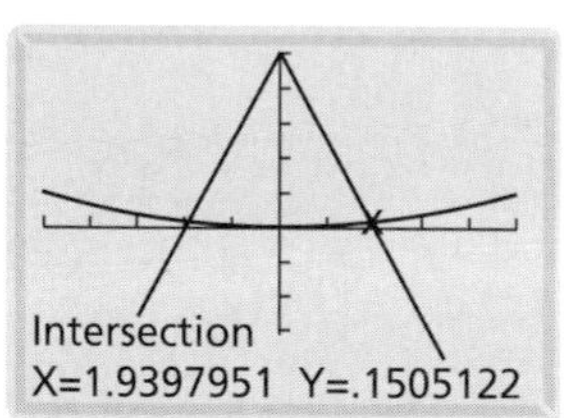

Xmin=−5 Ymin=−5
Xmax=5 Ymax=5
Xscl=1 Yscl=1

11. A; (−1, −2), (1, −2) **13.** C; no solution **15.** D

21. no solution;

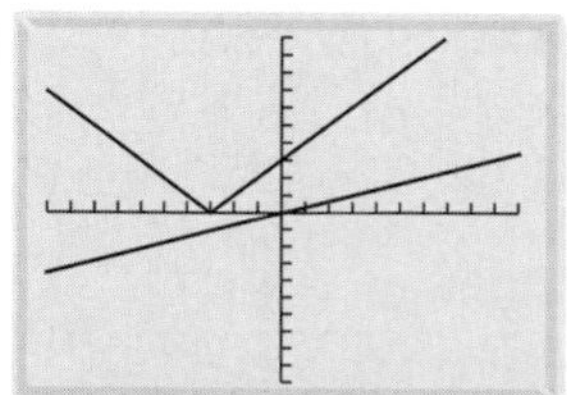

23. (−2, 3), (1, 0);

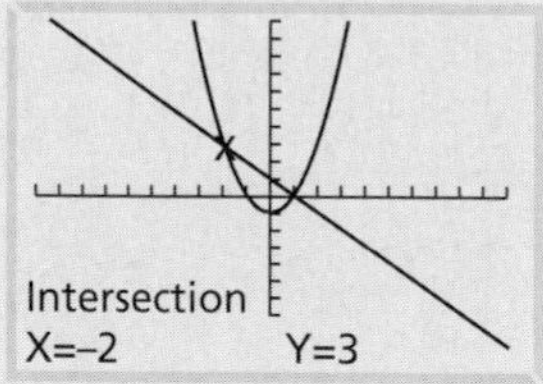

25. no solution;

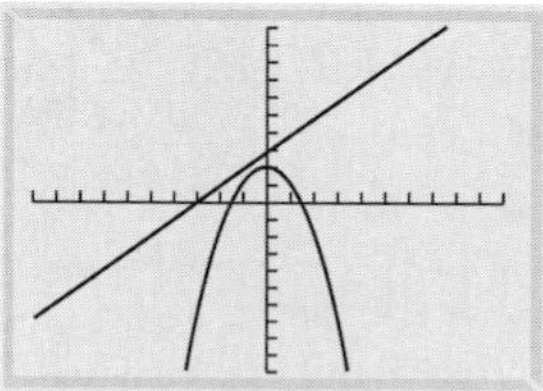

27. (−1, −2), (1, −2);

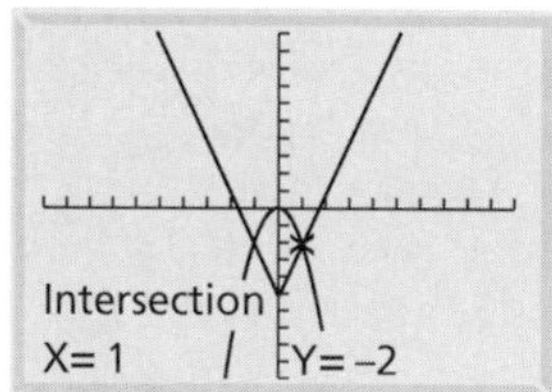

Selected Answers

29. no solution;

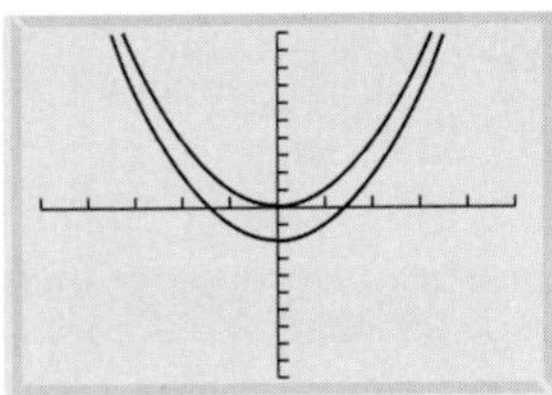

Xmin=–5 Ymin=–10
Xmax=5 Ymax=10
Xscl=1 Yscl=1

31. $(-2, 1), (4, 4)$;

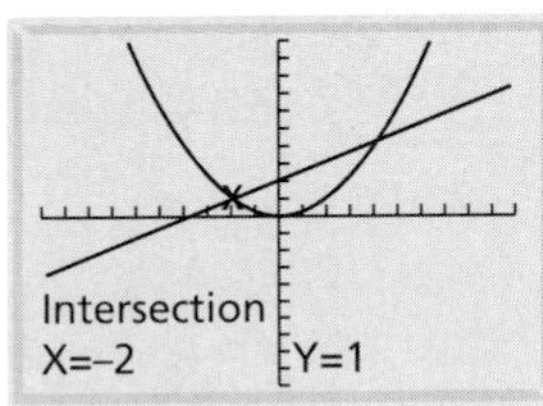

MIXED REVIEW **35.** 106.25% **37.** 6.5%

39. 91,800 **41.** $\begin{bmatrix} 7-x & x-5 \\ -3x & -y \\ 8z & 0 \end{bmatrix}$

43a. 1000000*B2/C2 **43b.** D2: 1576; D3: 2423

Wrap-Up pages 311–313

1. $x = 3, y = 1; (3, 1)$ **2.** $y = -\frac{3}{2}x - \frac{3}{2}, y = \frac{3}{2}x + \frac{3}{2}$; $(-1, 0)$ **3.** $y = x - 1, y = -x + 3; (2, 1)$
4. $x = -1, y = -x + 1; (-1, 2)$

5. $(1, 2)$;

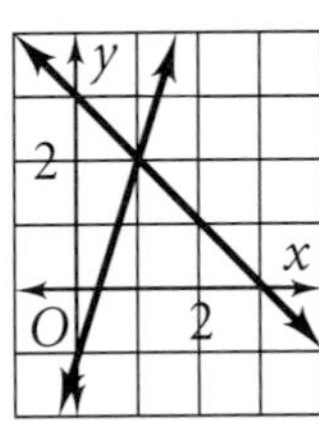

6. $(-1, 2)$;

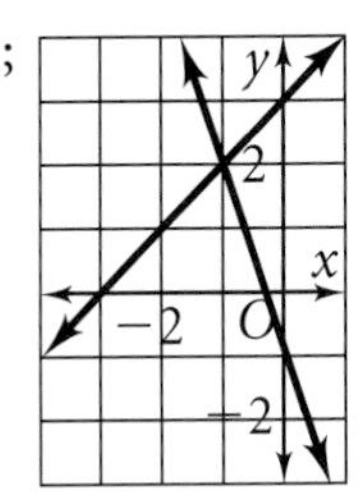

7. no solution;

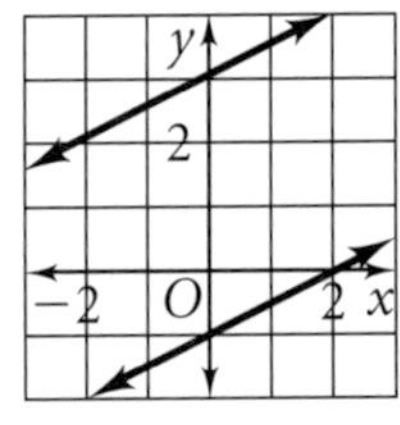

8. $(1, -1)$;

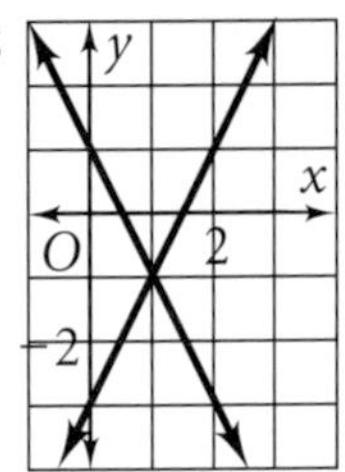

9. $(-2, 5)$ **10.** $(-4\frac{1}{2}, -6)$ **11.** $(2, 2)$
12. $(-1\frac{1}{9}, -\frac{5}{9})$ **14.** $(-6, 23)$ **15.** $(1, -1)$ **16.** $(6, 4)$
17. $(12, 6)$ **18.** $10\frac{2}{3}$ fl oz **19.** 63° and 27°

20.

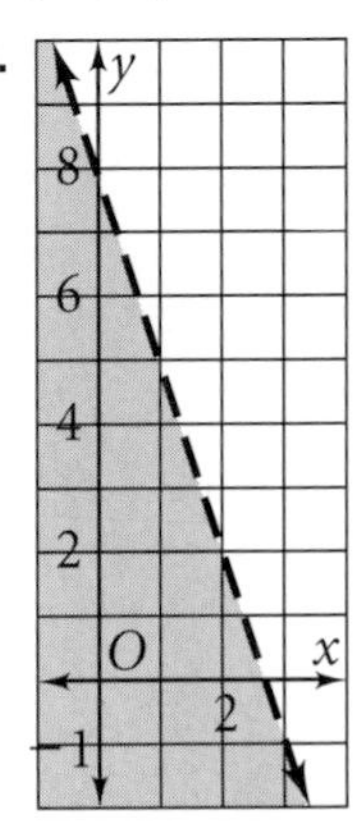

21.

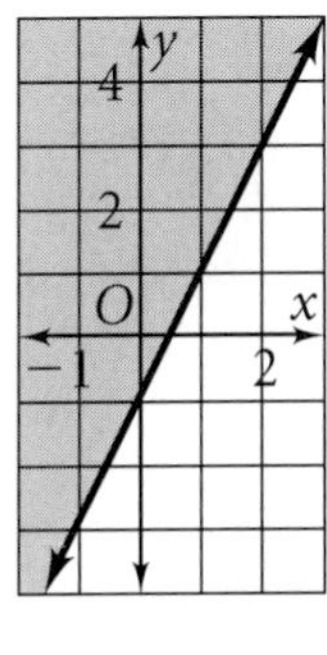

22.

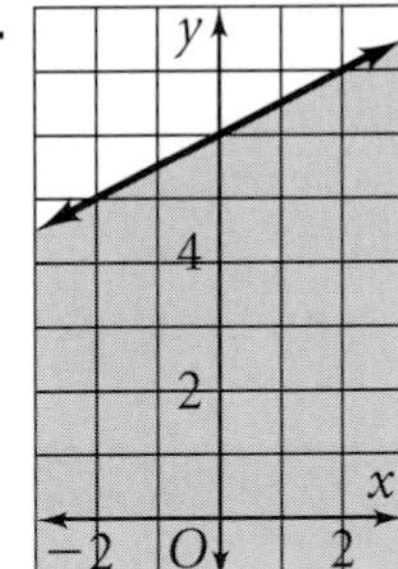

23.

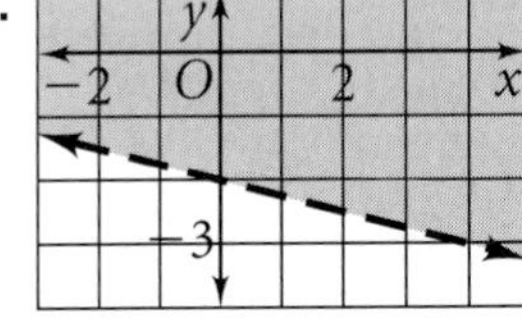

24.

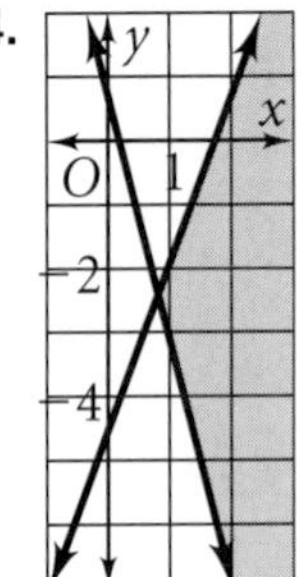

25.

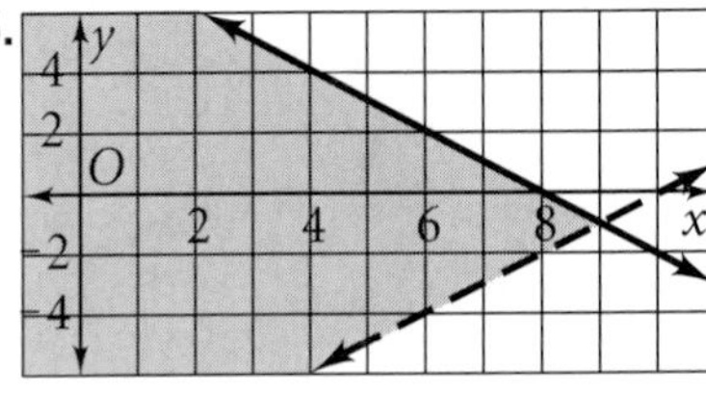

26.

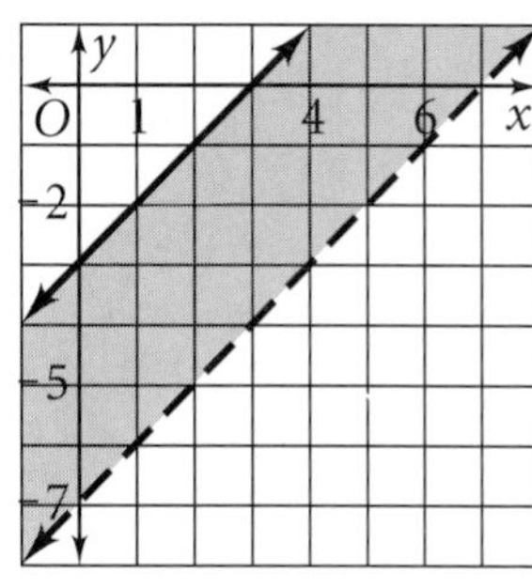

27.

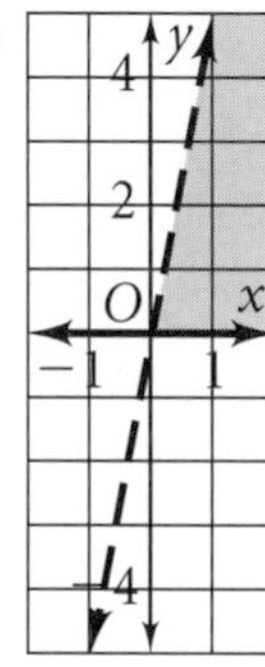

29. 0; 21;

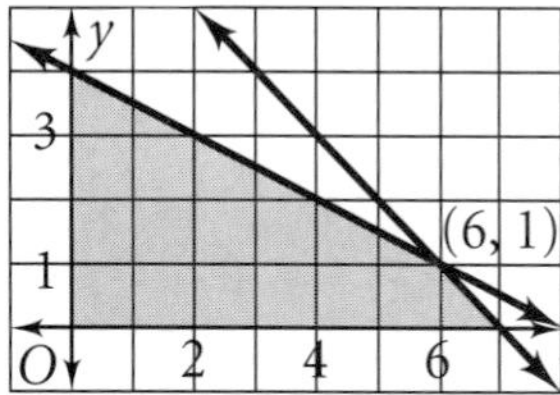

30. 3; 7.5;

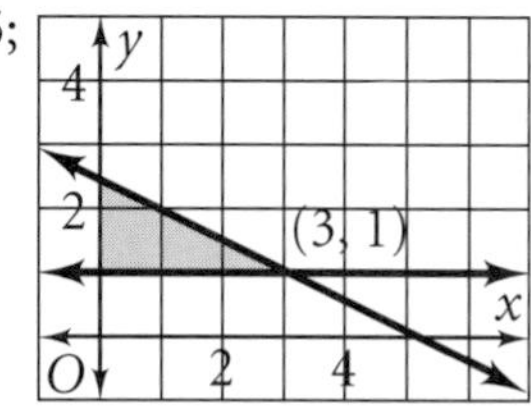

31. 0; 18;

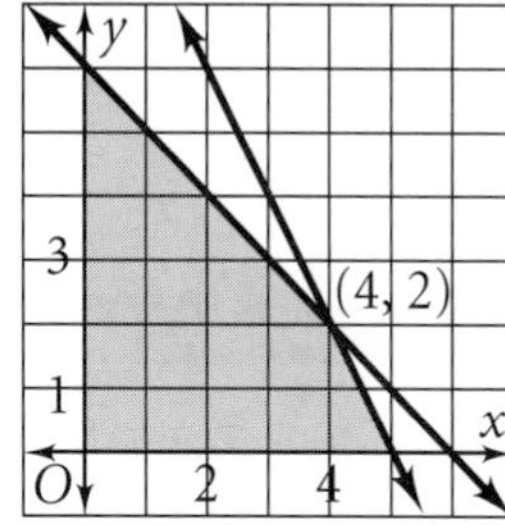

32. 7; 16;

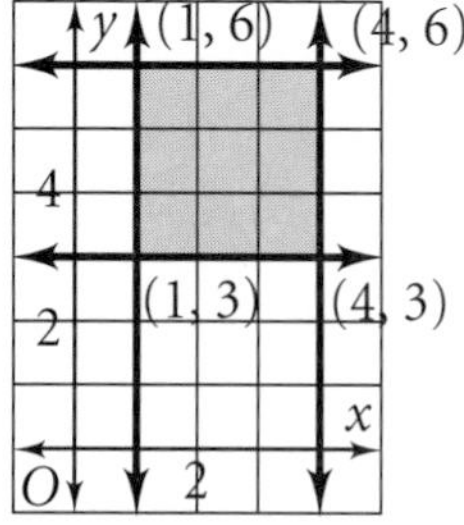

33. E

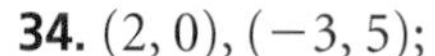

34. (2, 0), (−3, 5);

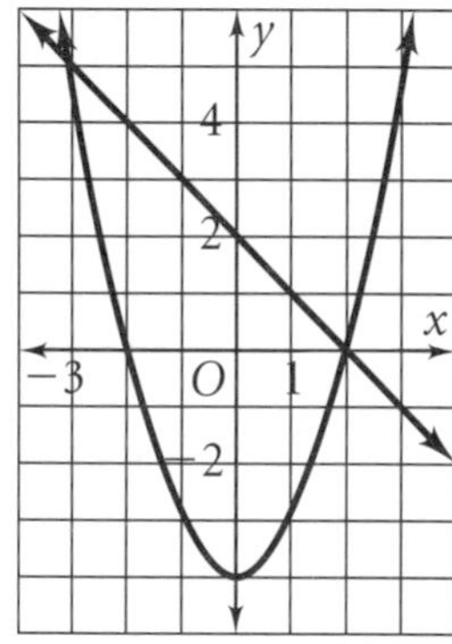

35. (2, 1), $(-\frac{2}{3}, -1\frac{2}{3})$;

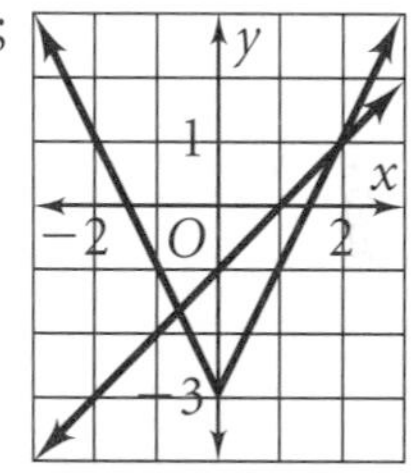

36. (0, 3), (2, 1);

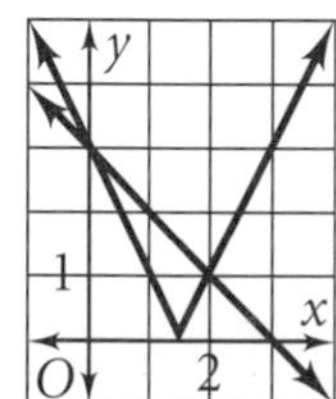

37. (−1, 4), (3, 12)

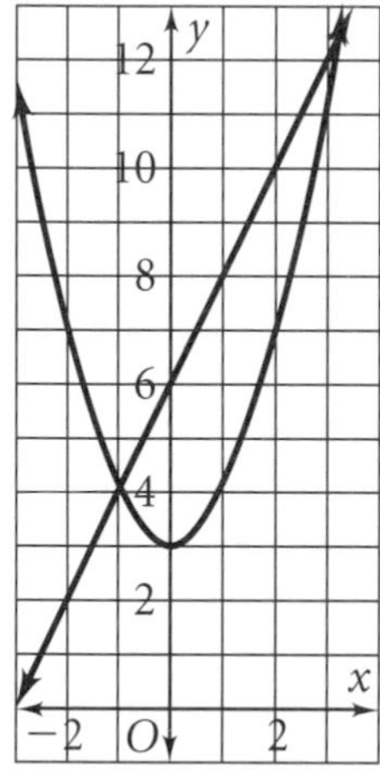

38. 0, 1, 2, 3, or 4; the number of solutions of a system with an absolute value equation and a quadratic equation correspond to the number of times the graphs of the equations intersect. It is possible for the graphs to intersect 0, 1, 2, 3, or 4 times. The graphs cannot intersect more than 4 times. **39.** 9 **40.** 49 **41.** 20.25 **42.** $\frac{1}{4}$ **43.** 121 **44.** 67.24

45. 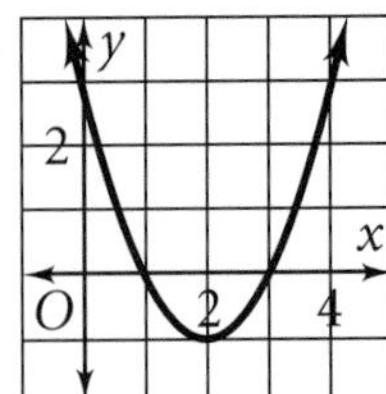

46. 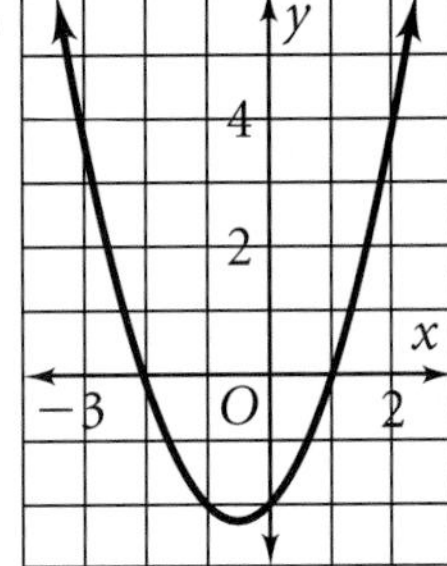

47. 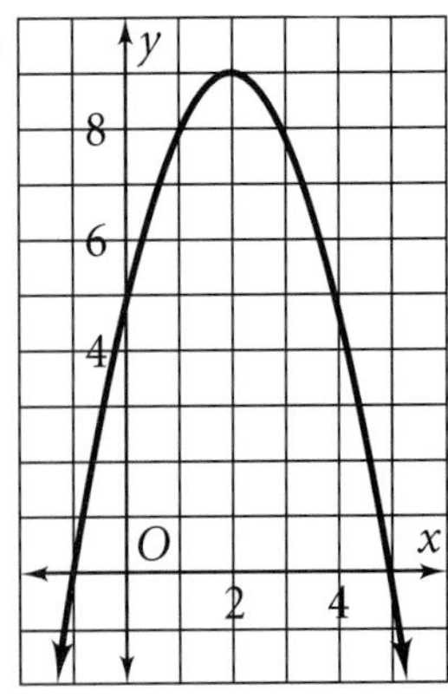

48. 1 **49.** 109 **50.** 64 **51.** 17 **52.** 11 **53.** 170.24

Cumulative Review page 315

1. E **3.** E **5.** A **7.** C **9.** E **11.** B
13. $y = -\frac{5}{2}x + 2$ **15.** about 3.4%

CHAPTER 7

Lesson 7-1 pages 318–322

ON YOUR OWN **1.** 1; 2; 4 **3.** −1, −3, −9
5. upward; min. **7.** downward; max.

9. 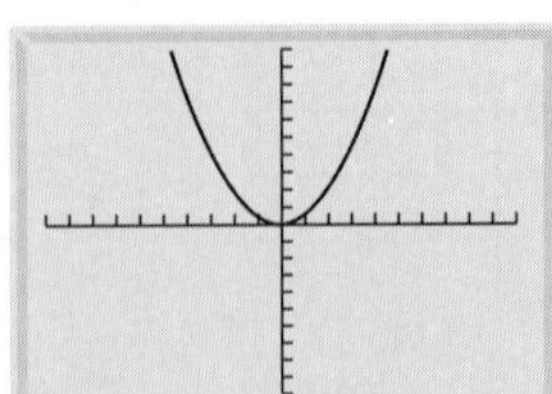

11. 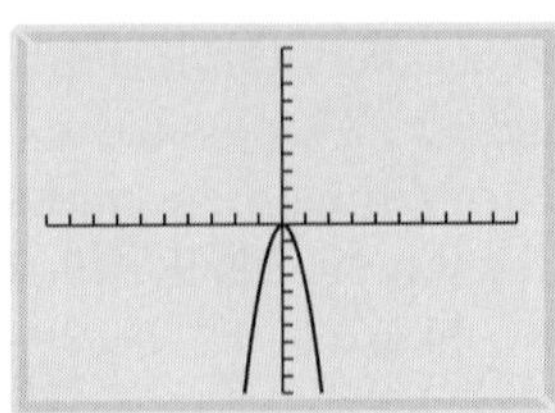

13. 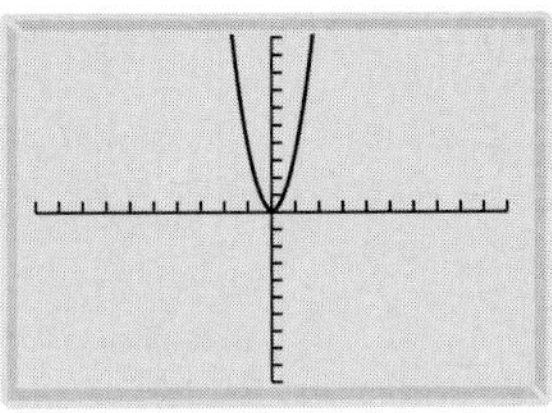

15. 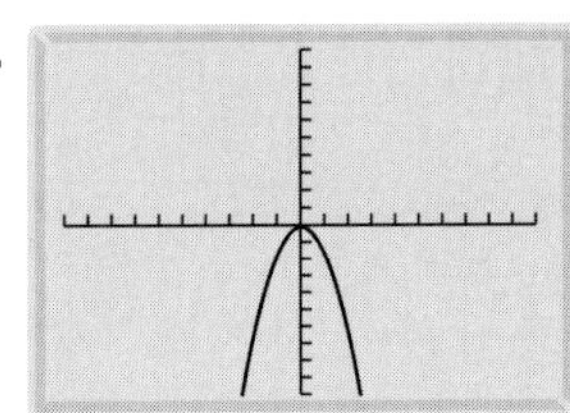

17. $y = x^2, y = 3x^2, y = 7x^2$ **19.** $y = -\frac{2}{3}x^2$, $y = -2x^2, y = -4x^2$ **21.** *K*; *L* **23.** *K*
29. narrower **31.** narrower **35.** E **37.** F **39.** C

MIXED REVIEW **41.** 40% increase
43a. 199,980,000 Slinkies **43b.** about 33 lb
43c. about 24,048 mi; about 7655 mi

45. 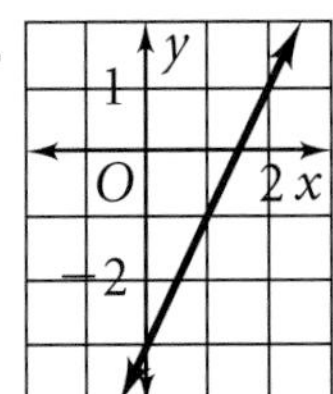

Lesson 7-2 pages 323–326

ON YOUR OWN **3.** maximum **5.** maximum

7. 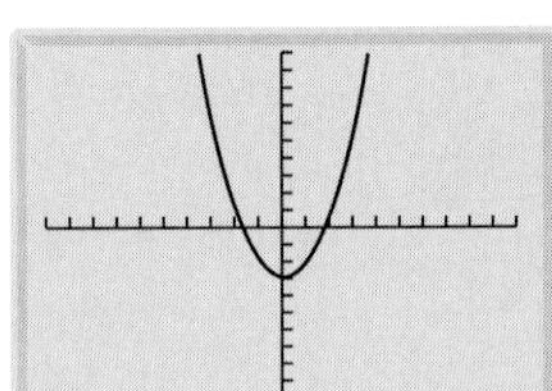

9. 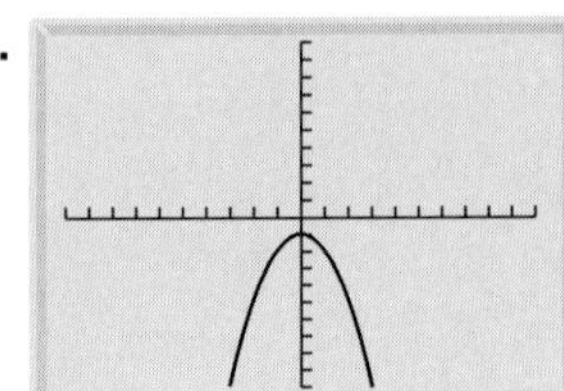

11.

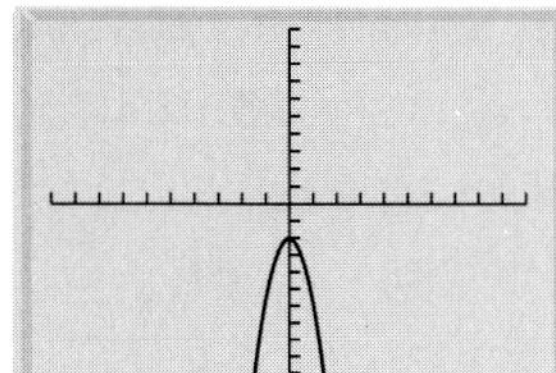

13.

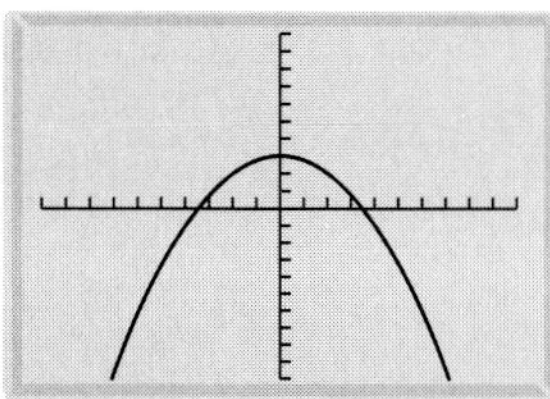

15.

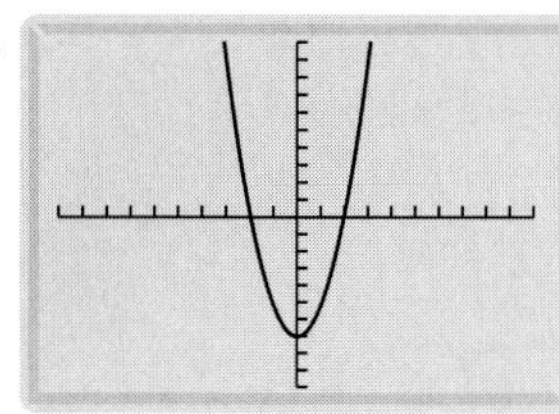

17.

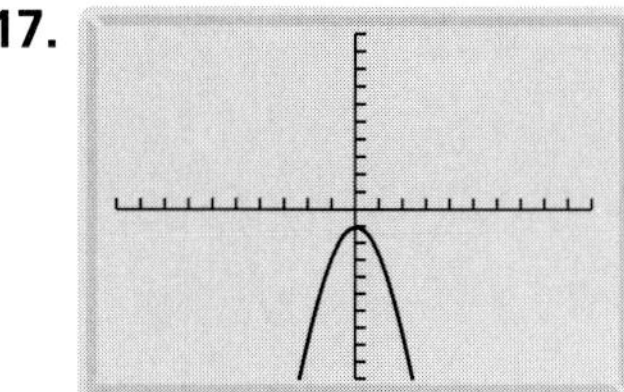

21. *E* **23.** *F* **25.** *C* **27.** *E* **29.** *E, F* **31.** *G*

33a.

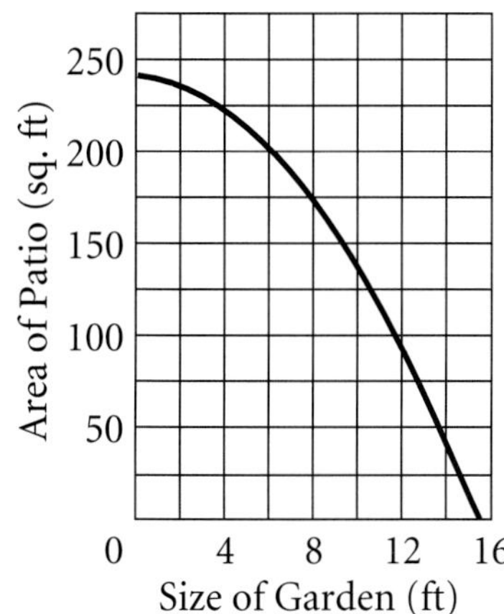

33b. $0 < x < 12$; the length of the side of the garden must be positive and shorter than 12 ft, the shorter side of the patio. **33c.** $96 < y < 240$; the larger the garden the smaller the area of the patio. As the length of the side of the garden changes from 0 to 12 ft, the value of the function changes from 240 to 96.

MIXED REVIEW **35.** $y = -\frac{1}{5}x + \frac{7}{5}$ **37.** $y = -2x - 18$ **39.** $y = -\frac{1}{4}x + 3$ **41.** about \$129,067 **43.** $\frac{1}{16}$

Lesson 7-3 pages 327–331

ON YOUR OWN **1.** $x = 0$; $(0, 4)$ **3.** $x = -1$; $(-1, -7)$ **5.** $x = 0$; $(0, -3)$ **7.** $x = -2$; $(-2, -1)$ **9.** $x = 0$; $(0, 12)$ **11.** E **13.** F **15.** D

17.

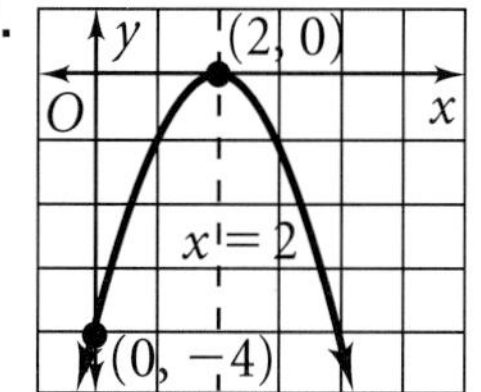

19.

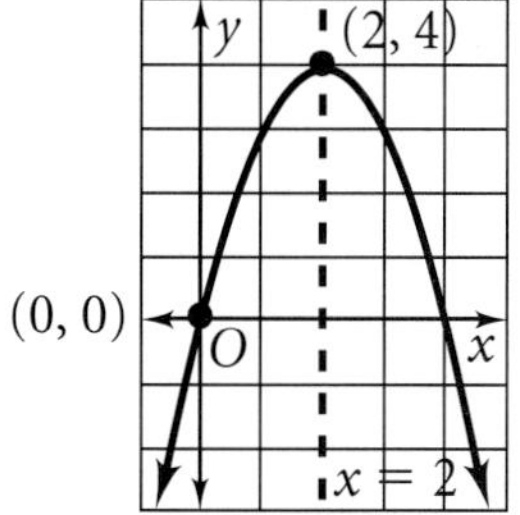

21.

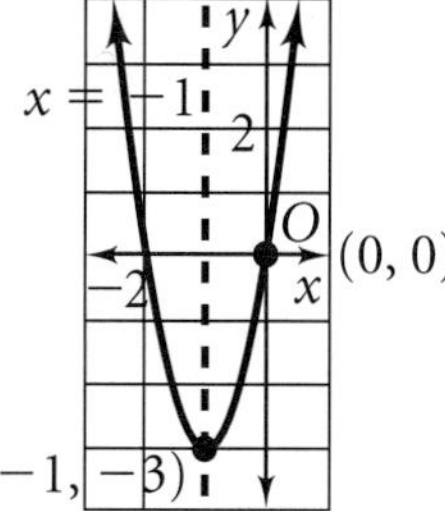

23.

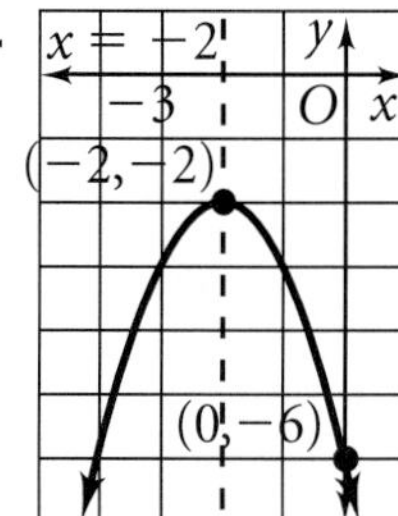

25.

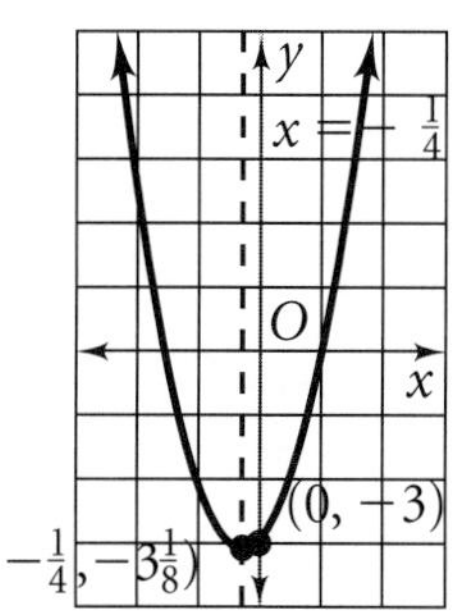

Selected Answers

27. 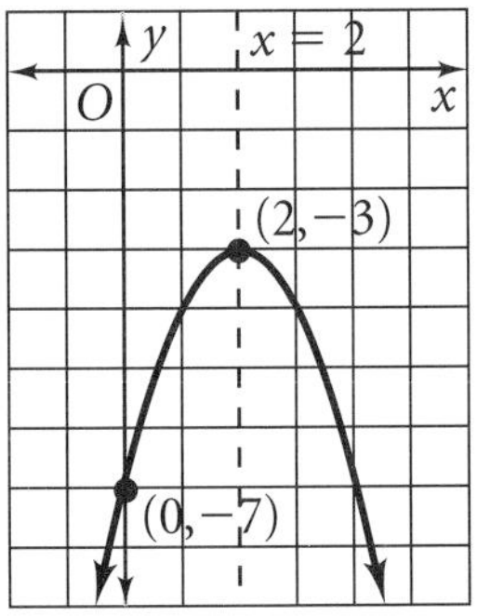

29. 20 ft; 400 ft^2 **31.** 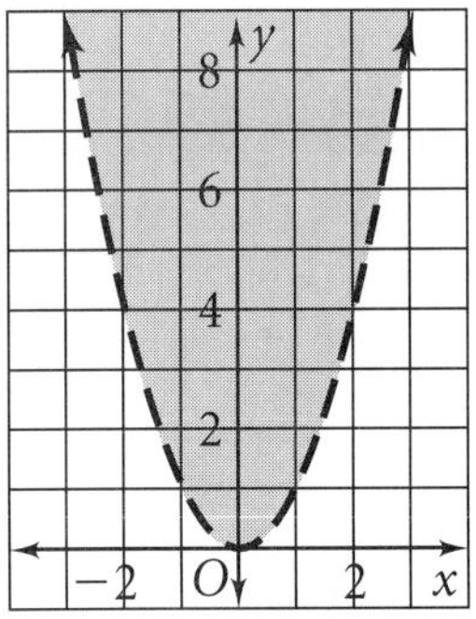

33. 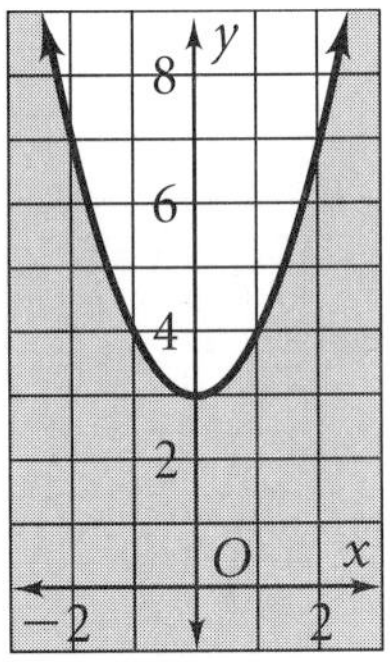

35. 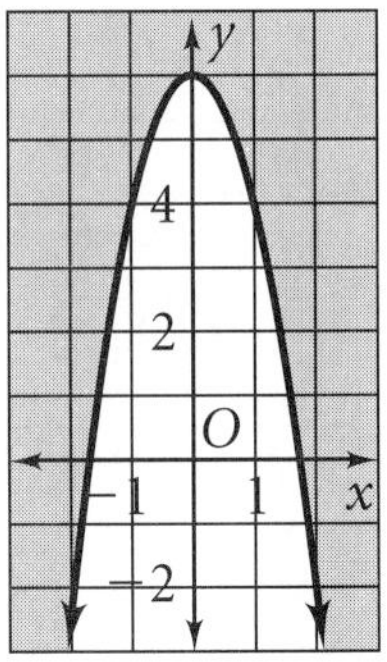

37. 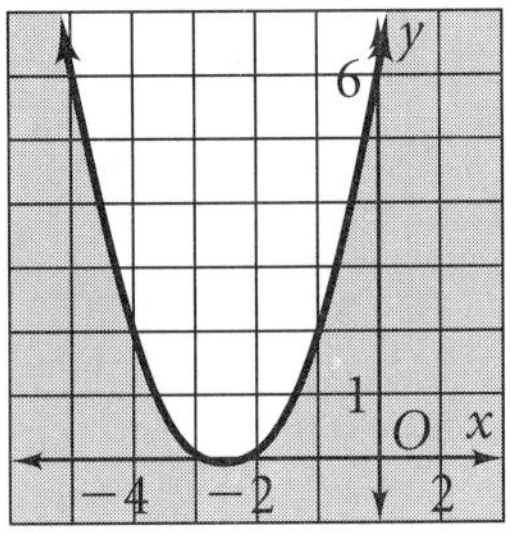

39. 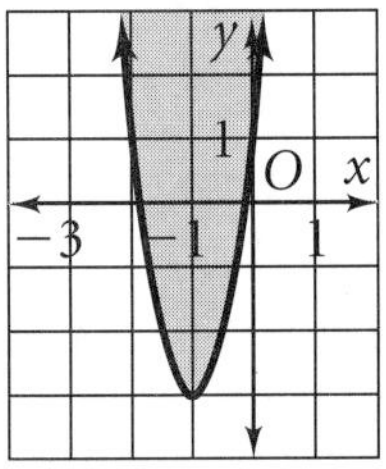

MIXED REVIEW **43.** $\frac{1}{4}$ **45.** $\frac{1}{4}$ **47a.** 10.1 mi/h **47b.** 569 strokes **49.** −1 **51.** −36

Lesson 7-4 pages 332–336

ON YOUR OWN **1.** ±13 **3.** $\pm\frac{1}{3}$ **5.** ±0.5 **7.** ±1.1 **9.** irrat. **11.** irrat. **13.** 5 and 6 **15.** −16 and −15

17. 3.46 **19.** 107.47 **21a.** about 0.93 **21b.** about 4.6 ft **23.** ±0.6 **25.** $\pm\frac{5}{4}$ **27.** ±20 **29.** ±25 **31.** $\pm\frac{1}{9}$ **33.** ±27 **35a.** about 8400 km **35b.** about 7700 km **37.** 4 **39.** $-\frac{2}{5}$ **41.** $\frac{1}{6}$ **43.** −12.53 **45.** −3.61 **47.** 33 **49.** 6.40 **53.** irrat. **55.** rat. **57.** irrat. **59.** undefined **61.** true **63.** false; $-5 < -\sqrt{17} < -4$ **65.** false; $-17 < -\sqrt{280} < -16$ **67.** false; $-37 < -\sqrt{1300} < -36$ **69.** true

MIXED REVIEW

71. $s < -2$; 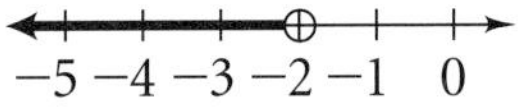

73. $b < -6$; 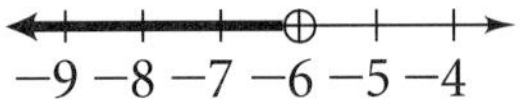

75. $c \leq \frac{1}{7}$; 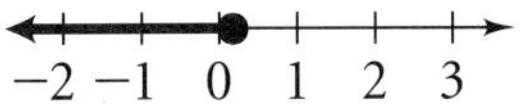

77. $t > 1\frac{2}{3}$; 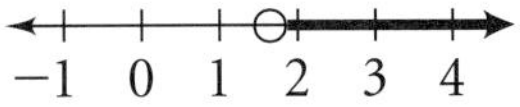

79. $13\frac{2}{3}$ **81.** 0

CHECKPOINT

1. (0, 0); 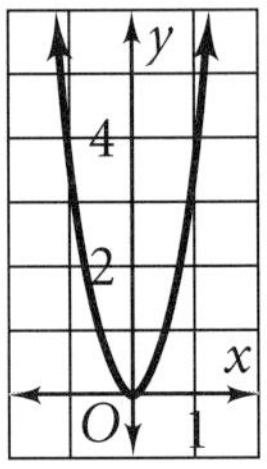

2. (0, 7); 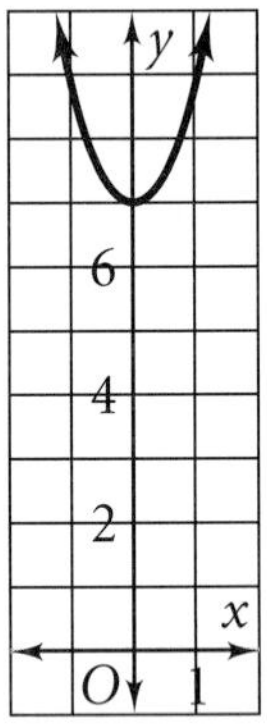

3. (−1, 11); 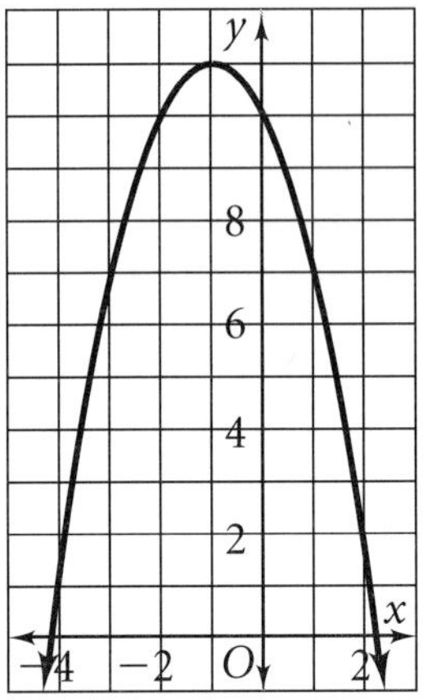

4. 2.65 **5.** −10 **6.** 4.80 **7.** 12 **8.** −12.25 **9.** $-\frac{1}{3}$

Lesson 7-5 pages 337–341

ON YOUR OWN **1.** $-2, 2$ **3.** no solution **5.** no solution **7.** $-\frac{3}{7}, \frac{3}{7}$ **9.** $-\frac{5}{2}, \frac{5}{2}$ **11.** 0 **13.** Sample: Michael used -5 and 5 as square roots of -25, which does not have a real number square root. **15.** $-2.8, 2.8$ **17.** $-1.4, 1.4$ **19.** $-4.6, 4.6$ **21.** 3.6 in. **23.** False; there are no solutions. **25.** False; there are two solutions **27.** true; $-8, 8$ **29.** true **31.** 11.2 ft **33.** 2.5 s **37.** $-2.5, 2.5$ **39.** $-2.4, 2.4$ **41.** $-2, 2$

MIXED REVIEW **43.** (2, 3) **45.** (15, −15) **47.** 3.16 **49.** 4.69

Toolbox page 342

1. about 10.78, 13.22 **3.** $-2, 1\frac{1}{2}$ **5.** about 0.28, 17.72 **7.** $-12, 6$

Lesson 7-6 pages 343–347

ON YOUR OWN **1.** $3x^2 + 13x - 10 = 0$ **3.** $x^2 - 5x - 7 = 0$ **5.** $12x^2 - 25x + 84 = 0$ **7.** $-1.67, 0.5$ **9.** $-4.65, 4.65$ **11.** $-2.2, 3$ **13.** 0, 0.56 **15.** $-1.78, 0.28$ **17.** $-1.5, -1$ **19b.** about 356.9 million **19c.** 2007 **21.** $-6, 6$ **23.** $-1.41, 1.41$ **25.** $-2, -3$ **27.** $-2, 3$ **29.** $-0.39, 1.72$ **31.** $-1.43, 2.23$ **35a.** 630 ft **35b.** 0 ft **35c.** about 6.3 s

MIXED REVIEW **37.** $\frac{1}{4}$ **39.** 0 **41.** 41 **43.** 24 **45.** 49

CHECKPOINT **1.** $-8.06, 8.06$ **2.** $-2, 2$ **3.** $-11, 11$ **4.** 1, 3 **5.** $-1, 0.4$ **6.** 0.23, 3.27 **7.** D

Toolbox page 348

1. $y = x^2 + 6x + 8$ **3.** $y = 2x^2 + 6x - 8$

Lesson 7-7 pages 349–353

ON YOUR OWN **1.** C **3.** A **5.** 1 **7.** 2 **9.** 2 **11.** 0 **13.** 1 **15.** 2 **17a.** no value of x **17b.** Yes; $266 = -x^2 + 3x + 270$ transforms to $-x^2 + 3x + 4 = 0$. The discriminant is positive. **19.** A **21.** Rational; the square root of the discriminant is a positive integer. **23.** 2 **25.** 2 **27.** 0 **29.** 0 **31.** B **33.** no **35.** yes; $(\frac{2}{3}, 0), (-1, 0)$ **37.** yes; $(-1, 0), (2\frac{1}{2}, 0)$ **39.** no **41a.** A2^2 − 4; A2^2 − 8 **41b.** for integer values ≤ -2 or ≥ 2 **41c.** integer values between -2 and 2

MIXED REVIEW **43.** **45.**

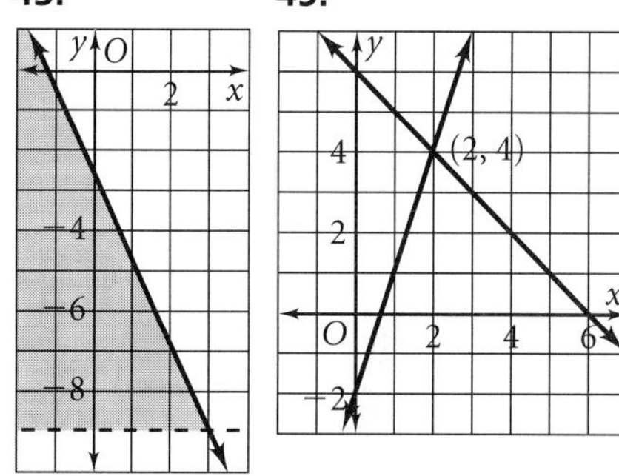

47. 3 **49.** -4

Wrap-Up pages 355–357

5. 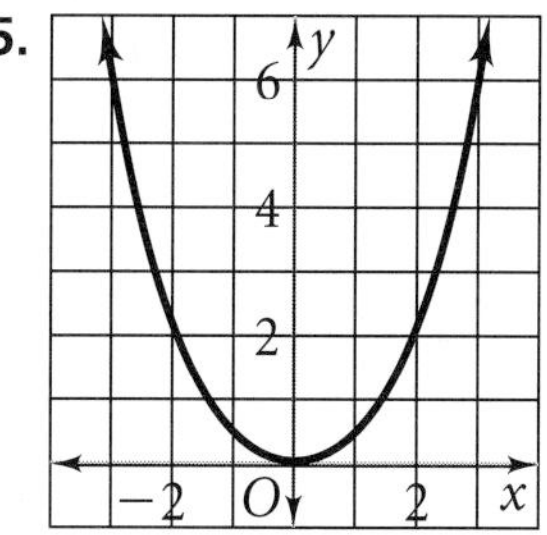

6. 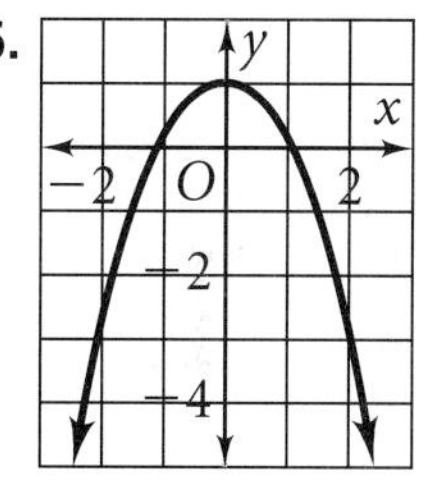

7. 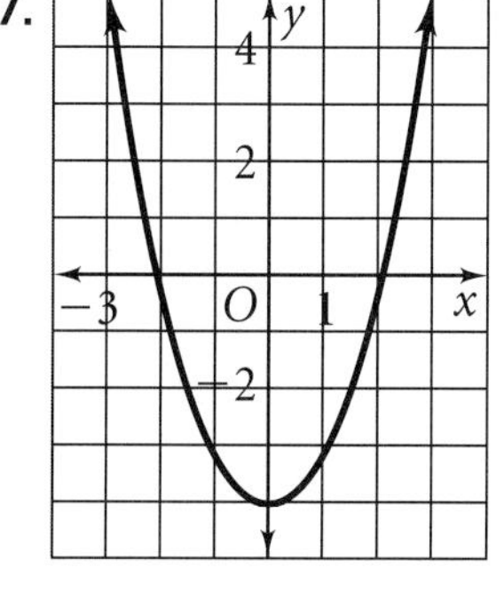

8. 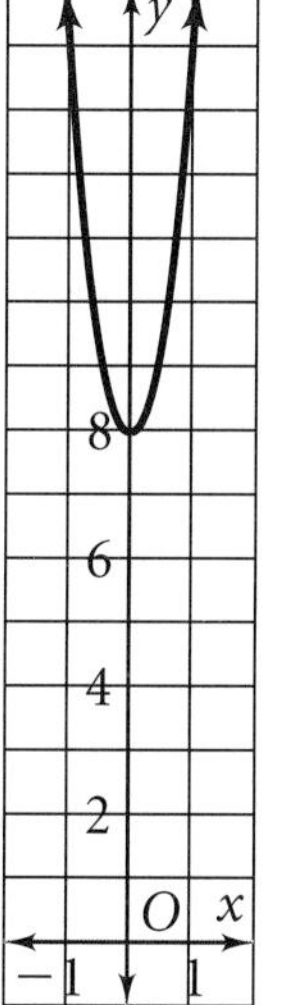

9. min. **10.** max. **11.** min. **12.** max.

Selected Answers

13.
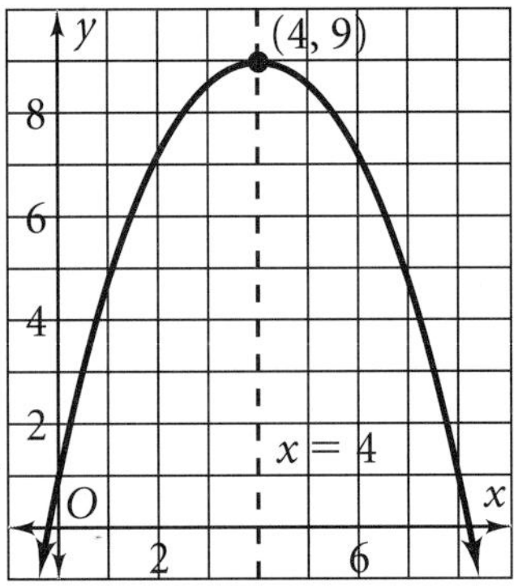

14.
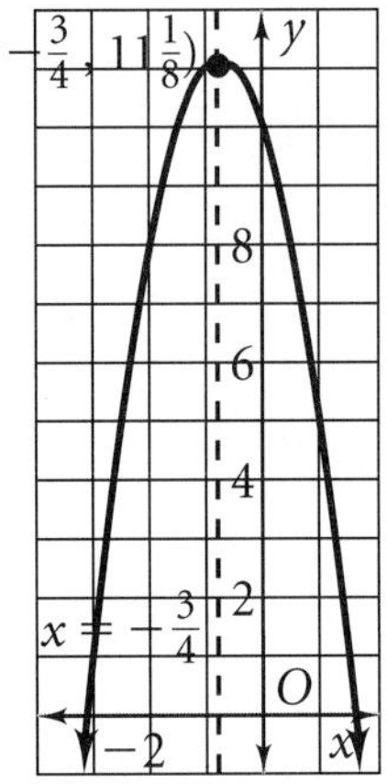

15.
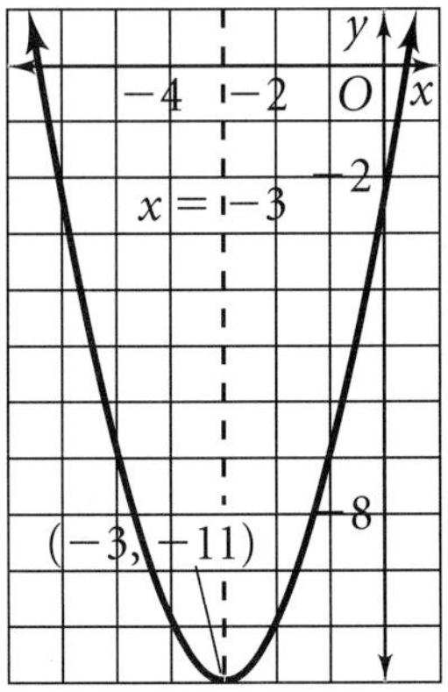

16.
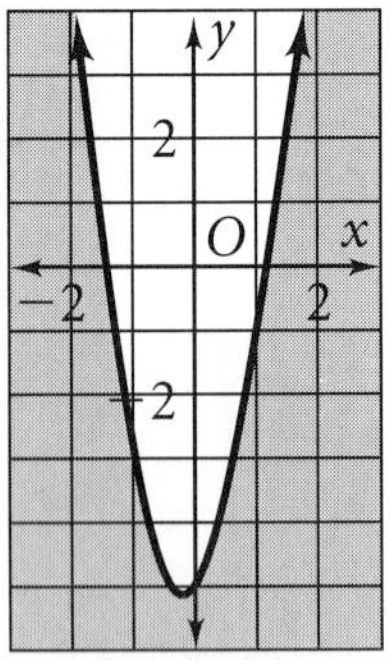

17.
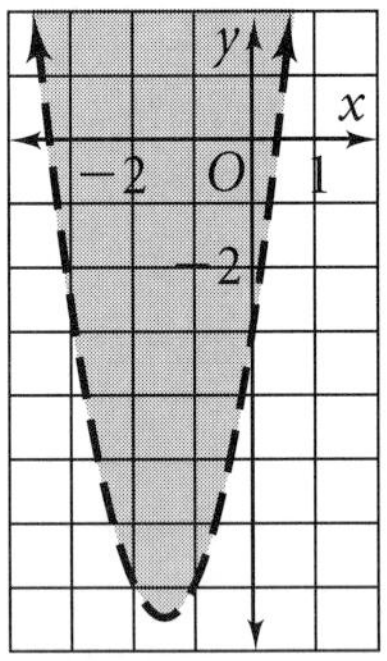

18.
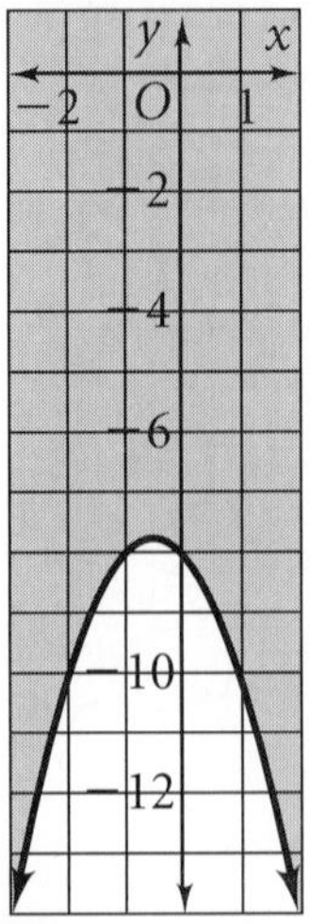

19. irrat. **20.** rat. **21.** irrat. **22.** rat. **23.** irrat. **24.** rat. **25.** 3 **26.** -6.86 **27.** 0.6 **28.** 11.83 **29.** -1 **30.** 14 **31.** B **32.** False; there are two solutions. **33.** true; $-3, 3$ **34.** $-2, 2$ **35.** $-5, 5$ **36.** 0 **37.** no solution **38.** 2.3 in. **39.** $-1.84, 1.09$ **40.** 0.5, 3 **41.** 0.13, 7.87 **42.** $-5.48, 5.48$ **43.** 1.5 s **44.** 49; 2 **45.** 112; 2 **46.** -39; 0 **48.** $3^2\,5^3$ **49.** $8^3\,x^4$ **50.** $h^5\,w^2$ **51.** 5000 **52.** 0 **53.** 80,000 **54.** 9 **55.** -720 **56.** 0.7 **57.** 36 **58.** 12 **59.** $\frac{1}{3}$

Preparing for Standardized Tests page 359

1. E **3.** C **5.** D **7.** A **9.** B **11.** B **13.** $\left(\frac{3}{8}, -\frac{9}{16}\right)$; $x = \frac{3}{8}$

15.
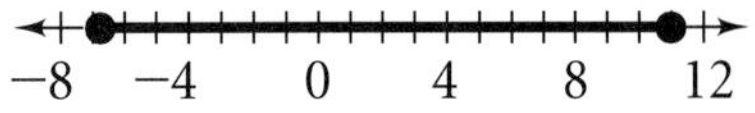

CHAPTER 8

Lesson 8-1 pages 362–366

ON YOUR OWN

1.

Time	Time Periods	Pattern	Number of Bacteria Cells
Initial	0	75	75
20 min	1	$75 \cdot 2$	$75 \cdot 2^1 = 150$
40 min	2	$75 \cdot 2 \cdot 2$	$75 \cdot 2^2 = 300$
60 min	3	$75 \cdot 2 \cdot 2 \cdot 2$	$75 \cdot 2^3 = 600$
80 min	4	$75 \cdot 2 \cdot 2 \cdot 2 \cdot 2$	$75 \cdot 2^4 = 1200$

There will be more than 30,000 bacteria cells after 3 h. **3.** equal **5.** $100x^2$ **7.** 4, 16, 64, 256, 1024; increasing **9.** 1, 1, 1, 1, 1; neither **11.** 0.5, 0.25, 0.125, 0.0625, 0.03125; decreasing **13.** 40, 400, 4000, 40,000, 400,000; increasing **15.** B **19.** 1.5625 **21.** 0.2 **23.** I: A; II: C; III. B

25a.

x	y
1	-2
2	4
3	-8
4	16
5	-32
6	64

25b. Sample: The positive and negative values alternate. The absolute values of the output are the same as the absolute values of the output of 2^x.
25c. No; the shape of the graph cannot be similar to the shape of the graph of an exponential function.

27.

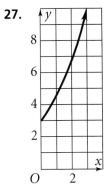

29.

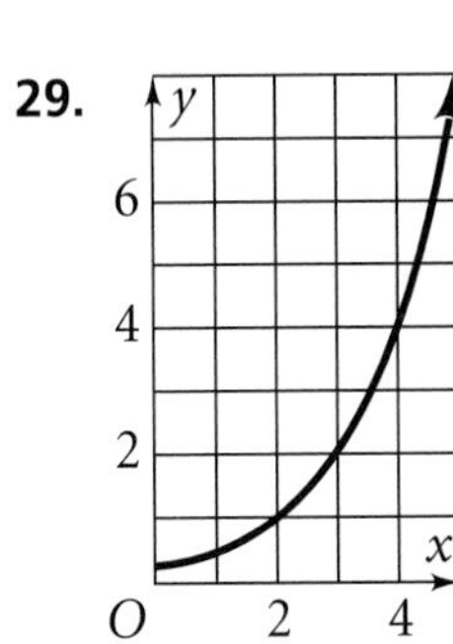

31.

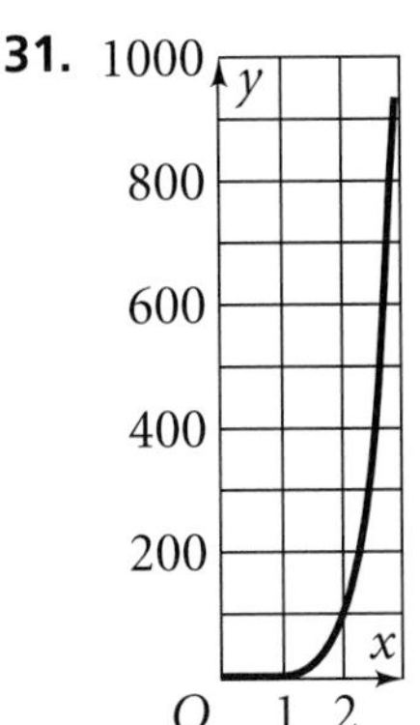

MIXED REVIEW **33.** 1, −4 **35.** 2, 3 **37.** {2, 4, 8, 16, 32} **39.** {1, 2, 4, 8, 16} **41.** {6, 12, 24, 48, 96}

Lesson 8-2 pages 367–372

ON YOUR OWN **1.** 20; 2 **3.** 10,000; 1.01 **5.** 50% **7.** 4% **9.** 1.04 **11.** 1.037 **13.** 1.005 **15.** x = number of years; y = population; $y = 130{,}000 \cdot 1.01^x$ **17.** x = number of months; y = deposit with interest; $y = 3000 \cdot \left(1 + \frac{0.05}{12}\right)^x$ **19a.** \$355 **19b.** 8% **19c.** about \$766 **21.** E

23. linear

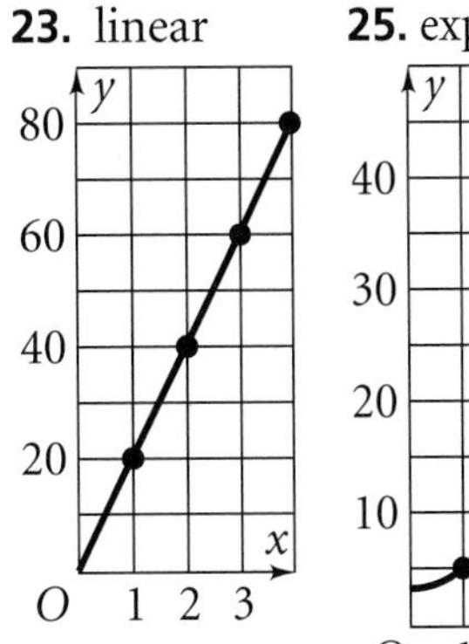

25. exponential

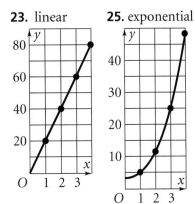

27. Linear; graph is a straight line. **29.** Exponential; graph curves upward. **31.** $y = 20{,}000 \cdot \left(1 + \frac{0.035}{4}\right)^{4x}$; \$28,338.18 **33.** $y = 2400 \cdot (1 + 0.07)^x$; \$4721.16

MIXED REVIEW **35.** $\left(-\frac{1}{3}, -8\frac{1}{3}\right)$; minimum **37.** (0, −11); minimum **39.** $\frac{1}{4}$ **41.** $\frac{3}{4}$ **43.** 0.9604

Lesson 8-3 pages 373–377

ON YOUR OWN **1.** exponential growth **3.** exponential growth **5.** 0.5 **7.** $\frac{2}{3}$ **9.** 10% **11.** 50% **13.** 4 da **15.** 2.5 yr

17. exponential decay

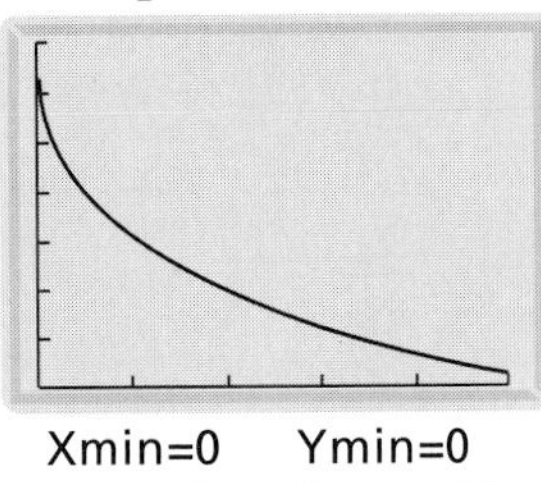

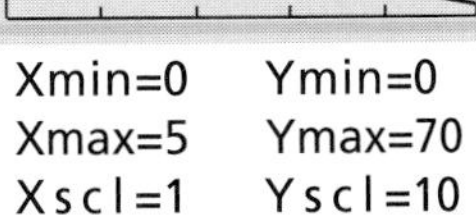

19. exponential decay

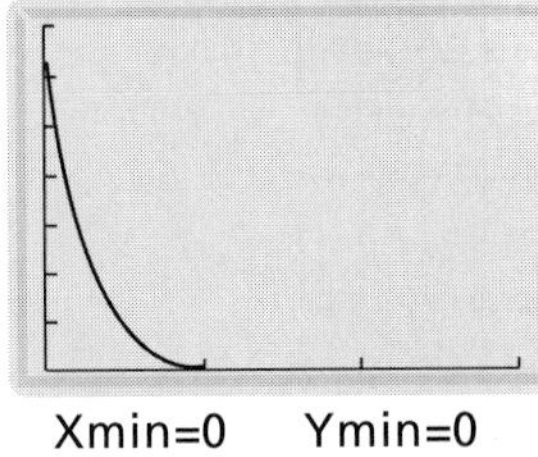

Xmin=0 Ymin=0
Xmax=3 Ymax=3.5
Xscl=1 Yscl=0.5

21. exponential decay **23.** exponential decay

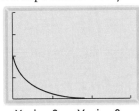

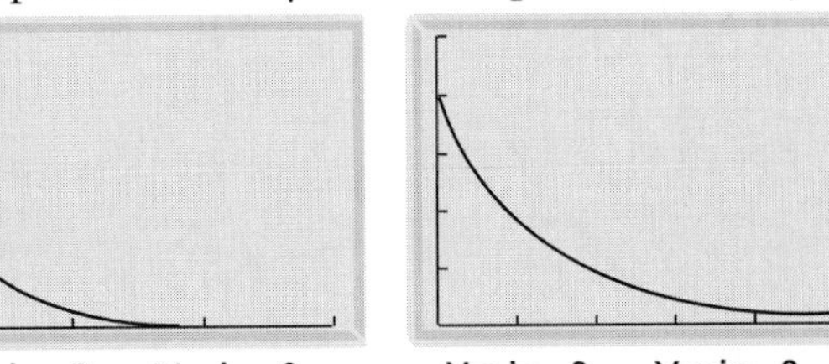

Xmin=0 Ymin=0
Xmax=3 Ymax=0.2
Xscl=1 Yscl=0.05

Xmin=0 Ymin=0
Xmax=5 Ymax=0.5
Xscl=1 Yscl=0.1

Selected Answers

27. $y = 900 \cdot 0.8^x$; \$235.93 **29a.** $y = 161{,}000 \cdot 0.99^x$ **29b.** 145,606 **29c.** 119,092 **31.** 0.97 **33.** 0.974 **35.** 0.993 **37a.** about 4 h **37b.** about $\frac{1}{4}$

37c. $\frac{15 \cdot 0.84^8}{15} = 0.247875891 \approx \frac{1}{4}$ **39.** 4 half-lives

MIXED REVIEW **41.** $x < -3$ **43.** $-3, 3$ **45.** 4 **47.** 4; 16; $\frac{1}{4}$

CHECKPOINT **1.** $y = 65{,}000 \cdot 1.032^x$; \$104,257.86 **2.** $y = 200{,}000 \cdot 0.95^x$; 71,697 **3.** $y = 300 \cdot 2^x$; x = ten-year period; \$9600 **4.** B

5. exponential growth

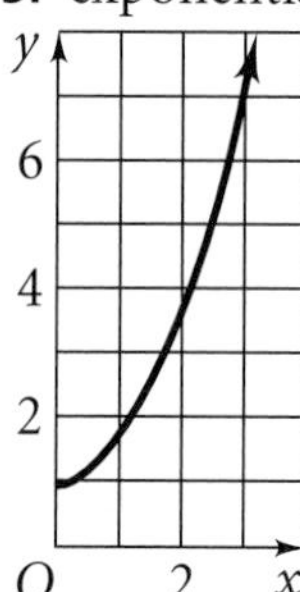

6. exponential decay

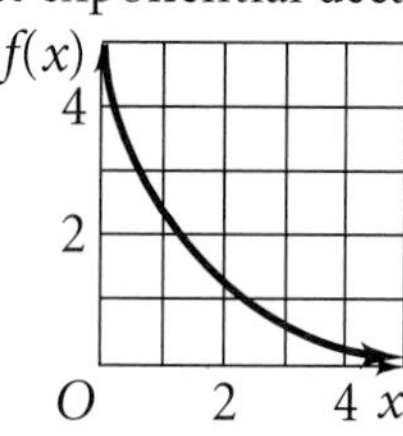

7. exponential growth

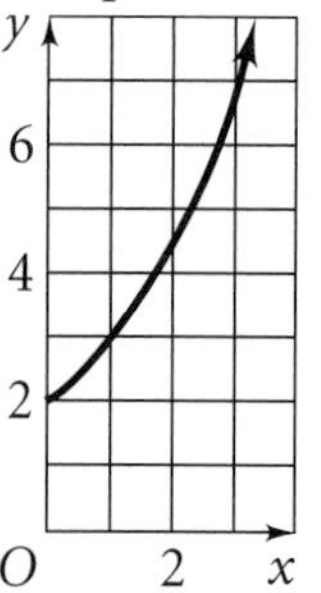

Toolbox page 378

1. $y = 13.65799901 \cdot 1.105628281^x$

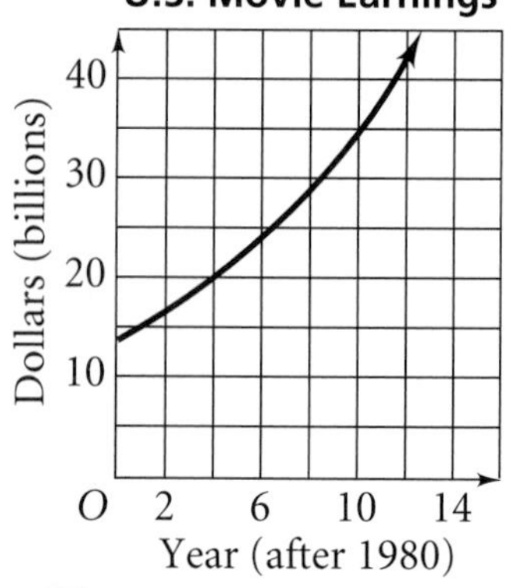

3a. Use $x = 0$ for 1970; $y = 1.040248033 \cdot 1.01999578^x$; 2.297 million

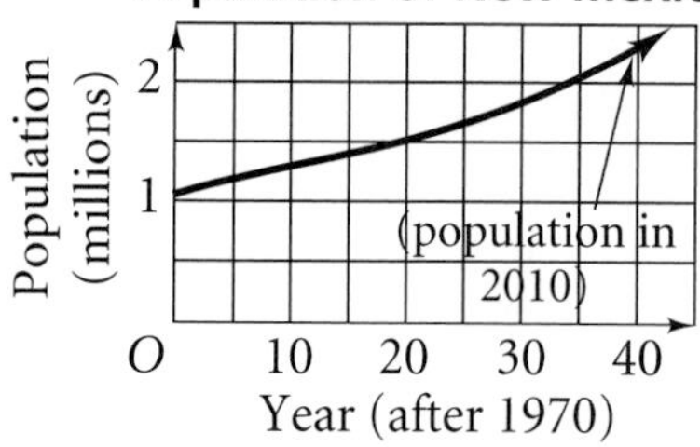

Lesson 8-4 pages 379–384

ON YOUR OWN **1.** -1 **3.** $-\frac{1}{5}$ **5.** 8 **7.** 9 **9.** $\frac{1}{64}$ **11.** 45 **13.** 6 **15.** $\frac{1}{20}$ **17.** $\frac{1}{4}$ **19a.** 5^{-2}; 5^{-1}; 5^0 or 1; 5^1; 5^2 **19b.** 5^4 **19c.** a^n **21.** x^7 **23.** $\frac{1}{625x^4}$

25. $\frac{1}{a^4}$ **27.** $\frac{12x}{y^3}$ **29.** $\frac{5a}{c^5}$ **31.** $\frac{8c^3}{a^5d^3}$ **33.** $\frac{7t^3}{5s^5}$ **35.** $\frac{a^3}{b^3}$ **37.** $\frac{mq^2}{n^4}$ **39.** $\frac{2}{9}$ **41.** $\frac{1}{16}$ **43.** -64

45.

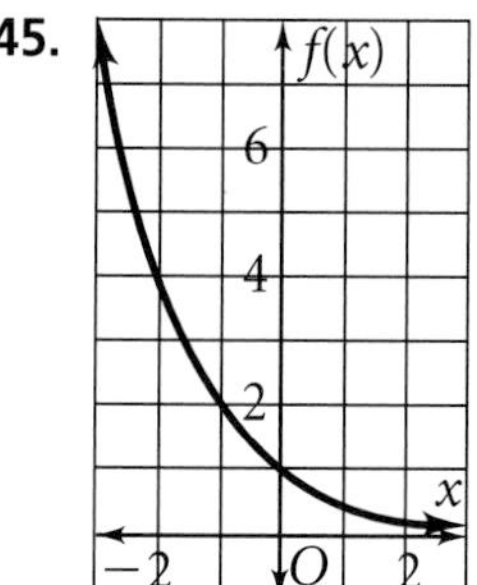

47. [graph]

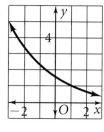

49. I

51.

a	4	0.2	$\frac{1}{3}$	6	$\frac{7}{8}$	2
a^{-1}	$\frac{1}{4}$	5	3	$\frac{1}{6}$	$\frac{8}{7}$	0.5

53. positive **55.** negative **57.** positive **59.** -3 **61.** 0; -3 **63.** -3; -2 **65.** -2; -3 **67.** A, B, D **69a.** 10^{-15} m **69b.** 10^{-6} m **69c.** 10^{-10} m **71.** about 2 students; about 16 students; about 29 students

73.

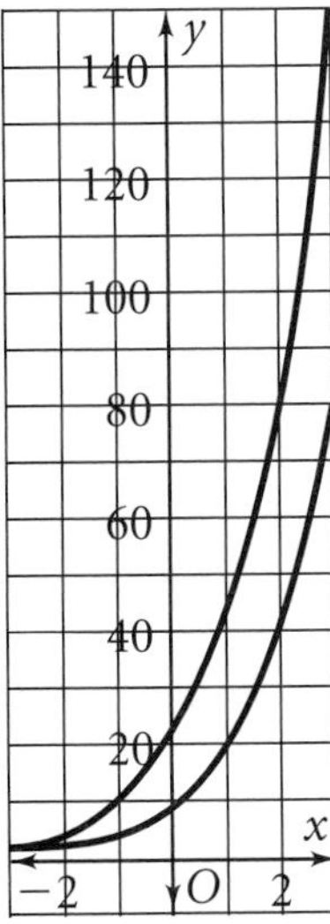

75a. $\frac{1}{2}, \frac{1}{4}, \frac{1}{8}, \frac{1}{16}$ **75b.** $2^{-1}, 2^{-2}, 2^{-3}, 2^{-4}$
75c. $r = 2^{-n}$ **75d.** 2^{-10} or $\frac{1}{2^{10}}$

MIXED REVIEW

77.

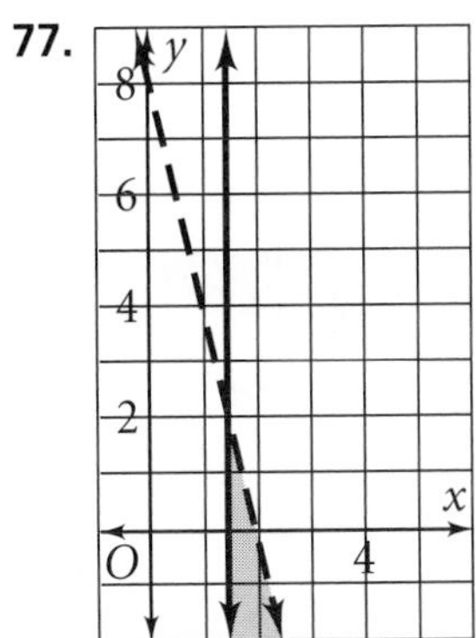

79a. $b = 31.17p$ **79b.** $124.68 **81.** 0.07
83. 0.003 **85.** 3067.85

Lesson 8-5 pages 385–389

ON YOUR OWN **1.** $10^{-3}, 10^{-1}, 10^{0}, 10^{1}, 10^{5}$
3. $4.1 \times 10^4, 4 \times 10^5, 4.02 \times 10^5, 4.1 \times 10^5$
5. 2.3×10^8 **7.** 2.7×10^{-7} **9.** 2.579×10^{-4}
11. 9.04×10^9 **13.** 9.2×10^{-4} **15.** 3.7×10^{11}
17. 4.18×10^{10} **19.** 6.29×10^{16} **21.** 3.3×10^{-8}
23. 8.35×10^{-5} **25.** 4.18×10^5 **27.** 1.28×10^{-2}
29. 4×10^{-6} **33.** 0.000 004 69 **35.** 50,000,000,000
37. 5.6×10^{-2} **39.** 6×10^2 **41.** 2×10^{-8}
43. about 1.5×10^{-4} **45.** about 5×10^2 s

47. 7×10^{-3} **49.** 9×10^1 **51.** 5×10^7 **53.** about $3426 per person

MIXED REVIEW **55.** $\begin{bmatrix} -3.2 & 2.4 \\ 4.1 & -1.2 \end{bmatrix}$ **57.** t^7
59. 5^3s^3

Toolbox page 390

1. 6 **3.** 3 **5.** 1.02×10^{-4} **7.** 2.53×10^5
9. 7.25×10^5

Lesson 8-6 pages 391–395

ON YOUR OWN **1.** $x^4 \cdot x^3 = x^7$ **3.** $x^{-2} \cdot x^{-5} = x^{-7}$ **5.** −4 **7.** 5 **9.** −4 **11.** 2; −3 **13.** 8×10^5
15. 6×10^9 **17.** 4×10^3 **21.** 1 **23.** $3r^5$ **25.** a^8b^3
27. $3x^4$ **29.** -0.99^3 **31.** b^3 **33.** −7 **35.** $-45a^4$
37. $\frac{b^2}{c^6}$ **39.** $12a^6c^8$ **41.** a^8b **43.** a^5 **45.** $6a^3 + 10a^2$
47. $-8x^5 + 36x^4$ **49a.** Jerome's work; Jeremy added exponents having different bases. **49b.** a^3b^6
51. $6x^3 + 2x^2$ **53.** $4y^5 + 8y^2$ **55.** $3(-2)x^{2+4} = -6x^6$ **57.** $x^{6+1+3} = x^{10}$ **59a.** about 10^{-7} m
59b. longer

MIXED REVIEW **61.** irrational **63.** rational; $\frac{1}{2}$
65. rational; $\frac{3}{4}$ **67.** 3^6 **69.** 5^{28}

CHECKPOINT **1.** 1 **2.** $\frac{1}{9}$ **3.** $-\frac{1}{8}$ **4.** 125 **5.** −16
6. $-\frac{1}{8}$ **7.** s^3 **8.** $21ab^2$ **9.** −1 **10.** $\frac{g^3}{h^4}$ **11.** $\frac{y^6}{x^5}$
12. 1.5×10^7 **13.** 8×10^{-8} **14.** 3×10^{11}
15. 2.4×10^4 **16a.** 3×10^6; 9×10^4
16b. about 462

18.

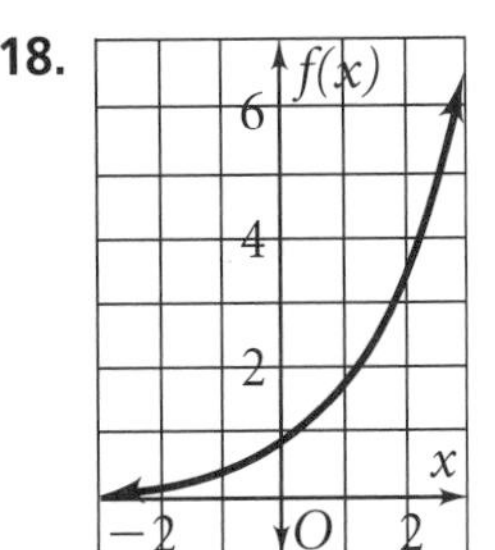

19.

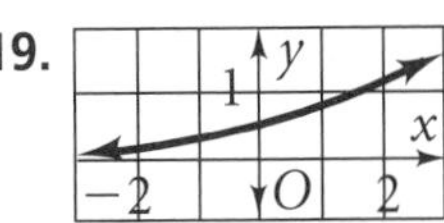

Selected Answers

20. 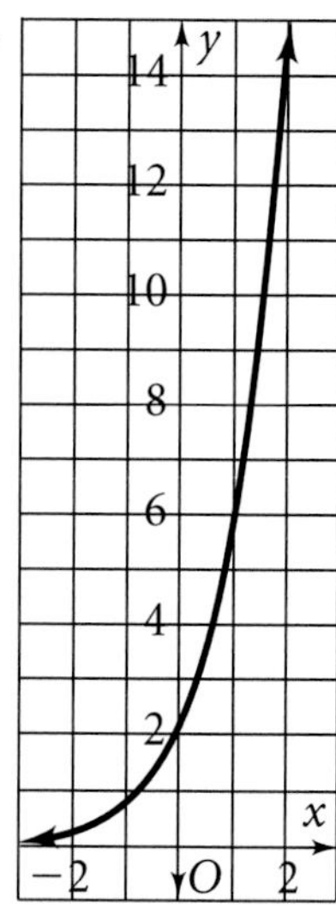

Lesson 8-7 pages 396–400

ON YOUR OWN **1.** x^9y^9 **3.** a^6b^{12} **5.** $\frac{1}{g^{40}}$ **7.** $x^{12}y^4$ **9.** 16 **11.** g^{10} **13.** s^{11} **15.** $\frac{m}{g^4}$ **17.** 1 **19.** $64a^9b^6$ **21.** 1 **23.** 10,000 **25.** b^{3n+2} **27.** 1 **29a.** about 5.15×10^{14} m^2 **29b.** about 3.6×10^{14} m^2 **29c.** about 1.37×10^{18} m^3 **31.** 8×10^{-9} **33.** 3.6×10^{25} **35.** 6.25×10^{-18} **41.** 3 **43.** 4 **45.** 0 **47.** 6 **49.** 3 **51.** 1.1×10^{18} insects **53.** $(ab)^5$ **55.** $(\frac{2}{xy})^2$

MIXED REVIEW **57.** -1 **59.** $\frac{1}{x}$ **61.** $\frac{1}{t^5}$

Lesson 8-8 pages 401–405

ON YOUR OWN **1.** $\frac{1}{4}$ **3.** $\frac{9}{16}$ **5.** $\frac{1}{9}$ **7.** y **9.** a^6 **11.** $-\frac{27}{8}$ **13.** $5^3 = 125$ **15.** $(2c)^4 = 16c^4$ **17.** $x^0 = 1$ **19.** 5×10^7 **21.** 9×10^2 **23.** about 1.52×10^{-6} **25a.** about 1642 h **25b.** about 4.5 h/da **27.** 4 **29.** 729 **31.** $2c^6$ **33.** $\frac{a^5}{b^3}$ **35.** $\frac{d^8}{c^5}$ **37.** $\frac{1}{25}$ **39.** $\frac{1}{c^{12}}$ **41.** $\frac{9}{25}$ **43.** $\frac{125n^3}{m^6}$ **45.** $\left(\frac{3}{5}\right)^5$ **47.** d^3 **49.** $\left(\frac{3x}{2y}\right)^3$ **51a.** about \$4013 **51b.** about \$17,846 **51c.** about 345% **53.** division and negative exponent properties; $\frac{1}{2^3}$ **55.** multiplication property; $\frac{1}{2^3}$

57a.

Mercury	≈ 1.52
Venus	≈ 1.01
Earth	≈ 1.03
Mars	≈ 1.21
Jupiter	≈ 1.10
Saturn	≈ 1.12
Uranus	≈ 1.10
Neptune	≈ 1.02
Pluto	≈ 1.67

57b. Pluto; its circularity is farthest from 1; Venus; its circularity is closest to 1.

MIXED REVIEW **59.** 0.6, -0.6 **61.** -6

63. **65.** 3.26×10^{11} gal

Wrap-Up pages 407–409

1. 6, 12, 24, 48 **2.** 7.5, 5.625, 4.21875 **3a.** 2430 bacteria **3b.** about 178 min **4.** growth; 3 **5.** growth; $\frac{3}{2}$ **6.** decay; 0.32 **7.** decay; $\frac{1}{4}$

8. 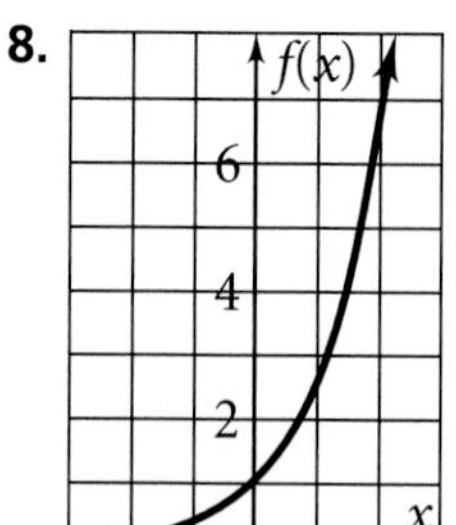

9. 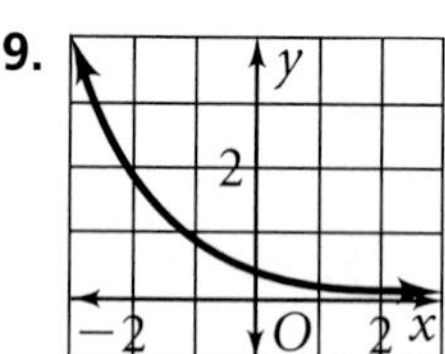

10.

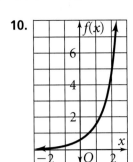

11.

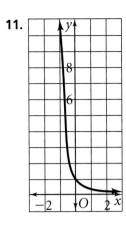

12. 2.5% inc. **13.** 25% dec. **14.** 100% inc. **15.** 10% dec. **16a.** $y = 100{,}000 \cdot 1.07^x$ **16a.** $y = 100{,}000 \cdot 1.07^x$ **16b.** 542,743 **17a.** \$1250.18; \$1267.37 **17b.** 6%; it pays more interest. **18.** 2.5 mCi **19.** $\frac{d^6}{b^4}$ **20.** $\frac{y^8}{x^2}$ **21.** $\frac{7h^3}{k^8}$ **22.** $\frac{q^4}{p^2}$ **23.** $\frac{3^4}{2^4}$ or $\frac{81}{16}$ **24.** Yes, if $b = 0$; no if $b \neq 0$. **25.** C **26.** 9.5×10^7 **27.** 7.235×10^9 **28.** yes **29.** 8.4×10^{-4} **30.** 2.6×10^{-4} **31.** 2.793×10^6 **32.** 1.89×10^8 **33.** 1.606×10^8 **34.** 4.6×10^{-9} **35.** 1.4168×10^7 **36.** 1×10^{-12} **37.** $2d^5$ **38.** $q^{12}r^4$ **39.** $-20c^4m^2$ **40.** 1.7956 **41.** $\frac{243}{64}x^2y^{14}$ **42.** Sample: about 7.8×10^3 pores **44.** $\frac{1}{w^3}$ **45.** $\frac{1}{64}$ **46.** yes **47.** $\frac{n^{35}}{v^{21}}$ **48.** $\frac{c^3}{e^{11}}$ **49.** $s^{15}x^{45}$ **50.** 2×10^{-3} **51.** 2.5×10^1 **52.** 5×10^{-5} **53.** 3×10^3 **55.** 2 **56.** 11 **57.** 6 **58.** $77r + 28rx$ **59.** $24m - 16mt$ **60.** $8b + 2b^2$ **61.** $5p + 6d$ **62.** n **63.** 61 **64.** 65 **65.** $13t^2$ **66.** $4y^2$ **67.** \$19; about \$48.86 **68.** 5 kg; 4.5 kg **69.** 0.4 min; 1.24 min

Cumulative Review — page 411

1. D **3.** D **5.** A **7.** A **9.** D **11.** A **13.** A

15.

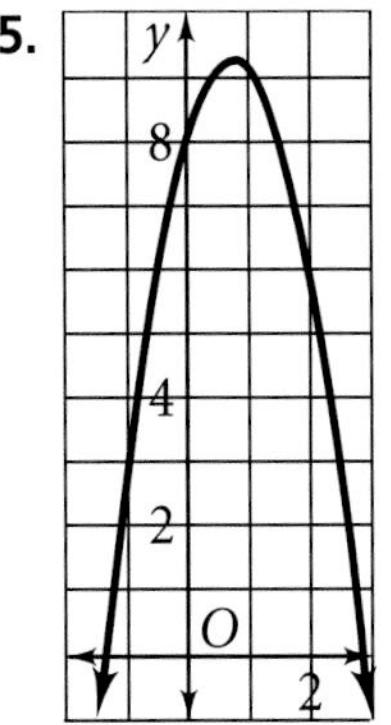

17. Yes; sides are parallel and meet in right angles.

CHAPTER 9

Lesson 9-1 — pages 414–418

ON YOUR OWN **1.** 10 **3.** 2.2 **5.** 7.1 **7.** 5.7 **9.** 20 **11.** 66.1 **13a.** $6^2 + 8^2 = 100$ and $10^2 = 100$

13b.

a	b	c
3	4	5
5	12	13
7	24	25
9	40	41

13c. Sample: 8, 15, 17 **15.** 9.7 **17.** 559.9 **19b.** 6 in., $\sqrt{10^2 - 8^2}$; about 12.8 in., $\sqrt{10^2 + 8^2}$ **21.** yes; $9^2 + 12^2 = 15^2$ **23.** no; $2^2 + 4^2 \neq 5^2$ **25.** no; $4^2 + 4^2 \neq 8^2$ **27.** yes; $1.25^2 + 3^2 = 3.25^2$ **29.** yes; $14^2 + 48^2 = 50^2$ **31.** no; $1^2 + 1.5^2 \neq 2^2$ **33.** no; $4^2 + 5^2 \neq 6^2$ **35.** yes; $18^2 + 80^2 = 82^2$ **37a.** about 3610 ft **37b.** about 180 ft/min; about 2 mi/h **39.** 4.3 cm

MIXED REVIEW **41.** $\frac{1}{2}, \frac{1}{2}$ **43.** 5 **45.** 8.5

Toolbox — page 419

1. yes **3.** yes **5.** yes **7.** yes **9.** no **11.** yes **13.** yes **15.** yes

Lesson 9-2 — pages 420–424

ON YOUR OWN **1.** 10.6 **3.** 8.2 **5.** 11.3 **7.** 2.2 **9.** 11.2 **11.** 8.2 **13.** 14 **15.** 1.4

17a.

17b. $(0, -0.5)$ **17c.** The meeting point is 0.5 mi south of the substation. **19.** $(1\frac{1}{2}, 7\frac{1}{2})$ **21.** $(-2\frac{1}{2}, 3)$ **23.** $(-4, 4)$ **25.** $(8\frac{1}{2}, -9)$ **27.** $(7, 7)$ **29.** $(0, 0)$ **31.** 16 **33.** 21.6 **35.** x-coordinates are opposites; y-coordinates are opposites.

MIXED REVIEW **37.** $2 - \frac{7}{2}y$ **39.** $\frac{V}{\pi r^2}$ **41.** \$720 **43.** $\frac{5}{13}, \frac{12}{13}, \frac{12}{5}$ **45.** 6.8 **47.** 7.28

Lesson 9-3 pages 425–429

ON YOUR OWN **1.** Sample: Kentucky and Virginia are adjacent states. **3.** $\frac{4}{5}$ **5.** $\frac{4}{5}$ **7.** $\frac{4}{3}$ **9.** 0.7660 **11.** 0.9962 **13.** $\frac{21}{29}, \frac{20}{29}, \frac{21}{20}$ **15.** $\frac{12}{13}, \frac{5}{13}, \frac{12}{5}$ **17.** 10.4 **19.** about 250 ft **21.** about 10,000 ft **23.** 78.4 **25.** 514.3

MIXED REVIEW

29.

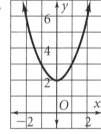

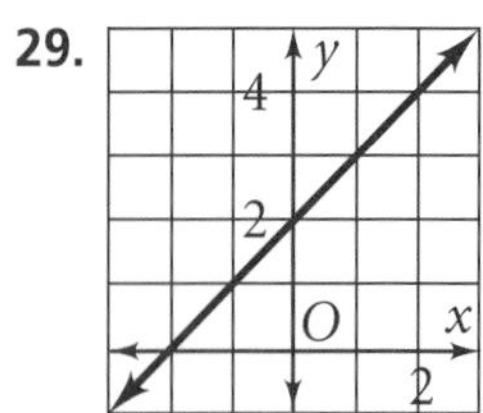

31.

33. 250 mi **35.** 13 **37.** -6

CHECKPOINT **1.** $c \approx 4.5$ **2.** $c \approx 5.8$ **3.** $c \approx 7.1$ **4.** $c = 5$ **5.** $b = 24$ **6.** $a \approx 8.5$ **7.** $b \approx 8.9$ **8.** $a = 15$ **10.** about 270 ft **11.** 3.2 **12.** 6.7 **13.** 9.8 **14.** 3.2 **16.** about 2.7 **17.** about 4.5

Lesson 9-4 pages 430–434

ON YOUR OWN **1.** no **3.** no **5.** no **7.** 16 **9.** 20 **11.** $10\sqrt{2}$ **13.** $875\sqrt{7}$ **15.** 72 **17.** $3\sqrt{17}$ **19.** $4\sqrt{6}$ **21.** 10 **23.** $5\sqrt{10}$ **25.** $\frac{3}{2}$ **27.** $\frac{5}{2}$ **29.** $\frac{2\sqrt{30}}{11}$ **31.** $\frac{3\sqrt{2}}{4}$ **33.** $\frac{13}{12}$ **35.** 1.2 m **37a.** $\sqrt{18} \cdot \sqrt{10} = \sqrt{180} = \sqrt{36 \cdot 5} = 6\sqrt{5}$ **39.** D **41.** $\frac{2\sqrt{a}}{a^2}$ **43.** $ab^2c\sqrt{abc}$ **45.** $2y^2$ **47.** $\frac{\sqrt{2x}}{3}$ **49.** $2\sqrt{3}$ **51.** $\frac{9\sqrt{2}}{4}$ **53.** $5\sqrt{5}$ **55.** $\frac{8\sqrt{6}}{3}$

MIXED REVIEW **57.** 3; 2 **59.** -5; 3 **61.** For $c =$ crab and $t =$ turkey, $5c + 3t \leq 30$. **63.** -1 **65.** 10

Lesson 9-5 pages 435–439

ON YOUR OWN **1.** 42 **3.** $3\sqrt{2} + \sqrt{3}$ **5.** $6 - 2\sqrt{3}$ **7.** $3\sqrt{3} - 3\sqrt{2}$ **9.** $\sqrt{7}$ **11.** $3\sqrt{5} + 2\sqrt{3}$ **13.** $2\sqrt{3} + 2\sqrt{6} - 6$ **15.** $4 - 4\sqrt{2}$ **17.** 3.1 **19.** 15.8 **21.** 6.0 **23.** 8.5 **25.** -1.0 **27.** $2\sqrt{3} + 4\sqrt{2}$ **29.** -24 **31.** $6\sqrt{2} + 6\sqrt{3}$ **33.** $2\sqrt{17} + 17$ **37a.** $2\sqrt{6} + 4\sqrt{3}$ **37b.** Bill simplified $\sqrt{48}$ as $2\sqrt{24}$ instead of $2\sqrt{12}$ or $4\sqrt{3}$. **39.** $8\sqrt{2}$ **41.** $6\sqrt{10}$ **43.** E

MIXED REVIEW **45.** -3; 5; rational **47.** 1 **49.** 0

Lesson 9-6 pages 440–444

ON YOUR OWN **1.** 3 **3.** 27 **5.** 625 **7a.** 25 **7b.** $11\frac{1}{4}$ **9.** no solution **11.** $-\frac{1}{4}$ **13.** 0, 12 **15.** 7 **17.** 3 **19.** about 98.2 in.^{3} **21.** 2 **23.** 3, 6 **25.** no solution **27.** 4 **29.** 1, 6 **31a.** $V = 10x^2$ **31b.** $x = \frac{\sqrt{10V}}{10}$ **33.** -4 **35.** $-\frac{1}{2}$ **37.** none

MIXED REVIEW **39.** $\frac{1}{a^5b^5}$ **41.** $\frac{2}{xy^2}$ **43.** 0 **45.** 2

Lesson 9-7 pages 445–449

ON YOUR OWN **1.** $x \geq 2$ **3.** $x \geq 0$ **5.** $x \geq -7$ **7.** $x \geq -3$ **9.** $x \geq 5$ **11.** B **13.** A

15. 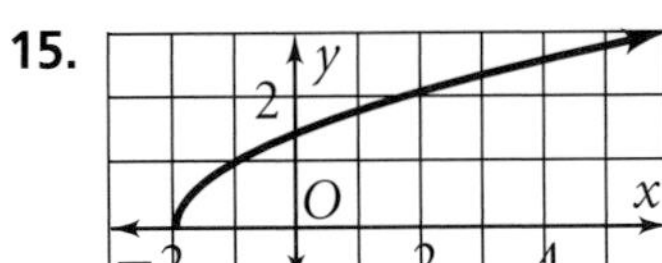

17. 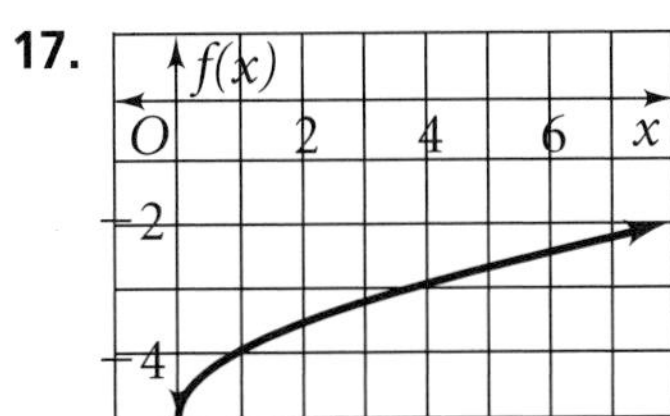

19. 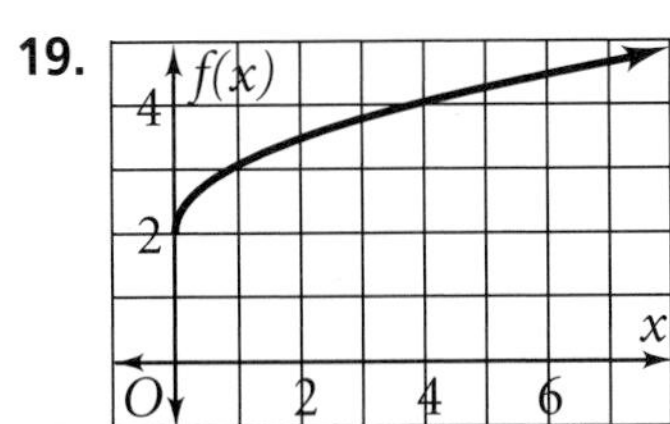

21. 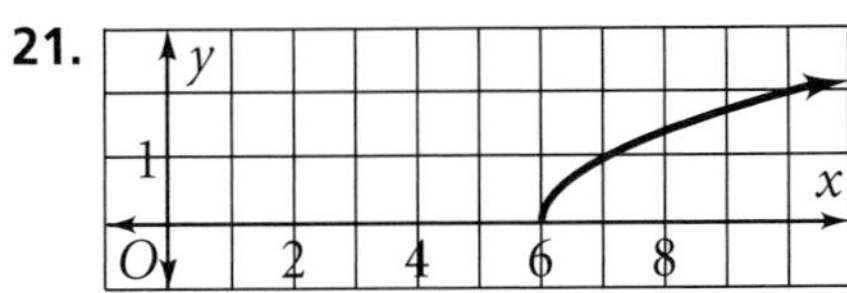

23. 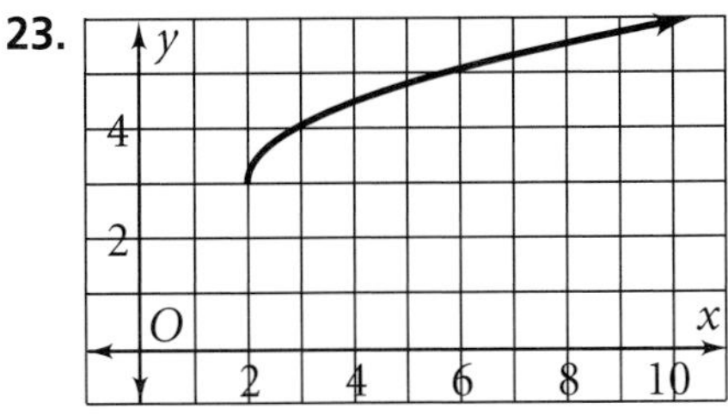

25. 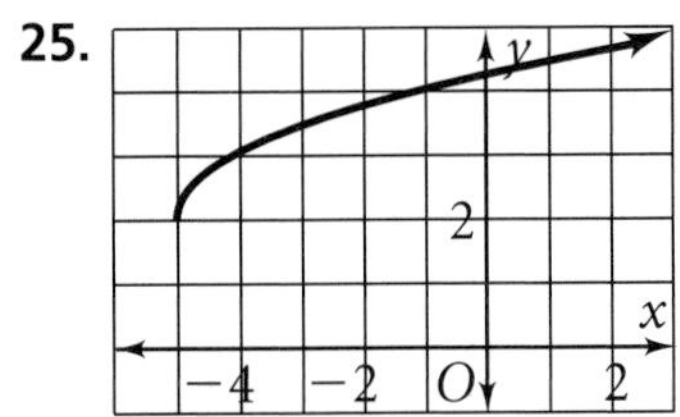

27. shift left 8 **29.** shift up 12

MIXED REVIEW

33. 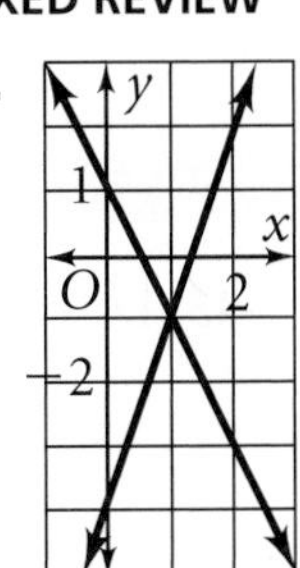 (1, −1) **35.** 7.8 **37.** −1.8

CHECKPOINT **1.** 9 **2.** 14 **3.** $8b^2\sqrt{b}$ **4.** $\sqrt{2}$ **5.** $3 + 4\sqrt{3}$ **6.** $2\sqrt{2}$ **7.** $\frac{x\sqrt{x}}{2}$ **8.** $2\sqrt{3}$ **9.** 68 **10.** 6 **11.** 8 **12.** 18

13. 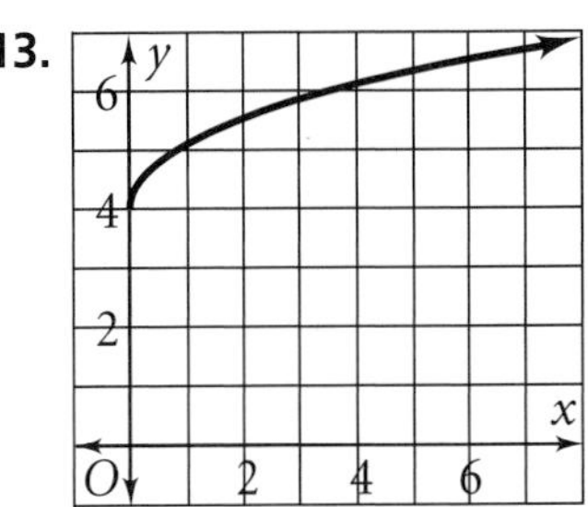

14. 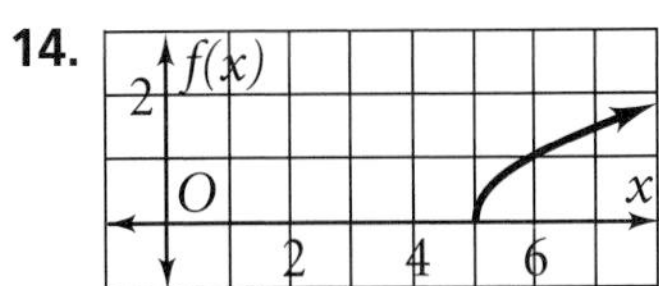

15. 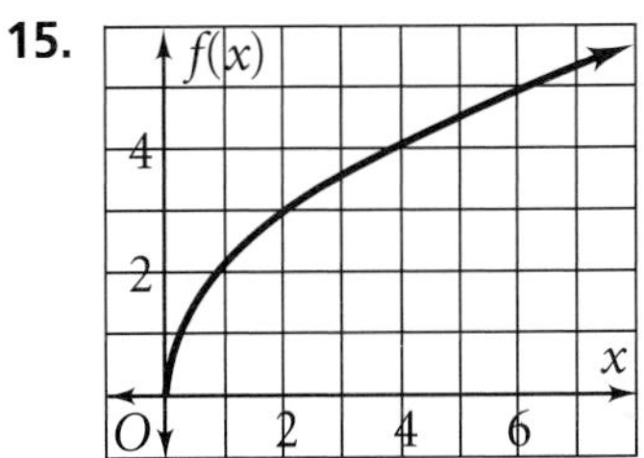

16. 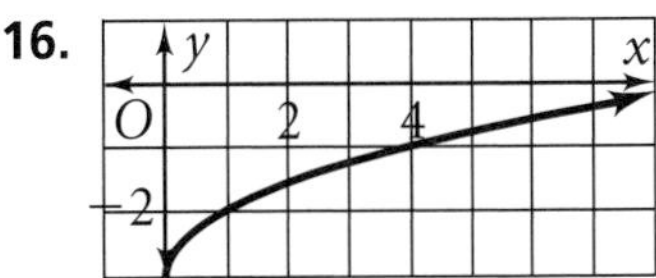

18. D

Toolbox page 450

1. 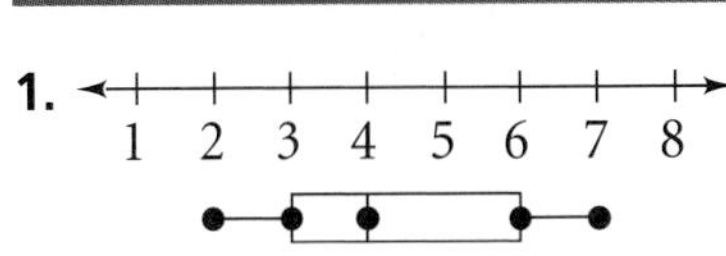

3. 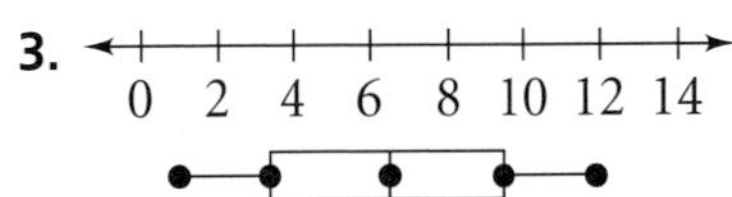

5. 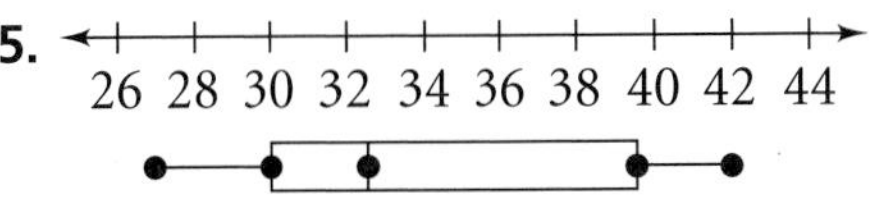

7. 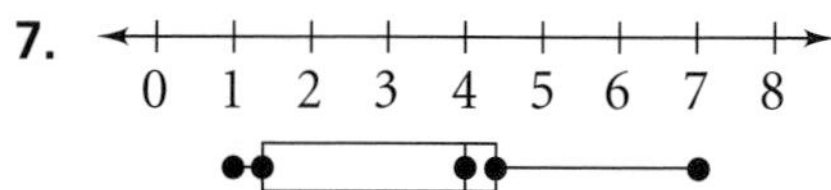

9b. 2; 33; 33 **9c.** 21 h; 23 h; both are much less than the typical 29-h week.

Lesson 9-8 pages 451–455

ON YOUR OWN

1.

x	$\overline{x}$	$x - \overline{x}$	$(x - \overline{x})^2$
5	5	0	0
3	5	−2	4
2	5	−3	9
5	5	0	0
10	5	5	25
		Sum:	38

standard deviation: about 2.8

3.

x	$\overline{x}$	$x - \overline{x}$	$(x - \overline{x})^2$
3.5	4	−0.5	0.25
4.5	4	0.5	0.25
6.0	4	2	4
4.0	4	0	0
2.5	4	−1.5	2.25
2.5	4	−1.5	2.25
5.0	4	1	1
		Sum:	10

standard deviation: about 1.2

5a. The data are spread far apart **5b.** Most data are near 25. **9a.** Sample: Lyman should have asked about the range and the standard deviation or the median salary and the mode. The range and the standard deviation would have told him that the salaries are widely distributed. The mode and the median, both \$265, would have told him that the mean does not represent the data well. **9b.** \$1165 **9c.** Large; all the data are far from the mean. **9d.** about 321.36 **11.** about 0.98 **13.** about 25.47 **15a.** \$20 **15b.** about 5.83 **15c.** 6; 39

MIXED REVIEW **17.** 3.47×10^{-3} **19.** 8.25×10^{-4} **21.** (1, 2) **23.** (5, 2) **25.** $x \geq 5$ **27.** \$14,961.04

Wrap-Up pages 457–459

1. 5.83 **2.** 17.80 **3.** 14.76 **4.** 9.85 **6.** (0.5, 5.5) **7.** (5.5, 6) **8.** (8.5, 3.5) **9.** (2.5, 13) **11.** $BC \approx 6.71$; $AC \approx 9.95$ **12.** $AC \approx 27.7$; $AB \approx 29.12$ **13.** $BC \approx 6.25$; $AB \approx 10.15$ **14.** C **15.** $48\sqrt{2}$ **16.** $\frac{2\sqrt{21}}{11}$ **17.** $20\sqrt{6}$ **18.** $\frac{10}{13}$ **19.** $10\sqrt{2}$ cm by $70\sqrt{2}$ cm **20.** $2\sqrt{7}$ **21.** $30\sqrt{5}$ **22.** $\sqrt{6}$ **23.** $2\sqrt{5}$ **24.** $10 - 10\sqrt{2}$ **25.** $25\sqrt{10}$ **26.** $18\sqrt{2}$ **27.** $17\sqrt{7}$ **28.** $\sqrt{29}$ in. **29.** 2 **30.** 16 **31.** 8 **32.** 81 **33.** 2.93 in.

34. $x \geq 0$; 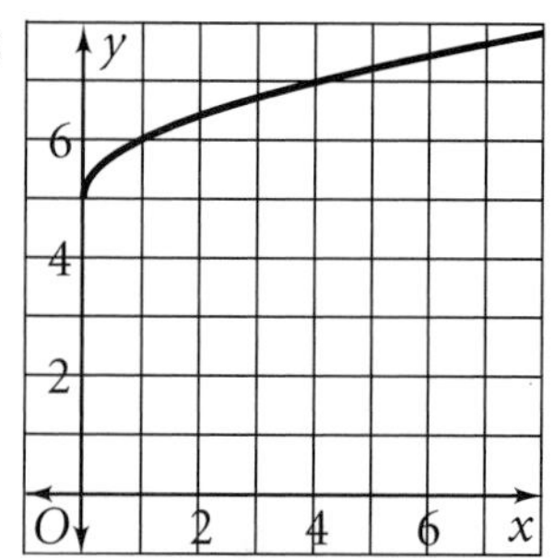

35. $x \geq 2$; 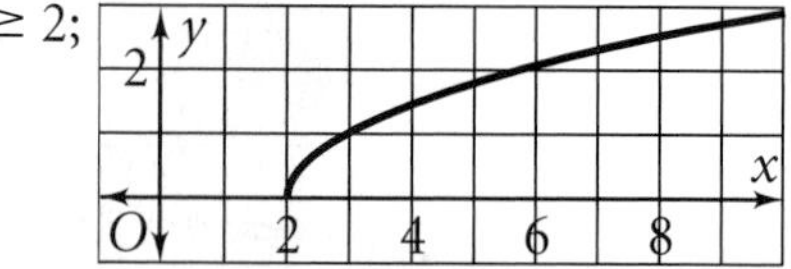

36. $x \geq -1$; 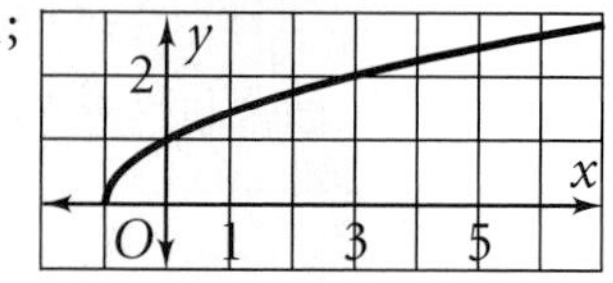

37. $x \geq 0$; 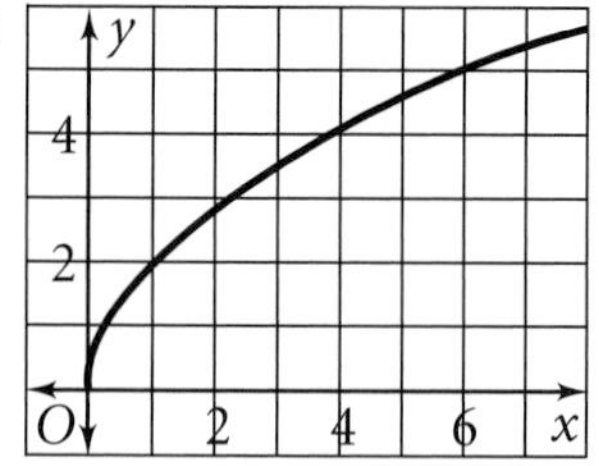

38. about 5.44 **39.** about 4.69 **40.** about 6.15 **41.** about 7.44 **42.** 0.64, −3.14 **43.** 1.90, −1.23 **44.** 4.70, −1.70 **45.** no solution **46.** 2, −1.2 **47.** 1.47, −1.75

Preparing for Standardized Tests page 461

1. B **3.** B **5.** A **7.** C **9.** A **11.** B **13.** D **15.** 85; 5.40 **17.** 31 or 32

CHAPTER 10

Lesson 10-1 pages 464–469

ON YOUR OWN **1.** C **3.** E **5.** A **7.** $4x + 9$; linear binomial **9.** $-11z^3 + 9z^2 + 5z - 5$; cubic with four terms **11.** $c^2 + 4c - 2$; quadratic trinomial **13.** $4q^4 + 3q^2 - 8q - 10$; fourth degree polynomial with four terms **15.** $x^2 - 1$ **17.** $-6x^3 + 3x^2 - x - 4$ **19.** $7a^3 + 11a^2 - 4a - 2$ **21.** $6x^2 - 12$ **25.** $8y$ **27.** $28c - 16$ **31.** $5x + 18$ **33.** $6y + 2$ **35.** $-2x^2 - 7x - 11$ **37.** $2r^2 - r - 7$ **39.** $9b^4 - 3b^2 + 7b - 6$

MIXED REVIEW **41.** 4^4 **43.** $\left(\frac{2}{3}\right)^4$ **45.** 5.0 **47.** 1.9 **49.** $2x - 6$ **51.** $15a - 21$

Lesson 10-2 pages 470–474

ON YOUR OWN **1.** $3x + 12$ **3.** $4x^2 + 2x$ **5.** $8x^2 + 12x$

7.

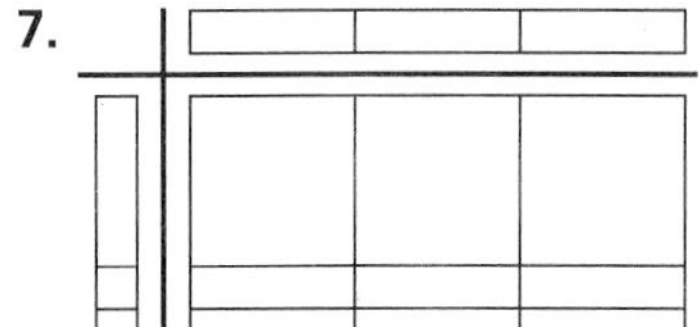

$(x + 2)(3x) = 3x^2 + 6x$

9. $8x + 28$ **11.** $-54x^4 + 36x^2 - 48x$ **13.** $-12a^3 + 15a^2 - 27a$ **15.** $6p^5 - 15p^3$ **17.** $-4x^2 + 13x$ **19.** $x^2 + x$ **21.** 3 **23.** 12 **25.** 5 **27.** $3x$ **29.** $5s$ **31.** $8x^2$ **35a.** $V = 64s^3$ **35b.** $V = 48\pi s^2$ **35c.** $V = 64s^3 - 48\pi s^2$ **35d.** $V = 16s^2(4s - 3\pi)$ **35e.** about 182,071 in.^{3} **37.** $s(s^3 + 4s^2 - 2)$ **39.** $2x^2(1 - 2x^2)$ **41.** $7k(k^2 - 5k + 10)$ **43.** $3x(3 + 4x)$ **45.** $6m^2(m^4 - 4m^2 + 1)$ **47.** $m^2(5m - 7)$ **49.** $(x^2 - 7)(2x + 1)$ **51a.** 7; 4 **51b.** $n - 3$ **51c.** $\frac{1}{2}n^2 - \frac{3}{2}n$

MIXED REVIEW **53.** $\frac{4}{5}$ **55.** $\frac{3}{5}$ **57.** $\frac{3}{4}$ **59.** $28x^3 - 48x^2 + 128x$

Lesson 10-3 pages 475–479

ON YOUR OWN **1.** $x - 4$; $-x + 2$; $-x^2 + 6x - 8$ **3.** $x - 3$; $-x + 3$; $-x^2 + 6x - 9$ **5.** $x^2 - x - 20$ **7.** 30 **9.** 7 **11.** $x^2 + x - 42$ **13.** $2y^2 - y - 15$ **15.** $5y^2 + 12y - 32$ **17.** $a^3 - 6a^2 + 9a - 4$ **19.** $4t^3 - 22t^2 + 36t - 15$ **23.** $x^2 + 8x + 15$ **25.** $a^2 - 8a + 7$ **27.** $5a^2 + 13a - 6$ **29.** $-6y^2 + 20y - 14$ **33.** 1; rational **35.** $26 + 10\sqrt{5}$; irrational

MIXED REVIEW **37.** 2, −2 **39.** 2, −1 **41.** $(2x + 4)(3x + 5)$ **43.** $(-3x + 5)(4x + 1)$

CHECKPOINT **1.** $3x^2 + 5x - 4$ **2.** $2a^3 + a^2 - 7$ **3.** $-2m^2 - 5m + 8$ **4.** $9x^2 - x - 8$ **5.** $-w^2 + 9$ **6.** $-6t^3 - 4t^2 + 12t$ **7.** $m^2 + m - 12$ **8.** $b^2 - 9b + 18$ **9.** $-3c(c^2 - 5c + 1)$ **10.** $5a(2a^2 + a + 1)$ **11.** $4p(2p^2 - 5p - 6)$ **12.** $x(x^2 + 4x + 7)$

Toolbox page 480

1.

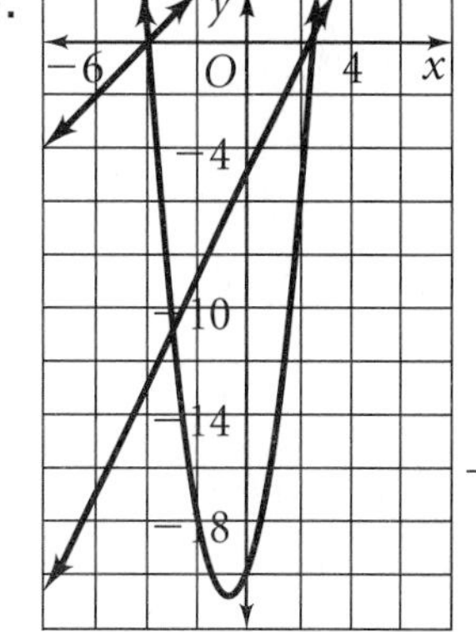

3.

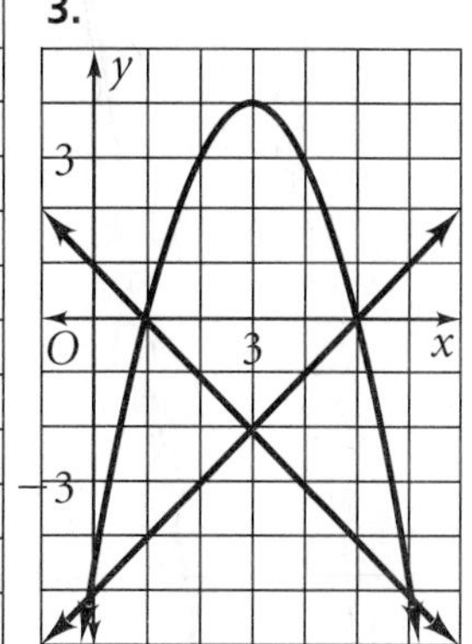

5.

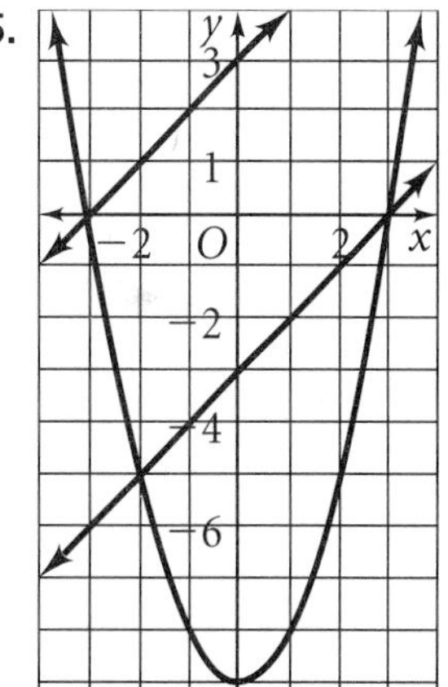

7. The x-intercepts are the same. **9.** $-x + 2$, $x - 2$; $-x^2 + 4x - 4$ **11.** $-2x - 6$, $\frac{1}{2}x - 1$; $-x^2 - x + 6$

Lesson 10-4 pages 481–485

ON YOUR OWN **1.** $x + 3$, $x + 2$; $x^2 + 5x + 6$ **3.** $x + 2$, $x + 2$; $x^2 + 4x + 4$ **5.** No; no two numbers with product 8 can have sum 5. **7.** Yes; $(x + 8)(x + 1) = x^2 + 9x + 8$

9.

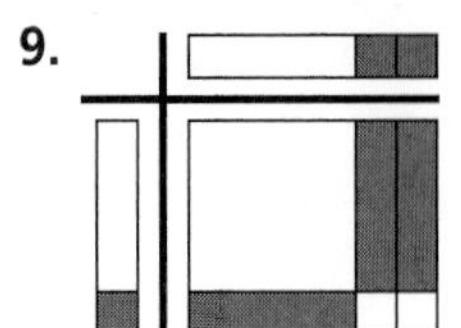

$(x-2)(x-1)$

11.

$(x-4)(x+2)$

13.

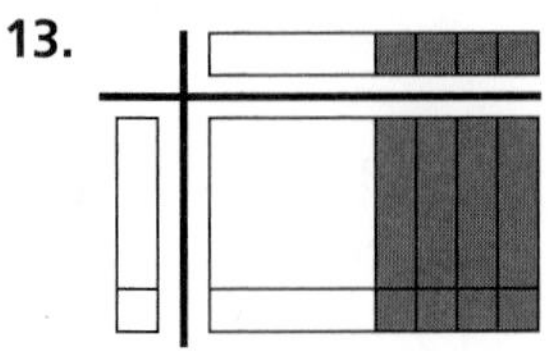

$(x-4)(x+1)$

15.

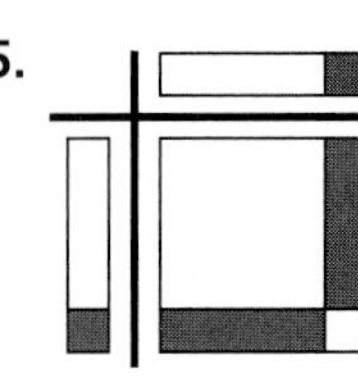

$(x-1)(x-1)$

17. 2 **19.** -1 **21.** -3 **23a.** $x^2+15x+56$ **23b.** $(x+7)(x+8)$ **25.** $(a-2)(a-3)$ **27.** $(k+1)(k+8)$ **29.** $(r-11)(r+1)$ **31.** $(x+5)(x-3)$ **33.** $(x+5)(x+7)$ **35.** $(a-7)(a-2)$ **37.** $(y+16)(y-3)$ **39.** $(w-6)(w+4)$ **43.** $(2x-1)(x-7)$ **45.** $(2x-3)(x+1)$ **47.** $(2x+3)(x-7)$ **49.** $(2x-1)(x-3)$ **51.** $(7x+1)(x-3)$ **53.** $(3x+5)(x+4)$

MIXED REVIEW **55.** 5 **57.** about 8.1

59.

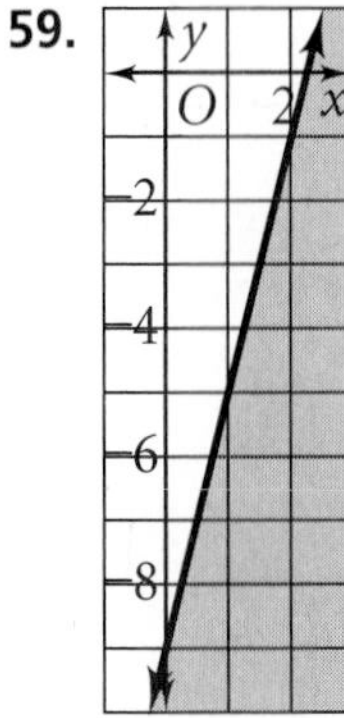

61. 84 **63.** $4x^2+12x+9$ **65.** x^2-64 **67.** $4x^2-49$ **69.** $4x^2-4x+1$

Lesson 10-5 pages 486–490

ON YOUR OWN **1.** $x^2+10x+25$; $x+5$, $x+5$ **3.** $9x^2+6x+1$; $3x+1$, $3x+1$ **5.** $(x+1)^2$ **7.** $(x-9)^2$ **9.** $3(x-1)^2$ **11.** $6(x+5)(x-5)$ **13.** $(x+7)(x-7)$ **15.** $(2x-1)^2$ **17.** $(3x+1)^2$ **19.** $(x+20)(x-20)$ **23a.** $3.14n^2-3.14m^2$; $3.14(n+m)(n-m)$ **23b.** 285.74 in.^{2} **25.** 891 **27.** 1591 **29.** 384 **31.** 396 **33.** $\left(\frac{1}{2}m+\frac{1}{3}\right)\left(\frac{1}{2}m-\frac{1}{3}\right)$ **35.** $\left(\frac{1}{3}n+\frac{1}{5}\right)\left(\frac{1}{3}n-\frac{1}{5}\right)$ **37a.** $t-3$; 4 **37b.** $(t+1)(t-7)$

MIXED REVIEW **39.** $5+6\sqrt{2}$ **41.** $\sqrt{41}$ **43.** 30% **45.** $-\frac{4}{3}$ **47.** $\frac{5}{3}$

Lesson 10-6 pages 491–495

ON YOUR OWN **1.** 3, 7 **3.** $-\frac{2}{7}, -\frac{4}{5}$ **5.** $-2, 7$ **7.** 5, 11 **9.** $-4, 3$ **11.** 0, 10 **13.** $-4, \frac{2}{5}$ **15.** $-1, 10$ **17.** 5 cm **19.** $x^2-10x+24=0$; 4, 6 **21.** $2q^2+22q+60=0$; $-6, -5$ **23.** $6n^2-5n-4=0$; $-\frac{1}{2}, \frac{4}{3}$ **25.** $20p^2-80=0$; $-2, 2$ **27.** $4n^2-100=0$; $5, -5$ **29.** $9c^2-36=0$; $2, -2$ **31.** 5 in. **33a.** 10 ft base; 22 ft height **33b.** about 24.2 ft **35.** 0, 4, 6 **37.** 0, 3 **39.** 0, 1, 9 **41.** 3, 4, 5 **43.** $0, -1$ **45.** 8 in. × 10 in.

MIXED REVIEW **47.** $\frac{1}{3y^3}$ **49.** 1 **51.** $\frac{25}{3}$ **53.** 60 students **55.** $\frac{1}{5}, -\frac{3}{2}$

CHECKPOINT **1.** $(x-3)(x-2)$ **2.** $(n-3)^2$ **3.** $(g-10)(g+2)$ **4.** $(3x+7)(3x-7)$ **5.** $-3, \frac{2}{3}$ **6.** $6, -\frac{3}{2}$ **7.** $-7, -2$ **8.** $2, -2$ **9.** $-\frac{4}{3}$ **10.** $\frac{3}{2}, -\frac{2}{5}$ **11.** A

Toolbox page 496

1. 4 **3.** 49 **5.** Sample: Divide the coefficient of the first degree term in half and square the result. **7.** $-6, -2$ **9.** $-8, 2$ **11.** $-6, 2$ **13.** $9, -5$ **15.** $-5 \pm \sqrt{35}$ **17.** $-4 \pm \sqrt{13}$

Lesson 10-7 pages 497–501

ON YOUR OWN **1.** $-0.08, -13$ **3.** $1.25, -1.33$ **5.** no real solutions **7.** $3, -3$ **9.** $2, -2$ **11a.** $-\frac{1}{2}, 3$ **11b.** $-\frac{1}{2}, 3$ **11c.** $(2x+1)(x-3)=0$, so $x=-\frac{1}{2}$ or $x=3$. **13.** $-4, 2$ **15.** no real solutions **17.** no real solutions **19.** 4 **21.** $0, \frac{4}{5}$ **23.** $-1.85, 4.85$ **25.** 1.75 **27.** $\frac{13}{7}, -\frac{13}{7}$ **29.** B **31.** about 167.7 ft

MIXED REVIEW **35.** 13; 28 **37.** the parabola $y = x^2$ shifted 2 units right, 1 unit down; $x = 2$; 3; 1 and 3.

Wrap-Up pages 503–505

1. $7x^3 + 8x^2 - 3x + 12$ **2.** $8g^4 - 5g^2 + 11g + 5$ **3.** $-b^5 + 2b^3 + 6$ **4.** $t^3 - 5t^2 + 12t - 8$ **6.** $-40x^2 + 16x$ **7.** $35g^3 + 15g^2 - 45g$ **8.** $-40t^4 + 24t^3 - 32t^2$ **9.** $5m^3 + 15m^2$ **10.** $-6w^4 - 8w^3 + 20w^2$ **11.** $-3b^3 + 5b^2 + 10b$ **12.** $3x$; $3x(3x^3 + 4x^2 + 2)$ **13.** $4t^2$; $4t^2(t^3 - 3t + 2)$ **14.** $10n^3$; $10n^3(4n^2 + 7n - 3)$ **15.** $x^2 + 8x + 15$ **16.** $15x^2 - 29x - 14$ **17.** $6x^2 + 11x - 10$ **18.** $-x^2 + 5x - 4$ **19.** $x^3 + 3x^2 + 3x + 2$ **20.** $4x^2 - 21x + 5$ **21.** $x^3 - 9x^2 + 18x + 8$ **22.** $3x^2 + 10x + 8$ **23.** $(2x + 1)(x + 4)$; $2x^2 + 9x + 4$ **24.** $(x + 2)(x + 1)$ **25.** $(y - 7)(y - 2)$ **26.** $(x - 5)(x + 3)$ **27.** $(2w - 3)(w + 1)$ **28.** $(-b + 4)(b - 3)$ **29.** $(2t - 1)(t + 2)$ **30.** $(x - 1)(x + 6)$ **31.** $2(3x + 2)(x + 1)$ **32.** A **33.** $(q + 1)^2$ **34.** $(b - 4)(b + 4)$ **35.** $(x - 2)^2$ **36.** $(2t + 11)(2t - 11)$ **37.** $(2d - 5)^2$ **38.** $(3c + 1)^2$ **39.** $(3k + 5)(3k - 5)$ **40.** $(x + 3)^2$ **41.** The factors are equal. **42.** -3, -4 **43.** 0, 2 **44.** 4, 5 **45.** $-3, \frac{1}{2}$ **46.** $-\frac{2}{3}, 1\frac{1}{2}$ **47.** 1, 4 **48.** 10 ft by 17 ft **49.** $-5, 5$ **50.** $-4.12, 0.78$ **51.** 0.18, 2.82 **52.** 324 ft^2 **53.** $\frac{57}{10}$ **54.** $-\frac{33}{4}$ **55.** $\frac{157}{100}$ **56.** $\frac{52}{5}$ **57.** $-\frac{1849}{1000}$ **58.** $\frac{767}{100}$ **59.** $\frac{1}{3}$ **60.** $-1\frac{1}{2}$ **61.** $-\frac{3}{7}$ **62.** $\frac{10}{13}$ **63.** $7\frac{1}{2}$ **64.** $2\frac{1}{3}$ **65.** $9\frac{1}{6}$ **66.** 26

Cumulative Review page 507

1. D **3.** D **5.** B **7.** D **9.** C **11.** A **13.** 5 and 9 **15.** 5 m by 7 m

CHAPTER 11

Lesson 11-1 pages 510–514

ON YOUR OWN **1a.** 16 h; 10 h; 8 h; 4 h **1b.** hourly wage and time worked **1c.** $xy = 80$ **3.** 8 **5.** 7 **7.** 96 **9.** $\frac{1}{6}$ **11.** 20 **13.** 130 **15.** D **17.** 1.1 **19.** 2.5 **21.** 375 **23a.** 120; distance from your house to the lake **23b.** 3 h **25.** 2.4 da **27.** $y = 70x$ **29.** $xy = 48$ **31.** Direct; as s increases, P increases. **33.** Inverse; as r increases, t decreases.

MIXED REVIEW **37.** $(x + 5)^2$ **39.** $(x - 3)^2$ **41.** $\frac{1}{5}$ **43.** $\frac{3}{8}$ **45.** -1

Toolbox page 515

1.

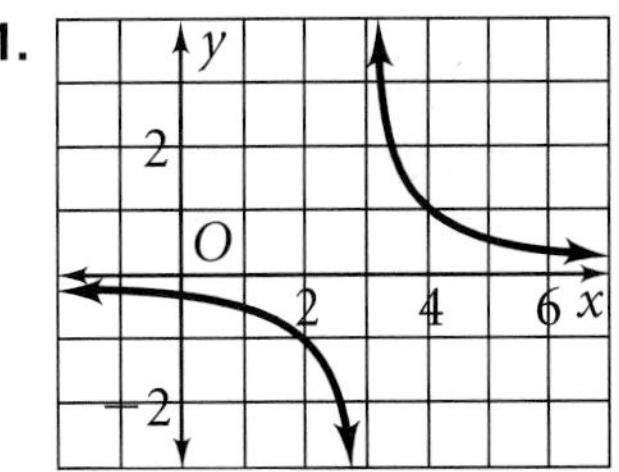

3.

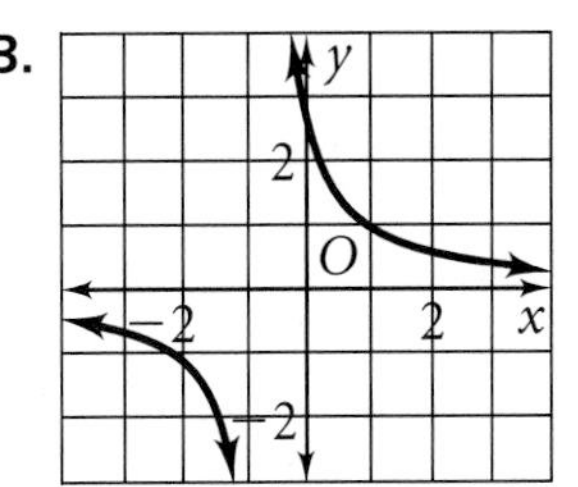

5.

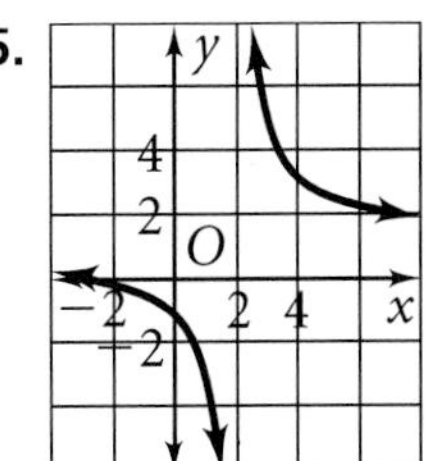

7.

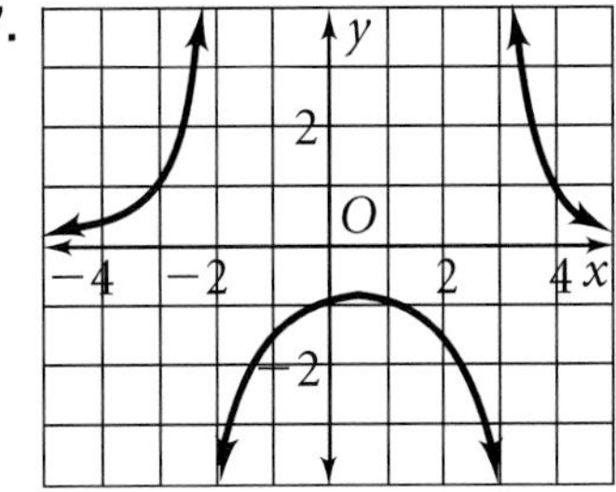

9.

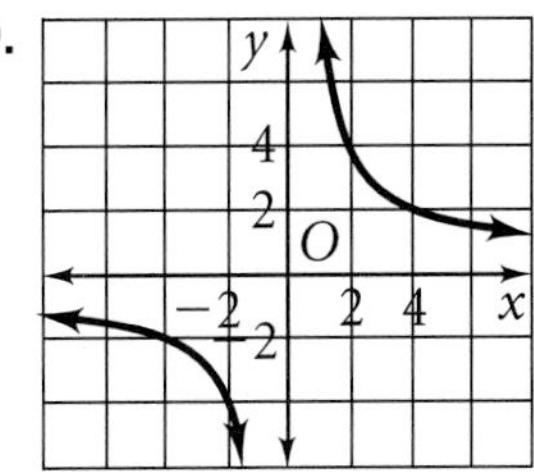

Selected Answers

11.

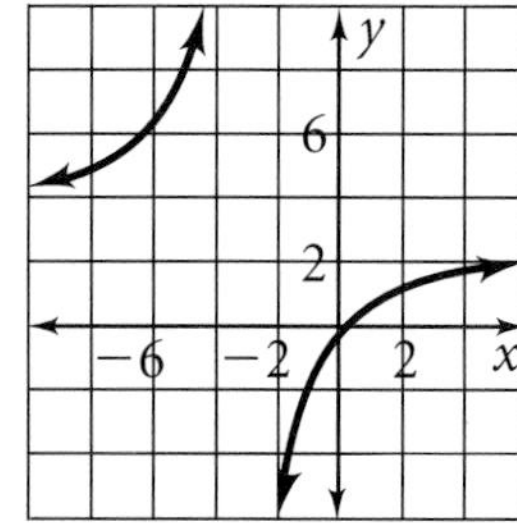

13a. The shapes of the graphs are the same, but they are in different positions along the x-axis. **13b.** The shapes of the graphs are the same, but they are in different positions along the y-axis.

Lesson 11-2 pages 516–521

ON YOUR OWN **1.** $3; 0; \frac{1}{2}$ **3.** $\frac{1}{2}; -4; 8$ **5.** 0 **7.** -2 **9.** $x = 2, y = 0$ **11.** $x = 1, y = -1$

13.

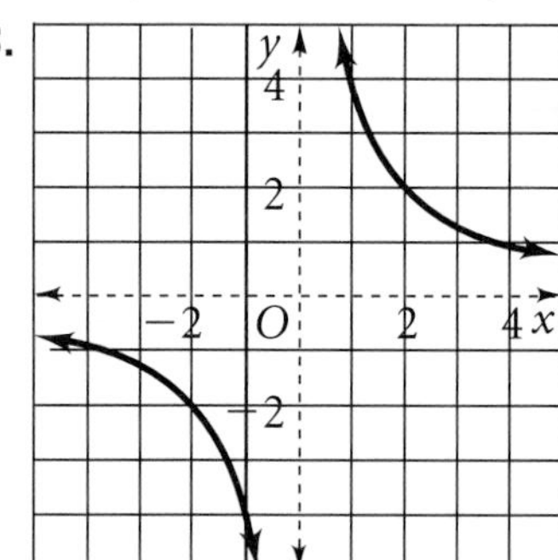

15.

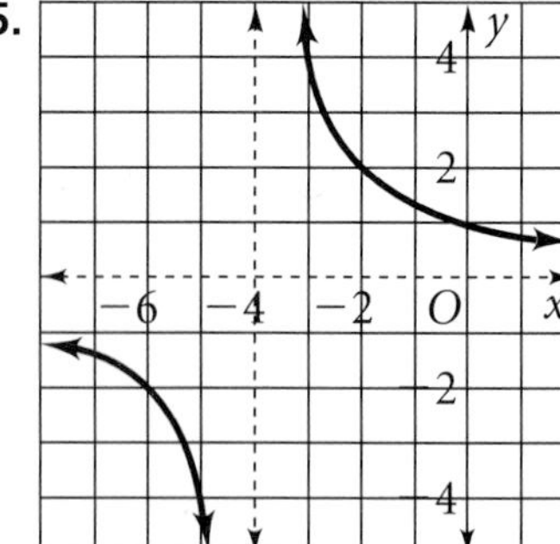

17.

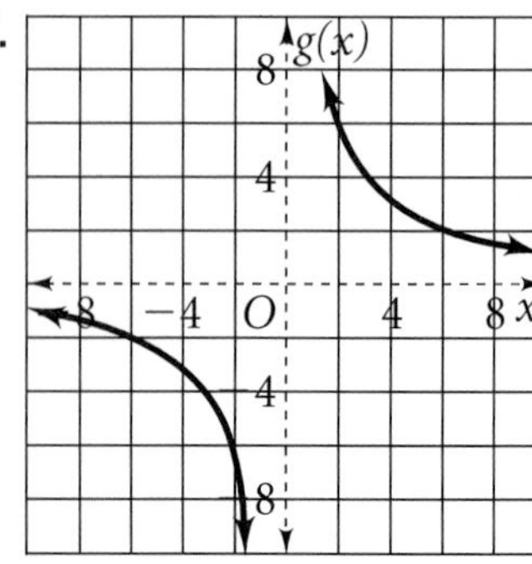

19.

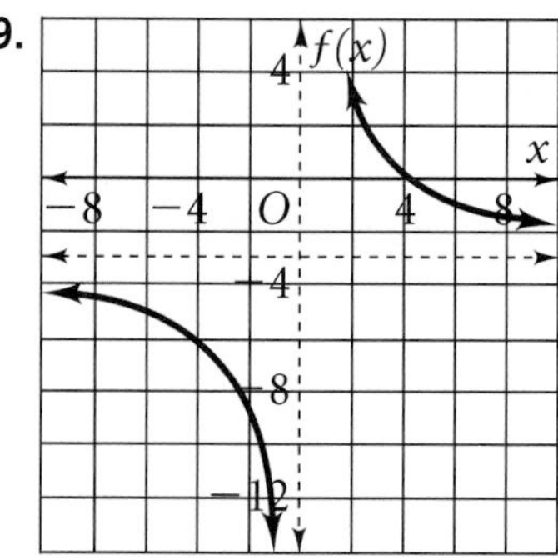

21.

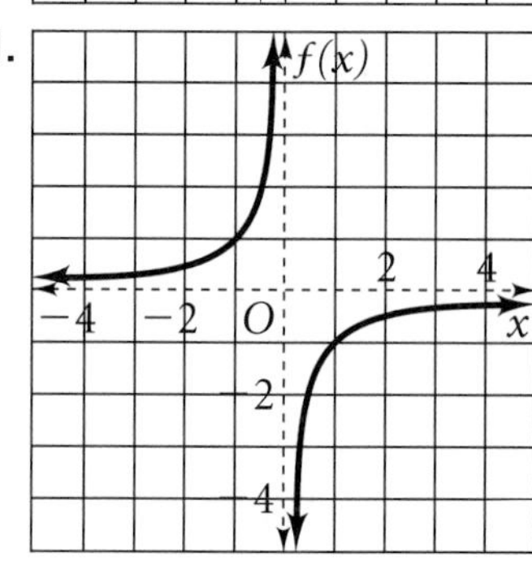

23.

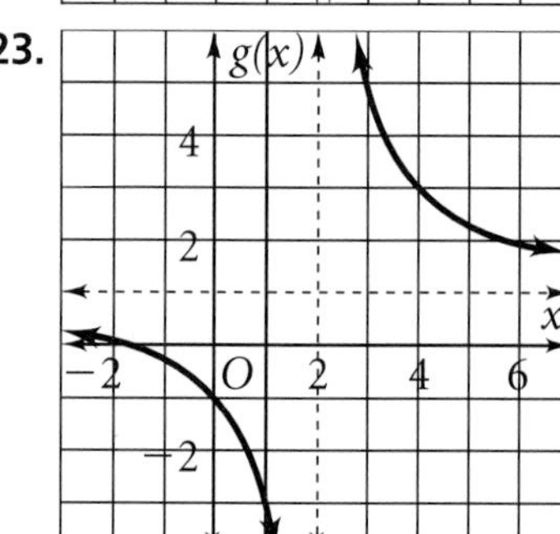

25a.

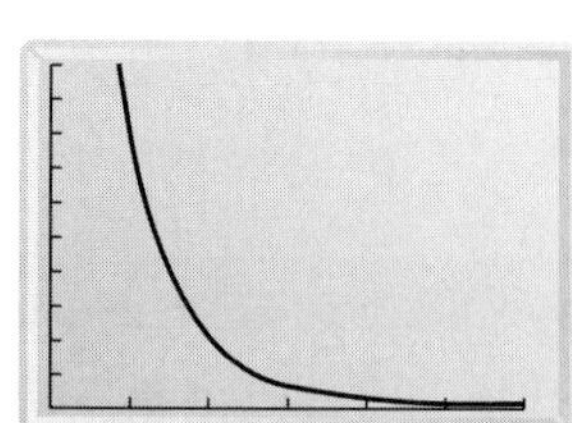

Xmin=0 Ymin=0
Xmax=6 Ymax=2000
Xscl=1 Yscl=200

; $d \geq 40$ **25b.** 16; 1600; 160,000

29.

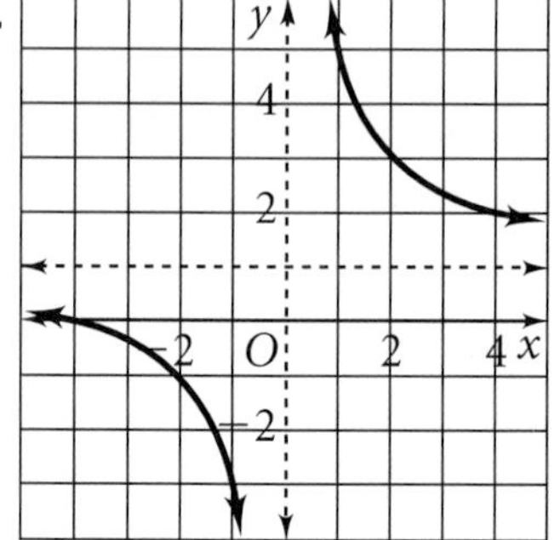

31.
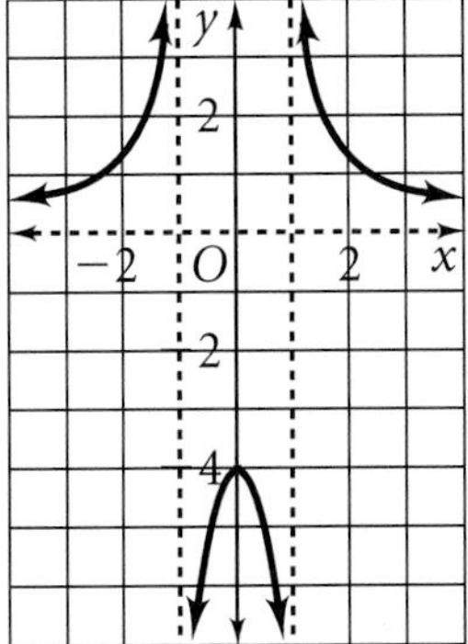

33.
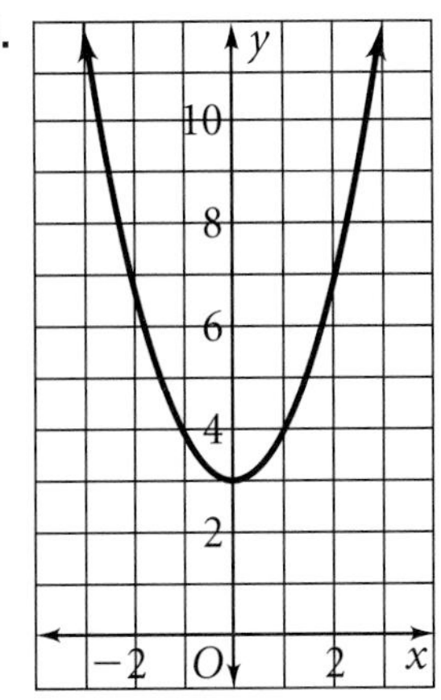

35.
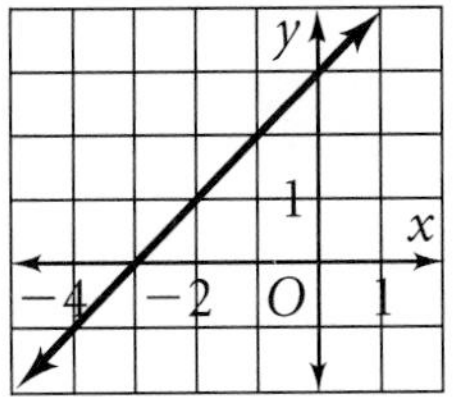

37.
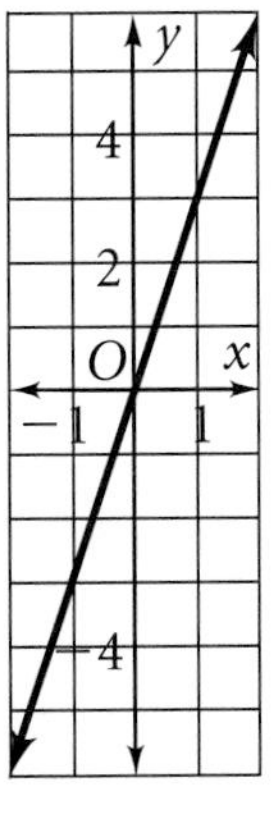

39.
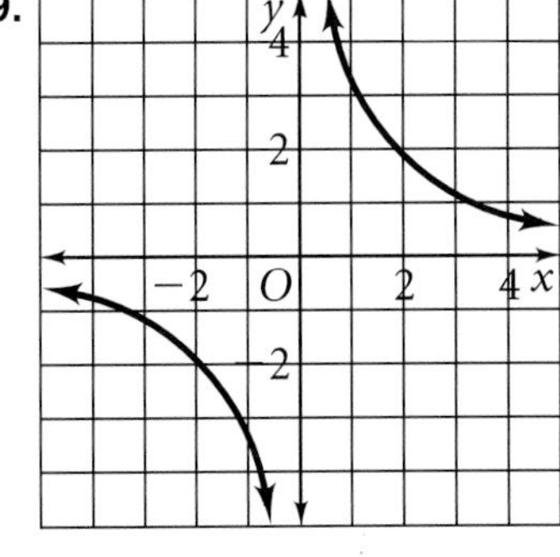

41.
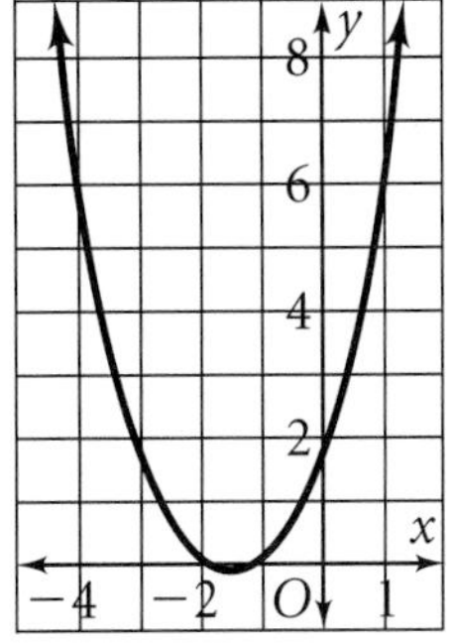

43.
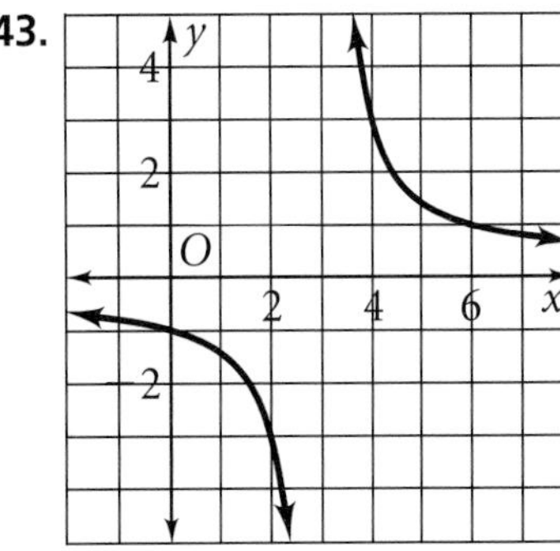

MIXED REVIEW **45.** $(g - 7)(g - 5)$ **47.** $(a + 7)(a - 1)$ **49.** \$10 **51.** 0, 3 **53.** $-4, 4$

CHECKPOINT **1.** 3 **2.** 2 **3.** 4

4.
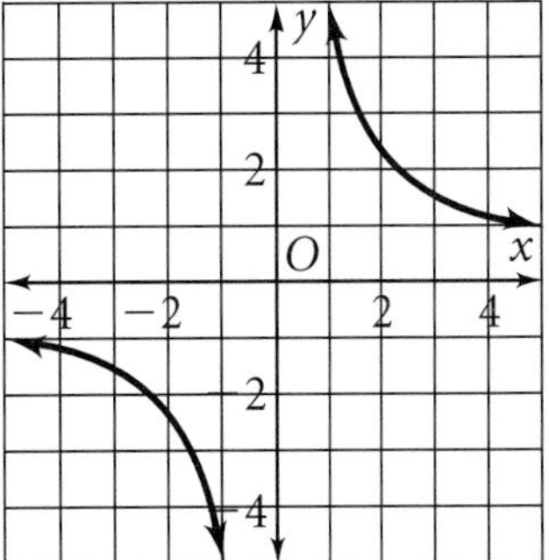

5.
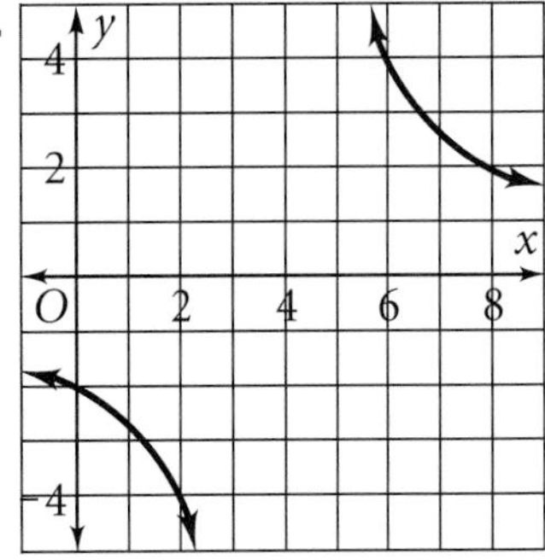

Selected Answers

6.

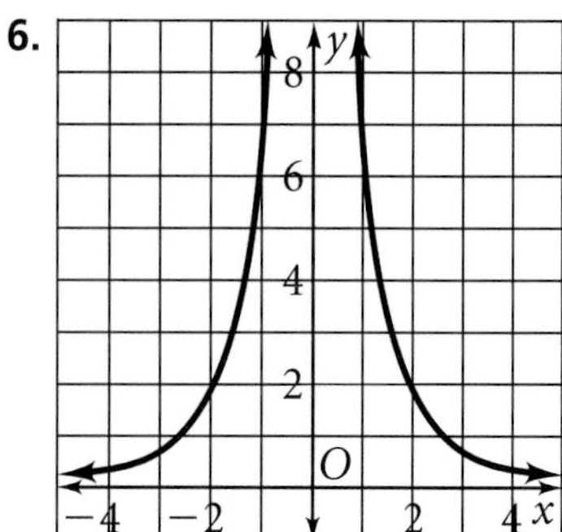

7.

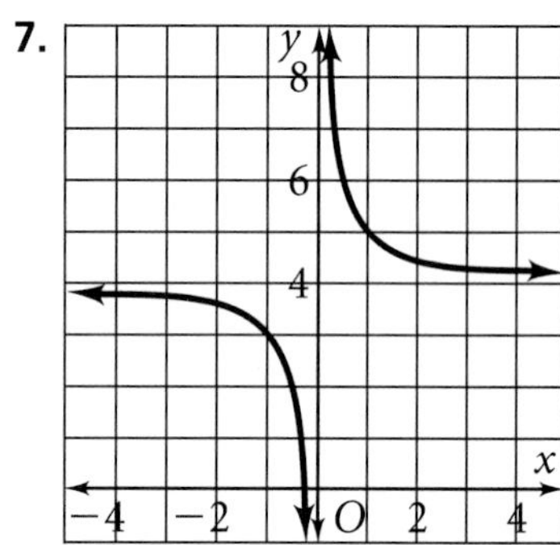

9. 91 lb

Lesson 11-3 pages 522–526

ON YOUR OWN **1.** $\frac{a}{4}$; $a \neq 0$ **3.** $\frac{x-2}{x+2}$; $x \neq -2$ **5.** $\frac{2a+3}{4}$ **7.** $\frac{1}{7x}$; $x \neq 0$ **9.** $\frac{1}{2}$; $p \neq 12$ **11.** $\frac{2}{3}$; $x \neq 0$, -1 **13.** $3x$; $x \neq 3$ **15.** $\frac{w}{w-7}$; $w \neq -7, 7$ **17.** $\frac{x^2-9}{x+3}$ does not have -3 in its domain. **21.** $-\frac{125}{16}$ **23.** $\frac{12}{x}$ **25.** $2x$ **27.** $\frac{3x^4}{2}$ **29.** 6 **31.** $-\frac{1}{2}$ **33.** $\frac{11}{7k-15}$ **35.** $\frac{\frac{4}{3}\pi r^3}{\pi r^2} = \frac{r}{3}$ **37.** $\frac{5w}{5w+6}$ **39.** $\frac{3y}{4(y+4)}$

MIXED REVIEW **41.** 3^{x+5} **43.** $-12m^4 - 18m$ **45.** $\frac{2}{3}$ **47.** $\frac{3}{5}$

Lesson 11-4 pages 527–531

ON YOUR OWN **1.** $\frac{7}{5}$ **3.** $-\frac{2}{b}$ **5.** $\frac{4}{11g}$ **7.** $\frac{2}{d}$ **9.** $\frac{5n}{7}$ **11.** $\frac{26r}{5}$ **13.** $4x^2$ **15.** $2m^2$ **17.** $6t^5$ **19.** $46d^4$ **21.** $5a$ **23.** $35b^3$ **25.** $\frac{35a^3+6}{15a^4}$ **27.** $\frac{18+20x^2}{15x^8}$ **29.** $\frac{b^3-4}{2b^4}$ **31.** $\frac{9+2m}{24m^3}$ **33.** $-\frac{77}{36k}$ **35.** $\frac{45+36x^2}{20x^2}$ **37a.** $\frac{17}{7r}$ **37b.** about 0.81 h, or 49 min **39.** $\frac{10}{m+1}$ **41.** $\frac{m+2}{m+3}$ **43.** $\frac{2}{t^2+1}$ **45.** $\frac{s+2}{4s^2+2}$ **47.** $\frac{1}{m+1}$ **49.** $\frac{5y-11}{(y+2)(y-3)}$

MIXED REVIEW **53.** about 12.2 **55.** about 10.8 **57.** 4 **59.** 6

Lesson 11-5 pages 532–536

ON YOUR OWN **1a.** 32 **1c.** no **3.** 12 **5.** -1 **7.** 2 **9.** no solution **11.** $-3\frac{1}{9}$ **13.** $-\frac{1}{3}$ **15.** $22\frac{1}{2}$ min **17.** 2 **19.** $\frac{1}{2}$ **21.** $-2, 4$ **23.** $5\frac{1}{3}$ **25.** 6 **27.** 5 **29.** A **31.** $a = 4$; $b = \frac{7}{27}$; $c = 11$; $d = -\frac{1}{3}$

MIXED REVIEW **33.** $-2, 2$ **35.** -5.5 **37.** 1, 2, 3, 4, 5, 6 **39.** H1, H2, H3, H4, H5, H6, T1, T2, T3, T4, T5, T6

CHECKPOINT **1.** $\frac{4}{m}$; $m \neq 0$ **2.** $6(x-2)$; $x \neq -2$ **3.** $\frac{c+3}{c-3}$; $c \neq 3$ **4.** $\frac{3z+12}{z^3}$; $z \neq 0$ **6.** $\frac{6}{7}$ **7.** -9 **8.** $\frac{5}{2}$ **9.** $-0.74, 10.74$ **10.** $\frac{9}{c}$ **11.** $\frac{5}{x-3}$ **12.** $\frac{2(7m-6)}{(m+2)(m-3)}$ **13.** $\frac{6t+3}{t^2}$ **14.** B

Toolbox page 537

1. symmetric **3.** reflexive **5a.** division property of equality **5b.** distributive property **5c.** subtraction property of equality

Lesson 11-6 pages 538–542

ON YOUR OWN **1.** 10 choices **3.** 30 ways **5a.** 24 different numbers **5b.** 6 even numbers **5d.** $\frac{1}{4}$ **7.** 210 **9.** 60 **11.** 6 **13.** 5040 **15.** 840 **17.** 7 **21.** 40,320 orders **23.** ${}_9P_7$ **25.** C **27a.** 2520 **27b.** $\frac{1}{2520}$

MIXED REVIEW

29. 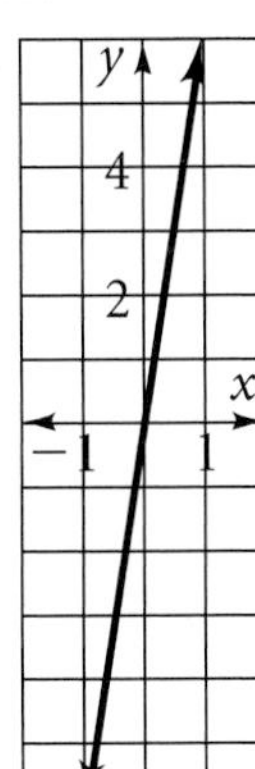

31. 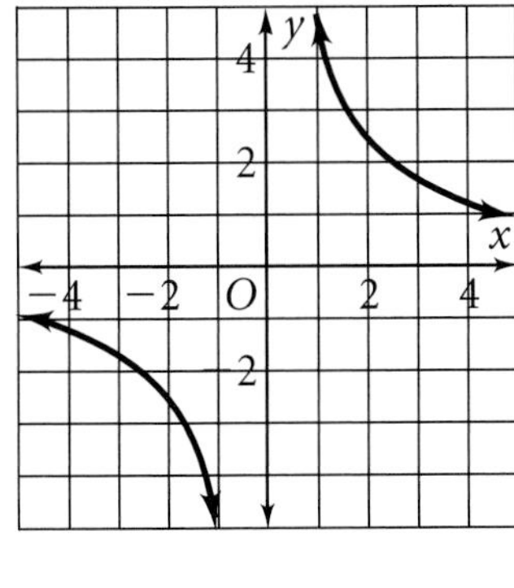

33. campsite \$20; family trail pass \$5 **35.** $\frac{5}{72}$

Lesson 11-7 pages 543–547

ON YOUR OWN **1a.** 14,886,690 different arrangements **1b.** about 1.94×10^{17} combinations **5.** 6 **7.** 20 **9.** 6 **11.** 1365 **13.** 56

15. 35 **17a.** 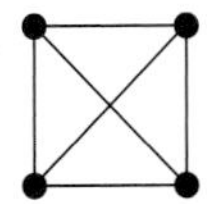 **17b–c.** 6 segments

17d. 45 segments **19.** 126 different combinations **21.** Permutation; the order of videos is important. **23.** Combination; the order of committee members is not important. **25.** 10 **27.** 35 **31a.** 792 different choices **31b.** 36 ways **31c.** $\frac{1}{22}$ **33a.** 45 possible combinations **33b.** 3 combinations **33c.** $\frac{1}{15}$ **33d.** $\frac{2}{15}$

MIXED REVIEW **35.** 12 **37.** 5040 **39.** 9 **41.** $\frac{4x^2 + 5}{3x}$ **43.** $\frac{13x - 8}{(x + 2)(x - 2)}$ **45.** $-\frac{27}{20n}$ **47a.** about 1143 times **47b.** 6 *t*

Wrap-Up pages 549–551

1. 6 **2.** 9 **3.** 4.4 **4.** no **5.** yes; $xy = 10.6$

6. 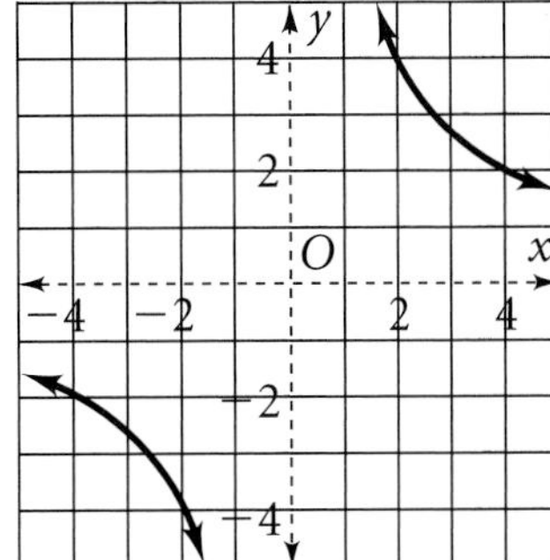

7. 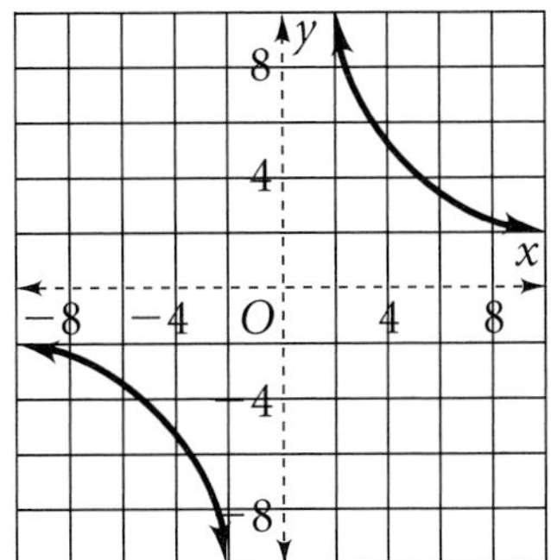

8. 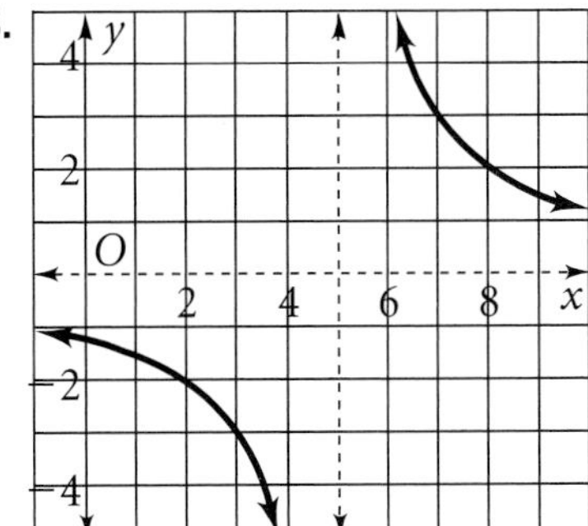

9. 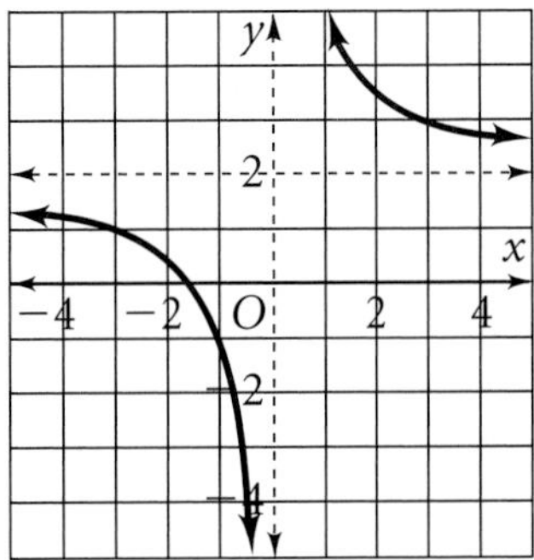

12. $x - 2; x \neq -2$ **13.** $\frac{x}{4x + 3}; x \neq -\frac{3}{4}$ **14.** $\frac{-3}{t(t - 1)}$; $t \neq 0, 1$ **15.** $\frac{1}{2z - 3}; z \neq -2, 1\frac{1}{2}$ **16.** $\frac{24m}{(m - 3)(m + 1)}$ **17.** $\frac{1}{2(2e + 1)}$ **18.** $\frac{5c + 3}{2c(c - 1)}$ **19.** $3(n + 2)$ **20.** $\frac{8}{k}$

Selected Answers

21. $\frac{4(2x-1)}{x-7}$ **22.** $\frac{15x^2+13x+27}{(3x-1)(2x+3)}$ **23.** $\frac{-3m+10}{(m-1)(m+1)}$

24. C **25.** 24 **26.** 9 **27.** -14 **28.** 6 min **29.** 60 **30.** 1680 **31.** 360 **32.** 20 **33.** 3024 **34.** 42 **35a.** 160 possible area codes **35b.** 640 new area codes **36.** 6 **37.** 210 **38.** 36 **39.** 165 **40.** 5 **41.** 15 **42.** 4 different combinations **43.** 45 ways

44. $\frac{3}{28}$

Preparing for Standardized Tests page 553

1. D **3.** C **5.** D **7.** B **9.** A **11.** B **13.** $(2x-3)^2$ **15.** $x = 2, y = 1; -3; -1\frac{1}{2}$

Cumulative Review pages 554–555

1. E **3.** E **5.** A **7.** D **9.** D **11.** A **13.** B **15.** D **17.** A **19.** B **21.** D **23a.** $2; \frac{1}{4}$ **29.** $-\frac{13}{3}$ **31.** \$1701 **33a.** 5.5

EXTRA PRACTICE

Chapter 1 page 556

1. 39.375; 38; 35 **3.** 6.3; 6; 5 and 8 **5a.** c = length of a car; $3c = 24$ **5b.** b = weight of a book, p = weight of a pen; $2b = 39p$ **7.** 28 **9.** 9 **11.** $4\frac{1}{9}$ **13.** -27.7 **15.** $-\frac{1}{2}$ **17.** -26 **19.** $10\frac{1}{2}$ **21.** -20 **23.** -59 **25.** 18

27. $\frac{7}{27}$ **29.** $\frac{22}{27}$

31. $\frac{23}{54}$ **33.** $\begin{bmatrix} -7 & 6 \\ 3 & 8 \end{bmatrix}$ **35.** $\begin{bmatrix} -1.6 & 4.1 \\ 1.5 & 4.6 \end{bmatrix}$

Chapter 2 page 557

1a.

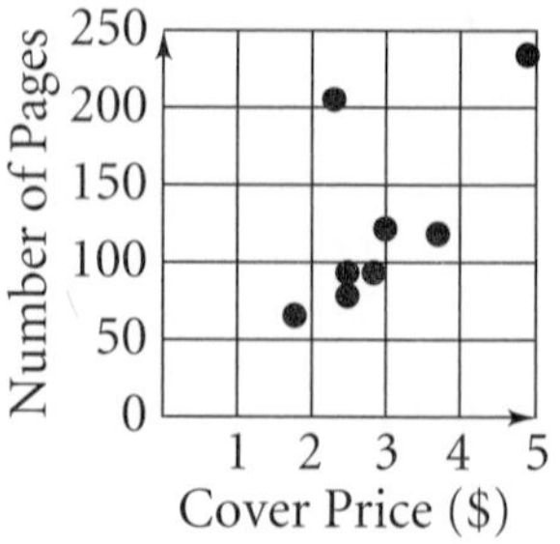

1b. The number of pages increases as the price increases. **1c.** About 75 pages; you can find the y-coordinate of the point on the line with x-coordinate 2.00.

7. $f(x) = 2x$

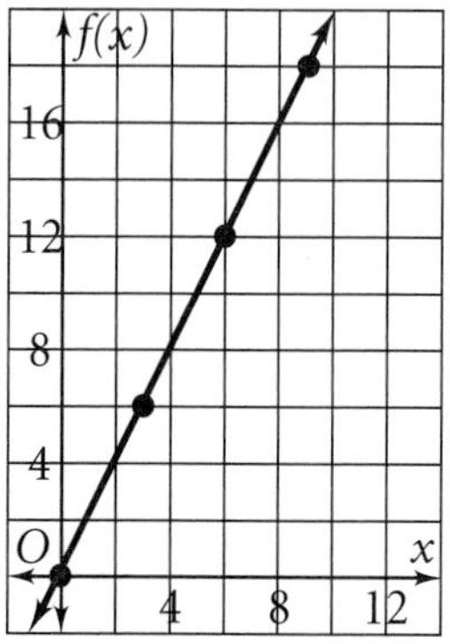

9. $f(x) = \frac{1}{2}x$

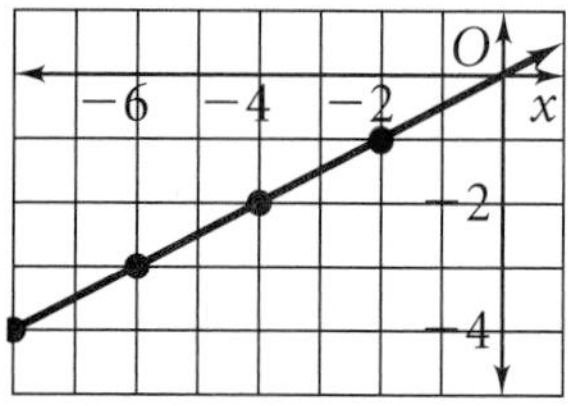

11. $\{-2, -1, 1, 2, 6\}$; absolute value **13.** $\{6, 7\frac{1}{2}, 8, 9\frac{1}{2}, 12\}$; linear **15.** $\{-\frac{8}{3}, -\frac{2}{3}, 0, 2, \frac{16}{3}\}$; linear **17.** $\{0, 3, 7, 52, 88\}$; quadratic **19.** $\{1, 4, 5, 8, 13\}$; linear **21.** $\left\{0, \frac{3}{5}, \frac{9}{5}, \frac{12}{5}, \frac{24}{5}\right\}$; absolute value **23.** 0 **25.** $\frac{2}{3}$ **27.** $\frac{1}{3}$ **29.** $\frac{1}{3}$

Chapter 3 page 558

1. 14 **3.** 8 **5.** -5.7 **7.** 2 **9.** 24 **11.** $\frac{18}{49}$ **13.** -2 **15.** 1 **17.** 10 **19.** -6 **21.** n = next test score; $\frac{87+84+85+n}{4} = 90$; no **23.** $\frac{5}{128}$ **25.** $\frac{9}{128}$ **27.** $\frac{1}{20}$ **29.** $\frac{1}{16}$ **31.** $n = 0.1 \times 94$; 9.4 **33.** $147 = 0.14 \times n$; 1050 **35.** $13.2 = 0.55 \times n$; 24 **37.** $n = 0.75 \times 68$; 51 **39.** $n \times 54 = 28$; 52% **41.** $n \times 20 = 31$; 155% **43.** about 11% increase **45.** about 33% decrease **47.** 38% decrease **49.** about 3% increase **51.** 125% increase **53.** about 11% increase **55.** about 46%

Chapter 4 page 559

1. -8 **3.** 48 **5.** $\frac{4}{3}$ **7.** $\frac{155}{2}$ **9.** $\frac{5}{3}$ **11.** 3 **13.** 8 ft × 12 ft **15.** 1 **17.** 1 **19.** -40 **21.** $9, -15$ **23.** $5, -5$ **25.** $-\frac{1}{3}$ **27.** identity **29.** The bus traveled 5 h; the car traveled 4 h. **31.** $cv - w$

33. $\frac{P-2w}{2}$ **35.** $m(b-a)$ **37.** $\frac{gr^2}{1.9}$

39. $p \leq 8$;

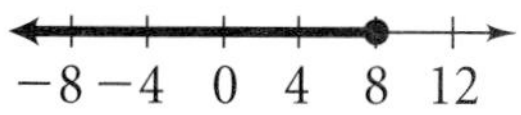

41. $y \leq -1\frac{3}{7}$;
−4 −2 0 2 4

43. $h > -12$;
−12 −8 −4 0 4 8

45. $s \leq 18$;
−12 −6 0 6 12 18

47. $l \geq -3.5$;
−4 −3 −2 −1 0 1

49. $m \leq -12$ or $m \geq 4$;
−12 −8 −4 0 4 8

51. $-2.5 \leq n \leq 14.5$;
−4 −2 0 2 4 6 8 10 12 14 16

53. $a < -11$
−12 −8 −4 0 4 8

55. $j \geq 5$;
0 2 4 6 8 10

57. no more than five balls

59. $\{1, 2, 3\}$;
−2 −1 0 1 2 3

61. integers > 0;
−2 −1 0 1 2 3 4

63. integers ≥ 1;
0 1 2 3

65. integers > 10;

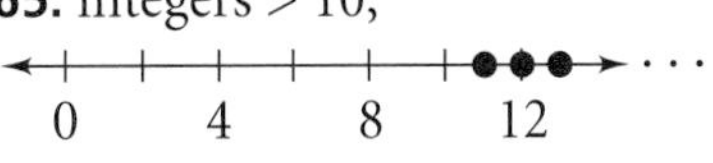

Chapter 5 page 560

1. $\frac{3}{2}$; $y = \frac{3}{2}x + 2$ **3.** 1; $y = x + 6$ **5.** $\frac{5}{2}$; $y = \frac{5}{2}x + 5\frac{1}{2}$
7. $-\frac{1}{7}$; $y = -\frac{1}{7}x$ **17.** 0.2 m/yr **19.** 0.2 blocks/min

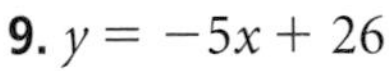

9. $y = -5x + 26$

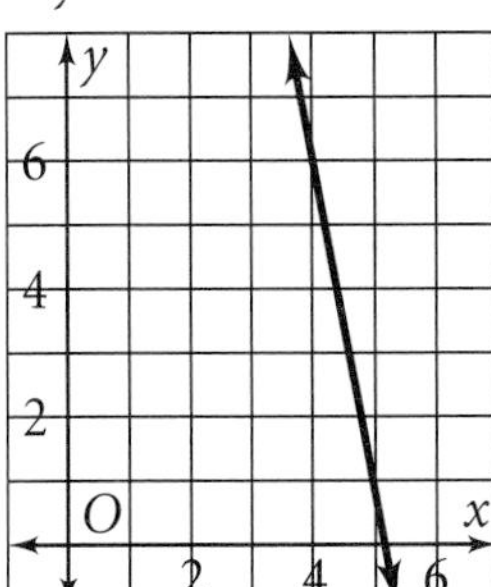

11. $y = \frac{1}{2}x + 1$

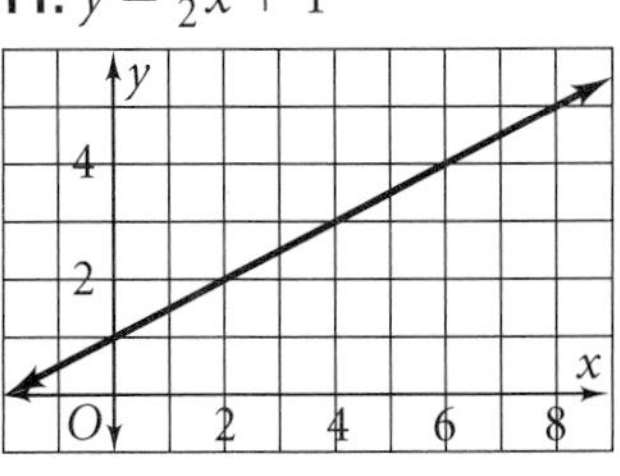

13. $y = 2x + 11$

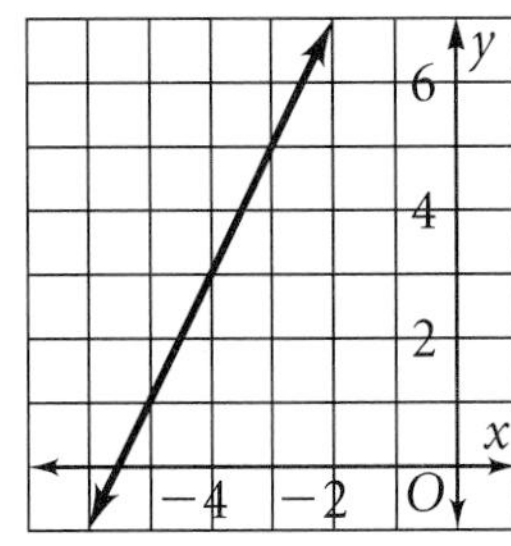

15. $y = 7x - 28$

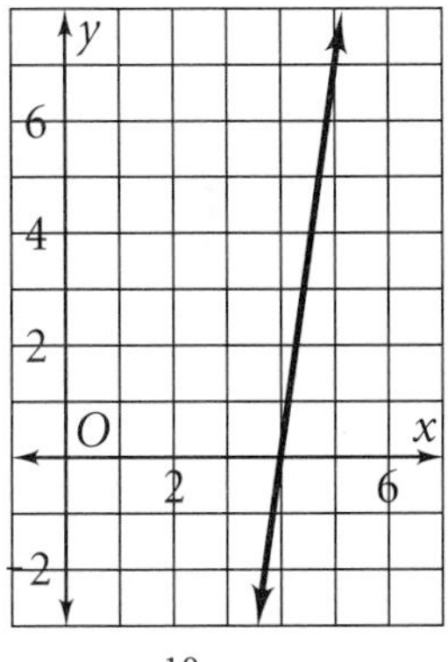

21. $y = \frac{4}{5}x$

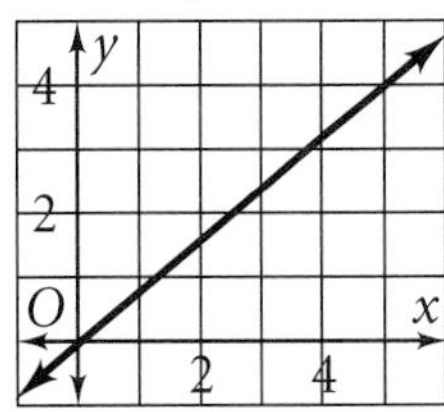

23. $y = \frac{10}{3}x$

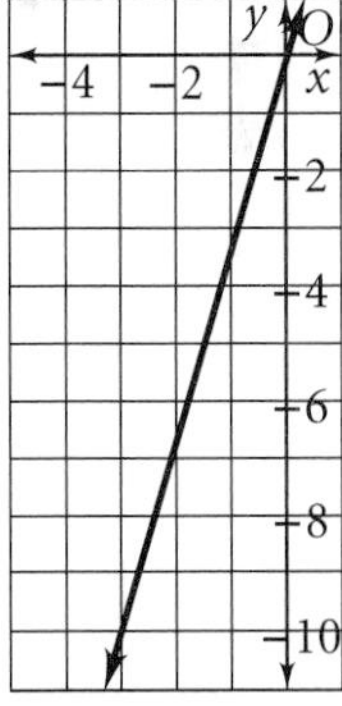

25. $y = -\frac{9}{2}x$

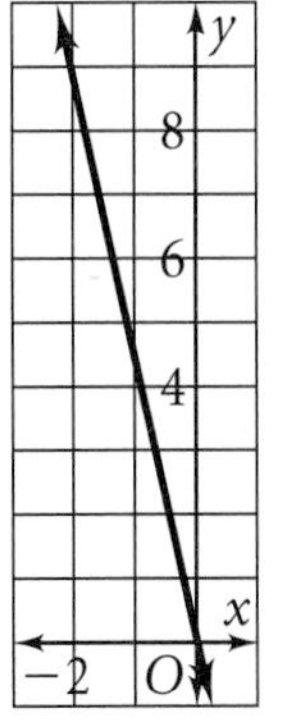

27. $y = -\frac{1}{4}x$

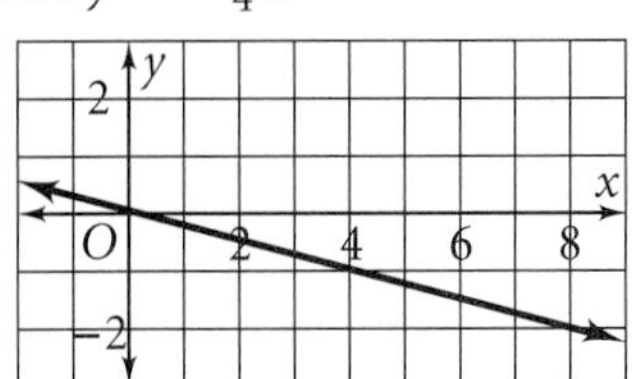

Selected Answers

29. $y = \frac{4}{3}x$

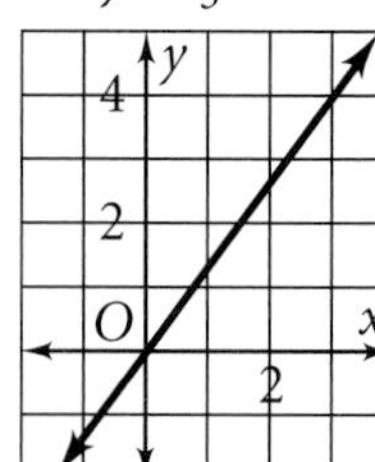

31. $y = -x$

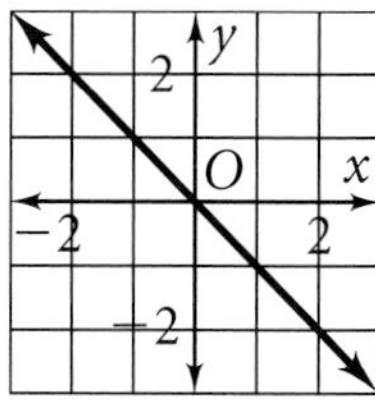

33. 6; 8;

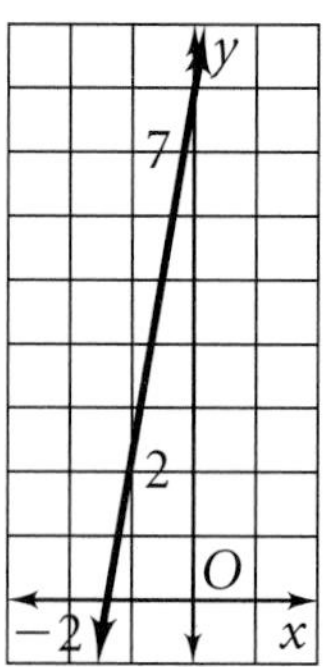

35. $-\frac{5}{2}$; 6;

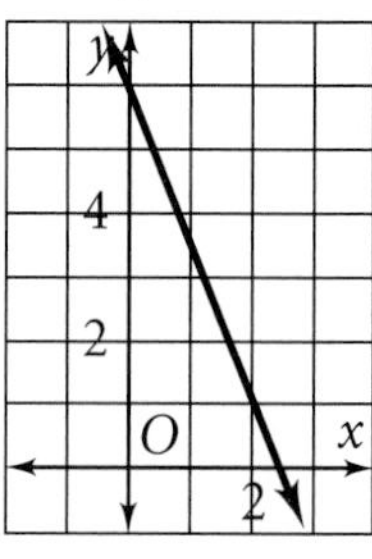

37. $-\frac{3}{4}$; −8;

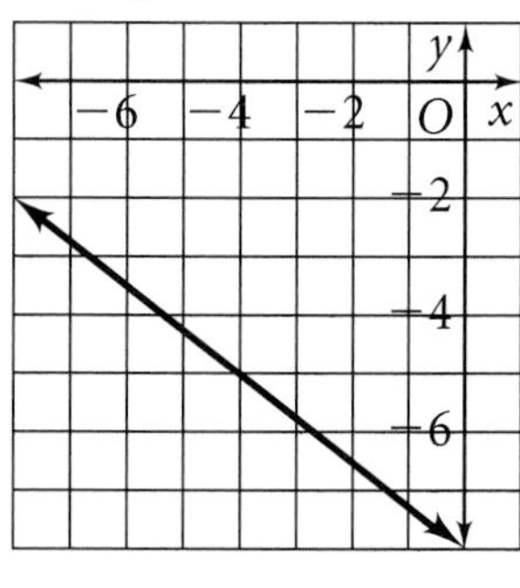

39. $\frac{1}{2}$; 3;

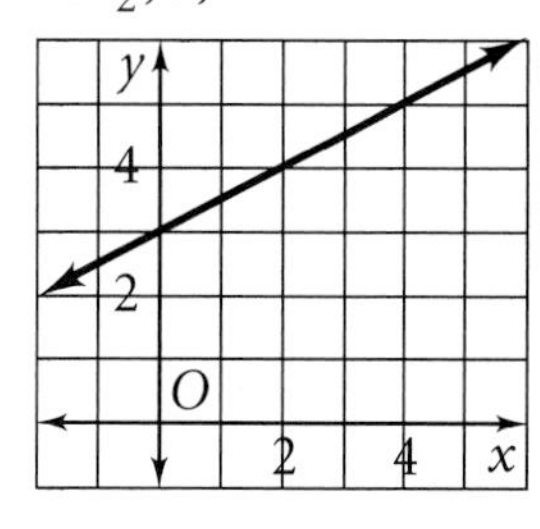

41a–b.

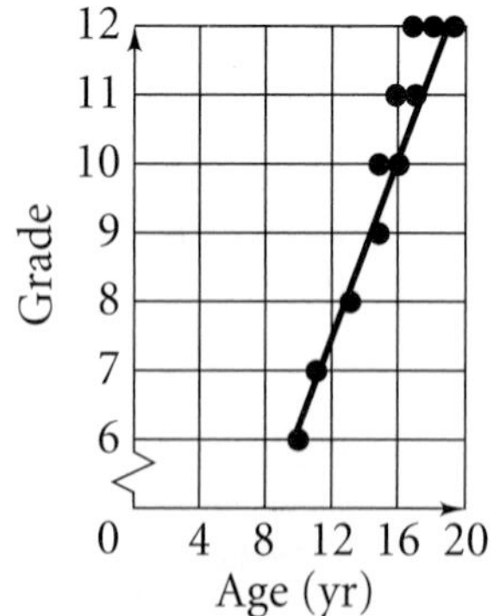

41c. $y = 0.7203196347x - 1.117579909$

43. $y = x$ **45.** $y = 2x + 3$ **47.** $y = \frac{5}{2}x - 6$

49. 1 **51.** − 2 **53.** − 3 **55.** 19

Chapter 6 page 561

1. (4, −3) **3.** (11, 7) **5.** (1, −1) **7.** (6, 13) **9.** (4, −5) **11.** (4, −9) **13.** $n + p = 12$, $5n + p = 32$

15.

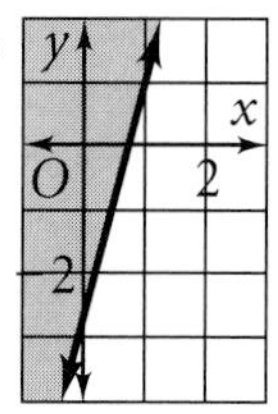

17.

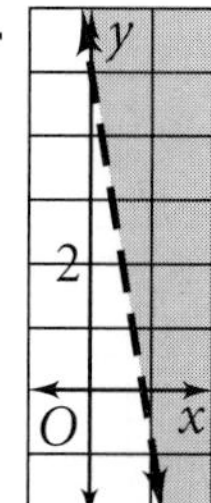

19.

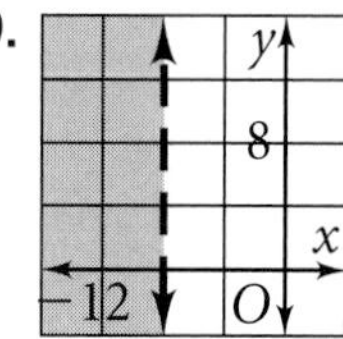

21.

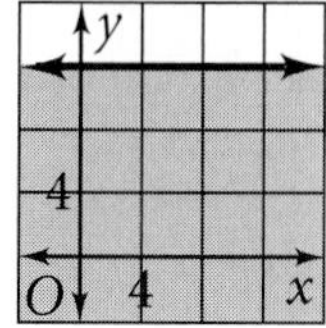

23.

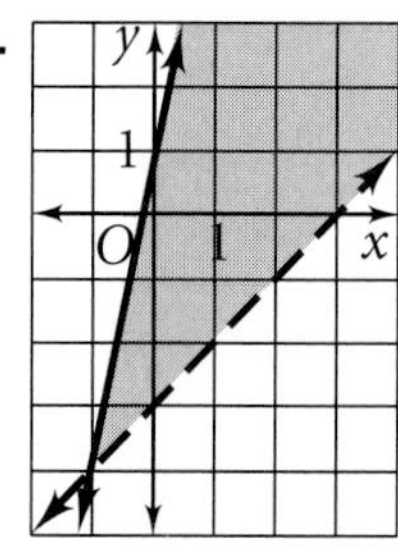

25.

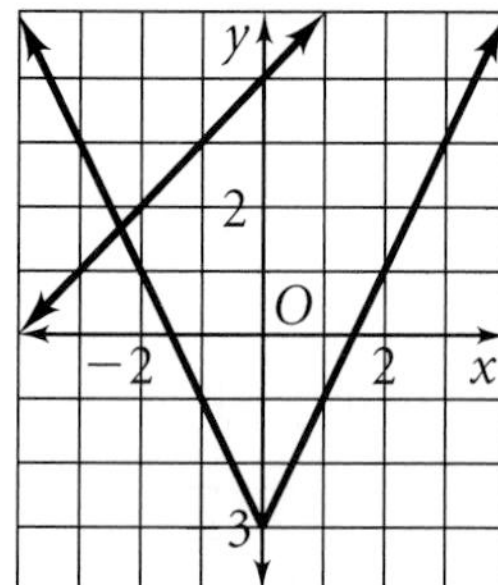

27.

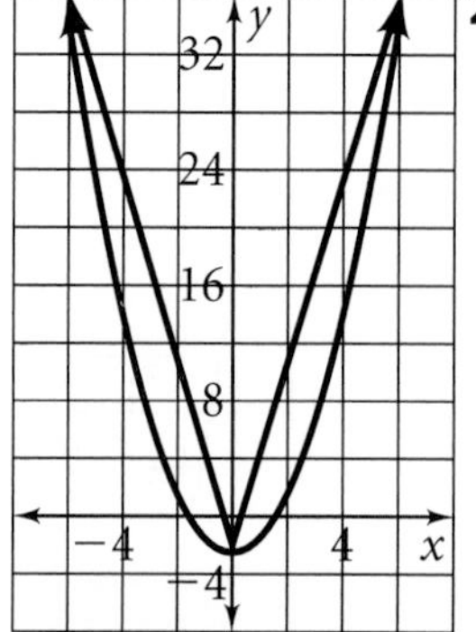

29.

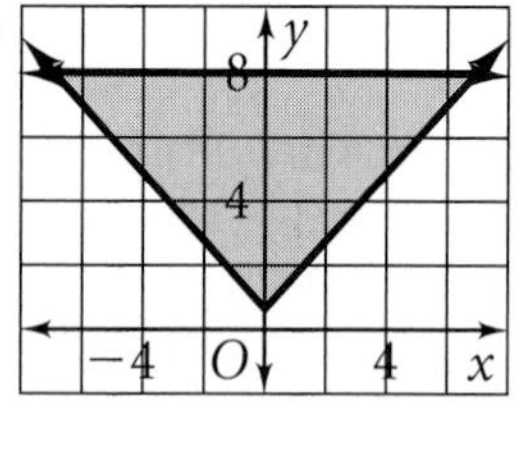

31.

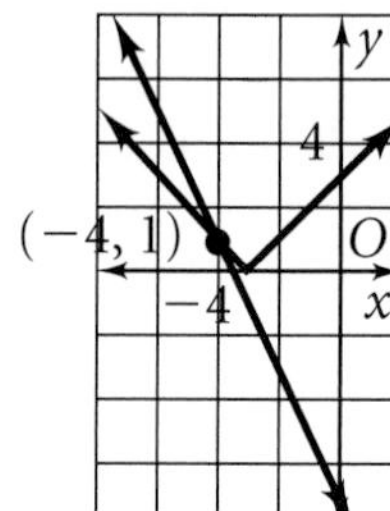

33.

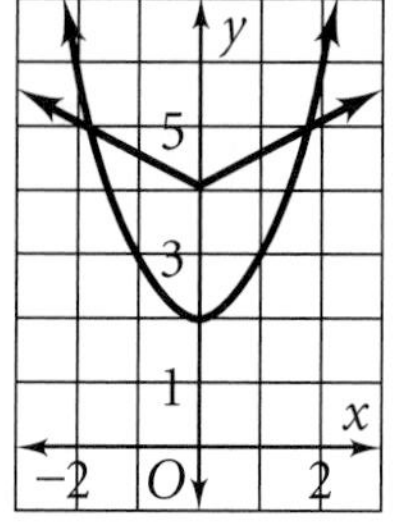

35. 30; 0

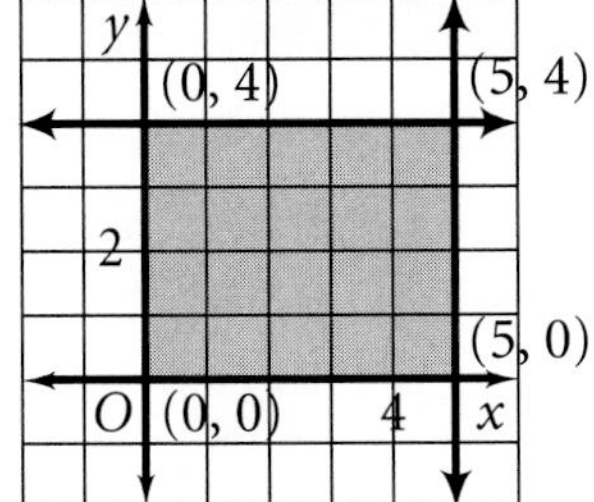

37. 29; 8

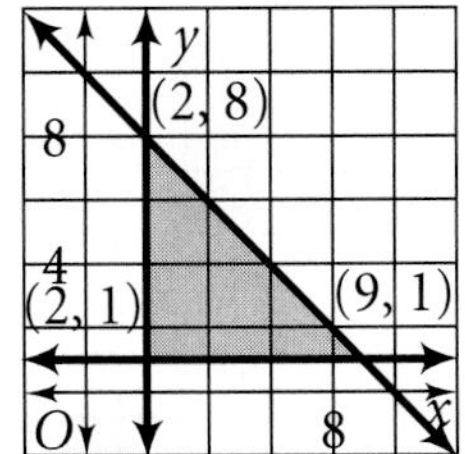

Chapter 7 page 562

1. narrower **3.** opens down, wider **5.** down 4 **7.** narrower, up 5

9.

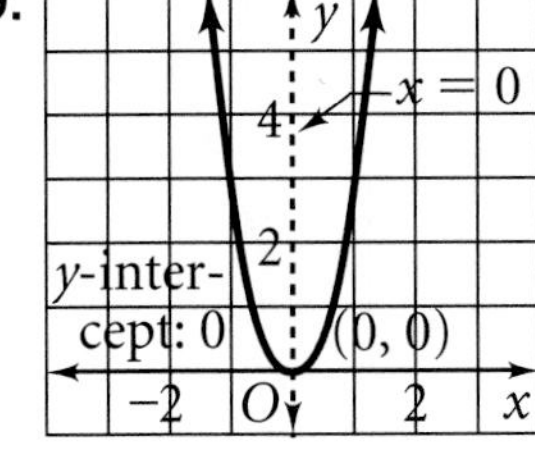

11.

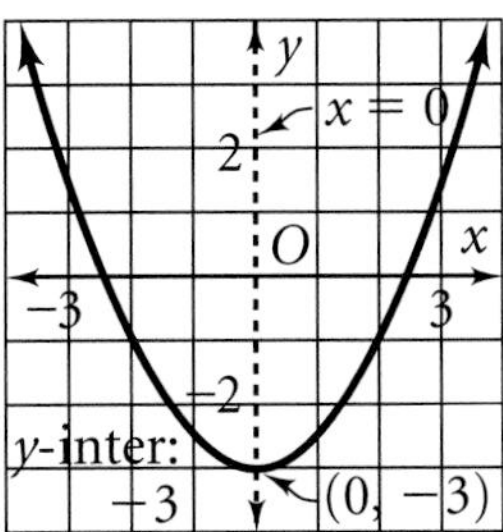

13.

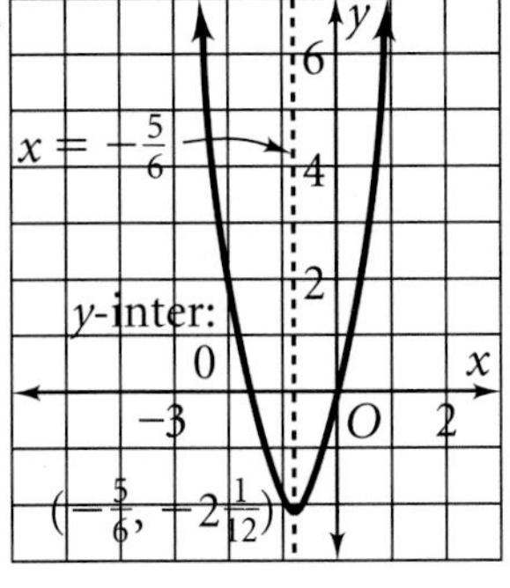

15.

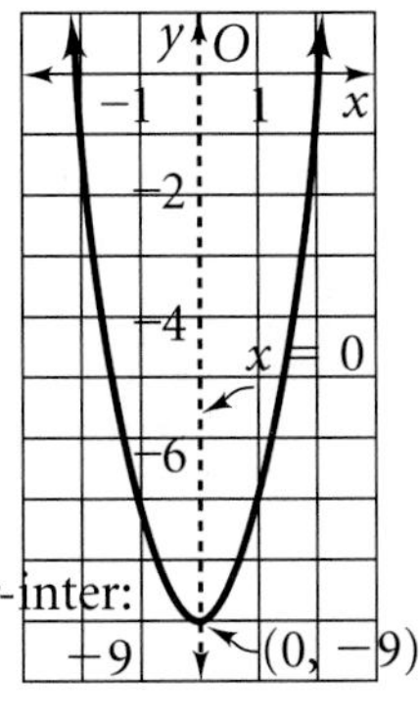

17.

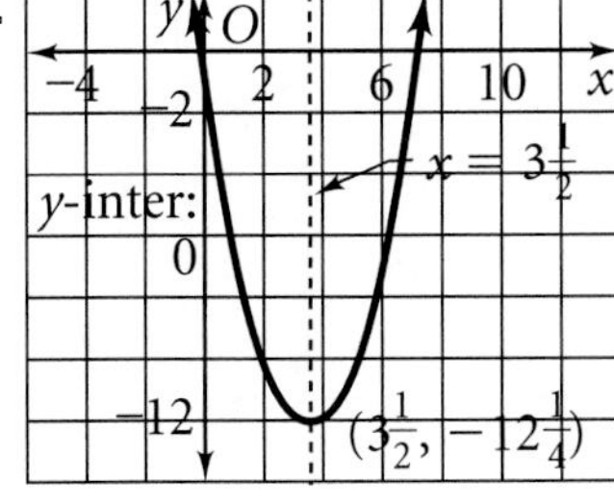

21.

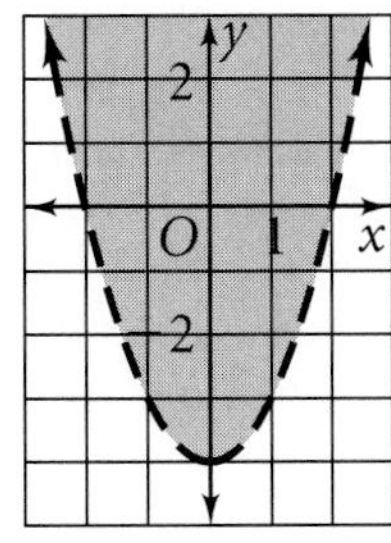

23.

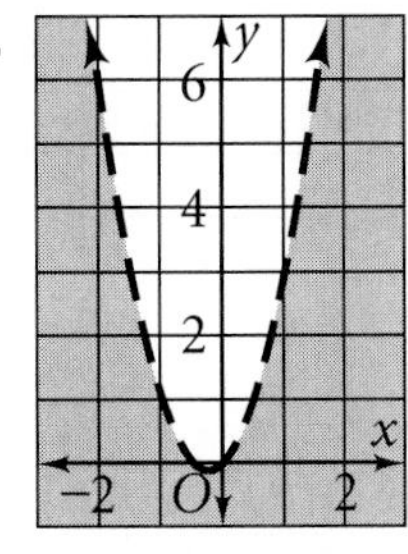

25.

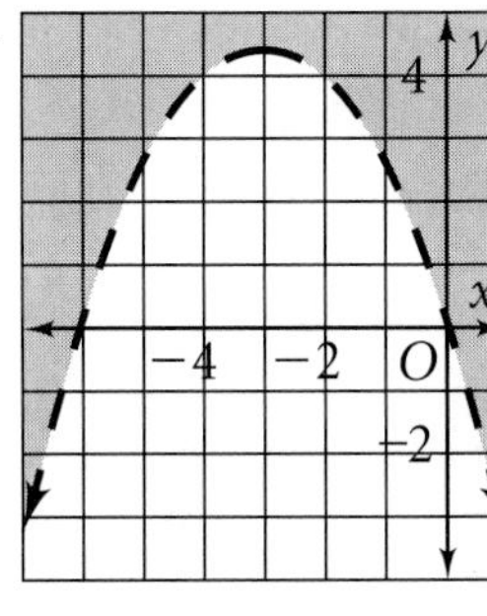

27. 5, −5 **29.** 8, −8 **31.** 0.9, −0.9 **33.** 1.5, −1.5 **35.** $\frac{1}{5}$, $-\frac{1}{5}$ **37.** $\frac{1}{3}$, $-\frac{1}{3}$ **39.** 6, −6 **41.** 10, −10 **43.** 14, −6 **45.** 13, −13 **47.** no real solution **49.** 6.14, −1.14 **51.** 1.71, 0.29 **53.** 8, −2 **55.** 3.65, −1.65 **57.** −19; 0 **59.** 57; 2 **61.** −24; 0 **63.** −27; 0 **65.** 21; 2

Chapter 8 page 563

1. exponential growth

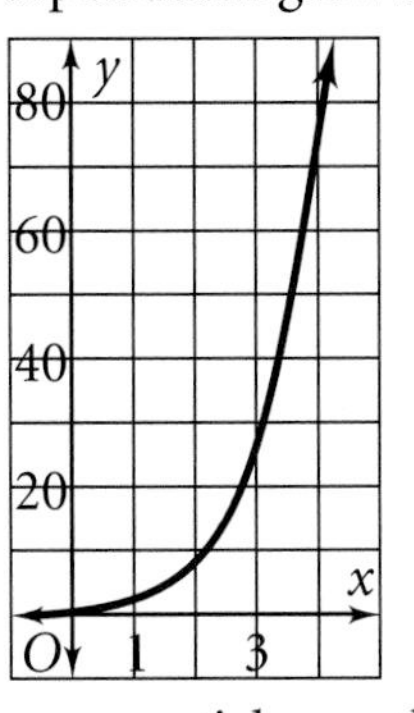

3. exponential growth

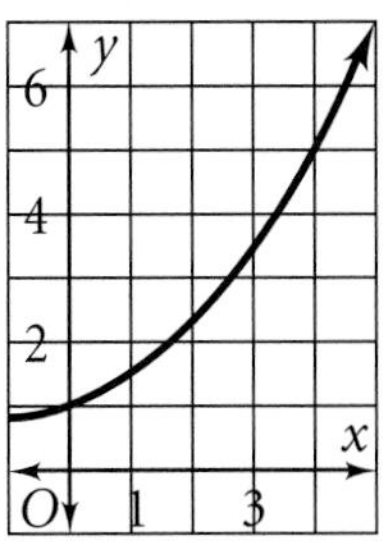

5. exponential growth

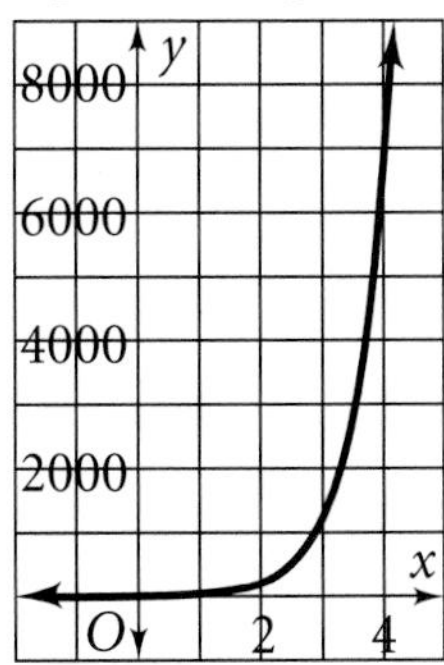

7. exponential decay

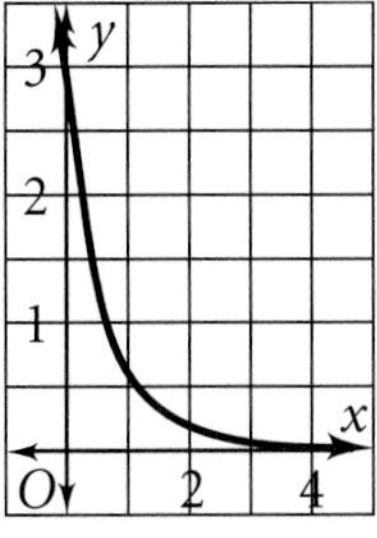

9. exponential growth

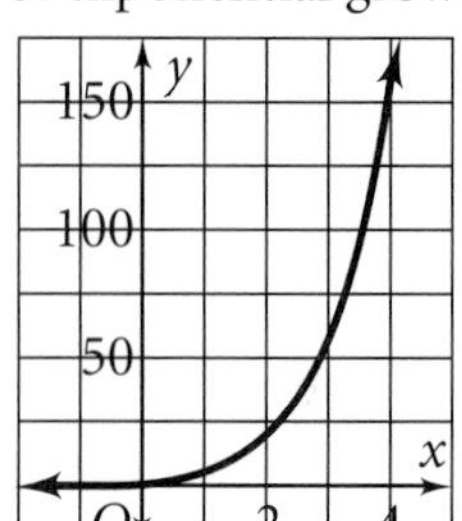

11. exponential growth

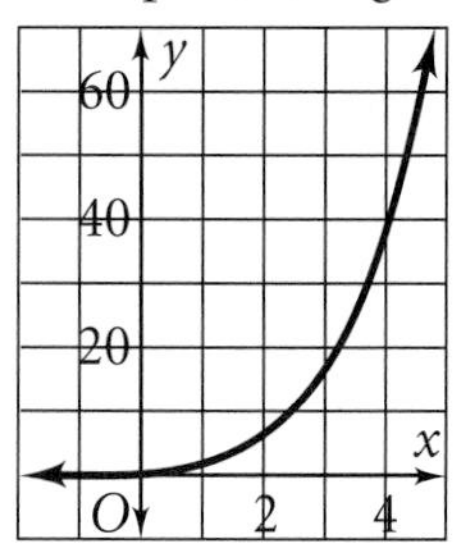

13. 8 **15.** $\frac{1}{2}$ **17.** 0.65 **19.** $\frac{1}{4}$ **21.** $y = 200 \cdot 1.04^x$; \$243.33 **23.** $y = 3000 \cdot 0.92^x$; \$2336.06 **25.** $\frac{5}{m^3}$
27. $\frac{m^{14}}{j^{10}}$ **29.** $w^6 j^{22}$ **31.** $9n^8$ **33.** a^4 **35.** $6t^4$
37. $\frac{2r^{15}}{t^7}$ **39.** $\frac{1}{c^{12}}$ **41.** $\frac{1}{9}$ **43.** 144 **45.** 16 **47.** $-\frac{64}{27}$
49. 6.3×10^{-4} **51.** 2×10^{-4} **53.** 6.2×10^9
55. 8.91×10^{-10} **57.** 3.8×10^{-1} **59.** 5.07×10^{12}
61. 0.000 000 32 **63.** 0.000 425

Chapter 9 page 564

1. no; $4^2 + 5^2 \neq 7^2$ **3.** no; $6^2 + 9^2 \neq 13^2$ **5.** yes; $15^2 + 36^2 = 39^2$ **7.** yes; $8^2 + 15^2 = 17^2$ **9.** 10
11. 10.8 **13.** 5.1; (1.5, 5.5) **15.** 1.4; (4.5, −0.5)
17. 25.5; (2, −2) **19.** 17.0; (−1.5, 1.5) **21.** 11.2; (2.5, 5) **23.** $\frac{3}{5}$ **25.** $\frac{3}{5}$ **27.** $\frac{3}{4}$ **29.** $\frac{5}{2}$ **31.** $\frac{6}{5}$
33. −10 **35.** $6 - 3\sqrt{6}$ **37.** 150 **39.** 9 **41.** 5
43. 4 **45.** 6

47. $x \geq 0$;

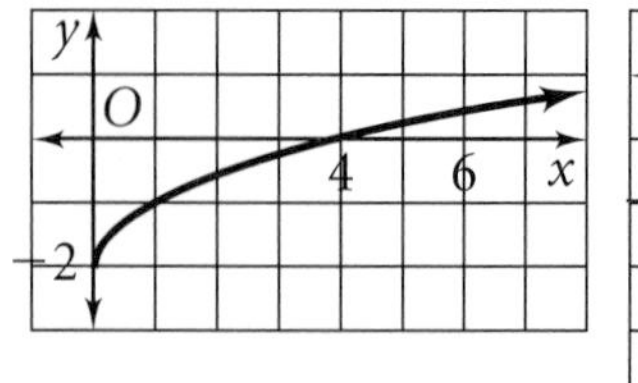

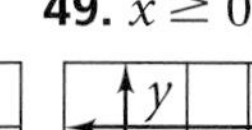
49. $x \geq 0$;

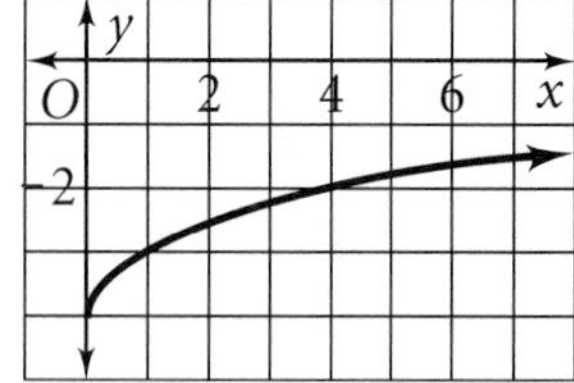

51. $x \geq 0$;

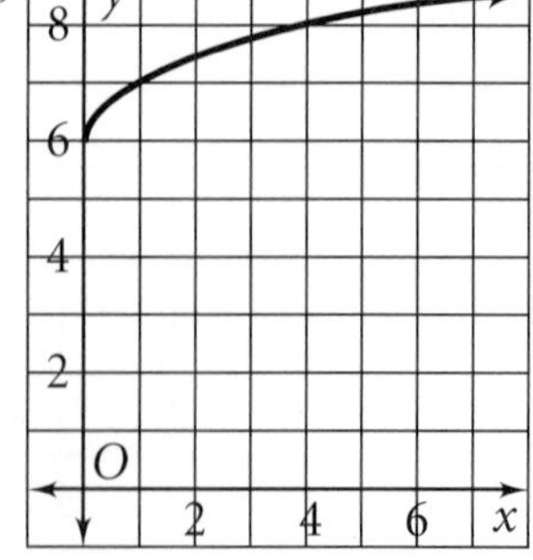

53. 1.6 **55.** 3.4 **57.** 3.2

Chapter 10 page 565

1. $2x^3 + 4x^2 - 11x + 11$ **3.** $6m^3 + m + 4$
5. $-10c^3 - c^2 - 9c - 7$ **7.** $-4s^4 - 2s^3 + 2s^2 + 4s$
9. $4b^3 + 12b$ **11.** $6t^2 + t - 1$ **13.** $32m^2 - 40m$
15. $5k^3 + 40k^2$ **17.** $4n^2 + 2n - 12$ **19.** $b^2 + 10b + 21$ **21.** $(3x - 1)(2x + 5), 6x^2 + 13x - 5$
23. 3 **25.** $2v^5$ **27.** $5r$ **29.** d^4 **31.** 4 **33.** w
35. $(x + 5)(x - 5)$ **37.** $(3c + 13)(3c - 13)$
39. $(t - 3)^2$ **41.** $(2d - 3)^2$ **43.** $(3v - 2)(v + 4)$
45. $(-w + 1)(w - 4)$ or $(-w + 4)(w - 1)$
47. $(4m + 1)(3m - 2)$ **49.** $(c - 5)^2$ **51.** 12, −12
53. 2, 3 **55.** −0.38, −2.62 **57.** 1.35, −1.85
59. 5, $-\frac{1}{2}$ **61.** −0.22, −2.28

Chapter 11 page 566

1. 70 **3.** 0.8 **5.** 0.6 **7.** 8.1 **9.** 2 **11.** 3 **13.** 5

15.

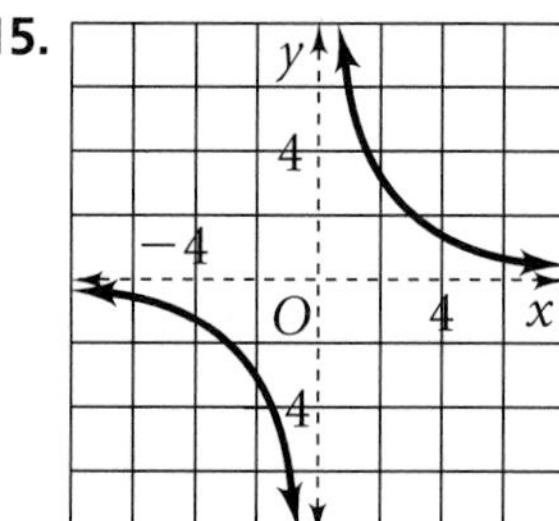

17.

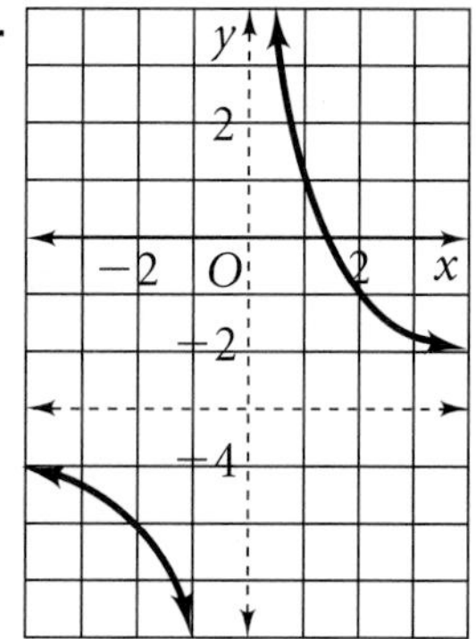

19.

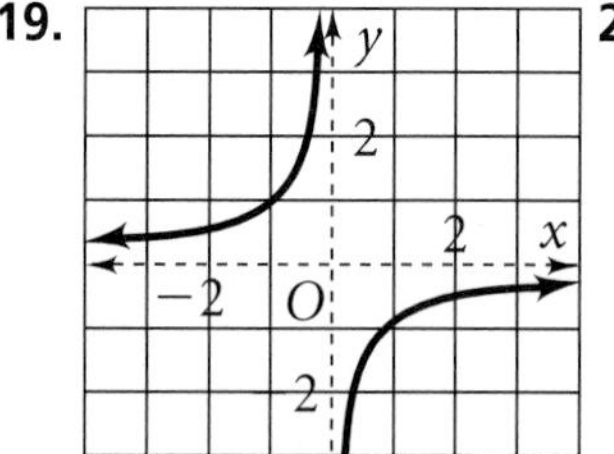

21.

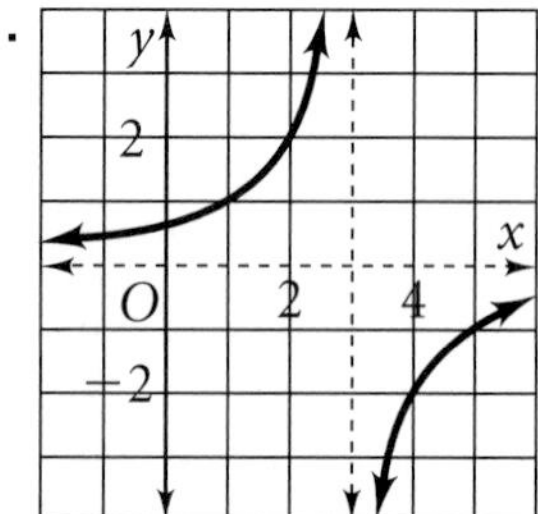

23.

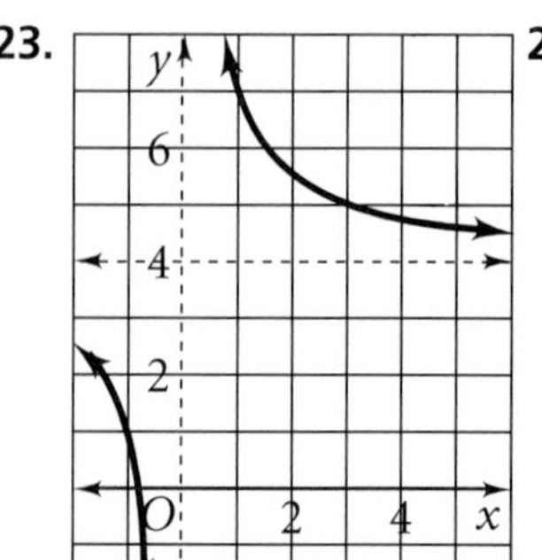

25.

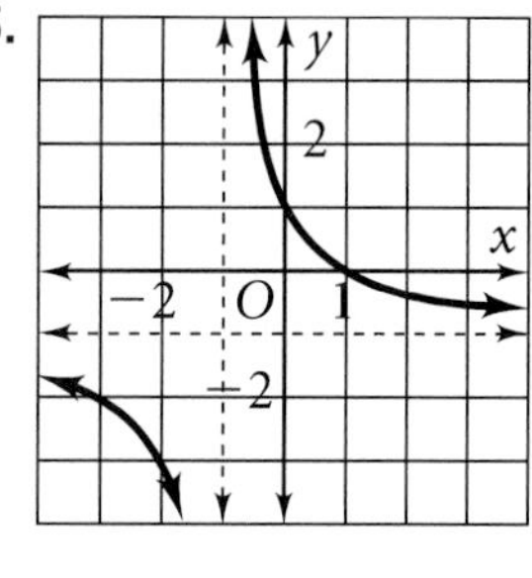

27. ; 0 **29.** 4; 3 **31.** ; 0 **33.** ; 0 **35.** $\frac{s}{2}$; 0 **37.** $12b^2$; 0, $\frac{1}{2}$ **39.** $\frac{8(t-1)}{(t-4)(t+4)}$; 4, -4 **41.** $\frac{y}{6}$; 0, 2 **43.** 8 **45.** -1 **47.** 9 **49.** 5, -5 **51.** -12 **53.** 6, -10 **55.** 42 **57.** 8 **59.** 36 **61.** 84 **63.** 1320 **65.** 5040 **67.** 8568 committees

SKILLS HANDBOOK

page 567

EXERCISES **1.** 6 games **3.** 9 tacks

page 568

EXERCISES **1.** 17, 19 or -19, -17 **3.** 24 **5.** mother 38, son 16, daughter 7

page 569

EXERCISES **1.** 81 books **3.** 36 stories **5.** 7.2 m **7.** 6 ways

page 570

EXERCISES **1.** 21 lockers **3.** about 370,000,000 times **5.** 62 games **7.** 32 and 33

page 571

EXERCISES **1.** dog K.C., horse Bo, bird Cricket, cat Tuffy **3.** Alexa, Karin, Heather, Annette, Tanya, Garo **5.** 126 players

page 572

EXERCISES **1.** 6 **3.** \$575 **5.** 6 tickets **7.** 7:25 A.M.

page 573

EXERCISES **1.** composite **3.** composite **5.** prime **7.** composite **9.** composite **11.** composite **13.** composite **15.** composite **17.** composite **19.** 1, 2, 23, 46 **21.** 1, 11 **23.** $2 \cdot 3 \cdot 3$ **25.** $2 \cdot 3 \cdot 3$ **27.** $3 \cdot 3 \cdot 3$ **29.** $2 \cdot 2 \cdot 2 \cdot 2 \cdot 2 \cdot 2$ **31.** $2 \cdot 2 \cdot 5 \cdot 5$ **33.** $2 \cdot 2 \cdot 3 \cdot 7$ **35.** $11 \cdot 11$

page 574

EXERCISES **1.** 2 **3.** 24 **5.** 3 **7.** 7 **9.** 14 **11.** 3 **13.** 5 **15.** 21 **17.** 80 **19.** 33 **21.** 60 **23.** 240 **25.** 2160 **27.** 50 **29.** 150 **31.** 40

page 575

EXERCISES **1.** 9 **3.** 48 **5.** 2 **7.** 9 **9.** 3 **11.** no **13.** no **15.** no **17.** $\frac{1}{2}$ **19.** $\frac{2}{3}$ **21.** $\frac{2}{5}$ **23.** $\frac{1}{3}$ **25.** $\frac{2}{5}$ **27.** $\frac{3}{4}$ **29.** $\frac{9}{11}$ **31.** $\frac{9}{17}$ **33.** $\frac{5}{6}$

page 576

EXERCISES **1.** 0.3 **3.** 0.2 **5.** $0.\overline{6}$ **7.** $\frac{1}{4}$ **9.** $\frac{13}{100}$ **11.** $\frac{7}{100}$ **13.** $1\frac{5}{7}$ **15.** $2\frac{1}{10}$ **17.** $4\frac{2}{5}$ **19.** $\frac{5}{2}$ **21.** $\frac{31}{6}$ **23.** $\frac{29}{7}$ **25.** 0.875

page 577

EXERCISES **1.** $\frac{5}{7}$ **3.** 3 **5.** $10\frac{7}{15}$ **7.** $6\frac{2}{9}$ **9.** $6\frac{7}{33}$ **11.** $\frac{1}{2}$ **13.** 3 **15.** $\frac{1}{11}$ **17.** $1\frac{7}{9}$ **19.** $7\frac{11}{12}$

page 578

EXERCISES **1.** $\frac{3}{10}$ **3.** $\frac{15}{32}$ **5.** $1\frac{1}{3}$ **7.** $8\frac{5}{8}$ **9.** 20 **11.** $1\frac{1}{5}$ **13.** $\frac{6}{7}$ **15.** $\frac{3}{7}$ **17.** $\frac{5}{7}$ **19.** $2\frac{4}{17}$

page 579

EXERCISES **1.** 56% **3.** 602% **5.** 820% **7.** 20% **9.** 11.1% **11.** 75% **13.** 0.07 **15.** 0.009 **17.** 0.83 **19.** $\frac{19}{100}$ **21.** $4\frac{1}{2}$ **23.** $\frac{16}{25}$

page 580

EXERCISES **1.** 6^4 **3.** $5 \cdot 2^4$ **5.** 64 **7.** 144 **9.** 3267 **11.** $(1 \cdot 10^3) + (2 \cdot 10^2) + (5 \cdot 10^1) + (4 \cdot 10^0)$ **13.** $(8 \cdot 10^4) + (3 \cdot 10^3) + (4 \cdot 10^2) + (1 \cdot 10^0)$

page 581

EXERCISES **1.** 100°; obtuse **3.** 180°; straight

page 582

EXERCISES **1.** 22 cm **3.** 24 cm^2 **5.** 216 cm^3 **7.** 351.68 cm^3

Index

Index

**ata**

Q

Acknowledgments

Cover Photos Globe and background, Bill Westheimer; jet plane, Joe Towers/Check Six

Technical Illustration ANCO/Outlook

Illustration

Leo Abbett: 67

ANCO/Outlook: 16, 18, 26, 82, 87, 95, 193, 227, 230, 249, 253, 270, 274, 279, 289, 326, 399, 439

David Frazier: 116, 117, 143, 167, 170

Kathleen Dempsey: 273, 298

Dave Garbot: 161

Barbara Goodchild: 12

Fran Jarvis: Technical Illustration Manager

Keith Kasnot: 392

Ellen Korey-Lie: 3, 57, 61, 107, 157, 213, 267, 317, 361, 413, 463, 509

Seymour Levy: 107, 150, 291, 346, 371, 455, 464, 489, 490, 513, 539

Andrea G. Maginnis: 147, 221, 241, 286, 287, 292, 298, 299, 302, 369, 429, 464, 468, 529, 546

Gary Phillips: 129

Matthew Pippin: 122, 124

Pond Productions: 9

Gary Torrisi: 276-277, 306

Feature Design Alan Lee Associates

Photography

Photo Research Toni Michaels

Abbreviations: KO = Ken O'Donoghue; MT = Mark Thayer; JC = Jon Chomitz; TSW = Tony Stone Images; SM = Stock Market; FPG = Freelance Photographer's Guild; SB = Stock Boston; PH = Prentice Hall File Photo

Front matter: Page vii, ©Markus Amon/TSW; **viii,** KO; **ix,** MT; **x,** ©Mark Burnett/SB; **xi,** ©Paramount Studios/The Kobal Collection; **xii,** ©David Young Wolff/TSW; **xiii,** Johnny Johnson/Animals Animals; **xiv,** ©Nigel Cattlin/Photo Researchers; **xv,** ©John Gilmoure/The Stock Market; **xvi,** MT; **xvii,** ©Charles West/SM; **xix,** FPG; **xxi,** JC; **xxii,** ©John Madere/SM; **xxv,** ©Andy Sacks/TSW.

Chapter 1: Pages 2-3, O. Louis Mazzatenta/National Geographic Image Collection; **3 inset,** JC; 4, ©David Noble/FPG; **5 t,** ©Tony Freeman/PhotoEdit; **5 b,** ©Marcel Ehrhard; **6, 8 t, 8 b,** ©Andy Sacks, Lonnie Duka, Darrell Gulin all TSW; **9,** Superstock, **12 l,** ©Markus Amon/TSW; **12 r,** KO; **14,** PH; **15,** NASA; **16,** ©Toni Michaels; **17,** KO; **19 l,** Karl Kreutz; **19 r,** ©Bruce Coleman; **20,** ©Uniphoto/Alan Lardman; **21,** ©Fotoconcept/Bertsch/Bruce Coleman; **23,** FRANK & ERNEST reprinted by permission of Newspaper Enterprise Association, Inc.; **23 t,** ©Janice Rubin/Black Star; **25,** NASA; **28,** Courtesy, Cedar Point/Photo by Dan Feicht; **30 all,** KO; **33,** ©Nicholas Devore III/Bruce Coleman; **34,** ©Michael Holford; **37,** ©Bob Daemmrich/The Image Works; **38,** ©Toni Michaels; **41,** ©Paul Souders/TSW; **42,** PH; **46,** KO; **48,** ©Gary Geer/TSW.

Chapter 2: Pages 56-7, ©Larry Lawfer; **57 inset, 59,** JC; **61,** PH; **62,** ©Leonard Lees Rue III/Bruce Coleman; **64,** ©Richard Wood/The Picture Cube; **66,** Courtesy, Professor Bernie Phinney, University of California; **69,** Martha Cooper/Peter Arnold; **71,** NASA; **72,** PH; **74-5,** Steve Greenberg; **77,** ©JC; **80,** The Computer Museum, Boston; **82,** JC; **84,** KO; **88 t,** PH; **88 b,** UPI/Bettmann; **90-1,** JC; **93 tl, br,** ©David McGlynn, Ralph Cowan both FPG; **95,** ©Winter/The Image Works; **96,** Courtesy, Wheel of Fortune; **98,** JC.

Chapter 3: Pages 106-7, JC; **108,** MT; **112,** ©Baloo/Rothco; **114, 115 all,** KO; **117,** PH; **120,** MT; **124,** ©Kevin Morris/Allstock; **126,** Schomburg Center for Research in Black Culture, New York Public Library; **130,** ©Michael Newman/Photo Edit; **135, 137,** MT; **140,** ©M. Siluk/The Image Works; **143,** ©David Young-Wolff/TSW; **144,** ©Jose L. Pelawz/SM; **146,** Courtesy, Dr. Graciela S. Alarcon; **147,** ©Arthur C. Smith III/Grant Heilman Photography; **148,** ©Charles Krebs/SM.

Chapter 4: Pages 156-57, ©Telegraph/FPG; **157 inset,** PH; **158 t,** ©Superstock; **158 b,** ©Bonnie Kamin/PhotoEdit; **160 l,** ©Fred Whitehead/Animals Animals; **160 r,** ©Mark Burnett/SB; **163, 164 all,** KO; **167,** ©Michelle Bridwell/PhotoEdit; **170 t,** ©Bob Daemmrich; **170 b,** ©Anthony Edgeworth/SM; **171,** MT; **173,** JC; **174,** ©Bob Daemmrich; **175,** ©Bill Luster/NCAA Photos; **176 all,** The Granger Collection; **177,** ©Guido Alberto Rossi/Photo Researchers; **179 br,** JC; **179 TR,** ©David Frazier/Photo Researchers; **179 l,** JC; **182,** PH; **184,** ©George Disarid/SM; **187,** JC; **189,** ©Stephen Dalton/Animals Animals; **190,** JC; **193,** TSW; **195,** ©Melinda Berge/Bruce Coleman; **196,** ©Bob Daemmrich/SB; **199,** ©Lawrence Migdale/Photo Researchers; **203,** ©John Madere/SM; **204,** Custom Medical Stock Photo.

Chapter 5: Pages 212-13, Larry Lawfer; **213 inset,** PH; **214 l,** ©Dean Siracusa/FPG; **214 r,** ©Chris Cheadle/TSW; **215 t,** ©Valder Tormey/Picture Perfect; **215 inset,** ©John

McGrail/FPG; **219,** ©E&P Bauer/Bruce Coleman; **220,** ©Gary Bigham/International Stock; **222,** ©Paul Silverman/Fundamental Photographs; **223,** ©Bruce Hands/TSW; **225,** JC; **226,** ©Telegraph/FPG; **229 tr,** ©David Madison/Bruce Coleman; **229 b,** Reprinted by permission: Tribune Media Services; **230 both,** ©Jean-Pierre/Sygma; **232,** MT; **234,** ©Peter Vanderworker/SB; **236,** ©LOL/FPG; **237,** PH; **239,** ©C. C. Lockwood/Bruce Coleman; **241,** ©Paramount Studios/The Kobal Collection; **244,** ©Chris Jones/SM; **247,** ©Nathan Bilow/Allsport; **248 l,** ©Lynn Karlin/FPG; **248 br,** Jeff Spielman/Stockphotos/The Image Bank; **250,** ©Tony Freeman/PhotoEdit; **257,** MT; **258,** ©The Granger Collection; **259,** NASA.

Chapter 6: Pages 266-67, ©David Austen/SB; **269,** ©Mary Kate Denny/TSW; **270,** ©Jose L. Pelaez/SM; **272,** Kim Barnes; **274,**©Robert Caputo/SB; **278,** ©David Young Wolff/TSW; **279,** Courtesy, Rubber Stamps of America; **281,** JC; **283,** PH; **284,** ©Will & Deni McIntyre/TSW; **285,** ©Bob Daemmrich/The Image Works; **286 tl,** JC; 286 br, ©Mark Burnett/SB; **286 tr,** ©David Young Wolff/PhotoEdit; **288,** ©Don Johnson/SM; **291 r,** Spencer Grant/The Picture Cube; **292,** ©D. Well/The Image Works; **296,** ©Stephen Kline/Bruce Coleman; **298 both,** PH; **300-301,** JC; **300 l,** ©Lawrence Migdale/Photo Researchers; **301 tr,** ©Bob Daemmrich; **301 b, 302,** ©John Eastcott, Frank Pedrick/The Image Works; **304,** ©Brian Smith/SB; **308,** From American Indian Design & Decoration by LeRoy H. Appleton, Dover Books; **309,** ©Charles Mercer Photography.

Chapter 7: Pages 316-17, Larry Lawfer; **317 inset,** Courtesy, Indiana Department of Motor Vehicles; **318,** ©Richard Megna/Fundamental Photographs; **321,** PH; **324,** ©Johnny Johnson/Animals Animals; **326,** ©Granitsas/The Image Works; **327 all,** JC; **328,** ©Mark Burnett/SB; **329,** ©Joe Szkodzinski/The Image Bank; **330,** ©Richard Pasley/SB; **333,** ©David Austen/TSW; **334,** NASA; **335,** Reprinted by permission: Tribune Media Services; **338,** ©Gene Peach/The Picture Cube; **340,** ©Nebraska State Historical Society; **341,** ©John Lund/TSW; **344 l, r** ©Chuck Savage, Jon Feingersh both SM; **346,** ©Hank del Espinasse/The Image Bank; **350 b,** ©Yellow Dog Productions/The Image Bank; **350 t,** ©Tony Page/TSW; **353 inset,** The Granger Collection; **353,** UPI/Corbis/Bettmann.

Chapter 8: Pages 360-61, ©Bob Daemmrich/SB; **361 inset,** ©Sidney Moulds/Science Photo Library/Photo Researchers; **363,** ©Andrew Henley/Auscape; **364,** PH; **365,** ©Chris Rogers/SM; **367,** ©Mark Burnett/SB; **371 l,** ©Alan McFee/FPG; **371 r,** ©Chip Henderson/TSW; **372,** ©Miro Vintoniv/SB; **373,** ©Corbis/Bettmann; **374** ©Grant Heilman Photography; **380 both,** ©Nigel Cattlin/Photo Researchers; **383,** ©Jack Stein Grove/Tom Stack and Assoc.; **385,** ©Bob Daemmrich/TSW; **386,** ©Telegraph/FPG; **387,** Martucci Studio; **388 tl,** Ray Ng; **388 br,** ©Paul S. Howell/Gamma Liaison; **389,** FOXTROT ©1991 Bill Amend. Reprinted with permission of UNIVERSAL PRESS SYNDICATE. All rights reserved; **390,** ©Dan McCoy/Rainbow; **392,** ©Nathan Benn/SB; **394,** ©Dr. Jeremy Burgess/Science Photo Library/Photo Researchers; **398,** The Granger Collection; **400,** Courtesy Dr. Jewel Plummer Cobb; **402 all,** MT.

Chapter 9: Pages 412-13, ©Paul Chesley/TSW; **415,** ©Spencer Jones/FPG; **417,** ©Jose Fuste Raga/SM; **418,** ©Mark Antman/The Image Works; **421,** ©Bob Daemmrich; **423,** ©Torleif Sënsson/SM; **424,** Cindy Loo/The Picture Cube; **426,** ©Joe McDonald/Bruce Coleman; **427,** T. Kevin Smyth/SM; **428,** D&J Heaton/SB; **431,** ©Dave Watters/TSW; **433,** ©Bob Daemmrich/The Image Works; **434,** PH; **436,** ©ABC/Mondrian Estate/Holtzman Trust/Haags Gemeentemuseum; **438,** Reprinted by permission: Tribune Media Services; **439 t,** ©Porterfield-Chickering/Photo Researchers; **439 b,** ©Ron Sherman/Stock Boston; **441,** ©Jim Tuten/FPG; **443,** ©Chris Jones/SM; **445,** ©John Gilmore/SM; **448,** KO; **451 tr,** ©James Shaffer/PhotoEdit; **451 bl,** ©Bob Daemmrich/SB; **453,** ©Anton Want/Allsport; **453 inset,** PH; **454,** ©Kindra Clineff/The Picture Cube; **455,** ©Jonathan Rawle/Stock Boston.

Chapter 10: Pages 462-63, ©Bob Daemmrich/TSW; **463 inset,** ©Don Mason/SM; **464 all,** MT; **472,** ©Patrick Ingrand/TSW; **476,** ©Bob Daemmrich; **479,** Courtesy, Southern Forest Products Association; **481,** ©Stacy Pick/SB; **484,** ©Kevin R. Morris/TSW; **485,** ©Tom & Pat Leeson/Photo Researchers; **486 both,** MT; **489,** ©Frank Gordon/FPG; **490,** ©Michael Newman/PhotoEdit; **492,** ©Robert Essel/SM; **493,** ©Henryk T. Kaiser/The Picture Cube; **494,** ©Michael Keller/FPG; **498,** Joachim Messerschmidt/FPG; **500,** CLOSE TO HOME copyright John McPherson. Reprinted with permission of UNIVERSAL PRESS SYNDICATE. All rights reserved; **501 t,** ©Mike Surowiak/TSW; **501 b,** ©Needham Research Institute.

Chapter 11: Pages 508-09, ©Jean-Claude Lejeune/SB; **509 inset,** ©Leonard Lessin/Peter Arnold; **510,** ©Ron Sherman/TSW; **513,** CLOSE TO HOME copyright John McPherson. Reprinted with permission of UNIVERSAL PRESS SYNDICATE. All rights reserved.; **514 r,** ©Lawrence Migdale/SB; **514 l,** ©Richard Laird/FPG; **516,** ©Michael Keller/SM; **518,** ©Michael Grecco/SB; **523,** ©Charles West/SM; **525 all,** KO; **530,** ©Bill Bachmann/PhotoEdit; **531 b,** ©Gerald Gscheidle/Peter Arnold; **531 t,** ©Greg Mancuso/Stock Boston; **533 c, l,** ©Spencer Jones/FPG; **533 r,** Lee Snider/The Image Works; **535,** Courtesy, Yield House; **540,** ©Steve Dunwell/The Image Bank; **541,** ©Christian Michaels/FPG; **544;** Ron Chapple/FPG.